McGraw-Hill Ryerson

Advanced Functions 12

 ## Authors

Wayne Erdman
B.Math., B.Ed.
Toronto District School Board

Antonietta Lenjosek
B.Sc., B.Ed.
Ottawa Catholic School Board

Roland W. Meisel
B.Sc., B.Ed., M.Sc.
Port Colborne, Ontario

Jacob Speijer
B.Eng., M.Sc.Ed., P.Eng.
District School Board of Niagara

Contributing Authors

Kirsten Boucher
Durham District School Board

Dan Ciarmoli
Hamilton-Wentworth District
School Board

Patrick Grew
Limestone District School Board

Jeff Irvine
Peel District School Board

Atul Kotecha
Limestone District School Board

 ## Consultants

Assessment Consultant
Jacqueline Hill
Durham District School Board

Technology Consultant
Dan Ciarmoli
Hamilton-Wentworth District
School Board

Mathematical Processes Consultant
Susan Siskind
Toronto, Ontario

Pedagogical Consultants
Wayne Erdman
Toronto District School Board

Larry Romano
Toronto Catholic District School Board

 ## Senior Advisors

John Santarelli
Stoney Creek, Ontario

Laura Tonin
District School Board of Niagara

Paula Thiessen
District School Board of Niagara

 ## Advisors

Kirsten Boucher
Durham District School Board

Karen Frazer
Ottawa-Carleton District School Board

Janine LeBlanc
Whitby, Ontario

Anthony Silva
York Region District School Board

Ken Stewart
York Region District School Board

Advisory Panel

Derrick Driscoll
Thames Valley District School Board

Roxanne Evans
Algonquin and Lakeshore Catholic
District School Board

Honi Huyck
Belle River, Ontario

Jeff Irvine
Peel District School Board

Colleen Morgulis
Durham Catholic District School Board

Terry Paradellis
Toronto District School Board

Barbara Vukets
Waterloo Region District School Board

Toronto • Montréal • Boston • Burr Ridge, IL • Dubuque, IA • Madison, WI • New York • San Francisco
St. Louis • Bangkok • Bogotá • Caracas • Kuala Lumpur • Lisbon • London • Madrid • Mexico City
Milan • New Delhi • Santiago • Seoul • Singapore • Sydney • Taipei

McGraw-Hill Ryerson Limited

*A Subsidiary of The **McGraw·Hill** Companies*

COPIES OF THIS BOOK
MAY BE OBTAINED BY
CONTACTING:
McGraw-Hill Ryerson Ltd.

E-MAIL:
orders@mcgrawhill.ca

TOLL-FREE FAX:
1-800-463-5885

TOLL-FREE CALL:
1-800-565-5758

OR BY MAILING YOUR
ORDER TO:
McGraw-Hill Ryerson
Order Department
300 Water Street
Whitby, ON L1N 9B6

Please quote the ISBN and
title when placing your order.

McGraw-Hill Ryerson
Advanced Functions 12

ISBN 10: 0-07-026636-0
ISBN 13: 978-0-07-026636-0

9   TCP   1 9 8 7 6 5 4 3

Printed and bound in Canada.

Care has been taken to trace ownership of copyright material contained in this text. The publishers will gladly take any information that will enable them to rectify any reference or credit in subsequent printings.

The information and activities in this textbook have been carefully developed and reviewed by professionals to ensure safety and accuracy. However, the publisher shall not be liable for any damages resulting, in whole or in part, from the reader's use of the material. The safety of students remains the responsibility of the classroom teacher, the principal, and the school board district.

The Geometer's Sketchpad® and *Fathom Dynamic Statistics™ Software*, Key Curriculum Press, 1150 65th Street, Emeryville, CA 94608, 1-800-995-MATH.

Statistics Canada information is used with the permission of Statistics Canada. Users are forbidden to copy the data and redisseminate them, in an original or modified form, for commercial purposes, without permission from Statistics Canada. Information on the availability of the wide range of data from Statistics Canada can be obtained from Statistics Canada's Regional Office, its World Wide Web site, and its toll-free access number 1-800-263-1136.

PUBLISHER: Linda Allison
ASSOCIATE PUBLISHER: Kristi Clark
PROJECT MANAGERS: Maggie Cheverie, Janice Dyer
DEVELOPMENTAL EDITORS: Richard Dupuis, Jackie Lacoursiere, Darren McDonald, Winnie Siu
MANAGER, EDITORIAL SERVICES: Crystal Shortt
SUPERVISING EDITOR: Shannon Martin
COPY EDITOR: Julia Cochrane
PHOTO RESEARCH/PERMISSIONS: Linda Tanaka
EDITORIAL ASSISTANT: Erin Hartley
ASSISTANT PROJECT COORDINATOR: Janie Reeson
MANAGER, PRODUCTION SERVICES: Yolanda Pigden
PRODUCTION COORDINATOR: Madeleine Harrington
COVER DESIGN: Valid Design
INTERIOR DESIGN: Michelle Losier
ELECTRONIC PAGE MAKE-UP: ArtPlus Limited
COVER IMAGE: Courtesy of Masterfile

Acknowledgements

Reviewers of *Advanced Functions 12*

The publishers, authors, and editors of *McGraw-Hill Ryerson Advanced Functions 12* wish to extend their sincere thanks to the students, teachers, consultants, and reviewers who contributed their time, energy, and expertise to the creation of this textbook. We are grateful for their thoughtful comments and suggestions. This feedback has been invaluable in ensuring that the text and related teacher's resource meet the needs of students and teachers.

Tracey Angelini
Hamilton-Wentworth District School Board

John A. Bradley
Ottawa Catholic District School Board

Dan Bruni
York Catholic District School Board

David Bukta
Upper Grand District School Board

Anita Casella
Hamilton-Wentworth District School Board

Karen Coveney
Ottawa Catholic District School Board

Emidio DiAntonio
Dufferin-Peel Catholic District School Board

John DiVizio
Durham Catholic District School Board

Doris Galea
Dufferin-Peel Catholic District School Board

Mark Gatti
York Region District School Board

Domenic Greto
York Catholic District School Board

Raymond Ho
Durham District School Board

Alison Kennedy
Halton District School Board

Karen Kokoski
Hamilton-Wentworth Catholic District School Board

Louis Lim
York Region District School Board

Steve Martinello
Peel District School Board

Susan Melville
Rainbow District School Board

Janet Moir
Toronto Catholic District School Board

Leo Moscone
Windsor-Essex Catholic District School Board

Donald Mountain
Thames Valley District School Board

Andrezj Pienkowski
Toronto District School Board

Rinaldo Schiabel
Toronto Catholic District School Board

Antonio Stancati
Toronto Catholic District School Board

Nancy Tsiobanos
Dufferin-Peel Catholic District School Board

Contents

Preface

McGraw-Hill Ryerson Advanced Functions 12 is designed for students planning to qualify for college or university. The book introduces new mathematical principles while providing a wide variety of applications linking the mathematical theory to real situations and careers.

Text Organization

- Chapter 1 generalizes concepts of polynomial functions and introduces the process of using secants and tangents to analyse rates of change. These concepts are then integrated as appropriate throughout other chapters of the text.

- In Chapter 2, you will combine your equation-solving skills with principles of polynomial functions to solve polynomial equations and inequalities. Chapter 3 focuses on properties of rational functions.

- Chapter 4 extends your understanding of trigonometry by defining trigonometric ratios of any angle using radians for angle measure. These concepts are then used in Chapter 5 to analyse trigonometric functions.

- Chapters 6 and 7 provide opportunities for you to explore and apply concepts of exponents and logarithms. In Chapter 8, concepts from all seven preceding chapters are integrated in the topic of combining functions.

Mathematical Processes

- This text integrates the seven mathematical processes: problem solving, reasoning and proving, reflecting, selecting tools and computational strategies, connecting, representing, and communicating. These processes are interconnected and are used throughout the course. Some examples and exercises are flagged with a mathematical processes graphic to show you which processes are involved in solving the problem.

Chapter Features

- The **Chapter Opener** introduces what you will learn in the chapters. It includes a list of the specific curriculum expectations that the chapter covers.

- **Prerequisite Skills** reviews key skills from previous mathematical courses and previous chapters in this book that are needed to be successful with the current chapter. Examples and further practice are given in the **Prerequisite Skills Appendix** on pages 484 to 504. The **Chapter Problem** is introduced at the end of the Prerequisite Skills. Questions related to this problem are identified in the exercises, and the **Chapter Problem Wrap-Up** is found at the end of the **Chapter Review**.

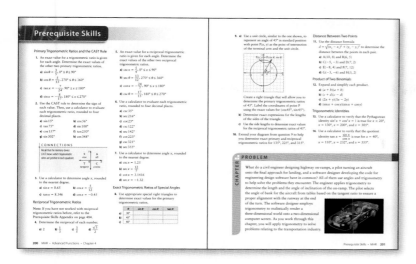

- Many numbered sections start with an **Investigate**, which allows you to construct your understanding of new concepts. Many of these investigations are best done using graphing calculators or dynamic geometry software, but in most instances a choice of tools is given.

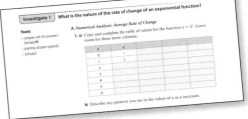

- Worked **Examples** provide model solutions that show how the new concepts are used. They often include more than one method, with and without technology. New mathematical terms are highlighted and defined in context. Refer to the **Glossary** on pages 586 to 594 for a full list of definitions of mathematical terms used in the text.

- The **Key Concepts** box summarizes the ideas in the lesson, and the **Communicate Your Understanding** questions allow you to reflect on the concepts of the section.

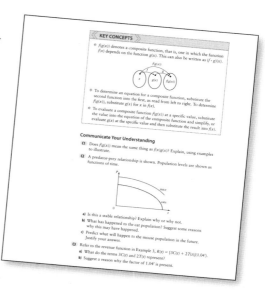

- Exercises are organized into three sections: **A: Practice, B: Connect and Apply,** and **C: Extend and Challenge**. Any questions that require technology tools are identified with **Use Technology**. Most C exercises end with a few **Math Contest** questions to provide extra challenge.

- Tasks are presented at the end of each chapter. These are more involved problems that require you to use several concepts from the preceding chapters. Some tasks may be assigned as either individual or group projects.

- Each chapter ends with a section-by-section **Chapter Review. Cumulative Reviews** occur after Chapters 3, 5, and 8.

- A **Practice Test** is also included at the end of each chapter.

- A **Course Review** follows the task at the end of Chapter 8. This comprehensive selection of questions will help you to determine if you are ready for the final examination.

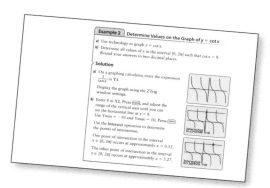

Assessment

- Some questions are designated as **Achievement Checks**. These questions provide you with an opportunity to demonstrate your knowledge and understanding, as well as your ability to apply, think about, and communicate what you have learned.

- The **Chapter Problem Wrap-Up** occurs at the end of the Chapter Review. It consists of a summary problem and may be assigned as a project.

Technology

- The text shows examples of the use of the TI-83 Plus and TI-84 Plus graphing calculators, *The Geometer's Sketchpad®*, and *Fathom Dynamic Statistics™* Software.

- The TI-89 Titanium calculator is used for computer algebra system (CAS) applications. For techniques that are new at the grade 12 level, detailed keystrokes are shown in worked examples.

Extension

- These optional features extend the concepts of the preceding section using technology or advanced mathematical techniques. They provide you with interesting activities to challenge and engage you in new mathematical ideas.

Connections

This margin item includes

- connections between topics in the course or to topics learned previously

- interesting facts related to topics in the examples and exercises

- suggestions for how to use the Internet to help you solve problems or to research or collect information—direct links are provided on the *Advanced Functions 12* page on the McGraw-Hill Ryerson Web site.

Answers

- Answers to the **Prerequisite Skills**, numbered sections, **Chapter Review**, and **Practice Test** are provided on pages 524 to 585.

- Responses for the **Investigate**, **Communicate Your Understanding**, and **Achievement Check** questions and **Chapter Problem Wrap-Up** are provided in the *McGraw-Hill Ryerson Advanced Functions 12 Teacher's Resource*.

- Full solutions to all questions, including proof questions, are on the *McGraw-Hill Ryerson Advanced Functions 12 Solutions CD-ROM*.

Chapter 1

Polynomial Functions

Linear and quadratic functions are members of a larger group of functions known as polynomial functions. In business, the revenue, profit, and demand can be modelled by polynomial functions. An architect may design bridges or other structures using polynomial curves, while a demographer may predict population trends using polynomial functions.

This chapter focuses on the properties and key features of graphs of polynomial functions and their transformations. You will also be introduced to the concepts of average and instantaneous rate of change.

By the end of this chapter, you will

- recognize a polynomial expression and the equation of a polynomial function, and identify linear and quadratic functions as examples of polynomial functions (C1.1)
- compare, through investigation, the numeric, graphical, and algebraic representations of polynomial functions (C1.2)
- describe key features of the graphs of polynomial functions (C1.3)
- distinguish polynomial functions from sinusoidal and exponential functions (C1.4)
- investigate connections between a polynomial function given in factored form and the x-intercepts of its graph, and sketch the graph of a polynomial function given in factored form using its key features (C1.5)
- investigate the roles of the parameters a, k, d, and c in functions of the form $y = af[k(x - d)] + c$ and describe these roles in terms of transformations on the functions $f(x) = x^3$ and $f(x) = x^4$ (C1.6)

- determine an equation of a polynomial function that satisfies a given set of conditions (C1.7)
- investigate properties of even and odd polynomial functions, and determine whether a given polynomial function is even, odd, or neither (C1.9)
- investigate and recognize examples of a variety of representations of average rate of change and instantaneous rate of change (D1.1, D1.2, D1.3, D1.6)
- calculate and interpret average rates of change of functions, given various representations of the functions (D1.4)
- make connections between average rate of change and the slope of a secant, and instantaneous rate of change and the slope of a tangent (D1.7)
- recognize examples of instantaneous rates of change arising from real-world situations, and make connections between instantaneous rates of change and average rates of change (D1.5)
- solve real-world problems involving average and instantaneous rate of change (D1.9)

Prerequisite Skills

Function Notation

1. Determine each value for the function
$f(x) = -4x + 7$.

  a) $f(0)$ **b)** $f(3)$ **c)** $f(-1)$

  d) $f\left(\dfrac{1}{2}\right)$ **e)** $f(-2x)$ **f)** $f(3x)$

2. Determine each value for the function
$f(x) = 2x^2 - 3x + 1$.

  a) $f(0)$ **b)** $f(3)$ **c)** $f(-1)$

  d) $f\left(\dfrac{1}{2}\right)$ **e)** $3f(2x)$ **f)** $f(3x)$

Slope and y-intercept of a Line

3. State the slope and the y-intercept of each line.

  a) $y = 3x + 2$ **b)** $4y = 6 - 2x$

  c) $5x - y + 7 = 0$ **d)** $y + 6 = -5(x + 1)$

  e) $-(x + 4) = 2(y - 3)$

Equation of a Line

4. Determine an equation for the line that
satisfies each set of conditions.

  a) The slope is 3 and the y-intercept is 5.

  b) The x-intercept is -1 and the y-intercept is 4.

  c) The slope is -4 and the line passes through
  the point $(7, 3)$.

  d) The line passes through the points $(2, -2)$
  and $(1, 5)$.

Finite Differences

5. Use finite differences to determine if each
function is linear, quadratic, or neither.

  a)

x	y
-2	-7
-1	-5
0	-3
1	-1
2	1
3	3
4	5

b)

x	y
-1	-8
0	-2
1	-1
2	5
3	7
4	13
5	20

c)

x	y
-4	-12
-3	-5
-2	0
-1	3
0	4
1	3
2	0

Domain and Range

6. State the domain and range of each function.
Justify your answer.

  a) $y = 2(x - 3)^2 + 1$

  b) $y = \dfrac{1}{x + 5}$

  c) $y = \sqrt{1 - 2x}$

Quadratic Functions

7. Determine the equation of a quadratic function
that satisfies each set of conditions.

  a) x-intercepts 1 and -1, y-intercept 3

  b) x-intercept 3, and passing through the
  point $(1, -2)$

  c) x-intercepts $-\dfrac{1}{2}$ and 2, y-intercept -4

8. Determine the x-intercepts, the vertex, the direction of opening, and the domain and range of each quadratic function. Then, graph the function.

a) $y = (x + 6)(2x - 5)$

b) $y = -2(x - 4)^2 + 1$

c) $y = -\dfrac{1}{4}(x - 3)^2 + 5$

d) $y = 5x^2 + 7x - 6$

e) $y = -3x^2 + 5x - 2$

Transformations

9. Identify each transformation of the function $y = f(x)$ as a vertical or horizontal translation, a stretch or compression, or a reflection in the x-axis or y-axis, or any combination of these.

a) $y = -4f(x)$

b) $y = \dfrac{1}{3}f(x)$

c) $y = f(2x)$

d) $y = f\left(-\dfrac{1}{3}x\right)$

e) $y = f(-x)$

10. **i)** Write an equation for the transformed function of each base function.

ii) Sketch a graph of each function.

iii) State the domain and range.

a) $f(x) = x$ is translated 2 units to the left and 3 units up.

b) $f(x) = x^2$ is stretched vertically by a factor of 5, reflected in the x-axis, and translated 2 units down and 1 unit to the left.

c) $f(x) = x$ is compressed horizontally by a factor of $\dfrac{1}{2}$, stretched vertically by a factor of 3, reflected in the x-axis, and translated 4 units to the left and 6 units up.

11. **i)** Describe the transformations that must be applied to the graph of each base function, $f(x)$, to obtain the given transformed function.

ii) Write an equation for the transformed function.

a) $f(x) = x$, $y = -2f(x + 3) + 1$

b) $f(x) = x^2$, $y = \dfrac{1}{3}f(x) - 2$

12. Describe the transformations that must be applied to the base function $y = x^2$ to obtain the function $y = 3\left[-\dfrac{1}{2}(x - 1)\right]^2 + 2$.

PROBLEM

Mathematical shapes and curves surround us. They are found in the designs of buildings, bridges, vehicles, furniture, containers, jewellery, games, cake decorations, fabrics, amusement parks, golf courses, art, and almost everywhere else! Some careers that involve working with mathematical designs are civil engineering, architectural design, computer graphics design, interior design, and landscape architecture.

Throughout this chapter, you will explore how the curves represented by polynomial functions are applied in various design-related fields.

Power Functions

A rock that is tossed into the water of a calm lake creates ripples that move outward in a circular pattern. The area, A, spanned by the ripples can be modelled by the function $A(r) = \pi r^2$, where r is the radius. The volume, V, of helium in a spherical balloon can be modelled by the function $V(r) = \frac{4}{3}\pi r^3$, where r is again the radius. The functions that represent each situation are called **power functions**. A power function is the simplest type of **polynomial function** and has the form $f(x) = ax^n$, where x is a variable, a is a real number, and n is a whole number.

CONNECTIONS

Polynomials are the building blocks of algebra. Polynomial functions can be used to create a variety of other types of functions and are important in many areas of mathematics, including calculus and numerical analysis. Outside mathematics, the basic equations in economics and many physical sciences are polynomial equations.

A polynomial expression is an expression of the form

$$a_n x^n + a_{n-1} x^{n-1} + a_{n-2} x^{n-2} + \ldots + a_3 x^3 + a_2 x^2 + a_1 x + a_0,$$

where

- n is a whole number
- x is a variable
- the **coefficients** $a_0, a_1, \ldots, a_n$ are real numbers
- the **degree** of the function is n, the exponent of the greatest power of x
- a_n, the coefficient of the greatest power of x, is the **leading coefficient**
- a_0, the term without a variable, is the **constant term**

A **polynomial function** has the form
$$f(x) = a_n x^n + a_{n-1} x^{n-1} + a_{n-2} x^{n-2} + \ldots + a_3 x^3 + a_2 x^2 + a_1 x + a_0$$

Polynomial functions are typically written in descending order of powers of x. The exponents in a polynomial do not need to decrease consecutively; that is, some terms may have zero as a coefficient. For example, $f(x) = 4x^3 + 2x - 1$ is still a polynomial function even though there is no x^2-term. A constant function, of the form $f(x) = a_0$, is also a type of polynomial function (where $n = 0$), as you can write the constant term a_0 in the form $a_0 x^0$.

1. Match each graph with the corresponding function. Justify your choices. Use a graphing calculator if necessary.

Tools
• graphing calculator

a) $y = x$

b) $y = x^2$

c) $y = x^3$

d) $y = x^4$

e) $y = x^5$

f) $y = x^6$

i)

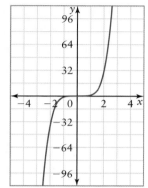

ii)

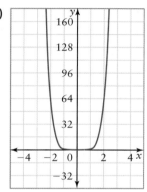

CONNECTIONS

Some power functions have special names that are associated with their degree.

Power Function	Degree	Name
$y = a$	0	constant
$y = ax$	1	linear
$y = ax^2$	2	quadratic
$y = ax^3$	3	cubic
$y = ax^4$	4	quartic
$y = ax^5$	5	quintic

iii)

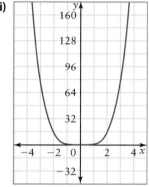

iv)

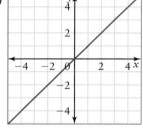

v)

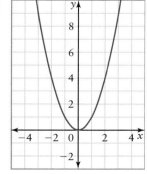

vi)

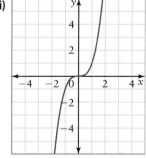

Recall that a relation is a function if for every x-value there is only one y-value. The graph of a relation represents a function if it passes the vertical line test, that is, if a vertical line drawn anywhere along the graph intersects that graph at no more than one point.

The **end behaviour** of the graph of a function is the behaviour of the y-values as x increases (that is, as x approaches positive infinity, written as $x \rightarrow \infty$) and as x decreases (that is, as x approaches negative infinity, written as $x \rightarrow -\infty$).

CONNECTIONS

• A graph has **line symmetry** if there is a line $x = a$ that divides the graph into two parts such that each part is a reflection of the other in the line $x = a$.

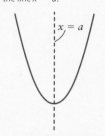

• A graph has **point symmetry** about a point (a, b) if each part of the graph on one side of (a, b) can be rotated 180° to coincide with part of the graph on the other side of (a, b).

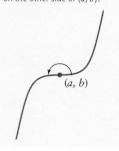

2. a) **Reflect** Decide whether each graph in step 1 represent a linear, a quadratic, a cubic, a quartic, or a quintic function. Justify your answer.

   b) **Reflect** Explain why each graph in step 1 represents a function.

3. a) State these key features for each graph:

   i) the domain

   ii) the range

   iii) the intercepts

   b) Describe the end behaviour of each graph as

   i) $x \rightarrow \infty$

   ii) $x \rightarrow -\infty$

4. a) Which graphs have both ends extending upward in quadrants 1 and 2 (that is, start high and end high)?

   b) Decide whether each graph has line symmetry or point symmetry. Explain.

   c) **Reflect** Describe how the graphs are similar. How are the equations similar?

5. a) Which graphs have one end extending downward in quadrant 3 (start low) and the other end extending upward in quadrant 1 (end high)?

   b) Decide whether each graph has line symmetry or point symmetry. Explain.

   c) **Reflect** Describe how the graphs are similar. How are the equations similar?

6. **Reflect** Summarize your findings for each group of power functions in a table like this one.

Key Features of the Graph	$y = x^n$, n is odd	$y = x^n$, n is even
Domain		
Range		
Symmetry		
End Behaviour		

7. a) Graph the function $y = x^n$ for $n = 2$, 4, and 6.

   b) Describe the similarities and differences between the graphs.

   c) **Reflect** Predict what will happen to the graph of $y = x^n$ for larger even values of n.

   d) Check your prediction in part c) by graphing two other functions of this form.

8. a) Graph the function $y = x^n$ for $n = 1$, 3, and 5.

   b) Describe the similarities and differences between the graphs.

   c) **Reflect** Predict what will happen to the graph of $y = x^n$ for larger odd values of n.

   d) Check your prediction in part c) by graphing two more functions of this form.

Determine which functions are polynomials. Justify your answer. State the degree and the leading coefficient of each polynomial function.

a) $g(x) = \sin x$

b) $f(x) = 2x^4$

c) $y = x^3 - 5x^2 + 6x - 8$

d) $g(x) = 3^x$

Solution

a) $g(x) = \sin x$

This a trigonometric function, not a polynomial function.

b) $f(x) = -2x^4$

This is a polynomial function of degree 4. The leading coefficient is -2.

c) $y = x^3 - 5x^2 + 6x - 8$

This is a polynomial function of degree 3. The leading coefficient is 1.

d) $g(x) = 3^x$

This is not a polynomial function but an exponential function, since the base is a number and the exponent is a variable.

Interval Notation

In this course, you will often describe the features of the graphs of a variety of types of functions in relation to real-number values. Sets of real numbers may be described in a variety of ways:

- as an inequality, $-3 < x \leq 5$

- in interval (or bracket) notation $(-3, 5]$

- graphically, on a number line

Intervals that are infinite are expressed using the symbol ∞ (infinity) or $-\infty$ (negative infinity).

Square brackets indicate that the end value is included in the interval, and round brackets indicate that the end value is not included.

A round bracket is used at infinity since the symbol ∞ means "without bound."

Below is a summary of all possible intervals for real numbers a and b, where $a < b$.

Bracket Interval	Inequality	Number Line	In Words
			The set of all real numbers x such that
(a, b)	$a < x < b$		x is greater than a and less than b
$(a, b]$	$a < x \leq b$		x is greater than a and less than or equal to b
$[a, b)$	$a \leq x < b$		x is greater than or equal to a and less than b
$[a, b]$	$a \leq x \leq b$		x is greater than or equal to a and less than or equal to b
$[a, \infty)$	$x \geq a$		x is greater than or equal to a
$(-\infty, a]$	$x \leq a$		x is less than or equal to a
(a, ∞)	$x > a$		x is greater than a
$(-\infty, a)$	$x < a$		x is less than a
$(-\infty, \infty)$	$-\infty < x < \infty$		x is an element of the real numbers

Example 2 | Connect the Equations and Features of the Graphs of Power Functions

For each function
i) state the domain and range
ii) describe the end behaviour
iii) identify any symmetry

a)
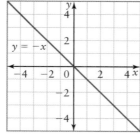

$y = -x$

b)
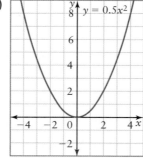

$y = 0.5x^2$

c)
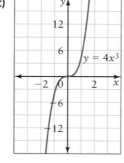

$y = 4x^3$

> **Solution**

a) $y = -x$

  i) domain $\{x \in \mathbb{R}\}$ or $(-\infty, \infty)$; range $\{y \in \mathbb{R}\}$ or $(-\infty, \infty)$

  ii) The graph extends from quadrant 4 to quadrant 2.
  Thus, as $x \to -\infty$, $y \to \infty$, and as $x \to \infty$, $y \to -\infty$.

  iii) The graph has point symmetry about the origin $(0, 0)$.

b) $y = 0.5x^2$

  i) domain $\{x \in \mathbb{R}\}$ or $(-\infty, \infty)$; range $\{y \in \mathbb{R}, y \geq 0\}$ or $[0, \infty)$

  ii) The graph extends from quadrant 2 to quadrant 1.
  Thus, as $x \to -\infty$, $y \to \infty$, and as $x \to \infty$, $y \to \infty$.

  iii) The graph has line symmetry in the y-axis.

c) $y = 4x^3$

  i) domain $\{x \in \mathbb{R}\}$ or $(-\infty, \infty)$; range $\{y \in \mathbb{R}\}$ or $(-\infty, \infty)$

  ii) The graph extends from quadrant 3 to quadrant 1.
  Thus, as $x \to -\infty$, $y \to -\infty$, and as $x \to \infty$, $y \to \infty$.

  iii) The graph has point symmetry about the origin.

Example 3	Describe the End Behaviour of Power Functions

Write each function in the appropriate row of the second column of the table. Give reasons for your choices.

$y = 2x$ $y = 5x^6$ $y = -3x^2$ $y = x^7$

$y = -\dfrac{2}{5}x^9$ $y = -4x^5$ $y = x^{10}$ $y = -0.5x^8$

End Behaviour	Function	Reasons
Extends from quadrant 3 to quadrant 1		
Extends from quadrant 2 to quadrant 4		
Extends from quadrant 2 to quadrant 1		
Extends from quadrant 3 to quadrant 4		

> **Solution**

End Behaviour	Function	Reasons
Extends from quadrant 3 to quadrant 1	$y = 2x$, $y = x^7$	odd exponent, positive coefficient
Extends from quadrant 2 to quadrant 4	$y = -\dfrac{2}{5}x^9$, $y = -4x^5$	odd exponent, negative coefficient
Extends from quadrant 2 to quadrant 1	$y = 5x^6$, $y = x^{10}$	even exponent, positive coefficient
Extends from quadrant 3 to quadrant 4	$y = -3x^2$, $y = -0.5x^8$	even exponent, negative coefficient

| Example 4 | Connecting Power Functions and Volume |

Helium is pumped into a large spherical balloon designed to advertise a new product. The volume, V, in cubic metres, of helium in the balloon is given by the function $V(r) = \frac{4}{3}\pi r^3$, where r is the radius of the balloon, in metres, and $r \in [0, 5]$.

a) Graph $V(r)$.

b) State the domain and range in this situation.

c) Describe the similarities and differences between the graph of $V(r)$ and the graph of $y = x^3$.

> **Solution**

a) Make a table of values, plot the points, and connect them using a smooth curve.

r (m)	$V(r) = \frac{4}{3}\pi r^3$ (m³)
0	$\frac{4}{3}\pi(0)^3 = 0$
1	$\frac{4}{3}\pi(1)^3 \doteq 4.2$
2	$\frac{4}{3}\pi(2)^3 \doteq 33.5$
3	$\frac{4}{3}\pi(3)^3 \doteq 113.1$
4	$\frac{4}{3}\pi(4)^3 \doteq 268.1$
5	$\frac{4}{3}\pi(5)^3 \doteq 523.6$

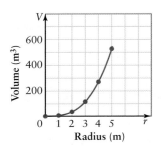

b) The domain is $r \in [0, 5]$. The range is approximately $V \in [0, 523.6]$.

c) The graph of $y = x^3$ is shown.

Similarities: The functions $V(r) = \frac{4}{3}\pi r^3$ and $y = x^3$ are both cubic, with positive leading coefficients. Both graphs pass through the origin $(0, 0)$ and have one end that extends upward in quadrant 1.

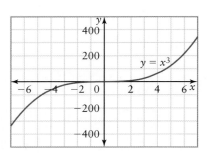

Differences: the graph of $V(r)$ has a restricted domain. Since the two functions are both cubic power functions that have different leading coefficients, all points on each graph, other than $(0, 0)$, are different.

- A polynomial expression has the form
$$a_n x^n + a_{n-1} x^{n-1} + a_{n-2} x^{n-2} + \ldots + a_3 x^3 + a_2 x^2 + a_1 x + a_0$$
where

  - n is a whole number
  - x is a variable
  - the coefficients $a_0, a_1, \ldots, a_n$ are real numbers
  - the degree of the function is n, the exponent of the greatest power of x
  - a_n, the coefficient of the greatest power of x, is the leading coefficient
  - a_0, the term without a variable, is the constant term

- A polynomial function has the form
$$f(x) = a_n x^n + a_{n-1} x^{n-1} + a_{n-2} x^{n-2} + \ldots + a_2 x^2 + a_1 x + a_0$$

- A power function is a polynomial of the form $y = ax^n$, where n is a whole number.

- Power functions have similar characteristics depending on whether their degree is even or odd.

- Even-degree power functions have line symmetry in the y-axis, $x = 0$.

- Odd-degree power functions have point symmetry about the origin, $(0, 0)$.

Communicate Your Understanding

C1 Explain why the function $y = 3$ is a polynomial function.

C2 How can you use a graph to tell whether the leading coefficient of a power function is positive or negative?

C3 How can you use a graph to tell whether the degree of a power function is even or odd?

C4 State a possible equation for a power function whose graph extends

    a) from quadrant 3 to quadrant 1

    b) from quadrant 2 to quadrant 1

    c) from quadrant 2 to quadrant 4

    d) from quadrant 3 to quadrant 4

A   Practise

For help with questions 1 and 2, refer to Example 1.

1. Identify whether each is a polynomial function. Justify your answer.

    a) $p(x) = \cos x$ **b)** $h(x) = -7x$

    c) $f(x) = 2x^4$ **d)** $y = 3x^5 - 2x^3 + x^2 - 1$

    e) $k(x) = 8^x$ **f)** $y = x^{-3}$

2. State the degree and the leading coefficient of each polynomial.

    a) $y = 5x^4 - 3x^3 + 4$ **b)** $y = -x + 2$

    c) $y = 8x^2$ **d)** $y = -\dfrac{x^3}{4} + 4x - 3$

    e) $y = -5$ **f)** $y = x^2 - 3x$

For help with question 3, refer to Example 2.

3. Consider each graph.

   i) Does it represent a power function of even degree? odd degree? Explain.

   ii) State the sign of the leading coefficient. Justify your answer.

   iii) State the domain and range.

   iv) Identify any symmetry.

   v) Describe the end behaviour.

a)

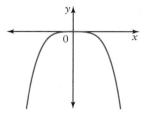

b)

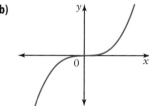

c)

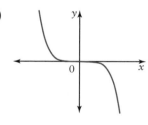

d)

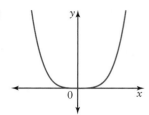

e)

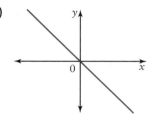

For help with question 4, refer to Example 3.

4. Copy and complete the table for the following functions.

$$y = -x^3 \qquad y = \frac{3}{7}x^2 \qquad y = 5x$$

$$y = 4x^5 \qquad y = -x^6 \qquad y = -0.1x^{11}$$

$$y = 2x^4 \qquad y = -9x^{10}$$

End Behaviour	Function	Reasons
Extends from quadrant 3 to quadrant 1		
Extends from quadrant 2 to quadrant 4		
Extends from quadrant 2 to quadrant 1		
Extends from quadrant 3 to quadrant 4		

B **Connect and Apply**

For help with questions 5 and 6, refer to Example 4.

5. As a tropical storm intensifies and reaches hurricane status, it takes on a circular shape that expands outward from the eye of the storm. The area, A, in square kilometres, spanned by a storm with radius, r, in kilometres, can be modelled by the function $A(r) = \pi r^2$.

   a) Graph $A(r)$ for $r \in [0, 10]$.

   b) State the domain and range.

   c) Describe the similarities and differences between the graph of $A(r)$ and the graph of $y = x^2$.

6. The circumference, C, in kilometres, of the tropical storm in question 5 can be modelled by the function $C(r) = 2\pi r$.

   a) Graph $C(r)$ for $r \in [0, 10]$.

   b) State the domain and range.

   c) Describe the similarities and differences between the graph of $C(r)$ and the graph of $y = x$.

7. Determine whether each graph represents a power function, an exponential function, a periodic function, or none of these. Justify your choice.

CONNECTIONS

You worked with periodic functions when you studied trigonometric functions in grade 11. Periodic functions repeat at regular intervals.

a)

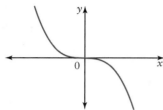

b)

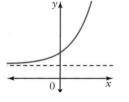

c)

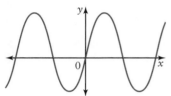

d)

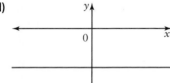

e)

f)

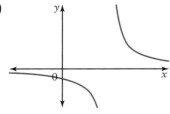

g)

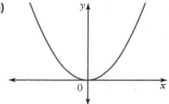

8. Use Technology

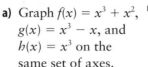

a) Graph $f(x) = x^3 + x^2$, $g(x) = x^3 - x$, and $h(x) = x^3$ on the same set of axes.

b) Compare and describe the key features of the graphs of these functions.

9. Use Technology

a) Graph $f(x) = x^4 + x$, $g(x) = x^4 - x^2$, and $h(x) = x^4$ on the same set of axes.

b) Compare and describe the key features of the graphs of these functions.

10. Describe the similarities and differences between the line $y = x$ and power functions with odd degree greater than one. Use graphs to support your answer.

11. Describe the similarities and differences between the parabola $y = x^2$ and power functions with even degree greater than two. Use graphs to support your answer.

12. a) Graph the functions $y = x^3$, $y = x^3 - 2$, and $y = x^3 + 2$ on the same set of axes. Compare the graphs. Describe how the graphs are related.

b) Repeat part a) for the functions $y = x^4$, $y = x^4 - 2$, and $y = x^4 + 2$.

c) Make a conjecture about the relationship between the graphs of $y = x^n$ and $y = x^n + c$, where $c \in \mathbb{R}$ and n is a whole number.

d) Test the accuracy of your conjecture for different values of n and c.

13. **Chapter Problem** Part of a computer graphic designer's job may be to create and manipulate electronic images found in video games. Power functions define curves that are useful in the design of characters, objects, and background scenery. Domain restrictions allow two or more curves to be combined to create a particular form. For example, a character's eye could be created using parabolas with restricted domains.

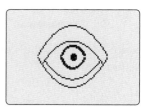

Describe the type(s) of power function(s) that could be used to design two of the following in a new video game. Provide equations and sketches of your functions. Include the domain and range of the functions you use.

• the path of a river that extends from the southwest to the northeast part of a large forest

• the cross-section of a valley that lies between two mountain ranges

• a deep canyon where the river flows

• characters' facial expressions

• a lightning bolt

• horseshoe tracks in the sand

C Extend and Challenge

14. **Use Technology**

   a) Graph each pair of functions. What do you notice? Provide an algebraic explanation for what you observe.

   i) $y = (-x)^2$ and $y = x^2$

   ii) $y = (-x)^4$ and $y = x^4$

   iii) $y = (-x)^6$ and $y = x^6$

   b) Repeat part a) for each of the following pairs of functions.

   i) $y = (-x)^3$ and $y = -x^3$

   ii) $y = (-x)^5$ and $y = -x^5$

   iii) $y = (-x)^7$ and $y = -x^7$

   c) Describe what you have learned about functions of the form $y = (-x)^n$, where n is a non-negative integer. Support your answer with examples.

15. a) Make a conjecture about the relationship between the graphs of $y = x^n$ and $y = ax^n$ for $a \in \mathbb{R}$.

   b) Test your conjecture using different values of n and a.

16. a) Describe the relationship between the graph of $y = x^2$ and the graph of $y = 2(x - 3)^2 + 1$.

   b) Predict the relationship between the graph of $y = x^4$ and the graph of $y = 2(x - 3)^4 + 1$.

   c) Verify the accuracy of your prediction by sketching the graphs in part b).

17. a) Use the results of question 16 to predict a relationship between the graph of $y = x^3$ and the graph of $y = a(x - h)^3 + k$.

   b) Verify the accuracy of your prediction in part a) by sketching two functions of the form $y = a(x - h)^3 + k$.

18. **Math Contest** Determine the number of digits in the expansion of $(2^{120})(5^{125})$ without using a calculator or computer.

19. **Math Contest** Find the coordinates of the two points that trisect the line segment with endpoints A(2, 3) and B(8, 2).

Characteristics of Polynomial Functions

In Section 1.1, you explored the features of power functions, which are single-term polynomial functions. Many polynomial functions that arise from real-world applications such as profit, volume, and population growth are made up of two or more terms. For example, the function $r = -0.7d^3 + d^2$, which relates a patient's reaction time, $r(d)$, in seconds, to a dose, d, in millilitres, of a particular drug is polynomial.

In this section, you will explore and identify the characteristics of the graphs and equations of general polynomial functions and establish the relationship between finite differences and the equations of polynomial functions.

Investigate 1 **What are the key features of the graphs of polynomial functions?**

A: *Polynomial Functions of Odd Degree*

1. a) Graph each cubic function on a different set of axes using a graphing calculator. Sketch the results.

Group A

i) $y = x^3$

ii) $y = x^3 + x^2 - 4x - 4$

iii) $y = x^3 + 5x^2 + 3x - 9$

Group B

i) $y = -x^3$

ii) $y = -x^3 - x^2 + 4x + 4$

iii) $y = -x^3 - 5x^2 - 3x + 9$

b) Compare the graphs in each group. Describe their similarities and differences in terms of

 i) end behaviour

 ii) number of minimum points and number of maximum points

 iii) number of **local minimum** and number of **local maximum** points, that is, points that are minimum or maximum points on some interval around that point

 iv) number of x-intercepts

c) Compare the two groups of graphs. Describe their similarities and differences as in part b).

Tools

• graphing calculator

Optional

• computer with *The Geometer's Sketchpad®*

CONNECTIONS

In this graph, the point $(-1, 4)$ is a local maximum, and the point $(1, -4)$ is a local minimum.

Notice that the point $(-1, 4)$ is not a maximum point of the function, since other points on the graph of the function are greater. Maximum or minimum points of a function are sometimes called absolute, or global, to distinguish them from local maximum and minimum points.

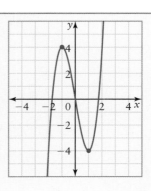

d) **Reflect** Which group of graphs is similar to the graph of

    i) $y = x$?

    ii) $y = -x$?

  Explain how they are similar.

2. **a)** Graph each quintic function on a different set of axes using a graphing calculator. Sketch the results.

    i) $y = x^5$

    ii) $y = x^5 + 3x^4 - x^3 - 7x^2 + 4$

    iii) $y = -x^5 + x^4 + 9x^3 - 13x^2 - 8x + 12$

  b) Compare the graphs. Describe their similarities and differences.

3. **Reflect** Use the results from steps 1 and 2 to answer each question.

  a) What are the similarities and differences between the graphs of linear, cubic, and quintic functions?

  b) What are the minimum and the maximum numbers of x-intercepts of graphs of cubic polynomial functions?

  c) Describe the relationship between the number of minimum and maximum points, the number of local minimum and local maximum points, and the degree of a polynomial function.

  d) What is the relationship between the sign of the leading coefficient and the end behaviour of graphs of polynomial functions with odd degree?

  e) Do you think the results in part d) are true for all polynomial functions with odd degree? Justify your answer.

B: Polynomial Functions of Even Degree

1. **a)** Graph each quartic function.

    Group A

    i) $y = x^4$

    ii) $y = x^4 - x^3 - 6x^2 + 4x + 8$

    iii) $y = x^4 - 3x^3 - 3x^2 + 11x - 4$

    Group B

    i) $y = -x^4$

    ii) $y = -x^4 - 5x^3 + 5x + 10$

    iii) $y = -x^4 + 3x^3 + 3x^2 - 11x + 4$

  b) Compare the graphs in each group. Describe their similarities and differences in terms of

    i) end behaviour

    ii) number of maximum and number of minimum points

    iii) number of local minimum and number of local maximum points

    iv) number of x-intercepts

  c) Compare the two groups of graphs. Describe their similarities and differences as in part b).

  d) **Reflect** Explain which group has graphs that are similar to the graph of

    i) $y = x^2$

    ii) $y = -x^2$

2. Reflect Use the results from step 1 to answer each question.

a) Describe the similarities and differences between the graphs of quadratic and quartic polynomial functions.

b) What are the minimum and the maximum numbers of x-intercepts of graphs of quartic polynomials?

c) Describe the relationship between the number of minimum and maximum points, the number of local maximum and local minimum points, and the degree of a polynomial function.

d) What is the relationship between the sign of the leading coefficient and the end behaviour of the graphs of polynomial functions with even degree?

e) Do you think the above results are true for all polynomial functions with even degree? Justify your answer.

| Investigate 2 | What is the relationship between finite differences and the equation of a polynomial function? |

1. Construct a finite difference table for $y = x^3$.

Tools

• graphing calculator

Method 1: *Use Pencil and Paper*

		Differences		
x	**y**	**First**	**Second**	**...**
−3				
−2				
−1				
0				
1				
2				
3				
4				

a) Create a finite difference table like this one.

b) Use the equation to determine the y-values in column 2.

c) Complete each column and extend the table as needed, until you get a constant difference.

Method 2: *Use a Graphing Calculator*

To construct a table of finite differences on a graphing calculator, press (STAT) **1**.

Enter the x-values in **L1**.

To enter the y-values for the function $y = x^3$ in **L2**, scroll up and right to select **L2**.

Enter the function, using **L1** to represent the variable x, by pressing (ALPHA) ["] (2nd) [L1] (^) 3 (ALPHA) ["].

- Press $\boxed{\text{ENTER}}$.

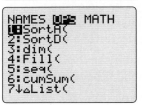

To determine the first differences, scroll up and right to select **L3**.
- Press $\boxed{\text{ALPHA}}$ ["] and then $\boxed{\text{2nd}}$ [LIST].
- Cursor right to select **OPS**.

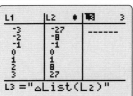

- Press 7 to select **ΔList(**.
- Press $\boxed{\text{2nd}}$ [L2] $\boxed{)}$ and then $\boxed{\text{ALPHA}}$ ["].

- Press $\boxed{\text{ENTER}}$.

The first differences are displayed in **L3**.

Determine the second differences and the third differences in a similar way.

2. Construct a finite difference table for

   a) $y = -2x^3$

   b) $y = x^4$

   c) $y = -2x^4$

3. a) What is true about the third differences of a cubic function? the fourth differences of a quartic function?

   b) How is the sign of the leading coefficient related to the sign of the constant value of the finite differences?

   c) How is the value of the leading coefficient related to the constant value of the finite differences?

   d) **Reflect** Make a conjecture about the relationship between constant finite differences and

   i) the degree of a polynomial function

   ii) the sign of the leading coefficient

   iii) the value of the leading coefficient

   e) Verify your conjectures by constructing finite difference tables for the polynomial functions $f(x) = 3x^3 - 4x^2 + 1$ and $g(x) = -2x^4 + x^3 + 3x - 1$.

Example 1 | Match a Polynomial Function With Its Graph

Determine the key features of the graph of each polynomial function. Use these features to match each function with its graph. State the number of x-intercepts, the number of maximum and minimum points, and the number of local maximum and local minimum points for the graph of each function. How are these features related to the degree of the function?

a) $f(x) = 2x^3 - 4x^2 + x + 1$ **b)** $g(x) = -x^4 + 10x^2 + 5x - 4$

c) $h(x) = -2x^5 + 5x^3 - x$ **d)** $p(x) = x^6 - 16x^2 + 3$

i)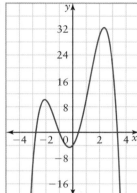

ii)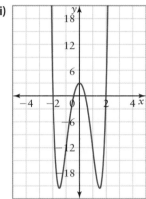

iii)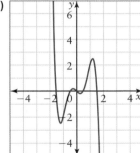

iv)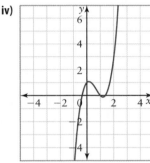

Solution

a) The function $f(x) = 2x^3 - 4x^2 + x + 1$ is cubic, with a positive leading coefficient. The graph extends from quadrant 3 to quadrant 1. The y-intercept is 1. Graph iv) corresponds to this equation.

There are three x-intercepts and the degree is three. The function has one local maximum point and one local minimum point, a total of two, which is one less than the degree. There is no maximum point and no minimum point.

b) The function $g(x) = -x^4 + 10x^2 + 5x - 4$ is quartic, with a negative leading coefficient. The graph extends from quadrant 3 to quadrant 4. The y-intercept is -4. Graph i) corresponds to this equation.

There are four x-intercepts and the degree is four. There is one maximum point and no minimum point. The graph has two local maximum points and one local minimum point, for a total of three, which is one less than the degree.

c) The function $h(x) = -2x^5 + 5x^3 - x$ is quintic, with a negative leading coefficient. The graph extends from quadrant 2 to quadrant 4. The y-intercept is 0. Graph iii) corresponds to this equation.

There are five x-intercepts and the degree is five. There is no maximum point and no minimum point. The graph has two local maximum points and two local minimum points, for a total of four, which is one less than the degree.

d) The function $p(x) = x^6 - 16x^2 + 3$ is a function of degree five with a positive leading coefficient. The graph extends from quadrant 2 to quadrant 1. The y-intercept is 3. Graph ii) corresponds to this equation.

There are four x-intercepts and the degree is six. The graph has two minimum points and no maximum point. The graph has one local maximum point and two local minimum points, for a total of three (three less than the degree).

CONNECTIONS

For any positive integer n, the product

$n \times (n - 1) \times \ldots \times 2 \times 1$

may be expressed in a shorter form as $n!$, read " **n factorial** ."

$5! = 5 \times 4 \times 3 \times 2 \times 1$
$\quad = 120$

Finite Differences

For a polynomial function of degree n, where n is a positive integer, the nth differences

- are equal (or constant)
- have the same sign as the leading coefficient
- are equal to $a[n \times (n - 1) \times \ldots \times 2 \times 1]$, where a is the leading coefficient

Example 2	Identify Types of Polynomial Functions From Finite Differences

Each table of values represents a polynomial function. Use finite differences to determine

i) the degree of the polynomial function

ii) the sign of the leading coefficient

iii) the value of the leading coefficient

a)

x	y
−3	−36
−2	−12
−1	−2
0	0
1	0
2	4
3	18
4	48

b)

x	y
−2	−54
−1	−8
0	0
1	6
2	22
3	36
4	12
5	−110

Solution

Construct a finite difference table. Determine finite differences until they are constant.

a)   i)

x	y	First Differences	Second Differences	Third Differences
-3	-36			
-2	-12	$-12 - (-36) = 24$		
-1	-2	$-2 - (-12) = 10$	$10 - 24 = -14$	
0	0	$0 - (-2) = 2$	$2 - 10 = -8$	$-8 - (-14) = 6$
1	0	$0 - 0 = 0$	$0 - 2 = -2$	$-2 - (-8) = 6$
2	4	$4 - 0 = 4$	$4 - 0 = 4$	$4 - (-2) = 6$
3	18	$18 - 4 = 14$	$14 - 4 = 10$	$10 - 4 = 6$
4	48	$48 - 18 = 30$	$30 - 14 = 16$	$16 - 10 = 6$

The third differences are constant. So, the table of values represents a cubic function. The degree of the function is three.

ii) The leading coefficient is positive, since 6 is positive.

iii) The value of the leading coefficient is the value of a such that
$$6 = a[n \times (n - 1) \times \ldots \times 2 \times 1].$$

Substitute $n = 3$:
$$6 = a(3 \times 2 \times 1)$$
$$6 = 6a$$
$$a = 1$$

CONNECTIONS

You will learn why the constant finite differences of a degree-n polynomial with leading coefficient a are equal to $a \times n!$ if you study calculus.

b)   i)

x	y	First Differences	Second Differences	Third Differences	Fourth Differences
-2	-54				
-1	-8	46			
0	0	8	-38		
1	6	6	-2	36	
2	22	16	10	12	-24
3	36	14	-2	-12	-24
4	12	-24	-38	-36	-24
5	-110	-122	-98	-60	-24

Since the fourth differences are equal and negative, the table of values represents a quartic function. The degree of the function is four.

ii) This polynomial has a negative leading coefficient.

iii) The value of the leading coefficient is the value of a such that
$$-24 = a[n \times (n - 1) \times \ldots \times 2 \times 1].$$

Substitute $n = 4$:
$$-24 = a(4 \times 3 \times 2 \times 1)$$
$$-24 = 24a$$
$$a = -1$$

Example 3 | Application of a Polynomial Function

A new antibacterial spray is tested on a bacterial culture. The table shows the population, P, of the bacterial culture t minutes after the spray is applied.

t (min)	P
0	800
1	799
2	782
3	737
4	652
5	515
6	314
7	37

a) Use finite differences to

   i) identify the type of polynomial function that models the population growth

   ii) determine the value of the leading coefficient

b) Use the regression feature of a graphing calculator to determine an equation for the function that models this situation.

Solution

- Press (STAT) 1. Enter the t-values in **L1** and the P-values in **L2**.

Use the calculator to calculate the first differences in **L3** as follows.

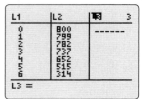

- Press (ALPHA) ['] and then (2nd) [LIST].
- Scroll right to select **OPS**.

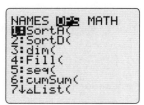

- Press 7 to select **ΔList(**.
- Press (2nd) [L2] ( ) and then (ALPHA) ['].

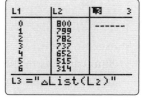

- Press (ENTER).

The first differences are displayed in **L3**.

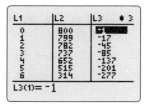

Repeat the steps to determine the second differences in **L4** and the third differences in **L5**.

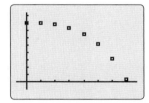

a) **i)** Since the third differences are constant, the population models a cubic function.

ii) The value of the leading coefficient is the value of a such that
$$-12 = a[n \times (n-1) \times \ldots \times 2 \times 1].$$
Substitute $n = 3$:
$$-12 = a(3 \times 2 \times 1)$$
$$-12 = 6a$$
$$a = -2$$

b) Create a scatter plot as follows.

- Press $\boxed{\text{2nd}}$ [STAT PLOT] **1** $\boxed{\text{ENTER}}$.

Turn on **Plot 1** by making sure **On** is highlighted, **Type** is set to the graph type you prefer, and **L1** and **L2** appear after **Xlist** and **Ylist**.

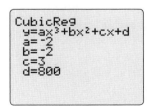

Display the graph as follows.

- Press $\boxed{\text{ZOOM}}$ **9** for **ZoomStat**.

Determine the equation of the curve of best fit as follows.

- Press $\boxed{\text{STAT}}$.

Move the cursor to **CALC**, and then press **6** to select a cubic regression function, since we know $n = 3$.

- Press $\boxed{\text{2nd}}$ [L1], $\boxed{\text{2nd}}$ [L2] $\boxed{,}$ $\boxed{\text{VARS}}$.

- Cursor over to **Y-VARS**.

- Press **1** twice to store the equation of the curve of best fit in **Y1** of the equation editor.

- Press $\boxed{\text{ENTER}}$ to display the results.

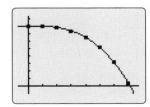

Substitute the values of a, b, c, and d into the general cubic equation as shown on the calculator screen.

An equation that models the data is
$y = -2x^3 - 2x^2 + 3x + 800$.

- Press $\boxed{\text{GRAPH}}$ to plot the curve.

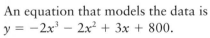

Key Features of Graphs of Polynomial Functions With Odd Degree

Positive Leading Coefficient

- the graph extends from quadrant 3 to quadrant 1 (similar to the graph of $y = x$)

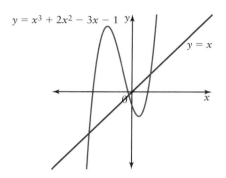

Negative Leading Coefficient

- the graph extends from quadrant 2 to quadrant 4 (similar to the graph of $y = -x$)

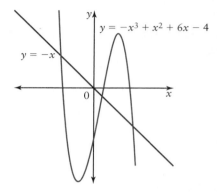

- Odd-degree polynomials have at least one x-intercept, up to a maximum of n x-intercepts, where n is the degree of the function.
- The domain of all odd-degree polynomials is $\{x \in \mathbb{R}\}$ and the range is $\{y \in \mathbb{R}\}$. Odd-degree functions have no maximum point and no minimum point.
- Odd-degree polynomials may have point symmetry.

Key Features of Graphs of Polynomial Functions With Even Degree

Positive Leading Coefficient

- the graph extends from quadrant 2 to quadrant 1 (similar to the graph of $y = x^2$)
- the range is $\{y \in \mathbb{R}, y \geq a\}$, where a is the minimum value of the function
- an even-degree polynomial with a positive leading coefficient will have at least one minimum point

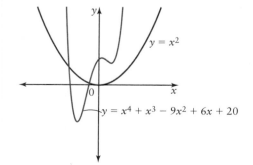

Negative Leading Coefficient

- the graph extends from quadrant 3 to quadrant 4 (similar to the graph of $y = -x^2$)
- the range is $\{y \in \mathbb{R}, y \leq a\}$, where a is the maximum value of the function
- an even-degree polynomial with a negative leading coefficient will have at least one maximum point

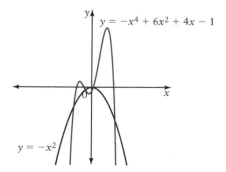

- Even-degree polynomials may have from zero to a maximum of n x-intercepts, where n is the degree of the function.
- The domain of all even-degree polynomials is $\{x \in \mathbb{R}\}$.
- Even-degree polynomials may have line symmetry.

Key Features of Graphs of Polynomial Functions

- A polynomial function of degree n, where n is a whole number greater than 1, may have at most $n - 1$ local minimum and local maximum points.
- For any polynomial function of degree n, the nth differences
  - are equal (or constant)
  - have the same sign as the leading coefficient
  - are equal to $a[n \times (n - 1) \times \ldots \times 2 \times 1]$, where a is the leading coefficient

Communicate Your Understanding

C1 Describe the similarities between

  a) the lines $y = x$ and $y = -x$ and the graphs of other odd-degree polynomial functions

  b) the parabolas $y = x^2$ and $y = -x^2$ and the graphs of other even-degree polynomial functions

C2 Discuss the relationship between the degree of a polynomial function and the following features of the corresponding graph:

  a) the number of x-intercepts

  b) the number of maximum and minimum points

  c) the number of local maximum and local minimum points

C3 Sketch the graph of a quartic function that

  a) has line symmetry

  b) does not have line symmetry

C4 Explain why even-degree polynomials have a restricted range. What does this tell you about the number of maximum or minimum points?

For help with questions 1 to 3, refer to Example 1.

1. Each graph represents a polynomial function of degree 3, 4, 5, or 6. Determine the least possible degree of the function corresponding to each graph. Justify your answer.

a)

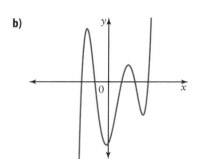

b)

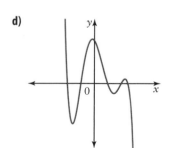

c)

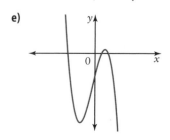

d)

e)

CONNECTIONS

The least possible degree refers to the fact that it is possible for the graphs of two polynomial functions with either odd degree or even degree to *appear* to be similar, even though one may have a higher degree than the other. For instance, the graphs of $y = (x - 2)^2(x + 2)^2$ and $y = (x - 2)^4(x + 2)^4$ have the same shape and the same x-intercepts, -2 and 2, but one function has a double root at each of these values, while the other has a quadruple root at each of these values.

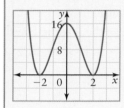

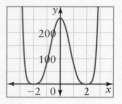

2. Refer to question 1. For each graph, do the following.

   a) State the sign of the leading coefficient. Justify your answer.

   b) Describe the end behaviour.

   c) Identify any symmetry.

   d) State the number of minimum and maximum points and local minimum and local maximum points. How are these related to the degree of the function?

3. Use the degree and the sign of the leading coefficient to

   i) describe the end behaviour of each polynomial function

   ii) state which finite differences will be constant

   iii) determine the value of the constant finite differences

   a) $f(x) = x^2 + 3x - 1$

   b) $g(x) = -4x^3 + 2x^2 - x + 5$

   c) $h(x) = -7x^4 + 2x^3 - 3x^2 + 4$

   d) $p(x) = 0.6x^5 - 2x^4 + 8x$

   e) $f(x) = 3 - x$

   f) $h(x) = -x^6 + 8x^3$

For help with question 4, refer to Example 2.

4. State the degree of the polynomial function that corresponds to each constant finite difference. Determine the value of the leading coefficient for each polynomial function.

a) second differences = -8

b) fourth differences = -48

c) third differences = -12

d) fourth differences = 24

e) third differences = 36

f) fifth differences = 60

B **Connect and Apply**

5. Determine whether each graph represents an even-degree or an odd-degree polynomial function. Explain your reasoning.

a)

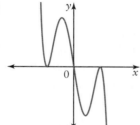

b)

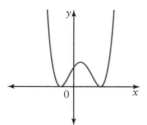

c)

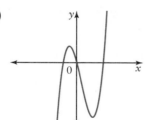

d)

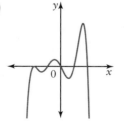

6. Refer to question 5. For each graph, do the following.

a) State the least possible degree.

b) State the sign of the leading coefficient.

c) Describe the end behaviour of the graph.

d) Identify the type of symmetry, if it exists.

For help with question 7, refer to Example 2.

7. Each table represents a polynomial function. Use finite differences to determine the following for each polynomial function.

i) the degree

ii) the sign of the leading coefficient

iii) the value of the leading coefficient

a)

x	y
−3	−45
−2	−16
−1	−3
0	0
1	−1
2	0
3	9
4	32

b)

x	y
−2	−40
−1	12
0	20
1	26
2	48
3	80
4	92
5	30

For help with questions 8 and 9, refer to Example 3.

8. A snowboard manufacturer determines that its profit, P, in thousands of dollars, can be modelled by the function $P(x) = x + 0.001\,25x^4 - 3$, where x represents the number, in hundreds, of snowboards sold.

a) What type of function is $P(x)$?

b) Without calculating, determine which finite differences are constant for this polynomial function. What is the value of the constant finite differences? Explain how you know.

c) Describe the end behaviour of this function, assuming that there are no restrictions on the domain.

d) State the restrictions on the domain in this situation.

e) What do the x-intercepts of the graph represent for this situation?

f) What is the profit from the sale of 3000 snowboards?

9. Use Technology The table shows the displacement, s, in metres, of an inner tube moving along a waterslide after time, t, in seconds.

t (s)	s (m)
0	10
1	34
2	42
3	46
4	58
5	90
6	154
7	262

a) Use finite differences to

   i) identify the type of polynomial function that models s

   ii) determine the value of the leading coefficient

b) Graph the data in the table using a graphing calculator. Use the regression feature of the graphing calculator to determine an equation for the function that models this situation.

10. a) Sketch graphs of $y = \sin x$ and $y = \cos x$.

b) Compare the graph of a periodic function to the graph of a polynomial function. Describe any similarities and differences. Refer to the end behaviour, local maximum and local minimum points, and maximum and minimum points.

11. The volume, V, in cubic centimetres, of a collection of open-topped boxes can be modelled by $V(x) = 4x^3 - 220x^2 + 2800x$, where x is the height of each box, in centimetres.

a) Graph $V(x)$. State the restrictions.

b) Fully factor $V(x)$. State the relationship between the factored form of the equation and the graph.

c) State the value of the constant finite differences for this function.

12. A medical researcher establishes that a patient's reaction time, r, in minutes, to a dose of a particular drug is $r(d) = -0.7d^3 + d^2$, where d is the amount of the drug, in millilitres, that is absorbed into the patient's blood.

a) What type of function is $r(d)$?

b) Without calculating the finite differences, state which finite differences are constant for this function. How do you know? What is the value of the constant differences?

c) Describe the end behaviour of this function if no restrictions are considered.

d) State the restrictions for this situation.

13. By analysing the impact of growing economic conditions, a demographer establishes that the predicted population, P, of a town t years from now can be modelled by the function $p(t) = 6t^4 - 5t^3 + 200t + 12\,000$.

a) Describe the key features of the graph represented by this function if no restrictions are considered.

b) What is the value of the constant finite differences?

c) What is the current population of the town?

d) What will the population of the town be 10 years from now?

e) When will the population of the town be approximately 175 000?

14. Consider the function $f(x) = x^3 + 2x^2 - 5x - 6$.

a) How do the degree and the sign of the leading coefficient correspond to the end behaviour of the polynomial function?

b) Sketch a graph of the polynomial function.

c) What can you tell about the value of the third differences for this function?

C ⟩ Extend and Challenge

15. Graph a polynomial function that satisfies each description.

a) a quartic function with a negative leading coefficient and three x-intercepts

b) a cubic function with a positive leading coefficient and two x-intercepts

c) a quadratic function with a positive leading coefficient and no x-intercepts

d) a quintic function with a negative leading coefficient and five x-intercepts

16. a) What possible numbers of x-intercepts can a quintic function have?

b) Sketch an example of a graph of a quintic function for each possibility in part a).

17. Use Technology

a) What type of polynomial function is each of the following? Justify your answer.

i) $f(x) = (x + 4)(x - 1)(2x + 5)$

ii) $f(x) = (x + 4)^2(x - 1)$

iii) $f(x) = (x + 4)^3$

b) Graph each function.

c) Describe the relationship between the x-intercepts and the equation of the function.

18. A storage tank is to be constructed in the shape of a cylinder such that the ratio of the radius, r, to the height of the tank is $1:3$.

a) Write a polynomial function to represent

i) the surface area of the tank in terms of r

ii) the volume of the tank in terms of r

b) Describe the key features of the graph that corresponds to each of the above functions.

19. Math Contest

a) Given the function $f(x) = x^3 - 2x$, sketch $y = f(|x|)$.

b) Sketch $g(x) = |x^2 - 1| - |x^2 - 4|$.

c) Sketch the region in the plane to show all points (x, y) such that $|x| + |y| \leq 2$.

CAREER CONNECTION

Davinder completed a 2-year course in mining engineering technology at a Canadian college. He works with an engineering and construction crew to blast openings in rock faces for road construction. In his job as the explosives specialist, he examines the structure of the rock in the blast area and determines the amounts and kinds of explosives needed to ensure that the blast is not only effective but also safe. He also considers environmental concerns such as vibration and noise. Davinder uses mathematical reasoning and a knowledge of physical principles to choose the correct formulas to solve problems. Davinder then creates a blast design and initiation sequence.

Equations and Graphs of Polynomial Functions

A rollercoaster is designed so that the shape of a section of the ride can be modelled by the function $f(x) = -0.000\,004x(x - 15)(x - 25)(x - 45)^2(x - 60) + 9$, $x \in [0, 60]$, where x is the time, in seconds, and $f(x)$ is the height of the ride above the ground, in metres, at time x.

What are the similarities and differences between this polynomial function and the ones studied in previous sections? What useful information does this form of the equation provide that can be used to sketch a graph to represent the path of the rollercoaster?

In this section, you will investigate the relationship between the factored form of a polynomial function and the x-intercepts of the corresponding graph. You will examine the effect of repeated factors on the graph of a polynomial function, and you will establish an algebraic method for determining whether a polynomial function has line symmetry or point symmetry.

| **Investigate 1** | **What is the connection between the factored form of a polynomial function and its graph?** |

Tools

• graphing calculator

Optional

• computer with *The Geometer's Sketchpad®*

1. a) Graph the function $y = x(x - 3)(x + 2)(x + 1)$.

b) From the graph, determine

   i) the degree of the polynomial function

   ii) the sign of the leading coefficient

   iii) the x-intercepts

   iv) the y-intercept

c) Refer to the graph in part a). The x-intercepts divide the x-axis into five intervals. Copy the table below and write the intervals in the first row. In the second row, indicate whether the function is positive (above the x-axis) or negative (below the x-axis) for the corresponding interval.

Interval					
Sign of $f(x)$					

d) Reflect

   i) How can you determine the degree and the sign of the leading coefficient from the equation?

   ii) What is the relationship between the x-intercepts and the equation of the function? the y-intercept and the equation of the function?

   iii) What happens to the sign of $f(x)$ near each x-intercept?

2. a) Graph each function on a separate set of axes. Sketch each graph in your notebook.

   i) $y = (x + 1)(x - 2)(x + 3)$

   ii) $y = (x - 2)^2(x + 3)$

   iii) $y = (x - 2)^3$

b) State the x-intercepts and the y-intercept of each graph in part a).

c) Reflect What is the relationship between the number of x-intercepts, the repeated factors in the equation of the function, and the sign of $f(x)$?

3. Repeat step 2 for the following polynomial functions:

   i) $y = -(x + 1)(x - 2)(x - 4)(x + 3)$

   ii) $y = -(x - 2)^2(x - 4)(x + 3)$

   iii) $y = -(x - 2)^4$

   iv) $y = -(x - 2)^2(x + 3)^2$

4. Reflect

a) Describe the effect on the graph of a polynomial function when a factor is repeated

   i) an even number of times

   ii) an odd number of times

b) What is the relationship between

   i) an even number of repeated factors and the sign of $f(x)$?

   ii) an odd number of repeated factors and the sign of $f(x)$?

5. a) Reflect Describe how a graph of a polynomial function can be sketched using the x-intercepts, the y-intercept, the sign of the leading coefficient, and the degree of the function.

b) Sketch a graph of $y = -2(x - 1)^2(x + 2)(x - 4)$. Use technology to verify your sketch.

c) Sketch a graph of each function. Use technology to verify your graph.

   i) $y = -(x + 4)(x - 1)^2$

   ii) $y = -(x - 1)^3$

   iii) $y = (x + 4)^2(x - 1)^2$

   iv) $y = (x + 4)^4$

The zeros of a polynomial function $y = f(x)$ correspond to the x-intercepts of the graph and to the roots of the corresponding equation $f(x) = 0$. For example, the function $f(x) = (x - 2)(x + 1)$ has zeros 2 and -1. These are the roots of the equation $(x - 2)(x + 1) = 0$.

If a polynomial function has a factor $(x - a)$ that is repeated n times, then $x = a$ is a zero of **order** n. The function $f(x) = (x - 2)(x + 1)^2$ has a zero of order 2 at $x = -1$ and the equation $(x - 2)(x + 1)^2 = 0$ has a double root at $x = -1$.

The graph of a polynomial function changes sign (from positive to negative or negative to positive) at zeros that are of odd order but does not change sign at zeros that are of even order.

$x = -2$ is a zero of order 1; the sign of the function changes from negative to positive at this intercept

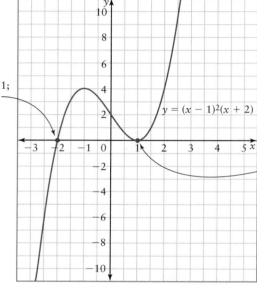

$y = (x - 1)^2(x + 2)$

$x = 1$ is a zero of order 2; the sign of the function does not change at this x-intercept but remains positive

Test values close to either side of an x-intercept to check if the function is positive or negative.

Consider the function $y = (x - 1)^2(x + 2)$ shown in the graph above.

To the left of -2, choose $x = -3$.

$f(-3) = (-3 - 1)^2(-3 + 2)$
$\quad = 16(-1)$
$\quad = -16$

Thus, $f(x) < 0$ to the left of -2.

To the right of -2, choose $x = -1$.

$f(-1) = (-1 - 1)^2(-1 + 2)$
$\quad = 4(1)$
$\quad = 4$

Thus, $f(x) > 0$ to the right of -2.

To the left of 1, choose $x = 0$.

$f(0) = (0 - 1)^2(0 + 2)$
$\quad = 1(2)$
$\quad = 2$

Thus, $f(x) > 0$ to the left of 1.

To the right of 1, choose $x = 2$.

$f(2) = (2 - 1)^2(2 + 2)$
$\quad = 1(4)$
$\quad = 4$

Thus, $f(x) > 0$ to the right of 1.

Example 1 **Analysing Graphs of Polynomial Functions**

For each graph of a polynomial function, determine

 i) the least possible degree and the sign of the leading coefficient

 ii) the x-intercepts and the factors of the function

 iii) the intervals where the function is positive and the intervals where it is negative

a)

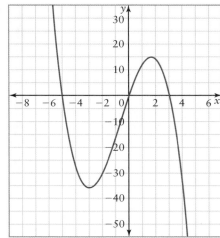

b)

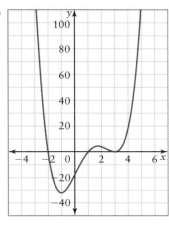

Solution

a) **i)** The three x-intercepts are of order one, so the least possible degree is 3. The graph extends from quadrant 2 to quadrant 4, so the leading coefficient is negative.

 ii) The x-intercepts are -5, 0, and 3. The factors are $x + 5$, x, and $x - 3$.

 iii)

Interval	$(-\infty, -5)$	$(-5, 0)$	$(0, 3)$	$(3, \infty)$
Sign of $f(x)$	+	−	+	−

 The function is positive for $x \in (-\infty, -5)$ and $x \in (0, 3)$.

 The function is negative for $x \in (-5, 0)$ and $x \in (3, \infty)$.

b) **i)** Two x-intercepts are of order one, and the third is of order two, so the least possible degree is four. The graph extends from quadrant 2 to quadrant 1, so the leading coefficient is positive.

 ii) The x-intercepts are -2, 1, and 3 (order 2). The factors are $x + 2$, $x - 1$, and $(x - 3)^2$.

 iii)

Interval	$(-\infty, -2)$	$(-2, 1)$	$(1, 3)$	$(3, \infty)$
Sign of $f(x)$	+	−	+	+

 The function is positive for $x \in (-\infty, -2)$, $x \in (1, 3)$, and $x \in (3, \infty)$ and negative for $x \in (-2, 1)$.

| | Example 2 | Analysing Equations to Sketch Graphs of Polynomial Functions |

Sketch a graph of each polynomial function.

a) $y = (x - 1)(x + 2)(x + 3)$

b) $y = -2(x - 1)^2(x + 2)$

c) $y = -(2x + 1)^3(x - 3)$

Solution

Use a table to organize information about each function. Then, use the information to sketch a graph.

a) $y = (x - 1)(x + 2)(x + 3)$

Degree	Leading Coefficient	End Behaviour	Zeros and x-intercepts	y-intercept
Each factor has one x. Their product is x^3. The function is cubic (degree 3).	The product of all the x-coefficients is 1.	A cubic with a positive leading coefficient extends from quadrant 3 to quadrant 1.	The zeros are 1, −2, and −3. These are the x-intercepts.	The y-intercept is $(0 - 2)(0 + 2)(0 + 3)$, or −6.

Mark the intercepts. Since the order of each zero is 1, the graph changes sign at each x-intercept. Beginning in quadrant 3, sketch the graph so that it passes up through $x = -3$ to the positive side of the x-axis, back down through $x = -2$ to the negative side of the x-axis, through the y-intercept −6, up through $x = 1$, and upward in quadrant 1.

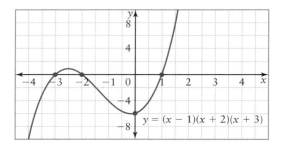

$y = (x - 1)(x + 2)(x + 3)$

b) $y = -2(x - 1)^2(x + 2)$

Degree	Leading Coefficient	End Behaviour	Zeros and x-intercepts	y-intercept
The product of all factors will give a multiple of x^3. The function is cubic (degree 3).	The product of all the x-coefficients is $-2 \times 1^2 \times 1$ or −2.	A cubic with a negative leading coefficient extends from quadrant 2 to quadrant 4.	The zeros are 1 (order 2) and −2. These are the x-intercepts.	The y-intercept is $-2(0 - 1)^2(0 + 2)$, or −4.

Mark the intercepts. The graph changes sign at $x = -2$ (order 1) but not at $x = 1$ (order 2). Begin in quadrant 2. Sketch the graph so that it passes through $x = -2$ to the negative side of the x-axis, through $y = -4$ and up to touch the x-axis at $x = 1$, and then down again, extending downward in quadrant 4.

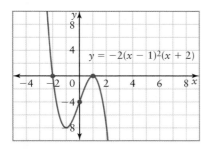

c) $y = -(2x + 1)^3(x - 3)$

Degree	Leading Coefficient	End Behaviour	Zeros and x-intercepts	y-intercept
The product of the x's in the factors is x^4. The function is quartic (degree 4).	The product of all the x-coefficients is $-1 \times 2^3 \times 1$, or -8.	A quartic with a negative leading coefficient extends from quadrant 3 to quadrant 4.	The zeros are $-\dfrac{1}{2}$ (order 3) and 3. These are the x-intercepts.	The y-intercept is $-(2(0) + 1)^3(0 - 3)$, or 3.

Mark the intercepts. Since the order of each zero is odd, the graph changes sign at both intercepts. Beginning in quadrant 3, sketch the graph so that it passes up through $x = -\dfrac{1}{2}$ (flatter near the x-axis, since this zero is of order 3) to the positive side of the x-axis, through $y = 3$ continuing upward, and then back down to pass through $x = 3$, extending downward in quadrant 4.

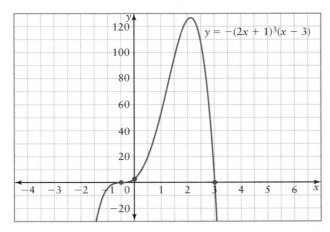

Tools

• graphing calculator

Optional

• computer with *The Geometer's Sketchpad®*

A: Even-Degree Polynomial Functions

1. a) Graph each function on a separate set of axes. Sketch each graph in your notebook.

    i) $f(x) = x^4$

    ii) $f(x) = x^4 - 8x^2$

    iii) $f(x) = -x^4 + 9x^2$

    iv) $f(x) = -x^6 + 7x^4 + 3x^2$

b) Reflect What type of symmetry does each graph have?

c) Reflect How can the exponents of the terms be used to identify these as even functions?

2. a) For each function in step 1a), determine $f(-x)$ by substituting $-x$ for x.

b) Reflect Compare $f(x)$ and $f(-x)$. What do you notice?

B: Odd-Degree Polynomial Functions

1. a) Graph each function on a separate set of axes. Sketch each graph in your notebook.

    i) $f(x) = x^3$

    ii) $f(x) = x^3 - 4x$

    iii) $f(x) = -x^5 + 16x^3$

    iv) $f(x) = -x^5 + 5x^3 + 6x$

b) Reflect What type of symmetry does each graph have?

c) Reflect How can the exponents of the terms be used to identify these as odd functions?

2. a) For each function in step 1a), determine $f(-x)$ and $-f(x)$.

b) Reflect Compare $-f(x)$ and $f(-x)$. What do you notice?

3. Reflect Use the results of parts A and B to describe two ways that the equation of a polynomial function can be used to determine the type of symmetry exhibited by the graph of that function.

An even-degree polynomial function is an **even function** if the exponent of each term of the equation is even. An even function satisfies the property $f(-x) = f(x)$ for all x in the domain of $f(x)$. An even function is symmetric about the y-axis.

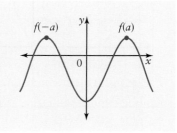

An odd-degree polynomial function is an **odd function** if each term of the equation has an odd exponent. An odd function satisfies the property $f(-x) = -f(x)$ for all x in the domain of $f(x)$. An odd function is rotationally symmetric about the origin.

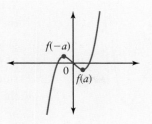

Example 3 | Identify Symmetry

Without graphing, determine if each polynomial function has line symmetry about the y-axis, point symmetry about the origin, or neither. Verify your response.

a) $f(x) = 2x^4 - 5x^2 + 4$

b) $f(x) = -3x^5 + 9x^3 + 2x$

c) $f(x) = 2x(x + 1)(x - 2)$

d) $f(x) = x^6 - 4x^3 + 6x^2 - 4$

Solution

a) Since the exponent of each term is even, $f(x) = 2x^4 - 5x^2 + 4$ is an even function and has line symmetry about the y-axis.

Verify that $f(-x) = f(x)$.

$$\begin{aligned} f(-x) &= 2(-x)^4 - 5(-x)^2 + 4 \qquad \text{Substitute } -x \text{ in the equation.} \\ &= 2x^4 - 5x^2 + 4 \\ &= f(x) \end{aligned}$$

b) Since the exponent of each term is odd, $f(x) = -3x^5 + 9x^3 + 2x$ is an odd function and has point symmetry about the origin. Verify that $f(-x) = -f(x)$.

$$\begin{aligned} f(-x) &= -3(-x)^5 + 9(-x)^3 + 2(-x) \qquad \text{Substitute } -x. \\ &= 3x^5 - 9x^3 - 2x \end{aligned}$$

$$\begin{aligned} -f(x) &= -(-3x^5 + 9x^3 + 2x) \qquad \text{Multiply } f(x) \text{ by } -1. \\ &= 3x^5 - 9x^3 - 2x \end{aligned}$$

The resulting expressions are equal, so $f(-x) = -f(x)$.

c) Since $f(x) = 2x(x + 1)(x - 2)$ is a cubic function, it may be odd and thus have point symmetry about the origin.

$$\begin{aligned} f(-x) &= 2(-x)(-x + 1)(-x - 2) \qquad \text{Substitute } -x. \\ &= -2x(-1)(x - 1)(-1)(x + 2) \qquad \text{Factor } -1 \text{ from each factor.} \\ &= -2x(x - 1)(x + 2) \end{aligned}$$

$$-f(x) = -2x(x + 1)(x - 2) \qquad \text{Multiply } f(x) \text{ by } -1.$$

The resulting expressions are not equal, so the function is not odd and does not have point symmetry about the origin.

d) Some exponents in $f(x) = x^6 - 4x^3 + 6x^2 - 4$ are even and some are odd, so the function is neither even nor odd and does not have line symmetry about the y-axis or point symmetry about the origin.

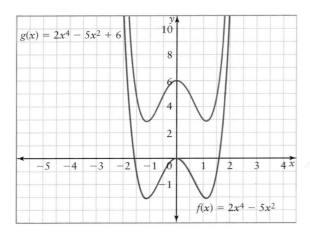

$g(x) = 2x^4 - 5x^2 + 6$

$f(x) = 2x^4 - 5x^2$

When a constant term is added to an even function, the function remains even. For example, the graph of $g(x) = 2x^4 - 5x^2 + 6$ represents a vertical translation of 6 units up of the graph of $f(x) = 2x^4 - 5x^2$. Thus, since $f(x) = 2x^4 - 5x^2$ is even and has line symmetry, the same is true for $g(x) = 2x^4 - 5x^2 + 6$.

CONNECTIONS

Recall that constant terms can be thought of as coefficients of x^0.

<< **KEY CONCEPTS** >>

- The graph of a polynomial function can be sketched using the x-intercepts, the degree of the function, and the sign of the leading coefficient.

- The x-intercepts of the graph of a polynomial function are the roots of the corresponding polynomial equation.

- When a polynomial function is in factored form, the zeros can be easily determined from the factors. When a factor is repeated n times, the corresponding zero has order n.

- The graph of a polynomial function changes sign only at x-intercepts that correspond to zeros of odd order. At x-intercepts that correspond to zeros of even order, the graph touches but does not cross the x-axis.

- An even function satisfies the property $f(-x) = f(x)$ for all x in its domain and is symmetric about the y-axis. An even-degree polynomial function is an even function if the exponent of each term is even.

- An odd function satisfies the property $f(-x) = -f(x)$ for all x in its domain and is rotationally symmetric about the origin. An odd-degree polynomial function is an odd function if the exponent of each term is odd.

Communicate Your Understanding

C1 Are all even-degree polynomial functions even? Are all odd-degree polynomial functions odd? Explain.

C2 Why is it useful to express a polynomial function in factored form?

C3 a) What is the connection between the order of the zeros of a polynomial function and the graph?

b) How can you tell from a graph if the order of a zero is 1, 2, or 3?

C4 How can symmetry be used to sketch a graph of a polynomial function?

For help with questions 1 and 2, refer to Example 1.

1. For each polynomial function:

   i) state the degree and the sign of the leading coefficient

   ii) describe the end behaviour of the graph of the function

   iii) determine the *x*-intercepts

   a) $f(x) = (x - 4)(x + 3)(2x - 1)$

   b) $g(x) = -2(x + 2)(x - 2)(1 + x)(x - 1)$

   c) $h(x) = (3x + 2)^2(x - 4)(x + 1)(2x - 3)$

   d) $p(x) = -(x + 5)^3(x - 5)^3$

2. For each graph, do the following.

   i) State the *x*-intercepts.

   ii) State the intervals where the function is positive and the intervals where it is negative.

   iii) Explain whether the graph might represent a polynomial function that has zeros of order 2 or of order 3.

a)

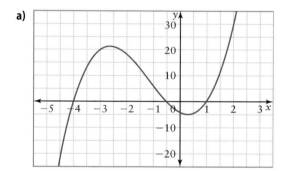

b)

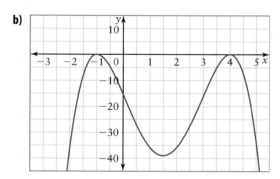

c)

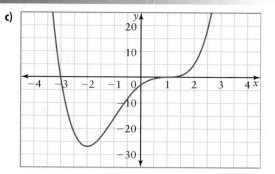

d)

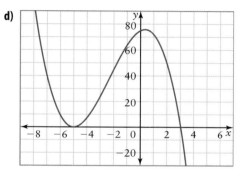

For help with question 3, refer to Example 2.

3. **a)** Determine the zeros of each polynomial function. Indicate whether they are of order 1, 2, or 3.

   i) $f(x) = -2(x - 3)(x + 2)(4x - 3)$

   ii) $g(x) = (x - 1)(x + 3)(1 + x)(3x - 9)$

   iii) $h(x) = -(x + 4)^2(x - 1)^2(x + 2)(2x - 3)$

   iv) $p(x) = 3(x + 6)(x - 5)^2(3x - 2)^3$

   b) Determine algebraically if each function is even or odd.

   c) Sketch a graph of each function in part a).

For help with questions 4 and 5, refer to Example 3.

4. Determine, algebraically, whether each function in question 1 has point symmetry about the origin or line symmetry about the *y*-axis. State whether each function is even, odd, or neither. Give reasons for your answer.

5. **i)** Determine whether each function even, odd, or neither. Explain.

   ii) Without graphing, determine if each polynomial function has line symmetry about the y-axis, point symmetry about the origin, or neither. Explain.

   a) $y = x^4 - x^2$

   b) $y = -2x^3 + 5x$

   c) $y = -4x^5 + 2x^2$

   d) $y = x(2x + 1)^2(x - 4)$

   e) $y = -2x^6 + x^4 + 8$

B **Connect and Apply**

6. Determine an equation for the polynomial function that corresponds to each graph.

   a)

   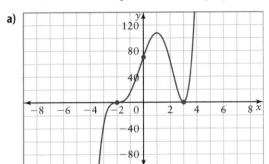

   b)

   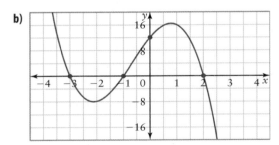

   c)

   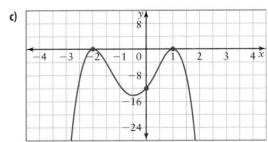

   d)

   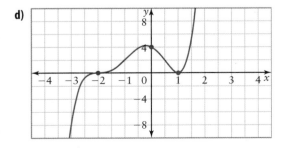

7. Determine an equation for each polynomial function. State whether the function is even, odd, or neither. Sketch a graph of each.

   a) a cubic function with zeros -2 (order 2) and 3 and y-intercept 9

   b) a quartic function with zeros -1 (order 3) and 1 and y-intercept -2

   c) a quintic function with zeros -1 (order 3) and 3 (order 2) that passes through the point $(-2, 50)$

   d) a quintic function with zeros -3, -2 (order 2), and 2 (order 2) that passes through the point $(1, -18)$

8. Without graphing, determine if each polynomial function has line symmetry, point symmetry, or neither. Verify your response using technology.

   a) $f(x) = -6x^5 + 2x$

   b) $g(x) = -7x^6 + 3x^4 + 6x^2$

   c) $h(x) = x^3 - 3x^2 + 5x$

   d) $p(x) = -5x^3 + 2x$

9. Each polynomial function has zeros at $-3, -1, 2$. Write an equation for each function. Then, sketch a graph of the function.

   Reasoning and Proving
   Representing · Selecting Tools
   Problem Solving
   Connecting · Reflecting
   Communicating

   a) a cubic function with a positive leading coefficient

   b) a quartic function that touches the x-axis at -1

   c) a quartic function that extends from quadrant 3 to quadrant 4

   d) a quintic function that extends from quadrant 3 to quadrant 1

10. **Chapter Problem** An engineer designs a rollercoaster so that a section of the ride can be modelled by the function $h(x) = -0.000\ 000\ 4x(x - 15)(x - 25)(x - 45)^2(x - 60)$, where x is the horizontal distance from the boarding platform, in metres; $x \in [0, 60]$; and h is the height, in metres, above or below the boarding platform.

a) What are the similarities and differences between this polynomial function and those studied in Sections 1.1 and 1.2?

b) What useful information does this form of the equation provide that can be used to sketch a graph of the path of the rollercoaster?

c) Use the information from part b) to sketch a graph of this section of the rollercoaster.

d) Estimate the maximum and the minimum height of the rollercoaster relative to the boarding platform.

11. a) Determine the zeros of $f(x) = (2x^2 - x - 1)(x^2 - 3x - 4)$.

b) Use graphing technology to verify your answer.

12. a) Determine the zeros of each polynomial function.

  i) $f(x) = x^4 - 13x^2 + 36$

  ii) $g(x) = 6x^5 - 7x^3 - 3x$

b) State whether each function is even, odd, or neither. Verify your answers algebraically.

c) Sketch a graph of each function.

C   Extend and Challenge

13. **Use Technology** Consider the polynomial function $f(x) = (x - 3)(x - 1)(x + 2)^2 + c$, where c is a constant. Determine a value of c such that the graph of the function has each number of x-intercepts. Justify your answer graphically.

a) four

b) three

c) two

d) one

e) zero

14. a) Write equations for two even functions with four x-intercepts, two of which are $\frac{2}{3}$ and 5.

Reasoning and Proving

Representing   Selecting Tools

Problem Solving

Connecting   Reflecting

Communicating

b) Determine an equation for a function with x-intercepts at $\frac{2}{3}$ and 5, passing through the point $(-1, -96)$.

c) Determine an equation for a function with x-intercepts at $\frac{2}{3}$ and 5 that is a reflection in the x-axis of the function in part b).

15. Explain algebraically why a polynomial that is an odd function is no longer an odd function when a nonzero constant is added.

16. **Math Contest** If the value of a continuous function $f(x)$ changes sign in an interval, there is a root of the equation $f(x) = 0$ in that interval. For example, $f(x) = x^3 - 4x - 2$ has a zero between 2 and 3. Evaluate the function at the endpoints and at the midpoint of the interval. This gives $f(2) = -2$, $f(2.5) = 3.625$, and $f(3) = 13$. The function changes sign between $x = 2$ and $x = 2.5$, so a root lies in this interval. Since $f(2.25) \doteq 0.39$, there is a root between $x = 2$ and $x = 2.25$. Continuing in this way gives increasingly better approximations of that root.

a) Determine, correct to two decimal places, the root of $x^3 - 3x + 1 = 0$ that lies between 0 and 1.

b) Calculate the greatest root of $2x^3 - 4x^2 - 3x + 1 = 0$, to three decimal places.

1.4 Transformations

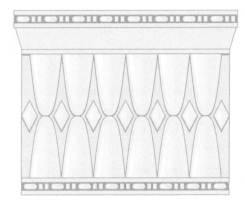

In the architectural design of a new hotel, a pattern is to be carved in the exterior crown moulding. What power function forms the basis of the pattern? What transformations are applied to the power function to create the pattern?

In this section, you will investigate the roles of the parameters a, k, d, and c in polynomial functions of the form $y = a[k(x - d)]^n + c$. You will determine equations to model given transformations. You will also apply transformations to the graphs of basic power functions of the form $y = x^n$ to sketch the graphs of functions of the form $y = a[k(x - d)]^n + c$.

Investigate | What are the roles of a, k, d, and c in polynomial functions of the form $y = a[k(x - d)]^n + c$, where $n \in \mathbb{N}$?

Tools
- graphing calculator

Optional
- computer with *The Geometer's Sketchpad®*

Apply your prior knowledge of transformations to predict the roles of the parameters a, k, d, and c in polynomial functions of the form $y = a[k(x - d)]^n + c$. Complete each part to verify the accuracy of your prediction.

A: *Describe the Roles of d and c in Polynomial Functions of the Form $y = a[k(x - d)]^n + c$*

1. a) Graph each group of functions on one set of axes. Sketch the graphs in your notebook.

   Group A
   i) $y = x^3$
   ii) $y = x^3 + 2$
   iii) $y = x^3 - 2$

   Group B
   i) $y = x^4$
   ii) $y = (x + 2)^4$
   iii) $y = (x - 2)^4$

   b) Compare the graphs in group A. For any constant c, describe the relationship between the graphs of $y = x^3$ and $y = x^3 + c$.

   c) Compare the graphs in group B. For any constant d, describe the relationship between the graphs of $y = x^4$ and $y = (x - d)^4$.

2. **Reflect** Describe the roles of the parameters c and d in functions of the form $y = a[k(x - d)]^n + c$. Summarize your results in tables like these.

Value of c in $y = a[k(x - d)]^n + c$	Effect on the Graph of $y = x^n$
$c > 0$	
$c < 0$	

Value of d in $y = a[k(x - d)]^n + c$	Effect on the Graph of $y = x^n$
$d > 0$	
$d < 0$	

B: *Describe the Roles of a and k in Polynomial Functions of the Form*
$y = a[k(x - d)]^n + c$

1. a) Graph each group of functions on one set of axes. Sketch the graphs in your notebook.

Group A

i) $y = x^3$

ii) $y = 3x^3$

iii) $y = -3x^3$

Group B

i) $y = x^4$

ii) $y = \dfrac{1}{3}x^4$

iii) $y = -\dfrac{1}{3}x^4$

b) Compare the graphs in group A. For any integer value *a*, describe the relationship between the graphs of $y = x^3$ and $y = ax^3$.

c) Compare the graphs in group B. For any rational value *a* such that $a \in (-1, 0)$ or $a \in (0, 1)$, describe the relationship between the graphs of $y = x^4$ and $y = ax^4$.

d) Reflect Describe the role of the parameter *a* in functions of the form $y = a[k(x - d)]^n + c$.

2. a) Graph each group of functions on one set of axes. Sketch the graphs in your notebook.

Group A

i) $y = x^3$

ii) $y = (3x)^3$

iii) $y = (-3x)^3$

Group B

i) $y = x^4$

ii) $y = \left(\dfrac{1}{3}x\right)^4$

iii) $y = \left(-\dfrac{1}{3}x\right)^4$

b) Compare the graphs in group A. For any integer value *k*, describe the relationship between the graphs of $y = x^3$ and $y = (kx)^3$.

c) Compare the graphs in group B. For any value $k \in (-1, 0)$ or $k \in (0, 1)$, describe the relationship between the graphs of $y = x^4$ and $y = (kx)^4$.

d) Reflect Describe the role of the parameter *k* in functions of the form $y = a[k(x - d)]^n + c$.

3. Summarize your results in tables like these.

Value of *a* in $y = a[k(x - d)]^n + c$	Effect on the Graph of $y = x^n$
$a > 1$	
$0 < a < 1$	
$-1 < a < 0$	
$a < 1$	

Value of *k* in $y = a[k(x - d)]^n + c$	Effect on the Graph of $y = x^n$
$k > 1$	
$0 < k < 1$	
$-1 < k < 0$	
$k < -1$	

The Roles of the Parameters a, k, d, and c in Polynomial Functions of the Form $y = a[k(x - d)]^n + c$, where $n \in \mathbb{N}$		
Value of c in $y = a[k(x - d)]^n + c$	**Transformation of the Graph of $y = x^n$**	**Example Using the Graph of $y = x^4$**
$c > 0$	Translation c units up	$c = 2$ $\qquad$ $y = x^4 + 2$
$c < 0$	Translation $|c|$ units down	$c = -2$ $\qquad$ $y = x^4 - 2$
Value of d in $y = a[k(x - d)]^n + c$		
$d > 0$	Translation d units right	$d = 2$ $\qquad$ $y = (x - 2)^4$
$d < 0$	Translation $|d|$ units left	$d = -2$ $\qquad$ $y = (x + 2)^4$
Value of a in $y = a[k(x - d)]^n + c$		
$a > 1$	Vertical stretch by a factor of a	$a = 4$ $\qquad$ $y = 4x^4$
$0 < a < 1$	Vertical compression by a factor of a	$a = 0.25$ $\qquad$ $y = 0.25x^4$

The Roles of the Parameters a, k, d, and c in Polynomial Functions of the Form $y = a[k(x - d)]^n + c$, where $n \in \mathbb{N}$		
Value of a in $y = a[k(x - d)]^n + c$	Transformation of the Graph of $y = x^n$	Example Using the Graph of $y = x^4$
$-1 < a < 0$	Vertical compression by a factor of $|a|$ and a reflection in the x-axis	$a = -0.25$ $\qquad$ $y = -0.25x^4$
$a < -1$	Vertical stretch by a factor of $|a|$ and a reflection in the x-axis	$a = -4$ $\qquad$ $y = -4x^4$
Value of k in $y = a[k(x - d)]^n + c$	Transformation of the Graph of $y = x^n$	Example Using the Graph of $y = x^3$
$k > 1$	Horizontal compression by a factor of $\dfrac{1}{k}$	$k = 2$ $\qquad$ $y = (2x)^3$
$0 < k < 1$	Horizontal stretch by a factor of $\dfrac{1}{k}$	$k = 0.5$ $\qquad$ $y = (0.5x)^3$
$-1 < k < 0$	Horizontal stretch by a factor of $\left\|\dfrac{1}{k}\right\|$ and a reflection in the y-axis	$k = -0.5$ $\qquad$ $y = (-0.5x)^3$
$k < -1$	Horizontal compression by a factor of $\left\|\dfrac{1}{k}\right\|$ and a reflection in the y-axis	$k = -2$ $\qquad$ $y = (-2x)^3$

The graph of a function of the form $y = a[k(x - d)]^n + c$ is obtained by applying transformations to the graph of the power function $y = x^n$. An accurate sketch of the transformed graph is obtained by applying the transformations represented by a and k *before* the transformations represented by c and d.

The order of transformations coincides with the order of operations on numerical expressions. Multiplication and division (represented by reflections, stretches, and compressions) are applied before addition and subtraction (translations). Transformations represented by a and k may be applied at the same time, followed by c and d together.

Example 1 Applying Transformations to Sketch a Graph

The graph of $y = x^3$ is transformed to obtain the graph of $y = -3[2(x + 1)]^3 + 5$.

a) State the parameters and describe the corresponding transformations.

b) Complete the table.

$y = x^3$	$y = (2x)^3$	$y = -3(2x)^3$	$y = -3[2(x + 1)]^3 + 5$
$(-2, -8)$			
$(-1, -1)$			
$(0, 0)$			
$(1, 1)$			
$(2, 8)$			

c) Sketch a graph of $y = -3[2(x + 1)]^3 + 5$.

d) State the domain and range.

Solution

a) The base power function is $f(x) = x^3$.

Compare $y = -3[2(x + 1)]^3 + 5$ to $y = a[k(x - d)]^n + c$.

- $k = 2$ corresponds to a horizontal compression of factor $\frac{1}{2}$. Divide the x-coordinates of the points in column 1 by 2.

- $a = -3$ corresponds to a vertical stretch of factor 3 and a reflection in the x-axis. Multiply the y-coordinates of the points in column 2 by -3.

- $d = -1$ corresponds to a translation of 1 unit to the left and $c = 5$ corresponds to a translation of 5 units up.

b)

$y = x^3$	$y = (2x)^3$	$y = -3(2x)^3$	$y = -3[2(x + 1)]^3 + 5$
$(-2, -8)$	$(-1, -8)$	$(-1, 24)$	$(-2, 29)$
$(-1, -1)$	$(-0.5, -1)$	$(-0.5, 3)$	$(-1.5, 8)$
$(0, 0)$	$(0, 0)$	$(0, 0)$	$(-1, 5)$
$(1, 1)$	$(0.5, 1)$	$(0.5, -3)$	$(-0.5, 2)$
$(2, 8)$	$(1, 8)$	$(1, -24)$	$(0, -19)$

c) To sketch the graph, plot the points from column 4 and draw a smooth curve through them.

d) There are no restrictions on the domain or range.

The domain is $\{x \in \mathbb{R}\}$ and the range is $\{y \in \mathbb{R}\}$.

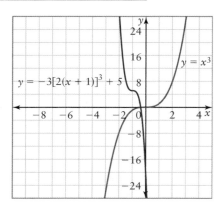

When n is even, the graphs of polynomial functions of the form $y = a[k(x - d)]^n + c$ are even functions and have a vertex at (d, c). The axis of symmetry is $x = d$.

For $a > 0$, the graph opens upward. The vertex is the minimum point on the graph and c is the minimum value. The range of the function is $\{y \in \mathbb{R}, y \geq c\}$.

For $a < 0$, the graph opens downward. The vertex is the maximum point on the graph and c is the maximum value. The range of the function is $\{y \in \mathbb{R}, y \leq c\}$.

Example 2 | Describing Transformations From an Equation

i) Describe the transformations that must be applied to the graph of each power function, $f(x)$, to obtain the transformed function. Then, write the corresponding equation.

ii) State the domain and range. State the vertex and the equation of the axis of symmetry for functions that are even.

a) $f(x) = x^4$, $y = 2f\left[\frac{1}{3}(x - 5)\right]$ b) $f(x) = x^5$, $y = \frac{1}{4}f[-2x + 6] + 4$

Solution

Compare the transformed equation with $y = af[k(x - d)]^n + c$ to determine the values of a, k, d, and c.

a) i) For $y = 2f\left[\frac{1}{3}(x - 5)\right]$, the parameters are $a = 2$, $k = \frac{1}{3}$, $d = 5$, and $c = 0$.

The function $f(x) = x^4$ is stretched vertically by a factor of 2, stretched horizontally by a factor of 3, and translated 5 units to the right, so the equation of the transformed function is $y = 2\left[\frac{1}{3}(x - 5)\right]^4$.

ii) This is a quartic function with $a = 2$, so it opens upward.
vertex $(5, 0)$; axis of symmetry $x = 5$; domain $\{x \in \mathbb{R}\}$; range $\{y \in \mathbb{R}, y \geq 0\}$

b) i) $y = \frac{1}{4}f(-2x + 6) + 4$ is not in the form $y = af[k(x - d)]^n + c$ since $-2x + 6$ is not expressed in the form $k(x - d)$. To determine the value of k, factor -2 from the expression $-2x + 6$:

$y = \frac{1}{4}f[-2(x - 3)] + 4$

This is now in the desired form. The parameters are $a = \frac{1}{4}$, $k = -2$, $d = 3$, and $c = 4$. The function $f(x) = x^5$ is compressed vertically by a factor of $\frac{1}{4}$, compressed horizontally by a factor of $\frac{1}{2}$, reflected in the y-axis, translated 3 units to the right, and translated 4 units up, so the equation of the transformed function is $y = \frac{1}{4}[-2(x - 3)]^5 + 4$.

ii) This is a quintic function.
domain $\{x \in \mathbb{R}\}$; range $\{y \in \mathbb{R}\}$

Example 3

Determine an Equation Given the Graph of a Transformed Function

Recall the crown moulding pattern introduced at the beginning of this section. Determine equations that could make up this pattern.

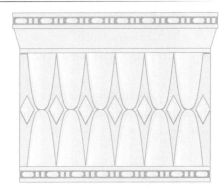

> **Solution**

Overlay the pattern on a grid and identify features of the graphs. The pattern is created by transforming a single polynomial function. Use points to identify the main power function. Then, determine the transformations that need to be applied to create the other graphs, and hence the entire pattern.

Examine graph ①. Since the graph extends from quadrant 3 to quadrant 1, it represents an odd-degree function with a positive leading coefficient. Some points on this graph are $(-2, -8)$, $(-1, -1)$, $(0, 0)$, $(1, 1)$, and $(2, 8)$. These points satisfy $y = x^3$, so an equation for this graph is $y = x^3$.

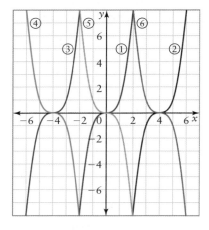

Consider graphs ② and ③. Each of these is a horizontal translation of graph ①. The point $(0, 0)$ on graph ① corresponds to the point $(4, 0)$ on graph ②. Thus, to obtain graph ②, translate the graph of $y = x^3$ to the right 4 units. An equation for graph ② is $y = (x - 4)^3$. To obtain graph ③, translate the graph of $y = x^3$ to the left 4 units. An equation for graph ③ is $y = (x + 4)^3$.

To obtain graph ⑤, reflect the graph of $y = x^3$ in the x-axis. An equation for graph ⑤ is $y = -x^3$.

To obtain graph ⑥, translate graph ⑤ to the right 4 units. Its equation is $y = -(x - 4)^3$.

To obtain graph ④, translate graph ⑤ to the left 4 units. Its equation is $y = -(x + 4)^3$.

Thus, the pattern is created by graphing the functions $y = x^3$, $y = (x - 4)^3$, $y = (x + 4)^3$, $y = -x^3$, $y = -(x - 4)^3$, and $y = -(x + 4)^3$.

- The graph of a polynomial function of the form $y = a[k(x - d)]^n + c$ can be sketched by applying transformations to the graph of $y = x^n$, where $n \in \mathbb{N}$. The transformations represented by a and k must be applied before the transformations represented by c and d.

- The parameters a, k, d, and c in polynomial functions of the form $y = a[k(x - d)]^n + c$, where n is a non-negative integer, correspond to the following transformations:

  - a corresponds to a vertical stretch or compression and, if $a < 0$, a reflection in the x-axis

  - k corresponds to a horizontal stretch or compression and, if $k < 0$, a reflection in the y-axis

  - c corresponds to a vertical translation up or down

  - d corresponds to a horizontal translation to the left or right

Communicate Your Understanding

C1 a) Which parameters cause the graph of a power function to become wider or narrower?

   b) Describe what values of the parameters in part a) make a graph

   i) wider   **ii)** narrower

C2 Which parameters do not change the shape of a power function? Provide an example.

C3 Which parameters can cause the graph of a power function to be reflected? Describe the type of reflections.

C4 a) Describe the order in which the transformations should be applied to obtain an accurate graph.

   b) What sequences of transformations produce the same result?

A ⟩ Practise

For help with question 1, refer to Example 1.

1. a) The graph of $y = x^4$ is transformed to obtain the graph of $y = 4[3(x + 2)]^4 - 6$. State the parameters and describe the corresponding transformations.

   b) Copy and complete the table.

$y = x^4$	$y = (3x)^4$	$y = 4(3x)^4$	$y = 4[3(x + 2)]^4 - 6$
$(-2, 16)$			
$(-1, 1)$			
$(0, 0)$			
$(1, 1)$			
$(2, 16)$			

   c) Sketch a graph of $y = 4[3(x + 2)]^4 - 6$.

   d) State the domain and range, the vertex, and the equation of the axis of symmetry.

For help with questions 2 to 4, refer to Example 2.

2. Match each function with the corresponding transformation of $y = x^n$.

   a) $y = -x^n$

   b) $y = (-x)^n + 2$

   c) $y = -(-x)^n$

   d) $y = x^n$

       i) no reflection

       ii) reflection in the x-axis

       iii) reflection in the x-axis and the y-axis

       iv) reflection in the y-axis

3. Match each function with the corresponding transformation of $y = x^n$.

   a) $y = 2x^n$

   b) $y = (2x)^n$

   c) $y = \frac{1}{2}x^n$

   d) $y = \left(\frac{1}{2}x\right)^n$

       i) horizontally stretched by a factor of 2

       ii) vertically compressed by a factor of $\frac{1}{2}$

       iii) vertically stretched by a factor of 2

       iv) horizontally compressed by a factor of $\frac{1}{2}$

4. Compare each polynomial function with the equation $y = a[k(x - d)]^n + c$. State the values of the parameters a, k, d, and c and the degree n, assuming that the base function is a power function. Describe the transformation that corresponds to each parameter.

   a) $y = (3x)^3 - 1$

   b) $y = 0.4(x + 2)^2$

   c) $y = x^3 + 5$

   d) $y = \frac{3}{4}[-(x - 4)]^3 + 1$

   e) $y = 2\left(\frac{1}{3}x\right)^4 - 5$

   f) $y = 8[(2x)^3 + 3]$

For help with question 5, refer to Example 3.

5. Match each graph with the corresponding function. Justify your choice.

   i) $y = -\frac{1}{4}x^3$

   ii) $y = x^3 - 1$

   iii) $y = \left(-\frac{1}{4}x\right)^5$

   iv) $y = -x^4$

a)

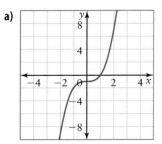

b)

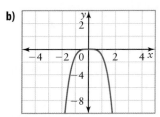

c)

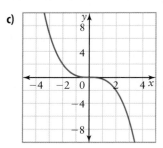

d)

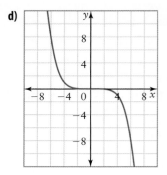

For help with questions 6 to 8, refer to Example 2.

6. Describe the transformations that must be applied to the graph of each power function $f(x)$ to obtain the transformed function. Write the transformed equation.

   a) $f(x) = x^2$, $y = f(x + 2) - 1$

   b) $f(x) = x^3$, $y = f(x - 4) + 5$

7. a) Given a base function of $y = x^4$, list the parameters of the polynomial function

   $$y = -3\left[\frac{1}{2}(x + 4)\right]^4 + 1.$$

   b) Describe how each parameter in part a) transforms the graph of the function $y = x^4$.

   c) Determine the domain, range, vertex, and equation of the axis of symmetry for the transformed function.

   d) Describe two possible orders in which the transformations can be applied to the graph of $y = x^4$ in order to sketch the graph of

   $$y = -3\left[\frac{1}{2}(x + 4)\right]^4 + 1.$$

8. Describe the transformations that must be applied to the graph of each power function, $f(x)$, to obtain the transformed function. Write the full equation of the transformed function.

   a) $f(x) = x^3$, $y = -0.5f(x - 4)$

   b) $f(x) = x^4$, $y = -f(4x) + 1$

   c) $f(x) = x^3$, $y = 2f\left[\frac{1}{3}(x - 5)\right] - 2$

9. a) For each pair of polynomial functions in question 8, sketch the original and transformed functions on the same set of axes.

   b) State the domain and range of the functions in each pair. For even functions, give the vertex and the equation of the axis of symmetry.

10. i) Transformations are applied to each power function to obtain the resulting graph. Determine an equation for the transformed function.

   ii) State the domain and range. For even functions, give the vertex and the equation of the axis of symmetry.

   a)
   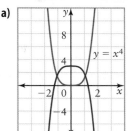

   b)
   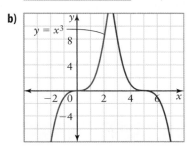

   c)
   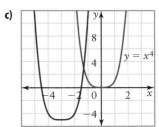

11. **Chapter Problem** A mechanical engineer is experimenting with new designs of fibreglass furnace filters to improve air quality. One of the patterns being considered for the new design is shown, superimposed on a grid. Determine equations for the polynomial functions used to create this pattern.

   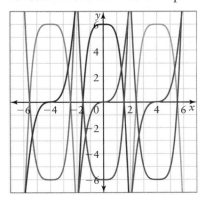

12. i) Write an equation for the function that results from the given transformations.

ii) State the domain and range. For even functions, give the vertex and the equation of the axis of symmetry.

a) The function $f(x) = x^4$ is translated 2 units to the left and 3 units up.

b) The function $f(x) = x^5$ is stretched horizontally by a factor of 5 and translated 12 units to the left.

c) The function $f(x) = x^4$ is stretched vertically by a factor of 3, reflected in the x-axis, and translated 6 units down and 1 unit to the left.

d) The function $f(x) = x^6$ is reflected in the x-axis, stretched horizontally by a factor of 5, reflected in the y-axis, and translated 3 units down and 1 unit to the right.

e) The function $f(x) = x^6$ is compressed horizontally by a factor of $\frac{4}{5}$, stretched vertically by a factor of 7, reflected in the x-axis, and translated 1 unit to the left and 9 units up.

✔ Achievement Check

13. a) The graph of $y = x^4$ is transformed to obtain the graph of $y = \frac{1}{4}[-2(x - 1)]^4 + 2$. List the parameters and describe the corresponding transformations.

b) Sketch a graph of $y = \frac{1}{4}[-2(x - 1)]^4 + 2$.

C Extend and Challenge

14. a) Predict the relationship between the graph of $y = x^3 - x^2$ and the graph of $y = (x - 2)^3 - (x - 2)^2$.

b) Use Technology Graph each function using technology to verify the accuracy of your prediction.

c) Factor each function in part a) to determine the x-intercepts.

15. Use Technology

a) Describe the transformations that must be applied to the graph of $y = x^4 - x^3 + x^2$ to obtain the graph of $y = -3\left(\left[\frac{1}{2}(x + 4)\right]^4 - \left[\frac{1}{2}(x + 4)\right]^3 + \left[\frac{1}{2}(x + 4)\right]^2\right)$.

b) Sketch each graph using technology.

c) Factor each function in part a) to determine the x-intercepts.

16. a) The function $h(x) = 3(x - 3)(x + 2)(x - 5)$ is translated 4 units to the left and 5 units down. Write an equation for the transformed function.

b) Suppose the transformed function is then reflected in the x-axis and vertically compressed by a factor of $\frac{2}{5}$. Write an equation for the new transformed function.

17. Math Contest A farm has a sale on eggs, selling 13 eggs for the usual price of a dozen eggs. As a result, the price of eggs is reduced by 24 cents a dozen. What was the original price for a dozen eggs?

18. Math Contest Given $f(x) = x^2$ and $f_{n + 1} = f_0(f_n(x))$, where n is any whole number

a) determine $f_1(x)$, $f_2(x)$, and $f_3(x)$

b) determine a formula for $f_n(x)$ in terms of n

1.5 Slopes of Secants and Average Rate of Change

Change occurs in many aspects of everyday life. A person's height and mass change from birth to adulthood. The distance that a car travels in a period of time changes according to its speed. Temperature fluctuations occur daily and with each season. The value of a house or antique may increase, or appreciate, over a period of time. The cost of a train ticket varies with the distance travelled. Some things change over a long period of time, while others change in an instant. Being able to understand and predict the rate at which a change occurs can provide useful information.

A **rate of change** is a measure of the change in one quantity (the dependent variable) with respect to a change in another quantity (the independent variable). There are two types of rates of change, average and instantaneous. An **average rate of change** is a change that takes place over an interval, while an instantaneous rate of change is a change that takes place in an instant. Instantaneous rates of change will be examined more closely in the next section of this chapter.

Consider the following scenario.

A car leaves Ottawa at 12 p.m. and arrives in Toronto at 4 p.m. after travelling a distance of 400 km. The average rate of change of distance with respect to time—the average velocity—is determined as shown:

$$\text{Average velocity} = \frac{\text{change in distance}}{\text{change in time}}$$
$$= \frac{\Delta d}{\Delta t}$$
$$= \frac{400}{4}$$
$$= 100$$

Therefore, the average velocity of the car is 100 km/h.

How can you connect average rate of change and slope?

1. Seismic activity at a certain point on the ocean floor creates a wave that spreads in a circular pattern over the calm surface of the ocean. The table shows the radius of the circular pattern during the first 10 s as the wave moves outward.

Time, t (s)	Radius, r (m)
0	0
1	2
2	4
3	6
4	8
5	10
6	12
7	14
8	16
9	18
10	20

a) Identify the independent variable and the dependent variable. Justify your choice.

b) Determine $\dfrac{\Delta r}{\Delta t} = \dfrac{\text{change in radius}}{\text{change in time}}$ for each time interval.

 i) [0, 10]   ii) [0, 1]   iii) [9, 10]

c) **Reflect** Interpret the values found in part b). State the units for these values.

d) Graph the data. What type of polynomial function does the graph represent? Explain.

e) A **secant** is a line that connects two points on a curve. Draw a secant on the graph to connect the pair of points associated with each time interval in part b). What is the slope of each secant line?

f) **Reflect** What is the relationship between the values found in part b) and the graph? Explain.

2. This table shows the total area covered by the wave during the first 10 s.

Radius, r (m)	Area, A (m²)
0	0
2	12.57
4	50.27
6	113.10
8	201.06
10	314.16
12	452.39
14	615.75
16	804.25
18	1017.88
20	1256.64

a) Identify the independent variable and the dependent variable. Justify your choice.

b) Determine $\dfrac{\Delta A}{\Delta r} = \dfrac{\text{change in area}}{\text{change in radius}}$ for each radius interval.

   i) [0, 20]

   ii) [0, 4]

   iii) [6, 12]

   iv) [0, 2]

   v) [14, 16]

c) Reflect Interpret the values found in part b). State the units for these values.

d) Graph the data. What type of polynomial function does the graph represent? Explain.

e) On the graph, draw a secant to connect the pair of points associated with each radius interval in part b). What is the slope of each secant line?

f) Reflect What is the relationship between the values found in part b) and the secant lines? How are these related to the shape of the graph? Explain.

The average rate of change between two points corresponds to the slope of the secant between the points. For example, the average rate of change of y with respect to x between the points $P_1(x_1, y_1)$ and $P_2(x_2, y_2)$ is determined as follows:

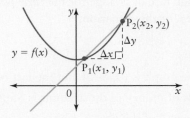

$$
\begin{aligned}
\text{Average rate of change} &= \frac{\Delta y}{\Delta x} \\[2mm]
&= \frac{\text{change in } y}{\text{change in } x} \\[2mm]
&= \frac{y_2 - y_1}{x_2 - x_1}
\end{aligned}
$$

Example 1	Calculate and Interpret Average Rates of Change From a Graph

The graph represents the amount of money in a bank account over a 1-year period.

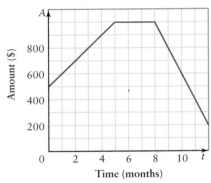

Amount of Money in a Bank Account

a) How much money was in the account
   i) at the start of the year?
   ii) at the end of the year?
b) What does the graph tell you about the average rate of change of the amount of money in the account in the following intervals:
   i) month 0 to month 5
   ii) month 5 to month 8
   iii) month 8 to month 12
c) Determine the average rate of change for the time periods in part b). Interpret these values for this situation.

> **Solution**

a) The first point on the graph is (0, 500) and the last point is (12, 200), so
   i) the initial amount of money in the account is $500
   ii) the amount at the end of the year is $200
b) **i)** Between month 0 and month 5, the graph is a line with positive slope. The average rate of change is constant and positive. The amount of money in the account is increasing by the same amount each month.
   ii) Between month 5 and month 8, the graph is a horizontal line with zero slope. The average rate of change is 0. The amount of money in the account does not change.
   iii) Between month 8 and month 12, the graph is a line with negative slope. The average rate of change is constant and negative. The amount of money in the account is decreasing by the same amount each month.

c) i) The points that correspond to month 0 and month 5 are (0, 500) and (5, 1000).

$$\text{Average rate of change} = \frac{\text{change in amount}}{\text{change in time}}$$

$$= \frac{1000 - 500}{5 - 0}$$

$$= \frac{500}{5}$$

$$= 100$$

The amount of money in the account is increasing on average by $100 per month.

ii) The points that correspond to month 5 and month 8 are (5, 1000) and (8, 1000).

$$\text{Average rate of change} = \frac{1000 - 1000}{8 - 5}$$

$$= \frac{0}{3}$$

$$= 0$$

No change occurs. The amount of money in the account remains the same.

iii) The points that correspond to month 8 and month 12 are (8, 1000) and (12, 200).

$$\text{Average rate of change} = \frac{200 - 1000}{12 - 8}$$

$$= \frac{-800}{4}$$

$$= -200 \qquad \text{The negative value indicates that the amount of money is decreasing.}$$

The amount of money in the account is decreasing on average by $200 per month.

Notice that the average rate of change and the slope are the same for each time period.

Example 2

Calculate and Interpret the Average Rate of Change From a Table of Values

Recall the problem from Example 3 in Section 1.2, page 22.

A new antibacterial spray is tested on a bacterial culture. The table shows the population, P, of the bacterial culture t minutes after the spray is applied.

t (min)	P
0	800
1	799
2	782
3	737
4	652
5	515
6	314
7	37

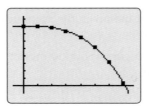

a) How can you tell that the average rate of change is negative by examining
   i) the table of values?   ii) the graph?

b) Determine the average rate of change of the number of bacteria over the entire time period shown in the table. Interpret this value for this situation.

c) Compare the average rate of change of the number of bacteria in the first 3 min and in the last 3 min. Explain any similarities and differences.

d) How can you tell that this situation involves a non-constant rate of change by examining
   i) the table of values?   ii) the graph?   iii) the average rate of change?

> **Solution**

a) i) From the table, the value of the dependent variable, P, is decreasing as the value of the independent variable, t, is increasing. So, the average rate of change will be negative.

   ii) The graph decreases from left to right, so the slope of any secant will be negative.

b) From the table, the points are (0, 800) and (7, 37).

$$\text{Average rate of change} = \frac{\Delta P}{\Delta t}$$
$$= \frac{37 - 800}{7 - 0}$$
$$= \frac{-763}{7}$$
$$= -109$$

During the entire 7 min, the number of bacteria decreases on average by 109 bacteria per minute.

c) From the table, the endpoints of the first interval are (0, 800) and (3, 737).

$$\text{Average rate of change} = \frac{\Delta P}{\Delta t}$$
$$= \frac{737 - 800}{3 - 0}$$
$$= \frac{-63}{3}$$
$$= -21$$

During the first 3 min, the number of bacteria decreases on average by 21 bacteria per minute.

From the table, the endpoints of the last interval are (4, 652) and (7, 37).

$$\text{Average rate of change} = \frac{\Delta P}{\Delta t}$$
$$= \frac{37 - 652}{7 - 4}$$
$$= \frac{-615}{3}$$
$$= -205$$

During the last 3 min, the number of bacteria decreases on average by 205 bacteria per minute.

Similarity: The average rates of change in the number of bacteria are decreasing.

Difference: The average rate of decrease is greater in the last 3 min than in the first 3 min. This may be because more bacteria are exposed to the spray as time passes.

d) **i)** From the table, the number of bacteria is decreasing at a different rate. The change in the dependent variable varies for each 1-min increase in the independent variable.

ii) The graph is a curve rather than a straight line, so the rate of change is not constant.

iii) The value of the average rate of change varies, which indicates that the bacteria population decreases at a non-constant rate. In the first 3 min, the average rate of decrease in the bacteria population is 21 bacteria per minute, while in the last 3 min it is 205 bacteria per minute.

Example 3	**Calculate and Interpret an Average Rate of Change From an Equation**

A football is kicked into the air such that its height, h, in metres, after t seconds can be modelled by the function $h(t) = -4.9t^2 + 14t + 1$.

a) Determine the average rate of change of the height of the ball for each time interval.

   i) $[0, 0.5]$ **ii)** $[2, 2.5]$

b) Consider the graph of $h(t) = -4.9t^2 + 14t + 1$ with secant lines AB and CD. Describe the relationship between the values in part a), the secant lines, and the graph.

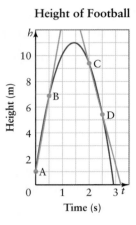

Height of Football

Solution

a) Use the equation to determine the endpoints corresponding to each interval.

   i) For $[0, 0.5]$:

Substitute $t = 0$ to find the height at 0 s.

$h(0) = -4.9(0)^2 + 14(0) + 1$
$\quad\;\, = 1$

Substitute $t = 0.5$ to find the height at 0.5 s.

$h(0.5) = -4.9(0.5)^2 + 14(0.5) + 1$
$\quad\quad\; = 6.775$

The points that correspond to 0 s and 0.5 s are $(0, 1)$ and $(0.5, 6.775)$.

$$\text{Average rate of change} = \frac{\Delta h}{\Delta t}$$

$$= \frac{6.775 - 1}{0.5 - 0}$$

$$= 11.55$$

The average rate of change of the height of the football from 0 s to 0.5 s is 11.55 m/s.

   ii) For $[2, 2.5]$:

Substitute $t = 2$ to find the height at 2 s.

$h(2) = -4.9(2)^2 + 14(2) + 1$
$\quad\;\, = 9.4$

Substitute $t = 2.5$ to find the height at 2.5 s.

$h(2.5) = -4.9(2.5)^2 + 14(2.5) + 1$
$\quad\quad\; = 5.375$

The points that correspond to 2 s and 2.5 s are $(2, 9.4)$ and $(2.5, 5.375)$.

Average rate of change $= \dfrac{\Delta h}{\Delta t}$

$$= \dfrac{5.375 - 9.4}{2.5 - 2}$$

$$= -8.05$$

The average rate of change of the height of the football from 2 s to 2.5 s is -8.05 m/s.

b) The average rate of change of the height of the football for $t \in [0, 0.5]$ corresponds to the slope of secant AB. The average rate of change is positive, as is the slope of AB. The height of the football is increasing. The average rate of change of the height of the football for $t \in [2, 2.5]$ corresponds to the slope of secant CD. The average rate of change is negative, as is the slope of the secant. The height of the football is decreasing.

KEY CONCEPTS

- A rate of change is a measure of how quickly one quantity (the dependent variable) changes with respect to another quantity (the independent variable).

- Average rates of change
  - represent the rate of change over a specified interval
  - correspond to the slope of a secant between two points $P_1(x_1, y_1)$ and $P_2(x_2, y_2)$ on a curve

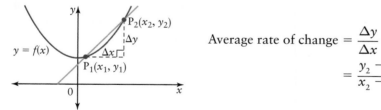

Average rate of change $= \dfrac{\Delta y}{\Delta x}$

$$= \dfrac{y_2 - y_1}{x_2 - x_1}$$

- An average rate of change can be determined by calculating the slope between two points given in a table of values or by using an equation.

Communicate Your Understanding

C1 Describe a situation for which the average rate of change is
    a) constant and positive   **b)** constant and negative   **c)** zero

C2 State the average rate of change for this situation. When the change in the independent variable is -3, the change in the dependent variable is 12.

C3 **a)** What information is provided by the sign (positive or negative) of an average rate of change?

    b) How can you tell from a graph if the average rate of change over an interval is positive or negative? Is it always possible to do so? Explain.

1. Which of the following does not represent a situation that involves an average rate of change? Justify your answer.

   a) A child grows 8 cm in 6 months.

   b) The temperature at a 750-m-high ski hill is 2°C at the base and −8°C at the top.

   c) A speedometer shows that a vehicle is travelling at 90 km/h.

   d) A jogger ran 23 km in 2 h.

   e) The laptop cost $750.

   f) A plane travelled 650 km in 3 h.

For help with questions 2 and 3, refer to Example 1.

2. Identify if the average rate of change for pairs of points along each graph is constant and positive, constant and negative, zero, or non-constant. Justify your response.

   a)

   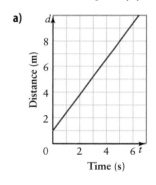

b)

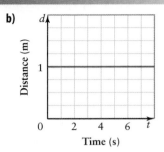

c)

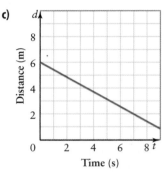

3. Determine the average rate of change for two points on each line segment in question 2.

4. In 1990, 16.2% of households had a home computer, while 66.8% of households had a home computer in 2003. Determine the average rate of change of the percent of households that had a home computer over this time period.

   Source: Statistics Canada, Canada at a Glance 2006, page 9, Household facilities.

B   **Connect and Apply**

For help with question 5, refer to Example 2.

5. The table shows the percent of Canadian households that used e-mail from 1999 to 2003.

Year	Households (%)
1999	26.3
2000	37.4
2001	46.1
2002	48.9
2003	52.1

   Source: Statistics Canada, Canada at a Glance, 2006, page 9, Household Internet use at home by Internet activity.

   a) Determine the average rate of change of the percent of households using e-mail from 1999 to 2003. What are the units for this average rate of change?

   b) Why might someone want to know the average rate of change found in part a)?

   c) Determine the average rate of change of the percent of households using e-mail for each pair of consecutive years from 1999 to 2003.

   d) Compare the values found in part c). Which value is the greatest? the least? What is the significance of these values?

   e) Compare the values found in part a) with those in part c). Explain any similarities or differences.

For help with questions 6 to 8, refer to Example 3.

6. Use Technology The purchase price, P, of one share in a company at any time, t, in years, can be modelled by the function
$P(t) = -0.2t^3 + 2t^2 + 8t + 2, t \in [0, 13]$.

a) Graph the function.

b) Use the graph to describe when the rate of change is positive, when it is zero, and when it is negative.

c) Determine the average rate of change of the purchase price from

i) year 0 to year 5

ii) year 5 to year 8

iii) year 8 to year 10

iv) year 8 to year 13

d) When was the best time to buy shares? sell shares? Justify your answers.

7. As a large snowball melts, its size changes. The volume, V, in cubic centimetres, is given by the equation
$V = \frac{4}{3}\pi r^3$, where r is the radius, in centimetres, and $r \in [0, 30]$. The surface area, S, in square centimetres, is given by the equation $S = 4\pi r^2$.

a) What type of polynomial function does each formula represent? Sketch a graph of each function. State the domain and range.

b) Determine the average rate of change of the surface area and of the volume as the radius decreases from
i) 30 cm to 25 cm   **ii)** 25 cm to 20 cm
Compare the change in surface area to the change in volume. Describe any similarities and differences.

c) Determine the average rate of change of the surface area when the surface area decreases from 2827.43 cm² to 1256.64 cm².

d) Determine the average rate of change of the volume when the volume decreases from 1675.52 cm³ to 942.48 cm³.

e) Interpret your answers in parts c) and d).

8. A cyclist riding a bike at a constant speed along a flat road decelerates to climb a hill. At the top of the hill the cyclist accelerates and returns to the constant cruising speed along another flat road, and then accelerates down a hill. Finally, the cyclist comes to another hill and coasts to a stop. Sketch a graph of the cyclist's speed versus time and a graph of distance travelled versus time. Justify your sketches.

9. Chapter Problem A structural engineer designs a bridge to be built over a river. The following design, consisting of a parabola and crossbeams, represents the bridge's metal support structure.

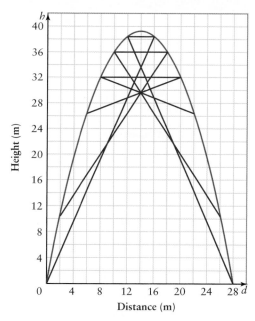

a) Determine an equation for the parabola in the design.

b) What type of line does each crossbeam represent?

c) Determine the slope of each crossbeam in the design. Describe your method.

d) What do the slopes of the crossbeams represent?

e) How is the symmetry of the parabola shown by the slopes of the crossbeams?

10. As water drains out of a 2000-L hot tub, the amount of water remaining in the tub can be modelled by the function $V = 0.000\,02(100 - t)^4$, where t is the time, in minutes, $0 \le t \le 100$, and $V(t)$ is the volume of water, in litres, remaining in the tub at time t.

a) Determine the average rate of change of the volume of water during

   i) the entire 100 min

   ii) the first 30 min

   iii) the last 30 min

b) What do the values from part a) tell you about the rate at which water drains from the tub?

c) **Use Technology** Graph the function $V(t) = 0.000\,02(100 - t)^4$. Sketch the function in your notebook.

d) On your drawing, sketch the secant lines that correspond to the time intervals in part a).

C) Extend and Challenge

11. **Use Technology**
The table shows the amount of water remaining in a swimming pool as it is being drained.

Reasoning and Proving
Representing — *Selecting Tools*
Problem Solving
Connecting — *Reflecting*
Communicating

Time (h)	Amount of Water (L)
0	18 750
1	17 280
2	15 870
3	14 520
4	13 230
5	12 000
6	10 830
7	9 720
8	8 670
9	7 680
10	6 750

a) Determine the average rate of change of the volume of water for consecutive hours.

b) Compare the values in part a). When is the rate of change the greatest? the least?

c) Create a table of finite differences for the data. Use the finite differences to determine the type of polynomial function that best models this situation.

d) Is there a relationship between the finite differences and the average rates of change? Explain.

e) Enter the data in a graphing calculator. Use the regression feature to obtain the equation of the curve of best fit for the data.

f) Graph the equation in part e).

g) How long will it take the pool to fully drain? Justify your answer.

12. The height, h, in metres, of a ball above the ground after t seconds can be modelled by the function $h(t) = -4.9t^2 + 20t$.

a) What does the average rate of change represent for this situation?

b) Determine the average rate of change of the height of the ball for each time interval.

   i) [1, 2]   **ii)** [1, 1.5]   **iii)** [1, 1.1]

   iv) [1, 1.01] **v)** [1, 1.001] **vi)** [1, 1.0001]

c) Compare the values in part b). Describe their relationship.

d) Explain how the values in part b) can be used to estimate the instantaneous rate of change of the ball at 1 s.

13. **Math Contest** A right triangle has an area of 25 cm². Express the hypotenuse, h, of this triangle as a function of its perimeter, p. Hint: Consider the square of the perimeter.

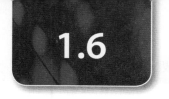
Slopes of Tangents and Instantaneous Rate of Change

When you hit or kick a ball, the height, h, in metres, of the ball can be modelled by the equation $h(t) = -4.9t^2 + v_0 t + c_0$. In this equation, t is the time, in seconds; c_0 represents the initial height of the ball, in metres; and v_0 represents the initial vertical velocity of the ball, in metres per second. In Section 1.5, you learned how to calculate the average rate of change of the height of the ball, or the average velocity of the ball, over an interval of time. What if you want to know the velocity of the ball 1 s after it was hit? To determine how fast the ball is travelling at a specific time, that is, to determine the **instantaneous rate of change** of the height of the ball, other methods are required. In this section, you will investigate the connection between average and instantaneous rates of change and learn how the slope of a tangent is used to determine an instantaneous rate of change.

Investigate **What is the connection between the slopes of secants, the slope of a tangent, and the instantaneous rate of change?**

1. A golf ball lying on the grass is hit so that its initial vertical velocity is 25 m/s. The height, h, in metres, of the ball after t seconds can be modelled by the quadratic function $h(t) = -4.9t^2 + 25t$. Copy and complete the table for $h(t)$.

Interval	Δh	Δt	Average rate of change, $\dfrac{\Delta h}{\Delta t}$
$1 \le t \le 2$	$h(2) - h(1)$ $= [-4.9(2)^2 + 25(2)] - [-4.9(1)^2 + 25(1)]$ $= 30.4 - 20.1$ $= 10.3$	$2 - 1 = 1$	
$1 \le t \le 1.5$			
$1 \le t \le 1.1$			
$1 \le t \le 1.01$			
$1 \le t \le 1.001$			

2. Explain how the time intervals in the first column are changing.

3. **Reflect** Describe how the average rate of change values in the fourth column are changing in relation to the time intervals.

4. **a)** Graph the function.

   b) Reflect On the graph, sketch the secants that correspond to the average rates of change in the table. How do the secants illustrate the relationship you described in step 3?

5. **a)** Sketch a tangent line, a line that touches the graph only at the point that corresponds to $t = 1$ s. Describe how the values of the average rate of change in your table could be used to estimate the slope of the tangent at $t = 1$ s.

   b) Reflect What does the slope of the tangent represent in this situation? Explain.

   c) What would happen if you approached $t = 1$ from below, that is, using $t = 0.9$, $t = 0.99$, $t = 0.999$, and so on? Explain.

6. **Reflect** Explain the relationship between

   a) the slopes of secants near a point on a curve and the slope of the tangent at that point

   b) the slope of a tangent at a point on a curve and the instantaneous rate of change

---

Relationship Between the Slope of Secants and the Slope of a Tangent

As a point Q becomes very close to a tangent point P, the slope of the secant line becomes closer to (approaches) the slope of the tangent line.

Often an arrow is used to denote the word "approaches." So, the above statement may be written as follows:

As Q → P, the slope of secant PQ → the slope of the tangent at P.

Thus, the average rate of change between P and Q becomes closer to the value of the instantaneous rate of change at P.

When the graph of a function is given, an approximate value for the instantaneous rate of change at a point on the curve may be determined using either of two methods: by calculating the slope of a line passing through the given point and another point on the curve that is very close to the given point, or by sketching the tangent line at the point and calculating the average rate of change over an interval between the tangent point and another point on the tangent line.

<table>
<tr><td>**Example 1**</td><td>**Estimate an Instantaneous Rate of Change From a Graph**</td></tr>
</table>

The graph shows the approximate distance travelled by a parachutist in the first 5 s after jumping out of a helicopter. How fast was the parachutist travelling 2 s after jumping out of the helicopter?

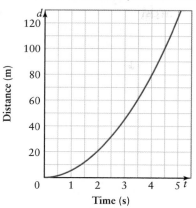

Distance Travelled by a Parachutist

Solution

The parachutist's velocity at 2 s corresponds to the instantaneous rate of change at $t = 2$ s. Calculate an approximate value for the instantaneous rate of change. Let P be the point on the graph at $t = 2$ s.

Method 1: *Use the Slope of a Secant*

Determine the slope of a secant passing through P and another point on the curve that is very close to P.

Select the point Q(3, 45), which is close to P and easy to read from the graph.

The slope of the secant PQ is

$$m_{PQ} = \frac{\Delta d}{\Delta t}$$

$$= \frac{45 - 20}{3 - 2}$$

$$= 25$$

Using a secant, the parachutist's velocity after falling for 2 s is approximately 25 m/s.

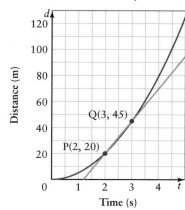

Distance Travelled by a Parachutist

Method 2: *Use Two Points on an Approximate Tangent Line*

Another way to estimate the slope of a tangent at a point from a graph is to sketch an approximate tangent line through that point and then select a second point on that line. Select the point (3, 40). Label it S.

The slope of PS is

$$m_{PS} = \frac{\Delta d}{\Delta t}$$

$$= \frac{40 - 20}{3 - 2}$$

$$= 20$$

Using points on the approximate tangent line, the parachutist's velocity after falling for 2 s is approximately 20 m/s.

Distance Travelled by a Parachutist

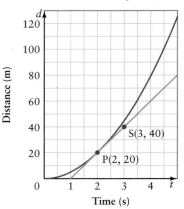

Note that both methods give an approximate value of the slope of the tangent because the calculations depend on either

- the accuracy of the coordinates of the selected point on the curve
- the accuracy of the approximate tangent line, as well as the accuracy of the coordinates of the second point on this approximate tangent line

In both methods, the closer the selected point is to P the better is the approximation of the slope of the tangent line.

Example 2	Estimate an Instantaneous Rate of Change From a Table of Values

In the table, the distance of the parachutist in Example 1 is recorded at 0.5-s intervals. Estimate the parachutist's velocity at 2 s.

Solution

To estimate an instantaneous rate of change from a table, calculate the average rate of change over a short interval by using points in the table that are closest to the tangent point.

The table shows that at 2 s the parachutist has travelled a distance of 20 m. This corresponds to the tangent point (2, 20) on the graph shown in Example 1. A point that is close to (2, 20) is the point (2.5, 31.25).

t (s)	d (m)
0	0
0.5	1.25
1.0	5.00
1.5	11.25
2.0	20.00
2.5	31.25
3.0	45.00
3.5	61.25
4.0	80.00

The average rate of change between (2, 20) and (2.5, 31.25) is

Average rate of change $= \dfrac{\Delta d}{\Delta t}$

$\qquad\qquad = \dfrac{31.25 - 20}{2.5 - 2}$

$\qquad\qquad = \dfrac{11.25}{0.5}$

$\qquad\qquad = 22.5$

The parachutist's velocity at 2 s is approximately 22.5 m/s.

Notice that we also could have chosen the point (1.5, 11.25).

| Example 3 | Estimate an Instantaneous Rate of Change From an Equation |

The function $d(t) = 5t^2$ may be used to model the approximate distance travelled by the parachutist in Examples 1 and 2. Use the equation to estimate the velocity of the parachutist after 2 s.

Solution

Determine the average rate of change over shorter and shorter intervals.

Interval	Δd	Δt	$\dfrac{\Delta d}{\Delta t}$
$2 \le t \le 3$	$d(3) - d(2) = 5(3)^2 - 5(2)^2$ $= 45 - 20$ $= 25$	$3 - 2 = 1$	$\dfrac{25}{1} = 25$
$2 \le t \le 2.5$	$d(2.5) - d(2) = 5(2.5)^2 - 5(2)^2$ $= 31.25 - 20$ $= 11.25$	$2.5 - 2 = 1$	$\dfrac{11.25}{0.5} = 22.5$
$2 \le t \le 2.1$	$d(2.1) - d(2) = 5(2.1)^2 - 5(2)^2$ $= 22.05 - 20$ $= 2.05$	$2.1 - 2 = 0.1$	$\dfrac{2.05}{0.1} = 20.5$
$2 \le t \le 2.01$	$d(2.01) - d(2) = 5(2.01)^2 - 5(2)^2$ $= 20.2005 - 20$ $= 0.2005$	$2.01 - 2 = 0.01$	$\dfrac{0.2005}{0.01} = 20.05$
$2 \le t \le 2.001$	$d(2.001) - d(2) = 5(2.001)^2 - 5(2)^2$ $= 20.020\ 005 - 20$ $= 0.020\ 005$	$2.001 - 2 = 0.001$	$\dfrac{0.020\ 005}{0.001} = 20.005$

As the time intervals decrease, the average rate of change (which corresponds to the slope of a secant line), becomes closer to (or approaches) 20. Thus, the velocity of the parachutist after 2 s is approximately 20 m/s. You also could have used values of t less than 2.

Communicate Your Understanding

C1 **a)** Does the speedometer of a car measure average speed or instantaneous speed? Explain.

b) Describe situations in which the instantaneous speed and the average speed would be the same.

C2 State if each situation represents average rate of change or instantaneous rate of change. Give reasons for your answer.

a) At 3 p.m., the plane was travelling at 850 km/h.

b) The average speed travelled by the train during the 10-h trip was 130 km/h.

c) The fire was spreading at a rate of 2 ha/h.

d) 5 s after an antiseptic spray is applied, the bacteria population is decreasing at a rate of 60 bacteria per second.

e) He lost 4 kg per month over a 5-month period.

f) After being heated for 2 min, the water temperature was rising at 1°C/min.

C3 Which method from Examples 1, 2, and 3 is the most accurate for finding the instantaneous rate of change? Explain.

For help with question 1, refer to Example 1.

1. Consider the graph shown.

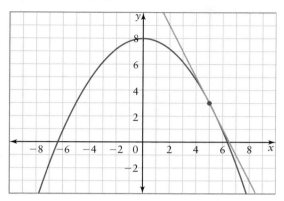

a) State the coordinates of the tangent point.

b) State the coordinates of another point on the tangent line.

c) Use the points you found in parts a) and b) to determine the slope of the tangent line.

d) What does the value you found in part c) represent?

2. a) At each of the indicated points on the graph, is the instantaneous rate of change positive, negative, or zero? Explain.

Height of a Tennis Ball

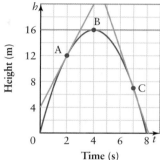

b) Estimate the instantaneous rate of change at points A and C.

c) Interpret the values in part b) for the situation represented by the graph.

For help with question 3, refer to Example 3.

3. A firework is shot into the air such that its height, h, in metres, after t seconds can be modelled by the function $h(t) = -4.9t^2 + 27t + 2$.

a) Copy and complete the table.

Interval	Δh	Δt	$\dfrac{\Delta h}{\Delta t}$
$3 \leq t \leq 3.1$			
$3 \leq t \leq 3.01$			
$3 \leq t \leq 3.001$			

b) Use the table to estimate the velocity of the firework after 3 s.

4. Use two different methods to estimate the slope of the tangent at the point indicated on the graph.

Distance Travelled by a Bungee Jumper

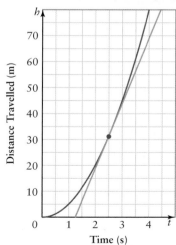

5. The data show the percent of households that play games over the Internet.

Year	% Households
1999	12.3
2000	18.2
2001	24.4
2002	25.7
2003	27.9

Source: Statistics Canada, Canada at a Glance 2006, page 9, Household Internet use at home by Internet activity.

a) Determine the average rate of change, in percent, of households that played games over the Internet from 1999 to 2003.

b) Estimate the instantaneous rate of change in percent of households that played games over the Internet

    i) in 2000   **ii)** in 2002

c) Compare the values found in parts a) and b). Explain any similarities and differences.

6. The table shows the consumer price index (CPI) every 5 years from 1955 to 2005.

Year	CPI
1955	16.8
1960	18.5
1965	20.0
1970	24.2
1975	34.5
1980	52.4
1985	75.0
1990	93.3
1995	104.2
2000	113.5
2005	127.3

Source: Statistics Canada, CANSIM Table 326-0002.

a) Determine the average rate of change in the CPI from 1955 to 2005.

b) Estimate the instantaneous rate of change in the CPI for

    i) 1965   **ii)** 1985   **iii)** 2000

c) Compare the values found in parts a) and b). Explain any similarities and differences.

7. A soccer ball is kicked into the air such that its height, h, in metres, after t seconds can be modelled by the function $h(t) = -4.9t^2 + 12t + 0.5$.

a) Determine the average rate of change of the height of the ball from 1 s to 2 s.

b) Estimate the instantaneous rate of change of the height of the ball after 1 s.

c) Sketch the curve and the tangent.

d) Interpret the average rate of change and the instantaneous rate of change for this situation.

8. On Earth, the height, h, in metres, of a free-falling object after t seconds can be modelled by the function $h(t) = -4.9t^2 + k$, while on Venus, the height can be modelled by $h(t) = -4.45t^2 + k$, where $t \geq 0$ and k is the height, in metres, from which the object is dropped. Suppose a rock is dropped from a height of 60 m on each planet.

a) Determine the average rate of change of the height of the rock in the first 3 s after it is dropped.

b) Estimate the instantaneous rate of change of the height of the rock 3 s after it is dropped.

c) Interpret the values in parts a) and b) for this situation.

9. A manufacturer estimates that the cost, C, in dollars, of producing x MP3 players can be modelled by $C(x) = 0.000\,15x^3 + 100x$.

a) Determine the average rate of change of the cost of producing from 100 to 200 MP3 players.

b) Estimate the instantaneous rate of change of the cost of producing 200 MP3 players.

c) Interpret the values found in parts a) and b) for this situation.

d) Does the cost ever decrease? Explain.

CONNECTIONS

The CPI measures the average price of consumer goods and services purchased by households. The percent change in the CPI is one measure of inflation.

10. Suppose the revenue, R, in dollars, from the sales of x MP3 players described in question 9 is given by $R(x) = x(350 - 0.000\,325x^2)$.

a) Determine the average rate of change of revenue from selling from 100 to 200 MP3 players.

b) Estimate the instantaneous rate of change of revenue from the sale of 200 MP3 players.

c) Interpret the values found in parts a) and b) for this situation.

d) The profit, P, in dollars, from the sale of x MP3 players is given by the profit function $P(x) = R(x) - C(x)$. Determine an equation for the profit function.

e) Determine the average rate of change of profit on the sale of from 100 to 200 MP3 players.

f) Estimate the instantaneous rate of change of profit on the sale of 200 MP3 players.

g) Interpret the values found in parts e) and f) for this situation.

11. A worldwide distributor of basketballs determines that the yearly profit, P, in thousands of dollars, earned on the sale of x thousand basketballs can be modelled by the function $P(x) = -0.09x^3 + 1.89x^2 + 9x$, where $x \in [0, 25]$.

a) Determine the average rate of change of profit earned on the sale of from

   i) 2000 to 6000 basketballs

   ii) 16 000 to 20 000 basketballs

b) What conclusions can you make by comparing the values in part b)? Explain your reasoning.

c) Estimate the instantaneous rate of change of profit earned on the sale of

   i) 5000 basketballs

   ii) 18 000 basketballs

d) What conclusions can you make from the values found in parts c)? Explain your reasoning.

e) **Use Technology** Graph the function. How does the graph support your answers in parts a) and c)?

C Extend and Challenge

12. The population, P, of a small town after t years can be modelled by the function $P(t) = 0.5t^3 + 150t + 1200$, where $t = 0$ represents the beginning of this year.

a) Write an expression for the average rate of change of the population from $t = 8$ to $t = 8 + h$.

b) Use the expression in part a) to determine the average rate of change of the population when

   i) $h = 2$ **ii)** $h = 4$ **iii)** $h = 5$

c) What do the values you found in part b) represent?

d) Describe how the expression in part a) could be used to estimate the instantaneous rate of change of the population after 8 years.

e) Use the method you described in part d) to estimate the instantaneous rate of change of the population after 8 years.

13. Math Contest Determine the exact value of
$$\sqrt{10 + \sqrt{10 + \sqrt{10 + \ldots}}}\,.$$

14. Math Contest Find $|m|$ given
$$\sqrt[3]{m + 9} = 3 + \sqrt[3]{m - 9}.$$

1.1 Power Functions

1. i) Which functions are polynomial functions? Justify your answer.

ii) State the degree and the leading coefficient of each polynomial function.

a) $f(x) = 3x^4 - 5x + 1$

b) $g(x) = x(4 - x)$

c) $h(x) = 3x + 2x$

d) $m(x) = x^{-2}$

e) $r(x) = 5(x - 1)^3$

2. For each graph, do the following.

i) State whether the corresponding function has even degree or odd degree.

ii) State whether the leading coefficient is positive or negative.

iii) State the domain and range.

iv) Describe the end behaviour.

v) Identify the type of symmetry.

a)

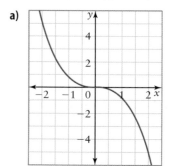

b)

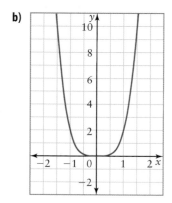

3. Set up a table as shown. Write each function in the appropriate row of column 2. Give reasons for your choices.

$$y = -x^5, \ y = \frac{2}{3}x^4, \ y = 4x^3, \ y = 0.2x^6$$

End Behaviour	Function	Reasons
Extends from quadrant 3 to quadrant 1		
Extends from quadrant 2 to quadrant 4		
Extends from quadrant 2 to quadrant 1		
Extends from quadrant 3 to quadrant 4		

1.2 Characteristics of Polynomial Functions

4. Match each graph of a polynomial function with the corresponding equation. Justify your choice.

i) $g(x) = 0.5x^4 - 3x^2 + 5x$

ii) $h(x) = x^5 - 7x^3 + 2x - 3$

iii) $p(x) = -x^6 + 5x^3 + 4$

a)

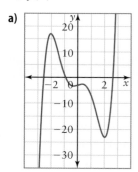

b)

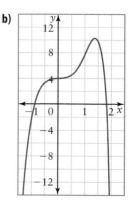

c)

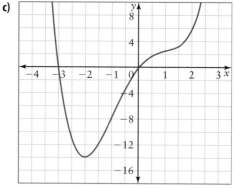

5. For each polynomial function in question 4, do the following.

  a) Determine which finite differences are constant.

  b) Find the value of the constant finite differences.

  c) Identify the type of symmetry, if it exists.

6. a) State the degree of the polynomial function that corresponds to each constant finite difference.

    i) first differences $= -5$

    ii) fifth differences $= -60$

    iii) fourth differences $= 36$

    iv) second differences $= 18$

    v) third differences $= 42$

    vi) third differences $= -18$

  b) Determine the value of the leading coefficient of each polynomial function in part a).

7. Each table of values represents a polynomial function. Use finite differences to determine the following for each:

  i) the degree

  ii) the sign of the leading coefficient

  iii) the value of the leading coefficient

a)

x	y
−3	124
−2	41
−1	8
0	1
1	−4
2	−31
3	−104
4	−247

b)

x	y
−2	−229
−1	−5
0	3
1	−7
2	−53
3	−129
4	35
5	1213

8. A parachutist jumps from a plane 3500 m above the ground. The height, h, in metres, of the parachutist above the ground t seconds after the jump can be modelled by the function $h(t) = 3500 - 4.9t^2$.

  a) What type of function is $h(t)$?

  b) Without calculating the finite differences, determine

    i) which finite differences are constant for this polynomial function

    ii) the value of the constant finite differences

    Explain how you found your answers.

  c) Describe the end behaviour of this function assuming there are no restrictions on the domain.

  d) Graph the function. State any reasonable restrictions on the domain.

  e) What do the t-intercepts of the graph represent for this situation?

1.3 Equations and Graphs of Polynomial Functions

9. Use each graph of a polynomial function to determine

  i) the least possible degree and the sign of the leading coefficient

  ii) the x-intercepts and the factors of the function

  iii) the intervals where the function is positive and the intervals where it is negative

a)

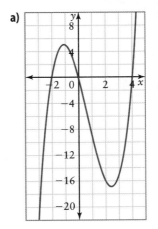

b)

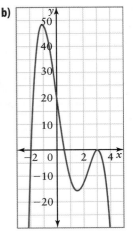

10. Sketch a graph of each polynomial function.

   a) $y = (x + 1)(x - 3)(x + 2)$

   b) $y = -x(x + 1)(x + 2)^2$

   c) $y = (x - 4)^2(x + 3)^3$

11. The zeros of a quartic function are -3, -1, and 2 (order 2). Determine

   a) equations for two functions that satisfy this condition

   b) an equation for a function that satisfies this condition and passes through the point $(1, 4)$

12. Without graphing, determine if each polynomial function has line symmetry about the y-axis, point symmetry about the origin, or neither. Graph the functions to verify your answers.

   a) $f(x) = -x^5 + 7x^3 + 2x$

   b) $f(x) = x^4 + 3x^2 + 1$

   c) $f(x) = 4x^3 - 3x^2 + 8x + 1$

13. Determine an equation for the polynomial function that corresponds to each graph.

a)

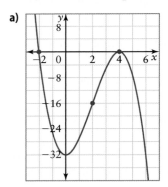

b)

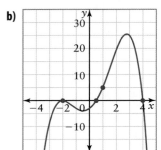

1.4 Transformations

14. i) Describe the transformations that must be applied to the graph of each power function, $f(x)$, to obtain the transformed function. Then, write the corresponding equation.

   ii) State the domain and range of the transformed function. For even functions, state the vertex and the equation of the axis of symmetry.

   a) $f(x) = x^3$, $y = -\dfrac{1}{4}f(x) - 2$

   b) $f(x) = x^4$, $y = 5f\left[\dfrac{2}{5}(x - 3)\right] + 1$

15. i) Write an equation for the function that results from each set of transformations.

   ii) State the domain and range. For even functions, state the vertex and the equation of the axis of symmetry.

   a) $f(x) = x^4$ is compressed vertically by a factor of $\dfrac{3}{5}$, stretched horizontally by a factor of 2, reflected in the y-axis, and translated 1 unit up and 4 units to the left.

   b) $f(x) = x^3$ is compressed horizontally by a factor of $\dfrac{1}{4}$, stretched vertically by a factor of 5, reflected in the x-axis, and translated 2 units to the left and 7 units up.

1.5 Slopes of Secants and Average Rate of Change

16. Which are not examples of average rates of change? Explain why.

   a) The average height of the players on the basketball team is 2.1 m.

   b) The temperature of water in the pool decreased by 5°C over 3 days.

   c) The snowboarder raced across the finish line at 60 km/h.

   d) The class average on the last math test was 75%.

   e) The value of the Canadian dollar increased from $0.75 U.S. to $1.01 U.S. in 8 months.

   f) Approximately 30 cm of snow fell over a 5-h period.

17. The graph represents the approximate value of a stock over 1 year.

Value of Stock

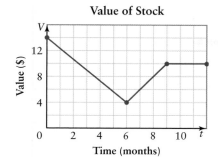

a) What was the value of the stock at the start of the year? at the end of the year?

b) What does the graph tell you about the average rate of change of the value of the stock in each interval?

   i) month 0 to month 6

   ii) month 6 to month 9

   iii) month 9 to month 12

c) Determine the average rate of change of the value of the stock for the time periods in part b). Interpret these values for this situation.

1.6 Slopes of Tangents and Instantaneous Rate of Change

18. The table shows the percent of Canadian households that used the Internet for electronic banking.

Year	Households (%)
1999	8.0
2000	14.7
2001	21.6
2002	26.2
2003	30.8

Source: Statistics Canada, Canada at a Glance 2006, page 9, Household Internet use at home by Internet activity.

a) Determine the average rate of change, in percent, of households that used the Internet for electronic banking from 1999 to 2003.

b) Estimate the instantaneous rate of change in the percent of households that used the Internet for electronic banking in the year 2000, and also in 2002.

c) Compare the values you found in parts a) and b). Explain any similarities and differences.

PROBLEM WRAP-UP

CHAPTER

Throughout this chapter, you have seen how polynomial functions can be used in different careers involving design. Create a design that uses polynomial functions. The design could be for items such as furniture, vehicles, games, clothing, or jewellery.

Provide a report on the design you select that includes the following:

- a description of the item the design relates to and why you selected it
- a drawing of the design using appropriate colours
- an explanation of how the design integrates the graphs of a variety of polynomial functions

Include the following information about each function you used to create the design:

- the equation, domain and range, and end behaviour
- the value of the constant finite differences
- any transformations used
- any symmetry
- any connections to average and instantaneous rate of change

You may wish to do some research on the Internet for ideas and you may want to use technology to help you create your design.

For questions 1 to 3, select the best answer.

1. Which statement is true? For those that are false, provide a counterexample.

   A All odd-degree polynomial functions are odd functions.

   B Even-degree polynomial functions have an even number of x-intercepts.

   C Odd-degree polynomial functions have at least one x-intercept.

   D All even-degree polynomial functions are even.

2. Which statement is true? For those that are false, provide a counterexample.

   A A polynomial function with constant third differences has degree four.

   B A polynomial function with a negative leading coefficient may extend from quadrant 3 to quadrant 4.

   C A power function with even degree has point symmetry.

   D A polynomial function with four x-intercepts has degree four.

3. Which statement is true? For those that are false, provide a counterexample.

   A A vertical compression of factor $\frac{1}{3}$ is the same as a horizontal stretch of factor 3.

   B When applying transformations, translations are applied before stretches and compressions.

   C Stretches must be applied before compressions.

   D A negative k-value in $y = a[k(x - d)]^n + c$ results in a reflection in the x-axis.

   E The equation of a transformed polynomial function can be written in the form $y = a[k(x - d)]^n + c$.

4. Match each graph of a polynomial function with the corresponding equation. Justify your choice.

   i) $f(x) = -2x^3 + 7x + 1$

   ii) $h(x) = x^5 - 7x^3 + 2x + 1$

   iii) $p(x) = -x^6 + 5x^2 + 1$

a)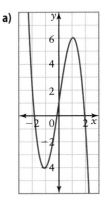

b)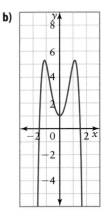

c)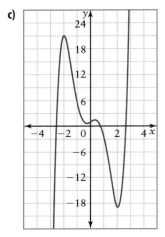

5. For each polynomial function in question 4, answer the following.

   a) Which finite differences are constant?

   b) Find the values of the constant finite differences.

   c) Identify any symmetry. Verify your answer algebraically.

6. A quartic function has zeros -1, 0, and 3 (order 2).

   a) Write equations for two distinct functions that satisfy this description.

   b) Determine an equation for a function satisfying this description that passes through the point $(2, -18)$.

   c) Sketch the function you found in part b). Then, determine the intervals on which the function is positive and the intervals on which it is negative.

7. Determine an equation for the polynomial function that corresponds to this graph.

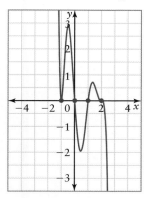

8. a) Identify the parameters a, k, d, and c in the polynomial function $y = \frac{1}{3}[-2(x + 3)]^4 - 1$. Describe how each parameter transforms the base function $y = x^4$.

b) State the domain and range, the vertex, and the equation of the axis of symmetry of the transformed function.

c) Describe two possible orders in which the transformations can be applied to the graph of $y = x^4$ to produce the graph of $y = \frac{1}{3}[-2(x + 3)]^4 - 1$.

d) Sketch graphs of the base function and the transformed function on the same set of axes.

9. Transformations are applied to $y = x^3$ to obtain the graph shown. Determine its equation.

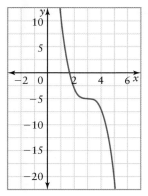

10. Describe a real-life situation that corresponds to

a) a constant, positive average rate of change

b) a constant, negative average rate of change

c) a non-constant average rate of change

d) a zero average rate of change

11. In 1990, 15.5% of households had a CD player, while 76.1% of households had a CD player in 2003. Determine the average rate of change of the percent of households that had a CD player over this time period.

Source: Statistics Canada, Canada at a Glance 2006, page 9, Household facilities.

12. An oil tank is being drained. The volume, V, in litres, of oil remaining in the tank after t minutes can be modelled by the function $V(t) = 0.2(25 - t)^3$, where $t \in [0, 25]$.

a) How much oil is in the tank initially?

b) Determine the average rate of change of volume during

   i) the first 10 min   **ii)** the last 10 min

c) Compare the values you found in part b). Explain any similarities and differences.

d) Sketch a graph to represent the volume.

e) What do the values found in part b) represent on the graph?

13. The distance, d, in metres travelled by a boat from the moment it leaves shore can be modelled by the function $d(t) = 0.002t^3 + 0.05t^2 + 0.3t$, where t is the time, in seconds.

a) Determine the average rate of change of the distance travelled during the first 10 s after leaving the shore.

b) Estimate the instantaneous rate of change 10 s after leaving the shore.

c) Interpret each value in parts a) and b) for this situation.

TASK

Create Your Own Water Park

Apply your knowledge of polynomial functions to create a design for a water park, with a minimum of two appropriate rides per age group:

- under 6 years old
- ages 6 to 12
- over age 12

a) Sketch a graph representing the height versus horizontal distance for each ride.

b) Describe each ride and explain why it is appropriate for the age group.

c) Create a polynomial equation for each ride. Explain how each equation represents the ride.

d) Create a map, diagram, or model of your park.

e) Share your design and equations with a partner.

Chapter **2**

Polynomial Equations and Inequalities

Many real-life problems can be modelled by equations or inequalities. For instance, a manufacturer of electronic games models the profit on its latest device using a polynomial function in one variable. How many devices must be sold to break even, or make a profit? Solving a polynomial equation enables such questions to be answered.

By the end of this chapter, you will

- recognize that there may be more than one polynomial function that can satisfy a given set of conditions (C1.7)
- determine the equation of the family of polynomial functions with a given set of zeros and of the member of the family that passes through another given point (C1.8)
- make connections, through investigation using technology, between the polynomial function $f(x)$, the divisor $x - a$, the remainder from the division $\frac{f(x)}{x-a}$, and $f(a)$ to verify the remainder theorem and factor theorem (C3.1)
- factor polynomial expressions in one variable, of degree no higher than four, by selecting and applying strategies (C3.2)
- determine, through investigation using technology, the connection between the real roots of a polynomial equation and the x-intercepts of the graph of the corresponding polynomial function, and describe this connection (C3.3)
- solve polynomial equations in one variable, of degree no higher than four, by selecting and applying strategies, and verify solutions using technology (C3.4)
- solve problems involving applications of polynomial and equations (C3.7)
- explain, for polynomial functions, the difference between the solution to an equation in one variable and the solution to an inequality in one variable, and demonstrate that given solutions satisfy an inequality (C4.1)
- determine solutions to polynomial inequalities in one variable by graphing the corresponding functions, using graphing technology, and identifying intervals for which x satisfies the inequalities (C4.2)
- solve linear inequalities and factorable polynomial inequalities in a variety of ways, and represent the solutions on a number line or algebraically (C4.3)

Prerequisite Skills

Use Long Division

1. Use long division to find each quotient. Write the remainder.

    a) $3476 \div 28$

    b) $5973 \div 37$

    c) $2508 \div 17$

    d) $6815 \div 19$

Evaluate Functions

2. Given $P(x) = x^3 - 5x^2 + 7x - 9$, evaluate.

    a) $P(-1)$

    b) $P(3)$

    c) $P(-2)$

    d) $P\left(-\dfrac{1}{2}\right)$

    e) $P\left(\dfrac{2}{3}\right)$

Simplify Expressions

3. Expand and simplify.

    a) $(x^3 + 3x^2 - x + 1)(x - 2) + 5$

    b) $(2x^3 - 4x^2 + x - 3)(x + 4) - 7$

    c) $(x^3 + 4x^2 - x + 8)(3x - 1) + 6$

    d) $(x - \sqrt{2})(x + \sqrt{2})$

    e) $(x - 3\sqrt{5})(x + 3\sqrt{5})$

    f) $(x - 1 + \sqrt{3})(x - 1 - \sqrt{3})$

Factor Expressions

4. Factor each difference of squares. Look for common factors first.

    a) $x^2 - 4$

    b) $25m^2 - 49$

    c) $16y^2 - 9$

    d) $12c^2 - 27$

    e) $2x^4 - 32$

    f) $3n^4 - 12$

5. Factor each trinomial.

    a) $x^2 + 5x + 6$

    b) $x^2 - 9x + 20$

    c) $b^2 + 5b - 14$

    d) $2x^2 - 7x - 15$

    e) $4x^2 - 12x + 9$

    f) $6a^2 - 7a + 2$

    g) $9m^2 - 24m + 16$

    h) $3m^2 - 10m + 3$

Solve Quadratic Equations

6. Solve by factoring.

    a) $x^2 - 2x - 15 = 0$

    b) $4x^2 + x - 3 = 0$

    c) $16x^2 - 36 = 0$

    d) $9x^2 = -15 + 48x$

    e) $20 - 12x = 8x^2$

    f) $21x^2 + 1 = 10x$

7. Use the quadratic formula to solve. Round answers to one decimal place.

    a) $5x^2 + 6x - 1 = 0$

    b) $2x^2 - 7x + 4 = 0$

    c) $4x^2 = -2x + 3$

    d) $7x + 20 = 6x^2$

Determine Equations of Quadratic Functions

8. Determine an equation for the quadratic function, with the given zeros, and that passes through the given point.

    a) zeros: -4 and 1; point: $(-1, 2)$

    b) zeros: 0 and 3; point: $(2, 6)$

    c) zeros: -3 and 4; point: $(3, 24)$

    d) zeros: 5 and -1; point: $(4, -10)$

    e) zeros: $\dfrac{3}{2}$ and $-\dfrac{1}{2}$; point: $(0, 9)$

Determine Intervals From Graphs

9. For the graph of each polynomial function,

   i) identify the x-intercepts

   ii) write the intervals for which the graph is above the x-axis and the intervals for which the graph is below the x-axis

a)

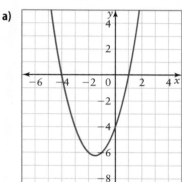

b)

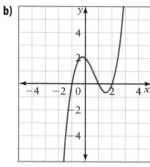

c)

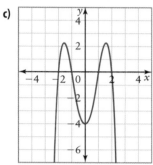

CHAPTER

PROBLEM

Best of U is a company that manufactures personal care products. Much of the company's recent success is due to the hard work of three key teams. The package design team is responsible for creating attractive, practical, and low-cost containers. The marketing team keeps in close touch with up-to-date trends and consumer demands for various products. Finally, the finance team analyses production costs, revenue, and profits to ensure that the company achieves its financial goals.

   Throughout this chapter, you will discover how polynomial functions may be used to model and solve problems related to some of the aspects of running this company.

2.1

The Remainder Theorem

A manufacturer of cardboard boxes receives an order for gift boxes. Based on cost calculations, the volume, V, of each box to be constructed can be modelled by the polynomial function $V(x) = x^3 + 7x^2 + 14x + 8$, where x is a positive integer such that $10 \leq x \leq 20$. The height, h, of each box is a linear function of x such that $h(x) = x + 2$. How can this information be used to determine the dimensions of the boxes in terms of polynomials?

In this section, you will apply the method of long division to divide a polynomial by a binomial. You will also learn to use the remainder theorem to determine the remainder of a division without dividing.

Investigate 1 | **How do you divide using long division?**

1. Examine these two long divisions.

a)
$$\begin{array}{r} 34 \\ 22\overline{)753} \\ 66 \\ \overline{93} \\ 88 \\ \overline{5} \end{array}$$

b)
$$\begin{array}{r} x + 3 \\ x + 2\overline{)x^2 + 5x + 7} \\ x^2 + 2x \\ \overline{3x + 7} \\ 3x + 6 \\ \overline{1} \end{array}$$

For each division, identify the expression or value that corresponds to

   i) the dividend   **ii)** the divisor

   iii) the quotient   **iv)** the remainder

2. Reflect

   a) Describe how long division is used to divide the numbers in step 1 a).

   b) Describe how long division is used to divide the trinomial in step 1 b).

   c) Describe similarities between the use of long division with numbers and with trinomials.

3. a) How can you check that the result of a long division is correct?

   b) Write the corresponding statement that can be used to check each division.

| Example 1 | Divide a Polynomial by a Binomial |

a) Divide $-3x^2 + 2x^3 + 8x - 12$ by $x - 1$. Express the result in quotient form.

b) Identify any restrictions on the variable.

c) Write the corresponding statement that can be used to check the division.

d) Verify your answer.

Solution

Write the polynomial in order of descending powers, just as numbers are written in order of place value: $2x^3 - 3x^2 + 8x - 12$.

a) Method 1: *Use Long Division*

$$
\begin{array}{r}
2x^2 - x + 7 \\
x - 1 \overline{\smash{)}\, 2x^3 - 3x^2 + 8x - 12} \\
\underline{2x^3 - 2x^2} \\
-x^2 + 8x \\
\underline{-x^2 + x} \\
7x - 12 \\
\underline{7x - 7} \\
-5
\end{array}
$$

Divide $2x^3$ by x to get $2x^2$.
Multiply $x - 1$ by $2x^2$ to get $2x^3 - 2x^2$.
Subtract. Bring down the next term, $8x$. Then, divide $-x^2$ by x to get $-x$.
Multiply $x - 1$ by $-x$ to get $-x^2 + x$.
Subtract. Bring down the next term, -12. Then, divide $7x$ by x to get 7.
Multiply $x - 1$ by 7 to get $7x - 7$.
Subtract. The remainder is -5.

$$\frac{-3x^2 + 2x^3 + 8x - 12}{x - 1} = 2x^2 - x + 7 + \frac{-5}{x - 1}$$

Method 2: *Use a Computer Algebra System (CAS)*

Press $\boxed{\text{HOME}}$ to display the CAS home screen and clear its memory using the **Clean Up** menu.

- From the F6 menu, select **2:NewProb**.
- Press $\boxed{\text{ENTER}}$.
- From the F2 menu, select **7:propFrac**. Enter the division expression.
- Press $\boxed{\text{ENTER}}$.

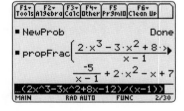

So, $\dfrac{-3x^2 + 2x^3 + 8x - 12}{x - 1} = 2x^2 - x + 7 + \dfrac{-5}{x - 1}$

b) Since division by zero is not defined, the divisor cannot be zero:
$x - 1 \neq 0$, or $x \neq 1$.

c) The corresponding statement is
$-3x^2 + 2x^3 + 8x - 12 = (x - 1)(2x^2 - x + 7) - 5$.

d) To check: Multiply the divisor by the quotient and add the remainder.

$$
\begin{aligned}
(x - 1)(2x^2 - x + 7) - 5 &= 2x^3 - x^2 + 7x - 2x^2 + x - 7 - 5 \\
&= 2x^3 - 3x^2 + 8x - 12 \\
&= -3x^2 + 2x^3 + 8x - 12
\end{aligned}
$$

The result of the division of a polynomial $P(x)$ by a binomial of the form $x - b$ is $\dfrac{P(x)}{x - b} = Q(x) + \dfrac{R}{x - b}$, where $Q(x)$ is the quotient and R is the remainder. The corresponding statement, that can be used to check the division, is $P(x) = (x - b)Q(x) + R$.

Example 2 — Divide a Polynomial by a Binomial of the Form $ax - b$

a) Divide $4x^3 + 9x - 12$ by $2x + 1$. Identify any restrictions on the variable.

b) Write the corresponding statement that can be used to check the division.

Solution

a) The polynomial does not have an x^2 term, so insert $0x^2$ as a placeholder.

$$
\begin{array}{r}
2x^2 - x + 5 \\
2x + 1\,\overline{)\,4x^3 + 0x^2 + 9x - 12} \\
\underline{4x^3 + 2x^2} \\
-2x^2 + 9x \\
\underline{-2x^2 - x} \\
10x - 12 \\
\underline{10x + 5} \\
-17
\end{array}
$$

Divide $4x^3$ by $2x$ to get $2x^2$.
Multiply $2x + 1$ by $2x^2$ to get $4x^3 + 2x^2$.
Subtract. Bring down the next term, $9x$.

$$\frac{4x^3 + 9x - 12}{2x + 1} = 2x^2 - x + 5 + \frac{-17}{2x + 1}$$

Restriction: $2x + 1 \neq 0$, or $x \neq -\dfrac{1}{2}$

b) The corresponding statement is $4x^3 + 9x - 12 = (2x + 1)(2x^2 - x + 5) - 17$.

Example 3 — Apply Long Division to Solve for Dimensions

The volume, V, in cubic centimetres, of a rectangular box is given by $V(x) = x^3 + 7x^2 + 14x + 8$.

Determine expressions for possible dimensions of the box if the height, h, in centimetres, is given by $x + 2$.

Solution

CONNECTIONS

The formula for the volume of a rectangular box is $V = lwh$.

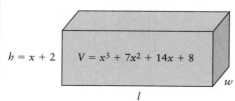

$h = x + 2$ $V = x^3 + 7x^2 + 14x + 8$

w

l

Divide the volume by the height to obtain an expression for the area of the base of the box. That is, $\dfrac{V}{h} = lw$, where lw is the area of the base.

$$
\begin{array}{r}
x^2 + 5x + 4 \\
x + 2\overline{)\,x^3 + 7x^2 + 14x + 8} \\
\underline{x^3 + 2x^2\phantom{{}+14x+8}} \\
5x^2 + 14x\phantom{{}+8} \\
\underline{5x^2 + 10x\phantom{{}+8}} \\
4x + 8 \\
\underline{4x + 8} \\
0
\end{array}
$$

Since the remainder is 0, the volume $x^3 + 7x^2 + 14x + 8$ can be expressed as $(x + 2)(x^2 + 5x + 4)$.

The quotient $x^2 + 5x + 4$ represents the area of the base of the box. This expression can be factored as $(x + 1)(x + 4)$. The factors represent the possible width and length of the base of the box.

Expressions for the possible dimensions of the box, in centimetres, are $x + 1$, $x + 2$, and $x + 4$.

Investigate 2   **How can you determine a remainder without dividing?**

Method 1: *Use Pencil and Paper*

1. a) Compare each binomial to $x - b$. Write the value of b.

   i) $x - 1$ **ii)** $x + 1$ **iii)** $x - 2$ **iv)** $x + 2$

   b) Given a polynomial $P(x)$, what is the value of x in each?

   i) $P(1)$ **ii)** $P(-1)$ **iii)** $P(2)$ **iv)** $P(-2)$

   Compare these values with those found in part a). What do you notice?

2. a) Evaluate parts i) to iv) of step 1b) for the polynomial $P(x) = x^3 + 6x^2 + 2x - 4$. What do the results represent?

   b) Use long division to divide $P(x) = x^3 + 6x^2 + 2x - 4$ by each binomial. Write the remainder.

   i) $x - 1$ **ii)** $x + 1$ **iii)** $x - 2$ **iv)** $x + 2$

   c) Compare the remainders in part b) to the values found in part a). What do you notice?

   d) Reflect Make a conjecture about how a remainder can be found without using division.

3. a) Use your conjecture from step 2 to predict the remainder when $P(x) = x^3 + 4x^2 - 3x + 1$ is divided by each binomial.

   i) $x + 1$ **ii)** $x + 2$ **iii)** $x - 3$ **iv)** $x + 3$

   b) Verify your predictions using long division.

4. Reflect Describe the relationship between the remainder when a polynomial $P(x)$ is divided by $x - b$ and the value of $P(b)$. Why is it appropriate to call this relationship the **remainder theorem**?

Tools

• calculator with a computer algebra system (CAS)

Method 2: *Use a CAS*

1. Define $P(x) = x^3 + 6x^2 + 2x - 4$.

  • From the **F4** menu, select **1:Define**. Enter the polynomial expression.

2. Determine $P(1)$.

  • Type **P(1)** and then press (ENTER).

3. Calculate $\dfrac{x^3 + 6x^2 + 2x - 4}{x - 1}$, or $\dfrac{P(x)}{x - 1}$.

  • From the **F2** menu, select **7:propFrac**.

  • Type **P(X) ÷ (X − 1))** and then press (ENTER). Write the remainder.

4. a) Reflect Is there a relationship between $P(1)$, the linear factor $x - 1$, and the polynomial division?

  b) Investigate for other values of x. Let $x = -1$, $x = 2$, and $x = -2$, and find $P(x)$.

  c) Calculate $\dfrac{P(x)}{x + 1}$, $\dfrac{P(x)}{x + 2}$, and $\dfrac{P(x)}{x - 2}$.

  d) Compare the remainders in part c) to the values found in part b). What do you notice?

  e) Reflect Make a conjecture about how a remainder can be found without using division.

5. a) Use your conjecture in step 4 to predict the remainder when $P(x) = x^3 + 4x^2 - 3x + 1$ is divided by each binomial.

  i) $x + 1$ **ii)** $x + 2$ **iii)** $x - 3$ **iv)** $x + 3$

  b) Verify your predictions using a CAS.

6. Reflect Describe the relationship between the remainder when a polynomial $P(x)$ is divided by $x - b$ and the value of $P(b)$. Why is it appropriate to call this relationship the **remainder theorem**?

Remainder Theorem

When a polynomial function $P(x)$ is divided by $x - b$, the remainder is $P(b)$; and when it is divided by $ax - b$, the remainder is $P\left(\dfrac{b}{a}\right)$, where a and b are integers, and $a \neq 0$.

Example 4 Apply and Verify the Remainder Theorem

a) Use the remainder theorem to determine the remainder when $P(x) = 2x^3 + x^2 - 3x - 6$ is divided by $x + 1$.

b) Verify your answer using long division.

c) Use the remainder theorem to determine the remainder when $P(x) = 2x^3 + x^2 - 3x - 6$ is divided by $2x - 3$.

Solution

a) Since $x + 1 = x - (-1)$, the remainder is $P(-1)$.

$$P(-1) = 2(-1)^3 + (-1)^2 - 3(-1) - 6$$
$$= -2 + 1 + 3 - 6$$
$$= -4$$

When $P(x) = 2x^3 + x^2 - 3x - 6$ is divided by $x + 1$, the remainder is -4.

b)

$$
\begin{array}{r}
2x^2 - x - 2 \\
x + 1 \overline{\smash{)}2x^3 + x^2 - 3x - 6} \\
\underline{2x^3 + 2x^2} \\
-x^2 - 3x \\
\underline{-x^2 - x} \\
-2x - 6 \\
\underline{-2x - 2} \\
-4
\end{array}
$$

Using long division, the remainder is -4. This verifies the answer in part a).

c) Comparing $2x - 3$ to $ax - b$, gives $a = 2$ and $b = 3$.

The remainder $P\left(\dfrac{b}{a}\right)$ is $P\left(\dfrac{3}{2}\right)$.

$$P\left(\frac{3}{2}\right) = 2\left(\frac{3}{2}\right)^3 + \left(\frac{3}{2}\right)^2 - 3\left(\frac{3}{2}\right) - 6$$

$$= 2\left(\frac{27}{8}\right) + \left(\frac{9}{4}\right) - 3\left(\frac{3}{2}\right) - 6$$

$$= \frac{27}{4} + \frac{9}{4} - \frac{18}{4} - \frac{24}{4}$$

$$= -\frac{6}{4}$$

$$= -\frac{3}{2}$$

When $P(x) = 2x^3 + x^2 - 3x - 6$ is divided by $2x - 3$, the remainder is $-\dfrac{3}{2}$.

Example 5 | **Solve for an Unknown Coefficient**

Determine the value of k such that when $3x^4 + kx^3 - 7x - 10$ is divided by $x - 2$, the remainder is 8.

> **Solution**

Let $P(x) = 3x^4 + kx^3 - 7x - 10$.

By the remainder theorem, when $P(x)$ is divided by $x - 2$, the remainder is $P(2)$. Solve $P(2) = 8$.

$$3(2)^4 + k(2)^3 - 7(2) - 10 = 8$$
$$48 + 8k - 14 - 10 = 8$$
$$24 + 8k = 8$$
$$8k = -16$$
$$k = -2$$

The value of k is -2.

« KEY CONCEPTS »

- Long division can be used to divide a polynomial by a binomial.

- The result of the division of a polynomial function $P(x)$ by a binomial of the form $x - b$ can be written as $P(x) = (x - b)Q(x) + R$ or $\dfrac{P(x)}{x - b} = Q(x) + \dfrac{R}{x - b}$, where $Q(x)$ is the quotient and R is the remainder.

- To check the result of a division, use
  divisor × quotient + remainder = dividend.

- The remainder theorem states that when a polynomial function $P(x)$ is divided by $x - b$, the remainder is $P(b)$, and when it is divided by $ax - b$, the remainder is $P\left(\dfrac{b}{a}\right)$, where a and b are integers and $a \neq 0$.

Communicate Your Understanding

C1 Explain why there is a restriction on the divisor of a polynomial function. How is the restriction determined?

C2 When and why might it be necessary to use a placeholder when dividing a polynomial by a binomial?

C3 Describe the error in this statement:
$$\frac{x^3 + 3x^2 - 2x - 1}{x - 2} = (x^2 + 5x + 8) + 5$$

C4 Given a polynomial function $P(x)$ such that $P(-3) = 0$, what are the divisor and the remainder? What is the relationship between the divisor and $P(x)$?

C5 Identify the dividend, divisor, quotient, and remainder in each statement.

a) $\dfrac{6x^2 + 5x - 7}{3x + 1} = 2x + 1 - \dfrac{8}{3x + 1}$

b) $12x^3 + 2x^2 + 11x + 14 = (3x + 2)(4x^2 - 2x + 5) + 4$

c) $\dfrac{5x^3 - 7x^2 - x + 6}{x - 1} = 5x^2 - 2x - 3 + \dfrac{3}{x - 1}$

A ⟩ Practise

For help with questions 1 and 2, refer to Example 1.

1. a) Divide $x^3 + 3x^2 - 2x + 5$ by $x + 1$. Express the result in quotient form.

b) Identify any restrictions on the variable.

c) Write the corresponding statement that can be used to check the division.

d) Verify your answer.

2. a) Divide $3x^4 - 4x^3 - 6x^2 + 17x - 8$ by $3x - 4$. Express the result in quotient form.

b) Identify any restrictions on the variable.

c) Write the corresponding statement that can be used to check the division.

d) Verify your answer.

For help with question 3, refer to Example 2.

3. Perform each division. Express the result in quotient form. Identify any restrictions on the variable.

a) $x^3 + 7x^2 - 3x + 4$ divided by $x + 2$

b) $6x^3 + x^2 - 14x - 6$ divided by $3x + 2$

c) $10x^3 + 11 - 9x^2 - 8x$ divided by $5x - 2$

d) $11x - 4x^4 - 7$ divided by $x - 3$

e) $3 + x^2 + 7x + 6x^3$ divided by $3x + 2$

f) $8x^3 + 4x^2 - 31$ divided by $2x - 3$

g) $6x^2 - 6 + 8x^3$ divided by $4x - 3$

4. Determine the remainder R so that each statement is true.

a) $(2x - 3)(3x + 4) + R = 6x^2 - x + 15$

b) $(x + 2)(x^2 - 3x + 4) + R = x^3 - x^2 - 2x - 1$

c) $(x - 4)(2x^2 + 3x - 1) + R$
$= 2x^3 - 5x^2 - 13x + 2$

For help with questions 5 and 6, refer to Example 3.

5. The volume, in cubic centimetres, of a rectangular box can be modelled by the polynomial expression $2x^3 + 17x^2 + 38x + 15$. Determine possible dimensions of the box if the height, in centimetres, is given by $x + 5$.

Reasoning and Proving

Representing · Selecting Tools

Problem Solving

Connecting · Reflecting

Communicating

6. The volume, in cubic centimetres, of a square-based box is given by $9x^3 + 24x^2 - 44x + 16$. Determine possible dimensions of the box if the area of the base, in square centimetres, is $9x^2 - 12x + 4$.

For help with questions 7 to 9, refer to Example 4.

7. Use the remainder theorem to determine the remainder when $2x^3 + 7x^2 - 8x + 3$ is divided by each binomial. Verify your answer using long division.

a) $x + 1$ b) $x - 2$ c) $x + 3$

d) $x - 4$ e) $x - 1$

8. Determine the remainder when each polynomial is divided by $x + 2$.

a) $x^3 + 3x^2 - 5x + 2$

b) $2x^3 - x^2 - 3x + 1$

c) $x^4 + x^3 - 5x^2 + 2x - 7$

9. Use the remainder theorem to determine the remainder for each division.

a) $x^3 + 2x^2 - 3x + 9$ divided by $x + 3$

b) $2x^3 + 7x^2 - x + 1$ divided by $x + 2$

c) $x^3 + 2x^2 - 3x + 5$ divided by $x - 3$

d) $x^4 - 3x^2 - 5x + 2$ divided by $x - 2$

For help with questions 10 to 12, refer to Example 5.

10. a) Determine the value of k such that when $P(x) = kx^3 + 5x^2 - 2x + 3$ is divided by $x + 1$, the remainder is 7.

b) Determine the remainder when $P(x)$ is divided by $x - 3$.

11. a) Determine the value of c such that when $f(x) = x^4 - cx^3 + 7x - 6$ is divided by $x - 2$, the remainder is -8.

b) Determine the remainder when $f(x)$ is divided by $x + 2$.

c) **Use Technology** Verify your answer in part b) using a CAS.

12. For what value of b will the polynomial $P(x) = -2x^3 + bx^2 - 5x + 2$ have the same remainder when it is divided by $x - 2$ and by $x + 1$?

13. For what value of k will the polynomial $f(x) = x^3 + 6x^2 + kx - 4$ have the same remainder when it is divided by $x - 1$ and by $x + 2$?

14. a) Use the remainder theorem to determine the remainder when $2x^3 + 5x^2 - 6x + 4$ is divided by $2x + 1$.

b) Verify your answer in part a) using long division.

c) **Use Technology** Verify your answer in part a) using technology.

15. a) Use the remainder theorem to determine the remainder when $10x^4 - 11x^3 - 8x^2 + 7x + 9$ is divided by $2x - 3$.

b) **Use Technology** Verify your answer in part a) using long division or using a CAS.

16. a) Determine the remainder when $6x^3 + 23x^2 - 6x - 8$ is divided by $3x - 2$.

b) What information does the remainder provide about $3x - 2$? Explain.

c) Express $6x^3 + 23x^2 - 6x - 8$ in factored form.

17. Chapter Problem The packaging design team at Best of U has determined that a cost-efficient way of manufacturing cylindrical containers for their products is to have the volume, V, in cubic centimetres, modelled by $V(x) = 9\pi x^3 + 51\pi x^2 + 88\pi x + 48\pi$, where x is an integer such that $2 \le x \le 8$. The height, h, in centimetres, of each cylinder is a linear function given by $h(x) = x + 3$.

a) Determine the quotient $\dfrac{V(x)}{h(x)}$. Interpret this result.

b) Use your answer in part a) to express the volume of a container in the form $\pi r^2 h$.

c) What are the possible dimensions and volumes of the containers for the given values of x?

CONNECTIONS

The formula for the volume of a cylinder is $V = \pi r^2 h$, where r is the radius of the circular base and h is the height.

---

18. Jessica Zelinka, a Canadian heptathlete, won a gold medal in javelin throw at the Pan American games in 2007. Suppose $h(t) = -5t^2 + 15t + 1$ represents the approximate height, in metres, of a javelin t seconds after it is thrown.

Reasoning and Proving

Representing — Selecting Tools

Problem Solving

Connecting — Reflecting

Communicating

a) Write a statement that corresponds to the quotient $\dfrac{h(t)}{t - b}$, where b is a positive integer.

b) Show that the statement in part a) may be written as $Q(t) = \dfrac{h(t) - h(b)}{t - b}$.

c) What is the geometric interpretation of $\dfrac{h(t) - h(b)}{t - b}$? Support your answer with a diagram.

d) Use the result of part c) to explain the physical meaning of $Q(t)$ for this situation.

e) Determine the remainder when $h(t)$ is divided by $t - 3$. Interpret the remainder for this situation.

19. The shot-put is another event in a heptathlon. Suppose $h(t) = -5t^2 + 8.3t + 1.2$ represents the approximate height, h, in metres, of a shot-put t seconds after it is thrown.

a) Determine the remainder when $h(t)$ is divided by $t - 1.5$.

b) Use the results of question 18 to interpret your answer in part a) for this situation.

C **Extend and Challenge**

20. When the polynomial $mx^3 - 3x^2 + nx + 2$ is divided by $x + 3$, the remainder is -1. When it is divided by $x - 2$, the remainder is -4. Determine the values of m and n.

21. When the polynomial $3x^3 + ax^2 + bx - 9$ is divided by $x - 2$, the remainder is -5. When it is divided by $x + 1$, the remainder is -16. Determine the values of a and b.

22. When $3x^2 + 10x - 3$ is divided by $x + k$, the remainder is 5. Determine the values of k.

23. **Math Contest** When a number, x, is divided by 4, the remainder is 3. Determine the remainder when $5x$ is divided by 4.

24. **Math Contest** Determine the area, A, of a triangle with vertices A(4, 6), B(2, 3), and C(8, 4) by applying Heron's formula,
$$A = \sqrt{s(s - a)(s - b)(s - c)},$$
where a, b, and c are the side lengths and $s = \frac{1}{2}(a + b + c)$.

25. **Math Contest** In $\triangle$HKL, $\angle$HKL = 90°. Prove that HM = MK.

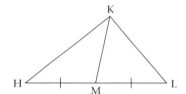

CAREER CONNECTION

Since graduating from a 4-year environmental science program at the University of Ottawa, Chantal has been working to become a licensed environmental engineer. She works in water resources management and ensures that social, economic, environmental, and technical concerns are taken into account when water resources, such as reservoirs, are built and maintained. Chantal creates mathematical models of the water resource she is studying and tests them for various factors. For example, she may test the maximum storage capacity of a new reservoir or optimize the amount of water an existing reservoir should release.

The Factor Theorem

Ice carvers from across Canada and around the world come to Ottawa every year to take part in the ice-carving competition at the Winterlude Festival. Some artists create gigantic ice sculptures from cubic blocks of ice with sides measuring as long as 3.7 m.

Suppose the forms used to make large rectangular blocks of ice come in different dimensions such that the volume of each block can be modelled by $V(x) = 3x^3 + 2x^2 - 7x + 2$. What dimensions, in terms of x, can result in this volume? You will see that the dimensions can be found by factoring $V(x)$.

Investigate | **How can you determine a factor of a polynomial?**

Tools

• calculator with a computer algebra system (optional)

1. a) Use the remainder theorem to determine the remainder when $x^3 + 2x^2 - x - 2$ is divided by $x - 1$.

b) Determine the quotient $\dfrac{x^3 + 2x^2 - x - 2}{x - 1}$. Write the corresonding statement that can be used to check the division.

c) Use your answer from part b) to write the factors of $x^3 + 2x^2 - x - 2$.

d) Reflect What is the connection between the remainder and the factors of a polynomial function?

2. a) Which of the following are factors of $P(x) = x^3 + 4x^2 + x - 6$? Justify your reasoning.

  A $x + 1$

  B $x - 1$

  C $x + 2$

  D $x - 2$

  E $x + 3$

b) Reflect Write a statement that describes the condition when a divisor $x - b$ is a factor of a polynomial $P(x)$. Why is it appropriate to call this the **factor theorem**? How is this related to the remainder theorem?

3. a) Reflect Describe a method you can use to determine the factors of a polynomial $f(x)$.

b) Use your method to determine the factors of $f(x) = x^3 - 2x^2 - x + 2$.

c) Verify your answer in part b).

Factor Theorem

$x - b$ is a factor of a polynomial $P(x)$ if and only if $P(b) = 0$.

Similarly, $ax - b$ is a factor of $P(x)$ if and only if $P\left(\dfrac{b}{a}\right) = 0$.

CONNECTIONS

"If and only if" is a term used in logic to say that the result works both ways. Here, both of the following are true:

- If $x - b$ is a factor, then $P(b) = 0$.
- If $P(b) = 0$, then $x - b$ is a factor of $P(x)$.

With the factor theorem, you can determine the factors of a polynomial without having to divide. For instance, to determine if $x - 3$ and $x + 2$ are factors of $P(x) = x^3 - x^2 - 14x + 24$, calculate $P(3)$ and $P(-2)$.

$P(3) = (3)^3 - (3)^2 - 14(3) + 24$
$\quad\ = 27 - 9 - 42 + 24$
$\quad\ = 0$

Since the remainder is zero, $P(x)$ is divisible by $x - 3$; that is, $x - 3$ divides evenly into $P(x)$, and $x - 3$ is a factor of $P(x)$.

$P(-2) = (-2)^3 - (-2)^2 - 14(-2) + 24$
$\quad\quad = -8 - 4 + 28 + 24$
$\quad\quad = 40$

Since the remainder is not zero, $P(x)$ is not divisible by $x + 2$. So, $x + 2$ is not a factor of $P(x)$.

In general, if $P(b) = 0$, then $x - b$ is a factor of $P(x)$, and, conversely, if $x - b$ is a factor of $P(x)$, then $P(b) = 0$. This statement leads to the factor theorem, which is an extension of the remainder theorem.

Example 1	**Use the Factor Theorem to Find Factors of a Polynomial**

a) Which binomials are factors of the polynomial $P(x) = 2x^3 + 3x^2 - 3x - 2$? Justify your answers.

   i) $x - 2$ **ii)** $x + 2$ **iii)** $x + 1$ **iv)** $x - 1$ **v)** $2x + 1$

b) Use your results in part a) to write $P(x) = 2x^3 + 3x^2 - 3x - 2$ in factored form.

Solution

a) Use the factor theorem to evaluate $P(b)$ or $P\left(\dfrac{b}{a}\right)$.

  Method 1: *Use Pencil and Paper*

   i) For $x - 2$, substitute $x = 2$ into the polynomial expression.

     $P(2) = 2(2)^3 + 3(2)^2 - 3(2) - 2$
          $= 16 + 12 - 6 - 2$
          $= 20$

   Since the remainder is not zero, $x - 2$ is not a factor of $P(x)$.

ii) For $x + 2$, substitute $x = -2$ into the polynomial expression.

$$P(-2) = 2(-2)^3 + 3(-2)^2 - 3(-2) - 2$$
$$= -16 + 12 + 6 - 2$$
$$= 0$$

Since the remainder is zero, $x + 2$ is a factor of $P(x)$.

iii) For $x + 1$, substitute $x = -1$ into the polynomial expression.

$$P(-1) = 2(-1)^3 + 3(-1)^2 - 3(-1) - 2$$
$$= -2 + 3 + 3 - 2$$
$$= 2$$

Since the remainder is not zero, $x + 1$ is not a factor of $P(x)$.

iv) For $x - 1$, substitute $x = 1$ into the polynomial expression.

$$P(1) = 2(1)^3 + 3(1)^2 - 3(1) - 2$$
$$= 2 + 3 - 3 - 2$$
$$= 0$$

Since the remainder is zero, $x - 1$ is a factor of $P(x)$.

v) For $2x + 1$, substitute $x = -\dfrac{1}{2}$ into the polynomial expression.

$$P\left(-\frac{1}{2}\right) = 2\left(-\frac{1}{2}\right)^3 + 3\left(-\frac{1}{2}\right)^2 - 3\left(-\frac{1}{2}\right) - 2$$
$$= -\frac{1}{4} + \frac{3}{4} + \frac{3}{2} - 2$$
$$= 0$$

Since the remainder is zero, $2x + 1$ is a factor of $P(x)$.

Method 2: *Use a Graphing Calculator*

Enter the function $y = 2x^3 + 3x^2 - 3x - 2$ in **Y1**.

- Press (2nd) (MODE) to return to the main screen.

i) For $x - 2$, substitute $x = 2$ and calculate Y1(2).

- Press (VARS) (▶). Select **1:Function**, and press (ENTER).
- Enter $Y_1(2)$ by pressing (( ) 2 ( )).
- Press (ENTER).

ii) For $x + 2$, substitute $x = -2$ and calculate $Y_1(-2)$.

Repeat the steps of part i). Enter $Y_1(-2)$ by pressing (( ) ((-)) 2 ( )).

iii) For $x + 1$, calculate $Y_1(-1)$.

iv) For $x - 1$, calculate $Y_1(1)$.

v) For $2x + 1 = 0$, substitute $x = -\dfrac{1}{2}$ and calculate $Y_1\left(-\dfrac{1}{2}\right)$.

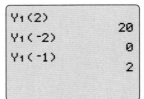

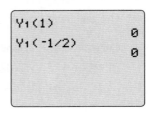

b) The factors of $P(x) = 2x^3 + 3x^2 - 3x - 2$ are $x + 2$, $x - 1$, and $2x + 1$.
In factored form, $2x^3 + 3x^2 - 3x - 2 = (x + 2)(x - 1)(2x + 1)$.

Technology Tip ∴

Another method of finding the y-values for specific x-values is to graph **Y1**. Then, press (TRACE), input a value, and press (ENTER).

CONNECTIONS

$P(x)$ is a cubic function, so it has at most three linear factors.

Consider the polynomial $P(x) = x^3 + 2x^2 - 5x - 6$.

A value $x = b$ that satisfies $P(b) = 0$ also satisfies $b^3 + 2b^2 - 5b - 6 = 0$, or $b^3 + 2b^2 - 5b = 6$. Factoring out the common factor b gives the product $b(b^2 + 2b - 5) = 6$.

For integer values of b, the value of $b^2 + 2b - 5$ is also an integer. Since the product $b(b^2 + 2b - 5)$ is 6, the possible integer values for the factors in the product are the factors of 6. They are ±1, ±2, ±3, and ±6.

The relationship between the factors of a polynomial and the constant term in the polynomial expression is stated in the **integral zero theorem** .

Integral Zero Theorem

If $x - b$ is a factor of a polynomial function $P(x)$ with leading coefficient 1 and remaining coefficients that are integers, then b is a factor of the constant term of $P(x)$.

CONNECTIONS

The word *integral* refers to integer values of b in a factor $x - b$. The word *zero* indicates the value of b being a zero of the polynomial function $P(x)$, that is, $P(b) = 0$.

Once one factor of a polynomial is found, division is used to determine the other factors. Synthetic division is an abbreviated form of long division for dividing a polynomial by a binomial of the form $x - b$. This method eliminates the use of the variable x and is illustrated in Example 2.

Example 2 | Two Division Strategies to Factor a Polynomial

Factor $x^3 + 2x^2 - 5x - 6$ fully.

Solution

Let $P(x) = x^3 + 2x^2 - 5x - 6$.

Find a value $x = b$ such that $P(b) = 0$.

By the integral zero theorem, test factors of -6, that is, ±1, ±2, ±3, and ±6.

Substitute $x = 1$ to test.

$$P(1) = (1)^3 + 2(1)^2 - 5(1) - 6$$
$$= 1 + 2 - 5 - 6$$
$$= -8$$

So, $x = 1$ is not a zero of $P(x)$ and $x - 1$ is not a factor.

Substitute $x = 2$ to test.

$$P(2) = (2)^3 + 2(2)^2 - 5(2) - 6$$
$$= 8 + 8 - 10 - 6$$
$$= 0$$

So, $x = 2$ is a zero of $P(x)$ and $x - 2$ is a factor.

Once one factor is determined, use one of the following methods to determine the other factors.

Method 1: *Use Long Division*

$$
\begin{array}{r}
x^2 + 4x + 3 \\
x - 2 \overline{)\, x^3 + 2x^2 - 5x - 6} \\
\underline{x^3 - 2x^2} \\
4x^2 - 5x \\
\underline{4x^2 - 8x} \\
3x - 6 \\
\underline{3x - 6} \\
0
\end{array}
$$

$x^3 + 2x^2 - 5x - 6 = (x - 2)(x^2 + 4x + 3)$

$x^2 + 4x + 3$ can be factored further to give $x^2 + 4x + 3 = (x + 3)(x + 1)$.

So, $x^3 + 2x^2 - 5x - 6 = (x - 2)(x + 3)(x + 1)$.

Method 2: *Use Synthetic Division*

Set up a division chart for the synthetic division of $P(x) = x^3 + 2x^2 - 5x - 6$ by $x - 2$ as shown.

List the coefficients of the dividend, $x^3 + 2x^2 - 5x - 6$, in the first row. To the left, write the value of -2 from the factor $x - 2$. Below -2, place a $-$ sign to represent subtraction. Use the $\times$ sign below the horizontal line to indicate multiplication of the divisor and the terms of the quotient.

$$
\begin{array}{c|cccc}
-2 & 1 & 2 & -5 & -6 \\
- &   &   &   &   \\
\hline
\times & & & &
\end{array}
$$

Perform the synthetic division.

Bring down the first coefficient, 1, to the right of the $\times$ sign.

$$
\begin{array}{c|cccc}
-2 & 1 & 2 & -5 & -6 \\
- & \downarrow & -2 & -8 & -6 \\
\hline
\times & 1 & 4 & 3 & 0
\end{array}
$$

Multiply -2 (top left) by 1 (right of $\times$ sign) to get -2.

Write -2 below 2 in the second column.

Subtract -2 from 2 to get 4.

Multiply -2 by 4 to get -8. Continue with $-5 - (-8) = 3$, $-2 \times 3 = -6$, and $-6 - (-6) = 0$.

1, 4, and 3 are the coefficients of the quotient, $x^2 + 4x + 3$.

0 is the remainder.

$x^3 + 2x^2 - 5x - 6 = (x - 2)(x^2 + 4x + 3)$

$x^2 + 4x + 3$ can be factored further to give $x^2 + 4x + 3 = (x + 3)(x + 1)$.

So, $x^3 + 2x^2 - 5x - 6 = (x - 2)(x + 3)(x + 1)$.

| Example 3 | Combine the Factor Theorem and Factoring by Grouping |

Factor $x^4 + 3x^3 - 7x^2 - 27x - 18$.

Solution

Let $P(x) = x^4 + 3x^3 - 7x^2 - 27x - 18$.

Find a value for x such that $P(x) = 0$.

By the integral zero theorem, test factors of -18, that is, ± 1, ± 2, ± 3, ± 6, ± 9, and ± 18.

Testing all 12 values for x can be time-consuming. Using a calculator will be more efficient.

Enter the function $y = x^4 + 3x^3 - 7x^2 - 27x - 18$ in **Y1**.

Test the factors ± 1, ± 2, ... by calculating $Y_1(1)$, $Y_1(-1)$, $Y_1(2)$, $Y_1(-2)$, ... until a zero is found.

> **Y1(1)**
>   -48
> **Y1(-1)**
>   0

Technology Tip ∴

Another method of finding a zero is to graph the polynomial function and use the **Zero** operation.

Since $x = -1$ is a zero of $P(x)$, $x + 1$ is a factor.

Use division to determine the other factor.

$$x^4 + 3x^3 - 7x^2 - 27x - 18 = (x + 1)(x^3 + 2x^2 - 9x - 18)$$

To factor $P(x)$ further, factor $x^3 + 2x^2 - 9x - 18$ using one of the following methods.

Method 1: *Apply the Factor Theorem and Division a Second Time*

Let $f(x) = x^3 + 2x^2 - 9x - 18$.

Test possible factors of -18 by calculating $Y_1(1)$, $Y_1(-1)$, $Y_1(2)$, $Y_1(-2)$, ... until a zero is found.

Since $Y_1(-2) = 0$, $x = -2$ is a zero of $f(x)$ and $x + 2$ is a factor.

Use division to determine the other factor.

$$\begin{aligned} f(x) &= x^3 + 2x^2 - 9x - 18 \\ &= (x + 2)(x^2 - 9) \\ &= (x + 2)(x + 3)(x - 3) \end{aligned}$$

So, $P(x) = x^4 + 3x^3 - 7x^2 - 27x - 18 = (x + 1)(x + 2)(x + 3)(x - 3)$.

Method 2: *Factor by Grouping*

$$\begin{aligned} f(x) &= x^3 + 2x^2 - 9x - 18 \\ &= x^2(x + 2) - 9(x + 2) \qquad && \text{Group the first two terms and factor out } x^2. \\ && \text{Then, group the second two terms and factor out } -9. \\ &= (x + 2)(x^2 - 9) \qquad && \text{Factor out } x + 2. \\ &= (x + 2)(x + 3)(x - 3) \qquad && \text{Factor the difference of squares } (x^2 - 9). \end{aligned}$$

So, $P(x) = x^4 + 3x^3 - 7x^2 - 27x - 18 = (x + 1)(x + 2)(x + 3)(x - 3)$.

CONNECTIONS

The method of factoring by grouping applies when pairs of terms of a polynomial can be grouped to factor out a common factor so that the resulting binomial factors are the same.

Consider a factorable polynomial such as $P(x) = 3x^3 + 2x^2 - 7x + 2$. Since the leading coefficient is 3, one of the factors must be of the form $3x - b$, where b is a factor of the constant term 2 and $P\left(\dfrac{b}{3}\right) = 0$.

To determine the values of x that should be tested to find b, the integral zero theorem is extended to include polynomials with leading coefficients that are not one. This extension is known as the $\boxed{\text{rational zero theorem}}$.

CONNECTIONS

A rational number is any number that can be expressed as a fraction.

Rational Zero Theorem

Suppose $P(x)$ is a polynomial function with integer coefficients and $x = \dfrac{b}{a}$ is a zero of $P(x)$, where a and b are integers and $a \neq 0$. Then,

- b is a factor of the constant term of $P(x)$
- a is a factor of the leading coefficient of $P(x)$
- $ax - b$ is a factor of $P(x)$

Example 4	Solve a Problem Using the Rational Zero Theorem

The forms used to make large rectangular blocks of ice come in different dimensions such that the volume, V, in cubic metres, of each block can be modelled by $V(x) = 3x^3 + 2x^2 - 7x + 2$.

a) Determine possible dimensions in terms of x, in metres, that result in this volume. Each dimension is a binomial of the form $ax + b$, where $a, b \in I$.

b) What are the dimensions of blocks of ice when $x = 1.5$?

Solution

a) Determine possible dimensions of the rectangular blocks of ice by factoring $V(x) = 3x^3 + 2x^2 - 7x + 2$.

Let b represent the factors of the constant term 2, which are ± 1 and ± 2.

Let a represent the factors of the leading coefficient 3, which are ± 1 and ± 3.

The possible values of $\dfrac{b}{a}$ are $\pm\dfrac{1}{1}$, $\pm\dfrac{1}{3}$, $\pm\dfrac{2}{1}$, and $\pm\dfrac{2}{3}$ or ± 1, ± 2, $\pm\dfrac{1}{3}$, and $\pm\dfrac{2}{3}$.

Test the values of $\dfrac{b}{a}$ for x to find the zeros. Use a graphing calculator.

Enter the function $y = 3x^3 + 2x^2 - 7x + 2$ in **Y1** and calculate $Y_1(1)$, $Y_1(-1)$, $Y_1(2)$, $Y_1(-2)$, ... to find the zeros.

Technology Tip   ∴

As a short cut, after one value has been found, press (2nd)(ENTER). The calculator will duplicate the previous calculation. Change the value in the brackets and press (ENTER).

Y1(1)		0
Y1(-1)		8
Y1(2)		20

Y1(-2)		0
Y1(-1/3)		4.444444444

Y1(1/3)		0
Y1(2/3)		-.8888888889

The zeros are 1, -2, and $\frac{1}{3}$. The corresponding factors are $x - 1$, $x + 2$, and $3x - 1$.

So, $3x^3 + 2x^2 - 7x + 2 = (x - 1)(x + 2)(3x - 1)$.

Possible dimensions of the rectangular block of ice, in metres, are $x - 1$, $x + 2$, and $3x - 1$.

b) For $x = 1.5$,

$$x - 1 = 1.5 - 1 \qquad x + 2 = 1.5 + 2 \qquad 3x - 1 = 3(1.5) - 1$$
$$= 0.5 \qquad\qquad\quad = 3.5 \qquad\qquad\quad = 4.5 - 1$$
$$\qquad\qquad\qquad\qquad\qquad\qquad\qquad\qquad\quad = 3.5$$

When $x = 1.5$, the dimensions are 0.5 m by 3.5 m by 3.5 m.

In Example 4, once one factor is determined for a polynomial whose leading coefficient is not 1, you can use division to determine the other factors.

≪ KEY CONCEPTS ≫

For integer values of a and b with $a \neq 0$,

- The factor theorem states that $x - b$ is a factor of a polynomial $P(x)$ if and only if $P(b) = 0$.

  Similarly, $ax - b$ is a factor of $P(x)$ if and only if $P\left(\dfrac{b}{a}\right) = 0$.

- The integral zero theorem states that if $x - b$ is a factor of a polynomial function $P(x)$ with leading coefficient 1 and remaining coefficients that are integers, then b is a factor of the constant term of $P(x)$.

- The rational zero theorem states that if $P(x)$ is a polynomial function with integer coefficients and $x = \dfrac{b}{a}$ is a rational zero of $P(x)$, then
  - b is a factor of the constant term of $P(x)$
  - a is a factor of the leading coefficient of $P(x)$
  - $ax - b$ is a factor of $P(x)$

Communicate Your Understanding

C1 a) Which of the following binomials are factors of the polynomial $P(x) = 2x^3 + x^2 - 7x - 6$? Justify your answers.

    A $x - 1$ **B** $x + 1$ **C** $x + 2$ **D** $x - 2$ **E** $2x + 1$ **F** $2x + 3$

   b) Use the results of part a) to write $P(x) = 2x^3 + x^2 - 7x - 6$ in factored form.

C2 When factoring a trinomial $ax^2 + bx + c$, you consider the product ac. How does this relate to the rational zero theorem?

C3 Describe the steps required to factor the polynomial $2x^3 - 3x^2 + 5x - 4$.

C4 Identify the possible factors of the expression $x^3 + 2x^2 - 5x - 4$. Explain your reasoning.

For help with questions 1 and 2, refer to Example 1.

1. Write the binomial factor that corresponds to the polynomial $P(x)$.

   a) $P(4) = 0$ b) $P(-3) = 0$

   c) $P\left(\dfrac{2}{3}\right) = 0$ d) $P\left(-\dfrac{1}{4}\right) = 0$

2. Determine if $x + 3$ is a factor of each polynomial.

   a) $x^3 + x^2 - x + 6$

   b) $2x^3 + 9x^2 + 10x + 3$

   c) $x^3 + 27$

For help with question 3, refer to Example 2.

3. List the values that could be zeros of each polynomial. Then, factor the polynomial.

   a) $x^3 + 3x^2 - 6x - 8$

   b) $x^3 + 4x^2 - 15x - 18$

   c) $x^3 - 3x^2 - 10x + 24$

For help with question 4, refer to Example 3.

4. Factor each polynomial by grouping terms.

   a) $x^3 + x^2 - 9x - 9$

   b) $x^3 - x^2 - 16x + 16$

   c) $2x^3 - x^2 - 72x + 36$

   d) $x^3 - 7x^2 - 4x + 28$

   e) $3x^3 + 2x^2 - 75x - 50$

   f) $2x^4 + 3x^3 - 32x^2 - 48x$

For help with question 5, refer to Example 4.

5. Determine the values that could be zeros of each polynomial. Then, factor the polynomial.

   a) $3x^3 + x^2 - 22x - 24$

   b) $2x^3 - 9x^2 + 10x - 3$

   c) $6x^3 - 11x^2 - 26x + 15$

   d) $4x^3 + 3x^2 - 4x - 3$

6. Factor each polynomial.

   a) $x^3 + 2x^2 - x - 2$

   b) $x^3 + 4x^2 - 7x - 10$

   c) $x^3 - 5x^2 - 4x + 20$

   d) $x^3 + 5x^2 + 3x - 4$

   e) $x^3 - 4x^2 - 11x + 30$

   f) $x^4 - 4x^3 - x^2 + 16x - 12$

   g) $x^4 - 2x^3 - 13x^2 + 14x + 24$

7. **Use Technology** Factor each polynomial.

   a) $8x^3 + 4x^2 - 2x - 1$

   b) $2x^3 + 5x^2 - x - 6$

   c) $5x^3 + 3x^2 - 12x + 4$

   d) $6x^4 + x^3 - 8x^2 - x + 2$

   e) $5x^4 + x^3 - 22x^2 - 4x + 8$

   f) $3x^3 + 4x^2 - 35x - 12$

   g) $6x^3 - 17x^2 + 11x - 2$

8. An artist creates a carving from a rectangular block of soapstone whose volume, V, in cubic metres, can be modelled by $V(x) = 6x^3 + 25x^2 + 2x - 8$. Determine possible dimensions of the block, in metres, in terms of binomials of x.

Reasoning and Proving

Representing — Selecting Tools

Problem Solving

Connecting — Reflecting

Communicating

9. Determine the value of k so that $x + 2$ is a factor of $x^3 - 2kx^2 + 6x - 4$.

10. Determine the value of k so that $3x - 2$ is a factor of $3x^3 - 5x^2 + kx + 2$.

11. Factor each polynomial.

   a) $2x^3 + 5x^2 - x - 6$

   b) $4x^3 - 7x - 3$

   c) $6x^3 + 5x^2 - 21x + 10$

   d) $4x^3 - 8x^2 + 3x - 6$

   e) $2x^3 + x^2 + x - 1$

   f) $x^4 - 15x^2 - 10x + 24$

12. a) Factor each difference of cubes.

    i) $x^3 - 1$

    ii) $x^3 - 8$

    iii) $x^3 - 27$

    iv) $x^3 - 64$

b) Use the results of part a) to predict a pattern for factoring $x^3 - a^3$.

c) Use your pattern from part b) to factor $x^3 - 125$. Verify your answer by expanding.

d) Factor each polynomial.

    i) $8x^3 - 1$ **ii)** $125x^6 - 8$

    iii) $64x^{12} - 27$ **iv)** $\dfrac{8}{125}x^3 - 64y^6$

13. a) Factor each sum of cubes.

    i) $x^3 + 1$ **ii)** $x^3 + 8$

    iii) $x^3 + 27$ **iv)** $x^3 + 64$

b) Use the results of part a) to predict a pattern for factoring $x^3 + a^3$.

c) Use your pattern from part b) to factor $x^3 + 125$. Verify your answer by expanding.

d) Factor each polynomial.

    i) $8x^3 + 1$ **ii)** $125x^6 + 8$

    iii) $64x^{12} + 27$ **iv)** $\dfrac{8}{125}x^3 + 64y^6$

14. Show that the polynomial $x^4 + x^2 + 1$ is not factorable into linear factors with integer coefficients.

15. Factor by letting $m = x^2$.

    a) $4x^4 - 37x^2 + 9$

    b) $9x^4 - 148x^2 + 64$

✓Achievement Check

16. Chapter Problem Best of U has produced a new body wash. The profit, P, in dollars, can be modelled by the function $P(x) = x^3 - 6x^2 + 9x$, where x is the number of bottles sold, in thousands.

a) Use the factor theorem to determine if $x - 1$ is a factor of $P(x)$.

b) Use the rational zero theorem to write the possible values of $\dfrac{b}{a}$ for the factored form: $P(x) = x(x^2 - 6x + 9)$

c) Use long division to check that $x - 3$ is a factor.

d) The company is happy with the profit and manufactured a similar body spray. The profit of this product can be modelled by the function $P(x) = 4x^3 + 12x^2 - 16x$. Find

C) Extend and Challenge

the factors of $P(x)$.

17. Factor each polynomial.

    a) $2x^5 + 3x^4 - 10x^3 - 15x^2 + 8x + 12$

    b) $4x^6 + 12x^5 - 9x^4 - 51x^3 - 30x^2 + 12x + 8$

18. Determine the values of m and n so that the polynomials $2x^3 + mx^2 + nx - 3$ and $x^3 - 3mx^2 + 2nx + 4$ are both divisible by $x - 2$.

19. Determine a polynomial function $P(x)$ that satisfies each set of conditions.

    a) $P(-4) = P\left(-\dfrac{3}{4}\right) = P\left(\dfrac{1}{2}\right) = 0$ and $P(-2) = 50$

    b) $P(3) = P(-1) = P\left(\dfrac{2}{3}\right) = P\left(-\dfrac{3}{2}\right) = 0$ and $P(1) = -18$

20. a) Factor each expression.

    i) $x^4 - 1$ **ii)** $x^4 - 16$

    iii) $x^5 - 1$ **iv)** $x^5 - 32$

b) Use the results of part a) to predict a pattern for factoring $x^n - a^n$.

c) Use your pattern from part b) to factor $x^6 - 1$. Verify your answer by expanding.

d) Factor each expression.

    i) $x^4 - 625$ **ii)** $x^5 - 243$

21. Is there a pattern for factoring $x^n + a^n$? Justify your answer.

22. Math Contest When a polynomial is divided by $(x + 2)$, the remainder is -19. When the same polynomial is divided by $(x - 1)$, the remainder is 2. Determine the remainder when the polynomial is divided by $(x - 1)(x + 2)$.

Polynomial Equations

Suppose the volume, V, in cubic centimetres, of a block of ice that a sculptor uses to carve the wings of a dragon can be modelled by $V(x) = 9x^3 + 60x^2 + 249x$, where x represents the thickness of the block, in centimetres. What maximum thickness of wings can be carved from a block of ice with volume 2532 cm^3? The solution to this problem can be determined by solving the cubic equation $9x^3 + 60x^2 + 249x = 2532$.

In this section, you will learn methods of solving polynomial equations of degree higher than two by factoring (using the factor theorem) and by using technology. You will also identify the relationship between the roots of polynomial equations, the x-intercepts of the graph of a polynomial function, and the zeros of the function.

CONNECTIONS

The Iranian mathematician Al-Khwarizmi (c. 780-850 A.D.) developed an algorithm for determining the roots of a quadratic equation in about 830 A.D. Methods for solving cubic and quartic equations were not discovered until about 700 years later. The Italian mathematician Scipione del Ferro (1465–1526) developed a method for solving cubic equations of the form $x^3 + mx = n$. In 1539, Niccolo Tartaglia (1499–1557) used an algorithm for solving cubic equations to win a challenge.

Investigate | **How are roots, x-intercepts, and zeros related?**

Tools

• graphing calculator

1. a) Graph the function $f(x) = x^4 - 13x^2 + 36$.

b) Determine the x-intercepts from the graph.

c) Factor $f(x)$. Then, use the factors to determine the zeros of $f(x)$.

d) Reflect What is the relationship between the zeros of the function and the x-intercepts of the corresponding graph?

2. a) Set the polynomial function $f(x) = x^4 - 13x^2 + 36$ equal to 0. Solve the equation $x^4 - 13x^2 + 36 = 0$ to determine the roots.

b) Compare the roots to the x-intercepts of the corresponding graph. What do you notice?

c) Reflect What is the relationship between the zeros of the function, the x-intercepts of the corresponding graph, and the roots of the polynomial equation?

In Chapter 1, you found that when a polynomial function is given in factored form, you can identify the zeros of the function and the x-intercepts of the corresponding graph. For a polynomial function $y = P(x)$, the roots are determined by letting $y = 0$ and solving the polynomial equation $P(x) = 0$. If the polynomial equation is factorable, then the values of the roots can be determined algebraically by solving each linear or quadratic factor. Polynomial equations of the form $P(x) = 0$ may also be solved graphically by examining the x-intercepts.

Example 1 | Solve Polynomial Equations by Factoring

Solve.

a) $x^3 - x^2 - 2x = 0$

b) $3x^3 + x^2 - 12x - 4 = 0$

Solution

a) $x^3 - x^2 - 2x = 0$

$\quad x(x^2 - x - 2) = 0$ Factor out the common factor x.

$\quad x(x - 2)(x + 1) = 0$ Factor the trinomial.

$\quad x = 0$ or $x - 2 = 0$ or $x + 1 = 0$

$\quad x = 0$ or $x = 2$ or $x = -1$

b) $3x^3 + x^2 - 12x - 4 = 0$ Factor by grouping.

$\quad x^2(3x + 1) - 4(3x + 1) = 0$ Factor out x^2 from the first two terms and -4 from the last two terms.

$\quad (3x + 1)(x^2 - 4) = 0$

$\quad (3x + 1)(x + 2)(x - 2) = 0$ Factor the difference of squares $x^2 - 4$.

$\quad 3x + 1 = 0$ or $x + 2 = 0$ or $x - 2 = 0$

$\quad x = -\dfrac{1}{3}$ or $x = -2$ or $x = 2$

Example 2 | Use the Factor Theorem to Solve a Polynomial Equation

a) Solve $2x^3 + 3x^2 - 11x - 6 = 0$.

b) What do the values of x in part a) represent in terms of the related polynomial function?

> **Solution**

a) Factor the polynomial $2x^3 + 3x^2 - 11x - 6$.

Use the rational zero theorem to determine the values that should be tested.

Let b represent the factors of the constant term -6, which are ± 1, ± 2, ± 3, and ± 6.

Let a represent the factors of the leading coefficient 2, which are ± 1 and ± 2.

The possible values of $\frac{b}{a}$ are $\pm\frac{1}{1}$, $\pm\frac{1}{2}$, $\pm\frac{2}{1}$, $\pm\frac{2}{2}$, $\pm\frac{3}{1}$, $\pm\frac{3}{2}$, $\pm\frac{6}{1}$, and $\pm\frac{6}{2}$, or ± 1, ± 2, ± 3, ± 6, $\pm\frac{1}{2}$, and $\pm\frac{3}{2}$.

Test the values of $\frac{b}{a}$ for x to find the zeros.

 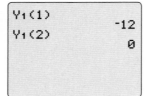

Since 2 is a zero of the function, $x - 2$ is a factor.

It is possible to begin with a different factor depending on which values are tested first.

Divide to determine the other factor.

$$\begin{array}{c|cccc} -2 & 2 & 3 & -11 & -6 \\ - & \downarrow & -4 & -14 & -6 \\ \hline \times & 2 & 7 & 3 & 0 \end{array}$$

$2x^3 + 3x^2 - 11x - 6 = (x - 2)(2x^2 + 7x + 3)$
$ = (x - 2)(2x + 1)(x + 3)$

Solve $2x^3 + 3x^2 - 11x - 6 = 0$.

$(x - 2)(2x + 1)(x + 3) = 0$

$x - 2 = 0$ or $2x + 1 = 0$ or $x + 3 = 0$

$x = 2$ or $x = -\frac{1}{2}$ or $x = -3$

b) The values 2, $-\frac{1}{2}$, and -3 are the roots of the equation $2x^3 + 3x^2 - 11x - 6 = 0$ and are the x-intercepts of the graph of the related function $y = 2x^3 + 3x^2 - 11x - 6$.

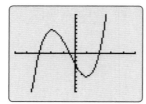

A polynomial equation may have real and non-real roots.

Consider the solution to the polynomial equation $(x - 3)(x^2 + 1) = 0$.

$(x - 3)(x^2 + 1) = 0$
$x - 3 = 0$ or $x^2 + 1 = 0$
$x = 3$ or $x^2 = -1$
$x = 3$ or $x = \pm\sqrt{-1}$

Since the square root of a negative number is not a real number, the only real root is $x = 3$.

The function $y = (x - 3)(x^2 + 1)$ has only one real zero, so the equation $(x - 3)(x^2 + 1) = 0$ has one real root. The x-intercept of the graph is 3.

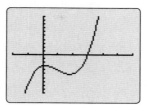

The x-intercepts of the graph of a polynomial function correspond to the real roots of the related polynomial equation.

| Example 3 | Solve a Problem by Determining the Roots of a Polynomial Equation |

The volume, V, in cubic centimetres, of a block of ice that a sculptor uses to carve the wings of a dragon can be modelled by $V(x) = 9x^3 + 60x^2 + 249x$, where x represents the thickness of the block, in centimetres. What maximum thickness of wings can be carved from a block of ice with volume 2532 cm³?

Solution

Determine the value of x that satisfies $V(x) = 2532$.

That is, solve the equation $9x^3 + 60x^2 + 249x = 2532$.

$9x^3 + 60x^2 + 249x - 2532 = 0$
$3(3x^3 + 20x^2 + 83x - 844) = 0$ Factor out the common factor 3.
$3x^3 + 20x^2 + 83x - 844 = 0$

Use the rational zero theorem to determine the values that should be tested.

Let b represent the factors of the constant term 844, which are $\pm1, \pm2, \pm4,$ $\pm211, \pm422,$ and $\pm844.$

Let a represent the factors of the leading coefficient 3, which are ±1 and ±3.

The possible values of $\dfrac{b}{a}$ are $\pm\dfrac{1}{1}, \pm\dfrac{1}{3}, \pm\dfrac{2}{1}, \pm\dfrac{2}{3}, \pm\dfrac{4}{1}, \pm\dfrac{4}{3}, \pm\dfrac{211}{1}, \pm\dfrac{211}{3},$

$\pm\dfrac{422}{1}, \pm\dfrac{422}{3}, \pm\dfrac{844}{1},$ and $\pm\dfrac{844}{3}$, or $\pm1, \pm2, \pm4, \pm211, \pm422, \pm844,$

$\pm\dfrac{1}{3}, \pm\dfrac{2}{3}, \pm\dfrac{4}{3}, \pm\dfrac{211}{3}, \pm\dfrac{422}{3},$ and $\pm\dfrac{844}{3}.$

CONNECTIONS

It is not necessary to list all the possible factors, unless a question asks for it. Do use a systematic method of checking possible factors starting with the simplest, $+/-1$.

Test only positive values of $\frac{b}{a}$ for x since x represents thickness.

 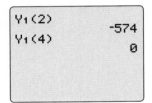

Since 4 is a zero of the function, $x - 4$ is a factor.

Divide to determine the other factor of $3x^3 + 20x^2 + 83x - 844$.

$3x^3 + 20x^2 + 83x - 844 = (x - 4)(3x^2 + 32x + 211)$

Solve $(x - 4)(3x^2 + 32x + 211) = 0$.

$x - 4 = 0$ or $3x^2 + 32x + 211 = 0$ The trinomial $3x^2 + 32x + 211$ cannot be factored.

$x = 4$ or $x = \dfrac{-32 \pm \sqrt{32^2 - 4(3)(211)}}{2(3)}$ Use the quadratic formula.

$x = \dfrac{-32 \pm \sqrt{-1508}}{6}$ These roots are not real.

Since the only positive real root is $x = 4$, the thickness of the wings is 4 cm.

A graph of the function verifies this solution.

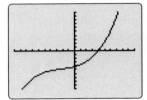

Example 4   ### Determine the Roots of a Non-Factorable Polynomial Equation

Solve $x^3 - 3x = -1$. Round the roots to one decimal place.

Solution

Write the equation as $x^3 - 3x + 1 = 0$.

The only factors of 1 are ± 1, neither of which makes the left side of the equation equal to 0 when tested.

Since the polynomial cannot be factored, determine the roots graphically using a graphing calculator.

Graph $y = x^3 - 3x + 1$.
Use the window
settings shown.

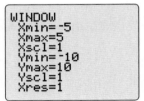 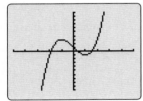

From the graph, there are three x-intercepts, one near -2, another near 0, and a third near 2.

Use the **Zero** operation.

CONNECTIONS

Another method of solving the equation with a graphing calculator is to find the points of intersection of the graphs of the two functions $y = x^3 - 3x$ and $y = -1$.

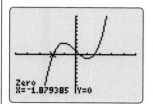
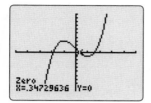
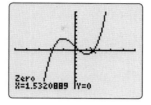

The three roots of the equation are -1.9, 0.3, and 1.5, to one decimal place.

KEY CONCEPTS

- The real roots of a polynomial equation $P(x) = 0$ correspond to the x-intercepts of the graph of the polynomial function $P(x)$.

- The x-intercepts of the graph of a polynomial function correspond to the real roots of the related polynomial equation.

- If a polynomial equation is factorable, the roots are determined by factoring the polynomial, setting its factors equal to zero, and solving each factor.

- If a polynomial equation is not factorable, the roots can be determined from the graph using technology.

Communicate Your Understanding

C1 Describe what is meant by a root, a zero, and an x-intercept. How are they related?

C2 Without solving, describe two ways to show that 2, -1, 3, and -2 are the roots of the polynomial equation $x^4 - 2x^3 - 7x^2 + 8x + 12 = 0$.

C3 A polynomial equation of degree four has exactly two distinct real roots. How many x-intercepts does the graph of the polynomial function have?

C4 Describe the different methods that can be used to factor a polynomial function.

C5 Suppose the degree of a polynomial function is n. What is the maximum number of real roots of the corresponding equation? Will the number of x-intercepts of the graph of the function be the same as the number of roots? Explain.

For help with question 1, refer to Example 1.

1. Solve.

a) $x(x + 2)(x - 5) = 0$

b) $(x - 1)(x - 4)(x + 3) = 0$

c) $(3x + 2)(x + 9)(x - 2) = 0$

d) $(x - 7)(3x + 2)(x + 1) = 0$

e) $(4x - 1)(2x - 3)(x + 8) = 0$

f) $(2x - 5)(2x + 5)(x - 7) = 0$

g) $(5x - 8)(x + 3)(2x - 1) = 0$

For help with question 2, refer to Example 2.

2. Use the graph to determine the roots of the corresponding polynomial equation. The roots are all integral values.

a) Window variables: $x \in [-4, 4]$, $y \in [-10, 10]$

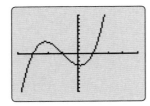

b) Window variables: $x \in [-5, 8]$, $y \in [-10, 20]$, Yscl = 2

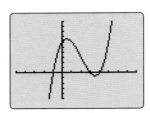

c) Window variables: $x \in [-5, 8]$, $y \in [-10, 20]$, Yscl = 2

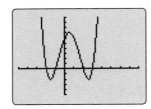

d) Window variables: $x \in [-8, 4]$, $y \in [-20, 20]$, Yscl = 2

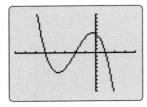

e) Window variables: $x \in [-4, 4]$, $y \in [-10, 10]$

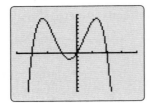

For help with question 3, refer to Example 3.

3. Determine the real roots of each polynomial equation.

a) $(x^2 + 1)(x - 4) = 0$

b) $(x^2 - 1)(x^2 + 4) = 0$

c) $(3x^2 + 27)(x^2 - 16) = 0$

d) $(x^4 - 1)(x^2 - 25) = 0$

e) $(4x^2 - 9)(x^2 + 16) = 0$

f) $(x^2 + 7x + 12)(x^2 - 49) = 0$

g) $(2x^2 + 5x - 3)(4x^2 - 100) = 0$

4. Determine the x-intercepts of the graph of each polynomial function.

a) $y = x^3 - 4x^2 - 45x$

b) $f(x) = x^4 - 81x^2$

c) $P(x) = 6x^3 - 5x^2 - 4x$

d) $h(x) = x^3 + x^2 - 4x - 4$

e) $g(x) = x^4 - 16$

f) $k(x) = x^4 - 2x^3 - x^2 + 2x$

g) $t(x) = x^4 - 29x^2 + 100$

5. Is each statement true or false? If the statement is false, reword it to make it true.

Reasoning and Proving

Representing • Selecting Tools • Problem Solving • Connecting • Reflecting • Communicating

a) If the graph of a quartic function has two x-intercepts, then the corresponding quartic equation has four real roots.

b) All the roots of a polynomial equation correspond to the x-intercepts of the graph of the corresponding polynomial function.

c) A polynomial equation of degree three must have at least one real root.

d) All polynomial equations can be solved algebraically.

e) All polynomial equations can be solved graphically.

6. Solve by factoring.

a) $x^3 - 4x^2 - 3x + 18 = 0$

b) $x^3 - 4x^2 - 7x + 10 = 0$

c) $x^3 - 5x^2 + 7x - 3 = 0$

d) $x^3 + x^2 - 8x - 12 = 0$

e) $x^3 - 3x^2 - 4x + 12 = 0$

f) $x^3 + 2x^2 - 7x + 4 = 0$

g) $x^3 - 3x^2 + x + 5 = 0$

7. Solve by factoring.

a) $2x^3 + 3x^2 - 5x - 6 = 0$

b) $2x^3 - 11x^2 + 12x + 9 = 0$

c) $9x^3 + 18x^2 - 4x - 8 = 0$

d) $5x^3 - 8x^2 - 27x + 18 = 0$

e) $8x^4 - 64x = 0$

f) $4x^4 - 2x^3 - 16x^2 + 8x = 0$

g) $x^4 - x^3 - 11x^2 + 9x + 18 = 0$

8. Solve by factoring.

a) $x^3 - 5x^2 + 8 = -2x$

b) $x^3 - x^2 = 4x + 6$

c) $2x^3 - 7x^2 + 10x - 5 = 0$

d) $x^4 - x^3 = 2x + 4$

e) $x^4 + 13x^2 = -36$

For help with question 9, refer to Example 4.

9. Use Technology Solve. Round answers to one decimal place.

a) $x^3 - 4x + 2 = 0$

b) $2x^3 + 9x^2 = x + 3$

c) $x^4 = 2$

d) $3x^3 + 6 = x$

e) $x^4 = x^3 + 7$

f) $4x^3 - 3x^2 - 5x + 2 = 0$

g) $x^4 + x^2 - x + 4 = 0$

10. The width of a square-based storage tank is 3 m less than its height. The tank has a capacity of 20 m³.

Reasoning and Proving

Representing • Selecting Tools • Problem Solving • Connecting • Reflecting • Communicating

If the dimensions are integer values in metres, what are they?

11. The passenger section of a train has width $2x - 7$, length $2x + 3$, and height $x - 2$, with all dimensions in metres. Solve a polynomial equation to determine the dimensions of the section of the train if the volume is 117 m³.

12. Is it possible for a polynomial equation to have exactly one irrational root? Use an example to justify your answer.

13. Is it possible for a polynomial equation to have exactly one non-real root? Use an example to justify your answer.

14. The distance, d, in kilometres, travelled by a plane after t hours can be represented by $d(t) = -4t^3 + 40t^2 + 500t$, where $0 \le t \le 10$. How long does the plane take to fly 4088 km?

15. A steel beam is supported by two vertical walls. When a 1000-kg weight is placed on the beam, x metres from one end, the vertical deflection, d, in metres, can be calculated using the formula $d(x) = 0.0005(x^4 - 16x^3 + 512x)$. How far from the end of the beam should the weight be placed for a deflection of 0 m?

16. Chapter Problem Based on research, the marketing team at Best of U predicts that when the price of a bottle of a new SPF 50 sunscreen is x dollars, the number, D, in hundreds, of bottles sold per month can be modelled by the function $D(x) = -x^3 + 8x^2 + 9x + 100$.

a) Graph the function $D(x)$. Write the domain for this situation.

b) How many bottles are sold per month when the price of each bottle is $5?

c) Determine the value(s) of x that will result in sales of 17 200 bottles of sunscreen per month. Interpret this answer.

17. Solve. Round answers to one decimal place if necessary.

a) $2(x - 1)^3 = 16$

b) $2(x^2 - 4x)^2 - 5(x^2 - 4x) = 3$

18. a) Determine the value of k such that -2 is one root of the equation $2x^3 + (k + 1)x^2 = 4 - x^2$.

b) Determine the other roots of the equation. Justify your answer.

19. Open-top boxes are constructed by cutting equal squares from the corners of cardboard sheets that measure 32 cm by 28 cm. Determine possible dimensions of the boxes if each has a volume of 1920 cm³.

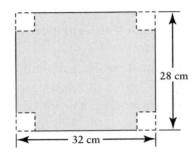

C   Extend and Challenge

20. A complex number is a number that can be written in the form $a + ib$, where a and b are real numbers and $i = \sqrt{-1}$. When the quadratic formula is used and the discriminant is negative, complex numbers result. See Example 3 of this section. The non-real roots $x = \dfrac{-32 \pm \sqrt{-1508}}{6}$ are complex roots. They may be written in terms of i, as shown below.

$$x = \frac{-32 \pm \sqrt{(-1)(1508)}}{6}$$

$$x = \frac{-32 \pm i\sqrt{1508}}{6}$$

a) Find all the real and complex solutions to $x^3 - 27 = 0$.

b) Determine a polynomial equation of degree three with roots $x = 3 \pm i$ and $x = -4$. Is this equation unique? Explain.

21. The dimensions of a gift box are consecutive positive integers such that the height is the least integer and the length is the greatest integer. If the height is increased by 1 cm, the width is increased by 2 cm, and the length is increased by 3 cm, then a larger box is constructed such that the volume is increased by 456 cm³. Determine the dimensions of each box.

22. The roots of the equation $6x^3 + 17x^2 - 5x - 6 = 0$ are represented by a, b, and c (from least to greatest). Determine an equation whose roots are $a + b$, $\dfrac{a}{b}$, and ab.

23. Math Contest AB is the diameter of a circle with centre O. P is a point on the circle, and AP is extended to C such that PC = OP. If $\angle COB = 45°$, what is the measure of $\angle POC$?

24. Math Contest Determine the product of all values of k for which the polynomial equation $2x^3 - 9x^2 + 12x - k = 0$ has a double root.

Families of Polynomial Functions

Crystal pieces for a large chandelier are to be cut according to the design shown. The graph shows how the design is created using polynomial functions. What do all the functions have in common? How are they different? How can you determine the equations that are used to create the design?

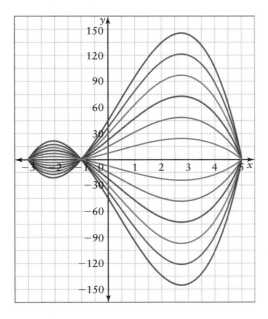

In this section, you will determine equations for a family of polynomial functions from a set of zeros. Given additional information, you will determine an equation for a particular member of the family.

How are polynomial functions with the same zeros related?

Tools

• graphing calculator

1. a) Examine each set of parabolas and the corresponding functions.

Set A   Set B

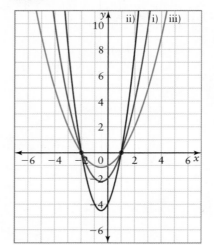   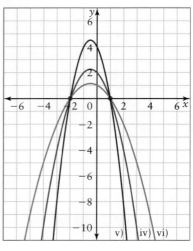

i) $y = (x - 1)(x + 2)$ **iv)** $y = -(x - 1)(x + 2)$

ii) $y = 2(x - 1)(x + 2)$ **v)** $y = -2(x - 1)(x + 2)$

iii) $y = \dfrac{1}{2}(x - 1)(x + 2)$ **vi)** $y = -\dfrac{1}{2}(x - 1)(x + 2)$

b) Reflect How are the graphs of the functions in part a) similar and how are they different?

2. Reflect Describe the relationship between the graphs of functions of the form $y = k(x - 1)(x + 2)$, where $k \in \mathbb{R}$. Why do you think this is called a **family of functions** ?

3. a) Examine the following functions. How are they similar? How are they different?

   i) $y = -2(x - 1)(x + 3)(x - 2)$ **ii)** $y = -(x - 1)(x + 3)(x - 2)$

   iii) $y = (x - 1)(x + 3)(x - 2)$ **iv)** $y = 2(x - 1)(x + 3)(x - 2)$

b) Reflect Predict how the graphs of the functions in part a) will be similar and how they will be different.

4. a) Use a graphing calculator to graph the functions in step 3 on the same set of axes.

b) Examine the graphs. Was your prediction accurate? If not, explain how it should be changed.

5. Reflect Describe the relationship between the graphs of polynomial functions of the form $y = k(x - r)(x - s)(x - t)$, where $k \in \mathbb{R}$. Why is it appropriate to call this a **family of polynomial functions** ?

A family of functions is a set of functions that have the same characteristics. Polynomial functions with the same zeros are said to belong to the same family. The graphs of polynomial functions that belong to the same family have the same x-intercepts but have different y-intercepts (unless zero is one of the x-intercepts).

An equation for the family of polynomial functions with zeros $a_1, a_2, a_3, \ldots, a_n$ is $y = k(x - a_1)(x - a_2)(x - a_3) \ldots (x - a_n)$, where $k \in \mathbb{R}$, $k \neq 0$.

Example 1 Represent a Family of Functions Algebraically

The zeros of a family of quadratic functions are 2 and -3.

a) Determine an equation for this family of functions.

b) Write equations for two functions that belong to this family.

c) Determine an equation for the member of the family that passes through the point $(1, 4)$.

Solution

a) The factor associated with 2 is $x - 2$ and the factor associated with -3 is $x + 3$.

An equation for this family is $y = k(x - 2)(x + 3)$, where $k \in \mathbb{R}$.

b) Use any two values for k to write two members of the family.

For $k = 8$, $y = 8(x - 2)(x + 3)$.
For $k = -3$, $y = -3(x - 2)(x + 3)$.

c) To find the member whose graph passes through $(1, 4)$, substitute $x = 1$ and $y = 4$ into the equation and solve for k.

$4 = k(1 - 2)(1 + 3)$
$4 = k(-1)(4)$
$4 = -4k$
$k = -1$

The equation is $y = -(x - 2)(x + 3)$.

Example 2 Determine an Equation for a Family of Cubic Functions Given Integral Zeros

The zeros of a family of cubic functions are -2, 1, and 3.

a) Determine an equation for this family.

b) Write equations for two functions that belong to this family.

c) Determine an equation for the member of the family whose graph has a y-intercept of -15.

d) Sketch graphs of the functions in parts b) and c).

> **Solution**

a) Since the zeros are -2, 1, and 3, then $x + 2$, $x - 1$, and $x - 3$ are factors of the family of cubic functions. An equation for this family is
$y = k(x + 2)(x - 1)(x - 3)$, where $k \in \mathbb{R}$.

b) Use any two values for k to write two members of the family.
For $k = 2$, $y = 2(x + 2)(x - 1)(x - 3)$.
For $k = -1$, $y = -(x + 2)(x - 1)(x - 3)$.

c) Since the y-intercept is -15, substitute $x = 0$ and $y = -15$ into
$y = k(x + 2)(x - 1)(x - 3)$.
$$-15 = k(0 + 2)(0 - 1)(0 - 3)$$
$$-15 = 6k$$
$$k = -2.5$$
The equation is $y = -2.5(x + 2)(x - 1)(x - 3)$.

d) From part a), the three functions have zeros, or x-intercepts, -2, 1, and 3.
From part c), the y-intercept of $y = -2.5(x + 2)(x - 1)(x - 3)$ is -15.

Substitute $x = 0$ to determine the y-intercepts of the functions from part b).

$y = 2(x + 2)(x - 1)(x - 3)$ $y = -(x + 2)(x - 1)(x - 3)$
$\quad = 2(0 + 2)(0 - 1)(0 - 3)$ $\quad = -(0 + 2)(0 - 1)(0 - 3)$
$\quad = 12$ $\quad = -6$

The y-intercept of   The y-intercept of
$y = 2(x + 2)(x - 1)(x - 3)$ is 12. $y = -(x + 2)(x - 1)(x - 3)$ is -6.

To sketch a graph of the functions, plot the common x-intercepts. Plot the y-intercept for each function.

The cubic function $y = 2(x + 2)(x - 1)(x - 3)$ has a positive leading coefficient, so its graph will extend from quadrant 3 to quadrant 1.

The cubic functions $y = -(x + 2)(x - 1)(x - 3)$ and
$y = -2.5(x + 2)(x - 1)(x - 3)$ have negative leading coefficients, so their graphs will extend from quadrant 2 to quadrant 4.

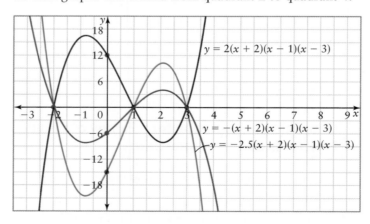

<table>
<tr><td>

Example 3

</td><td>

Determine an Equation for a Family of Quartic Functions Given Irrational Zeros

</td></tr>
</table>

a) Determine a simplified equation for the family of quartic functions with zeros ± 1 and $2 \pm \sqrt{3}$.

b) Determine an equation for the member of the family whose graph passes through the point $(2, 18)$.

Solution

a) The zeros are $1, -1, 2 + \sqrt{3}$, and $2 - \sqrt{3}$.

So, $(x - 1)$, $(x + 1)$, $(x - 2 - \sqrt{3})$, and $(x - 2 + \sqrt{3})$ are factors of the family of quartic functions. An equation for this family is

$$y = k(x - 1)(x + 1)(x - 2 - \sqrt{3})(x - 2 + \sqrt{3})$$
$$= k(x - 1)(x + 1)[(x - 2) - \sqrt{3}][(x - 2) + \sqrt{3}]$$
$$= k(x^2 - 1)[(x - 2)^2 - (\sqrt{3})^2]$$
$$= k(x^2 - 1)(x^2 - 4x + 4 - 3)$$
$$= k(x^2 - 1)(x^2 - 4x + 1)$$
$$= k(x^4 - 4x^3 + x^2 - x^2 + 4x - 1)$$
$$= k(x^4 - 4x^3 + 4x - 1)$$

> **CONNECTIONS**
>
> Each pair of factors has the difference of squares pattern:
> $(a - b)(a + b) = a^2 - b^2$.

b) To find the member whose graph passes through $(2, 18)$, substitute $x = 2$ and $y = 18$ into the equation and solve for k.

$$18 = k[(2)^4 - 4(2)^3 + 4(2) - 1]$$
$$18 = -9k$$
$$k = -2$$

The equation is $y = -2(x^4 - 4x^3 + 4x - 1)$, or $y = -2x^4 + 8x^3 - 8x + 2$.

<table>
<tr><td>

Example 4

</td><td>

Determine an Equation for a Quartic Function From a Graph

</td></tr>
</table>

Determine an equation for the quartic function represented by this graph.

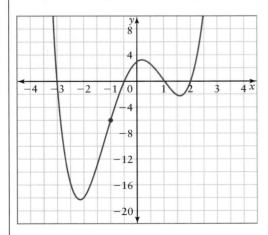

Solution

From the graph, the x-intercepts are -3, $-\frac{1}{2}$, 1, and 2.

The corresponding factors are $x + 3$, $2x + 1$, $x - 1$, and $x - 2$.

An equation for the family of polynomial functions with these zeros is
$y = k(x + 3)(2x + 1)(x - 1)(x - 2)$.

Select a point that the graph passes through, such as $(-1, -6)$.

Substitute $x = -1$ and $y = -6$ into the equation to solve for k.
$$-6 = k[(-1) + 3][2(-1) + 1][(-1) - 1][(-1) - 2]$$
$$-6 = k(2)(-1)(-2)(-3)$$
$$-6 = -12k$$
$$k = 0.5$$

The equation is $y = 0.5(x + 3)(2x + 1)(x - 1)(x - 2)$.

KEY CONCEPTS

- A family of functions is a set of functions with the same characteristics.

- Polynomial functions with graphs that have the same x-intercepts belong to the same family.

- A family of polynomial functions with zeros $a_1, a_2, a_3, \ldots, a_n$ can be represented by an equation of the form
$y = k(x - a_1)(x - a_2)(x - a_3) \ldots (x - a_n)$, where $k \in \mathbb{R}$, $k \neq 0$.

- An equation for a particular member of a family of polynomial functions can be determined if a point on the graph is known.

Communicate Your Understanding

C1 How many polynomial functions can have the same x-intercepts? Explain.

C2 What information is required to determine an equation for a family of polynomial functions?

C3 What information is required to determine an equation for a particular member of a family of polynomial functions?

C4 Describe how the graphs of the members of a family of polynomial functions are the same and how they are different.

For help with question 1, refer to Example 1.

1. The zeros of a quadratic function are -7 and -3.

   a) Determine an equation for the family of quadratic functions with these zeros.

   b) Write equations for two functions that belong to this family.

   c) Determine an equation for the member of the family that passes through the point $(2, 18)$.

For help with questions 2 to 4, refer to Example 2.

2. Examine the following functions. Which function does not belong to the same family? Explain.

   A $y = 1.5(x + 4)(x - 5)(x - 2)$

   B $y = -1.5(x - 2)(x - 5)(x + 4)$

   C $y = 1.5(x - 2)(x + 4)(x - 2)$

   D $y = 3(x - 5)(x - 2)(x + 4)$

3. The graphs of four polynomial functions are given. Which graphs represent functions that belong to the same family? Explain.

A

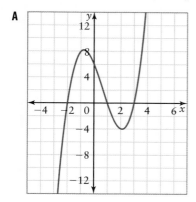

B

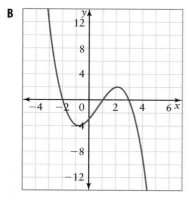

C

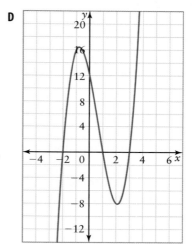

D

4. Which of the following polynomial functions belong to the same families? Explain. Sketch a graph of the functions in each family to verify your answer.

   A $f(x) = (x + 2)(x - 1)(x + 3)$

   B $h(x) = -(x - 2)(x + 1)(x - 3)$

   C $g(x) = 3(x + 2)(x - 1)(x + 3)$

   D $p(x) = 0.4(x - 3)(x + 1)(x - 2)$

   E $r(x) = -\dfrac{2}{5}(x - 1)(x + 2)(x + 3)$

   F $q(x) = -\sqrt{3}\,(x + 1)(x - 3)(x - 2)$

For help with question 5, refer to Example 3.

5. Write an equation for a family of polynomial functions with each set of zeros.

   a) $-5, 2, 3$ **b)** $1, 6, -3$

   c) $-4, -1, 9$ **d)** $-7, 0, 2, 5$

For help with question 6, refer to Example 4.

6. Determine an equation for the function that corresponds to each graph in question 3.

B Connect and Apply

7. **a)** Determine an equation for the family of cubic functions with zeros $-4, 0$, and 2.

   b) Write equations for two functions that belong to this family.

   c) Determine an equation for the member of the family whose graph passes through the point $(-2, 4)$.

   d) Sketch a graph of the functions in parts b) and c).

8. **a)** Determine an equation for the family of cubic functions with zeros $-2, -1$, and $\frac{1}{2}$.

   b) Write equations for two functions that belong to this family.

   c) Determine an equation for the member of the family whose graph has a y-intercept of 6.

   d) Sketch a graph of the functions in parts b) and c).

9. **a)** Determine an equation for the family of quartic functions with zeros $-4, -1, 2$, and 3.

   b) Write equations for two functions that belong to this family.

   c) Determine an equation for the member of the family whose graph has a y-intercept of -4.

   d) Sketch a graph of the functions in parts b) and c).

10. **a)** Determine an equation for the family of quartic functions with zeros $-\frac{5}{2}, -1, \frac{7}{2}$, and 3.

    b) Write equations for two functions that belong to this family.

    c) Determine an equation for the member of the family whose graph passes through the point $(-2, 25)$.

    d) Sketch a graph of the functions in parts b) and c).

11. **a)** Determine an equation, in simplified form, for the family of cubic functions with zeros $1 \pm \sqrt{2}$ and $-\frac{1}{2}$.

    b) Determine an equation for the member of the family whose graph passes through the point $(3, 35)$.

12. **a)** Determine an equation, in simplified form, for the family of quartic functions with zeros 3 (order 2) and $-4 \pm \sqrt{3}$.

    b) Determine an equation for the member of the family whose graph passes through the point $(1, -22)$.

13. **a)** Determine an equation, in simplified form, for the family of quartic functions with zeros $-1 \pm \sqrt{5}$ and $2 \pm \sqrt{2}$.

    b) Determine an equation for the member of the family whose graph has a y-intercept of -32.

14. Determine an equation for the cubic function represented by this graph.

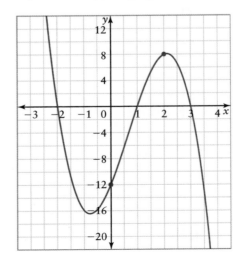

15. Determine an equation for the quartic function represented by this graph.

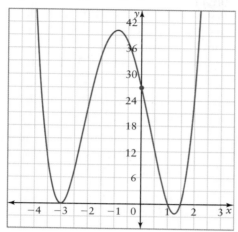

16. Determine an equation for the quartic function represented by this graph.

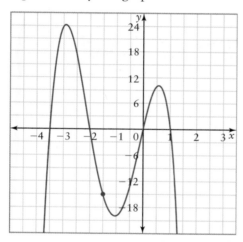

17. Use Technology Are the functions in each set a family? Justify your answer.

Set A

$y = (3x + 1)(2x - 1)(x + 3)(x - 2)$

$y = 2(3x + 1)(2x - 1)(x + 3)(x - 2) + 1$

$y = 3(3x + 1)(2x - 1)(x + 3)(x - 2) + 2$

$y = 4(3x + 1)(2x - 1)(x + 3)(x - 2) + 3$

Set B

$y = (3x + 1)(2x - 1)(x + 3)(x - 2)$

$y = (3x + 1)(4x - 2)(x + 3)(x - 2)$

$y = 3(3x + 1)(1 - 2x)(x + 3)(x - 2)$

$y = 4(3x + 1)(2x - 1)(x + 3)(6 - 3x)$

18. Chapter Problem Clear plastic sheets that measure 48 cm by 60 cm are to be used to construct gift boxes for Best of U personal care products. The boxes are formed by folding the sheets along the dotted lines, as shown in the diagram.

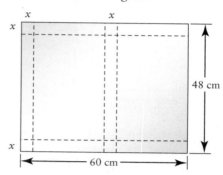

a) Express the volume of one of the boxes as a function of x.

b) Determine possible dimensions of the box if the volume of each box is to be 2300 cm³.

c) How does the volume function in part a) change if the height of the box is doubled? tripled? Describe the family of functions formed by multiplying the height by a constant.

d) Sketch graphs of two members of this family on the same coordinate grid.

19. The graph represents a section of the track of a rollercoaster. Write an equation for the family of functions that models the section of the track.

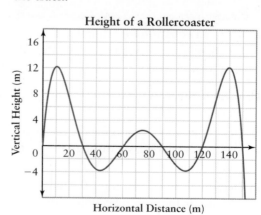

20. An open-top box is to be constructed from a piece of cardboard by cutting congruent squares from the corners and then folding up the sides. The dimensions of the cardboard are shown.

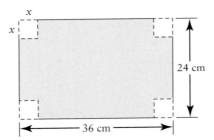

a) Express the volume of the box as a function of x.

b) Write an equation to represent a box with volume that is

  i) twice the volume of the box represented by the function in part a)

  ii) three times the volume of the box represented by the function in part a)

c) How are the equations in part b) related to the one in part a)?

d) Sketch graphs of all three functions on the same coordinate grid.

e) Determine possible dimensions of a box with volume 1820 cm³.

Reasoning and Proving
Representing   Selecting Tools
Problem Solving
Connecting   Reflecting
Communicating

✓ **Achievement Check**

21. a) The design for the crystal pieces of the chandelier at the beginning of this section is shown below. Determine an equation for the family of functions used to create the design.

b) Find equations for the members of the family that make up the design.

c) Create a design of your own. Write equations for the family of functions and the members used in your design.

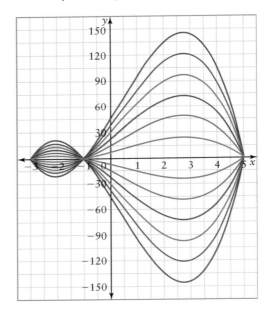

C Extend and Challenge

22. a) Write an equation for a family of even functions with four x-intercepts, two of which are $\dfrac{2}{3}$ and 5.

b) What is the least degree this family of functions can have?

c) Determine an equation for the member of this family that passes through the point $(-1, -96)$.

d) Determine an equation for the member of this family that is a reflection in the x-axis of the function in part c).

23. Refer to question 19. Design your own rollercoaster track using a polynomial function of degree six or higher. Sketch a graph of your rollercoaster.

24. Math Contest Two concentric circles have radii 9 cm and 15 cm. Determine the length of a chord of the larger circle that is tangent to the smaller circle.

25. Math Contest Given a function $g(x)$ such that $g(x^2 + 2) = x^4 + 5x^2 + 3$, determine $g(x^2 - 1)$.

Solve Inequalities Using Technology

An electronics manufacturer determines that the revenue, R, in millions of dollars, from yearly sales of MP3 players can be modelled by the function $R(t) = t^3 + 0.8t^2 - 2t + 1$, where t is the time, in years, since 2003. How can this model be used to determine when the yearly sales will be $100 million or more, that is, when will $t^3 + 0.8t^2 - 2t + 1 \geq 100$?

You have solved polynomial equations by determining the roots. In some problems, such as the one for MP3 players, the solution is a range of values. The equal sign in the equation is replaced with an inequality symbol. In this section, you will learn the meaning of a polynomial inequality and examine methods for solving polynomial inequalities using technology.

Investigate | **How are a polynomial inequality and the graph of a polynomial function related?**

1. Write an inequality that corresponds to the values of x shown on each number line.

a)

b)

c)

2. Graphs of two parabolas with their equations are given.

a) For graph A, write inequalities for the values of x for which the graph lies above the x-axis. What is the sign of the y-values of the graph for these values of x?

b) Reflect What is the relationship between the inequalities in part a) and $0.5(x - 3)(x + 5) > 0$?

Graph A

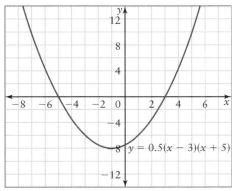

$y = 0.5(x - 3)(x + 5)$

c) For graph B, write inequalities for the values of x for which the graph is below the x-axis. What is the sign of the y-values of the graph for these values of x?

d) Reflect What is the relationship between the inequalities in part c) and $-(x - 5)(x + 4) < 0$?

Graph B

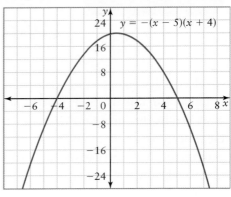

3. Reflect What is the relationship between the x-intercepts of the graphs and the inequalities determined in step 2?

4. Consider the cubic graph shown.

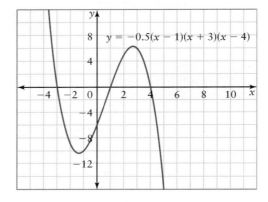

a) Write inequalities for the values of x such that $y \leq 0$.

b) Write inequalities for the values of x such that $y > 0$.

c) Reflect Explain how a graph can be used to solve each polynomial inequality.

   i) $-0.5(x - 1)(x + 3)(x - 4) \leq 0$

   ii) $-0.5(x - 1)(x + 3)(x - 4) > 0$

Examine the graph of $y = x^2 + 4x - 12$.

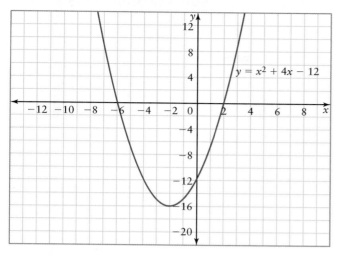

The x-intercepts are -6 and 2. These correspond to the zeros of the function $y = x^2 + 4x - 12$. By moving from left to right along the x-axis, we can make the following observations.

- The function is positive when $x < -6$ since the y-values are positive.
- The function is negative when $-6 < x < 2$ since the y-values are negative.
- The function is positive when $x > 2$ since the y-values are positive.

The zeros -6 and 2 divide the x-axis into three intervals: $x < -6$, $-6 < x < 2$, and $x > 2$. In each interval, the function is either positive or negative.

The information can be summarized in a table and is shown on the graph below.

Interval	$x < -6$	$-6 < x < 2$	$x > 2$
Sign of Function	+	−	+

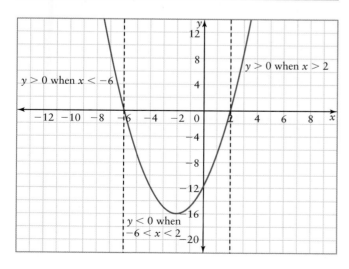

Example 1 **Solve a Polynomial Inequality Graphically**

Solve the polynomial inequality. Round answers to one decimal place.

$$2x^3 + x^2 - 6x - 2 \geq 0$$

Solution

Use a graphing calculator to graph the corresponding polynomial function.

Graph the function $y = 2x^3 + x^2 - 6x - 2$.

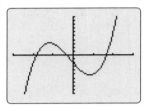

Use the **Zero** operation.

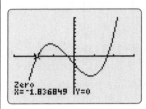 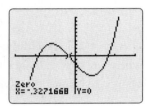 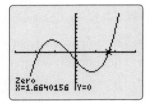

The three zeros are -1.8, -0.3, and 1.7, to one decimal place.

The values that satisfy the inequality $2x^3 + x^2 - 6x - 2 \geq 0$ are the values of x for which the graph is zero or positive (on or above the x-axis). From the graph, this occurs when $-1.8 \leq x \leq -0.3$ or $x \geq 1.7$.

A polynomial inequality may also be solved numerically by using the roots of the polynomial equation to determine the possible intervals on which the corresponding function changes from positive to negative and vice versa. Once the intervals are established, a value from each interval is used to test if the function is positive or negative in that interval.

Example 2 | **Solve Polynomial Inequalities Numerically Using a CAS**

Solve $x^4 - 5x^2 + 4 < 0$. Verify your answer graphically.

Solution

Use the CAS on a graphing calculator.

Determine the intervals using the roots of the polynomial equation and then numerically verify if the corresponding function is positive or negative within the intervals.

First, solve the equation $x^4 - 5x^2 + 4 = 0$.

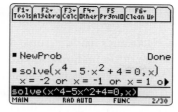

- From the F2 menu, select **1:solve**.

  Enter the equation to solve for x.

The roots are -2, -1, 1, and 2.

Arrange the roots in order from least to greatest on a number line.

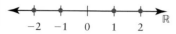

The intervals are $x < -2$, $-2 < x < -1$, $-1 < x < 1$, $1 < x < 2$, and $x > 2$.

To solve the inequality $x^4 - 5x^2 + 4 < 0$, use numerical values in each interval to test if the function is negative to determine if the values in that interval make the inequality true.

For $x < -2$, test $x = -3$.

- Press the key sequence

  $\boxed{X}\ \boxed{\char94}\ 4\ \boxed{-}\ 5\ \boxed{X}\ \boxed{\char94}\ 2\ \boxed{+}\ 4$
  $\boxed{2nd}\ 0\ 0\ \boxed{|}\ \boxed{X}\ \boxed{=}\ \boxed{(-)}\ 3.$

- Press $\boxed{ENTER}$.

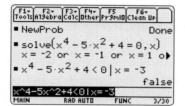

The inequality statement is false.

For $-2 < x < -1$, test $x = -1.5$.

The inequality statement is true.

For $-1 < x < 1$, test $x = 0$.

The inequality statement is false.

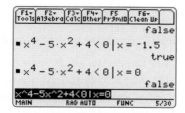

For $1 < x < 2$, test $x = 1.5$.

The inequality statement is true.

For $x > 2$, test $x = 3$.

The inequality statement is false.

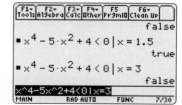

Since the inequality statement is true for the values tested in the two intervals $-2 < x < -1$ and $1 < x < 2$, the solutions to $x^4 - 5x^2 + 4 < 0$ are values of x such that $-2 < x < -1$ or $1 < x < 2$.

The graph of $y = x^4 - 5x^2 + 4$ verifies that $x^4 - 5x^2 + 4 < 0$ when $-2 < x < -1$ or $1 < x < 2$.

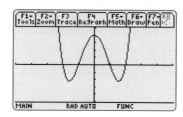

Example 3 | Solve a Problem Involving an Inequality

An electronics manufacturer determines that the revenue, R, in millions of dollars, from yearly sales of MP3 players can be modelled by the function $R(t) = t^3 + 0.8t^2 - 2t + 1$, where t is the time, in years, since 2003. Use this model to determine when the yearly sales will be $100 million or more, that is, when $t^3 + 0.8t^2 - 2t + 1 \geq 100$ will hold.

> ### Solution

Method 1: *Graph a Single Function*

Write the inequality as $t^3 + 0.8t^2 - 2t + 1 - 100 \geq 0$, or $t^3 + 0.8t^2 - 2t - 99 \geq 0$.

Graph the function $y = x^3 + 0.8x^2 - 2x - 99$.

Window variables: $x \in [-10, 10]$, $y \in [-200, 200]$, Yscl = 20

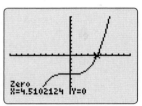

There is one x-intercept, which cannot be read easily from the graph. It is located between 4 and 5. Use the **Zero** operation to find its value.

The yearly sales will be $100 million or more approximately 4.5 years from 2003, or halfway through 2007.

Method 2: *Find the Intersection Point of Two Functions*

Consider the graphs of the two functions $y = t^3 + 0.8t^2 - 2t + 1$ and $y = 100$. The two functions are equal at their point(s) of intersection. Once this point is identified, determine where the y-values of $y = t^3 + 0.8t^2 - 2t + 1$ are greater than $y = 100$.

Graph $y = x^3 + 0.8x^2 - 2x + 1$ in **Y1** and $y = 100$ in **Y2**.

Window variables: $x \in [-10, 10]$, $y \in [-200, 200]$, Yscl = 20

Use the **Intersect** operation to find the coordinates of the point of intersection.

The point of intersection is approximately (4.5, 100).

From the graphs, the value of $y = x^3 + 0.8x^2 - 2x + 1$ is greater than or equal to $y = 100$ when $x \geq 4.5$. So, $t^3 + 0.8t^2 - 2t + 1 \geq 100$ when $t \geq 4.5$.

The yearly sales will be $100 million or more approximately 4.5 years from 2003, or halfway through 2007.

- A polynomial inequality results when the equal sign in a polynomial equation is replaced with an inequality symbol.

- The real zeros of a polynomial function, or x-intercepts of the corresponding graph, divide the x-axis into intervals that can be used to solve a polynomial inequality.

- Polynomial inequalities may be solved graphically by determining the x-intercepts and then using the graph to determine the intervals that satisfy the inequality.

- A CAS may be used to solve a polynomial inequality numerically by determining the roots of the polynomial equation and then testing values in each interval to see if they make the inequality true.

Communicate Your Understanding

C1 Explain the difference between a polynomial equation and a polynomial inequality. Support your answer with examples.

C2 Describe the connection between the solution to a polynomial inequality and the graph of the corresponding function.

C3 Describe the role of the real roots of a polynomial equation when solving the related inequality.

C4 Describe how technology can be used to solve the inequality $1.2x^3 - 5x^2 + 3.5x + 2 \le 0$.

A ⟩ Practise

1. Write inequalities for the values of x shown.

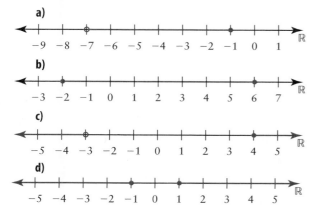

a)

b)

c)

d)

2. Write the intervals into which the x-axis is divided by each set of x-intercepts of a polynomial function.

a) $-1, 5$　　　　b) $-7, 2, 0$

c) $-6, 0, 1$　　　d) $-4, -2, \dfrac{2}{5}, 4.3$

For help with questions 3 to 5, refer to Example 1.

3. Sketch a graph of a cubic polynomial function $y = f(x)$ such that $f(x) < 0$ when $-4 < x < 3$ or $x > 7$ and $f(x) > 0$ when $x < -4$ or $3 < x < 7$.

4. Describe what the solution to each inequality indicates about the graph of $y = f(x)$.

a) $f(x) < 0$ when $-2 < x < 1$ or $x > 6$

b) $f(x) \ge 0$ when $x \le -3.6$ or $0 \le x \le 4.7$ or $x \ge 7.2$

5. For each graph, write

  i) the x-intercepts

  ii) the intervals of x for which the graph is positive

  iii) the intervals of x for which the graph is negative

a)

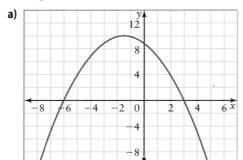

b)

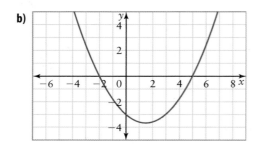

c)

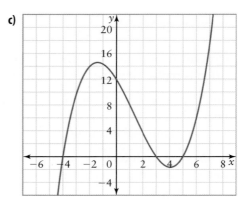

d)

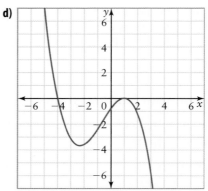

---

6. Solve each polynomial inequality by graphing the polynomial function.

  a) $x^2 - x - 12 < 0$

  b) $x^2 + 8x + 15 \leq 0$

  c) $x^3 - 6x^2 + 11x - 6 > 0$

  d) $x^3 + 8x^2 + 19x + 12 \geq 0$

  e) $x^3 - 2x^2 - 9x + 18 < 0$

  f) $x^3 + x^2 - 16x - 16 \leq 0$

For help with questions 7 to 9, refer to Example 2.

7. Solve each polynomial inequality. Use a CAS if available.

  a) $2x^2 + 7x - 4 \geq 0$

  b) $2x^2 - 5x - 3 < 0$

  c) $x^3 + 5x^2 + 2x - 8 \leq 0$

  d) $x^3 + 2x^2 - 19x - 20 > 0$

  e) $x^3 - 39x - 70 < 0$

  f) $x^3 - 3x^2 - 24x - 28 \leq 0$

8. Solve each polynomial inequality by first finding the approximate zeros of the related polynomial function. Round answers to two decimal places.

  a) $x^2 + 4x - 3 < 0$

  b) $-3x^2 - 4x + 8 > 0$

  c) $x^3 + x^2 - 3x - 1 \leq 0$

  d) $2x^3 + 4x^2 - x - 1 \geq 0$

  e) $3x^3 + 4x^2 - 5x - 3 < 0$

  f) $-x^4 + x^3 - 2x + 3 \geq 0$

9. Solve.

  a) $5x^3 - 7x^2 - x + 4 > 0$

  b) $-x^3 + 28x + 48 \geq 0$

  c) $3x^3 + 4x^2 - 35x - 12 \leq 0$

  d) $3x^3 + 2x^2 - 11x - 10 < 0$

  e) $-2x^3 + x^2 + 13x + 6 > 0$

  f) $2x^4 + x^3 - 26x^2 - 37x - 12 > 0$

10. The height, h, in metres, of a golf ball t seconds after it is hit can be modelled by the function $h(t) = -4.9t^2 + 32t + 0.2$. When is the height of the ball greater than 15 m?

11. The number, n, in hundreds, of tent caterpillars infesting a forested area after t weeks can be modelled by the function $n(t) = -t^4 + 5t^3 + 5t^2 + 6t$.

    a) When is the tent caterpillar population greater than 10 000?

    b) What will happen after 6 weeks?

12. Chapter Problem The Best of U marketing team has determined that the number, c, in thousands, of customers who purchase the company's products on-line from the Best of U Web site t years after 2003 can be modelled by the function $c(t) = 0.1t^3 - 2t + 8$.

    a) When will there be fewer than 8000 on-line customers?

    b) When will the number of on-line customers exceed 10 000?

13. a) Create a cubic polynomial inequality such that the corresponding equation has

    i) one distinct real root

    ii) two distinct real roots

    iii) three real roots, one of which is of order 2

    b) Solve the inequalities you created in part a).

14. a) Create a quartic inequality such that the corresponding quartic equation has

    i) no real roots

    ii) two distinct real roots

    iii) three distinct real roots

    iv) four real roots, two of which are of order 2

    b) Solve the inequalities you created in part a).

15. The solutions below correspond to inequalities involving a cubic function. For each solution, write two possible cubic polynomial inequalities, one with the less than symbol ($<$) and the other with the greater than symbol ($>$).

    a) $-\dfrac{2}{3} < x < \dfrac{4}{5}$ or $x > 3.5$

    b) $x < -1 - \sqrt{3}$ or $-1 + \sqrt{3} < x < 4$

C   Extend and Challenge

16. Solve $3x^4 + 2x^2 - 4x + 6 \geq 6x^4 - 5x^3 - x^2 - 9x + 2$.

17. Write the domain and range of each function.

    a) $f(x) = \sqrt{-x - x^2}$

    b) $g(x) = \dfrac{1}{\sqrt{x^2 - 1}}$

18. Math Contest Given a circle with centre O, PQ and PR are two tangents from a point P outside the circle. Prove that $\angle POQ = \angle POR$.

19. Math Contest Given that $3x - 5$ is a factor of the polynomial function $f(x) = kx^2 - bx + k$, determine the ratio $k : b$ in simplest form.

20. Math Contest In the figure, RS is perpendicular to PQ, PS = 4, and QS = 6. Find the exact length of RS.

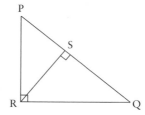

2.6 Solve Factorable Polynomial Inequalities Algebraically

A rectangular in-ground swimming pool is to be installed. The engineer overseeing the construction project estimates that at least 1408 m³ of earth and rocks needs to be excavated. What are the minimum dimensions of the excavation if the depth must be 2 m more than one quarter of the width, and the length must be 12 m more than four times the width? The solution to this problem can be found by solving a cubic polynomial inequality algebraically.

Example 1   Solve Linear Inequalities

Solve each inequality. Show the solution on a number line.

a) $x - 8 \geq 3$

b) $-4 - 2x < 12$

> ### Solution

a) $x - 8 \geq 3$

$$x \geq 3 + 8$$
$$x \geq 11$$

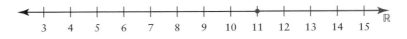

CONNECTIONS

Solving linear inequalities is similar to solving linear equations; however, when both sides of an inequality are multiplied or divided by a negative number, the inequality sign must be reversed.

b) $-4 - 2x < 12$

$$-2x < 12 + 4$$
$$-2x < 16$$
$$x > \frac{16}{-2} \qquad \text{Divide both sides by } -2. \text{ Reverse the inequality.}$$
$$x > -8$$

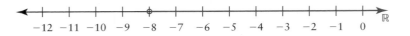

Example 2 **Solve Polynomial Inequalities Algebraically**

Solve each inequality.

a) $(x + 3)(2x - 3) > 0$

b) $-2x^3 - 6x^2 + 12x + 16 \leq 0$

Solution

a) $(x + 3)(2x - 3) > 0$

Method 1: *Consider All Cases*

$(x + 3)(2x - 3) > 0$

A product mn is positive when m and n are

- both positive or
- both negative

Case 1

$$x + 3 > 0 \qquad\qquad 2x - 3 > 0$$
$$x > -3 \qquad\qquad 2x > 3$$
$$x > \frac{3}{2}$$

$x > \frac{3}{2}$ is included in the inequality $x > -3$. So, the solution is $x > \frac{3}{2}$.

Case 2

$$x + 3 < 0 \qquad\qquad 2x - 3 < 0$$
$$x < -3 \qquad\qquad 2x < 3$$
$$x < \frac{3}{2}$$

$x < -3$ is included in the inequality $x < \frac{3}{2}$. So, the solution is $x < -3$.

Combining the results of the two cases, the solution is $x < -3$ or $x > \frac{3}{2}$.

Method 2: *Use Intervals*

$(x + 3)(2x - 3) > 0$

The roots of the equation $(x + 3)(2x - 3) = 0$ are $x = -3$ and $x = \frac{3}{2}$.

Use the roots to break the number line into three intervals.

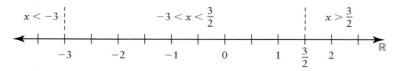

Test arbitrary values of x for each interval.

For $x < -3$, test $x = -4$.

$(-4 + 3)[2(-4) - 3] = 11$

Since $11 > 0$, $x < -3$ is a solution.

For $-3 < x < \dfrac{3}{2}$, test $x = 0$.

$(0 + 3)[2(0) - 3] = -9$

Since $-9 < 0$, $-3 < x < \dfrac{3}{2}$ is not a solution.

For $x > \dfrac{3}{2}$, test $x = 2$.

$(2 + 3)[2(2) - 3] = 5$

Since $5 > 0$, $x > \dfrac{3}{2}$ is a solution.

All of the information can be summarized in a table:

Interval Factor	$x < -3$	$x = -3$	$-3 < x < \dfrac{3}{2}$	$x = \dfrac{3}{2}$	$x > \dfrac{3}{2}$
$(x + 3)$	−	0	+	+	+
$(2x - 3)$	−	−	−	0	+
$(x + 3)(2x - 3)$	+	0	−	0	+

The solution is $x < -3$ or $x > \dfrac{3}{2}$. This can be shown on a number line.

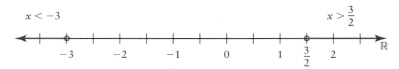

b) $-2x^3 - 6x^2 + 12x + 16 \le 0$

Factor $-2x^3 - 6x^2 + 12x + 16$ using the factor theorem.

$-2x^3 - 6x^2 + 12x + 16 = -2(x + 4)(x - 2)(x + 1)$

So, the inequality becomes $-2(x + 4)(x - 2)(x + 1) \le 0$.

CONNECTIONS

You will obtain the same final result if you divide the inequality by -2 and consider $(x + 4)(x - 2)(x + 1) \ge 0$.

Method 1: *Consider All Cases*

$-2(x + 4)(x - 2)(x + 1) \le 0$

Since -2 is a constant factor, it can be combined with $(x + 4)$ to form one factor.

Thus, the three factors of $-2(x + 4)(x - 2)(x + 1)$ are $-2(x + 4)$, $x - 2$, and $x + 1$.

A product abc is negative when all three factors, a, b, and c, are negative, or when two of the factors are positive and the third one is negative. There are four cases to consider.

Case 1

$-2(x + 4) \le 0$	$x - 2 \le 0$	$x + 1 \le 0$
$x + 4 \ge 0$	$x \le 2$	$x \le -1$
$x \ge -4$		

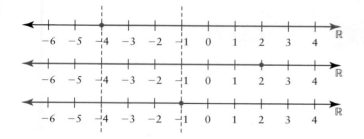

The broken lines indicate that $-4 \leq x \leq -1$ is common to all three intervals.

The values of x that are common to all three inequalities are $x \geq -4$ and $x \leq -1$.

So, $-4 \leq x \leq -1$ is a solution.

Case 2

$$
\begin{array}{lll}
-2(x + 4) \geq 0 & x - 2 \geq 0 & x + 1 \leq 0 \\
x + 4 \leq 0 & x \geq 2 & x \leq -1 \\
x \leq -4 & &
\end{array}
$$

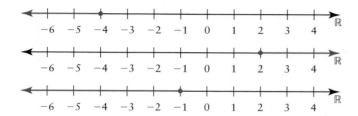

There are no x-values that are common to all three inequalities.

Case 2 has no solution.

Case 3

$$
\begin{array}{lll}
-2(x + 4) \geq 0 & x - 2 \leq 0 & x + 1 \geq 0 \\
x + 4 \leq 0 & x \leq 2 & x \geq -1 \\
x \leq -4 & &
\end{array}
$$

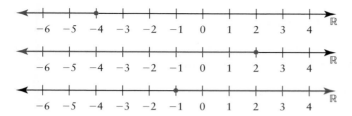

There are no x-values that are common to all three inequalities.

Case 3 has no solution.

Case 4

$$-2(x + 4) \leq 0 \qquad\qquad x - 2 \geq 0 \qquad\qquad x + 1 \geq 0$$
$$x + 4 \geq 0 \qquad\qquad\qquad x \geq 2 \qquad\qquad\qquad x \geq -1$$
$$x \geq -4$$

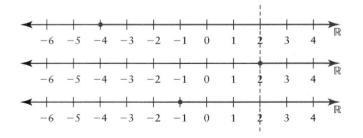

The broken line indicates that $x \geq 2$ is common to all three intervals.

$x \geq 2$ is included the intervals $x \geq -4$ and $x \geq -1$.

So, $x \geq 2$ is a solution.

Combining the results of the four cases, the solution is $-4 \leq x \leq -1$ or $x \geq 2$.

Method 2: *Use Intervals*

$$-2(x + 4)(x - 2)(x + 1) \leq 0$$

The roots of $-2(x + 4)(x - 2)(x + 1) = 0$ are $x = -4$, $x = -1$, and $x = 2$.

Use the roots to break the number line into four intervals.

Test arbitrary values of x in each interval.

For $x < -4$, test $x = -5$.
$$-2(-5 + 4)(-5 - 2)(-5 + 1) = 56$$
Since $56 > 0$, $x < -4$ is not a solution.

For $-4 < x < -1$, test $x = -3$.
$$-2(-3 + 4)(-3 - 2)(-3 + 1) = -20$$
Since $-20 < 0$, $-4 < x < -1$ is a solution.

For $-1 < x < 2$, test $x = 0$.
$$-2(0 + 4)(0 - 2)(0 + 1) = 16$$
Since $16 > 0$, $-1 < x < 2$ is not a solution.

For $x > 2$, test $x = 3$.
$$-2(3 + 4)(3 - 2)(3 + 1) = -56$$
Since $-56 < 0$, $x > 2$ is a solution.

Interval / Factor	$x < -4$	$x = -4$	$-4 < x < -1$	$x = -1$	$-1 < x < 2$	$x = 2$	$x > 2$
$-2(x + 4)$	+	0	−	−	−	−	−
$(x - 2)$	−	−	−	−	−	0	+
$(x + 1)(2x - 3)$	−	−	−	0	+	+	+
$-2(x + 4)(x - 2)(x + 1)$	+	0	−	0	+	0	−

The solution is $-4 \le x \le -1$ or $x \ge 2$.

This can be shown on a number line.

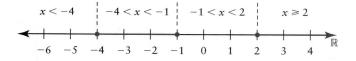

Example 3	Solve a Problem Involving a Factorable Polynomial Inequality

A rectangular in-ground pool is to be installed. The engineer overseeing the construction project estimates that at least 1408 m³ of earth and rocks needs to be excavated. What are the minimum dimensions of the excavation if the depth must be 2 m more than one quarter of the width, and the length must be 12 m more than four times the width?

Solution

From the given information, $h = \dfrac{1}{4}w + 2$ and $l = 4w + 12$, with $l > 0$, $w > 0$, and $h > 0$.

$$V = lwh$$
$$= (4w + 12)(w)\left(\dfrac{1}{4}w + 2\right)$$
$$= w^3 + 11w^2 + 24w$$

Since the volume must be at least 1408 m³, $V \ge 1408$; that is, $w^3 + 11w^2 + 24w \ge 1408$.

Solve $w^3 + 11w^2 + 24w - 1408 \ge 0$.

Factor the corresponding polynomial function.

$w^3 + 11w^2 + 24w - 1408 = (w - 8)(w^2 + 19w + 176)$

Then, solve $(w - 8)(w^2 + 19w + 176) \ge 0$. $w^2 + 19w + 176$ cannot be factored further.

Case 1

Both factors are non-negative.

$w - 8 \ge 0 \qquad\qquad w^2 + 19w + 176 \ge 0$
$w \ge 8$

$w^2 + 19w + 176 \ge 0$ is true for all values of w. These include values for $w \ge 8$.

So, $w \ge 8$ is a solution.

CONNECTIONS

The formula for the volume, V, of a rectangular prism is $V = lwh$, where l is the length, w is the width, and h is the height.

CONNECTIONS

The discriminant can be used to test for factors. If $b^2 - 4ac$ is a perfect square then the quadratic can be factored. Here $b^2 - 4ac = -343$, so the expression has no real roots.

Case 2

Both factors are non-positive, and w is positive (because w represents the width).

$0 < w \leq 8$ $\qquad\qquad$ $w^2 + 19w + 176 \leq 0$

$w^2 + 19w + 176 \leq 0$ is not possible for any values of w. There is no solution.

So, the possible solution is $w \geq 8$.

When $w = 8$, $h = \dfrac{1}{4}(8) + 2 = 4$ and $l = 4(2) + 12 = 20$.

The dimensions of the excavation that give a volume of at least 1408 cm^3 are width 8 m, depth 4 m, and length 20 m.

⟨⟨ KEY CONCEPTS ⟩⟩

- Factorable inequalities can be solved algebraically by
  - considering all cases
  - using intervals and then testing values in each interval

- Tables and number lines can help organize intervals to provide a visual clue to solutions.

Communicate Your Understanding

C1 Why is it necessary to reverse an inequality sign when each side is multiplied or divided by a negative value? Support your answer with examples.

C2 What are the similarities between solving a linear inequality and solving a polynomial inequality?

C3 Which method is more efficient for solving factorable inequalities algebraically, using cases or using intervals? Explain.

A ⟩ Practise

For help with question 1, refer to Example 1.

1. Solve each inequality. Show each solution on a number line.

  a) $x + 3 \leq 5$ $\qquad$ **b)** $2x + 1 > -4$

  c) $5 - 3x \geq 6$ $\qquad$ **d)** $7x < 4 + 3x$

  e) $2 - 4x > 5x + 20$ $\quad$ **f)** $2(1 - x) \leq x - 8$

For help with questions 2 to 4, refer to Example 2.

2. Solve by considering all cases. Show each solution on a number line.

  a) $(x + 2)(x - 4) > 0$

  b) $(2x + 3)(4 - x) \leq 0$

3. Solve using intervals. Show each solution on a number line.

  a) $(x + 3)(x - 2) > 0$

  b) $(x - 6)(x - 9) \leq 0$

  c) $(4x + 1)(2 - x) \geq 0$

4. Solve.

  a) $(x + 2)(3 - x)(x + 1) < 0$

  b) $(-x + 1)(3x - 1)(x + 7) \geq 0$

  c) $(7x + 2)(1 - x)(2x + 5) > 0$

  d) $(x + 4)(-3x + 1)(x + 2) \leq 0$

5. Solve by considering all cases. Show each solution on a number line.

a) $x^2 - 8x + 15 \geq 0$

b) $x^2 - 2x - 15 < 0$

c) $15x^2 - 14x - 8 \leq 0$

d) $x^3 - 2x^2 - 5x + 6 < 0$

e) $2x^3 + 3x^2 - 2x - 3 \geq 0$

6. Solve using intervals.

a) $x^3 + 6x^2 + 7x + 12 \geq 0$

b) $x^3 + 9x^2 + 26x + 24 < 0$

c) $5x^3 - 12x^2 - 11x + 6 \leq 0$

d) $6x^4 - 7x^3 - 4x^2 + 8x + 12 > 0$

7. Solve.

a) $x^2 + 4x - 5 \leq 0$

b) $-2x^3 + x^2 + 13x + 6 < 0$

c) $2x^3 + x^2 - 2x - 1 > 0$

d) $x^3 - 5x + 4 \geq 0$

For help with questions 8 and 9, refer to Example 3.

8. Cookies are packaged in boxes that measure 18 cm by 20 cm by 6 cm. A larger box is being designed by increasing the length, width, and height of the smaller box by the same length so that the volume is at least 5280 cm³. What are the minimum dimensions of the larger box?

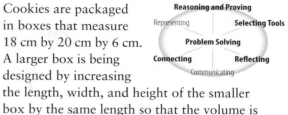
Reasoning and Proving
Representing — Selecting Tools
Problem Solving
Connecting — Reflecting
Communicating

9. The price, p, in dollars, of a stock t years after 1999 can be modelled by the function $p(t) = 0.5t^3 - 5.5t^2 + 14t$. When will the price of the stock be more than $90?

✔ **Achievement Check**

10. a) Solve the inequality $x^3 - 5x^2 + 2x + 8 < 0$ by

  i) using intervals

  ii) considering all cases

b) How are the two methods the same? How are they different?

11. a) How many cases must be considered when solving $(x + 4)(x - 2)(x + 1)(x - 1) \leq 0$? Justify your answer.

b) Would it be more efficient to solve this inequality using intervals? Justify your answer.

12. Solve $x^5 + 7x^3 + 6x < 5x^4 + 7x^2 + 2$.

13. A demographer develops a model for the population, P, of a small town n years from today such that $P(n) = -0.15n^5 + 3n^4 + 5560$.

a) When will the population of the town be between 10 242 and 25 325?

b) When will the population of the town be more than 30 443?

c) Will the model be valid after 20 years? Explain.

14. Write two possible quartic inequalities, one using the less than or equal to symbol ($\leq$) and the other using the greater than or equal to symbol ($\geq$), that correspond to the following solution:
$-6 - \sqrt{2} < x < -6 + \sqrt{2}$ or
$6 - \sqrt{2} < x < 6 + \sqrt{2}$

15. Math Contest Determine the exact length of PQ in the figure.

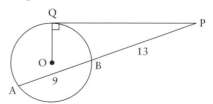

16. Math Contest Determine an equation for the line that is tangent to the circle with equation $x^2 + y^2 - 25 = 0$ and passes through the point $(4, -3)$.

2.1 The Remainder Theorem

1. **i)** Use the remainder theorem to determine the remainder for each division.

    ii) Perform each division. Express the result in quotient form. Identify any restrictions on the variable.

    a) $x^3 + 9x^2 - 5x + 3$ divided by $x - 2$

    b) $12x^3 - 2x^2 + x - 11$ divided by $3x + 1$

    c) $-8x^4 - 4x + 10x^3 - x^2 + 15$ divided by $2x - 1$

2. **a)** Determine the value of k such that when $f(x) = x^4 + kx^3 - 3x - 5$ is divided by $x - 3$, the remainder is -10.

    b) Determine the remainder when $f(x)$ is divided by $x + 3$.

    c) **Use Technology** Verify your answer in part b) using technology.

3. For what value of b will the polynomial $P(x) = 4x^3 - 3x^2 + bx + 6$ have the same remainder when it is divided by $x - 1$ and by $x + 3$?

2.2 The Factor Theorem

4. Factor each polynomial.

    a) $x^3 - 4x^2 + x + 6$

    b) $3x^3 - 5x^2 - 26x - 8$

    c) $5x^4 + 12x^3 - 101x^2 + 48x + 36$

5. Factor.

    a) $-4x^3 - 4x^2 + 16x + 16$

    b) $25x^3 - 50x^2 - 9x + 18$

    c) $2x^4 + 5x^3 - 8x^2 - 20x$

6. Rectangular blocks of limestone are to be cut up and used to build the front entrance of a new hotel. The volume, V, in cubic metres, of each block can be modelled by the function $V(x) = 2x^3 + 7x^2 + 2x - 3$.

    a) Determine the dimensions of the blocks in terms of x.

    b) What are the possible dimensions of the blocks when $x = 1$?

7. Determine the value of k so that $x + 3$ is a factor of $x^3 + 4x^2 - 2kx + 3$.

2.3 Polynomial Equations

8. Use the graph to determine the roots of the corresponding polynomial equation.

    Window variables: $x \in [-8, 8]$, $y \in [-40, 10]$, Yscl $= 2$

    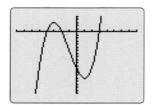

9. Determine the real roots of each equation.

    a) $(5x^2 + 20)(3x^2 - 48) = 0$

    b) $(2x^2 - x - 13)(x^2 + 1) = 0$

10. Solve. Round answers to one decimal place, if necessary.

    a) $7x^3 + 5x^2 - 5x - 3 = 0$

    b) $-x^3 + 9x^2 = x + 6$

11. The specifications for a cardboard box state that the width is 5 cm less than the length, and the height is 1 cm more than double the length. Write an equation for the volume of the box and find possible dimensions for a volume of 550 cm³.

2.4 Families of Polynomial Functions

12. Examine the following functions. Which function does not belong to the same family? Explain.

    A $y = 3.5(x + 2)(x - 1)(x - 3)$

    B $y = -0.2(x - 3)(2x + 4)(2x - 3)$

    C $y = (4x - 12)(x + 2)(x - 1)$

    D $y = -7(x - 1)(x - 3)(x + 2)$

13. **a)** Determine an equation, in simplified form, for the family of cubic functions with zeros $2 \pm \sqrt{5}$ and 0.

    b) Determine an equation for the member of the family with graph passing through the point (2, 20).

14. Determine an equation for the function represented by this graph.

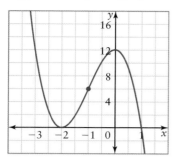

2.5 Solving Inequalities Using Technology

15. Use Technology Solve. Round the zeros to one decimal place, if necessary.

a) $x^2 + 3x - 5 \geq 0$

b) $2x^3 - 13x^2 + 17x + 12 > 0$

c) $x^3 - 2x^2 - 5x + 2 < 0$

d) $3x^3 + 4x^2 - 35x - 12 \leq 0$

e) $-x^4 - 2x^3 + 4x^2 + 10x + 5 < 0$

16. Use Technology A section of a water tube ride at an amusement park can be modelled by the function $h(t) = -0.002t^4 + 0.104t^3 - 1.69t^2 + 8.5t + 9$, where t is the time, in seconds, and h is the height, in metres, above the ground. When will the riders be more than 15 m above the ground?

2.6 Solving Factorable Polynomial Inequalities Algebraically

17. Solve each inequality. Show the solution on a number line.

a) $(5x + 4)(x - 4) < 0$

b) $-(2x + 3)(x - 1)(3x - 2) \leq 0$

c) $(x^2 + 4x + 4)(x^2 - 25) > 0$

18. Solve by factoring.

a) $12x^2 + 25x - 7 \geq 0$

b) $6x^3 + 13x^2 - 41x + 12 \leq 0$

c) $-3x^4 + 10x^3 + 20x^2 - 40x + 32 < 0$

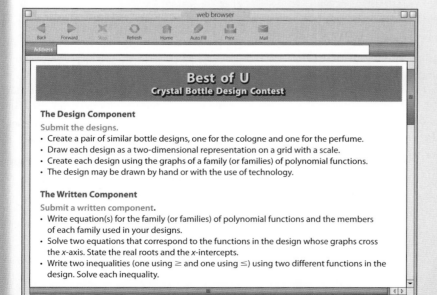

For questions 1 to 3, select the best answer.

1. Which statement is true for
   $P(x) = 5x^3 + 4x^2 - 3x + 2$?

   A When $P(x)$ is divided by $x + 1$, the remainder is 8.

   B $x + 2$ is a factor of $P(x)$.

   C $P(-2) = -16$

   D $P(x) = (x + 1)(5x^2 - x - 2) - 4$

2. Which of the following is not a factor of
   $2x^3 - 5x^2 - 9x + 18$?

   A $2x - 3$

   B $x + 2$

   C $x - 2$

   D $x - 3$

3. Which set of values for x should be tested to determine the possible zeros of
   $4x^3 + 5x^2 - 23x - 6$?

   A $\pm 1, \pm 2, \pm 3, \pm 4, \pm 6$

   B $\pm 1, \pm 2, \pm 3, \pm 4, \pm 6, \pm\frac{1}{2}, \pm\frac{2}{3}$

   C $\pm 4, \pm 6, \pm\frac{1}{2}, \pm\frac{3}{2}, \pm\frac{3}{4}, \pm\frac{1}{4}$

   D $\pm 1, \pm 2, \pm 3, \pm 6, \pm\frac{1}{2}, \pm\frac{3}{2}, \pm\frac{3}{4}, \pm\frac{1}{4}$

4. **a)** Divide $x^3 - 4x^2 + 3x - 7$ by $x + 3$. Express the result in quotient form.

   b) Identify any restrictions on the variable.

   c) Write the corresponding statement that can be used to check the division.

   d) Verify your answer.

5. **a)** Determine the value of k such that when $f(x) = x^4 + kx^3 - 2x^2 + 1$ is divided by $x + 2$, the remainder is 5.

   b) Determine the remainder when $f(x)$ is divided by $x + 4$.

   c) Verify your answer in part b) using long division.

6. Factor.

   a) $x^3 - 5x^2 + 2x + 8$

   b) $x^3 + 2x^2 - 9x - 18$

   c) $x^3 + 5x^2 - 2x - 24$

   d) $5x^3 + 7x^2 - 8x - 4$

   e) $x^3 + 9x^2 + 26x + 24$

   f) $2x^4 + 13x^3 + 28x^2 + 23x + 6$

7. Use the graph to determine the roots of the corresponding polynomial equation.
   Window variables: $x \in [-8, 8]$,
   $y \in [-40, 40]$, Yscl = 4

   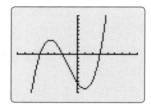

8. Determine the real roots of each equation.

   a) $(x^2 + 5)(x - 2) = 0$

   b) $(x^2 - 121)(x^2 + 16) = 0$

   c) $(x^2 - 2x + 3)(2x^2 - 50) = 0$

   d) $(3x^2 - 27)(x^2 - 3x - 10) = 0$

9. Solve by factoring.

   a) $x^3 + 4x^2 + 5x + 2 = 0$

   b) $x^3 - 13x + 12 = 0$

   c) $32x^3 - 48x^2 - 98x + 147 = 0$

   d) $45x^4 - 27x^3 - 20x^2 + 12x = 0$

10. **a)** Describe the similarities and differences between polynomial equations, polynomial functions, and polynomial inequalities. Support your answer with examples.

    b) What is the relationship between roots, zeros, and x-intercepts? Support your answer with examples.

11. a) Determine an equation for the quartic function represented by this graph.

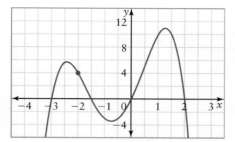

b) Use the graph to identify the intervals on which the function is below the x-axis.

12. a) Determine an equation, in simplified form, for the family of quartic functions with zeros 5 (order 2) and $-2 \pm \sqrt{6}$.

b) Determine an equation for the member of the family whose graph has a y-intercept of 20.

13. Boxes for chocolates are to be constructed from cardboard sheets that measure 36 cm by 20 cm. Each box is formed by folding a sheet along the dotted lines, as shown.

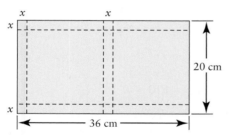

a) Express the volume of the box as a function of x.

b) Determine the possible dimensions of the box if the volume is to be 450 cm³. Round answers to the nearest tenth of a centimetre.

c) Write an equation for the family of functions that corresponds to the function in part a).

d) Sketch graphs of two members of this family on the same coordinate grid.

14. Use Technology Solve. Round answers to one decimal place.

a) $x^3 + 3x \le 8x^2 - 9$

b) $-x^4 + 3x^3 + 9x^2 > 5x + 5$

15. Use Technology Solve each inequality.

a) $x^3 + 3x^2 - 4x - 7 < 0$

b) $2x^4 + 5x^3 - 3x^2 - 15x - 9 \ge 0$

16. Solve by factoring.

a) $9x^2 - 16 < 0$

b) $-x^3 + 6x^2 - 9x > 0$

c) $2x^3 + 5x^2 - 18x - 45 \le 0$

d) $2x^4 + 5x^3 - 8x^2 - 17x - 6 \ge 0$

17. A open-top box is to be constructed from a piece of cardboard by cutting congruent squares from the corners and then folding up the sides. The dimensions of the cardboard are shown.

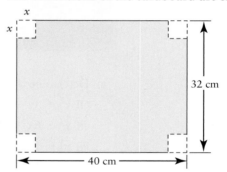

a) Express the volume of the box as a function of x.

b) Write an equation that represents the box with volume

  i) twice the volume of the box represented by the function in part a)

  ii) half the volume of the box represented by the function in part a)

c) How are the equations in part b) related to the one in part a)?

d) Use your function from part a) to determine the values of x that will result in boxes with a volume greater than 2016 cm³.

Can You Tell Just by Looking?

a) Determine the roots of each equation.

   i) $x^2 - 3x + 2 = 0$

   ii) $x^3 - 6x^2 + 11x - 6 = 0$

   iii) $x^4 - 10x^3 + 35x^2 - 50x + 24 = 0$

   iv) $x^5 - 15x^4 + 85x^3 - 225x^2 + 274x - 120 = 0$

b) Use technology to graph the function $y = f(x)$ that corresponds to each equation in part a). Confirm that the zeros of the function are the roots that you found for the corresponding equation.

c) Determine and explain patterns in the roots.

d) Conjecture clues in the equation that may help you predict the pattern in the roots.

e) Test your conjecture on the following equations.

   i) $x^3 - 7x + 6 = 0$

   ii) $x^4 - x^3 - 7x^2 + 13x - 6 = 0$

   iii) $x^6 - 21x^5 + 175x^4 - 735x^3 + 1624x^2 - 1764x + 720 = 0$

Chapter 3

Rational Functions

In most of your studies of functions to date, the graphs have been fairly predictable once you have found the x- and y-intercepts, calculated the slopes, and found any maximum or minimum points. Rational functions take the form $f(x) = \dfrac{P(x)}{Q(x)}$, where $P(x)$ and $Q(x)$ are both polynomial functions and $Q(x) \neq 0$. When $P(x)$ is divided by $Q(x)$, the results are not simple lines or parabolas. Special restrictions apply and some interesting and very complex graphs can result. In this chapter, you will investigate these functions, their graphs, and their rates of change and apply them to such fields as business, medicine, environmental studies, and electronics.

By the end of this chapter, you will

- determine key features of the graphs of rational functions that are the reciprocals of linear and quadratic functions, and make connections between their algebraic and graphical representations (C2.1)
- determine key features of the graphs of rational functions that have linear expressions in the numerator and denominator (C2.2)
- sketch the graph of a simple rational function using its key features, given the algebraic representation of the function (C2.3)
- determine and describe the connection between the real roots of a rational equation and the zeros of the corresponding rational function (C3.5)
- solve simple rational equations in one variable algebraically, and verify solutions using technology (C3.6)
- solve problems involving applications of polynomial and simple rational functions and equations (C3.7)
- explain the difference between the solution to a simple rational equation in one variable and the solution to an inequality, and demonstrate that given solutions satisfy an inequality (C4.1)

- solve graphically and numerically equations and inequalities whose solutions are not accessible by standard algebraic techniques (D4.2)
- recognize examples of rates of change, make connections between instantaneous and average rates of change, calculate approximate rates of change, sketch a graph that represents a rate of change, and solve related problems (D1.3, D1.4, D1.5, D1.6, D1.9)
- connect the slope of a secant with the slope of a tangent and the instantaneous rate of change, and determine the approximate slope of a tangent at a given point (D1.7, D1.8)
- recognize real-world applications of combinations of functions, and solve related problems graphically (D2.2)
- compare the characteristics of various functions, and apply concepts and procedures to solve problems (D3.1, D3.2)

Prerequisite Skills

Reciprocal Functions

1. Define the term *asymptote* and give an equation for the vertical asymptote of $f(x) = \frac{1}{x}$.

2. For each reciprocal function, write equations for the vertical and horizontal asymptotes. Use transformations to sketch each graph relative to the base function $f(x) = \frac{1}{x}$.

   a) $f(x) = \dfrac{1}{x - 3}$

   b) $f(x) = -\dfrac{1}{x + 4}$

   c) $f(x) = -\dfrac{3}{x - 8}$

   d) $f(x) = \dfrac{1}{2x - 10}$

Domain and Range

3. Write the domain and the range of each function.

   a) $f(x) = 4x - 2$

   b) $f(x) = 2(x - 1)^2 + 4$

   c) $f(x) = x^3$

   d) $f(x) = \dfrac{1}{x}$

   e) $f(x) = \dfrac{1}{x - 4}$

   f) $f(x) = -\dfrac{3}{x}$

Slope

4. Find the slope of the line passing through the points in each pair. Leave your answers in fraction form.

   a) $(3, -5)$ and $(2, 8)$

   b) $(-4, 0)$ and $(5, 3)$

   c) $(2, 2)$ and $(-7, 4)$

   d) $(0, 9)$ and $(1, 8)$

   e) $(1, 7)$ and $(2, -6)$

   f) $(3, 3)$ and $(-7, -9)$

5. Find the slope of the line passing through the points in each pair. Round your answers to two decimal places.

   a) $(7, 10)$ and $(-1, 7)$

   b) $(0, 6)$ and $(7, 11)$

   c) $(-4, 2)$ and $(7, 4)$

   d) $(-2, -1)$ and $(11, 4)$

   e) $(-6.6, -5.2)$ and $(1.5, -0.9)$

   f) $(5.8, -3.2)$ and $(10.1, -1.7)$

Factor Polynomials

6. Factor fully.

   a) $x^2 + 7x + 12$

   b) $5x^2 - 17x + 6$

   c) $6x^2 + 13x - 8$

   d) $x^3 + 2x^2 - 5x - 6$

   e) $12x^3 + 4x^2 - 5x - 2$

   f) $27x^3 - 64$

Solve Quadratic Equations

7. Find the roots of each quadratic equation.

   a) $x^2 - 4x - 32 = 0$

   b) $x^2 + 6x + 5 = 0$

   c) $2x^2 - 9x + 9 = 0$

   d) $6x^2 + 31x + 5 = 0$

   e) $2x^2 + 13x - 7 = 0$

   f) $3x^2 - 13x - 30 = 0$

8. Determine the *x*-intercepts. Express your answers in exact form.

   a) $y = x^2 - 4x + 2$

   b) $y = 2x^2 + 8x + 1$

   c) $y = -3x^2 + 5x + 4$

   d) $y = 5x^2 + 2x + 8$

   e) $y = 3x^2 + 8x + 2$

   f) $y = -x^2 + 2x + 7$

Solve Inequalities

9. Solve each inequality. Show your answers on a number line.

   a) $2x - 5 > 7$

   b) $4x + 9 \geq 6x - 2$

   c) $4x < 8x - 2$

   d) $2x + 1 > x - 4$

   e) $3x + 4 > x - 1$

   f) $x - 7 < 2x + 2$

10. Solve each inequality. Show your answers on a number line.

   a) $x^2 - 4 \leq 0$

   b) $x^2 - 3x - 18 > 0$

   c) $2x^2 + 4 < 30$

   d) $3x^2 + 5x - 12 > 2x^2 + 2x - 2$

   e) $2x^2 - x + 4 < x^2 - 9x - 3$

   f) $x^2 + 2x + 2 > -x^2 - 9x + 8$

CHAPTER PROBLEM

As we continue to discover the interconnectedness of our ecosystem with our environment and the world around us, care for the environment and knowledge of the effects of our actions have become increasingly important. Pollution can come in the form of chemical spills, carbon monoxide emissions, excess light in the night sky, loud sounds, and pesticides sprayed on our lawns. In this chapter, you will analyse some mathematical models of various types of pollution, including the costs of cleaning them up.

Reciprocal of a Linear Function

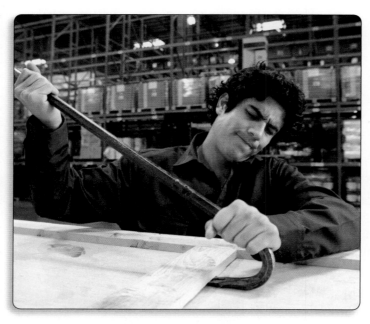

When you add, subtract, or multiply two polynomial functions, the result is another polynomial function. When you divide polynomial functions, the result is a **rational function**. Because division by zero is undefined, rational functions have special properties that polynomial functions do not have. These types of functions occur, for example, when expressing velocity, v, in terms of distance, d, and time, t, $v = \dfrac{d}{t}$, or with levers, where force is inversely proportional to the distance from the pivot point, $\text{Force} = \dfrac{\text{work}}{\text{distance}}$.

Investigate	**What is the nature of the graph of a reciprocal function?**

Tools

- grid paper
- graphing calculator

or

- computer with *The Geometer's Sketchpad®*

It is recommended that technology be used as a tool in this investigation, if available.

1. Consider the function $f(x) = \dfrac{1}{x}$.

   a) State the restriction on the domain. Explain your reasoning.

   b) Make a table of values and sketch a graph of $f(x) = \dfrac{1}{x}$.

   c) Describe what happens to the function as x approaches 0

      i) from the left

      ii) from the right

Technology Tip ∴

If you are using a graphing calculator, use a friendly window to avoid strange joining lines. Refer to the Extension on page 156.

   d) Describe what happens to the function as x approaches

      i) negative infinity $(-\infty)$

      ii) positive infinity $(+\infty)$

   e) Estimate the slope of the curve at $x = 0.1$, at $x = 1$, and at $x = 10$. Repeat for $x = -0.1$, $x = -1$, and $x = -10$.

CONNECTIONS

You learned how to estimate the slope of a curve at a chosen point in Chapter 1. See Section 1.5.

   f) **Reflect** Describe the graph in terms of asymptotes and slope.

2. Consider the function $g(x) = \dfrac{1}{2x - 3}$.

   a) State the restriction on the domain. Explain your reasoning.

b) Sketch a graph of $g(x) = \dfrac{1}{2x - 3}$.

c) Describe what happens to the function as x approaches the restricted value

  i) from the left

  ii) from the right

d) Describe what happens to the function

  i) as $x \to +\infty$

  ii) as $x \to -\infty$

e) Estimate the slope of the curve at $x = 1.6$, at $x = 2$, and at $x = 10$. Repeat for $x = 1.4$, $x = 0$, and $x = -10$.

f) Reflect Describe the graph in terms of asymptotes and slope.

3. Reflect Generalize your observations to describe the function $f(x) = \dfrac{1}{kx - c}$. Include the domain, range, and asymptotes in your description.

CONNECTIONS

"As $x \to +\infty$" is symbolic for "as x approaches positive infinity."

"As $x \to -\infty$" is symbolic for "as x approaches negative infinity."

Example 1 — Domain, Range, and Asymptotes

Consider the function $f(x) = \dfrac{1}{2x - 1}$.

a) State the domain.

b) Describe the behaviour of the function near the vertical asymptote.

c) Describe the end behaviour.

d) Sketch a graph of the function.

e) State the range.

Solution

a) Since division by zero is not defined, the denominator gives a restriction:

$$2x - 1 \neq 0$$
$$x \neq \frac{1}{2}$$

Domain: $\left\{ x \in \mathbb{R},\ x \neq \dfrac{1}{2} \right\}$

CONNECTIONS

The domain can also be written using interval notation as $x \in \left(-\infty, \dfrac{1}{2} \right) \cup \left(\dfrac{1}{2}, +\infty \right)$.

b) The tables show the behaviour of the function as $x \to \dfrac{1}{2}$ from the left and from the right.

As $x \to \dfrac{1}{2}^{-}$:

x	$f(x)$
0	-1
0.4	-5
0.45	-10
0.49	-50

As $x \to \dfrac{1}{2}^{+}$:

x	$f(x)$
1	1
0.6	5
0.55	10
0.51	50

CONNECTIONS

$x \to a^{+}$ means as x approaches a from the right.

$x \to a^{-}$ means as x approaches a from the left.

As $x \to \frac{1}{2}^{-}$, $f(x) \to -\infty$, and as

$x \to \frac{1}{2}^{+}$, $f(x) \to +\infty$. The function

approaches a vertical line at $x = \frac{1}{2}$,

but does not cross it. So, the curve is
discontinuous at this line. This line
is called a vertical asymptote.
An equation for the vertical

asymptote is $x = \frac{1}{2}$.

**Behaviour of $y = f(x)$
near the vertical asymptote $x = \frac{1}{2}$**

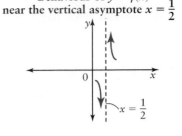

c) The tables show the end behaviour as $x \to -\infty$ and $x \to +\infty$.

As $x \to -\infty$:

x	$f(x)$
-10	$-\dfrac{1}{21}$
-100	$-\dfrac{1}{201}$
$-1\,000$	$-\dfrac{1}{2\,001}$
$-10\,000$	$-\dfrac{1}{20\,001}$

As $x \to +\infty$:

x	$f(x)$
10	$\dfrac{1}{19}$
100	$\dfrac{1}{199}$
$1\,000$	$\dfrac{1}{1\,999}$
$10\,000$	$\dfrac{1}{19\,999}$

As $x \to +\infty$, $f(x) \to 0$ from above, since
all values of $f(x)$ are positive. The graph
approaches a horizontal line at the x-axis,
but does not cross it. The horizontal
asymptote at $+\infty$ has equation $y = 0$.

As $x \to -\infty$, $f(x) \to 0$ from below, since
all values of $f(x)$ are negative.
The horizontal asymptote at $-\infty$
has equation $y = 0$.

**Behaviour of $y = f(x)$
as $x \to -\infty$ and as $x \to +\infty$**

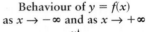

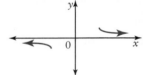

d)

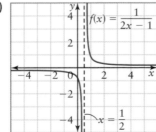

e) The graph of the function shows that $f(x)$ gets close to the line $y = 0$ but
never actually touches that line. Therefore, the only restriction on the
range of $f(x)$ is that $y \neq 0$.

Range: $\{y \in \mathbb{R}, y \neq 0\}$

Example 2 | Find Intercepts

Determine the x- and y-intercepts of the function $g(x) = \dfrac{2}{x + 5}$.

Solution

For the x-intercept, let $g(x) = 0$.

$$\frac{2}{x + 5} = 0$$

There is no value of x that makes this equation true. Therefore, there is no x-intercept.

For the y-intercept, let $x = 0$.

$$g(0) = \frac{2}{0 + 5}$$

$$= \frac{2}{5}$$

The y-intercept is $\dfrac{2}{5}$.

Example 3 | Rate of Change

Describe the intervals where the slope is increasing and the intervals where it is decreasing in the two branches of the rational function $h(x) = -\dfrac{1}{5x + 2}$.

Solution

The two branches of the function are on either side of the vertical asymptote. For the vertical asymptote, let the denominator equal zero.

$$5x + 2 = 0$$
$$x = -0.4$$

The vertical asymptote has equation $x = -0.4$.

Select a few points to the left and to the right of the asymptote and analyse the slope.

Select two points to the left of $x = -0.4$. Choosing consecutive x-values gives a denominator of 1. So, the slope is the difference in y-values.

At $x = -10$, $f(x) \doteq 0.021$.
At $x = -9$, $f(x) \doteq 0.023$.

$$\text{Slope} = \frac{y_2 - y_1}{x_2 - x_1}$$

$$\doteq \frac{(0.023) - (0.021)}{(-9) - (-10)}$$

$$= 0.002$$

Now, select two points closer to $x = -0.4$:

At $x = -4$, $f(x) \doteq 0.056$.
At $x = -3$, $f(x) \doteq 0.077$.
Slope $= f(-3) - f(-4)$
$ \doteq 0.021$

Because $0.021 > 0.002$ (the slope between the previous two points), the slope is positive and increasing within the interval $x < -0.4$.

Select two points to the right of $x = -0.4$:

At $x = 2$, $f(x) \doteq -0.083$.
At $x = 3$, $f(x) \doteq -0.059$.
Slope $= f(3) - f(2)$
$ \doteq 0.024$

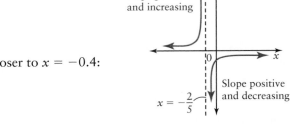

Now, select two points closer to $x = -0.4$:

At $x = 0$, $f(x) = -0.5$.
At $x = 1$, $f(x) \doteq -0.143$.
Slope $= f(1) - f(0)$
$ \doteq 0.357$

Because $0.357 > 0.024$, the slope is positive and decreasing within the interval $x > -0.4$.

KEY CONCEPTS

- The reciprocal of a linear function has the form $f(x) = \dfrac{1}{kx - c}$.

- The restriction on the domain of a reciprocal linear function can be determined by finding the value of x that makes the denominator equal to zero, that is, $x = \dfrac{c}{k}$.

- The vertical asymptote of a reciprocal linear function has an equation of the form $x = \dfrac{c}{k}$.

- The horizontal asymptote of a reciprocal linear function has equation $y = 0$.
  - If $k > 0$, the left branch of a reciprocal linear function has a negative, decreasing slope, and the right branch has a negative, increasing slope.
  - If $k < 0$, the left branch of a reciprocal function has positive, increasing slope, and the right branch has positive, decreasing slope.

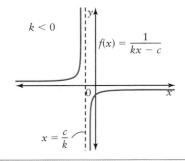

Communicate Your Understanding

C1 The calculator screen gives a table of values for the function $f(x) = \dfrac{4}{x-3}$. Explain why there is an error statement.

X	Y₁
2.99	-400
2.999	-4000
2.9999	-40000
3	ERROR
3.0001	40000
3.001	4000
3.01	400

X=2.99

C2 a) For the reciprocal of any linear function, as the denominator increases, what happens to the function value?

b) For the reciprocal of any linear function, as the denominator approaches zero, what happens to the function value?

C3 Can you find an example of a linear function whose reciprocal has no restrictions on either the domain or range? If yes, give an example. If no, explain.

A Practise

For questions 1 and 2, refer to Example 1.

1. Copy and complete each table to describe the behaviour of the function as x approaches each key value.

a) $f(x) = \dfrac{1}{x-2}$

As $x \rightarrow$	$f(x) \rightarrow$
2^+	
2^-	
$+\infty$	
$-\infty$	

b) $f(x) = \dfrac{1}{x+5}$

As $x \rightarrow$	$f(x) \rightarrow$
-5^+	
-5^-	
$+\infty$	
$-\infty$	

c) $f(x) = \dfrac{1}{x-8}$

As $x \rightarrow$	$f(x) \rightarrow$
8^+	
8^-	
$+\infty$	
$-\infty$	

2. a) Write equations to represent the horizontal and vertical asymptotes of each rational function.

i)

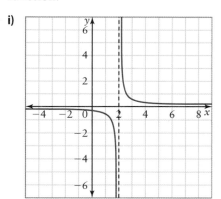

ii)

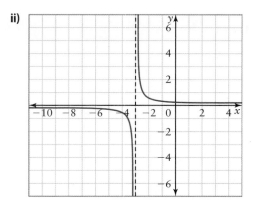

b) Write a possible equation for each function in part a).

For help with questions 3 to 5, refer to Example 2.

3. For each reciprocal function,
   i) write an equation to represent the vertical asymptote
   ii) write an equation to represent the horizontal asymptote
   iii) determine the y-intercept

   a) $f(x) = \dfrac{1}{x - 5}$ b) $g(x) = \dfrac{2}{x + 6}$

   c) $h(x) = \dfrac{5}{1 - x}$ d) $k(x) = -\dfrac{1}{x + 7}$

4. **Use Technology** Verify the vertical asymptotes in question 3 using technology.

5. Determine a possible equation to represent each function shown.

   a)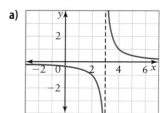

   b)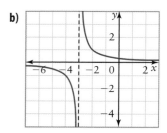

c)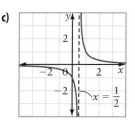

d)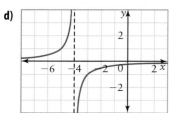

For help with question 6, refer to Example 3.

6. Sketch each function and then describe the intervals where the slope is increasing and the intervals where it is decreasing.

   a) $f(x) = \dfrac{1}{x - 3}$

   b) $k(x) = \dfrac{3}{2x + 7}$

   c) $m(x) = -\dfrac{2}{x + 4}$

   d) $p(x) = \dfrac{5}{3 - 2x}$

B Connect and Apply

7. Sketch a graph of each function. Label the y-intercept. State the domain, range, and equations of the asymptotes.

   a) $f(x) = \dfrac{1}{x - 1}$ b) $g(x) = \dfrac{1}{x + 4}$

   c) $h(x) = \dfrac{1}{2x + 1}$ d) $k(x) = -\dfrac{1}{x + 4}$

   e) $m(x) = -\dfrac{3}{2x - 5}$ f) $n(x) = \dfrac{4}{5 - x}$

   g) $p(x) = \dfrac{1}{\left(x - \dfrac{1}{4}\right)}$ h) $q(x) = -\dfrac{3}{\left(x + \dfrac{1}{2}\right)}$

8. Determine the equation in the form $f(x) = \dfrac{1}{kx - c}$ for the function with a vertical asymptote at $x = 1$ and a y-intercept at -1.

9. Determine the equation in the form $f(x) = \dfrac{1}{kx - c}$ for the function with a vertical asymptote at $x = -1$ and a y-intercept at -0.25.

10. The time required to fly from one location to another is inversely proportional to the average speed. When the average speed to fly from Québec City to Vancouver is 350 km/h, the flying time is 11 h.

a) Write a function to represent the time as a function of the speed.

b) Sketch a graph of this function.

c) How long would the trip from Québec to Vancouver take at an average speed of 500 km/h?

d) Describe the rate of change of the time as the average speed increases.

> **CONNECTIONS**
>
> If two variables, x and y, are inversely proportional, then $y = \frac{k}{x}$, where k is a constant.

11. a) Investigate a variety of functions of the form $f(x) = \frac{1}{bx + 2}$.

b) What is the effect on the graph when the value of b is varied?

12. Use the results from question 11 to sketch a graph of each function.

a) $f(x) = \frac{1}{x - 5}$

b) $g(x) = \frac{1}{2x - 5}$

c) $h(x) = \frac{1}{3x - 5}$

13. The force required to lift an object is inversely proportional to the distance of the force from the fulcrum of a lever. A force of 200 N is required at a point 3 m from the fulcrum to lift a certain object.

a) Determine a function to represent the force as a function of the distance.

b) Sketch a graph of this function.

c) How much force is required to lift this object at a point 2 m from the fulcrum?

d) What is the effect on the force needed as the distance from the fulcrum is doubled?

> **CONNECTIONS**
>
> A fulcrum is the pivot on which a lever turns.

C Extend and Challenge

14. Analyse the key features (domain, range, vertical asymptotes, and horizontal asymptotes) of each function, and then sketch the function.

a) $f(x) = \frac{1}{\sqrt{x}}$

b) $g(x) = \frac{1}{|x|}$

c) $f(x) = \frac{3}{x - 2} + 4$

15. Graph the line $y = 2x - 5$ and find the x-intercept. Analyse the reciprocals of the y-coordinates on either side of the x-intercept. How do these numbers relate to the key features of the function $f(x) = \frac{1}{2x - 5}$?

16. Math Contest Solve for x in terms of y and z:
$$\frac{1}{x} + \frac{1}{y} = \frac{1}{z}$$

17. Math Contest Given that $3a = 75b$, find the value of $\frac{3a - 5b}{5b}$.

18. Math Contest Two points are chosen on the unit circle with centre at the origin. What is the probability that the distance between these two points is at least 1?

A $\frac{1}{4}$ **B** $\frac{1}{2}$ **C** $\frac{3}{4}$ **D** $\frac{1}{3}$ **E** $\frac{2}{3}$

Extension

Asymptotes and the TI-83 Plus or TI-84 Plus Graphing Calculator

A: *Friendly Windows*

The viewing window on the TI-83 Plus or TI-84 Plus graphing calculator is 94 pixels by 62 pixels. If the graph has a vertical asymptote that falls between two consecutive plot points, the calculator draws an almost vertical drag line, or "joining line." This occurs because the calculator connects the two points that span the asymptote, one with a positive *y*-coordinate and the other with a negative *y*-coordinate.

You can avoid this by using a "friendly window." The *x*-axis is 94 pixels across. When the calculator divides the pixels evenly into negative and positive integers, each pixel represents one tick mark. Therefore, *x*-values can go from −47 to 47. The *y*-axis has 62 pixels vertically and stretches from −31 to 31. When you press `ZOOM` and select **4:ZDecimal**, you get a small friendly window.

You can obtain other friendly windows by multiplying 94 and 62 by the same constant.

1. Graph the function shown in the first screen in the margin using the friendly window shown in the second screen. Compare the two graphs.

2. Is each a friendly window? Explain why or why not.

a)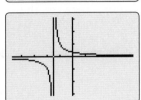

b)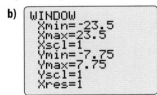

3. How can you obtain a friendly window that has Xmin = 0?

B: *Drawing in Asymptotes*

In some situations it may be helpful to actually draw in the asymptote(s) properly. This can be done using the **DRAW** feature.

- Press [2nd] `PRGM` to obtain the **DRAW** menu.
- Select **3:Horizontal** for a horizontal asymptote.
- Select **4:Vertical** for a vertical asymptote.
- Press `ENTER`.
- Move the cursor to the coordinate on the axis that the asymptote will pass though.
- Press `ENTER`.

You can clear the line by selecting **1:ClrDraw** from the **DRAW** menu.

For example, an asymptote for the function $f(x) = -\dfrac{1}{2x - 3}$ is shown.

1. Use a graphing calculator to check your answers for question 3 or 7 in Section 3.1.

Reciprocal of a Quadratic Function

In Section 3.1, the rational functions you analysed had linear denominators. However, rational functions can have polynomials of any degree, such as a quadratic (or second-degree polynomial), in the numerator and denominator. Because quadratics have possibly zero, one, or two x-intercepts, a parabolic shape, and a maximum or minimum point, plotting their reciprocals becomes fairly complex. In this section, you will analyse and graph functions such as $f(x) = -\dfrac{10}{x^2 - 2x - 15}$.

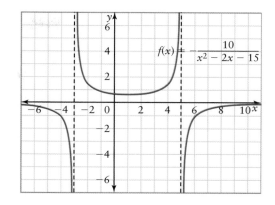

$$f(x) = -\frac{10}{x^2 - 2x - 15}$$

Investigate **What is the nature of the graph of the reciprocal of a quadratic function?**

It is recommended that technology be used as a tool in this investigation, if available.

1. Create a graph of the function $f(x) = \dfrac{1}{x^2}$. Describe the key features of the graph:

  a) horizontal asymptote

  b) vertical asymptote

  c) intercepts

  d) domain and range

  e) end behaviour

  f) positive and negative intervals

  g) increasing and decreasing intervals

2. Consider the function $g(x) = \dfrac{1}{(x - 2)(x + 1)}$.

  a) Determine the restrictions on x and state the domain of $g(x)$.

  b) **Use Technology** Graph the function using technology.

  c) Describe the behaviour of the graph to the left and to the right of each asymptote.

  d) Investigate the slope, and the change in slope, for the following intervals:

   i) to the left of the left-most vertical asymptote

   ii) to the right of the right-most vertical asymptote

  e) Devise a plan for determining the maximum point in the interval between the asymptotes.

  f) Use your plan from part e) to determine the coordinates of the maximum point between the asymptotes.

  g) State the range of the function.

  h) Explain how the graph of $g(x)$ is different from the graph of $f(x)$ in step 1.

Tools

• grid paper

• graphing calculator

or

• computer with *The Geometer's Sketchpad*®

3. Consider the function $h(x) = -\dfrac{2}{(x-1)^2}$.

   a) Determine the restrictions on x and state the domain of $h(x)$.

   b) **Use Technology** Graph the function using technology.

   c) Describe the behaviour of the graph to the left and to the right of the vertical asymptote.

   d) Investigate the slope, and the change in slope, for the following intervals:

   i) to the left of the vertical asymptote

   ii) to the right of the vertical asymptote

   e) State the range of the function.

   f) Explain how the graph of $h(x)$ is different from the graphs in steps 1 and 2.

4. a) Without using technology, analyse the graph of the function

   $k(x) = \dfrac{2}{x^2 + 3x + 2}$ under the following headings:

   i) Horizontal and vertical asymptotes

   ii) Domain and range

   iii) Behaviour of the slope
   - positive or negative
   - increasing or decreasing

   iv) End behaviour

   v) Intercepts

   b) Sketch a graph of the function.

   c) **Use Technology** Verify that your analysis and graph are correct using technology.

5. **Reflect** Describe how the graphs of reciprocals of quadratic functions behave differently from the graphs of reciprocals of linear functions.

Example 1 Find the Domain, Range, and Asymptotes

Consider the function $f(x) = \dfrac{2}{x^2 - 4}$.

a) State the domain.

b) Find the equations of the asymptotes. Describe the behaviour of the function near the asymptotes.

c) Determine the x- and y-intercepts.

d) Sketch a graph of the function.

e) State the range.

Solution

a) The function can be rewritten by factoring the difference of squares in the denominator.

$f(x) = \dfrac{2}{(x+2)(x-2)}$

Because the denominator cannot equal zero, there are restrictions at $x = 2$ and $x = -2$.

Domain: $\{x \in \mathbb{R}, x \neq -2, x \neq 2\}$

b) The vertical asymptotes have equations $x = -2$ and $x = 2$.

As $x \to \pm\infty$, the denominator approaches $+\infty$, so $f(x)$ approaches 0. Thus, $f(x)$ approaches a horizontal line at $y = 0$, but does not cross it.

The horizontal asymptote has equation $y = 0$.

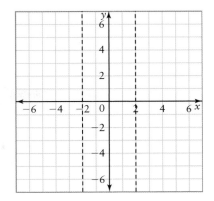

Check selected points near the vertical asymptotes.

As $x \to -2^-$, the function is positive and increasing toward $+\infty$.

As $x \to -2^+$, the function is negative and decreasing toward $-\infty$.

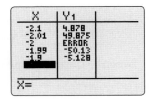

As $x \to 2^-$, the function is negative and decreasing toward $-\infty$ (i.e., negative slope).

As $x \to 2^+$, the function is positive and increasing toward $+\infty$ (i.e., negative slope).

A table can be used to summarize the above observations.

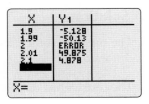

Interval of x	$x < -2$	$-2 < x < 2$	$x > 2$
Sign of $f(x)$	+	−	+
Sign of Slope	+	+ to −	−

c) For the x-intercepts, let $f(x) = 0$:

$$\frac{2}{(x + 2)(x - 2)} = 0$$

Since there is no value of x that makes this statement true, there is no x-intercept.

For the y-intercept, let $x = 0$:

$$f(0) = \frac{2}{(0 + 2)(0 - 2)}$$

$$= -0.5$$

Because of the symmetry of the function, since this point lies exactly halfway between the two vertical asymptotes, $(0, -0.5)$ is the maximum point for this interval.

d)

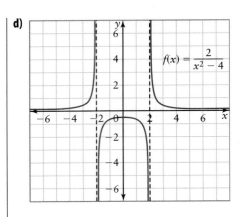

$$f(x) = \frac{2}{x^2 - 4}$$

e) Range: $y > 0$ or $y \leq -0.5$

Example 2	Rate of Change

Describe the increasing and decreasing intervals in the branches of the function $f(x) = -\dfrac{1}{2x^2 - x - 6}$. Then, graph the function.

Solution

The function can be rewritten as $f(x) = -\dfrac{1}{(2x + 3)(x - 2)}$ by factoring the denominator.

The restrictions on the domain occur at $x = -1.5$ and $x = 2$.

The intervals to be analysed are (i) $x < -1.5$, (ii) $-1.5 < x < 2$, and (iii) $x > 2$.

Select points in each interval and approximate the slope at each point.

i) Consider the interval $x < -1.5$.

At $x = -4$, $f(x) \doteq -0.033\,33$.

x	y	Slope of secant with $(-4, -0.033\,33)$
-3.9	$-0.035\,31$	$\dfrac{(-0.035\,31) - (-0.033\,33)}{(-3.9) - (-4)}$ $= -0.0198$
-3.99	$-0.033\,52$	-0.019
-3.999	$-0.033\,35$	-0.02

The slope is approximately -0.02 at the point $(-4, -0.033\,33)$.

At $x = -2$, $f(x) = -0.25$.

x	y	Slope of secant with $(-2, -0.25)$
-2.1	$-0.203\,25$	$-0.467\,5$
-2.01	$-0.244\,49$	-0.551
-2.001	$-0.249\,44$	-0.56

The slope is approximately -0.56 at the point $(-2, -0.25)$.

The slope is negative and decreasing on the interval $x < -1.5$.

ii) Consider the interval $x > 2$. At $x = 3$, $f(x) \doteq -0.111\,11$.

x	y	Slope of secant with $(3, -0.111\,11)$
3.1	$-0.098\,81$	0.123
3.01	$-0.109\,77$	0.134
3.001	$-0.110\,98$	0.13

The slope is approximately 0.13 at the point $(3, -0.111\,11)$.

At $x = 4$, $f(x) \doteq -0.045\,45$.

x	y	Slope of secant with $(4, -0.045\,45)$
4.1	$-0.042\,52$	$0.029\,3$
4.01	$-0.045\,15$	0.03
4.001	$-0.045\,42$	0.03

The slope is approximately 0.03 at the point $(4, -0.045\,45)$.

The slope is positive and decreasing on the interval $x > 2$.

iii) Consider the interval $-1.5 < x < 2$. As can be seen in the Investigate and Example 1, there will be a maximum or a minimum point between the asymptotes. Just as a quadratic has the x-coordinate of its maximum or minimum point exactly halfway between the x-intercepts, the reciprocal of a quadratic has the x-coordinate of its maximum or minimum point exactly halfway between the vertical asymptotes.

For the midpoint:

$$x = \frac{-1.5 + 2}{2}$$

$$= 0.25$$

$$f(0.25) = \frac{8}{49}$$

$$\doteq 0.163\,27$$

Consider points just to the left of $(0.25, 0.163\,27)$.

x	y	Slope of secant with $(0.25, 0.163\,27)$
0.23	$0.163\,29$	-0.001
0.24	$0.163\,27$	0

Consider points just to the right of (0.25, 0.163 27).

x	y	Slope of secant with (0.25, 0.163 27)
0.26	0.163 27	0
0.27	0.163 29	0.001

For the interval $-1.5 < x < 0.25$, the slope is negative and increasing.

For the interval $0.25 < x < 2$, the slope is positive and increasing.

At $x = 0.25$, the slope is 0.

This can all be summarized in a table.

Interval	$x < -1.5$	$-1.5 < x < 0.25$	$x = 0.25$	$0.25 < x < 2$	$x > 2$
Sign of $f(x)$	−	+	+	+	−
Sign of slope	−	−	0	+	+
Change in slope	− decreasing	+ increasing		+ increasing	− decreasing

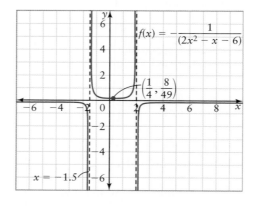

$$f(x) = -\frac{1}{(2x^2 - x - 6)}$$

$\left(\frac{1}{4}, \frac{8}{49}\right)$

$x = -1.5$

Example 3 | Describe the Key Features of a Function

Analyse the key features of the function $f(x) = \dfrac{1}{x^2 + 4}$ and sketch its graph.

Solution

For the domain and vertical asymptotes:

Consider the denominator $x^2 + 4$.

Since $x^2 \geq 0$, $x^2 + 4 > 0$ for all values of x.

Therefore, there is no restriction on the domain and there is no vertical asymptote.

Domain: $\mathbb{R}$

For the x-intercepts:

Let $f(x) = 0$.

$$\frac{1}{x^2 + 4} = 0$$

Because there are no values of x that make this statement true, there is no x-intercept.

For the horizontal asymptote:

As $x \to -\infty$, $f(x) \to 0$ and $f(x) > 0$.

As $x \to +\infty$, $f(x) \to 0$ and $f(x) > 0$.

The horizontal asymptote has equation $y = 0$ and the curve lies entirely above the asymptote.

For the y-intercept:

Let $x = 0$.

$$f(x) = \frac{1}{x^2 + 4}$$

$$f(0) = \frac{1}{(0)^2 + 4}$$

$$= 0.25$$

Range: $\{y \in \mathbb{R}, 0 < y \le 0.25\}$

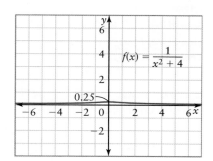

$$f(x) = \frac{1}{x^2 + 4}$$

KEY CONCEPTS

- Rational functions can be analysed using key features: asymptotes, intercepts, slope (positive or negative, increasing or decreasing), domain, range, and positive and negative intervals.

- Reciprocals of quadratic functions with two zeros have three parts, with the middle one reaching a maximum or minimum point. This point is equidistant from the two vertical asymptotes.

- The behaviour near asymptotes is similar to that of reciprocals of linear functions.

- All of the behaviours listed above can be predicted by analysing the roots of the quadratic relation in the denominator.

Communicate Your Understanding

C1 Describe the slope and change in slope for each graph.

a)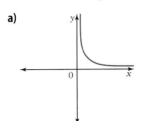

b)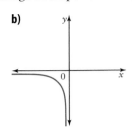

c)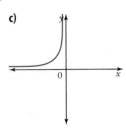

C2 A reciprocal of a quadratic function has the following summary table. Sketch a possible graph of the function.

Interval	$x < -3$	$-3 < x < 1$	$x = 1$	$1 < x < 5$	$x > 5$
Sign of $f(x)$	+	−	−	−	+
Sign of Slope	+	+	0	−	−
Change in Slope	+	−	−	−	+

C3 Describe the key features of the function shown.

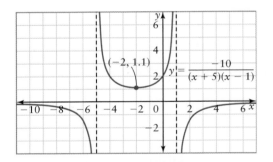

A Practise

For help with questions 1 and 2, refer to Example 1.

1. Copy and complete each table to describe the behaviour of the function as x approaches each key value.

a) $f(x) = \dfrac{1}{(x-3)(x-1)}$

As $x \to$	$f(x) \to$
3^-	
3^+	
1^-	
1^+	
$-\infty$	
$+\infty$	

b) $f(x) = \dfrac{1}{(x-5)(x+4)}$

As $x \to$	$f(x) \to$
-4^-	
-4^+	
5^-	
5^+	
$-\infty$	
$+\infty$	

c) $f(x) = -\dfrac{1}{(x+6)^2}$

As $x \to$	$f(x) \to$
-6^-	
-6^+	
$-\infty$	
$+\infty$	

2. Determine equations for the vertical asymptotes, if they exist, for each function. Then, state the domain.

a) $g(x) = \dfrac{1}{(x-4)^2}$

b) $f(x) = \dfrac{1}{(x-2)(x+7)}$

c) $v(x) = \dfrac{1}{x^2+1}$

d) $m(x) = \dfrac{3}{x^2-25}$

e) $h(x) = \dfrac{1}{x^2-4x+3}$

f) $k(x) = -\dfrac{2}{x^2+7x+12}$

g) $n(x) = -\dfrac{2}{3x^2+2x-8}$

h) $u(x) = -\dfrac{2}{2x^2+3x+8}$

For help with questions 3 and 4, refer to Example 2.

3. Make a summary table with the headings shown for each graph.

Interval	
Sign of Function	
Sign of Slope	
Change in Slope	

a)

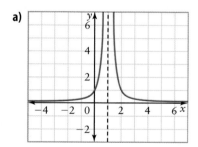

b)

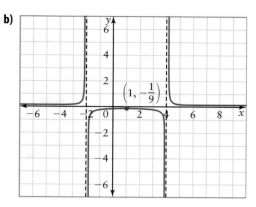

$\left(1, -\dfrac{1}{9}\right)$

c)

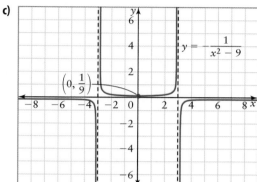

$y = -\dfrac{1}{x^2-9}$

$\left(0, \dfrac{1}{9}\right)$

d)

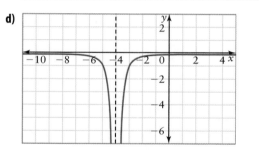

4. Determine a possible equation for each function in question 3.

B Connect and Apply

For help with question 5, refer to Example 3.

5. For each function,

i) give the domain

ii) determine equations for the asymptotes

iii) determine the y-intercepts

iv) sketch a graph of the function

v) include a summary table of the slopes

vi) give the range

a) $f(x) = \dfrac{1}{x^2-9}$

b) $t(x) = \dfrac{1}{x^2-2x-15}$

c) $p(x) = -\dfrac{1}{x^2+5x-21}$

d) $w(x) = \dfrac{1}{3x^2-5x-2}$

e) $q(x) = \dfrac{1}{x^2+2}$

6. For each function in question 5, approximate the instantaneous rate of change at each y-intercept.

7. Recall that a quadratic function with a double zero is tangent to the x-axis at its vertex. Describe the key features of the reciprocal of a perfect square quadratic function, after investigating the graphs of the following functions.

a) $f(x) = \dfrac{1}{x^2}$

b) $g(x) = \dfrac{1}{(x-1)^2}$

c) $h(x) = \dfrac{1}{(x+2)^2}$

8. Sketch each function. Then, determine the intervals where the function is increasing and those where it is decreasing.

a) $f(x) = \dfrac{1}{x^2 - 1}$

b) $c(x) = \dfrac{1}{x^2 + 8x + 15}$

c) $q(x) = \dfrac{4}{x^2 + x - 6}$

d) $h(x) = -\dfrac{1}{4x^2 - 4x - 3}$

e) $w(x) = \dfrac{8}{x^2 + 1}$

f) $g(x) = -\dfrac{1}{(x-6)^2}$

g) $k(x) = -\dfrac{1}{x^2 + 3}$

h) $m(x) = \dfrac{1}{9x^2 - 6x + 1}$

9. a) Describe how to find the vertex of the parabola defined by the function $f(x) = x^2 + 6x + 11$.

b) Explain how to use your method in part a) to find the maximum point of the function $g(x) = \dfrac{1}{x^2 + 6x + 11}$.

c) Use your technique to sketch a graph of each function.

i) $h(x) = \dfrac{4}{2x^2 - 8x + 9}$

ii) $k(x) = -\dfrac{5}{x^2 + 5x + 8}$

10. Without graphing, describe the similarities and differences between the graphs of the functions in each pair. Check your answers by graphing.

a) $f(x) = \dfrac{1}{x^2 - 7x + 12}$, $g(x) = -\dfrac{1}{x^2 - 7x + 12}$

b) $h(x) = \dfrac{1}{x^2 - 9}$, $k(x) = \dfrac{2}{x^2 - 9}$

c) $m(x) = \dfrac{1}{x^2 - 4}$, $n(x) = \dfrac{1}{x^2 - 25}$

11. Each function described below is the reciprocal of a quadratic function. Write an equation to represent each function.

Reasoning and Proving • Representing • Selecting Tools • Problem Solving • Connecting • Reflecting • Communicating

a) The horizontal asymptote is $y = 0$. The vertical asymptotes are $x = 2$ and $x = -3$. For the intervals $x < -3$ and $x > 2$, $y > 0$.

b) The horizontal asymptote is $y = 0$. There is no vertical asymptote. The maximum point is $(0, 0.5)$. Domain: $\mathbb{R}$

c) The horizontal asymptote is $y = 0$. The vertical asymptote is $x = -3$. Domain: $\{x \in \mathbb{R}, x \neq -3\}$

12. Chapter Problem Radiation from the Sun keeps us all alive, but with the thinning of the ozone layer, it is important to limit exposure. The intensity of radiation is inversely proportional to the square of the distance that the Sun's rays travel. The formula $I = \dfrac{k}{d^2}$ models the relationship between intensity, I, in watts per square metre (W/m²), and distance, d, in astronomical units (AU). The intensity of radiation from the Sun is 9140 W/m² on Mercury, which is 0.387 AU away.

a) Determine an equation relating the intensity of radiation and the distance from the Sun.

b) Sketch a graph of this relationship.

c) Determine the intensity of radiation and its rate of change on Earth, which is 1 AU from the Sun.

13. When astronauts go into space, they feel lighter. This is because weight decreases as a person rises above Earth's gravitational pull according to the formula $W(h) = \dfrac{W_e}{\left(1 + \dfrac{h}{6400}\right)^2}$ where W_e is the person's weight, in newtons, at sea level on Earth, and $W(h)$ is the weight at h kilometres above sea level.

a) Sketch a graph of this function for an astronaut whose weight is 820 N at sea level.

b) What is this astronaut's weight at each altitude?

   i) 10 km   **ii)** 4000 km

c) At what range of altitudes will this astronaut have a weight of less than 10 N?

14. Use your knowledge of transformations to sketch each function.

a) $f(x) = \dfrac{1}{x^2} + 3$

b) $g(x) = \dfrac{1}{x^2 - 9} - 4$

✔ Achievement Check

15. Consider the function $f(x) = \dfrac{3}{x^2 - 25}$.

a) Determine any restrictions on x.

b) State the domain and range.

c) State equation(s) for the asymptote(s).

d) Determine any x- and y-intercepts.

e) Sketch a graph of the function.

f) Describe the behaviour of the function as x approaches -5 and 5.

C   Extend and Challenge

16. One method of graphing rational functions that are reciprocals of polynomial functions is to sketch the polynomial function and then plot the reciprocals of the y-coordinates of key ordered pairs.

Use this technique to sketch $y = \dfrac{1}{f(x)}$ for each function.

a) $f(x) = 2x$

b) $f(x) = 4x^2$

c) $f(x) = x^2 - 1$

d) $f(x) = x^3$

17. Determine whether the graph of each function is symmetric about the x-axis, the y-axis, the origin, the line $y = x$, the line $y = -x$, or none of these.

a) $y = \dfrac{1}{x^3}$ **b)** $y = \dfrac{1}{x^4}$

18. Sketch each function. Compare your results to those in question 12 and explain the connection.

a) $f(x) = \dfrac{3x^2 + 1}{x^2}$

b) $g(x) = \dfrac{-4x^2 + 37}{x^2 - 9}$

19. Math Contest Write a rational equation that cannot have a or b as a root, given that $a, b \in \mathbb{R}$.

20. Math Contest The ratio of $a + 5$ to $2a - 1$ is greater than 40%. Solve for a.

21. Math Contest Consider the equation $g(z + 1) = \dfrac{g(z - 2)g(z - 1) + 1}{g(z)}$. Find $g(5)$, given that $g(1) = 1$, $g(2) = 2$, and $g(3) = 3$.

22. Math Contest A circle with centre O intersects another circle with centre P at points C and D. If $\angle COD = 30°$ and $\angle CPD = 60°$, what is the ratio of the area of the circle with centre O to the area of the circle with centre P?

A $9:1$

B $(\sqrt{6} + \sqrt{2}):1$

C $1:(2 - \sqrt{3})$

D $(6 + 2\sqrt{3}):1$

Rational Functions of the Form $f(x) = \dfrac{ax + b}{cx + d}$

In Sections 3.1 and 3.2, you investigated rational functions that are reciprocals of polynomial functions. In this section, you will look at polynomial functions in which both the numerator and the denominator are linear expressions. Because there is a variable in both the numerator and the denominator, there are effects on both the vertical and horizontal asymptotes and, as a result, the domain and range. You will see how these concepts are applied to pollutants flowing into a pond in question 10.

Investigate   **How can you determine the asymptotes of a rational function of the form $f(x) = \dfrac{ax + b}{cx + d}$?**

Tools

- grid paper
- graphing calculator

or

- computer with *The Geometer's Sketchpad®*

1. Investigate the key features of the family of functions of the form $f(x) = \dfrac{x}{cx - 3}$ for $c \in \mathbb{Z}$. Include both negative and positive values of c. Make a table using the headings shown.

c	Equation(s) of Vertical Asymptote(s)	Equation of Horizontal Asymptote	Comparison to $f(x) = \dfrac{x}{x - 3}$

2. a) Describe the nature of the vertical asymptote(s).

   b) Describe the nature of the horizontal asymptote.

   c) Develop a method for determining an equation for the horizontal asymptote.

3. Reflect Summarize the behaviour of the function $f(x) = \dfrac{x}{cx - 3}$ using the headings shown.

Interval	
Sign of Function	
Sign of Slope	
Change in Slope	

4. Sketch a graph of each function listed in your table.

Example 1 | Determine Key Features

Determine the key features of $f(x) = \dfrac{x}{x-2}$. Use the key features to graph the function.

Solution

The vertical asymptote has equation $x = 2$.

For the horizontal asymptote:

At $x \to \infty$, the numerator and denominator both approach infinity.

Divide each term by x.

$$f(x) = \dfrac{\dfrac{x}{x}}{\dfrac{x}{x} - \dfrac{2}{x}}$$

$$= \dfrac{1}{1 - \dfrac{2}{x}}$$

As $x \to +\infty$, $\dfrac{2}{x}$ gets very close to 0.

$$f(x) \to \dfrac{1}{1 - 0}$$

$$f(x) \to 1$$

As $x \to -\infty$, $\dfrac{2}{x}$ gets very close to 0.

$$f(x) \to \dfrac{1}{1 - 0}$$

$$f(x) \to 1$$

The function approaches the line $y = 1$ for both $x \to +\infty$ and $x \to -\infty$. So, $y = 1$ is the equation of the horizontal asymptote.

For the x-intercept, let $f(x) = 0$.

$$\dfrac{x}{x-2} = 0$$

$$x = 0$$

For the y-intercept, let $x = 0$.

$$f(0) = \dfrac{0}{0-2}$$

$$= 0$$

The y-intercept is 0.

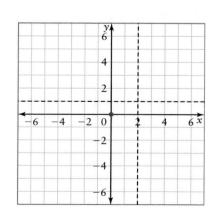

To determine where the slope is negative and where it is positive, select points in the interval to the left of the vertical asymptote and in the interval to the right of the vertical asymptote.

Select two points in the interval $x < 2$, say $x = -8$ and $x = 1$:
$f(-8) = 0.8$ and $f(1) = -1$.
$f(x)$ is decreasing, so the slope is negative.

Select two points in the interval $x > 2$, say $x = 3$ and $x = 10$:
$f(3) = 3$ and $f(10) = 1.25$.
$f(x)$ is decreasing, so the slope is negative.

There is a vertical asymptote at $x = 2$, but what is the sign of $f(x)$ on either side of this asymptote?

$f(1.99)$ will give a positive numerator and a negative denominator, so $f(1.99)$ is negative.

$f(2.01)$ will give a positive numerator and a positive denominator, so $f(2.01)$ is positive.

What is the end behaviour of this function?
Choose large positive and negative values of x.

$f(10\ 000) > 1$, so the function is above the asymptote.

$f(-10\ 000) < 1$, so the function is below the asymptote.

Summarize the intervals. At $x = 0$, $y = 0$, so the curve crosses the x-axis at the origin:

Interval	$x < 0$	$x = 0$	$0 < x < 2$	$x > 2$
$f(x)$	+	0	−	+
Slope	−	−	−	−

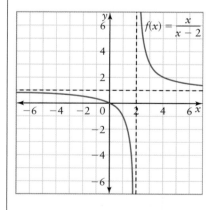

Domain: $\{x \in \mathbb{R}, x \neq 2\}$

Range: $\{y \in \mathbb{R}, y \neq 1\}$

Example 2 | Compare Rational Functions

a) Compare the graphs of the functions $f(x) = \dfrac{x-1}{2x+5}$, $g(x) = \dfrac{x-5}{2x+5}$, and $h(x) = \dfrac{x-10}{2x+5}$.

b) Explain the effects of the coefficient b in $f(x) = \dfrac{ax+b}{cx+d}$.

Reasoning and Proving
Representing · Selecting Tools
Problem Solving
Connecting · Reflecting
Communicating

Solution

a) The vertical asymptote for all three functions has equation $x = -\dfrac{5}{2}$.

For the horizontal asymptote, divide each term in the numerator and the denominator by x:

$$f(x) = \dfrac{\dfrac{x}{x} - \dfrac{1}{x}}{\dfrac{2x}{x} + \dfrac{5}{x}}$$

$$= \dfrac{1 - \dfrac{1}{x}}{2 + \dfrac{5}{x}}$$

As $x \to +\infty$, $\dfrac{1}{x} \to 0$ and $\dfrac{5}{x} \to 0$, so

$$f(x) \to \dfrac{1-0}{2+0}$$

$$f(x) \to \dfrac{1}{2}$$

As $x \to -\infty$, $\dfrac{1}{x} \to 0$ and $\dfrac{5}{x} \to 0$, so

$$f(x) \to \dfrac{1-0}{2+0}$$

$$f(x) \to \dfrac{1}{2}$$

The horizontal asymptote for $f(x)$ has equation $y = \dfrac{1}{2}$. By similar reasoning, the functions $g(x)$ and $h(x)$ have the same horizontal asymptote as $f(x)$.

Determine the intercepts.

Function	$f(x) = \dfrac{x-1}{2x+5}$	$g(x) = \dfrac{x-5}{2x+5}$	$h(x) = \dfrac{x-10}{2x+5}$
x-intercept	1	5	10
y-intercept	$-\dfrac{1}{5}$	-1	-2

To determine where the slope is negative and where it is positive, select points in each interval.

For the interval $x < -\dfrac{5}{2}$, $f(-10) = 0.7\overline{3}$ and $f(-5) = 1.2$.

The function f is increasing, so the slope is positive.

For the interval $x > -\dfrac{5}{2}$, $f(-2) = -3$ and $f(10) = 0.36$.

The function f is increasing, so the slope is positive.

Use the same reasoning to find where g and h are increasing and decreasing. Build an interval summary table.

	Interval	$x < -\dfrac{5}{2}$	$-\dfrac{5}{2} < x < x\text{-intercept}$	$x\text{-intercept}$	$x > x\text{-intercept}$
$f(x) = \dfrac{x-1}{2x+5}$	Sign of $f(x)$	+	−	0	+
	Sign of Slope	+	+	+	+
$g(x) = \dfrac{x-5}{2x+5}$	Sign of $g(x)$	+	−	0	+
	Sign of Slope	+	+	+	+
$h(x) = \dfrac{x-10}{2x+5}$	Sign of $h(x)$	+	−	0	+
	Sign of Slope	+	+	+	+

Graph the functions:

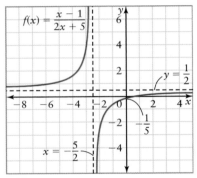

$$f(x) = \frac{x-1}{2x+5}$$

Domain: $\left\{x \in \mathbb{R}, x \neq -\dfrac{5}{2}\right\}$

Range: $\left\{y \in \mathbb{R}, y \neq \dfrac{1}{2}\right\}$

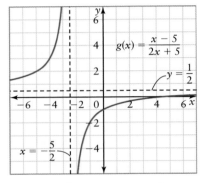

$$g(x) = \frac{x-5}{2x+5}$$

Domain: $\left\{x \in \mathbb{R}, x \neq -\dfrac{5}{2}\right\}$

Range: $\left\{y \in \mathbb{R}, y \neq \dfrac{1}{2}\right\}$

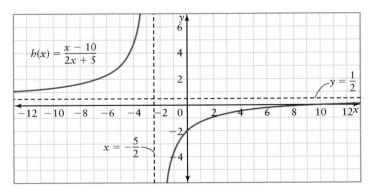

$$h(x) = \frac{x-10}{2x+5}$$

Domain: $\left\{x \in \mathbb{R}, x \neq \dfrac{1}{2}\right\}$

Range: $\left\{y \in \mathbb{R}, y \neq \dfrac{1}{2}\right\}$

The graphs have a similar shape, with the same horizontal and vertical asymptotes. The intervals have the same sign and slope analyses. The domain and range are the same. The graphs have different x- and y-intercepts.

b) The constant b in $f(x) = \dfrac{ax + b}{cx + d}$ has an effect that is similar to both a vertical and a horizontal stretch factor but does not affect the asymptotes, domain, or range.

KEY CONCEPTS

- A rational function of the form $f(x) = \dfrac{ax + b}{cx + d}$ has the following key features:

  - The equation of the vertical asymptote can be found by setting the denominator equal to zero and solving for x, provided the numerator does not have the same zero.

  - The equation of the horizontal asymptote can be found by dividing each term in both the numerator and the denominator by x and investigating the behaviour of the function as $x \rightarrow \pm\infty$.

  - The coefficient b acts to stretch the curve but has no effect on the asymptotes, domain, or range.

  - The coefficient d shifts the vertical asymptote.

  - The two branches of the graph of the function are equidistant from the point of intersection of the vertical and horizontal asymptotes.

Communicate Your Understanding

C1 Describe the end behaviour (that is, as $x \rightarrow \pm\infty$) of each function.

a) $f(x) = \dfrac{x - 1}{x + 3}$

b) $g(x) = \dfrac{2x}{4x - 7}$

c) $h(x) = \dfrac{3 - x}{2 + x}$

C2 Describe the roles of the numerator and the denominator in determining the key features of the graph of a rational function of the form $f(x) = \dfrac{ax + b}{cx + d}$.

For help with questions 1 to 3, refer to Example 1.

1. Determine an equation for the vertical asymptote of each function. Then, state the domain.

   a) $f(x) = \dfrac{x}{x - 7}$
   b) $g(x) = \dfrac{2x}{x + 5}$

   c) $h(x) = -\dfrac{x}{x + 8}$
   d) $k(x) = \dfrac{x}{3x - 1}$

   e) $m(x) = \dfrac{5x - 3}{4x + 9}$
   f) $n(x) = \dfrac{6 - x}{5 - x}$

2. Determine an equation for the horizontal asymptote of each function. Then, state the range.

   a) $p(x) = \dfrac{x}{x - 6}$
   b) $q(x) = \dfrac{3x}{x + 4}$

   c) $r(x) = \dfrac{x - 1}{x + 1}$
   d) $s(x) = \dfrac{5x - 2}{2x + 3}$

   e) $t(x) = \dfrac{x - 6}{4 - x}$
   f) $u(x) = \dfrac{3 - 4x}{1 - 2x}$

3. Sketch each function and then summarize the increasing and decreasing intervals.

   a) $f(x) = \dfrac{x}{x - 5}$
   b) $c(x) = \dfrac{4x}{x + 8}$

   c) $k(x) = \dfrac{x + 1}{4 - x}$
   d) $w(x) = \dfrac{x + 2}{4x - 5}$

   e) $d(x) = \dfrac{-2x - 3}{x + 5}$
   f) $m(x) = \dfrac{3x + 1}{2x + 1}$

For help with questions 4 to 6, refer to Example 2.

4. **a)** For the function $f(x) = \dfrac{2x}{x - 3}$, compare the slopes of the tangents

   i) at the points where $x = 3.5$ and $x = 20$

   ii) at the points where $x = 2.5$ and $x = -20$

   b) What do these results indicate about the key features of the graph?

5. **a)** Determine an equation for the horizontal asymptote of each function.

   i) $f(x) = \dfrac{x - 5}{2x + 1}$
   ii) $g(x) = \dfrac{3 - 5x}{2x + 1}$

   b) How do the equations of the horizontal asymptotes relate to the coefficients in each function?

   c) Summarize your findings to describe how to determine an equation for the horizontal asymptote of the function $f(x) = \dfrac{ax + b}{cx + d}$.

6. Use your results from question 5 to determine an equation for the horizontal asymptote of each function. Then, determine an equation for the vertical asymptote and graph the function. State the domain and range.

   a) $f(x) = \dfrac{x}{x - 9}$
   b) $g(x) = \dfrac{3x}{x + 2}$

   c) $h(x) = \dfrac{4x - 3}{2x + 1}$
   d) $k(x) = \dfrac{x - 3}{2x - 5}$

   e) $m(x) = \dfrac{4 - x}{5 + x}$
   f) $p(x) = \dfrac{6 - 8x}{3x - 4}$

7. Write an equation for the rational function shown on each graph.

   a)

   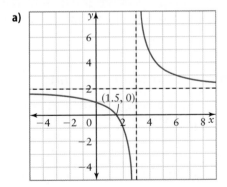

   b)

   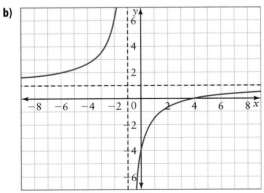

8. Write an equation for a rational function whose graph has all of the indicated features.

- x-intercept of -4
- y-intercept of -2
- vertical asymptote with equation $x = 2$
- horizontal asymptote with equation $y = 1$

9. Write an equation for a rational function whose graph has all of the indicated features.

- x-intercept of $\dfrac{3}{5}$
- y-intercept of -3
- vertical asymptote with equation $x = -\dfrac{1}{2}$
- horizontal asymptote with equation $y = \dfrac{5}{2}$

10. **Chapter Problem** After a train derailment in Northern Ontario, the concentration, C, in grams per litre, of a pollutant after t minutes in a 5 000 000-L pond can be modelled by the function $C(t) = \dfrac{30t}{200\,000 + t}$, when a pollutant concentration of 30 g/L flows into the pond at a rate of 25 L/min.

   a) Sketch a graph showing the concentration of the pollutant after t minutes.

   b) What happens as t becomes very large?

   c) When a concentration level of 0.05 g/L in the pond is reached, the fish stock will be irreversibly damaged. When will this occur?

11. a) Use long division to rewrite the function $f(x) = \dfrac{4x + 5}{2x - 1}$ as the sum of a constant and a rational function.

    b) Explain how this method could be used to graph rational functions.

    c) Use this method to sketch a graph of $f(x)$.

12. Use your method from question 11 to graph each function.

    a) $p(x) = \dfrac{2x + 3}{x + 1}$

    b) $t(x) = \dfrac{5x - 4}{2x + 5}$

✔ **Achievement Check**

13. Consider the function $g(x) = \dfrac{x}{x - 7}$.

    a) Determine an equation for the vertical asymptote.

    b) State the domain.

    c) Determine an equation for the horizontal asymptote.

    d) State the range.

    e) Sketch the function.

    f) Summarize the increasing and decreasing intervals.

    g) Compare the slopes of the tangents at the points where

       i) $x = 7.5$ and $x = 20$

       ii) $x = 6.5$ and $x = -20$

C **Extend and Challenge**

14. A golf ball of mass 4.6 g is struck by a golf club at a speed of 50 m/s. The ball has initial velocity, v, in metres per second, of $v(m) = \dfrac{83m}{m + 0.046}$, where m is the mass, in grams, of the golf club. Describe the rate of change of the initial velocity as the mass of the club increases.

15. Analyse the key features of the function $f(x) = \dfrac{\sqrt{x}}{\sqrt{x} - 1}$ and sketch its graph. How does it compare to the graph of $f(x) = \dfrac{x}{x - 1}$?

Reasoning and Proving

Representing — Selecting Tools

Problem Solving

Connecting — Reflecting

Communicating

16. Rational functions can have any polynomial in the numerator and denominator. Analyse the key features of each function and sketch its graph. Describe the common features of the graphs.

a) $f(x) = \dfrac{x}{x^2 - 1}$

b) $g(x) = \dfrac{x - 2}{x^2 + 3x + 2}$

c) $h(x) = \dfrac{x + 5}{x^2 - x - 12}$

Many rational functions have an asymptote that is not vertical or horizontal but on an angle or slant. These asymptotes are called slant or oblique asymptotes. Use this information to answer questions 17 to 19.

17. Math Contest Investigate when you can expect to have an oblique asymptote. Graph each function on a graphing calculator and determine what factor leads to an oblique asymptote.

a) $f(x) = \dfrac{x^3 + 1}{x^3}$

b) $f(x) = \dfrac{x^3 + 1}{x^2}$

c) $f(x) = \dfrac{x^2 + 1}{x}$

d) $f(x) = \dfrac{x^2 + 1}{x^3}$

18. Refer to question 17. Given the general function $f(x) = \dfrac{x^a + k}{x^b + m}$, a linear oblique asymptote will occur when

A $a > b$

B $b > a$

C $a - b = 1$

D $|a - b| = 1$

19. Math Contest Given the function $f(x) = \dfrac{x^2 - 2}{x}$:

a) Perform long division on $f(x)$ and state the quotient and the remainder.

b) Write $f(x)$ in terms of its quotient, remainder, and divisor in the form $f(x) = q(x) + \dfrac{r(x)}{d(x)}$.

c) Determine equations for all asymptotes of each function and graph the function without using technology.

i) $g(x) = \dfrac{x^2 - 3x - 4}{x - 2}$

ii) $f(x) = \dfrac{x^2 + x - 2}{2x - 4}$

iii) $z(x) = \dfrac{x^2 - 9}{x + 3}$

CAREER CONNECTION

Marissa graduated from the University of Ontario Institute of Technology after studying applied and industrial mathematics for 5 years. She now works in the field of mathematical modelling, helping an aircraft manufacturer to design faster, safer, and environmentally cleaner airplanes. Marissa uses her knowledge of fluid mechanics and software programs that can, for example, model a wind tunnel, to run experiments. Data from these tests help her to translate physical phenomena into equations. She then analyses and solves these complex equations and interprets the solutions. As computers become more powerful, Marissa will be able to tackle more complex problems and get answers in less time, thereby reducing research and development costs.

3.4 Solve Rational Equations and Inequalities

Proper lighting is of critical importance in surgical procedures. If a surgeon requires more illumination from a light source of fixed power, the light needs to be moved closer to the patient. By how much is the intensity increased if the distance between the light and the patient is halved? The intensity of illumination is inversely proportional to the square of the distance to the light source. The function $I = \dfrac{k}{d^2}$ relates the illumination, I, to the distance, d, from the light source. If a specific intensity is needed, the distance needs to be solved for in order to determine the placement of the light source.

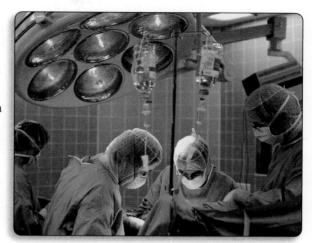

Example 1 Solve Rational Equations Algebraically

Solve.

a) $\dfrac{4}{3x - 5} = 4$

b) $\dfrac{x - 5}{x^2 - 3x - 4} = \dfrac{3x + 2}{x^2 - 1}$

> **Solution**

a) $\dfrac{4}{3x - 5} = 4$

$\qquad 4 = 4(3x - 5), \quad x \neq \dfrac{5}{3}$ Multiply both sides by $(3x - 5)$.

$\qquad 4 = 12x - 20$

$\quad 12x = 24$

$\qquad x = 2$

b) $\dfrac{x - 5}{x^2 - 3x - 4} = \dfrac{3x + 2}{x^2 - 1}$

$\dfrac{x - 5}{(x - 4)(x + 1)} = \dfrac{3x + 2}{(x - 1)(x + 1)}, \quad x \neq -1, x \neq 1, x \neq 4$ Factor the expressions in the denominators.

$(x - 5)(x - 1) = (3x + 2)(x - 4)$ Multiply both sides by $(x - 4)(x + 1)(x - 1)$.

$x^2 - 6x + 5 = 3x^2 - 10x - 8$

$2x^2 - 4x - 13 = 0$

$$x = \frac{4 \pm \sqrt{(-4)^2 - 4(2)(-13)}}{2(2)}$$

2x^2 − 4x − 13 cannot be factored.
Use the quadratic formula.

$$= \frac{4 \pm \sqrt{120}}{4}$$

$$= \frac{4 \pm 2\sqrt{30}}{4}$$

$$= \frac{2 \pm \sqrt{30}}{2}$$

Example 2 | Solve a Rational Equation Using Technology

Solve $\dfrac{x}{x - 2} = \dfrac{2x^2 - 3x + 5}{x^2 + 6}$.

Solution

$$\frac{x}{x - 2} = \frac{2x^2 - 3x + 5}{x^2 + 6}$$

$$x(x^2 + 6) = (x - 2)(2x^2 - 3x + 5), \ x \neq 2$$

Multiply both sides by $(x - 2)(x^2 + 6)$.

$$x^3 + 6x = 2x^3 - 7x^2 + 11x - 10$$

$$x^3 - 7x^2 + 5x - 10 = 0$$

Use technology to solve the equation.

CONNECTIONS

You can solve using technology directly from the initial equation. With a graphing calculator, you can graph both sides separately and find the point of intersection. With a CAS, you can use the **solve** operation directly. Other methods are possible.

Method 1: *Use a Graphing Calculator*

Graph the function $y = x^3 - 7x^2 + 5x - 10$.

Then, use the **Zero** operation.

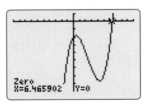

$x \doteq 6.47$ is the only solution.

Method 2: *Use a Computer Algebra System (CAS)*

Use the **solve** function or the **zero** function.

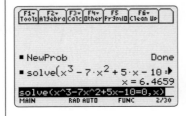

Example 3

Example 3 | **Solve a Simple Rational Inequality**

Solve $\dfrac{2}{x-5} < 10$.

Solution

Method 1: *Consider the Key Features of the Graph of a Related Rational Function*

$$\frac{2}{x-5} < 10$$

$$\frac{2}{x-5} - 10 < 0$$

$$\frac{2 - 10x + 50}{x-5} < 0 \qquad \text{Combine the terms using a common denominator of } x - 5.$$

$$\frac{-10x + 52}{x-5} < 0$$

Consider the function $f(x) = \dfrac{-10x + 52}{x-5}$.

The vertical asymptote has equation $x = 5$.

The horizontal asymptote has equation $y = -10$.

The x-intercept is 5.2.

The y-intercept is -10.4.

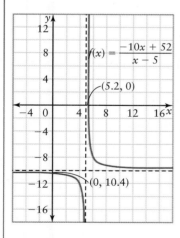

From the graph, the coordinates of all of the points below the x-axis satisfy the inequality $f(x) < 0$.

So, $\dfrac{-10x + 52}{x-5} < 0$, or $\dfrac{2}{x-5} < 10$, for $x < 5$ or $x > 5.2$.

In interval notation, $x \in (-\infty, 5) \cup (5.2, +\infty)$.

Method 2: *Solve Algebraically*

$$\frac{2}{x - 5} < 10$$

Because $x - 5 \neq 0$, either $x > 5$ or $x < 5$.

Case 1:

$x > 5$

$2 < 10(x - 5)$ Multiply both sides by $(x - 5)$, which is positive if $x > 5$.

$2 < 10x - 50$

$52 < 10x$

$5.2 < x$

$x > 5.2$

$x > 5.2$ is within the inequality $x > 5$, so the solution is $x > 5.2$.

Case 2:

$x < 5$

$$\frac{2}{x - 5} < 10$$

$2 > 10(x - 5)$ Change the inequality when multiplying by a negative.

$2 > 10x - 50$

$52 > 10x$

$5.2 > x$

$x < 5.2$

$x < 5$ is within the inequality $x < 5.2$, so the solution is $x < 5$.

Combining the two cases, the solution to the inequality is $x < 5$ or $x > 5.2$.

Example 4	Solve a Quadratic Over a Quadratic Rational Inequality

Solve $\dfrac{x^2 - x - 2}{x^2 + x - 12} \geq 0$.

Reasoning and Proving
Representing　**Selecting Tools**
Problem Solving
Connecting　　Reflecting
Communicating

Solution

Method 1: *Solve Using an Interval Table*

$$\frac{x^2 - x - 2}{x^2 + x - 12} \geq 0$$

$$\frac{(x - 2)(x + 1)}{(x - 3)(x + 4)} \geq 0$$

From the numerator, the zeros occur at $x = 2$ and $x = -1$, so solutions occur at these values of x.

From the denominator, the restrictions occur at $x = 3$ and $x = -4$.

A number line can be used to consider intervals.

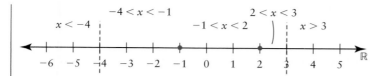

$-4 < x < -1$

$x < -4$

$2 < x < 3$

$-1 < x < 2$

$x > 3$

Use a table to consider the signs of the factors on each interval. Pick an arbitrary number in each interval. The number line is broken into five intervals, as shown. Select test values of x for each interval. Check whether the value of $\dfrac{(x - 2)(x + 1)}{(x - 3)(x + 4)}$ in each interval is greater than or equal to 0.

For example, for $x < -4$, test $x = -5$.

$\dfrac{(-5 - 2)(-5 + 1)}{(-5 - 3)(-5 + 4)} = \dfrac{28}{8} > 0$, so $x < -4$ is part of the solution.

Continue testing a selected point in each interval and record the results in a table.

Interval	Choice for x in the interval	Signs of Factors of $\dfrac{(x - 2)(x + 1)}{(x - 3)(x + 4)}$	Sign of $\dfrac{(x - 2)(x + 1)}{(x - 3)(x + 4)}$
$(-\infty, -4)$	$x = -5$	$\dfrac{(-)(-)}{(-)(-)}$	$+$
$(-4, -1)$	$x = -2$	$\dfrac{(-)(-)}{(-)(+)}$	$-$
-1	$x = 1$	$\dfrac{(-)(0)}{(-)(+)}$	0
$(-1, 2)$	$x = 0$	$\dfrac{(-)(+)}{(-)(+)}$	$+$
2	$x = 2$	$\dfrac{(0)(+)}{(-)(+)}$	0
$(2, 3)$	$x = 2.5$	$\dfrac{(+)(+)}{(-)(+)}$	$-$
$(3, +\infty)$	$x = 4$	$\dfrac{(+)(+)}{(+)(+)}$	$+$

The same data are shown in a different format below. The critical values of x are bolded, and test values are chosen within each interval.

x	-5	-4	-2	-1	0	2	2.5	3	4
$\dfrac{(x - 2)(x + 1)}{(x - 3)(x + 4)}$	$+$	∞	$-$	0	$+$	0	$-$	∞	$+$

CONNECTIONS

The critical values of x are those values where there is a vertical asymptote, or where the slope of the graph of the inequality changes sign.

For the inequality $\dfrac{x^2 - x - 2}{x^2 + x - 12} \geq 0$, the solution is $x < -4$ or $-1 \leq x \leq 2$ or $x > 3$.

In interval notation, the solution set is $x \in (-\infty, -4) \cup [-1, 2] \cup (3, +\infty)$.

The solution can be shown on a number line.

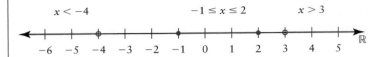

A graph of the related function, $f(x) = \dfrac{x^2 - x - 2}{x^2 + x - 12}$, confirms this solution.

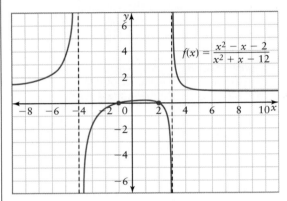

Method 2: *Use a Graphing Calculator*

Enter the function $f(x) = \dfrac{x^2 - x - 2}{x^2 + x - 12}$ and view its graph.

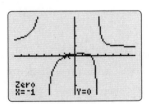

Either visually or by checking the table, you can see that there are asymptotes at $x = -4$ and $x = 3$, so there are no solutions there.

Use the **Zero** operation to find that the zeros are at $x = -1$ and $x = 2$.

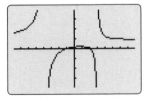

Using the graph and the zeros, you can see that $f(x) \geq 0$ for $x < -4$, for $-1 \leq x \leq 2$, and for $x > 3$.

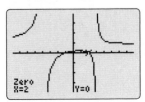

Communicate Your Understanding

C1 Describe the process you would use to solve $\dfrac{2}{x-1} = \dfrac{3}{x+5}$.

C2 Explain why $\dfrac{1}{x^2 + 2x + 9} < 0$ has no solution.

C3 Explain the difference between the solution to the equation $\dfrac{4}{x-5} = \dfrac{3}{x+4}$ and the solution to the inequality $\dfrac{4}{x-5} < \dfrac{3}{x+4}$.

A) Practise

For help with questions 1 and 2, refer to Example 1.

1. Determine the x-intercept(s) for each function. Verify using technology.

a) $y = \dfrac{x+1}{x}$

b) $y = \dfrac{x^2 + x - 12}{x^2 - 3x + 5}$

c) $y = \dfrac{2x - 3}{5x + 1}$

d) $y = \dfrac{x}{x^2 - 3x + 2}$

2. Solve algebraically. Check each solution.

a) $\dfrac{4}{x-2} = 3$

b) $\dfrac{1}{x^2 - 2x - 7} = 1$

c) $\dfrac{2}{x-1} = \dfrac{5}{x+3}$

d) $x - \dfrac{5}{x} = 4$

e) $\dfrac{1}{x} = \dfrac{x - 34}{2x^2}$

f) $\dfrac{x-3}{x-4} = \dfrac{x+2}{x+6}$

For help with question 3, refer to Example 2.

3. **Use Technology** Solve each equation using technology. Express your answers to two decimal places.

a) $\dfrac{5x}{x-4} = \dfrac{3x}{2x+7}$

b) $\dfrac{2x+3}{x-6} = \dfrac{5x-1}{4x+7}$

c) $\dfrac{x}{x-2} = \dfrac{x^2-4x+1}{x-3}$

d) $\dfrac{x^2-1}{2x^2-3} = \dfrac{2x^2+3}{x^2+1}$

For help with question 4, refer to Example 3.

4. Solve each inequality without using technology. Illustrate the solution on a number line.

a) $\dfrac{4}{x-3} < 1$ b) $\dfrac{7}{x+1} > 7$

c) $\dfrac{5}{x+4} \le \dfrac{2}{x+1}$ d) $\dfrac{(x-2)(x+1)^2}{(x-4)(x+5)} \ge 0$

e) $\dfrac{x^2-16}{x^2-4x-5} > 0$ f) $\dfrac{x-2}{x} < \dfrac{x-4}{x-6}$

For help with question 5, refer to Example 4.

5. Solve each inequality using an interval table. Check using technology.

a) $\dfrac{x^2+9x+14}{x^2-6+5} > 0$

b) $\dfrac{2x^2+5x-3}{x^2+8x+16} < 0$

c) $\dfrac{x^2-3x-4}{x^2+11x+30} \le 0$

d) $\dfrac{3x^2-8x+4}{2x^2-9x-5} \ge 0$

B   Connect and Apply

6. Write a rational equation that cannot have $x = 3$ or $x = -5$ as a solution. Explain your reasoning.

7. Solve $\dfrac{x}{x+1} < \dfrac{2x}{x-2}$ by graphing the functions $f(x) = \dfrac{x}{x+1}$ and $g(x) = \dfrac{2x}{x-2}$ with or without using technology. Determine the points of intersection and when $f(x) < g(x)$.

8. Use the method from question 7 to solve $\dfrac{x}{x-3} > \dfrac{3x}{x+5}$.

9. Solve and check.

a) $\dfrac{1}{x} + 3 = \dfrac{2}{x}$ b) $\dfrac{2}{x+1} + 5 = \dfrac{1}{x}$

c) $\dfrac{12}{x} + x = 8$ d) $\dfrac{x}{x-1} = 1 - \dfrac{1}{1-x}$

e) $\dfrac{2x}{2x+3} - \dfrac{2x}{2x-3} = 1$

f) $\dfrac{7}{x-2} - \dfrac{4}{x-1} + \dfrac{3}{x+1} = 0$

10. Solve. Illustrate graphically.

a) $\dfrac{2}{x} + 3 > \dfrac{29}{x}$ b) $\dfrac{16}{x} - 5 < \dfrac{1}{x}$

c) $\dfrac{5}{6x} + \dfrac{2}{3x} > \dfrac{3}{4}$ d) $6 + \dfrac{30}{x-1} < 7$

11. The ratio of $x + 2$ to $x - 5$ is greater than $\dfrac{3}{5}$. Solve for x.

12. Compare the solutions to $\dfrac{2x-1}{x+7} > \dfrac{x+1}{x+3}$ and $\dfrac{2x-1}{x+7} < \dfrac{x+1}{x+3}$.

13. Compare the solutions to $\dfrac{x+1}{x-4} \le \dfrac{x-3}{x+5}$ and $\dfrac{x-4}{x+1} \le \dfrac{x+5}{x-3}$.

14. A number x is the harmonic mean of two numbers a and b if $\dfrac{1}{x}$ is the mean of $\dfrac{1}{a}$ and $\dfrac{1}{b}$.

a) Write an equation to represent the harmonic mean of a and b.

b) Determine the harmonic mean of 12 and 15.

c) The harmonic mean of 6 and another number is 1.2. Determine the other number.

15. Chapter Problem Light pollution is caused by many lights being on in a concentrated area. Think of the night sky in the city compared to the night sky in the country. Light pollution can be a problem in cities, as more and more bright lights are used in such things as advertising and office buildings. The intensity of illumination is inversely proportional to the square of the distance to the light source and is defined by the formula $I = \dfrac{k}{d^2}$, where I is the intensity, in lux; d is the distance from the source, in metres; and k is a constant. When the distance from a certain light source is 10 m, the intensity is 900 lux.

a) Determine the intensity when the distance is

   i) 5 m   **ii)** 200 m

b) What distance, or range of distance, results in an intensity of

   i) 4.5 lux?   **ii)** at least 4500 lux?

16. The relationship between the object distance, d, and image distance, I, both in centimetres, for a camera with focal length 2.0 cm is defined by the relation $d = \dfrac{2.0I}{I - 2.0}$. For what values of I is d greater than 10.0 cm?

✓ Achievement Check

17. Consider the functions $f(x) = \dfrac{1}{x} + 4$ and $g(x) = \dfrac{2}{x}$. Graph f and g on the same grid.

a) Determine the points of intersection of the two functions.

b) Show where $f(x) < g(x)$.

c) Solve the equation $\dfrac{1}{x} + 4 = \dfrac{2}{x}$ to check your answer to part a).

d) Solve the inequality $\dfrac{1}{x} + 4 < \dfrac{2}{x}$ to check your answer to part b).

C) Extend and Challenge

18. a) A rectangle has perimeter 64 cm and area 23 cm². Solve the following system of equations to find the rectangle's dimensions.

$$l = \frac{23}{w}$$

$$l + w = 32$$

b) Solve the system of equations.

$$x^2 + y^2 = 1$$

$$xy = 0.5$$

19. Use your knowledge of exponents to solve.

a) $\dfrac{1}{2^x} = \dfrac{1}{x + 2}$

b) $\dfrac{1}{2^x} > \dfrac{1}{x^2}$

20. Determine the region(s) of the Cartesian plane for which

a) $y > \dfrac{1}{x^2}$

b) $y \le x^2 + 4$ and $y \ge \dfrac{1}{x^2 + 4}$

21. Math Contest In some situations, it is convenient to express a rational expression as the sum of two or more simpler rational expressions. These simpler expressions are called *partial fractions*. Partial fractions are used when, given $\dfrac{P(x)}{D(x)}$, the degree of $P(x)$ is less than the degree of $D(x)$.

Decompose each of the following into partial fractions. Check your solutions by graphing the equivalent function on a graphing calculator. Hint: Start by factoring the denominator, if necessary.

a) $f(x) = \dfrac{5x + 7}{x^2 + 2x - 3}$

b) $g(x) = \dfrac{7x + 6}{x^2 - x - 6}$

c) $h(x) = \dfrac{6x^2 - 14x - 27}{(x + 2)(x - 3)^2}$

Making Connections With Rational Functions and Equations

Most of us know that getting closer in a concert means getting a better view, but it also means more exposure to potentially damaging sound levels. Just how much more intense can sound levels become as you move closer and closer to the source? The intensity, I, increases by what is known as the inverse square law, or the reciprocal of the square of the distance, d, from the sound source, so that $I = \frac{k}{d^2}$. This law also applies to gravitational force and light intensity.

Example 1 | Intensity of Sound

Reasoning and Proving
Representing · Selecting Tools
Problem Solving
Connecting · Reflecting
Communicating

The intensity of sound, in watts per square metre, varies inversely as the square of the distance, in metres, from the source of the sound. The intensity of the sound from a loudspeaker at a distance of 2 m is 0.001 W/m².

a) Determine a function to represent this relationship.

b) Graph this function.

c) What is the effect of halving the distance from the source of the sound?

Solution

a) Let I represent the intensity of sound. Let d represent the distance from the source of the sound. I varies inversely as the square of d.

So, $I = \frac{k}{d^2}$, where k is a constant.

Substitute $I = 0.001$ and $d = 2$ into the equation to find k.

$$0.001 = \frac{k}{2^2}$$
$$k = 0.004$$
$$I = \frac{0.004}{d^2}, \, d > 0$$

b)

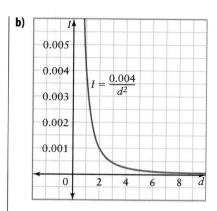

$$I = \frac{0.004}{d^2}$$

c) Substitute $\frac{1}{2}d$ for d.

$$I = \frac{0.004}{\left(\frac{1}{2}d\right)^2}$$

$$= \frac{0.004}{\left(\frac{d^2}{4}\right)}$$

$$= 4 \times \frac{0.004}{d^2}$$

If the distance is halved, the sound is four times as intense.

Example 2 | Diving Time

The maximum time, T, in minutes, a scuba diver can rise without stopping for decompression on the way up to the surface is defined by the equation $T(d) = \dfrac{525}{d - 10}$, $d > 10$, where d is the depth of the dive, in metres. For the maximum time to be less than 30 min, how deep can the diver dive?

Solution

$$\frac{525}{d - 10} < 30$$

Since $d > 10$, there is only one case.

$525 < 30(d - 10)$ Multiply both sides by $d - 10$.

$$\frac{525}{30} < d - 10$$

$$d > \frac{525}{30} + 10$$

$$d > 27.5$$

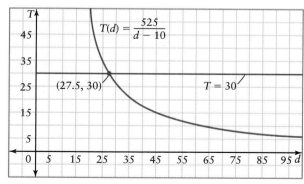

This can be illustrated graphically.

If the diver dives deeper than 27.5 m, the time without decompression stops will be less than 30 min.

| Example 3 | Special Cases |

Sketch a graph of each function. Explain how these are special cases.

a) $f(x) = \dfrac{x^2 - x - 6}{x + 2}$

b) $g(x) = \dfrac{2x^2 - 7x - 4}{2x^2 + 5x + 2}$

> **Solution**

a) $f(x) = \dfrac{x^2 - x - 6}{x + 2}$

$ = \dfrac{(x - 3)(x + 2)}{x + 2}$

$ = x - 3,\ x \neq -2$

Notice that $f(x)$ simplifies to a linear relationship. So, even though the function is undefined at $x = -2$, we can find what value f approaches as $x \to -2$. From the simplified form, as $x \to -2, f \to -5$.

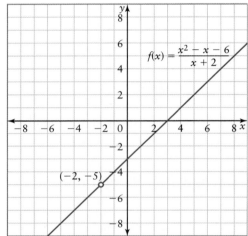

This is a special case of a line that is **discontinuous** at $x = -2$. This is a value at which the function is undefined. Here, the discontinuity is not an asymptote, but the point $(-2, -5)$. This type of discontinuity is called a hole or a gap.

b) $g(x) = \dfrac{2x^2 - 7x - 4}{2x^2 + 5x + 2}$

$ = \dfrac{(2x + 1)(x - 4)}{(2x + 1)(x + 2)},\ x \neq -2,\ x \neq -\dfrac{1}{2}$

$ = \dfrac{x - 4}{x + 2}$

This is a special case because there is a hole at the point $\left(-\dfrac{1}{2}, -3\right)$.

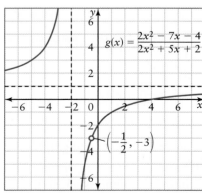

- When solving a problem, it is important to read carefully to determine whether a function is being analysed or an equation or inequality is to be solved.

- A full analysis will involve four components:
  - numeric (tables, ordered pairs, calculations)
  - algebraic (formulas, solving equations)
  - graphical
  - verbal (descriptions)

- When investigating special cases of functions, factor and reduce where possible. Indicate the restrictions on the variables in order to identify hidden discontinuities.

- When investigating new types of rational functions, consider what is different about the coefficients and the degree of the polynomials in the numerator and denominator. These differences could affect the stretch factor of the curve and the equations of the asymptotes and they could cause other discontinuities.

Communicate Your Understanding

C1 Other than at asymptotes, describe when a discontinuity can occur in a rational function.

C2 The maximum height, h, in kilometres, of a rocket launched with initial velocity, v, in kilometres per hour, is given by the formula $h = \dfrac{6400v^2}{125\,440 - v^2}$, ignoring air resistance. Explain why the velocity at the vertical asymptote is considered the escape velocity of the rocket.

CONNECTIONS

Escape velocity is the speed at which the magnitude of the kinetic energy of an object is equal to the magnitude of its gravitational potential energy. It is commonly described as the speed needed to "break free" from a gravitational field.

A   Practise

For help with question 1, refer to Example 1.

1. The intensity of illumination is inversely proportional to the square of the distance to the light source. It is modelled by the formula $I = \dfrac{k}{d^2}$, where I is the intensity, in lux; d is the distance, in metres, from the source; and k is a constant. When the distance from a certain light source is 50 m, the intensity is 6 lux.

   a) Sketch a graph of this relation.

   b) Describe what happens to the light intensity as the distance becomes greater.

   c) Comment on the model for values of d close to 0.

For help with questions 2 and 3, refer to Example 2.

2. According to Boyle's law, under constant temperature, the volume of gas varies inversely with the pressure. A tank holds 10 L of hydrogen gas at a pressure of 500 kPa.

   a) Determine a function to relate volume and pressure for this gas.

   b) Sketch a graph of this relation, showing the volume of gas for different atmospheric pressures.

   c) What is the effect of doubling the pressure?

3. When connected in parallel, a resistor of x ohms and a resistor of $1\ \Omega$ will have a total resistance defined by the function $R(x) = \dfrac{x}{1 + x}$.

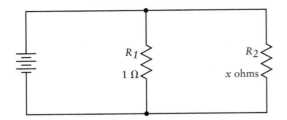

a) For the total resistance to be $0.5\ \Omega$, what does the resistance x need to be?

b) For the total resistance to be less than $0.25\ \Omega$, what does the resistance x need to be?

For help with question 4, refer to Example 3.

4. Sketch a graph of each function. Describe each special case.

a) $f(x) = \dfrac{x}{x^2 - 2x}$

b) $g(x) = \dfrac{x - 4}{x^2 + x - 20}$

c) $h(x) = \dfrac{x^2 + 7x + 12}{x^2 + 2x - 3}$

d) $k(x) = \dfrac{3x^2 + x - 2}{2x^2 + 7x + 5}$

e) $m(x) = \dfrac{x}{x^3 - 4x^2 - 12x}$

f) $n(x) = \dfrac{x^2 - 3x + 2}{x^3 - 7x + 6}$

B Connect and Apply

5. The profit, P, in thousands of dollars, from the sale of x kilograms of coffee can be modelled by the function $P(x) = \dfrac{4x - 200}{x + 400}$.

a) Sketch a graph of this relation.

b) The average profit for a given sales level, x, can be found by drawing a secant from the origin to the point $(x, P(x))$. Explain how average profit is related to the slope of a secant.

c) Estimate where the average profit is the greatest. Verify using slopes.

d) Determine the rate of change of the profit at a sales level of 1000 kg.

6. The electrical resistance, R, in ohms, of a wire varies directly with its length, l, in metres, and inversely with the square of the diameter, d, in millimetres, of its cross section according to the function $R = \dfrac{kl}{d^2}$.

a) If 1000 m of 4-mm-diameter wire has a resistance of $40\ \Omega$, determine an equation to model length and cross section.

b) Sketch a graph of the function for the electrical resistance of 1000 m of wire at various cross sections.

7. A bus company models its cost, C, in dollars, per person for a bus charter trip with the equation $C(x) = \dfrac{10\,000}{10 + x}$, where x is the number of passengers over its minimum number of 10. Describe the change in the cost model represented by each of the following, and accompany each with a graph.

a) $C(x) = \dfrac{10\,000}{8 + x}$

b) $C(x) = \dfrac{20\,000}{10 + x}$

c) $C(x) = \dfrac{15\,000}{12 + x}$

8. A function has equation $f(x) = \dfrac{x^2 - 2x - 5}{x - 1}$. In addition to a vertical asymptote, it has an oblique, or slant, asymptote, which is neither vertical nor horizontal.

a) **Use Technology** Graph the function using technology.

b) Describe what is meant by the term *oblique asymptote*.

c) Use long division to rewrite this function.

d) How can the new form of the equation be used to determine an equation for the slant asymptote?

9. Refer to question 8 to graph each function.

a) $f(x) = \dfrac{x^2 + 5x - 2}{x + 3}$

b) $g(x) = \dfrac{2x^2 - 5x + 3}{x + 2}$

10. In the event of a power failure, a computer model estimates the temperature, T, in degrees Celsius, in a food-processing plant's freezer to be $T = \dfrac{2t^2}{t + 1} - 15$, where t is the time, in hours, after the power failure.

a) Sketch a graph of this function. Use technology or the method from question 8.

b) How long would it take for the temperature to reach 0°C?

c) A generator starts up when the temperature is -5°C. How long would it take for this to happen?

11. A cylindrical tank is to have a volume of 100 000 cm³.

a) Write a formula for the height in terms of the radius.

b) Sketch a graph of the relationship between height and radius.

12. Use Technology As blood moves away from the heart, the systolic pressure, P, in millimetres of mercury (mmHg), after t seconds, changes according to the function $P(t) = \dfrac{25t^2 + 125}{t^2 + 1}$, $0 \le t \le 10$.

Reasoning and Proving
Representing · Selecting Tools
Problem Solving
Connecting · Reflecting
Communicating

a) Graph this function using technology.

b) Describe what happens to the systolic pressure over the first 10 s.

c) To measure the rate of change in systolic pressure, you can use the function $R(t) = -\dfrac{200t}{(t^2 + 1)^2}$. Graph this function using technology. Describe the rate of change.

d) Compare the rate of change at $t = 5$ s, using the slope of a tangent of $P(t)$, to the rate of change function $R(t)$ at $t = 5$ s.

C Extend and Challenge

13. For $x > 0$, what value of x gives the least sum of x and its reciprocal?

14. The function $C(t) = \dfrac{0.16t}{t^2 + t + 2}$ models the concentration, C, in milligrams per cubic centimetre, of a drug in the bloodstream after time, t, in minutes.

a) Sketch a graph of the function, without using technology.

b) Explain the shape of the graph in the context of the concentration of the drug in the bloodstream.

15. A generator produces electrical power, P, in watts, according to the function $P(R) = \dfrac{120R}{(0.4 + R)^2}$, where R is the resistance, in ohms. Determine the intervals on which the power is increasing.

16. Math Contest Is the following statement true or false? The function $g(x) = \dfrac{x^n - n^2}{x^{n-1} - n}$, $n \in \mathbb{N}$, has a slant asymptote for all values of n. Give a reason for your answer.

17. Math Contest When the polynomial $5x^4 + 4x^3 + 3x^2 + Px + Q$ is divided by $x^2 - 1$, the remainder is 0. What is the value of $P + Q$?

A -12 **B** 212 **C** 26 **D** 12 **E** 6

18. Math Contest Solve the equation $\sqrt{3} \sin x + \cos x = 2$ for x.

3.1 Reciprocal of a Linear Function

1. Determine equations for the vertical and horizontal asymptotes of each function.

   a) $f(x) = \dfrac{1}{x - 2}$

   b) $g(x) = \dfrac{3}{x + 7}$

   c) $h(x) = -\dfrac{4}{x - 5}$

2. Determine an equation to represent each function.

   a)
   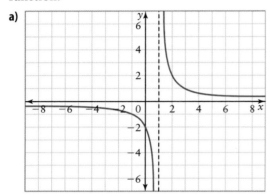

   b)
   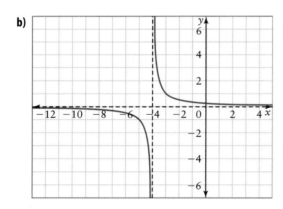

3. Sketch a graph of each function. State the domain, range, y-intercepts, and equations of the asymptotes.

   a) $f(x) = \dfrac{5}{x - 3}$ b) $g(x) = -\dfrac{1}{x - 4}$

   c) $h(x) = \dfrac{1}{2x - 3}$ d) $k(x) = -\dfrac{8}{5x + 4}$

3.2 Reciprocal of a Quadratic Function

4. Determine equations for the vertical asymptotes of each function. Then, state the domain.

   a) $f(x) = \dfrac{1}{(x - 3)(x + 4)}$

   b) $g(x) = -\dfrac{2}{(x + 3)^2}$

   c) $h(x) = \dfrac{1}{x^2 + 8x + 12}$

5. For each function,

   i) determine equations for the asymptotes

   ii) determine the y-intercepts

   iii) sketch a graph

   iv) describe the increasing and decreasing intervals

   v) state the domain and range

   a) $f(x) = \dfrac{1}{x^2 + 6x + 5}$

   b) $g(x) = \dfrac{1}{x^2 - 5x - 24}$

   c) $h(x) = -\dfrac{1}{x^2 - 6x + 9}$

   d) $k(x) = -\dfrac{2}{x^2 + 5}$

6. Analyse the slope, and change in slope, for the intervals of the function $f(x) = \dfrac{1}{2x^2 + 3x - 5}$ by sketching a graph of the function.

7. Write an equation for a function that is the reciprocal of a quadratic and has the following properties:

   - The horizontal asymptote is $y = 0$.
   - The vertical asymptotes are $x = -4$ and $x = 5$.
   - For the intervals $x < -4$ and $x > 5$, $y < 0$.

3.3 Rational Functions of the Form $f(x) = \dfrac{ax + b}{cx + d}$

8. Determine an equation for the horizontal asymptote of each function.

   a) $a(x) = \dfrac{x}{x + 5}$

   b) $b(x) = -\dfrac{2x}{x - 3}$

   c) $c(x) = \dfrac{x + 2}{x - 2}$

9. Summarize the key features of each function. Then, sketch a graph of the function.

a) $f(x) = \dfrac{x}{x - 2}$

b) $g(x) = -\dfrac{3x}{x + 1}$

c) $h(x) = \dfrac{x - 2}{x + 4}$

d) $k(x) = \dfrac{6x + 2}{2x - 1}$

10. Write an equation of a rational function of the form $f(x) = \dfrac{ax + b}{cx + d}$ whose graph has all of the following features:

- x-intercept of $\dfrac{1}{4}$
- y-intercept of $-\dfrac{1}{2}$
- vertical asymptote with equation $x = -\dfrac{2}{3}$
- horizontal asymptote with equation $y = \dfrac{4}{3}$

3.4 Solve Rational Equations and Inequalities

11. Solve algebraically. Check each solution.

a) $\dfrac{7}{x - 4} = 2$

b) $\dfrac{3}{x^2 + 6x - 24} = 1$

12. Use Technology Solve each equation using technology. If necessary, express your answers to two decimal places.

a) $\dfrac{4x}{x + 2} = \dfrac{5x}{3x + 1}$

b) $\dfrac{5x + 2}{2x - 9} = \dfrac{3x - 1}{x + 2}$

c) $\dfrac{x^2 - 3x + 1}{2 - x} = \dfrac{x^2 + 5x + 4}{x - 6}$

13. Solve each inequality without using technology. Illustrate the solution on a number line. Check your solutions using technology.

a) $\dfrac{3}{x + 5} < 2$

b) $\dfrac{3}{x + 2} \le \dfrac{4}{x + 3}$

c) $\dfrac{x^2 - x - 20}{x^2 - 4x - 12} > 0$

d) $\dfrac{x}{x + 5} > \dfrac{x - 1}{x + 7}$

14. Use Technology Solve each inequality using technology.

a) $\dfrac{x^2 + 5x + 4}{x^2 - 5x + 6} < 0$

b) $\dfrac{x^2 - 6x + 9}{2x^2 + 17x + 8} > 0$

3.5 Making Connections With Rational Functions and Equations

15. A manufacturer is predicting profit, P, in thousands of dollars, on the sale of x tonnes of fertilizer according to the equation $P(x) = \dfrac{600x - 15000}{x + 100}$.

a) Sketch a graph of this relation.

b) Describe the predicted profit as sales increase.

c) Compare the rates of change of the profit at sales of 100 t and 500 t of fertilizer.

16. Sketch a graph of each function. Describe each special case.

a) $f(x) = \dfrac{x}{x^2 + 5x}$

b) $g(x) = \dfrac{x^2 - 2x - 35}{x^2 - 3x - 28}$

■■ PROBLEM WRAP-UP

CHAPTER

The cost, C, in millions of dollars, of cleaning up an oil spill can be modelled by the function $C(p) = \dfrac{20}{100 - p}$, where p is the percent of the oil that was spilled. The rate of change of the cost, in millions of dollars, is given by $R(p) = \dfrac{20}{(100 - p)^2}$.

a) State the domain and range of each function, and explain what they mean.

b) Calculate the rate of change at $p = 50$, using the slope of the tangent to $C(p)$.

c) Compare the rate of change from part b) to that using the rate of change function $R(p)$ for $p = 50$.

d) Write a report outlining the cost of cleaning up the oil spill. Include the following:

- graphs of $C(p)$ and $R(p)$
- the total cost to clean up 25%, 50%, and 90% of the spill
- the rate of change of the cost at 25%, 50%, and 90% of the spill

For questions 1 to 3, select the best answer.

1. Which graph represents $f(x) = \dfrac{1}{x^2 - 1}$?

A

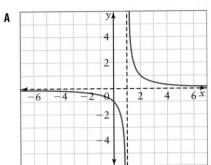

B

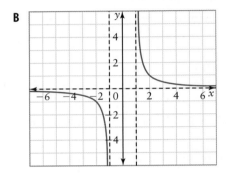

C

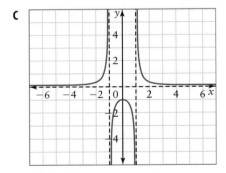

D

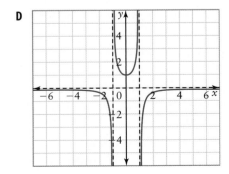

2. For the function $f(x) = \dfrac{2}{x + 5}$, which statement is correct?

A As $x \to +\infty$, $f(x) \to +\infty$.

B As $x \to +\infty$, $f(x) \to 0$.

C As $x \to 5^+$, $f(x) \to +\infty$.

D As $x \to 5^-$, $f(x) \to +\infty$.

3. For the function $f(x) = \dfrac{x + 2}{x - 5}$, which statement is true?

A Domain: $\{x \in \mathbb{R}, x \neq 5\}$,
Range: $\{y \in \mathbb{R}, y \neq 1\}$

B Domain: $\{x \in \mathbb{R}, x \neq -2\}$,
Range: $\{y \in \mathbb{R}, y \neq 1\}$

C Domain: $\{x \in \mathbb{R}, x \neq 5\}$,
Range: $\{y \in \mathbb{R}, y \neq 0\}$

D Domain: $\{x \in \mathbb{R}, x > 5\}$,
Range: $\{y \in \mathbb{R}, y > 0\}$

4. Write a possible equation for the function in each graph.

a)

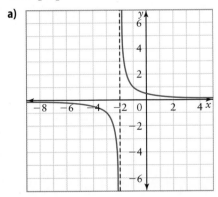

b)

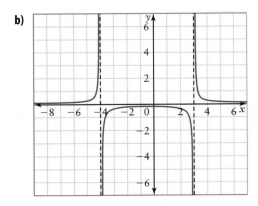

5. Consider the function $f(x) = -\dfrac{4}{x^2 + 2}$.

  a) Determine the following key features of the function:

    i) domain and range

    ii) intercepts

    iii) asymptotes

    iv) intervals where the function is increasing and intervals where it is decreasing

  b) Sketch a graph of the function.

6. If $f(x)$ is a polynomial function, does $\dfrac{1}{f(x)}$ always have a horizontal asymptote? If yes, explain why. If no, provide a counterexample.

7. Solve each equation. Provide an exact solution.

  a) $\dfrac{3x + 5}{x - 4} = \dfrac{1}{2}$

  b) $\dfrac{20}{x^2 - 4x + 7} = x + 2$

8. Solve each inequality. Illustrate your solution on a number line.

  a) $\dfrac{5}{2x + 3} < 4$

  b) $\dfrac{x + 1}{x - 2} > \dfrac{x + 7}{x + 1}$

9. a) Determine an equation of the form $f(x) = \dfrac{ax + b}{cx + d}$ for the rational function with x-intercept 2, vertical asymptote at $x = -1$, and horizontal asymptote at $y = -\dfrac{1}{2}$.

  b) Is it possible for another function to have the same key features? If not, explain why not. If so, provide an example.

10. The acceleration due to gravity is inversely proportional to the square of the distance from the centre of Earth. The acceleration due to gravity for a satellite orbiting 7000 km above the centre of Earth is 8.2 m/s².

  a) Write a formula for this relationship.

  b) Sketch a graph of the relation.

  c) At what height will the acceleration due to gravity be 6.0 m/s²?

11. When a saw is used to cut wood, a certain percent is lost as sawdust, depending on the thickness of the saw-blade. The wood lost is called the kerf. The percent lost, $P(t)$, can be modelled by the function $P(t) = \dfrac{100t}{t + W}$, where t is the thickness of the blade and W is the thickness of the wood, both in millimetres. Consider a saw cutting a 30-mm-thick piece of wood.

  a) Sketch a graph of the function, in the context of this situation.

  b) State the domain and range.

  c) Explain the significance of the horizontal asymptote.

12. The electric power, P, in watts, delivered by a certain battery is given by the function $P = \dfrac{100R}{(2 + R)^2}$, where R is the resistance, in ohms.

  a) Sketch a graph of this function.

  b) Describe the power output as the resistance increases from 0 Ω to 20 Ω.

  c) Show that the rate of change is 0 at $R = 2$. What does this indicate about the power?

13. Investigate the graphs of functions of the form $f(x) = \dfrac{1}{x^n}$, where $n \in \mathbb{N}$. Summarize what happens to the asymptotes and slopes as n increases. Consider, also, when n is even or odd.

Chapter 1

1. Sketch a graph of each polynomial function. Determine the x- and y-intercepts.

   a) $y = x^3 - 2x^2 - x + 2$

   b) $y = x^4 - 2x^3 - 8x^2 + 12x - 16$

2. Describe the symmetry and the end behaviour of each function.

   a) $f(x) = 5x^4 - 2x^3 + x^2 - 3x + 1$

   b) $g(x) = 4x^3 - 5x^2 + 7x - 3$

3. a) Determine the average rate of change of the cubic function $f(x) = -4x^3$ for the intervals

   i) $x = 2.0$ to $x = 2.5$

   ii) $x = 1.5$ to $x = 2.0$

   b) Find the average of these two rates of change and describe what the result approximates.

4. Sketch graphs of the functions in each pair on the same set of axes. Label fully.

   a) $f(x) = x^3$ and $g(x) = 0.5(x - 1)^3 + 3$

   b) $f(x) = x^4$ and $g(x) = -(2x + 6)^4$

5. A function is represented by the table of values.

x	y
−5	−288
−4	−50
−3	0
−2	−18
−1	−32
0	−18
1	0
2	−50
3	−288

   a) Sketch a graph of the function, assuming that all zeros are given in the table and that they are each of order 2.

   b) Determine the degree of the function.

   c) Write an equation in factored form to represent the function.

   d) Explain what effect the leading coefficient has on the graph.

6. Consider the function $f(x) = x^3 - 5x^2 + 4x - 5$.

   a) Determine the instantaneous rate of change at the point where $x = 2$.

   b) Determine the instantaneous rate of change at the point where $x = 4$.

   c) What special kind of point occurs between the points in parts a) and b)? Explain.

7. A section of rollercoaster can be modelled by $h(x) = 0.0025x(x - 8)(x - 16)(x - 32)$, $0 \le x \le 32$, where x is the horizontal distance and h is the height relative to the platform, with all measurements in metres.

   a) Determine the maximum and minimum height of each hill and valley. Round answers to two decimal places.

   b) What is the average rate of change of the rollercoaster between each pair of maximum and minimum points?

   c) Where would the instantaneous rate of change of the rollercoaster be the greatest? Justify your answer using appropriate calculations.

Chapter 2

8. Write two possible equations for a quartic function with zeros at $x = -7$ and $x = 0$ and a zero of order two at $x = 3$.

9. Write an equation representing the family of curves defined by the graph shown. Provide two possible examples of specific functions that are members of this family and give the y-intercept for each.

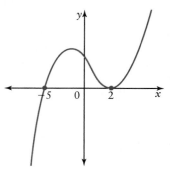

10. Use long division to divide. State the restriction on the variable.

   a) $4x^3 - 5x^2 + 6x + 2$ divided by $2x + 1$

   b) $3x^4 - 5x^2 - 28$ divided by $x - 2$

11. Use the remainder theorem to determine the remainder of each division.

a) $6x^3 - 7x^2 + 5x + 8$ divided by $x - 2$

b) $3x^4 + x^3 - 2x + 1$ divided by $3x + 4$

12. Use the factor theorem to determine whether the second polynomial is a factor of the first.

a) $4x^5 - 3x^3 - 2x^2 + 5$, $x + 5$

b) $3x^3 - 15x^2 + 10x + 8$, $x - 4$

13. Determine the value of k so that, when $3x^4 - 4x^3 + kx - 3x + 6$ is divided by $x - 2$, the remainder is 3.

14. Factor fully.

a) $x^3 - 27$

b) $2x^3 + 4x^2 - 13x - 6$

15. Find the real roots of each equation.

a) $x^3 - 2x^2 - 19x + 20 = 0$

b) $5x^3 + 23x^2 = 9 - 21x$

16. Solve each inequality.

a) $x^2 - 7x + 6 \geq 0$

b) $x^3 + 3x^2 - 4x - 12 < 0$

17. The mass, m, in tonnes, of fuel in a rocket t minutes after it is launched is given by $m = -t^2 - 140t + 2000$. During what period of time is the mass of the fuel greater than 500 t?

Chapter 3

18. Which graph represents $f(x) = \dfrac{1}{(x - 1)^2}$?

A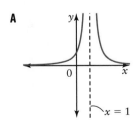

$x = 1$

B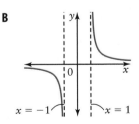

$x = -1$ $x = 1$

C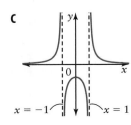

$x = -1$ $x = 1$

D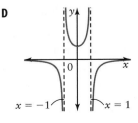

$x = -1$ $x = 1$

19. Describe what happens to the function $f(x) = \dfrac{4}{x - 3}$ as x approaches each value.

a) $+\infty$ b) $-\infty$ c) 3^+ d) 3^-

20. State the domain and the range of the function $f(x) = \dfrac{x - 2}{x + 1}$.

21. i) State the key features of each function:
- domain and range
- x- and y-intercepts
- equations of the asymptotes
- slope of the function in each interval
- change in slope for each interval

ii) Sketch a graph of each function.

a) $f(x) = \dfrac{6x + 1}{2x - 4}$ b) $f(x) = \dfrac{1}{x^2 - 9}$

22. Determine an equation for the rational function of the form $f(x) = \dfrac{ax + b}{cx + d}$ that has an x-intercept of -2, a vertical asymptote at $x = 1$, and a horizontal asymptote at $y = 3$.

23. Solve each equation.

a) $\dfrac{2x + 3}{x - 2} = \dfrac{1}{3}$

b) $\dfrac{10}{x^2 - 3x + 5} = x + 1$

24. Solve each inequality. Show your solution on a number line.

a) $\dfrac{3}{2x + 4} > -2$

b) $\dfrac{x + 3}{x - 1} \leq \dfrac{x + 4}{x - 2}$

25. The profit, in thousands of dollars, from the sale of x kilograms of tuna fish can be modelled by the function $P(x) = \dfrac{5x - 400}{x + 600}$.

a) Sketch a graph of this function.

b) State the domain and the range.

c) Explain the significance of the horizontal asymptote.

26. The current, I, in ohms (Ω), in an electrical circuit after t milliseconds is given by $I = \dfrac{11 - t}{10 - t}$. What is an appropriate domain for this function? Explain your reasoning.

TASK

ZENN and Now

The ZENN (Zero Emissions, No Noise) car is an environmentally friendly commuter car invented in Canada. The current model is powered by six 12-volt rechargeable batteries, and has a top speed of 40 km/h.

The batteries have the following discharge characteristics:

Fully charged: 72 V

Totally discharged (0 V) with constant usage: 12 h

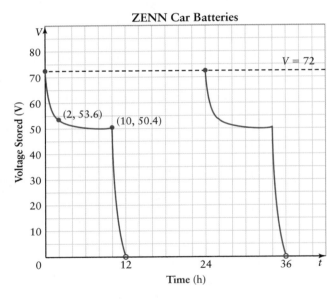

The battery discharge is not constant. The graph shows the discharge pattern of the batteries.

- During the first two hours, the batteries discharge exponentially to approximately 80% of original charge. The function for this period has the form $V = a(10^{-kt})$, where V is the remaining voltage, t is the time in hours, and a and k are constants.

- The batteries then discharge nonlinearly over the next 8 h to 70% of original charge. The function for this period has the form $V = b + \sqrt{c - t}$, where b and c are constants.

- During the last 2 h the charge drops on a steep curve to 0 V. The function for this part is $V = n(t - p)^2 + q$, where n, p and q are constants.

a) Justify in writing that the graph meets all the conditions described.

b) What happened between 12 h and 24 h?

c) Find the equations for the three parts of the curve, for the time interval [0, 12]. Specify any restrictions on domain and range, using appropriate mathematical notation.

d) If a new rechargeable battery has a discharge time of 20 h, describe how this would effect the graph and change your answers to part c).

e) Use the Internet to research how the cost to run this battery-powered car compares to the costs to run a compact gasoline-powered car. Write a brief report to a courier company that is planning to purchase a fleet of small cars for city deliveries.

Chapter 4

Trigonometry

You may be surprised to learn that scientists, engineers, designers, and other professionals who use angles in their daily work generally do not measure the angles in degrees. In this chapter, you will investigate another method of measuring angles known as radian measure. You will extend the use of radian measure to trigonometric ratios and gain an appreciation for the simpler representations that occur when using radian measure. You will develop trigonometric formulas for compound angles and investigate equivalent trigonometric expressions using a variety of approaches. You will develop techniques for identifying and proving trigonometric identities.

By the end of this chapter, you will

- recognize the radian as an alternative unit to the degree for angle measurement, define the radian measure of an angle as the length of the arc that subtends this angle at the centre of a unit circle, and develop and apply the relationship between radian and degree measure (B1.1)
- represent radian measure in terms of π and as a rational number (B1.2)
- determine, with technology, the primary trigonometric ratios and the reciprocal trigonometric ratios of angles expressed in radian measure (B1.3)
- determine, without technology, the exact values of the primary trigonometric ratios and the reciprocal trigonometric ratios for the special angles $0, \frac{\pi}{6}, \frac{\pi}{4}, \frac{\pi}{3}, \frac{\pi}{2}$, and their multiples less than or equal to 2π (B1.4)

- recognize equivalent trigonometric expressions, and verify equivalence using graphing technology (B3.1)
- explore the algebraic development of the compound angle formulas and use the formulas to determine exact values of trigonometric ratios (B3.2)
- recognize that trigonometric identities are equations that are true for every value in the domain; prove trigonometric identities through the application of reasoning skills, using a variety of relationships; and verify identities using technology (B3.3)

Prerequisite Skills

Primary Trigonometric Ratios and the CAST Rule

1. An exact value for a trigonometric ratio is given for each angle. Determine the exact values of the other two primary trigonometric ratios.

   a) $\sin \theta = \frac{3}{5}, 0° \leq \theta \leq 90°$

   b) $\cos \theta = \frac{5}{13}, 270° \leq \theta \leq 360°$

   c) $\tan x = -\frac{7}{24}, 90° \leq x \leq 180°$

   d) $\sin x = -\frac{8}{17}, 180° \leq x \leq 270°$

2. Use the CAST rule to determine the sign of each value. Then, use a calculator to evaluate each trigonometric ratio, rounded to four decimal places.

   a) $\sin 15°$ b) $\cos 56°$

   c) $\tan 75°$ d) $\sin 100°$

   e) $\cos 157°$ f) $\tan 250°$

   g) $\sin 302°$ h) $\cos 348°$

   CONNECTIONS

   Recall that the memory device CAST shows which trigonometric ratios are positive in each quadrant.

   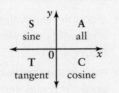

3. Use a calculator to determine angle x, rounded to the nearest degree.

   a) $\sin x = 0.65$ b) $\cos x = \frac{5}{12}$

   c) $\tan x = 8.346$ d) $\cos x = -0.45$

Reciprocal Trigonometric Ratios

Note: If you have not worked with reciprocal trigonometric ratios before, refer to the Prerequisite Skills Appendix on page 484.

4. Determine the reciprocal of each number.

   a) 2 b) $\frac{1}{3}$ c) $\frac{3}{5}$ d) $\frac{\sqrt{3}}{2}$

5. An exact value for a reciprocal trigonometric ratio is given for each angle. Determine the exact values of the other two reciprocal trigonometric ratios.

   a) $\csc x = \frac{5}{4}, 0° \leq x \leq 90°$

   b) $\sec \theta = \frac{13}{12}, 270° \leq \theta \leq 360°$

   c) $\cot x = -\frac{24}{7}, 90° \leq x \leq 180°$

   d) $\csc \theta = -\frac{17}{15}, 180° \leq \theta \leq 270°$

6. Use a calculator to evaluate each trigonometric ratio, rounded to four decimal places.

   a) $\csc 35°$

   b) $\sec 216°$

   c) $\cot 25°$

   d) $\csc 122°$

   e) $\sec 142°$

   f) $\cot 223°$

   g) $\csc 321°$

   h) $\sec 355°$

7. Use a calculator to determine angle x, rounded to the nearest degree.

   a) $\csc x = 1.25$

   b) $\sec x = \frac{12}{7}$

   c) $\cot x = 3.1416$

   d) $\sec x = -1.32$

Exact Trigonometric Ratios of Special Angles

8. Use appropriate special right triangles to determine exact values for the primary trigonometric ratios.

	θ	$\sin \theta$	$\cos \theta$	$\tan \theta$
a)	30°			
b)	45°			
c)	60°			

9. a) Use a unit circle, similar to the one shown, to represent an angle of 45° in standard position with point P(x, y) as the point of intersection of the terminal arm and the unit circle.

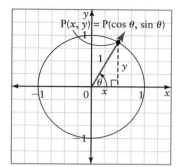

Create a right triangle that will allow you to determine the primary trigonometric ratios of 45°. Label the coordinates of point P using the exact values for (cos 45°, sin 45°).

b) Determine exact expressions for the lengths of the sides of the triangle.

c) Use the side lengths to determine exact values for the reciprocal trigonometric ratios of 45°.

10. Extend your diagram from question 9 to help you determine exact primary and reciprocal trigonometric ratios for 135°, 225°, and 315°.

Distance Between Two Points

11. Use the distance formula $d = \sqrt{(x_2 - x_1)^2 + (y_2 - y_1)^2}$ to determine the distance between the points in each pair.

a) A(10, 8) and B(6, 5)

b) C(−5, −3) and D(7, 2)

c) E(−8, 4) and F(7, 12)

d) G(−3, −6) and H(3, 2)

Product of Two Binomials

12. Expand and simplify each product.

a) $(a + b)(a + b)$

b) $(c + d)(c - d)$

c) $(2x + y)(3x - 2y)$

d) $(\sin x + \cos y)(\sin x + \cos y)$

Trigonometric Identities

13. Use a calculator to verify that the Pythagorean identity $\sin^2 x + \cos^2 x = 1$ is true for $x = 20°$, $x = 130°$, $x = 200°$, and $x = 305°$.

14. Use a calculator to verify that the quotient identity $\tan x = \dfrac{\sin x}{\cos x}$ is true for $x = 40°$, $x = 110°$, $x = 232°$, and $x = 355°$.

▚ PROBLEM

What do a civil engineer designing highway on-ramps, a pilot turning an aircraft onto the final approach for landing, and a software designer developing the code for engineering design software have in common? All of them use angles and trigonometry to help solve the problems they encounter. The engineer applies trigonometry to determine the length and the angle of inclination of the on-ramp. The pilot selects the angle of bank for the aircraft from tables based on the tangent ratio to ensure a proper alignment with the runway at the end of the turn. The software designer employs trigonometry to realistically render a three-dimensional world onto a two-dimensional computer screen. As you work through this chapter, you will apply trigonometry to solve problems relating to the transportation industry.

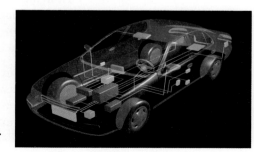

Radian Measure

Ancient Babylonian astronomers are credited with inventing degree measure and for choosing 360 as the number of degrees in a complete turn. They noted that the stars in the night sky showed two kinds of movement. They would "rise" and "set" during the course of a single night, moving in arcs centred on the North Star. However, they also noted a change in the position of a given star from night to night of about $\frac{1}{360}$ of a circle, taking about a year to complete one revolution. This long-term motion of the stars is thought to be the basis for choosing 360° as one complete revolution.

In this section, you will investigate and learn to use another way of measuring angles, known as radian measure.

Investigate How can you determine the meaning of radian measure?

Tools

- a large wheel, such as a bicycle wheel
- a length of heavy string
- masking tape
- protractor
- scissors

Method 1: *Use a Wheel and a String*

1. Measure and cut a length of string equal to the radius of the wheel.

2. Lay the string along the outside circumference of the wheel to form an arc. Use tape to hold the string on the wheel.

3. Measure and cut two more lengths, each equal to the radius. Tape these lengths of string from each end of the arc to the centre of the wheel. The two radii and the arc form an area known as a **sector**.

4. The angle θ formed at the centre of the wheel by the two radii is the **central angle**. The arc **subtends**, or is opposite to, this central angle. Estimate the measure of the central angle, in degrees. Then, use a protractor to measure the angle. Record the measurement.

5. One **radian** is the measure of the angle subtended at the centre of a circle by an arc that has the same length as the radius of the circle. Since you used an arc with the same length as the radius, the angle θ measures 1 radian. Estimate how many degrees are equivalent to 1 radian.

6. Estimate the number of arcs of length one radius that it would take to go once around the outside circumference of the wheel. Explain how you made the estimate.

7. Use a length of string to make a more accurate measure of the number of arcs of length one radius that it takes to go once around the wheel. If you have a fraction of an arc left over, estimate the fraction, and convert to a decimal.

8. **Reflect** What is the relationship between the radius of a circle and its circumference? How does this relationship compare to your measurement in step 7?

Method 2: *Use The Geometer's Sketchpad®*

1. Open *The Geometer's Sketchpad®*. Turn on the grid display. Adjust the scale on the axes so that 1 unit in each direction fills most of the workspace, as shown.

2. Construct a circle with centre at the origin A and radius 1 unit.

3. Select the circle. From the **Construct** menu, choose **Point On Circle** to create point B. Move point B to (1, 0). Construct a line segment AB from the origin to (1, 0). Use the **Display** menu to adjust the line width to thick.

4. Select the circle. From the **Construct** menu, choose **Point On Circle** to create point C. Move point C on the circle to the first quadrant, if necessary. Join C to A with a thick line segment.

5. Select points B and C, in that order, and the circle. From the **Construct** menu, choose **Arc On Circle**.

6. CA, AB, and the arc BC form an area known as a sector . Measure the length of the arc and the length of the radius.

7. Calculate the ratio of the length of the arc to the length of the radius.

Tools

• computer with *The Geometer's Sketchpad®*

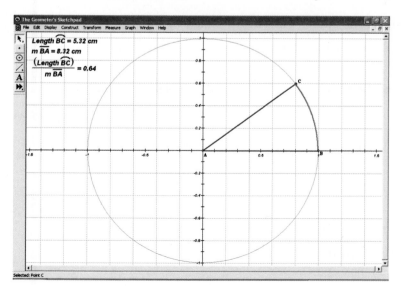

8. The angle formed at the centre of the circle by the two radii is the central angle . Drag point C along the circle until the ratio from step 7 equals 1. When the length of the arc is equal to the radius, the central angle subtended by the arc, ∠BAC, measures 1 radian .

9. Measure ∠BAC. How many degrees make up 1 radian? Record the measurement.

10. Estimate the number of arcs of length one radius that it would take to go once around the circumference of the circle. Explain how you made the estimate.

11. Make a more accurate measure of the number of arcs of length one radius that it takes to go once around the circumference by continuing to drag point C around the circle until you have completed one revolution.

12. **Reflect** What is the relationship between the radius of a circle and its circumference? How does this relationship compare to your measurement in step 11?

13. Save your sketch for later use.

The radian measure of an angle θ is defined as the length, a, of the arc that subtends the angle divided by the radius, r, of the circle.

$$\theta = \frac{a}{r}$$

For one complete revolution, the length of the arc equals the circumference of the circle, $2\pi r$.

$$\theta = \frac{2\pi r}{r}$$
$$= 2\pi$$

One complete revolution measures 2π radians.

You can determine the relationship between radians and degrees.

Radians to Degrees

$2\pi \text{ rad} = 360°$

$1 \text{ rad} = \left(\frac{360}{2\pi}\right)°$ Divide both sides by 2π.

$1 \text{ rad} = \left(\frac{180}{\pi}\right)°$ Simplify.

Degrees to Radians

$360° = 2\pi \text{ rad}$ The abbreviation rad means radian.

$1° = \frac{2\pi}{360} \text{ rad}$ Divide both sides by 360.

$1° = \frac{\pi}{180} \text{ rad}$ Simplify.

One radian is $\left(\frac{180}{\pi}\right)°$, or approximately 57.3°. One degree is $\frac{\pi}{180}$ rad, or approximately 0.0175.

In practice, the term *radian* or its abbreviation, rad, is often omitted. An angle with a degree symbol, such as 30°, is understood to be measured in degrees. An angle with no symbol, such as 6.28, is understood to be measured in radians.

Exact angles in radians are usually written in terms of π. For example, a straight angle is referred to as π radians.

Example 1 | Degree Measure to Radian Measure

Determine an exact and an approximate radian measure, to the nearest hundredth, for an angle of 30°.

Solution

To convert a degree measure to a radian measure, multiply the degree measure by $\dfrac{\pi}{180}$ radians.

Method 1: *Use Pencil, Paper, and Scientific Calculator*

$$30° = 30 \times \frac{\pi}{180}$$
$$= \frac{\pi}{6}$$

30° is exactly $\dfrac{\pi}{6}$ radians.

Use a calculator to determine the approximate radian measure.

$$\frac{\pi}{6} \doteq 0.52$$

30° is approximately 0.52 radians.

Note: Whenever possible, you should leave angle measures in exact form, to preserve accuracy.

Method 2: *Use a Computer Algebra System (CAS)*

On a TI-89 calculator, press MODE and ensure that the **Angle** measure is set to **RADIAN**. While in the **MODE** menu, scroll down to **Exact/Approx** and ensure that it is set to **AUTO**.

In the Home screen, type $30 \times \pi \div 180$, and press ENTER. Note that the CAS will display the exact answer.

30° is exactly $\dfrac{\pi}{6}$ radians.

From the **F2** menu, select **5:approx(.**
Type $30 \times \pi \div 180$, and press) ENTER.
Notice that the CAS returns the approximate answer.

30° is approximately 0.52 radians.

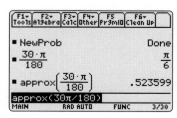

CONNECTIONS

$\dfrac{\pi}{6}$ is usually read "pi over six."

Technology Tip   ⁚⁚

You can use a TI-83 Plus or TI-84 Plus graphing calculator to convert degree measure to approximate radian measure. Ensure that the calculator is in Radian mode.
Type the angle, in degrees.
- For example, type 30.
- Press 2nd APPS to access the **ANGLE** menu.
- Select **1:°**.
- Press ENTER.
The measure of the angle is displayed in radians.

30°   .5235987756

Technology Tip   ⁚⁚

Instead of using the **approx(** operation of a CAS, you can press MODE and set the accuracy to **APPROXIMATE** or press ◆ ENTER for ≈, which is an approximation symbol.

Technology Tip ∴

You can use a TI-83 Plus or TI-84 Plus graphing calculator to convert radian measure to degree measure.

Ensure that the calculator is in Degree mode.

Type the angle, in radians.

- For example, type (π ÷ 4).
- Press 2nd APPS to access the **ANGLE** menu.
- Select **3:ʳ**.
- Press ENTER.

The measure of the angle is displayed in degrees.

```
(π/4)ʳ
              45
```

Example 2 Radian Measure to Degree Measure

Determine the degree measure, to the nearest tenth, for each radian measure.

a) $\dfrac{\pi}{4}$

b) 5.86

Solution

a) To convert radian measure to degree measure, multiply the radian measure by $\left(\dfrac{180}{\pi}\right)^\circ$.

$$\frac{\pi}{4} = \frac{\pi}{4} \times \left(\frac{180}{\pi}\right)^\circ$$
$$= 45^\circ$$

$\dfrac{\pi}{4}$ radians is exactly 45°.

b) $5.86 = 5.86 \times \left(\dfrac{180}{\pi}\right)^\circ$
$$\doteq 335.8^\circ$$

5.86 radians is approximately 335.8°.

Example 3 Arc Length for a Given Angle

Suzette chooses a camel to ride on a carousel. The camel is located 9 m from the centre of the carousel. If the carousel turns through an angle of $\dfrac{5\pi}{6}$, determine the length of the arc travelled by the camel, to the nearest tenth of a metre.

CONNECTIONS

The invention of radian measure is credited to Roger Cotes as early as 1714, although he did not use the term *radian*. This term first appeared in an examination paper set by James Thomson at Queen's College, Belfast, in 1873.

Solution

The radius, r, is 9 m, and the measure of angle θ is $\dfrac{5\pi}{6}$ radians.

$$\text{Angle measure in radians} = \frac{\text{length of arc subtended by the angle}}{\text{radius}}$$

$$\theta = \frac{a}{r}$$
$$a = r\theta$$
$$a = 9 \times \frac{5\pi}{6}$$
$$a \doteq 23.6$$

The camel travels approximately 23.6 m.

Example 4 | Angular Velocity of a Rotating Object

The angular velocity of a rotating object is the rate at which the central angle changes with respect to time. The hard disk in a personal computer rotates at 7200 rpm (revolutions per minute). Determine its angular velocity, in

a) degrees per second

b) radians per second

Solution

a) The hard disk rotates through an angle of 7200 × 360°, or 2 592 000°, in 1 min.

$$\text{Angular velocity} = \frac{2\ 592\ 000°}{60\ \text{s}}$$

$$= 43\ 200°/\text{s}$$

The angular velocity of the hard disk is 43 200°/s.

b) The hard disk rotates through an angle of 7200 × 2π, or 14 400π rad, in 1 min.

$$\text{Angular velocity} = \frac{14\ 400\pi\ \text{rad}}{60\ \text{s}}$$

$$= 240\pi\ \text{rad/s}$$

The angular velocity of the hard disk is 240π rad/s.

《 KEY CONCEPTS 》

- The radian measure of angle θ is defined as the length, a, of the arc that subtends the angle divided by the radius, r, of the circle: $\theta = \frac{a}{r}$.

- 2π rad = 360° or π rad = 180°.

- To convert degree measure to radian measure, multiply the degree measure by $\frac{\pi}{180}$ radians.

- To convert radian measure to degree measure, multiply the radian measure by $\left(\frac{180}{\pi}\right)°$.

Communicate Your Understanding

C1 Determine mentally the degree measure of an angle of π radians. Justify your answer.

C2 Determine mentally the radian measure of a right angle. Justify your answer.

C3 As described in the introduction, the Babylonian method of measuring angles in degrees is based on the division of a complete revolution into an arbitrary number of units. Why is radian measure a more suitable method of measuring angles than degree measure?

A Practise

For help with questions 1 to 6, refer to Example 1.

1. Determine mentally the exact radian measure for each angle, given that 30° is exactly $\frac{\pi}{6}$ rad.

a) 60°   **b)** 90°   **c)** 120°   **d)** 150°

2. Determine mentally the exact radian measure for each angle, given that 30° is exactly $\frac{\pi}{6}$ rad.

a) 15°   **b)** 10°   **c)** 7.5°   **d)** 5°

3. Determine mentally the exact radian measure for each angle, given that 45° is exactly $\frac{\pi}{4}$ rad.

a) 90°   **b)** 135°   **c)** 180°   **d)** 225°

4. Determine mentally the exact radian measure for each angle, given that 45° is exactly $\frac{\pi}{4}$ rad.

a) 22.5°   **b)** 15°   **c)** 9°   **d)** 3°

5. Determine the exact radian measure for each angle.

a) 40°   **b)** 10°   **c)** 315°
d) 210°   **e)** 300°   **f)** 75°

6. Determine the approximate radian measure, to the nearest hundredth, for each angle.

a) 23°   **b)** 51°   **c)** 82°
d) 128°   **e)** 240°   **f)** 330°

For help with questions 7 and 8, refer to Example 2.

7. Determine the exact degree measure for each angle.

a) $\frac{\pi}{5}$ **b)** $\frac{\pi}{9}$ **c)** $\frac{5\pi}{12}$

d) $\frac{5\pi}{18}$ **e)** $\frac{3\pi}{4}$ **f)** $\frac{3\pi}{2}$

8. Determine the approximate degree measure, to the nearest tenth, for each angle.

a) 2.34   **b)** 3.14   **c)** 5.27
d) 7.53   **e)** 0.68   **f)** 1.72

For help with question 9, refer to Example 3.

9. A circle of radius 25 cm has a central angle of 4.75 radians. Determine the length of the arc that subtends this angle.

B Connect and Apply

For help with question 10, refer to Example 4.

10. Kumar rides his bicycle such that the back wheel rotates 10 times in 5 s. Determine the angular velocity of the wheel in

a) degrees per second

b) radians per second

11. The measure of one of the equal angles in an isosceles triangle is twice the measure of the remaining angle. Determine the exact radian measures of the three angles in the triangle.

12. Use Technology Refer to *The Geometer's Sketchpad®* sketch from Method 2 of the Investigate. Right-click on point C, and select **Animate**. Use a stopwatch to determine the length of time required for five complete revolutions of C about the origin. Calculate the angular velocity of point C about the origin in

a) degrees per second

b) radians per second

13. Aircraft and ships use nautical miles for measuring distances. At one time, a nautical mile was defined as one minute of arc, or $\frac{1}{60}$ of a degree, along a meridian of longitude, following Earth's surface.

a) Determine the radian measure of one minute of arc, to six decimal places.

b) The radius of Earth is about 6400 km. Determine the length of a nautical mile, using the old definition, to the nearest metre.

c) The length of a nautical mile is no longer calculated in this way. In 1929, the International Extraordinary Hydrographic Conference adopted a definition of exactly 1852 m. Suggest reasons why a calculation using the radius of Earth might not be the best way to define the nautical mile.

14. A milliradian (mrad) is $\frac{1}{1000}$ of a radian. Milliradians are used in artillery to estimate the distance to a target.

a) Show that an arc of length 1 m subtends an angle of 1 mrad at a distance of 1 km.

b) A target scope shows that a target known to be 2 m high subtends an angle of 0.25 mrad. How far away is the target, in kilometres?

15. The Moon has a diameter of about 3480 km and an orbital radius of about 384 400 km from the centre of Earth. Suppose that the Moon is directly overhead. What is the measure of the angle subtended by the diameter to the Moon as measured by an astronomer on the surface of Earth? Answer in both radians and degrees.

16. David made a swing for his niece Sarah using ropes 2.4 m long, so that Sarah swings through an arc of length 1.2 m. Determine the angle through which Sarah swings, in both radians and degrees.

17. An engine on a jet aircraft turns at about 12 000 rpm. Find an exact value, as well as an approximate value, for the angular velocity of the engine in radians per second.

18. **Chapter Problem** Two highways meet at an angle measuring $\frac{\pi}{3}$ rad, as shown. An on-ramp in the shape of a circular arc is to be built such that the arc has a radius of 80 m.

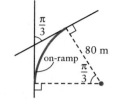

a) Determine an exact expression for the length of the on-ramp.

b) Determine the length of the on-ramp, to the nearest tenth of a metre.

19. Satellites that are used for satellite television must stay over the same point on Earth at all times, so that the receiving antenna

is always pointed at the satellite. This is known as a geostationary orbit and requires an orbit at a distance of approximately 35 900 km above Earth's surface.

a) Explain how such a satellite could remain over the same point on Earth as it orbits the planet.

b) How long would such an orbit require for one complete revolution of Earth?

c) What is the angular velocity of such a satellite, in radians per second?

d) How does the angular velocity of the satellite compare to the angular velocity of the point on Earth that it is hovering over? Justify your answer.

20. When the metric system was developed in France, it was suggested to change the measure of one revolution from 360° to 400 grads. This was known as gradian measure. Gradian measure has not enjoyed wide popularity, but most calculators can handle angles measured in gradians. Look for a key marked DRG on your scientific calculator. Alternatively, look for a MODE key, as it may be an option in the mode menu.

a) What is the measure of a right angle in gradians?

b) Determine the radian measure of an angle of 150 grads.

Achievement Check

21. The London Eye is a large Ferris wheel located on the banks of the Thames River in London, England. Each sealed and air-conditioned passenger capsule holds about 25 passengers. The diameter of the wheel is 135 m, and the wheel takes about half an hour to complete one revolution.

a) Determine the exact angle, in radians, that a passenger will travel in 5 min.

b) How far does a passenger travel in 5 min?

c) How long would it take a passenger to travel 2 radians?

d) What is the angular velocity of a passenger, in radians per second?

e) What is the angular velocity of a passenger, in degrees per second?

C Extend and Challenge

22. Refer to question 19. Determine the orbital speed of a geostationary satellite.

23. In the days of sailing ships, the speed of a ship was determined by tying knots in a rope at regular intervals, attaching one end of the rope to a log, and tossing the log overboard. A sailor would count how many knots followed the log in 30 s, giving the speed of the ship in knots. If the speed in knots is the same as the speed in nautical miles per hour, how far apart would the knots in the rope need to be tied?

> C O N N E C T I O N S
>
> The speed of the ship was recorded in a book, which came to be known as the ship's log.

24. Consider your angular velocity due to the rotation of Earth. How does your angular velocity compare to that of an African living on the equator? an Inuit living on the Arctic Circle? Justify your answers.

25. The following proportion is true:

$$\frac{\text{sector area}}{\text{area of circle}} = \frac{\text{central angle}}{\text{one revolution angle}}$$

a) Use this proportion to derive a formula for the sector area, A, in terms of the central angle θ and the radius, r, of the circle.

b) Determine the area of a sector with a central angle of $\frac{\pi}{5}$ and a radius of 12 cm.

26. **Math Contest** You can locate a point in a plane using the Cartesian coordinate system and a unique ordered pair (x, y). You can also locate a point in a plane by using its distance, r, from the origin and its direction angle, θ, from the positive x-axis. This form of coordinates, (r, θ), is known as polar coordinates.

a) Give the polar coordinates of the points A, B, C, and D for $0 \le \theta \le 2\pi$.

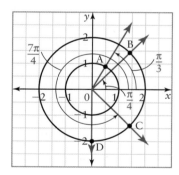

b) Determine the polar coordinates of each point.

   i) $(1, 1)$

   ii) $(-3, 4)$

   iii) $(0, -5)$

4.2 Trigonometric Ratios and Special Angles

Scientists, engineers, and other professionals work with radians in many ways. For example, the variety of sounds possible in electronic music is created using trigonometric models. The electricity produced by a power plant follows a trigonometric relation. In this section, you will learn how to use technology to determine trigonometric ratios of angles expressed in radian measure and how to determine exact trigonometric ratios of special angles.

Investigate 1

How can you use technology to evaluate trigonometric ratios for angles measured in radians?

Method 1: *Use a Scientific Calculator*

Tools
- scientific calculator

1. The angle mode is usually displayed on the screen of a scientific calculator. Possible displays are DEG, RAD, GRAD, or D, R, G. Often, there is a key marked DRG that can be pressed to cycle through the angle modes.

   a) Set the angle mode to degrees.

   b) Evaluate sin 45°. Record the answer, to four decimal places.

2. **a)** What is the exact equivalent of 45° in radian measure?

   b) Set the angle mode to radians.

   c) To evaluate $\sin\frac{\pi}{4}$, press the key sequence $\boxed{\pi}$ $\boxed{\div}$ $\boxed{4}$ $\boxed{=}$ $\boxed{\text{SIN}}$. How does the answer compare to the answer from step 1b)?

3. Evaluate $\cos\frac{\pi}{4}$ and $\tan\frac{\pi}{4}$.

4. You can evaluate the reciprocal trigonometric ratios using the reciprocal key, which is usually marked x^{-1} or $\frac{1}{x}$. To find $\csc\frac{\pi}{4}$, press the key sequence for $\sin\frac{\pi}{4}$ from step 2c). Then, press the reciprocal key.

5. Evaluate $\sec\frac{\pi}{4}$ and $\cot\frac{\pi}{4}$.

6. Consider an angle of 1.5 radians. Determine the six trigonometric ratios for this angle.

7. **Reflect** Compare sin 1.5 and sin 1.5°. Explain why they are not equal.

Technology Tip

Scientific calculators will vary. If the instructions shown do not match your calculator, refer to your calculator manual.

Tools

• graphing calculator

Technology Tip ∴

Using a calculator in the wrong angle mode is a common source of error in assignments and on tests and exams. It is wise to develop the habit of checking the mode before using any calculator for calculations involving angles.

Method 2: *Use a Graphing Calculator*

1. a) Press [MODE]. Ensure that the calculator is set to Degree mode.

b) Return to the calculation screen.

c) Evaluate sin 45°. Record the answer, to four decimal places.

2. a) What is the exact equivalent of 45° in radian measure?

b) Set the angle mode to radians.

c) To evaluate $\sin\frac{\pi}{4}$, press the key sequence [SIN] [2nd] [π] [÷] 4 [ )] [ENTER]. How does the answer compare to the answer from step 1c)?

3. Evaluate $\cos\frac{\pi}{4}$ and $\tan\frac{\pi}{4}$.

4. You can evaluate the reciprocal trigonometric ratios using the reciprocal key, [x⁻¹]. To find $\csc\frac{\pi}{4}$, press the sequence for $\sin\frac{\pi}{4}$ from step 2c). Then, press [x⁻¹] [ENTER].

5. Evaluate $\sec\frac{\pi}{4}$ and $\cot\frac{\pi}{4}$.

6. Consider an angle of 1.5 radians. Determine the six trigonometric ratios for this angle.

7. Reflect Compare sin 1.5 and sin 1.5°. Explain why they are not equal.

Tools

• computer algebra system

Technology Tip ∴

Notice that the CAS displays an equivalent expression for a radical expression that does not have a radical in the denominator. This is because the denominator has been rationalized as follows:

$$\sin 45° = \frac{1}{\sqrt{2}}$$
$$= \frac{1}{\sqrt{2}} \times \frac{\sqrt{2}}{\sqrt{2}}$$
$$= \frac{\sqrt{2}}{2}$$

Method 3: *Use a Computer Algebra System (CAS)*

1. a) Press [MODE]. Ensure that the **Angle** mode is set to **DEGREE**.

b) Return to the Home screen.

c) Evaluate sin 45°. Notice that the CAS returns the exact answer of $\frac{\sqrt{2}}{2}$.

d) To obtain the approximate decimal equivalent, use the **approx(** operation from the F2 menu. Record the answer, to four decimal places.

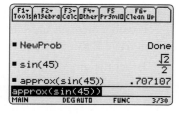

2. a) What is the exact equivalent of 45° in radian measure?

b) Set the angle mode to radians.

c) To evaluate $\sin\frac{\pi}{4}$, press the key sequence [2nd] [SIN] [2nd] [π] [÷] 4 [ )]. Note that the CAS returns the exact answer. Use the **approx(** operation to obtain the approximate decimal equivalent. How does the answer compare to the answer from step 1d)?

3. Evaluate $\cos\frac{\pi}{4}$ and $\tan\frac{\pi}{4}$.

4. You can evaluate the reciprocal trigonometric ratios by using the exponent key, [^], followed by −1. To find $\csc\frac{\pi}{4}$, press the sequence for $\sin\frac{\pi}{4}$ from step 2c). Then, press [^] [(−)] 1 [ENTER]. Note that the CAS returns the exact answer. Use the **approx(** operation to obtain the approximate decimal equivalent.

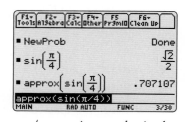

5. Evaluate $\sec\dfrac{\pi}{4}$ and $\cot\dfrac{\pi}{4}$.

6. Consider an angle of 1.5 radians. Determine the six trigonometric ratios for this angle.

7. Reflect Compare sin 1.5 and sin 1.5°. Explain why they are not equal.

| **Investigate 2** | **How can you determine trigonometric ratios for special angles without using technology?** |

1. a) Draw a unit circle on grid paper. Draw the terminal arm for an angle $\theta = 45°$ in standard position.

b) Mark the intersection of the terminal arm and the circle as point P.

c) Create a triangle by drawing a vertical line from point P to point A on the *x*-axis.

d) Consider the special relationships among the sides of △POA to determine an exact value for sides PA and OA. Alternatively, recall that the terminal arm of an angle θ in standard position intersects the unit circle at $P(x, y) = P(\cos\theta, \sin\theta)$.

e) Use the measures from part d) to write exact values for sin 45°, cos 45°, and tan 45°.

f) What is the exact equivalent of 45° in radian measure?

g) Record your results in a table like this one.

Tools

• compasses
• grid paper
• protractor

Special Angles and Trigonometric Ratios				
θ (degrees)	θ (radians)	$\sin\theta$	$\cos\theta$	$\tan\theta$
0°				
30°				
45°				
60°				
90°				

2. Use your unit circle to help you complete the table from step 1.

3. Consider the angles 120°, 135°, 150°, and 180°. Use the unit circle, the CAST rule, and the results from step 2 to extend the table for these angles.

4. Consider the angles 210°, 225°, 240°, and 270°. Use the unit circle, the CAST rule, and the results from step 2 to extend the table for these angles.

5. Consider the angles 300°, 315°, 330°, and 360°. Use the unit circle, the CAST rule, and the results from step 2 to extend the table for these angles.

6. Reflect Select two special angles from each quadrant. Use a calculator set to Radian mode to evaluate the three trigonometric ratios for each angle. Compare the results to those in your table.

CONNECTIONS

The triangles found in a geometry set are a 45°-45°-90° triangle and a 30°-60°-90° triangle. These triangles can be used to construct similar triangles with the same special relationships among the sides.

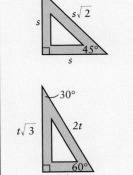

Example 1 Apply Trigonometric Ratios for Special Angles

Ravinder is flying his kite at the end of a 50-m string. The sun is directly overhead, and the string makes an angle of $\frac{\pi}{6}$ with the ground. The wind speed increases, and the kite flies higher until the string makes an angle of $\frac{\pi}{3}$ with the ground.

a) Determine an exact expression for the horizontal distance that the shadow of the kite moves between the two positions of the kite.

b) Determine the distance in part a), to the nearest tenth of a metre.

Solution

a) Draw a diagram to represent the situation. Place Ravinder at the origin.

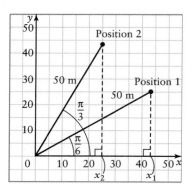

Use the exact values of the trigonometric ratios for $\frac{\pi}{6}$ and $\frac{\pi}{3}$ to write expressions for the two x-coordinates.

Position 1

$$\cos\frac{\pi}{6} = \frac{x_1}{50}$$

$$\frac{\sqrt{3}}{2} = \frac{x_1}{50}$$

$$\frac{50\sqrt{3}}{2} = x_1$$

$$x_1 = 25\sqrt{3}$$

Position 2

$$\cos\frac{\pi}{3} = \frac{x_2}{50}$$

$$\frac{1}{2} = \frac{x_2}{50}$$

$$\frac{50}{2} = x_2$$

$$x_2 = 25$$

Subtract the x-coordinates to determine the horizontal distance, d, that the shadow moves.

$$d = 25\sqrt{3} - 25$$
$$= 25(\sqrt{3} - 1)$$

An exact expression for the distance that the shadow of the kite moves is $25(\sqrt{3} - 1)$ m.

b) $25(\sqrt{3} - 1) \doteq 18.3$

The shadow of the kite moves approximately 18.3 m.

Example 2

Trigonometric Ratios for a Multiple of a Special Angle

Use the unit circle to determine exact values of the six trigonometric ratios for an angle of $\frac{3\pi}{4}$.

Solution

Sketch the angle in standard position. Let P be the point of intersection of the terminal arm and the unit circle. Create a triangle by drawing a perpendicular from point P to the x-axis. The angle between the terminal arm and the x-axis is $\frac{\pi}{4}$. The terminal arm of an angle of $\frac{\pi}{4}$ intersects the unit circle at a point with coordinates $\left(\frac{1}{\sqrt{2}}, \frac{1}{\sqrt{2}}\right)$. Since the terminal arm of an angle of $\frac{3\pi}{4}$ is in the second quadrant, the coordinates of the point of intersection are $P\left(-\frac{1}{\sqrt{2}}, \frac{1}{\sqrt{2}}\right)$.

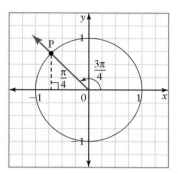

$$\sin\frac{3\pi}{4} = y$$
$$= \frac{1}{\sqrt{2}}$$

$$\cos\frac{3\pi}{4} = x$$
$$= -\frac{1}{\sqrt{2}}$$

$$\tan\frac{3\pi}{4} = \frac{y}{x}$$
$$= \frac{\frac{1}{\sqrt{2}}}{-\frac{1}{\sqrt{2}}}$$
$$= -1$$

$$\csc\frac{3\pi}{4} = \frac{1}{y}$$
$$= \frac{1}{\frac{1}{\sqrt{2}}}$$
$$= \sqrt{2}$$

$$\sec\frac{3\pi}{4} = \frac{1}{x}$$
$$= \frac{1}{-\frac{1}{\sqrt{2}}}$$
$$= -\sqrt{2}$$

$$\cot\frac{3\pi}{4} = \frac{x}{y}$$
$$= \frac{-\frac{1}{\sqrt{2}}}{\frac{1}{\sqrt{2}}}$$
$$= -1$$

≪ KEY CONCEPTS ≫

- You can use a calculator to calculate trigonometric ratios for an angle expressed in radian measure by setting the angle mode to radians.

- You can determine the reciprocal trigonometric ratios for an angle expressed in radian measure by first calculating the primary trigonometric ratios and then using the reciprocal key on a calculator.

- You can use the unit circle and special triangles to determine exact values for the trigonometric ratios of the special angles 0, $\frac{\pi}{6}$, $\frac{\pi}{4}$, $\frac{\pi}{3}$, and $\frac{\pi}{2}$.

- You can use the unit circle along with the CAST rule to determine exact values for the trigonometric ratios of multiples of the special angles.

Communicate Your Understanding

C1 Use a calculator to evaluate $\tan \frac{\pi}{2}$. Explain why the calculator returns this answer. Predict another trigonometric ratio that will return the same answer. Check your prediction with a calculator.

C2 Ancient mathematicians tried to represent π as a rational number. A fraction that is very close to π is $\frac{355}{113}$. Use a calculator to determine the decimal approximation of this fraction. Is it close enough to π to yield the same value for $\sin \pi$, to the limit of the accuracy of your calculator? Use a calculator to check.

C3 Does $\sin \frac{\pi}{2} = \frac{1}{2} \sin \pi$? Explain why or why not.

A) Practise

For help with questions 1 to 6, refer to Investigate 1.

1. a) Use a calculator to evaluate each trigonometric ratio, to four decimal places.

  i) $\sin 25°$ **ii)** $\cos 72°$

  iii) $\tan 115°$ **iv)** $\sin 165°$

  b) Use a calculator to evaluate each trigonometric ratio, to four decimal places.

  i) $\sin 0.436$ **ii)** $\cos 1.257$

  iii) $\tan 2.007$ **iv)** $\sin 2.880$

  c) Note any similarities between the answers to parts a) and b). Explain why they occur.

2. a) Use a calculator to evaluate each trigonometric ratio, to four decimal places.

  i) $\sin 1.21$ **ii)** $\cos 2.53$

  iii) $\tan 3.05$ **iv)** $\cos 4.72$

  b) Use a calculator to evaluate each trigonometric ratio, to four decimal places.

  i) $\sin 69°$ **ii)** $\cos 145°$

  iii) $\tan 175°$ **iv)** $\cos 270°$

  c) Note any similarities between the answers to parts a) and b). Explain why they occur.

3. Use a calculator to evaluate each trigonometric ratio, to four decimal places.

  a) $\sin \frac{\pi}{4}$ **b)** $\cos \frac{\pi}{7}$

  c) $\tan \frac{5\pi}{6}$ **d)** $\tan \frac{9\pi}{8}$

4. Use a calculator to evaluate each trigonometric ratio, to four decimal places.

  a) $\csc 15°$ **b)** $\sec 52°$

  c) $\cot 124°$ **d)** $\csc 338°$

5. Use a calculator to evaluate each trigonometric ratio, to four decimal places.

  a) $\csc 0.97$ **b)** $\sec 1.84$

  c) $\cot 3.21$ **d)** $\sec 5.95$

6. Use a calculator to evaluate each trigonometric ratio, to four decimal places.

  a) $\csc \frac{7\pi}{6}$ **b)** $\sec \frac{3\pi}{11}$

  c) $\cot \frac{13\pi}{5}$ **d)** $\cot \frac{17\pi}{9}$

For help with questions 7 and 8, refer to Example 2.

7. Use the unit circle to determine exact values of the primary trigonometric ratios for each angle.

  a) $\frac{2\pi}{3}$ **b)** $\frac{5\pi}{6}$

  c) $\frac{3\pi}{2}$ **d)** $\frac{7\pi}{4}$

8. Use the unit circle to determine exact values of the six trigonometric ratios for each angle.

  a) $\frac{7\pi}{6}$ **b)** $\frac{4\pi}{3}$

  c) $\frac{5\pi}{4}$ **d)** π

For help with questions 9 and 10, refer to Example 1.

9. Lynda is flying her kite at the end of a 40-m string. The string makes an angle of $\frac{\pi}{4}$ with the ground. The wind speed increases, and the kite flies higher until the string makes an angle of $\frac{\pi}{3}$ with the ground.

   a) Determine an exact expression for the horizontal distance that the kite moves between the two positions.

   b) Determine an exact expression for the vertical distance that the kite moves between the two positions.

   c) Determine approximate answers for parts a) and b), to the nearest tenth of a metre.

10. Refer to question 9. Suppose that the length of string is 40 m at an angle of $\frac{\pi}{4}$, but then Lynda lets out the string to a length of 60 m as the angle changes to $\frac{\pi}{3}$.

   a) Determine an exact expression for the horizontal distance that the kite moves between the two positions.

   b) Does the kite move closer to Lynda, horizontally, or farther away? Justify your answer.

   c) Determine an exact expression for the vertical distance that the kite moves between the two positions. Does the altitude of the kite above the ground increase or decrease? Justify your answer.

   d) Determine approximate answers for parts a) and c), to the nearest tenth of a metre.

11. a) Determine an exact value for each expression.

   i) $\dfrac{\sin \frac{\pi}{3} \tan \frac{\pi}{6}}{\cos \frac{\pi}{4}}$ ii) $\tan \frac{\pi}{4} + \tan \frac{\pi}{6} \tan \frac{\pi}{3}$

   b) Use a calculator to check your answers to part a).

12. a) Determine an exact value for each expression.

   i) $\dfrac{\cos \frac{4\pi}{3} \tan \frac{5\pi}{6}}{\sin \frac{3\pi}{4}}$

   ii) $\cot \frac{5\pi}{4} + \tan \frac{11\pi}{6} \tan \frac{5\pi}{3}$

   b) Use a calculator to check your answers to part a).

13. Two triangular building lots, ABC and ACD, have side AC in common. ∠ABC and ∠ACD are right angles. $\angle CAB = \frac{\pi}{6}$ and $\angle DAC = \frac{\pi}{4}$. Side DA measures 60 m.

   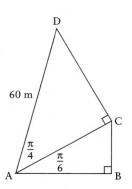

   a) Determine an exact expression for the length of side AC.

   b) Determine an exact expression for the length of side AB.

14. When Sunita received her bachelor's degree in mathematics, her friends presented her with a "radian watch." Her friends repainted the face of the watch. Instead of the usual numbers around the face, they replaced the 12 with 0 and the 6 with π. The hour and minute hands of the watch run in the usual clockwise direction. A radian time of π is shown in the diagram.

   a) What radian time corresponds to 3:00?

   b) What radian time corresponds to 4:00?

   c) What normal time corresponds to a radian time of $\frac{3\pi}{2}$?

   d) What normal time corresponds to a radian time of $\frac{11\pi}{6}$?

   e) What radian time corresponds to 7:30?

15. Use Technology You can set the angle units in *The Geometer's Sketchpad®* to radians and then calculate trigonometric ratios for angles measured in radians.

a) Open *The Geometer's Sketchpad®*. From the **Edit** menu, choose **Preferences…**. Click on the **Units** tab. Set the angle units to radians and the precision to thousandths for all measurements. Click on **OK**.

b) Construct a right $\triangle ABC$ such that $\angle B$ is a right angle. Measure $\angle B$. If it does not appear to be a right angle, adjust your diagram until it is. How is radian measure expressed in *The Geometer's Sketchpad®*?

c) Measure $\angle A$ and $\angle C$. Taking care not to change $\angle B$, adjust the triangle until $\angle A = \frac{\pi}{6}$ and $\angle C = \frac{\pi}{3}$.

d) Use the **Measure** menu to calculate values for sin $\angle A$, cos $\angle A$, and tan $\angle A$. Compare these calculations with your Special Angles and Trigonometric Ratios table from Investigate 2.

Technology Tip   ⠂⠂

When it is in radian mode, *The Geometer's Sketchpad®* uses directed angles (angles with signs). If an angle measurement is negative, select the points that define the angle in the opposite order.

---

16. a) Determine an exact value for each expression.

i) $\sin \dfrac{4\pi}{3} \cos \dfrac{5\pi}{3} + \sin \dfrac{5\pi}{3} \cos \dfrac{4\pi}{3}$

ii) $\sin \dfrac{5\pi}{4} \cos \dfrac{3\pi}{4} - \sin \dfrac{3\pi}{4} \cos \dfrac{5\pi}{4}$

b) Use a calculator to verify your answers to part a).

17. a) Determine an exact value for each expression.

i) $\cos \dfrac{11\pi}{6} \cos \dfrac{\pi}{6} - \sin \dfrac{11\pi}{6} \sin \dfrac{\pi}{6}$

ii) $\cos \dfrac{7\pi}{4} \cos \dfrac{\pi}{4} + \sin \dfrac{7\pi}{4} \sin \dfrac{\pi}{4}$

b) Use a calculator to verify your answers to part a).

18. a) Determine an exact value for each expression.

i) $\dfrac{\tan \dfrac{\pi}{4} + \tan \dfrac{3\pi}{4}}{1 - \tan \dfrac{\pi}{4} \tan \dfrac{3\pi}{4}}$

ii) $\dfrac{\tan \dfrac{5\pi}{3} - \tan \dfrac{7\pi}{6}}{1 + \tan \dfrac{5\pi}{3} \tan \dfrac{7\pi}{6}}$

b) Use a calculator to verify your answers to part a).

19. Chapter Problem The engineering software used to design modern vehicles must include routines to render models of three-dimensional objects onto a two-dimensional computer screen. The software constructs the model in a three-dimensional world, represented by a box, and then projects the model onto the computer screen, represented by the front of the box.

To get an idea of how this works, consider a three-dimensional model that includes line segment OA, as shown. OA lies along an angle of $\frac{\pi}{4}$ from the plane of the screen, and upward at an angle of $\frac{\pi}{6}$ from the bottom plane. The line segment OD is the rendering of OA in the plane of the screen. If OA is 10 cm long, show that the length of OC is given by the expression $10 \cos \dfrac{\pi}{6} \cos \dfrac{\pi}{4}$.

20. Consider the equation
$2 \sin x \cos y = \sin (x + y) + \sin (x - y)$.
Emilio claims that substituting $x = \dfrac{5\pi}{4}$ and
$y = \dfrac{3\pi}{4}$ makes the equation true.

a) Determine an exact value for the left side using Emilio's solution.

b) Determine an exact value for the right side using Emilio's solution.

c) Is Emilio correct?

d) Is $x = \dfrac{5\pi}{6}$ and $y = \dfrac{\pi}{6}$ a solution? Justify your answer.

e) Based on the answers to parts c) and d), is it reasonable to conclude that the equation is true no matter what angles are substituted for x and y? Justify your answer.

C   Extend and Challenge

21. Another way to measure angles is to use gradians. These units were intended to replace degree measure when the metric system was developed in France in the 1790s. A complete revolution is 400 grads.

a) Determine the six trigonometric ratios of an angle measuring 150 grads.

b) Explain why, in general, conversions of angle measures from degrees to gradians or from radians to gradians is difficult.

22. Use Technology For small angles, the measure of an angle in radians and the sine of that angle are approximately equal. Investigate the domain over which this approximation is accurate to two decimal places. The instructions below assume the use of a graphing calculator. You can also use a spreadsheet or a CAS.

a) Set a graphing calculator to Radian mode, and set the accuracy to two decimal places.

b) Clear all lists. In list **L1**, enter the numbers 0, 0.1, 0.2, ..., 1.0.

c) In list **L2**, enter the formula sin(L1).

d) Over what domain does the approximation seem to be accurate to two decimal places?

e) Modify this method to determine the domain over which the approximation is valid to three decimal places.

23. a) Determine an expression using trigonometric ratios of special angles that simplifies to an answer of $\dfrac{1}{2}$. You must use three different angles and three different ratios.

b) Trade expressions with a classmate and simplify.

c) Trade solutions and resolve any concerns.

24. Math Contest $0 = \dfrac{-5}{13}$, then which of the following is a possible value of $\sin\left(\dfrac{\theta}{2}\right)$?

A $\dfrac{\sqrt{26}}{26}$ **B** $\dfrac{\sqrt{3}}{3}$ **C** $\dfrac{2\sqrt{2}}{13}$ **D** $\dfrac{\sqrt{3}}{12}$

25. Math Contest The term *inverse sine* is confusing to some students who have studied functions and their inverses as reflections in the line $y = x$. In this case, inverse sine indicates that you are looking for the angle that gives the indicated ratio. Another term that is sometimes used to mean the same as $\sin^{-1}$ is *arcsin*. Determine the exact value of
$\tan\left(\arcsin\left(\dfrac{-4}{5}\right)\right)$ for $\dfrac{\pi}{2} \le \theta \le \dfrac{3\pi}{2}$.

A $\dfrac{5}{4}$ **B** $\dfrac{4}{3}$ **C** $\dfrac{1}{\sqrt{3}}$ **D** $\dfrac{\sqrt{3}}{2}$

4.3

Equivalent Trigonometric Expressions

When trigonometry is used to model a real-world application, such as a system of gears for an automobile transmission or the acoustic response of a concert hall, the expressions and equations generated can become very complicated. These expressions can often be simplified by substituting **equivalent trignometric expressions**, which are expressions that yield the same value for all values of the variable. In this section, you will learn how to show that certain trigonometric expressions are equivalent, and you will assemble a table of equivalent expressions for use in subsequent sections.

Investigate 1	**How can you use a right triangle to determine equivalent trigonometric expressions?**

1. Sketch $\triangle ABC$ such that $\angle B$ is a right angle. Mark $\angle B$ as $\frac{\pi}{2}$.

2. Mark $\angle A$ as x. Use the sum of the interior angles of a triangle to derive an expression for the measure of $\angle C$ in terms of x.

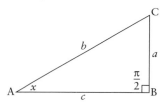

3. Determine an expression for $\sin x$ in terms of the sides of the triangle, a, b, and c.

4. Determine expressions for the sine, cosine, and tangent of $\angle C$ in terms of the sides of the triangle. Which of these is equal to $\sin x$?

5. **Reflect**

   a) You have shown that $\sin x$ and $\cos\left(\frac{\pi}{2} - x\right)$ are equivalent trigonometric expressions. Does the relationship between these equivalent expressions depend on the value of x? Justify your answer.

   b) What is the sum of x and $\left(\frac{\pi}{2} - x\right)$? What name is given to a pair of angles such as x and $\left(\frac{\pi}{2} - x\right)$?

6. Use $\triangle ABC$ to determine equivalent trigonometric expressions for $\cos x$ and $\tan x$.

7. Use △ABC to determine equivalent trigonometric expressions for $\csc x$, $\sec x$, and $\cot x$.

8. Summarize the six relations among trigonometric functions in a table like the one shown. The first line has been entered for you.

Trigonometric Identities
$\sin x = \cos\left(\frac{\pi}{2} - x\right)$

9. Reflect An identity is an equation that is true for all values of the variable for which the expressions on both sides of the equation are defined. An identity involving trigonometric expressions is called a **trigonometric identity**. The trigonometric identities in step 8 are known as the cofunction identities. Why are they called *cofunction* identities? Suggest an easy way to remember these identities.

CONNECTIONS

Sometimes the cofunction identities are referred to as the *co-related angle identities*.

Investigate 2	**How can you use transformations to determine equivalent trigonometric expressions?**

1. Draw a unit circle with centre O.

2. Draw the terminal arm for an angle x in standard position in the first quadrant, $x \in \left[0, \frac{\pi}{2}\right]$. Let the intersection of the unit circle and the terminal arm of angle x be represented by point P. Label the coordinates of point P in terms of the appropriate trigonometric functions of angle x.

3. Transform P to P′ by applying a rotation of $\frac{\pi}{2}$ counterclockwise about the origin. Label the coordinates of P′ in terms of the appropriate trigonometric functions of angle $\left(x + \frac{\pi}{2}\right)$.

4. Create △PQO by drawing a vertical line from point P to point Q on the x-axis. Similarly, create △OQ′P′.

Tools

- compasses and protractor
  OR
- computer with *The Geometer's Sketchpad*®

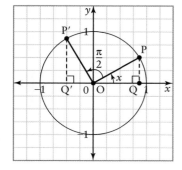

CONNECTIONS

The symbol ≅ means "is congruent to." Congruent geometric figures have exactly the same shape and size.

5. Explain why $\triangle PQO \cong \triangle OQ'P'$.

6. Use the coordinates of points P and P′ to show that $\cos\left(x + \dfrac{\pi}{2}\right)$ and $-\sin x$ are equivalent trigonometric expressions.

7. Determine an equivalent trigonometric expression of angle x for $\sin\left(x + \dfrac{\pi}{2}\right)$.

8. Determine an equivalent trigonometric expression of angle x for $\tan\left(x + \dfrac{\pi}{2}\right)$.

9. Determine an equivalent trigonometric expression of angle x for each of $\csc\left(x + \dfrac{\pi}{2}\right)$, $\sec\left(x + \dfrac{\pi}{2}\right)$, and $\cot\left(x + \dfrac{\pi}{2}\right)$.

10. Extend your table from step 8 of Investigate 1 to summarize these six relations among trigonometric functions.

11. Reflect You now have 12 trigonometric identities in your table, which all feature the angle $\dfrac{\pi}{2}$. Similar identities are possible using other angles, such as π, $\dfrac{3\pi}{2}$, and 2π. Use the unit circle to derive an equivalent trigonometric expression for $\cos(\pi - x)$ in terms of angle x.

CONNECTIONS

After a rotation of $\dfrac{\pi}{2}$, or 90°, counterclockwise about the origin, the coordinates of the point (x, y) become $(-y, x)$.

| Example 1 | **Use Equivalent Trigonometric Expressions to Evaluate Primary Trigonometric Expressions** |

Given that $\sin\dfrac{\pi}{5} \doteq 0.5878$, use equivalent trigonometric expressions to evaluate the following, to four decimal places.

a) $\cos\dfrac{3\pi}{10}$

b) $\cos\dfrac{7\pi}{10}$

Solution

a) Since an angle of $\dfrac{3\pi}{10}$ lies in the first quadrant, it can be expressed as a difference between $\dfrac{\pi}{2}$ and an angle a. Find the measure of angle a.

$$\dfrac{3\pi}{10} = \dfrac{\pi}{2} - a$$

$$a = \dfrac{\pi}{2} - \dfrac{3\pi}{10}$$

$$a = \dfrac{5\pi}{10} - \dfrac{3\pi}{10}$$

$$a = \dfrac{2\pi}{10}$$

$$a = \dfrac{\pi}{5}$$

Now apply a cofunction identity.

$$\cos\dfrac{3\pi}{10} = \cos\left(\dfrac{\pi}{2} - \dfrac{\pi}{5}\right)$$

$$= \sin\dfrac{\pi}{5}$$

$$\doteq 0.5878$$

b) Since an angle of $\dfrac{7\pi}{10}$ lies in the second quadrant, it can be expressed as a sum of $\dfrac{\pi}{2}$ and an angle a.

$$a + \dfrac{\pi}{2} = \dfrac{7\pi}{10}$$

$$a = \dfrac{7\pi}{10} - \dfrac{\pi}{2}$$

$$a = \dfrac{7\pi}{10} - \dfrac{5\pi}{10}$$

$$a = \dfrac{2\pi}{10}$$

$$a = \dfrac{\pi}{5}$$

Now apply a trigonometric identity.

$$\cos \dfrac{7\pi}{10} = \cos\left(\dfrac{\pi}{5} + \dfrac{\pi}{2}\right)$$

$$= -\sin\dfrac{\pi}{5}$$

$$\doteq -0.5878$$

Example 2	**Use an Equivalent Trigonometric Expression to Evaluate a Reciprocal Trigonometric Expression**

Given that $\csc \dfrac{2\pi}{7} \doteq 1.2790$, use an equivalent trigonometric expression to determine $\sec \dfrac{3\pi}{14}$, to four decimal places.

Solution

An angle of $\dfrac{3\pi}{14}$ lies in the first quadrant. Express $\dfrac{3\pi}{14}$ as a difference between $\dfrac{\pi}{2}$ and an angle a. Then, apply a cofunction identity.

$$\dfrac{3\pi}{14} = \dfrac{\pi}{2} - a$$

$$a = \dfrac{\pi}{2} - \dfrac{3\pi}{14}$$

$$a = \dfrac{7\pi}{14} - \dfrac{3\pi}{14}$$

$$a = \dfrac{4\pi}{14}$$

$$a = \dfrac{2\pi}{7}$$

Therefore,

$$\sec \dfrac{3\pi}{14} = \sec\left(\dfrac{\pi}{2} - \dfrac{2\pi}{7}\right)$$

$$= \csc\dfrac{2\pi}{7}$$

$$\doteq 1.2790$$

Example 3	Use Graphing Technology to Verify Equivalent Trigonometric Expressions

Use a graphing calculator to verify that $\sin x = \cos\left(\frac{\pi}{2} - x\right)$.

> **Solution**

Ensure that your calculator is set to Radian mode and that all stat plots are turned off.

Use the **Y=** editor to enter $\sin x$ in **Y1** and $\cos\left(\frac{\pi}{2} - x\right)$ in **Y2**.

Change the line display for **Y2** to heavy.

- Cursor left to the slanted line beside **Y2**.

- Press (ENTER) to change the line style.

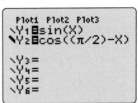

From the **ZOOM** menu, select **6:ZStandard**. The graph of $\sin x$ will be drawn first. Then, the graph of $\cos\left(\frac{\pi}{2} - x\right)$ will be drawn with a heavier line. You can pause the plot by pressing (ENTER). Pressing (ENTER) again will resume the plot.

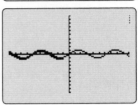

CONNECTIONS

You have graphed trigonometric functions in degree measure before. You can also graph these functions in radian measure.

Technology Tip ∴

If you want to watch the plot again, you cannot just press (GRAPH). The graphing calculator will simply display the completed plot. To see the plot again, return to the **Y=** editor, clear **Y1**, and then re-enter $\sin x$. When you press (GRAPH), both curves will be re-plotted.

KEY CONCEPTS

- You can use a right triangle to derive equivalent trigonometric expressions that form the cofunction identities, such as $\sin x = \cos\left(\frac{\pi}{2} - x\right)$.

- You can use the unit circle along with transformations to derive equivalent trigonometric expressions that form other trigonometric identities, such as $\cos\left(\frac{\pi}{2} + x\right) = -\sin x$.

- Given a trigonometric expression of a known angle, you can use equivalent trigonometric expressions to evaluate trigonometric expressions of other angles.

- You can use graphing technology to demonstrate that two trigonometric expressions are equivalent.

Trigonometric Identities Featuring $\frac{\pi}{2}$			
Cofunction Identities			
$\sin x = \cos\left(\frac{\pi}{2} - x\right)$	$\cos x = \sin\left(\frac{\pi}{2} - x\right)$	$\sin\left(x + \frac{\pi}{2}\right) = \cos x$	$\cos\left(x + \frac{\pi}{2}\right) = -\sin x$
$\tan x = \cot\left(\frac{\pi}{2} - x\right)$	$\cot x = \tan\left(\frac{\pi}{2} - x\right)$	$\tan\left(x + \frac{\pi}{2}\right) = -\cot x$	$\cot\left(x + \frac{\pi}{2}\right) = -\tan x$
$\csc x = \sec\left(\frac{\pi}{2} - x\right)$	$\sec x = \csc\left(\frac{\pi}{2} - x\right)$	$\csc\left(x + \frac{\pi}{2}\right) = \sec x$	$\sec\left(x + \frac{\pi}{2}\right) = -\csc x$

Communicate Your Understanding

C1 Is $\cos(x + \pi)$ an equivalent trigonometric expression for $\cos x$? Justify your answer using the unit circle. Check your answer with graphing technology.

C2 Does $\cos\left(\dfrac{\pi}{2} - x\right) = \cos\dfrac{\pi}{2} - \cos x$? Investigate using the unit circle. Check your answer with a calculator.

C3 Does $\cos\left(\dfrac{\pi}{2} - x\right) = -\cos\left(x - \dfrac{\pi}{2}\right)$? Investigate using the unit circle. Check your answer with a calculator.

A) Practise

For help with questions 1 and 2, refer to Investigate 1.

1. Given that $\sin\dfrac{\pi}{6} = \dfrac{1}{2}$, use an equivalent trigonometric expression to show that $\cos\dfrac{\pi}{3} = \dfrac{1}{2}$.

2. Given that $\cos\dfrac{\pi}{4} = \dfrac{1}{\sqrt{2}}$, use an equivalent trigonometric expression to show that $\sin\dfrac{\pi}{4} = \dfrac{1}{\sqrt{2}}$.

For help with questions 3 and 4, refer to Investigate 2.

3. Given that $\sin\dfrac{\pi}{6} = \dfrac{1}{2}$, use an equivalent trigonometric expression to show that $\cos\dfrac{2\pi}{3} = -\dfrac{1}{2}$.

4. Given that $\csc\dfrac{\pi}{4} = \sqrt{2}$, use an equivalent trigonometric expression to show that $\sec\dfrac{3\pi}{4} = -\sqrt{2}$.

For help with questions 5 to 10, refer to Examples 1 and 2.

5. Given that $\cos\dfrac{\pi}{7} = \sin y$, first express $\dfrac{\pi}{7}$ as a difference between $\dfrac{\pi}{2}$ and an angle, and then apply a cofunction identity to determine the measure of angle y.

6. Given that $\cot\dfrac{4\pi}{9} = \tan z$, first express $\dfrac{4\pi}{9}$ as a difference between $\dfrac{\pi}{2}$ and an angle, and then apply a cofunction identity to determine the measure of angle z.

7. Given that $\cos\dfrac{13\pi}{18} = -\sin y$, first express $\dfrac{13\pi}{18}$ as a sum of $\dfrac{\pi}{2}$ and an angle, and then apply a trigonometric identity to determine the measure of angle y.

8. Given that $\cot\dfrac{13\pi}{14} = -\tan z$, first express $\dfrac{13\pi}{14}$ as a sum of $\dfrac{\pi}{2}$ and an angle, and then apply a trigonometric identity to determine the measure of angle z.

9. Given that $\cos\dfrac{3\pi}{11} \doteq 0.6549$, use equivalent trigonometric expressions to evaluate the following, to four decimal places.

   a) $\sin\dfrac{5\pi}{22}$ **b)** $\sin\dfrac{17\pi}{22}$

10. Given that $\tan\dfrac{2\pi}{9} \doteq 0.8391$, use equivalent trigonometric expressions to evaluate the following, to four decimal places.

   a) $\cot\dfrac{5\pi}{18}$ **b)** $\cot\dfrac{13\pi}{18}$

11. Given that $\csc a = \sec 1.45$ and that a lies in the first quadrant, use a cofunction identity to determine the measure of angle a, to two decimal places.

12. Given that $\sec b = \csc 0.64$ and that b lies in the first quadrant, use a cofunction identity to determine the measure of angle b, to two decimal places.

13. Given that $\csc a = \sec 0.75$ and that a lies in the second quadrant, determine the measure of angle a, to two decimal places.

14. Given that $-\sec b = \csc 1.34$ and that b lies in the second quadrant, determine the measure of angle b, to two decimal places.

For help with questions 15 to 19, refer to Investigate 2.

15. Use the unit circle to investigate equivalent expressions involving the six trigonometric functions of $(\pi - x)$, where x lies in the first quadrant. Add these to your trigonometric identities table from Investigate 2.

16. Use the unit circle to investigate equivalent expressions involving the six trigonometric functions of $(x + \pi)$, where x lies in the first quadrant. Add these to your trigonometric identities table from Investigate 2.

17. Use the unit circle to investigate equivalent expressions involving the six trigonometric functions of $\left(\dfrac{3\pi}{2} - x\right)$, where x lies in the first quadrant. Add these to your trigonometric identities table from Investigate 2.

18. Use the unit circle to investigate equivalent expressions involving the six trigonometric functions of $\left(x + \dfrac{3\pi}{2}\right)$, where x lies in the first quadrant. Add these to your trigonometric identities table from Investigate 2.

19. Use the unit circle to investigate equivalent expressions involving the six trigonometric functions of $(2\pi - x)$, where x lies in the first quadrant. Add these to your trigonometric identities table from Investigate 2.

For help with question 20, refer to Example 3.

20. **Use Technology** Select one trigonometric identity from each of questions 15 to 19. Use graphing technology to verify the identities.

21. Charmaine finds that the [SIN] key on her calculator is not working. Determine two different ways that she can find $\sin \dfrac{9\pi}{13}$ without using the [SIN] key.

Reasoning and Proving
Representing — Selecting Tools
Problem Solving
Connecting — Reflecting
Communicating

22. **Chapter Problem**

   a) When a pilot banks an aircraft moving at a speed v, in metres per second, at an angle θ, the radius of the turn that results is given by the formula $r = \dfrac{v^2}{g} \tan\left(\dfrac{\pi}{2} - \theta\right)$, where g is the acceleration due to gravity, or 9.8 m/s². Use an appropriate equivalent trigonometric expression to show that this formula can be simplified to $r = \dfrac{v^2}{g \tan \theta}$.

   b) A pilot is flying an aircraft at a speed of 50 m/s, and banks at an angle of $\dfrac{\pi}{4}$. Determine the radius of the turn, to the nearest metre.

✓ **Achievement Check**

23. Determine an exact value for angle a such that $\sec a = \csc (3a)$.

   a) Write the cofunction identity related to this problem.

   b) In the cofunction identity, what is the sum of the arguments on the left side and the right side?

   c) Write an equation relating the sum in part b) to the sum of the arguments on the left side and the right side of the given equation. Then, solve for a.

   d) Check your solution.

24. a) Determine an exact value of b such that
$$\csc\left(6b + \frac{\pi}{8}\right) = \sec\left(2b - \frac{\pi}{8}\right).$$

   b) Check your answer.

25. a) Determine an exact value of c such that
$$\cot\left(4c - \frac{\pi}{4}\right) + \tan\left(2c + \frac{\pi}{4}\right) = 0.$$

   b) Check your answer.

26. a) Use one of the equivalent trigonometric expressions from questions 15 to 19 to develop a problem similar to question 24 or 25.

   b) Exchange problems with a classmate. Solve each other's problem.

   c) Return the solutions, and check. Resolve any concerns.

27. Given $\triangle ABC$ with sides a, b, and c, show that the area of the triangle is given by
$$A = \frac{a^2 \sin B \sin C}{2 \sin (B + C)}.$$

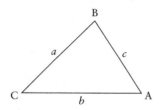

28. **Math Contest** Refer to Section 4.1, question 27.

   a) Determine the polar coordinates, (r, θ), of each point given in Cartesian coordinates. Use the domain $-\pi \le \theta \le \pi$.

   i) $\left(\frac{1}{2}, \frac{\sqrt{3}}{2}\right)$ ii) $\left(\frac{5\sqrt{3}}{2}, -\frac{5}{2}\right)$

   b) Determine the Cartesian coordinates, (x, y), of each point given in polar form.

   i) $\left(3, \frac{\pi}{6}\right)$ ii) $(4, 3\pi)$

   c) Give the general form of all terminal rays that pass from O (the origin) through point A, where

   i) $\theta = \frac{\pi}{6}$ ii) $\theta = -\frac{\pi}{3}$

29. **Math Contest** Use the unit circle shown to prove that $\tan\frac{1}{2}\theta = \frac{\sin\theta}{1 + \cos\theta}$.

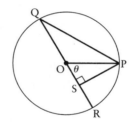

CAREER CONNECTION

Rapid advances in computer technology are mainly a result of the research efforts of computer hardware engineers. Lucas completed a 4-year bachelor's degree in computer engineering at McMaster University. This program gave him the skills to research, design, develop, and test computer equipment for scientific use. In his job as a computer hardware engineer, he does research in the field of neural networks and assists in the design of robots that mimic the behaviour of the human brain. Lucas needs to have an expert understanding of how all parts of a computer work. A good knowledge of trigonometry is vital when designing an efficient robot.

4.4 Compound Angle Formulas

The electromagnetic waves that are used to broadcast radio and television signals can be modelled using trigonometric expressions. Since these waves are moving away from the broadcasting antenna, they depend on both position x and time t. A possible modelling expression looks like $\sin(x + 2\pi ft)$. A trigonometric expression that depends on two or more angles is known as a **compound angle expression**. In this section, you will see how compound angle formulas are developed and learn how to apply them.

Investigate | How can you verify a compound angle formula?

1. The compound angle addition formula for cosine is
$\cos(x + y) = \cos x \cos y - \sin x \sin y$. Suppose that $x = \dfrac{\pi}{6}$ and $y = \dfrac{\pi}{3}$. Substitute these angles into the formula. Simplify the expression for $x + y$.

2. Use your Special Angles and Trigonometric Ratios table from Section 4.2 to evaluate the trigonometric ratios and simplify both sides. Is the formula true for these values of x and y?

3. a) Suppose that $x = \dfrac{\pi}{5}$ and $y = \dfrac{\pi}{7}$. Substitute these angles into the formula given in step 1.

   b) Use a calculator to evaluate each side of the formula. Is the formula true for these values of x and y?

4. Repeat step 3 with $x = \dfrac{2\pi}{9}$ and $y = \dfrac{\pi}{8}$.

5. **Reflect** Based on your results, can you conclude that the formula is valid for any choice of angles? Justify your answer.

6. **Reflect** It is tempting to conjecture that $\cos(x + y) = \cos x + \cos y$. Show that this is not generally true for angles x and y.

Addition Formula for Cosine

The unit circle can be used to show that the formula
$\cos(x + y) = \cos x \cos y - \sin x \sin y$ is valid for all angles. Consider the unit circle shown.

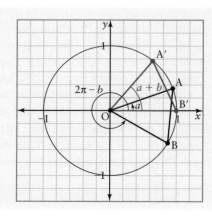

Point A is on the terminal arm of angle a, and point B is on the terminal arm of angle $2\pi - b$.

Rotate OA and OB counterclockwise about the origin through an angle b.
Point A' is on the terminal arm of angle $a + b$, and point B' is on the x-axis.

Join A to B and A' to B'.

The coordinates of the four points are
A($\cos a$, $\sin a$)
A'($\cos(a + b)$, $\sin(a + b)$)
B'(1, 0)
B($\cos(2\pi - b)$, $\sin(2\pi - b)$)

You can use equivalent trigonometric expressions from Section 4.3 to write the coordinates of point B as
B($\cos b$, $-\sin b$)

Since lengths are preserved under a rotation, A'B' = AB.

Apply the distance formula $d = \sqrt{(x_2 - x_1)^2 + (y_2 - y_1)^2}$ to A'B' and AB.

$$\sqrt{[\cos(a + b) - 1]^2 + [\sin(a + b) - 0]^2} = \sqrt{(\cos a - \cos b)^2 + [\sin a - (-\sin b)]^2}$$

$[\cos(a + b) - 1]^2 + [\sin(a + b) - 0]^2 = (\cos a - \cos b)^2 + [\sin a - (-\sin b)]^2$ Square both sides.

$\cos^2(a + b) - 2\cos(a + b) + 1 + \sin^2(a + b) = \cos^2 a - 2\cos a\cos b + \cos^2 b + \sin^2 a + 2\sin a \sin b + \sin^2 b$ Expand the binomials.

$\sin^2(a + b) + \cos^2(a + b) + 1 - 2\cos(a + b) = \sin^2 a + \cos^2 a + \sin^2 b + \cos^2 b - 2\cos a\cos b + 2\sin a \sin b$ Rearrange the terms.

$1 + 1 - 2\cos(a + b) = 1 + 1 - 2\cos a\cos b + 2\sin a \sin b$ Apply the Pythagorean identity, $\sin^2 x + \cos^2 x = 1$.

$-2\cos(a + b) = -2\cos a\cos b + 2\sin a \sin b$

$\cos(a + b) = \cos a\cos b - \sin a \sin b$ Divide both sides by -2.

The addition formula for cosine is usually written as $\cos(x + y) = \cos x\cos y - \sin x \sin y$.

Subtraction Formula for Cosine

The subtraction formula for cosine can be derived from the addition formula for cosine.

$\cos(x + y) = \cos x\cos y - \sin x \sin y$

$\cos(x + (-y)) = \cos x\cos(-y) - \sin x \sin(-y)$ Substitute $-y$ for y.

$\cos(x - y) = \cos x\cos(2\pi - y) - \sin x \sin(2\pi - y)$ From the unit circle, angle $-y$ is the same as angle $(2\pi - y)$.

$\cos(x - y) = \cos x\cos y - \sin x(-\sin y)$ $\cos(2\pi - y) = \cos y$; $\sin(2\pi - y) = -\sin y$

$\cos(x - y) = \cos x\cos y + \sin x \sin y$

Addition Formula for Sine

Recall the cofunction identities $\sin x = \cos\left(\frac{\pi}{2} - x\right)$ and $\cos x = \sin\left(\frac{\pi}{2} - x\right)$.

Apply these and the subtraction formula for cosine.

$$\sin(x + y) = \cos\left[\frac{\pi}{2} - (x + y)\right]$$ Apply a cofunction identity.

$$= \cos\left[\left(\frac{\pi}{2} - x\right) - y\right]$$ Regroup the terms in the argument.

$$= \cos\left(\frac{\pi}{2} - x\right)\cos y + \sin\left(\frac{\pi}{2} - x\right)\sin y$$ Apply the subtraction formula for cosine.

$$= \sin x \cos y + \cos x \sin y$$ Apply cofunction identities.

Subtraction Formula for Sine

The subtraction formula for sine can be derived from the addition formula for sine, following the approach used for the subtraction formula for cosine.

$$\sin(x + (-y)) = \sin x \cos(-y) + \cos x \sin(-y)$$ Substitute $-y$ for y.

$$\sin(x - y) = \sin x \cos y + \cos x(-\sin y)$$

$$\sin(x - y) = \sin x \cos y - \cos x \sin y$$

Example 1   Test Compound Angle Formulas

a) Show that the formula $\cos(x - y) = \cos x \cos y + \sin x \sin y$ is true for $x = \frac{\pi}{3}$ and $y = \frac{\pi}{6}$.

b) Show that the formula $\sin(x + y) = \sin x \cos y + \cos x \sin y$ is true for $x = \frac{\pi}{2}$ and $y = \frac{3\pi}{4}$.

Solution

a) Consider the left side and right side separately and verify that they are equal.

$$\begin{aligned}
\text{L.S.} &= \cos(x - y) & \text{R.S.} &= \cos x \cos y + \sin x \sin y\\
&= \cos\left(\frac{\pi}{3} - \frac{\pi}{6}\right) & &= \cos\frac{\pi}{3}\cos\frac{\pi}{6} + \sin\frac{\pi}{3}\sin\frac{\pi}{6}\\
&= \cos\left(\frac{2\pi}{6} - \frac{\pi}{6}\right) & &= \frac{1}{2} \times \frac{\sqrt{3}}{2} + \frac{\sqrt{3}}{2} \times \frac{1}{2}\\
&= \cos\left(\frac{\pi}{6}\right) & &= \frac{\sqrt{3}}{4} + \frac{\sqrt{3}}{4}\\
&= \frac{\sqrt{3}}{2} & &= \frac{2\sqrt{3}}{4}\\
& & &= \frac{\sqrt{3}}{2}
\end{aligned}$$

$$\text{L.S.} = \text{R.S.}$$

The formula is valid for $x = \frac{\pi}{3}$ and $y = \frac{\pi}{6}$.

b) L.S. $= \sin(x + y)$

$$= \sin\left(\frac{\pi}{2} + \frac{3\pi}{4}\right)$$

$$= \sin\left(\frac{2\pi}{4} + \frac{3\pi}{4}\right)$$

$$= \sin\left(\frac{5\pi}{4}\right)$$

$$= -\frac{1}{\sqrt{2}}$$

R.S. $= \sin x \cos y + \cos x \sin y$

$$= \sin\frac{\pi}{2}\cos\frac{3\pi}{4} + \cos\frac{\pi}{2}\sin\frac{3\pi}{4}$$

$$= 1 \times \left(-\frac{1}{\sqrt{2}}\right) + 0 \times \frac{1}{\sqrt{2}}$$

$$= -\frac{1}{\sqrt{2}} + 0$$

$$= -\frac{1}{\sqrt{2}}$$

L.S. = R.S.

The formula is valid for $x = \dfrac{\pi}{2}$ and $y = \dfrac{\pi}{4}$.

Example 2	Determine Exact Trigonometric Ratios for Angles Other Than Special Angles

a) Use an appropriate compound angle formula to determine an exact value for $\sin\dfrac{\pi}{12}$.

b) Check your answer using a calculator.

Solution

a) First, express the non-special angle as a sum or difference of two special angles. In this case,

$$\frac{\pi}{3} - \frac{\pi}{4} = \frac{4\pi}{12} - \frac{3\pi}{12}$$

$$= \frac{\pi}{12}$$

$$\sin\frac{\pi}{12} = \sin\left(\frac{\pi}{3} - \frac{\pi}{4}\right) \qquad \text{Write the given angle as a difference.}$$

$$= \sin\frac{\pi}{3}\cos\frac{\pi}{4} - \cos\frac{\pi}{3}\sin\frac{\pi}{4} \qquad \text{Apply the subtraction formula for sine.}$$

$$= \frac{\sqrt{3}}{2} \times \frac{1}{\sqrt{2}} - \frac{1}{2} \times \frac{1}{\sqrt{2}}$$

$$= \frac{\sqrt{3} - 1}{2\sqrt{2}} \qquad \text{Simplify.}$$

b) Use a calculator to determine that $\sin\dfrac{\pi}{12} \doteq 0.2588$

and $\dfrac{\sqrt{3} - 1}{2\sqrt{2}} \doteq 0.2588$. So, the answer in part a) checks.

- You can develop compound angle formulas using algebra and the unit circle.

- Once you have developed one compound angle formula, you can develop others by applying equivalent trigonometric expressions.

- The compound angle, or addition and subtraction, formulas for sine and cosine are

  $\sin(x + y) = \sin x \cos y + \cos x \sin y$

  $\sin(x - y) = \sin x \cos y - \cos x \sin y$

  $\cos(x + y) = \cos x \cos y - \sin x \sin y$

  $\cos(x - y) = \cos x \cos y + \sin x \sin y$

- You can apply compound angle formulas to determine exact trigonometric ratios for angles that can be expressed as sums or differences of special angles.

Communicate Your Understanding

C1 In the proof on pages 228–229, angle $(a + b)$ was drawn in the first quadrant. Would it make any difference to the development of the compound angle formula if the angle was in the second quadrant? If so, explain what difference it would make. If not, explain why not.

C2 It is sometimes tempting to conclude that $\sin(x + y) = \sin x + \sin y$. Identify one pair of angles x and y that shows that it is not generally true. Explain why it is not generally true.

C3 Are there any angles x and y that satisfy $\sin(x + y) = \sin x + \sin y$? If so, determine one example, and show that it works. If not, explain why not.

A) Practise

For help with questions 1 to 3, refer to Example 1.

1. Use an appropriate compound angle formula to express as a single trigonometric function, and then determine an exact value for each.

a) $\sin \dfrac{\pi}{4} \cos \dfrac{\pi}{12} + \cos \dfrac{\pi}{4} \sin \dfrac{\pi}{12}$

b) $\sin \dfrac{\pi}{4} \cos \dfrac{\pi}{12} - \cos \dfrac{\pi}{4} \sin \dfrac{\pi}{12}$

c) $\cos \dfrac{\pi}{4} \cos \dfrac{\pi}{12} - \sin \dfrac{\pi}{4} \sin \dfrac{\pi}{12}$

d) $\cos \dfrac{\pi}{4} \cos \dfrac{\pi}{12} + \sin \dfrac{\pi}{4} \sin \dfrac{\pi}{12}$

2. Use an appropriate compound angle formula to express as a single trigonometric function, and then determine an exact value for each.

a) $\sin \dfrac{3\pi}{5} \cos \dfrac{\pi}{15} + \cos \dfrac{3\pi}{5} \sin \dfrac{\pi}{15}$

b) $\sin \dfrac{7\pi}{5} \cos \dfrac{\pi}{15} - \cos \dfrac{7\pi}{5} \sin \dfrac{\pi}{15}$

c) $\cos \dfrac{2\pi}{9} \cos \dfrac{5\pi}{18} - \sin \dfrac{2\pi}{9} \sin \dfrac{5\pi}{18}$

d) $\cos \dfrac{10\pi}{9} \cos \dfrac{5\pi}{18} + \sin \dfrac{10\pi}{9} \sin \dfrac{5\pi}{18}$

3. Apply a compound angle formula, and then determine an exact value for each.

a) $\sin\left(\dfrac{\pi}{3} + \dfrac{\pi}{4}\right)$ **b)** $\cos\left(\dfrac{\pi}{3} + \dfrac{\pi}{4}\right)$

c) $\cos\left(\dfrac{2\pi}{3} - \dfrac{\pi}{4}\right)$ **d)** $\sin\left(\dfrac{2\pi}{3} - \dfrac{\pi}{4}\right)$

For help with questions 4 to 7, refer to Example 2.

4. Use an appropriate compound angle formula to determine an exact value for each.

a) $\sin\dfrac{7\pi}{12}$ **b)** $\sin\dfrac{5\pi}{12}$

5. Use an appropriate compound angle formula to determine an exact value for each.

a) $\cos\dfrac{11\pi}{12}$ **b)** $\cos\dfrac{5\pi}{12}$

6. Use an appropriate compound angle formula to determine an exact value for each.

a) $\sin\dfrac{13\pi}{12}$ **b)** $\cos\dfrac{17\pi}{12}$

7. Use an appropriate compound angle formula to determine an exact value for each.

a) $\sin\dfrac{19\pi}{12}$ **b)** $\cos\dfrac{23\pi}{12}$

B   Connect and Apply

8. Angles x and y are located in the first quadrant such that $\sin x = \dfrac{3}{5}$ and $\cos y = \dfrac{5}{13}$.
a) Determine an exact value for $\cos x$.
b) Determine an exact value for $\sin y$.

9. Refer to question 8. Determine an exact value for each of the following.
a) $\sin(x + y)$
b) $\sin(x - y)$
c) $\cos(x + y)$
d) $\cos(x - y)$

10. Angle x is in the second quadrant and angle y is in the first quadrant such that $\sin x = \dfrac{5}{13}$ and $\cos y = \dfrac{3}{5}$.
a) Determine an exact value for $\cos x$.
b) Determine an exact value for $\sin y$.

11. Refer to question 10. Determine an exact value for each of the following.
a) $\sin(x + y)$
b) $\sin(x - y)$
c) $\cos(x + y)$
d) $\cos(x - y)$

12. Use a compound angle formula for sine to show that $\sin 2\theta = 2\sin\theta\cos\theta$.

13. Use a compound angle formula for cosine to show that $\cos 2x = \cos^2 x - \sin^2 x$.

CONNECTIONS
The formulas in questions 12 and 13 are known as the double angle formulas.

14. Use the Pythagorean identity to show that the double angle formula for cosine can be written as
a) $\cos 2x = 1 - 2\sin^2 x$
b) $\cos 2x = 2\cos^2 x - 1$

15. Angle θ lies in the second quadrant and $\sin\theta = \dfrac{7}{25}$.
a) Determine an exact value for $\cos 2\theta$.
b) Determine an exact value for $\sin 2\theta$.
c) Use a calculator to determine an approximate measure for θ in radians.
d) Use a calculator to check your answers to parts a) and b).

16. Use Technology Use a graphing calculator to check the formulas in questions 12, 13, and 14 by graphing the left side and then the right side. Refer to the method used in Section 4.3, Example 3.

17. Chapter Problem The wings on an airplane are usually angled upward relative to the body, or fuselage, of the aircraft.

This is known as a dihedral, and makes the aircraft more stable in flight, especially during turbulence.

a) An aircraft wing is 12 ft long and has a dihedral angle x. Determine an expression for the vertical displacement, h_1, above the bottom of the fuselage, in terms of x.

b) Some aircraft have a double dihedral. Suppose that a wing is designed as shown, with an initial dihedral angle of x for the first 6 ft, and an additional angle x for the next 6 ft. Show that $h_2 = 6\sin x(1 + 2\cos x)$.

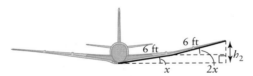

18. At the winter solstice (on or about December 21), the power, in watts, received from the Sun on each square metre of Earth's surface can be modelled by the formula $P = 1000\sin(x + 113.5°)$, where x represents the angle of latitude in the northern hemisphere.

a) Determine the angle of latitude at which the power level drops to 0. Suggest a reason why this happens at this latitude. Justify your answer.

b) Determine the angle of latitude at which the power level is a maximum. Explain what is meant by the negative sign. Suggest a reason why this happens at this latitude. Justify your answer.

✓ Achievement Check

19. The angle $2x$ lies in the fourth quadrant such that $\cos 2x = \dfrac{8}{17}$.

a) Sketch the location of angle $2x$.

b) Which quadrant contains angle x?

c) Determine an exact value for $\cos x$.

d) Use a calculator to determine the measure of x, in radians.

e) Use a calculator to verify your answer for part c).

C) Extend and Challenge

20. Recall the quotient identity $\tan x = \dfrac{\sin x}{\cos x}$.

a) Use the quotient identity and the compound angle formulas for $\sin(x + y)$ and $\cos(x + y)$ to write a formula for $\tan(x + y)$.

b) Show that the formula in part a) can be written as $\tan(x + y) = \dfrac{\tan x + \tan y}{1 - \tan x \tan y}$.

c) Use your Special Angles and Trigonometric Ratios table from Section 4.2 to show that the formula in part b) is valid for $x = \dfrac{2\pi}{3}$ and $y = \dfrac{\pi}{6}$.

21. a) Use the formula in question 20, part b), and appropriate equivalent trigonometric expressions to show that $\tan(x - y) = \dfrac{\tan x - \tan y}{1 + \tan x \tan y}$.

b) Use your Special Angles and Trigonometric Ratios table from Section 4.2 to show that the formula in part a) is valid for $x = \dfrac{\pi}{3}$ and $y = \dfrac{\pi}{6}$.

22. a) Use the formula from question 20, part b), to derive a formula for $\tan 2x$.

b) Use Technology Use a graphing calculator to check the formula in part a) by graphing the left side and then the right side.

c) Use a calculator to show that the formula in part a) is valid for $x = 0.52$.

23. The compound angle formulas can be used to derive many other formulas. One of these is the sum formula

$$\sin x + \sin y = 2 \sin\left(\frac{x+y}{2}\right)\cos\left(\frac{x-y}{2}\right).$$

a) Show that the formula is valid for $x = \frac{2\pi}{3}$ and $y = \frac{\pi}{3}$.

b) Use appropriate equivalent trigonometric expressions to derive a similar formula for $\sin x - \sin y$.

24. a) Derive the half-angle formula for sine,

$$\sin\frac{x}{2} = \pm\sqrt{\frac{1-\cos x}{2}}\,,$$ from a double angle formula for cosine.

b) Derive the half-angle formula for cosine,

$$\cos\frac{x}{2} = \pm\sqrt{\frac{1+\cos x}{2}}\,,$$ from a double angle formula for cosine.

25. Math Contest Find the acute angle θ of intersection between the lines $y = 4x - 1$ and $y = -2x + 5$.

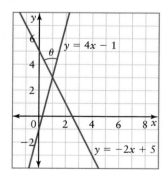

26. Math Contest If A, B, and C are angles in a triangle, by expanding $\tan(A + B + C)$, show that $\tan A \tan B \tan C = \tan A + \tan B + \tan C$.

27. Math Contest An interesting area of mathematics revolves around the study of approximation. An example is the approximation of π in the form of a rational number, $\pi \doteq \frac{22}{7}$. Both sine and cosine have approximations in polynomial form:

$\sin\theta \doteq \theta - \frac{\theta^3}{6}$ and $\cos\theta \doteq 1 - \frac{\theta^2}{2}$, where θ is an angle measure in radians ($\theta \in \mathbb{R}$) and is a value near zero.

a) Calculate each value, and then copy and complete the table.

θ	0.01	0.05	0.10	0.15	0.25	0.35
$\theta - \dfrac{\theta^3}{6}$						
$\sin\theta$						

b) Calculate each value, and then copy and complete the table.

θ	0.01	0.05	0.10	0.15	0.25	0.35
$1 - \dfrac{\theta^2}{2}$						
$\cos\theta$						

28. Math Contest Trigonometric functions can be approximated by using an expanded power series, where θ is measured in radians and is close to zero. Determine an approximation in simplified form for $\sin\theta$, $\cos\theta$, and $\tan\theta$ given the equivalent power series for each.

a) $\sin\theta = \theta - \dfrac{\theta^3}{3!} + \dfrac{\theta^5}{5!} - \dfrac{\theta^7}{7!} + \cdots$

b) $\cos\theta = 1 - \dfrac{\theta^2}{2!} + \dfrac{\theta^4}{4!} - \dfrac{\theta^6}{6!} + \cdots$

c) $\tan\theta = \theta + \dfrac{\theta^3}{3} + \dfrac{2\theta^5}{15} + \dfrac{17\theta^7}{315} + \cdots$

4.5 Prove Trigonometric Identities

To simulate a weightless environment to train astronauts, an aircraft is flown along a trajectory in the shape of a parabolic arc. The width of the parabola to be flown can be modelled by the relation $w = \dfrac{2v^2}{g} \sin\theta\cos\theta$, where v is the speed of the aircraft entering the parabola, in metres per second; g is the acceleration due to gravity, 9.8 m/s²; and θ is the initial climb angle selected by the pilot of the aircraft.

This equation can be simplified using the double angle formula $\sin 2\theta = 2\sin\theta\cos\theta$ to get $w = \dfrac{2v^2}{g}\sin 2\theta$.

This form is easier to work with. For example, suppose that the pilot wishes to maximize the width of the parabola flown. The maximum value of $\sin 2\theta$ is 1, when $2\theta = \dfrac{\pi}{2}$, or $\theta = \dfrac{\pi}{4}$. The pilot should use an initial climb angle of $\dfrac{\pi}{4}$ to maximize the width of the parabola flown.

CONNECTIONS

A company called Zero-G, based in Florida, offers the weightless experience to the general public on a modified Boeing 727 aircraft.

| Investigate | **How can you determine whether an equation is an identity?** |

Tools

• graphing calculator

1. Consider the equation $\tan\left(x + \dfrac{\pi}{4}\right) = \sin x + \cos x$. Substitute $x = 0$ in both sides. Is the equation true for this value of x?

2. **Reflect** Can you conclude that the equation is an identity? Justify your answer.

3. One way to show that an equation is not an identity is to find a value of x for which the equation is not true. This is known as finding a counterexample. Use your Special Angles and Trigonometric Ratios table from Section 4.2 to determine a counterexample for the equation in step 1.

4. Another way to check is to graph each side of the equation individually using a graphing calculator.

   a) Ensure that your calculator is set to Radian mode and all stat plots are turned off.

   b) Use the **Y=** editor to enter $\tan\left(x + \dfrac{\pi}{4}\right)$ in **Y1** and $\sin x + \cos x$ in **Y2**.

   c) Change the line display for **Y2** to heavy.

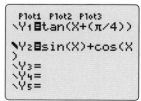

d) From the **ZOOM** menu, select **6:ZStandard**. The graph of $\tan\left(x + \frac{\pi}{4}\right)$ will be drawn first with a light line. Then, the graph of $\sin x + \cos x$ will be drawn with a heavier line. You can pause the plot by pressing $\boxed{\text{ENTER}}$. Pressing $\boxed{\text{ENTER}}$ again will resume the plot.

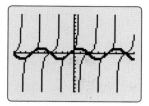

5. Reflect

a) How do the graphs demonstrate that the equation is not an identity?

b) Take note of the points where the graphs cross. What do these points signify?

6. a) Consider the equation $\sin x = \cos x \tan x$. Is the equation true for $x = \frac{\pi}{4}$?

b) Attempt to find a counterexample to show that the equation is not an identity. Report your findings.

c) Graph both sides of the equation on a graphing calculator.

7. Reflect Does the equation in step 6 appear to be an identity? Justify your answer.

Graphing both sides of an equation can make an equation appear to be an identity. However, this approach does not constitute a proof. Some graphs appear identical in a particular domain, but then diverge when the domain is extended. To prove an identity, show that one side of the equation is equivalent to the other side. Start by writing down the left side (**L.S.**) and right side (**R.S.**) separately. Then, transform the expression for one side into the exact form of the expression on the other side.

In the remainder of this section, you will use the basic trigonometric identities shown to prove other identities.

Pythagorean Identity

$\sin^2 x + \cos^2 x = 1$

Quotient Identity

$\tan x = \dfrac{\sin x}{\cos x}$

Reciprocal Identities

$\csc x = \dfrac{1}{\sin x} \qquad \sec x = \dfrac{1}{\cos x} \qquad \cot x = \dfrac{1}{\tan x}$

Compound Angle Formulas

$\sin(x + y) = \sin x \cos y + \cos x \sin y$

$\sin(x - y) = \sin x \cos y - \cos x \sin y$

$\cos(x + y) = \cos x \cos y - \sin x \sin y$

$\cos(x - y) = \cos x \cos y + \sin x \sin y$

Example 1 · Use a Compound Angle Formula to Prove a Double Angle Formula

a) Prove that $\sin 2x = 2\sin x \cos x$.

b) Illustrate the identity by graphing.

> **Solution**

a) $\text{L.S.} = \sin 2x$ $\qquad\qquad\qquad\qquad$ $\text{R.S.} = 2\sin x \cos x$

$\qquad\quad = \sin(x + x)$

$\qquad\quad = \sin x \cos x + \cos x \sin x$

$\qquad\quad = 2\sin x \cos x$

$$\text{L.S.} = \text{R.S.}$$

Therefore, $\sin 2x = 2\sin x \cos x$ is an identity.

b) Use the **Y=** editor of a graphing calculator to enter $\sin 2x$ in **Y1** and $2\sin x \cos x$ in **Y2**. Then, observe the graphs being drawn.

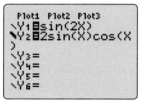 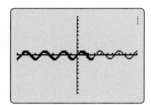

Example 2 · Use a Compound Angle Formula to Prove a Cofunction Identity

Prove that $\cos\left(\dfrac{\pi}{2} - x\right) = \sin x$.

> **Solution**

$\text{L.S.} = \cos\left(\dfrac{\pi}{2} - x\right)$ $\qquad\qquad\qquad$ $\text{R.S.} = \sin x$

$\qquad\quad = \cos\dfrac{\pi}{2}\cos x + \sin\dfrac{\pi}{2}\sin x$

$\qquad\quad = 0 \times \cos x + 1 \times \sin x$

$\qquad\quad = \sin x$

$$\text{L.S.} = \text{R.S.}$$

Therefore, $\cos\left(\dfrac{\pi}{2} - x\right) = \sin x$ is an identity.

Example 3

Prove an Identity Involving Reciprocal Trigonometric Ratios

Prove that $\csc 2x = \dfrac{\csc x}{2\cos x}$.

Solution

$$\text{L.S.} = \csc 2x$$

$$= \frac{1}{\sin 2x} \qquad \text{Use a reciprocal identity.}$$

$$= \frac{1}{2\sin x \cos x} \qquad \text{Use the double angle formula from Example 1.}$$

$$= \frac{1}{2} \times \frac{1}{\sin x} \times \frac{1}{\cos x} \qquad \text{Write as separate rational expressions.}$$

$$= \frac{1}{2} \times \csc x \times \frac{1}{\cos x} \qquad \text{Use a reciprocal identity.}$$

$$= \frac{\csc x}{2\cos x} \qquad \text{Combine into one term.}$$

$$\text{R.S.} = \frac{\csc x}{2\cos x}$$

$$\text{L.S.} = \text{R.S.}$$

Therefore, $\csc 2x = \dfrac{\csc x}{2\cos x}$ is an identity.

Example 4 Prove a More Complex Identity

Prove $\cos(x + y)\cos(x - y) = \cos^2 x + \cos^2 y - 1$.

Reasoning and Proving

Representing   **Selecting Tools**

Problem Solving

Connecting   Reflecting

Communicating

Solution

$$\text{L.S.} = \cos(x + y)\cos(x - y)$$

$$= (\cos x \cos y - \sin x \sin y)(\cos x \cos y + \sin x \sin y) \qquad \text{Use the compound angle formulas for cosine.}$$

$$= \cos^2 x \cos^2 y - \sin^2 x \sin^2 y \qquad \text{Expand the binomials and collect like terms.}$$

$$= \cos^2 x \cos^2 y - (1 - \cos^2 x)(1 - \cos^2 y) \qquad \text{Use the Pythagorean identity.}$$

$$= \cos^2 x \cos^2 y - (1 - \cos^2 y - \cos^2 x + \cos^2 x \cos^2 y) \qquad \text{Expand the binomials.}$$

$$= \cos^2 x \cos^2 y - 1 + \cos^2 y + \cos^2 x - \cos^2 x \cos^2 y$$

$$= \cos^2 y + \cos^2 x - 1 \qquad \text{Collect like terms.}$$

$$\text{R.S.} = \cos^2 x + \cos^2 y - 1$$

$$\text{L.S.} = \text{R.S.}$$

Therefore, $\cos(x + y)\cos(x - y) = \cos^2 x + \cos^2 y - 1$ is an identity.

- A trigonometric identity is an equation with trigonometric expressions that is true for all angles in the domain of the expressions on both sides.

- One way to show that an equation is not an identity is to determine a counterexample.

- To prove that an equation is an identity, treat each side of the equation independently and transform the expression on one side into the exact form of the expression on the other side.

- The basic trigonometric identities are the Pythagorean identity, the quotient identity, the reciprocal identities, and the compound angle formulas. You can use these identities to prove more complex identities.

- Trigonometric identities can be used to simplify solutions to problems that result in trigonometric expressions. This is important in understanding solutions for problems in mathematics, science, engineering, economics, and other fields.

Communicate Your Understanding

C1 Explain the difference between a general equation that involves trigonometric expressions and an equation that is an identity.

C2 a) Show that $\sin^2 2x = 4\sin x \cos x - 1$ is true for $x = \dfrac{\pi}{4}$.

b) How can you determine whether the equation in part a) is an identity? Carry out your method, and report on your findings.

C3 Construct a trigonometric equation that is true for at least one value of x. Then, determine whether or not it is an identity. Justify your conclusion.

A) Practise

For help with questions 1 and 2, refer to Example 1.

1. Prove that $\cos 2x = 2\cos^2 x - 1$.

2. Prove that $\cos 2x = 1 - 2\sin^2 x$.

For help with questions 3 to 6, refer to Example 2.

3. Prove that $\sin(x + \pi) = -\sin x$.

4. Prove that $\sin\left(\dfrac{3\pi}{2} - x\right) = -\cos x$.

5. Prove that $\cos(\pi - x) = -\cos x$.

6. Prove that $\cos\left(\dfrac{3\pi}{2} + x\right) = \sin x$.

For help with questions 7 and 8, refer to Example 3.

7. Prove that $\cos x = \sin x \cot x$.

8. Prove that $1 + \sin x = \sin x(1 + \csc x)$.

9. a) Prove that
$$1 - 2\cos^2 x = \sin x \cos x (\tan x - \cot x).$$

b) **Use Technology** Illustrate the identity by graphing with technology.

10. a) Prove that $\csc^2 x = 1 + \cot^2 x$.

b) Prove that $\sec^2 x = 1 + \tan^2 x$.

11. Prove that $\dfrac{1 - \sin^2 x}{\cos x} = \dfrac{\sin 2x}{2 \sin x}$.

12. Prove that $\dfrac{\csc^2 x - 1}{\csc^2 x} = 1 - \sin^2 x$.

13. Prove that $\dfrac{\csc x}{\cos x} = \tan x + \cot x$.

14. The software code that renders three-dimensional images onto a two-dimensional screen uses trigonometric expressions.

Any simplification that can be made to the calculations decreases processing time and smoothes the motion on the screen. Trigonometric identities can be used to simplify calculations. To get a feel for the usefulness of identities, you will time how long it takes to calculate each side of the identity $\sin (x + y) = \sin x \cos y + \cos x \sin y$.

a) Let $x = \dfrac{\pi}{12}$ and $y = \dfrac{\pi}{8}$. Ask a classmate to time how long it takes you to evaluate $\sin (x + y)$ using a calculator.

b) Determine how long it takes you to evaluate $\sin x \cos y + \cos x \sin y$.

c) Compare the times in parts a) and b). Express the time saved as a percent.

d) Let $x = \dfrac{3\pi}{4}$. How much time can you save using $\sin 2x$ rather than $2 \sin x \cos x$?

15. Prove that $2 \sin x \sin y = \cos (x - y) - \cos (x + y)$.

16. Prove that
$$\sin 2x + \sin 2y = 2 \sin (x + y) \cos (x - y).$$

17. a) **Use Technology** Use graphing technology to determine whether it is reasonable to conjecture that $\cos 2x = \dfrac{1 - \tan^2 x}{1 + \tan^2 x}$ is an identity.

b) If the equation is an identity, prove that it is an identity. If it is not, determine one counterexample.

18. a) Show that $\sin x = \sqrt{1 - \cos^2 x}$ is not an identity.

b) Explain why it cannot be an identity.

✓ Achievement Check

19. Use an appropriate compound angle formula to determine an expression for $\sin 3x$ in terms of $\sin x$ and $\cos x$.

a) Write $3x$ as the sum of two terms involving x.

b) Substitute the expression from part a) into $\sin 3x$.

c) Use an appropriate compound angle formula to expand the expression from part b).

d) Use an appropriate double angle formula to expand any terms involving $2x$ in the expanded expression from part c). Simplify as much as possible.

e) Select a value for x, and show that your expression in part d) holds true for that value.

f) **Use Technology** Use graphing technology to illustrate your identity.

20. a) **Use Technology** Use graphing technology to determine whether it is reasonable to conjecture that
$$\sin^6 x + \cos^6 x = 1 - 3 \sin^2 x \cos^2 x$$
is an identity.

b) If it appears to be an identity, prove the identity. If not, determine a counterexample.

21. Prove that $\cos^4 x - \sin^4 x = \cos 2x$.

22. Refer to question 20 in Section 4.4. Use the addition formula for tangents to derive the double angle formula for tangents.

23. **Math Contest** Prove.

a) $\cos (\sin^{-1} x) = \sqrt{1 - x^2}$

b) $\cos^{-1} a + \cos^{-1} b$
$= \cos^{-1}(ab - \sqrt{1 - a^2} \sqrt{1 - b^2})$,
for a, b > = 0

Extension

Use *The Geometer's Sketchpad®* to Sketch and Manipulate Three-Dimensional Structures in a Two-Dimensional Representation

Tools

- computer with *The Geometer's Sketchpad®*

You can use *The Geometer's Sketchpad®* to get a feel for the operation of the kind of software used for engineering design or computer graphics imaging. This software makes heavy use of trigonometry to render three-dimensional objects on a two-dimensional computer screen, as you have seen in some parts of the Chapter Problem.

Although *The Geometer's Sketchpad®* is a two-dimensional program, it can be used to represent and animate three-dimensional representations in a limited way.

Part 1: *Make an Object Fly and Turn*

1. Open *The Geometer's Sketchpad®*. Use the **Line Tool** to construct a representation of a cube, as shown, near the upper left of the work area.

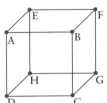

2. Construct a quadrilateral interior for the left (ADHE) and right (BCGF) faces and assign each a different colour.

CONNECTIONS

If the final object is different from the initial object, the initial object will appear to transform into the final object. In computer graphics imaging, this is known as *morphing*.

3. You will move the structure to the lower right corner of the work space, causing it to rotate and dilate on the way. Construct a representation of the desired final form of the structure, as shown.

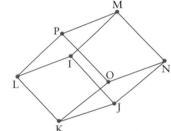

4. Point A will move to point I, B to J, and so on. To achieve this, select the points in the order A, I, B, J, C, K, D, L, E, M, F, N, G, O, H, and P. This process maps point A to point I, point B to point J, and so on.

5. From the **Edit** menu, choose **Action Buttons**. Choose **Movement….** Click on **OK**. Select the button marked **Move Points**. From the **Edit** menu, choose **Properties**, and then choose the **Label** tab. Change the label to **Fly**. Click on **OK**.

6. Hide the destination points I to P, as well as the line segments that join them.

7. Click on the button labelled **Fly**. Observe the movement. Notice that the original structure appears to move toward you as it rotates.

8. To return the structure to the starting location, hold the ⌃ key, and press **Z**.

Part 2: *Fold Up a Box*

1. Start with the representation of the cube from Part 1. Map A to F, B to E, D to G, and C to H.

2. From the **Edit** menu, choose **Action Buttons**. Choose **Movement....** Click on **OK**. Right-click on the button marked **Move Points**, and change the label to **Fold**.

3. Click on the button labelled **Fold**. Observe the movement.

Part 3: *Combine Actions*

You can combine the actions in Parts 1 and 2. You can make them occur simultaneously or sequentially.

1. Select the **Fly** button and the **Fold** button.

2. From the **Edit** menu, choose **Action Buttons** and then **Presentation....** Ensure that the **Simultaneously** radio button is selected. Click on **OK**. Rename the button **Simultaneous**.

3. Click on the **Simultaneous** button. Observe what happens.

4. Repeat steps 1 and 2, but this time select the **Sequentially** radio button. Rename the button **Sequential**.

5. Click on the **Sequential** button. Observe what happens.

Part 4: *Experiment*

1. Delete all points, segments, and buttons except the original cube.

2. Construct two different sets of destination points. Create an action button for each set.

3. What happens if you try to combine the action buttons simultaneously? sequentially?

4. Drag your sets of destination points to form patterns of interest to you. Experiment with the action buttons to produce interesting movements.

5. Create a third and fourth set of destination points, as well as action buttons. Experiment with different combinations of movements.

6. Use *The Geometer's Sketchpad*® to represent and manipulate a three-dimensional object of your own design. Features of your sketch can include, but are not limited to,
- rotations
- dilations
- translations
- colour
- multiple movements
- simultaneous and sequential movements
- morphing to a different shape

7. Reflect What are some of the limitations of a two-dimensional program like *The Geometer's Sketchpad*® in representing three-dimensional objects? Describe some of the features that a true three-dimensional dynamic geometry program would need.

4.1 Radian Measure

1. Determine the approximate radian measure, to the nearest hundredth, for each angle.

  a) 33°   **b)** 138°   **c)** 252°   **d)** 347°

2. Determine the approximate degree measure, to the nearest tenth, for each angle.

  a) 1.24   **b)** 2.82   **c)** 4.78   **d)** 6.91

3. Determine the exact radian measure of each angle.

  a) 75°   **b)** 20°   **c)** 12°   **d)** 9°

4. Determine the exact degree measure of each angle.

  a) $\dfrac{2\pi}{5}$ **b)** $\dfrac{4\pi}{9}$ **c)** $\dfrac{7\pi}{12}$ **d)** $\dfrac{11\pi}{18}$

5. The turntable in a microwave oven rotates 12 times per minute while the oven is operating. Determine the angular velocity of the turntable in

  a) degrees per second

  b) radians per second

6. Turntables for playing vinyl records have four speeds, in revolutions per minute (rpm): 16, $33\frac{1}{3}$, 45, and 78. Determine the angular velocity for each speed in

  a) degrees per second

  b) radians per second

  Summarize your results in a table.

4.2 Trigonometric Ratios and Special Angles

7. Use a calculator to determine the six trigonometric ratios of the angle $\dfrac{4\pi}{11}$. Round your answers to four decimal places.

8. Determine an exact value for each expression.

  a) $\dfrac{\cot \dfrac{\pi}{4}}{\cos \dfrac{\pi}{3}\csc \dfrac{\pi}{2}}$

  b) $\cos \dfrac{\pi}{6}\csc \dfrac{\pi}{3} + \sin \dfrac{\pi}{4}$

9. A ski lodge is constructed with one side along a vertical cliff such that it has a height of 15 m, as shown. Determine an exact measure for the base of the lodge, b.

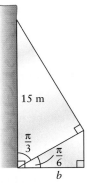

4.3 Equivalent Trigonometric Expressions

10. Given that $\cot \dfrac{2\pi}{7} = \tan z$, first express $\dfrac{2\pi}{7}$ as a difference between $\dfrac{\pi}{2}$ and an angle, and then apply a cofunction identity to determine the measure of angle z.

11. Given that $\cos \dfrac{5\pi}{9} = -\sin y$, first express $\dfrac{5\pi}{9}$ as a sum of $\dfrac{\pi}{2}$ and an angle, and then apply a trigonometric identity to determine the measure of angle y.

12. Given that $\tan \dfrac{4\pi}{9} \doteq 5.6713$, determine the following, to four decimal places, without using a calculator. Justify your answers.

  a) $\cot \dfrac{\pi}{18}$ **b)** $\tan \dfrac{13\pi}{9}$

13. Given that $\sin x = \cos \dfrac{3\pi}{11}$ and that x lies in the second quadrant, determine the measure of angle x.

4.4 Compound Angle Formulas

14. Use an appropriate compound angle formula to express as a single trigonometric function, and then determine an exact value of each.

  a) $\sin \dfrac{5\pi}{12}\cos \dfrac{\pi}{4} + \cos \dfrac{5\pi}{12}\sin \dfrac{\pi}{4}$

  b) $\sin \dfrac{5\pi}{12}\cos \dfrac{\pi}{4} - \cos \dfrac{5\pi}{12}\sin \dfrac{\pi}{4}$

  c) $\cos \dfrac{5\pi}{12}\cos \dfrac{\pi}{4} - \sin \dfrac{5\pi}{12}\sin \dfrac{\pi}{4}$

  d) $\cos \dfrac{5\pi}{12}\cos \dfrac{\pi}{4} + \sin \dfrac{5\pi}{12}\sin \dfrac{\pi}{4}$

15. Angles x and y are located in the first quadrant such that $\sin x = \dfrac{4}{5}$ and $\cos y = \dfrac{7}{25}$.

  a) Determine an exact value for $\cos x$.

  b) Determine an exact value for $\sin y$.

  c) Determine an exact value for $\sin(x + y)$.

16. Angle x lies in the third quadrant, and $\tan x = \dfrac{7}{24}$.

  a) Determine an exact value for $\cos 2x$.

  b) Determine an exact value for $\sin 2x$.

17. Determine an exact value for $\cos \dfrac{13\pi}{12}$.

4.5 Prove Trigonometric Identities

18. Prove that $\sin(2\pi - x) = -\sin x$.

19. a) Prove that $\sec x = \dfrac{2(\cos x \sin 2x - \sin x \cos 2x)}{\sin 2x}$.

  b) Use Technology Use graphing technology to illustrate the identity in part a).

20. Prove that $2\sin x \cos y = \sin(x + y) + \sin(x - y)$.

21. a) Use Technology Use graphing technology to determine whether it is reasonable to conjecture that $\cos 3x = \cos^3 x - 3\cos x \sin x$.

  b) Outline a method that you could use to develop a formula for $\cos 3x$ in terms of $\sin x$ and $\cos x$.

22. Consider the equation $\cos 2x = 2\sin x \sec x$. Either prove that it is an identity, or determine a counterexample to show that it is not an identity.

23. Prove that $(\sin 2x)(\tan x + \cot x) = 2$.

■ PROBLEM WRAP-UP

CHAPTER

In Section 4.1, question 18; Section 4.2, question 19; Section 4.3, question 22; and Section 4.4, question 17, you solved problems involving trigonometry in the context of transportation and transportation engineering.

a) A highway enters a city and runs east for 2 km. Then, the highway turns southward through an angle of $\dfrac{\pi}{12}$ and runs for another 2 km before it leaves the city. To divert through traffic around the city, the highway engineers will design an arc-shaped bypass road with its centre at the bend in the highway and a radius of 2 km.

  i) Sketch a diagram of the old highway and the bypass. Mark all given information.

  ii) Determine the length of the bypass, to the nearest hundredth of a kilometre.

b) The bypass road in part a) runs over a ravine bridged by a cable suspension bridge with a central tower 50 m high. The top of the tower is connected to each end of the bridge by two cables. The angle of inclination of the first cable is x. The angle of inclination of the second cable is twice that of the first cable.

  i) Sketch the bridge, the tower, and the four cables. Mark all given information.

  ii) Show that the total length of the two cables on one side of the central tower is given by the expression
$$l = \dfrac{50(1 + 2\cos x)}{\sin 2x}.$$

For questions 1 to 7, select the best answer.

1. The exact radian measure of 105° is

A $\dfrac{5\pi}{12}$

B $\dfrac{7\pi}{12}$

C $\dfrac{15\pi}{24}$

D $\dfrac{13\pi}{12}$

2. The exact degree measure of $\dfrac{13\pi}{24}$ is

A 22.5°

B 75°

C 97.5°

D 142.5°

3. Use a calculator to determine $\sin\dfrac{15\pi}{17}$, rounded to four decimal places.

A −0.9325

B 0.0484

C 0.3612

D 0.9988

4. Which of these is an equivalent trigonometric expression for $\sin x$?

A $-\cos\left(\dfrac{\pi}{2} - x\right)$

B $\sin\left(\dfrac{\pi}{2} - x\right)$

C $\cos\left(x + \dfrac{\pi}{2}\right)$

D $-\cos\left(x + \dfrac{\pi}{2}\right)$

5. The exact value of $\cos\dfrac{5\pi}{3}$ is

A $\dfrac{\sqrt{3}}{2}$

B $\dfrac{1}{2}$

C $-\dfrac{\sqrt{3}}{2}$

D $-\dfrac{2}{\sqrt{3}}$

6. Given that $\cot\theta = -1$ and angle θ lies in the second quadrant, what is $\sec\theta$?

A $\dfrac{1}{\sqrt{2}}$

B $-\dfrac{1}{\sqrt{2}}$

C $-\sqrt{2}$

D $\sqrt{2}$

7. Simplify $\cos\dfrac{\pi}{5}\cos\dfrac{\pi}{6} - \sin\dfrac{\pi}{5}\sin\dfrac{\pi}{6}$.

A $\cos\dfrac{11\pi}{30}$

B $\sin\dfrac{11\pi}{30}$

C $\cos\dfrac{\pi}{30}$

D $\sin\dfrac{\pi}{30}$

8. a) The Moon orbits Earth every 27.3 days. Determine the angular velocity of the Moon, in degrees per day and in radians per day.

b) The radius of the orbit of the Moon is about 384 400 km. How far does the Moon move along an arc of its orbit every day?

9. Determine an exact value for the expression

$$\dfrac{\sin\dfrac{\pi}{3} - \cos\dfrac{5\pi}{6}}{1 - \tan\dfrac{3\pi}{4}\cot\dfrac{\pi}{4}}.$$

10. An irregular building lot in a subdivision has the shape shown.

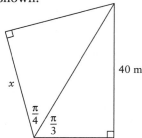

a) Determine an exact expression for the length of side x.

b) Determine an approximation for x, to the nearest tenth of a metre.

11. Given that $\cos \dfrac{7\pi}{18} \doteq 0.3420$, determine the following, to four decimal places, without using a calculator. Justify your answers.

a) $\sin \dfrac{\pi}{9}$

b) $\sin \dfrac{8\pi}{9}$

12. a) Determine an exact value for $\sin \dfrac{17\pi}{12}$.

b) Determine the answer to part a) using a different method.

13. Angle x is in the second quadrant and angle y is in the first quadrant such that $\sin x = \dfrac{7}{25}$ and $\cos y = \dfrac{5}{13}$.

a) Determine an exact value for $\cos x$.

b) Determine an exact value for $\sin y$.

c) Determine an exact value for $\cos(x - y)$.

14. The manufacturer of a propeller for a small aircraft mandates a maximum operating angular velocity of 300 rad/s. Determine whether it is safe to install this propeller on an aircraft whose engine is expected to run at a maximum of 2800 rpm.

15. A cruise ship sailed north for 50 km. Then, the captain turned the ship eastward through an angle of $\dfrac{\pi}{6}$ and sailed an additional 50 km. Without using a calculator, determine an exact expression for the direct distance from the start to the finish of the cruise.

16. Prove that $(\cos x - \sin x)^2 = 1 - \sin 2x$.

17. Prove that $2\cos x \cos y = \cos(x + y) + \cos(x - y)$.

18. Use a counterexample to show that $\cos 2x + \sin 2y = 2\sin(x + y)\cos(x - y)$ is not an identity.

19. Prove that $(\csc x - \cot x)^2 = \dfrac{1 - \cos x}{1 + \cos x}$.

20. A truss is used to hold up a heavy sign on a building, as shown. The truss is attached to the building along side AB, which measures 2.4 m. Determine an exact expression for the length CD.

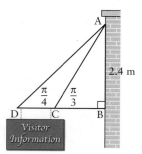

21. Use Technology A graphing calculator or graphing software can be used to deduce equivalent trigonometric expressions.

a) Ensure that your graphing calculator is set to Radian mode. Graph $y = \cos x$. From the **ZOOM** menu, select **7:ZTrig**. Determine the angle that is represented by each tick on the horizontal axis.

b) Plot a horizontal line at $y = 0.5$. Determine the coordinates of two successive points A and B where the line intersects the cosine graph. Deduce an equivalent trigonometric expression for the cosine ratio from these coordinates.

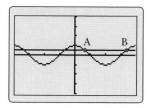

c) Clear the horizontal line graph. Graph $y = \sin x$. Inspect the intersection of the sine and cosine graphs. Use the intersection points to deduce one of the trigonometric identities for sine and cosine.

d) Does this method of deducing the identities constitute a proof of each identity? Justify your answer.

TASK

Make Your Own Identity

$$\sec^2 x = \frac{1 - \cos^2 x}{1 - \sin^2 x} + \csc^2 x - \cot^2 x$$

Make your own trigonometric identity and then challenge your friends to prove that it is true.

- Start with a statement you know is true for all values of x: for example $\sin^2 x = \sin^2 x$.

- Progressively change each side into an equivalent, but more complex form: for example
  $1 - \cos^2 x = -\cos 2x + \cos^2 x$.

- Continue replacing terms with equivalent expressions until you decide that your identity is sufficiently complex.

- **Use Technology** Graph the left side of your identity with a thin line, and the right side with a thick line. Do the two overlap? How is this evidence, but not proof, that you have an identity?

- Check your work by proving your identity in your notebook.

- Trade identities with a partner, and prove your partner's identity.

- Work with your partner to develop a "Hints For Proving Identities" list.

Chapter 5

Trigonometric Functions

In this chapter, you will extend your knowledge of trigonometric ratios to develop trigonometric functions expressed in radian measure.

You will investigate the properties of the sine, cosine, tangent, cosecant, secant, and cotangent functions. You will develop models for real-world applications such as theme park rides using trigonometric functions.

By the end of this chapter, you will

- sketch the graphs of $f(x) = \sin x$ and $f(x) = \cos x$ for angle measures expressed in radians, and determine and describe some key properties in terms of radians (B2.1)
- make connections between the tangent ratio and the tangent function by using technology to graph the relationship between angles in radians and their tangent ratios and defining this relationship as the function $f(x) = \tan x$, and describe key properties of the tangent function (B2.2)
- graph, with technology and using the primary trigonometric functions, the reciprocal trigonometric functions for angle measures expressed in radians, determine and describe key properties of the reciprocal functions, and recognize notations used to represent the reciprocal functions (B2.3)
- determine the amplitude, period, and phase shift of sinusoidal functions whose equations are given in the form $f(x) = a \sin [k(x - d)] + c$ or $f(x) = a \cos [k(x - d)] + c$, with angles expressed in radians (B2.4)
- sketch graphs of $y = a \sin [k(x - d)] + c$ and $y = a \cos [k(x - d)] + c$ by applying transformations to the graphs of $f(x) = \sin x$ and $f(x) = \cos x$ with angles expressed in radians, and state the period, amplitude, and phase shift of the transformed functions (B2.5)
- represent a sinusoidal function with an equation, given its graph or its properties, with angles expressed in radians (B2.6)
- pose problems based on applications involving a trigonometric function with domain expressed in radians, and solve these and other such problems by using a given graph or a graph generated with or without technology from a table of values or from its equation (B2.7)
- solve linear and quadratic trigonometric equations, with and without graphing technology, for the domain of real values from 0 to 2π, and solve related problems (B3.4)
- recognize rates of change, make connections between instantaneous rates of change and average rates of change, and solve related real-world problems (D1.5, D1.6, D1.8, D1.9)
- solve problems, using a variety of tools and strategies, including problems arising from real-world applications, by reasoning with functions and by applying concepts and procedures involving functions (D3.3)

Prerequisite Skills

Trigonometric Ratios of Angles Using Radian Measure

Note: Ensure that your calculator is set to Radian mode.

1. Use a calculator to evaluate each trigonometric ratio, to four decimal places.

   a) $\sin \dfrac{\pi}{5}$

   b) $\cos \dfrac{\pi}{12}$

   c) $\tan \dfrac{5\pi}{9}$

   d) $\tan \dfrac{7\pi}{8}$

2. Use a calculator to evaluate each trigonometric ratio, to four decimal places.

   a) $\csc 0.17$

   b) $\sec 1.54$

   c) $\cot 1.21$

   d) $\sec 3.95$

Exact Trigonometric Ratios of Special Angles Using Radian Measure

3. Determine the exact value of each trigonometric ratio.

   a) $\sin \dfrac{5\pi}{4}$

   b) $\cos \dfrac{\pi}{6}$

   c) $\tan \dfrac{3\pi}{4}$

   d) $\sin \dfrac{5\pi}{6}$

   e) $\cos \dfrac{5\pi}{3}$

   f) $\tan \dfrac{4\pi}{3}$

4. Determine the exact value of each reciprocal trigonometric ratio.

   a) $\csc \dfrac{5\pi}{3}$

   b) $\sec \dfrac{7\pi}{6}$

   c) $\cot \dfrac{7\pi}{4}$

   d) $\sec 2\pi$

   e) $\cot \dfrac{3\pi}{2}$

   f) $\csc \dfrac{\pi}{4}$

Graphs and Transformations of Sinusoidal Functions Using Degree Measure

5. Sketch the graph of $y = \sin x$ on the interval $x \in [-360°, 360°]$.

6. Sketch the graph of $y = \cos x$ on the interval $x \in [-360°, 360°]$.

7. Explain why the graphs of the functions $y = \sin x$ and $y = \cos x$ are periodic.

8. Consider the function $f(x) = 3\sin[2(x - 30°)] - 1$.

   a) Determine the amplitude, period, phase shift, and vertical translation with respect to $y = \sin x$.

   b) What are the maximum and minimum values of the function?

   c) Determine the first three x-intercepts to the right of the origin, rounded to the nearest tenth of a degree.

   d) Determine the y-intercept of the function, to one decimal place.

9. Consider the function $f(x) = 2\cos(x + 90°) + 1$.

   a) Determine the amplitude, period, phase shift, and vertical translation with respect to $y = \cos x$.

   b) What are the maximum and minimum values of the function?

   c) Determine the first three x-intercepts to the right of the origin.

   d) Determine the y-intercept of the function.

Angles From Trigonometric Ratios

10. Use a calculator to find the measure of each angle x, to the nearest tenth of a degree.

    a) $\sin x = 0.52$

    b) $\cos x = -0.78$

    c) $\tan x = 3.56$

    d) $\csc x = 2.14$

11. Use a calculator to find the measure of each angle x, to the nearest tenth of a radian.

    a) $\sin x = 0.15$

    b) $\cos x = -0.64$

    c) $\tan x = 1.36$

    d) $\csc x = 5.44$

Vertical and Horizontal Asymptotes

12. Consider the reciprocal function $y = \dfrac{1}{x^2 + x - 2}$.

a) Determine the equations of the vertical asymptotes.

b) Determine the equation of the horizontal asymptote.

c) Graph the function. Use dotted lines for asymptotes where appropriate.

Rates of Change for Linear Functions

13. a) What is the instantaneous rate of change of the function $y = 3x + 1$ at $x = 2$? Justify your answer.

b) How does this compare to the average rate of change?

CONNECTIONS

Recall from Chapter 1 that the instantaneous rate of change of a function at a point is given by the slope of the tangent to the function at that point.

14. Justine starts 6 km from home. She rides her bicycle and arrives home 25 min later. Determine the average rate of change, in kilometres per hour, of her distance from home during the ride.

Rates of Change for Polynomial Functions

15. The height, h, in metres, of a baseball as it flies through the air can be modelled by the function $h = 20t - 5t^2$, where t is the time, in seconds.

a) Determine the average rate of change of the height from $t = 0.1$ s to $t = 0.5$ s.

b) Estimate the instantaneous rate of change of the height at $t = 0.5$ s.

c) What quantity is represented by the instantaneous rate of change in part b)?

PROBLEM

CHAPTER

Many theme park rides involve circular motion or pendulum motion. Rollercoasters are constructed from sections of track with hills and valleys. These motions and track sections can be modelled with trigonometric functions. In this chapter, you will use trigonometric functions to solve problems that involve modelling several such rides and then use the models to make engineering calculations. You will finish by designing and modelling your own ride, using a combination of trigonometric, polynomial, and rational functions.

Graphs of Sine, Cosine, and Tangent Functions

Trigonometric ratios are typically first introduced using right triangles. Trigonometric ratios can be extended to define trigonometric functions, which can be applied to model real-world processes that are far removed from right triangles. One example is the business cycle, which models the periodic expansion and contraction of the economy.

Business Cycle

Economy

Time

Investigate **How can you use graphs to represent trigonometric functions?**

Tools

• scientific calculator
• grid paper

Optional

• graphing calculator
OR
• graphing software

1. a) Copy and complete the table. Use your knowledge of special angles to determine exact values for each trigonometric ratio. Then, use a scientific calculator set to Radian mode to determine approximate values, to two decimal places. One row has been completed for you.

Angle, x	$y = \sin x$	$y = \cos x$	$y = \tan x$
0			
$\dfrac{\pi}{6}$	$\dfrac{1}{2} = 0.50$	$\dfrac{\sqrt{3}}{2} \doteq 0.87$	$\dfrac{1}{\sqrt{3}} \doteq 0.58$
$\dfrac{\pi}{4}$			
$\dfrac{\pi}{3}$			
$\dfrac{\pi}{2}$			

b) Extend the table to include multiples of the special angles in the other three quadrants.

2. a) Graph $y = \sin x$ on the interval $x \in [0, 2\pi]$.

  b) Create a table to summarize the following characteristics of the function $y = \sin x$. Include two additional columns, one for $y = \cos x$ and the other for $y = \tan x$, to be filled in later.
   - the maximum value, the minimum value, and the amplitude
   - the period, in radian measure
   - the zeros in the interval $x \in [0, 2\pi]$
   - the y-intercept
   - the domain and range

Technology Tip ∴

If you are using a graphing calculator, you can press ZOOM and select **7:ZTrig**. This will set the window variables appropriately for this graph.

3. a) Graph $y = \cos x$ on the interval $x \in [0, 2\pi]$.

  b) Determine the following characteristics of the function $y = \cos x$. Add the results to your table from step 2b).
   - the maximum value, the minimum value, and the amplitude
   - the period, in radian measure
   - the zeros in the interval $x \in [0, 2\pi]$
   - the y-intercept
   - the domain and range

4. Reflect

  a) Suppose that you extended the graph of $y = \sin x$ to the right of 2π. Predict the shape of the graph. Use a calculator to investigate a few points to the right of 2π. At what value of x will the next cycle end?

  b) Suppose that you extended the graph of $y = \sin x$ to the left of 0. Predict the shape of the graph. Use a calculator to investigate a few points to the left of 0. At what value of x will the next cycle end?

5. Reflect Repeat step 4 for $y = \cos x$.

6. a) Inspect the column for $y = \tan x$ in your table from step 1. Why are some values undefined?

  b) Use a calculator to investigate what happens to $\tan x$ as $x \to \dfrac{\pi}{2}^{-}$.

  Then, investigate what happens to the value of $\tan x$ as $x \to \dfrac{\pi}{2}^{+}$.

  Report your findings, and explain why this happens.

7. a) Graph $y = \tan x$ on the interval $x \in [0, 2\pi]$. Use your results from step 6 to determine how the graph should be drawn close to $x = \dfrac{\pi}{2}$ and $x = \dfrac{3\pi}{2}$. Sketch vertical dotted lines at these locations. What name is given to these lines?

  b) Determine the following characteristics of the function $y = \tan x$. Add the results to your table from step 2b).
   - the maximum value, the minimum value, and the amplitude
   - the period, in radian measure
   - the zeros in the interval $x \in [0, 2\pi]$
   - the y-intercept
   - the domain and range

8. Reflect

a) Suppose that you extended the graph of $y = \tan x$ to the right of 2π. Predict the shape of the graph. Use a calculator to investigate a few points to the right of 2π.

b) Suppose that you extended the graph of $y = \tan x$ to the left of 0. Predict the shape of the graph. Use a calculator to investigate a few points to the left of 0.

c) Explain how you know that $y = \tan x$ is a function.

| Example 1 | Graphs of the Form $y = \sin x + c$ |

a) Predict the effect on the graph of $y = \sin x$ of adding a constant c to the right side.

b) Transform the graph of $y = \sin x$ to sketch $y = \sin x + 2$ and $y = \sin x - 3$.

Solution

a) Adding a constant c to $\sin x$ changes the y-coordinate of every point on the graph of $y = \sin x$ by the same amount. This appears as a vertical translation upward if c is positive and downward if c is negative.

b) Method 1: *Use Pencil and Paper*

Start by sketching the graph of $y = \sin x$.

Use the fact that one cycle of the sine function includes a maximum, a minimum, and three zeros to help you select points along the curve.

To obtain the graph of $y = \sin x + 2$, add 2 to the y-coordinate of each point.

To obtain the graph of $y = \sin x - 3$, subtract 3 from the y-coordinate of each point.

Sketch a smooth curve through each set of translated points.

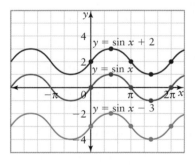

Technology Tip ⠶

Ensure that the graphing calculator is in Radian mode.

Technology Tip ⠶

The window settings for ZTrig on a graphing calculator in Radian mode are

$Xmin = -\dfrac{47\pi}{24}$

$Xmax = \dfrac{47\pi}{24}$

$Xscl = \dfrac{\pi}{2}$

$Ymin = -4$

$Ymax = 4$

$Yscl = 1$

Method 2: *Use a Graphing Calculator*

Use the **Y=** editor to enter the functions, as shown.

Change the line style of **Y1**.

• Cursor left to the slanted line beside **Y1**.

• Press ⏎ to change the line style to heavy.

Press ☐ZOOM and select **7:ZTrig**.

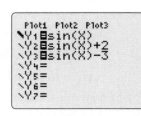

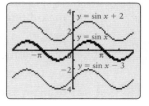

Example 2 **Graphs of the Form $y = a\sin x$**

a) Predict the effect on the graph of $y = \sin x$ of multiplying the right side by a constant a.

b) Transform the graph of $y = \sin x$ to sketch

   i) $y = 2\sin x$

   iii) $y = -3\sin x$

Solution

a) Multiplying $\sin x$ by a constant a changes the y-coordinate of each point by a factor a. Negative values of a cause a reflection in the x-axis. The amplitude of the graph changes from 1 to $|a|$.

CONNECTIONS

Remember that $|a|$ means the absolute value of a.

b) **i)**

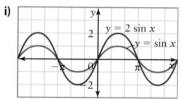 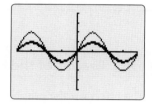

ii)

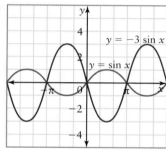 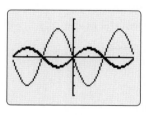

Example 3 **Graphs of the Form $y = \sin(x - d)$**

a) Predict the effect on the graph of $y = \sin x$ of subtracting a constant d from the angle x.

b) Transform the graph of $y = \sin x$ to sketch

   i) $y = \sin\left(x - \dfrac{\pi}{4}\right)$

   ii) $y = \sin\left(x + \dfrac{\pi}{6}\right)$

Solution

a) Since the function $y = \sin x$ has a zero at $x = 0$, the function $y = \sin(x - d)$ will have a zero at $x - d = 0$, or $x = d$.

If d is positive, the argument of the function becomes $x - (+d)$, or $x - d$, and the shift is to the right. If d is negative, the argument of the function becomes $x - (-d)$, or $x + d$, and the shift is to the left.

b) i)

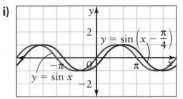

ii)

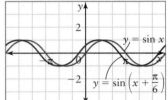

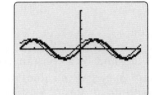

Example 4 | Graphs of the Form $y = \sin kx$

a) Predict the effect on the graph of $y = \sin x$ of multiplying the angle x by a constant k.

b) Transform the graph of $y = \sin x$ to sketch

i) $y = \sin 2x$

ii) $y = \sin \dfrac{1}{2}x$

Solution

a) The period of $y = \sin x$ is 2π radians. Multiplying the angle by a constant k changes the period to $\dfrac{2\pi}{k}$.

b) i) The period of $y = \sin 2x$ is $\dfrac{2\pi}{2}$, or π.

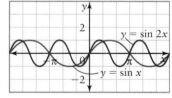

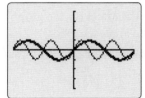

ii) The period of $y = \sin \dfrac{1}{2}x$ is $\dfrac{2\pi}{\dfrac{1}{2}}$, or 4π.

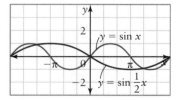

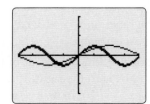

● The graphs of $y = \sin x$, $y = \cos x$, and $y = \tan x$ are periodic.

● The graphs of $y = \sin x$ and $y = \cos x$ are similar in shape and have an amplitude of 1 and a period of 2π.

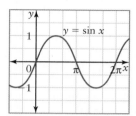 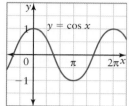

● The graph of $y = \sin x$ can be transformed into graphs modelled by equations of the form $y = \sin x + c$, $y = a \sin x$, $y = \sin (x - d)$, and $y = \sin kx$. Similarly, the graph of $y = \cos x$ can be transformed into graphs modelled by equations of the form $y = \cos x + c$, $y = a \cos x$, $y = \cos (x - d)$, and $y = \cos kx$.

● The graph of $y = \tan x$ has no amplitude because it has no maximum or minimum values. It is undefined at values of x that are odd multiples of $\frac{\pi}{2}$, such as $\frac{\pi}{2}$ and $\frac{3\pi}{2}$. The graph becomes asymptotic as the angle approaches these values from the left and the right. The period of the function is π.

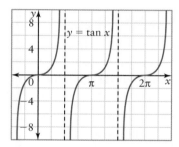

Communicate Your Understanding

C1 Compare the graphs of $y = \sin x$ and $y = \cos x$. How can you use a phase shift to map the sine function onto the cosine function? the cosine function onto the sine function? Is there more than one way to do each of these? Explain your answer.

C2 Compare the graphs of $y = \cos x$ and $y = \tan x$. How does the location of the asymptotes on the tangent graph relate to the value of the cosine graph for the same angle?

For help with questions 1 and 2, refer to Example 1.

1. Predict the maximum value, the minimum value, and the values of x where they occur for each function on the interval $x \in [-2\pi, 2\pi]$.

   a) $y = \sin x + 4$ c) $y = \sin x - 2$

   b) $y = \cos x - 5$ d) $y = \cos x + 1$

2. Sketch a graph of each function in question 1 on the interval $x \in [-2\pi, 2\pi]$.

For help with questions 3 and 4, refer to Example 2.

3. Write an equation for each function.

   a) sine function with an amplitude of 3

   b) cosine function with an amplitude of 5

   c) sine function with an amplitude of 4, reflected in the x-axis

   d) cosine function with an amplitude of 2, reflected in the x-axis

4. Sketch a graph of each function in question 3 on the interval $x \in [-2\pi, 2\pi]$.

For help with questions 5 and 6, refer to Example 3.

5. Write an equation for each function.

   a) sine function with a phase shift of $-\dfrac{\pi}{3}$

   b) cosine function with a phase shift of $+\dfrac{5\pi}{6}$

   c) sine function with a phase shift of $-\dfrac{3\pi}{4}$

   d) cosine function with a phase shift of $+\dfrac{4\pi}{3}$

6. Sketch a graph of each function in question 5 on the interval $x \in [-2\pi, 2\pi]$.

For help with questions 7 and 8, refer to Example 4.

7. Write an equation for each function.

   a) sine function with a period of $\dfrac{\pi}{2}$

   b) cosine function with a period of $\dfrac{3\pi}{2}$

   c) sine function with a period of 6π

   d) cosine function with a period of π

8. Sketch a graph of each function in question 7 on the interval $x \in [-2\pi, 2\pi]$.

9. A sine function has an amplitude of 3 and a period of π.

   a) Write the equation of the function in the form $y = a \sin kx$.

   b) Graph the function over two cycles.

10. A cosine function has a maximum value of 7 and a minimum value of -3.

    a) Determine the amplitude of the function.

    b) Determine the vertical translation.

    c) Graph the function over two cycles.

11. One cycle of a sine function begins at $x = -\dfrac{\pi}{6}$ and ends at $x = \dfrac{\pi}{3}$.

    a) Determine the period of the function.

    b) Determine the phase shift of the function.

    c) Write the equation of the function in the form $y = \sin[k(x - d)]$.

    d) Graph the function over two cycles.

12. The frequency of a periodic function is defined as the number of cycles completed in 1 s and is typically measured in hertz (Hz). It is the reciprocal of the period of a periodic function.

    a) One of the A-notes from a flute vibrates 440 times in 1 s. It is said to have a frequency of 440 Hz. What is the period of the A-note?

    b) The sound can be modelled using a sine function of the form $y = \sin kx$. What is the value of k?

13. The voltage of the electricity supply in North America can be modelled using a sine function. The maximum value of the voltage is about 120 V. The frequency is 60 Hz.

    a) What is the amplitude of the model?

    b) What is the period of the model?

    c) Determine the equation of the model in the form $y = a \sin kx$.

    d) Graph the model over two cycles.

14. A function is said to be even if $f(-x) = f(x)$ for all values of x. A function is said to be odd if $f(-x) = -f(x)$ for all values of x.

a) Is the function $y = \sin x$ even, odd, or neither? Justify your answer.

b) Is the function $y = \cos x$ even, odd, or neither? Justify your answer.

c) Is the function $y = \tan x$ even, odd, or neither? Justify your answer.

15. Recall the quotient identity $\tan x = \dfrac{\sin x}{\cos x}$. Use the graphs of $y = \sin x$ and $y = \cos x$ in conjunction with the quotient identity to explain the shape of the graph of $y = \tan x$.

Reasoning and Proving

Representing · Selecting Tools

Problem Solving

Connecting · Reflecting

Communicating

16. Use Technology You can use the animation features in *The Geometer's Sketchpad®* to dynamically vary the properties of a function. Refer to the Technology Appendix on page 506 for detailed instructions on using *The Geometer's Sketchpad®*.

a) Open *The Geometer's Sketchpad®* and turn on the grid.

b) Draw a unit circle.

c) Draw a point A on the circle.

d) Measure the x-coordinate, or abscissa, x_A, of the point.

e) Plot a new function of the form $x_A * \sin(x)$. Accept the change to radian measure.

f) Right-click on point A, and choose **Animate Point**. The motion controller will appear. Experiment with the controls.

g) Explain why the plot moves as it does.

h) Predict what will happen if you use a circle other than a unit circle. Check your prediction.

i) Use x_A to control other properties of the sine plot.

j) Measure the y-coordinate, or ordinate, y_A. Use x_A to control one property and y_A to control another property.

17. Chapter Problem The Octopus ride at an amusement park completes one revolution every 60 s. The cars reach a maximum of 4 m above the ground and a minimum of 1 m above the ground. The height, h, in metres, above the ground can be modelled using a sine function of the form $h = a \sin(kt) + c$, where t represents the time, in seconds.

a) Determine the amplitude of the function.

b) Determine the vertical translation of the function.

c) What is the desired period of the function?

d) Determine the value of k that results in the period desired in part c).

18. A popular attraction in many water theme parks is the wave pool. Suppose that the wave generator moves back and forth 20 complete cycles every minute to produce waves measuring 1.2 m from the top of the crest to the bottom of the trough.

a) Model the displacement, d, in metres, of the wave from the mean pool level as a function of time, t, in seconds.

b) Sketch a graph of the model over two cycles.

c) If the operator increases the speed of the wave generator to 30 complete cycles every minute, what change or changes would you expect to see in the waves? How would your model change? Justify your answer.

19. The graph of a cosine function is shown.

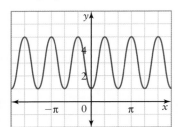

a) What is the maximum value? the minimum value?

b) What is the amplitude?

c) What is the vertical translation?

d) What is the period?

e) What value of k in the formula Period $= \dfrac{2\pi}{k}$ will result in the required period?

f) Explain why the phase shift can have more than one value. Suggest at least three possible values for the phase shift.

C Extend and Challenge

20. Consider the relation $y = |\sin x|$.

a) Predict the form of the graph of this relation.

b) Graph the relation on the interval $x \in [-2\pi, 2\pi]$.

c) Is the relation a function? Justify your answer.

d) Is the relation even, odd, or neither? Justify your answer.

21. Use Technology

a) Predict the form of the graph of $y = \tan x + 2$. Verify your prediction using graphing technology.

b) Predict the form of the graph of $y = 3 \tan x$. Verify your prediction using graphing technology.

c) Predict the form of the graph of $y = \tan\left(x - \dfrac{\pi}{4}\right)$. Verify your prediction using graphing technology.

d) Predict the form of the graph of $y = \tan 3x$. Verify your prediction using graphing technology.

22. Consider the graph of $y = \dfrac{x}{7}$.

a) How many times will this graph intersect the graph of $y = \sin x$ if both are graphed on the same set of axes with no limits on the domain? Justify your answer.

b) Illustrate your answer graphically.

23. The $\sin^{-1}$ key on a calculator returns the angle in the interval $\left[-\dfrac{\pi}{2}, \dfrac{\pi}{2}\right]$ that has a given sine ratio. For example, $\sin^{-1}\left(\dfrac{1}{\sqrt{2}}\right)$ will return an answer of $\dfrac{\pi}{4}$, or 0.785 398…. Predict the answer for each of the following. Then, use a calculator to verify the answer. Explain any discrepancies.

a) $\sin^{-1}\left(\dfrac{\sqrt{3}}{2}\right)$ **b)** $\cos^{-1}\left(\dfrac{\sqrt{3}}{2}\right)$

c) $\tan^{-1}(1)$ **d)** $\cos^{-1}\left(-\dfrac{1}{\sqrt{2}}\right)$

24. Math Contest A point P on a Cartesian plane has coordinates $P(x, y)$. In the polar coordinate system, the coordinates of the same point are given by $P(r, \theta)$. If a ray is drawn from the origin through point P, then r is the distance from the origin to point P and θ is the direction angle from the positive x-axis to the ray.

a) Rewrite each Cartesian equation in polar form.

   i) $x^2 + y^2 = 4$

   ii) $3x + 4y = 5$

   iii) $x^2 + y^2 - 4y = \sqrt{x^2 + y^2}$

b) Rewrite each polar equation in Cartesian form.

   i) $r = 6$

   ii) $r = 3 \cos \theta$

   iii) $r = 2 \sin \theta + 2 \cos \theta$

5.2

Graphs of Reciprocal Trigonometric Functions

The reciprocal trigonometric functions are related to the primary trigonometric functions. They appear in various engineering applications. For example, the cosecant function is used in modelling the radiation pattern of a radar antenna array to ensure that radar energy is not wasted in airspace, where there is little chance of finding an aircraft.

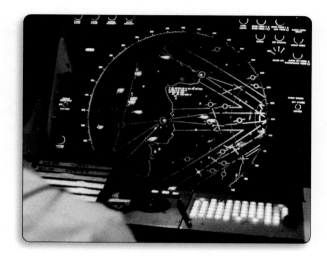

Investigate | **How can you use graphs of the primary trigonometric functions to deduce the shape of the graphs of the reciprocal trigonometric functions?**

1. a) To investigate the graph of $y = \csc x$, begin by sketching a graph of $y = \sin x$ on the interval $x \in [0, 2\pi]$.

   b) Since $\csc x = \dfrac{1}{\sin x}$, the two graphs will intersect whenever $\sin x = \pm 1$. Mark all such points on your graph.

   c) For what values of x will the value of $\csc x$ be undefined? Determine where these values are on the graph, and draw vertical dotted lines to represent the asymptotes at these values.

2. a) Consider the value of $y = \sin x$ at $x = \dfrac{\pi}{2}$, and move toward $x = 0$. What happens to the value of $\sin x$? What happens to the value of $\csc x$? Sketch the expected shape of the graph of $y = \csc x$ as the value of x moves from $\dfrac{\pi}{2}$ to 0.

   b) Consider the value of $y = \sin x$ at $x = \dfrac{\pi}{2}$, and move toward $x = \pi$. What happens to the value of $\sin x$? What happens to the value of $\csc x$? Sketch the expected shape of the graph of $y = \csc x$ as the value of x moves from $\dfrac{\pi}{2}$ to π.

   c) Consider the value of $y = \sin x$ at $x = \dfrac{3\pi}{2}$, and move toward $x = \pi$. What happens to the value of $\sin x$? What happens to the value of $\csc x$? Sketch the expected shape of the graph of $y = \csc x$ as the value of x moves from $\dfrac{3\pi}{2}$ to π.

Tools

- scientific calculator
- grid paper

Optional

- graphing calculator

OR

- graphing software

d) Consider the value of $y = \sin x$ at $x = \dfrac{3\pi}{2}$, and move toward $x = 2\pi$. What happens to the value of $\sin x$? What happens to the value of $\csc x$? Sketch the expected shape of the graph of $y = \csc x$ as the value of x moves from $\dfrac{3\pi}{2}$ to 2π.

3. a) Inspect the shape of the graph of $y = \csc x$. Determine the domain, range, and period of the graph.

b) Describe the values of x where the asymptotes occur. Why do these asymptotes occur?

c) Consider the tangent lines at $x = \dfrac{\pi}{4}$ for the graphs of $y = \sin x$ and $y = \csc x$. How does the sign of the slope of the tangent on the sine graph at this point compare to the sign of the slope of the tangent on the cosecant graph? Consider other values of x. Is this relationship always true?

d) Consider the slope of the tangent to the sine graph as x varies from $\dfrac{\pi}{4}$ to $\dfrac{\pi}{2}$. Does the slope increase or decrease? What happens to the slope of the tangent to the cosecant graph over this same interval? Consider other intervals of x. Is this relationship always true?

4. Reflect Suppose that the graphs of $y = \sin x$ and $y = \csc x$ are extended to the interval $x \in [2\pi, 4\pi]$. Predict where the asymptotes will occur. Sketch the graphs you expect on this interval.

5. Apply the method in steps 1 to 4 to the graph of $y = \cos x$ to deduce the shape of the graph of $y = \sec x$.

6. Reflect Compare the graph of $y = \sec x$ to the graph of $y = \csc x$. How are they similar? How are they different?

7. a) To investigate the graph of $y = \cot x$, begin by sketching a graph of $y = \tan x$ on the interval $x \in [0, 2\pi]$.

b) Inspect the graph of $y = \tan x$. For what values of x do you expect the value of $\cot x$ to be undefined? Sketch vertical asymptotes for these values on another set of axes.

c) For what values of x will the graph of $y = \cot x$ intersect the x-axis? Justify your answer. Mark these points on your graph.

d) Consider the value of $y = \tan x$ at $x = 0$, and move toward $x = \dfrac{\pi}{2}$. What happens to the value of $\tan x$? What happens to the value of $\cot x$? Sketch the expected shape of the graph of $y = \cot x$ as the value of x moves from 0 to $\dfrac{\pi}{2}$.

e) Consider the value of $y = \tan x$ at $x = \dfrac{\pi}{2}$, and move toward $x = \pi$. What happens to the value of $\tan x$? What happens to the value of $\cot x$? Sketch the expected shape of the graph of $y = \cot x$ as the value of x moves from $\dfrac{\pi}{2}$ to π.

f) Consider the value of $y = \tan x$ at $x = \pi$, and move toward $x = \dfrac{3\pi}{2}$. What happens to the value of $\tan x$? What happens to the value of $\cot x$? Sketch the expected shape of the graph of $y = \cot x$ as the value of x moves from π to $\dfrac{3\pi}{2}$.

g) Consider the value of $y = \tan x$ at $x = \dfrac{3\pi}{2}$, and move toward $x = 2\pi$. What happens to the value of $\tan x$? What happens to the value of $\cot x$? Sketch the expected shape of the graph of $y = \cot x$ as the value of x moves from $\dfrac{3\pi}{2}$ to 2π.

8. a) Inspect the shape of the graph of $y = \cot x$. Determine the domain, range, and period of the graph.

b) What are the values of x where the asymptotes occur? Why do these asymptotes occur?

9. Reflect Compare the graph of $y = \tan x$ to the graph of $y = \cot x$. How are they similar? How are they different?

10. Copy and complete the summary table.

Property	$y = \csc x$	$y = \sec x$	$y = \cot x$
Domain			
Range			
Period			
Equations of asymptotes on the interval $x \in [0, 2\pi]$			
Sketch of graph			

Example 1   Determine Values on the Graph of $y = \csc x$

a) Use technology to graph $y = \sin x$ and $y = \csc x$.

b) Determine all values of x in the interval $[0, 2\pi]$ such that $\csc x = 3$. Round your answers to two decimal places.

c) What happens when $\csc x = \pm 1$? Why does this happen?

Solution

a) Ensure that the graphing calculator is in Radian mode.

Press $\boxed{Y=}$. Enter $\sin x$ in **Y1** and $\dfrac{1}{\sin x}$ in **Y2**.

Press $\boxed{\text{ZOOM}}$ and select **7:ZTrig**.

The graphs will display as shown.

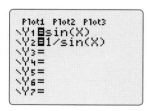
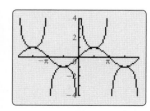

b) Use the **Intersect** operation to determine the points of intersection of the horizontal line $y = 3$ and the graph of $y = \csc x$ on the interval $x \in [0, 2\pi]$.

- Press $\boxed{\text{Y=}}$, and enter 3 in **Y3**. Press $\boxed{\text{GRAPH}}$.
- Press $\boxed{\text{2nd}}$ [CALC] to display the **CALCULATE** menu, and select **5:intersect**.
- Use the cursor keys to select the first relation, the second relation, and guess, pressing $\boxed{\text{ENTER}}$ after each.

One point of intersection occurs at approximately $x = 0.34$.

In a similar manner, determine that the other point of intersection in the interval $x \in [0, 2\pi]$ occurs at approximately $x = 2.80$.

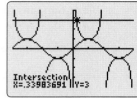

c) When $\csc x = \pm 1$, the cosecant graph intersects the sine graph. This happens because the cosecant function is the reciprocal of the sine function.

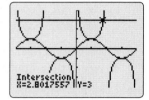

Example 2 **Determine Values on the Graph of $y = \cot x$**

a) Use technology to graph $y = \cot x$.

b) Determine all values of x in the interval $[0, 2\pi]$ such that $\cot x = 8$. Round your answers to two decimal places.

Solution

a) On a graphing calculator, enter the expression $\dfrac{1}{\tan x}$ in **Y1**.

Display the graph using the ZTrig window settings.

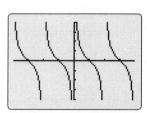

b) Enter 8 in **Y2**. Press $\boxed{\text{WINDOW}}$, and adjust the range of the vertical axis until you can see the horizontal line at $y = 8$. Use Ymin $= -10$ and Ymax $= 10$. Press $\boxed{\text{GRAPH}}$.

Use the **Intersect** operation to determine the points of intersection.

One point of intersection in the interval $x \in [0, 2\pi]$ occurs at approximately $x = 0.12$.

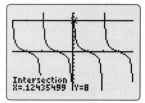

The other point of intersection in the interval $x \in [0, 2\pi]$ occurs at approximately $x = 3.27$.

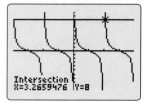

Example 3   Modelling Absorption of Sunlight

When the Sun is directly overhead, its rays pass through the atmosphere as shown. Call this 1 unit of atmosphere. When the Sun is not overhead, but is inclined at angle x to the surface of Earth, its rays pass through more air before they reach sea level. Call this y units of atmosphere. The value of y affects the temperature at the surface of Earth.

a) Use the diagram to determine an expression for y in terms of angle x.

b) Graph $y = f(x)$ on the interval $x \in \left[0, \dfrac{\pi}{2}\right]$.

c) Describe what happens to the value of y as x approaches 0.

d) Explain why the answer to part c) makes sense.

e) What assumptions did you make when constructing the model in part a)?

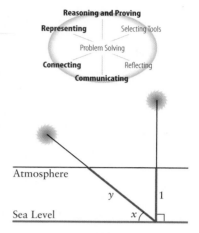

Solution

a) Use parallel lines:

$$\sin x = \frac{1}{y}$$

$$y = \frac{1}{\sin x}$$

$$y = \csc x$$

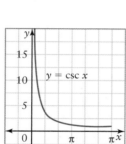

b) The graph is shown.

c) As x approaches 0, the value of y becomes very large.

d) The answer to part c) makes sense because the Sun's rays must travel through increasing amounts of air as angle x approaches 0.

e) The surface of Earth is assumed to be flat when constructing the model in part a). The atmosphere is assumed to be uniform and to end at a particular height above the surface of Earth.

CONNECTIONS

Many factors affect the temperature at the surface of Earth, such as particulate pollution, winds, and cloud cover. Climate scientists take these into account and build mathematical models that are used to predict temperatures. Since there are so many variables, many of which are difficult to model, the temperature predictions lose accuracy quickly with time.

Example 4   Reciprocal and Inverse Notation

a) Explain the difference between $\csc \dfrac{1}{2}$ and $\sin^{-1}\left(\dfrac{1}{2}\right)$.

b) Use a calculator to illustrate the difference between the expressions in part a).

Solution

a) The cosecant function is the reciprocal of the sine function.

$$\csc \frac{1}{2} = \frac{1}{\sin \dfrac{1}{2}}$$

$$= \left[\sin \frac{1}{2}\right]^{-1}$$

The inverse sine is the opposite operation of sine. The expression $\sin^{-1}\left(\dfrac{1}{2}\right)$ asks you to determine an angle whose sine is $\dfrac{1}{2}$.

b) $\csc\dfrac{1}{2} = \dfrac{1}{\sin\dfrac{1}{2}}$ $\sin^{-1}\left(\dfrac{1}{2}\right) = \dfrac{\pi}{6}$

$\phantom{\csc\dfrac{1}{2}} \doteq \dfrac{1}{0.4794}$

$\phantom{\csc\dfrac{1}{2}} \doteq 2.0858$

Technology Tip ∴

To evaluate csc x, use the [SIN] key and the reciprocal key, usually x^{-1} or $\dfrac{1}{x}$.

To evaluate $\sin^{-1}x$, use the $\sin^{-1}$ key. You will usually need to press the [2nd] key first.

Note: The reciprocal trigonometric ratio $\csc\dfrac{1}{2}$ can have only one possible answer. Since $\dfrac{1}{2}$ represents an angle measure in radians, the value of the cosecant is fixed. The inverse trigonometric expression $\sin^{-1}\left(\dfrac{1}{2}\right)$ has only one possible answer. On the other hand, $\sin x = \dfrac{1}{2}$ can have many possible solutions. Another is $\dfrac{5\pi}{6}$.

KEY CONCEPTS

- The graphs of $y = \csc x$, $y = \sec x$, and $y = \cot x$ are periodic. They are related to the graphs of the primary trigonometric functions as reciprocal graphs.

- Reciprocal trigonometric functions are different from inverse trigonometric functions.

  - $\csc x$ means $\dfrac{1}{\sin x}$, while $\sin^{-1}x$ asks you to find an angle that has a sine ratio equal to x

  - $\sec x$ means $\dfrac{1}{\cos x}$, while $\cos^{-1}x$ asks you to find an angle that has a cosine ratio equal to x

  - $\cot x$ means $\dfrac{1}{\tan x}$, while $\tan^{-1}x$ asks you to find an angle that has a tangent ratio equal to x

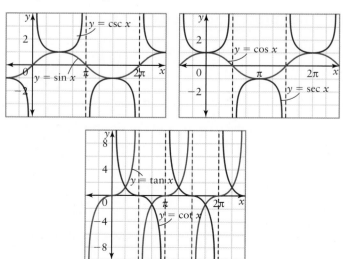

Communicate Your Understanding

C1 Determine an angle x in the interval $[0, 2\pi]$ such that $\cos x = \sec x$. Is this the only angle on this interval where this occurs? Justify your answer. If not, determine all other angles in the interval that satisfy this condition.

C2 For what values of x will the graph of $y = \tan x$ intersect the graph of $y = \cot x$ on the interval $[0, 2\pi]$? If there are no such intersections, explain why not.

C3 Consider the graph of $y = \csc 2x$. Predict the values of x in the interval $[0, 2\pi]$ at which asymptotes will occur. Justify your answer.

A) Practise

For help with questions 1 to 3, refer to Examples 1 and 2.

1. **Use Technology** Use graphing technology to determine all values of x in the interval $[0, 2\pi]$ such that $\csc x = 5$. Round your answers to two decimal places.

2. **Use Technology** Use graphing technology to determine all values of x in the interval $[0, 2\pi]$ such that $\sec x = 2$. Round your answers to two decimal places.

3. **Use Technology** Use graphing technology to determine all values of x in the interval $[0, 2\pi]$ such that $\cot x = -4$. Round your answers to two decimal places.

For help with questions 4 to 6, refer to Example 4.

4. **a)** Explain the difference between $\csc \dfrac{1}{\sqrt{2}}$ and $\sin^{-1}\left(\dfrac{1}{\sqrt{2}}\right)$.

   b) Determine a value for each expression in part a).

5. **a)** Explain the difference between $\sec \dfrac{\sqrt{3}}{2}$ and $\cos^{-1}\left(\dfrac{\sqrt{3}}{2}\right)$.

   b) Determine a value for each expression in part a).

6. **a)** Explain the difference between $\cot 1$ and $\tan^{-1}(1)$.

   b) Determine a value for each expression in part a).

B) Connect and Apply

7. **a)** Describe the graph of $y = \sec x$ in terms of a transformation of the graph of $y = \csc x$.

   b) Is there more than one transformation that will accomplish this? Explain your answer.

8. **Use Technology**

   a) Use graphing technology to show that there is at least one value of x such that $\csc x = \sin^{-1} x$.

   b) Determine a value of x that makes the equation in part a) true.

   c) Verify your value from part b).

9. A lifeguard at position L spots a swimmer in trouble at one corner of the pool, S. She runs down the length of the pool to position P, and then dives in and swims a distance d from P to S.

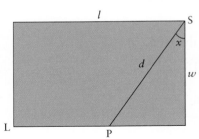

a) Show that the swimming distance is given by the relation $d = w \sec x$.

b) If $l = 2w$, determine the range of values that x may take on, given that P can be anywhere along the length of the pool.

c) Determine the range of values that d may take on.

d) Sketch a graph of $d = w \sec x$ over the appropriate interval.

e) Suggest reasons why the lifeguard might choose to swim, rather than run down the length and width, to reach the swimmer.

10. An awning is used to shade a window of height 2 m. It projects a distance d from the wall such that it completely shades the window when the Sun is at its maximum angle of elevation on the summer solstice.

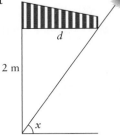

a) Show that the value of d is given by the relation $d = 2 \cot x$.

b) If $x = \dfrac{\pi}{3}$, how far must the awning project from the wall?

c) Sketch a graph of $d = 2 \cot x$ on the interval $x \in \left[0, \dfrac{\pi}{2}\right]$.

d) Interpret the meaning of the graph as x approaches 0 and as x approaches $\dfrac{\pi}{2}$.

11. Chapter Problem A variant on the carousel at a theme park is the swing ride. Swings are suspended from a rotating platform and move outward to form an angle x with the vertical as the ride rotates. The angle is related to the radial distance, r, in metres, from the centre of rotation; the acceleration, $g = 9.8$ m/s², due to gravity; and the speed, v, in metres per second, of the swing, according to the formula $\cot x = \dfrac{rg}{v^2}$.

a) Determine the angle x for a swing located 3.5 m from the centre of rotation and moving at 5.4 m/s, to the nearest hundredth of a radian.

b) If the distance from the centre of rotation is doubled, but the speed is kept the same, does the angle double? Justify your answer.

c) If the speed is doubled while keeping the distance from the centre of rotation the same, is the angle halved? Justify your answer.

12. Use Technology

a) Use graphing technology to determine whether it is reasonable to conjecture that $\csc^2 x = \cot^2 x$. If so, justify your conclusion. If not, use the graphs to determine a similar equation that is an identity.

b) Prove that your conjecture in part a) is true for all values of x for which the expressions on both sides are defined.

13. A lighthouse with a rotating beam is located 500 m south of a coastal cliff that runs west to east.

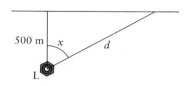

a) Determine a relation for the distance from the lighthouse to the point the light strikes the cliff in terms of the angle of rotation x.

b) Determine an exact expression for this distance when $x = \dfrac{5\pi}{12}$.

c) Sketch a graph of the relation in part a) on the interval $x \in \left[0, \dfrac{\pi}{2}\right]$.

✓ Achievement Check

14. A road is built up the slope of a hill with a height of h metres and an angle of inclination of x. The length of the road is d.

a) Sketch a diagram of this situation. Label all quantities.

b) Show that the length of the road is represented by the relation $d = h \csc x$.

c) Determine the length of a road that ascends a hill of height 100 m at an angle of 0.3. Round your answer to the nearest tenth of a metre.

d) Sketch a graph of $d = h \csc x$ for a hill of height 100 m and on the interval $x \in \left[0, \dfrac{\pi}{4}\right]$.

e) Interpret the meaning of the graph as x approaches 0.

C Extend and Challenge

15. a) Sketch the function $y = \csc x$.

b) Predict the shape of each function, and then check by graphing.

    i) $y = 3 \csc x$ ii) $y = \csc 2x$

    iii) $y = \csc x + 1$ iv) $y = \csc (x - 3)$

16. a) Sketch the function $y = \tan x$.

b) Predict the shape of each function, and then check by graphing.

    i) $y = 2 \tan x$ ii) $y = \tan 2x$

    iii) $y = \tan x + 3$ iv) $y = \tan (x + 1)$

17. Consider the equation $\sin^{-1}(\sin x) = x$ on the interval $x \in [0, 1]$.

a) Show that the equation is true for $x = 0.5$.

b) Is the equation true for any value of x such that $x \in \mathbb{R}$? Justify your answer.

18. Determine an exact value for $\sin\left[\cos^{-1}\left(\dfrac{4}{5}\right)\right]$ if $x \in \left[0, \dfrac{\pi}{2}\right]$.

19. **Math Contest** Refer to Section 5.1, question 24.

a) Sketch a graph of $r = 2\cos\theta$ by copying and completing the table of values.

θ	$r = 2\cos\theta$	(r, θ)
0		
$\dfrac{\pi}{6}$		
$\dfrac{\pi}{4}$		
$\dfrac{\pi}{3}$		
$\dfrac{\pi}{2}$		
$\dfrac{2\pi}{3}$		
$\dfrac{3\pi}{4}$		
$\dfrac{5\pi}{6}$		
π		

b) Sketch a graph of each polar equation.

    i) $r = 6$ ii) $r = 1 - \sin\theta$ iii) $r = \tan\theta$

Sinusoidal Functions of the Form $f(x) = a \sin [k(x - d)] + c$ and $f(x) = a \cos [k(x - d)] + c$

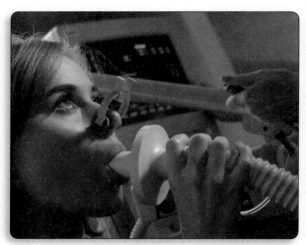

Many real-world applications can be modelled with sinusoidal functions. However, the construction of the model usually requires one or more transformations to fit the function to the data. One example is the volume of air contained in your lungs during normal breathing. The air inhaled and exhaled can be measured using a spirometer.

In this section, you will learn how to transform the sine and cosine functions so that you can use them as models for real-world applications later in the chapter.

Investigate | **How can you model the volume of air in your lungs using a sine function?**

Tools
- 2-L plastic bottle
- measuring cup or graduated cylinder
- flexible tube
- sink or basin with water
- grid paper or graphing technology

Optional
- spirometer
- computer with capture and graphing software such as Logger Pro® installed

OR

- graphing calculator with CBL 2™ Calculator-Based Laboratory

Note: The instructions that follow assume the use of a plastic bottle to capture exhaled air. If you are using laboratory technology, refer to the instructions that accompany the technology.

1. Time your normal breathing for several minutes, starting when you have finished exhaling, and counting the number of complete breaths. Determine the period of your breathing cycle when resting, in seconds.

2. Fill a 2-L plastic bottle with water. Invert the bottle in a sink or basin half full of water.

3. Breathe in normally. Then, exhale through a tube and capture the exhaled air in the bottle. Stop when you reach your normal minimum.

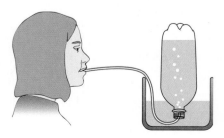

4. Refill the bottle using a measuring cup to determine the volume of air that you breathed out, in millilitres.

5. The model you will use to represent the volume, V, in millilitres, of air in your lungs, versus time, t, in seconds, has the form $V = a\sin[k(t - d)] + c$.

   a) Use the volume from step 4 to determine the amplitude, a, of the function.

   b) The value of c is derived from the volume of air that remains in your lungs after a normal exhalation. This is difficult to measure directly. A reasonable estimate for the value of c is to add 2.4 L to your value of a.

   c) Explain why the value of the phase shift, d, is $\frac{\pi}{2}$. Refer to step 1.

   d) Use the period you calculated in step 1 to determine the value of k.

   e) Write an equation to model the volume of air in your lungs.

6. Graph at least two cycles of the model you constructed in step 5.

7. **Reflect** Inspect the graph from step 6. Explain how it correctly shows the period, the maximum value, the minimum value, and the phase shift of your breathing cycle.

CONNECTIONS

It is not possible to expel all of the air from your lungs. Depending on the size of your lungs, about 1.2 L of air remain even when you think your lungs are empty.

Example 1 | Transform a Cosine Function

a) Transform the function $f(x) = \cos x$ to $g(x)$ such that $g(x)$ has an amplitude of 4, a period of π, a phase shift of $\frac{\pi}{6}$ rad to the left, and a vertical translation of 2 units upward.

b) Graph $g(x)$ over at least two cycles.

Solution

a) The function $g(x)$ will have the form $g(x) = a\cos[k(x - d)] + c$.

The desired amplitude is 4. Therefore, $a = 4$.

The desired period is π.

$$\pi = \frac{2\pi}{k} \qquad \text{Determine the value of } k \text{ required for a period of } \pi.$$

$$\pi k = 2\pi$$

$$k = 2$$

The phase shift is $\frac{\pi}{6}$ rad to the left. Therefore, $d = -\frac{\pi}{6}$.

The vertical translation is 2 units upward. Therefore, $c = 2$.

Substitute these values into the model for $g(x)$.

$$g(x) = 4\cos\left[2\left(x + \frac{\pi}{6}\right)\right] + 2$$

b) **Method 1:** *Use Pencil and Paper*

Start by sketching a cosine curve with an amplitude of 4 and a period of π: $y = 4\cos 2x$.

Use the fact that one cycle of a sinusoidal function includes a maximum, a minimum, and three zeros to help you select points along the curve.

Then, apply the phase shift of $\dfrac{\pi}{6}$ rad to the left and the vertical translation of 2 units upward to each point.

Sketch a smooth curve through the translated points.

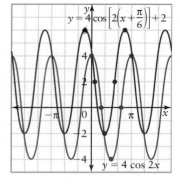

Method 2: *Use a Graphing Calculator*

On a graphing calculator, enter the function $g(x)$ using [Y=].

Press [ZOOM] and select **7:ZTrig**. Adjust the range of the vertical axis to display the graph properly. Use Ymin $= -4$ and Ymax $= 8$.

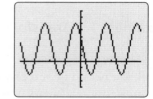

Example 2	**Transform a Sine Function to Match Data Not Given in Terms of π**

a) Transform the function $f(x) = \sin x$ to $g(x)$ such that $g(x)$ has an amplitude of 2, a period of 1, a phase shift of 0.5 rad to the left, and a vertical translation of 3 units upward.

b) Graph $g(x)$ over at least two cycles.

Solution

a) The function $g(x)$ will have the form $g(x) = a\sin[k(x - d)] + c$.

The desired amplitude is 2. Therefore, $a = 2$.

The desired period is 1.

$1 = \dfrac{2\pi}{k}$ Determine the value of k required for a period of 1.

$k = 2\pi$

The phase shift is 0.5 rad to the left. Therefore, $d = -0.5$.

The vertical translation is 3 units upward. Therefore, $c = 3$.

Substitute these values into the model for $g(x)$.

$g(x) = 2\sin[2\pi(x + 0.5)] + 3$

b) Method 1: *Use Pencil and Paper*

Start by sketching a sine curve with an amplitude of 2 and a period of 1: $y = 2 \sin 2\pi x$.

Use the fact that one cycle of a sinusoidal function includes a maximum, a minimum, and three zeros to help you select points along the curve.

Then, apply the phase shift of 0.5 rad to the left and the vertical translation of 3 units upward to each point.

Sketch a smooth curve through the translated points.

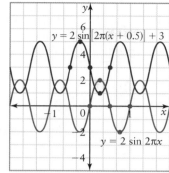

Method 2: *Use a Graphing Calculator*

On a graphing calculator, enter the function $g(x)$ using ⟨ Y= ⟩.

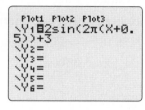

Press ⟨ZOOM⟩ and select **6:ZStandard**. Adjust the window variables to display the graph properly. Use Xmin = -2, Xmax = 2, Xscl = 1, Ymin = -4, and Ymax = 6.

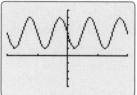

| Example 3 | **Model the Round-Up** |

The Round-Up is a popular ride at many theme parks. It consists of a large wheel that starts in a horizontal position. As the ride picks up rotational speed, the wheel tilts up to an angle of about $\frac{\pi}{4}$.

Reasoning and Proving
Representing — Selecting Tools
Problem Solving
Connecting — Reflecting
Communicating

a) Determine a sine function model for the vertical position, h, in metres, of a rider on the Round-Up after time, t, in seconds, with the following specifications:

The maximum height above the ground is 7.5 m and the minimum height is 1.5 m.

The wheel completes one turn in 5 s.

The model predicts the highest point at $t = 0$ s.

b) Graph the model and verify that it matches the requirements in part a).

Solution

a) The model will have the form $h = a\sin[k(t - d)] + c$. Determine the values of a, k, d, and c.

In this situation, the amplitude is half the difference between the maximum and minimum heights.

$$a = \frac{7.5 - 1.5}{2}$$

$$= 3$$

The desired period is 5 s.

$$5 = \frac{2\pi}{k} \qquad \text{Determine the value of } k \text{ required for a period of 5 s.}$$

$$5k = 2\pi$$

$$k = 0.4\pi$$

The maximum value of the sine function normally occurs at $\frac{1}{4}$ of a period. In this case, one quarter of a period is $\frac{5}{4}$, or 1.25 s.

However, in this model the highest point is to occur at $t = 0$ s.

Find the phase shift, d.

$$t - d = 1.25$$
$$0 - d = 1.25$$
$$d = -1.25$$

The phase shift is one and one-quarter period to the left.

The vertical translation is the average of the maximum and minimum heights.

$$c = \frac{7.5 + 1.5}{2}$$

$$= 4.5$$

A sine function that models the Round-Up is $h = 3\sin[0.4\pi(t + 1.25)] + 4.5$.

b) On a graphing calculator, enter the model equation.

Press [ZOOM] and select **6:ZStandard**.

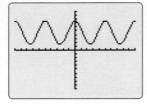

Use the [TRACE] key to help you verify that the graph matches the requirements from part a).

- The transformation of a sine or cosine function $f(x)$ to $g(x)$ has the general form $g(x) = af[k(x - d)] + c$, where $|a|$ is the amplitude, d is the phase shift, and c is the vertical translation.

- The period of the transformed function is given by $\dfrac{2\pi}{k}$.

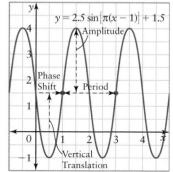

Communicate Your Understanding

C1 Consider the transformation of the cosine function represented by $g(x) = 2\cos(3x - 2) + 5$. Explain why the phase shift is not 2 rad to the right and determine the actual phase shift.

C2 Consider the transformation of the sine function represented by $g(x) = 3\sin\left[2\left(x - \dfrac{3\pi}{4}\right)\right] + 4$. Explain why $g(x)$ has no zeros. Check by graphing.

C3 Consider Example 3. Is it possible to model the Round-Up using a cosine function? If so, describe what changes would need to be made in the equation of the transformation. If not, explain why not.

A Practise

For help with questions 1 to 6, refer to Examples 1 and 2.

1. Determine the amplitude and the period of each sinusoidal function. Then, transform the graph of $y = \sin x$ to sketch a graph of each function.

a) $y = 5\sin 3x$

b) $y = -3\cos \dfrac{4}{3}x$

c) $y = 3\sin \pi x$

d) $y = \dfrac{1}{2}\cos \dfrac{1}{4}x$

e) $y = -1.5\sin 0.2\pi x$

f) $y = 0.75\cos 0.8\pi x$

2. Determine an equation in the form $y = a\sin kx$ or $y = a\cos kx$ for each graph.

a)

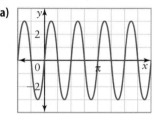

b)

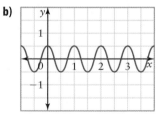

3. Consider the function $y = 4 \sin \left[3 \left(x + \frac{\pi}{3} \right) \right] - 2$.

   a) What is the amplitude?

   b) What is the period?

   c) Describe the phase shift.

   d) Describe the vertical translation.

   e) Sketch a graph of the function for two cycles.

4. Consider the function $y = 3 \cos \left[\pi(x + 2) \right] - 1$.

   a) What is the amplitude?

   b) What is the period?

   c) Describe the phase shift.

   d) Describe the vertical translation.

   e) Sketch a graph of the function for two cycles.

5. Determine the amplitude, the period, the phase shift, and the vertical translation for each function with respect to $y = \sin x$. Then, sketch a graph of the function for two cycles.

   a) $y = 3 \sin \left(x + \frac{\pi}{4} \right) - 1$

   b) $y = -2 \sin \left[\frac{1}{2} \left(x - \frac{5\pi}{6} \right) \right] + 4$

   c) $y = 2 \sin \left[2\pi(x + 3) \right] - 2$

6. Determine the amplitude, the period, the phase shift, and the vertical translation for each function with respect to $y = \cos x$. Then, sketch a graph of the function for two cycles.

   a) $y = 3 \cos \left(x - \frac{\pi}{4} \right) + 6$

   b) $y = -5 \cos \left[\frac{1}{4} \left(x + \frac{4\pi}{3} \right) \right] - 5$

   c) $y = 7 \cos \left[3\pi(x - 2) \right] + 7$

7. a) Refer to Example 3. Determine a model for the Round-Up using a cosine function.

   b) Graph the model and verify that it matches the requirements in part a).

8. Model the graph shown using a sine function.

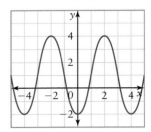

   a) From the graph, determine the amplitude, the period, the phase shift, and the vertical translation.

   b) Write an equation for the function.

   c) Graph the equation of the function.

   d) Compare the graph in part c) to the given graph, and verify that the graphs match.

9. Model the graph shown using a cosine function.

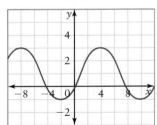

   a) From the graph, determine the amplitude, the period, the phase shift, and the vertical translation.

   b) Write an equation for the function.

   c) Graph the equation of the function.

   d) Compare the graph in part c) to the given graph, and verify that the graphs match.

10. Determine an equation for each sine function. Check by graphing.

a)

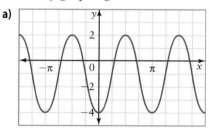

b)

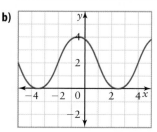

11. Determine an equation for each cosine function. Check by graphing.

a)

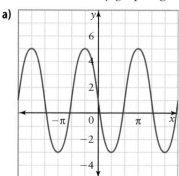

b)

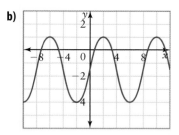

12. A sine function has a maximum value of 7, a minimum value of -1, a phase shift of $\frac{3\pi}{4}$ rad to the left, and a period of $\frac{\pi}{2}$.

a) Write an equation for the function.

b) Graph the function and verify that it has the properties given.

13. A cosine function has a maximum value of 1, a minimum value of -5, a phase shift of 2 rad to the right, and a period of 3.

a) Write an equation for the function.

b) Graph the function and verify that it has the properties given.

14. A sine function is transformed such that it has a single x-intercept in the interval $[0, \pi]$, a period of π, and a y-intercept of 3.

Reasoning and Proving
Representing   **Selecting Tools**
Problem Solving
Connecting   **Reflecting**
Communicating

a) Determine an equation for a function that satisfies the properties given.

b) Graph the equation and verify that the given properties are satisfied.

c) Are there any other sine functions that match the given properties? If not, explain why not. If so, provide one example and its graph.

15. A cosine function has twice the period of $y = \cos x$. All other parameters are the same between the two functions.

a) Predict the number of points of intersection if the two functions are graphed on the interval $x \in [0, 2\pi]$. Justify your answer.

b) **Use Technology** Use technology to determine the coordinates of all points of intersection in part a). Was your prediction correct? If not, explain why not.

16. a) Write an equation for a transformed cosine function that includes at least three transformations. Generate a minimum number of clues to the transformation. Solve your problem to ensure that the clues are adequate to deduce the transformation.

b) Trade clues with a classmate. Determine the transformations required to match the clues. If more than one answer is possible, explain why.

c) Trade solutions, and discuss any observations or concerns.

17. Use Technology

a) Search the Internet for data on the fraction of the Moon that is illuminated at midnight every day for the current month.

b) Plot the data on a graph.

c) Use the graph to determine a sinusoidal model for the data.

d) Graph the model and compare it to the data. Comment on the accuracy of the fit.

18. Chapter Problem A popular ride at many theme parks is the Gravitron, which pins riders to the walls of the ride as it spins and then drops the floor to leave them suspended by friction and centrifugal effects. Suppose that such a ride is designed with a radius of 4 m and a period of 2 s, with the origin at the centre of rotation.

a) Model the x-position as a function of time, t, using a sine function.

b) Model the y-position as a function of time, t, using a cosine function.

c) Graph the x and y models.

d) Show that $x^2 + y^2 = 16$ for all values of t.

e) Explain why the relation in part d) is always true.

19. A buoy bobs up and down in the lake. The distance between the highest and lowest points is 1.5 m. It takes 6 s for the buoy to move from its highest point to its lowest point and back to its highest point.

a) Model the vertical displacement, v, in metres, of the buoy as a function of time, t, in seconds. Assume that the buoy is at its equilibrium point at $t = 0$ s and that the buoy is on its way down at that time.

b) Sketch a graph of v versus t over two cycles.

20. The piston in the engine of a small aircraft moves horizontally relative to the crankshaft, from a minimum distance of 25 cm to a maximum distance of 75 cm. During normal cruise power settings, the piston completes 2100 rpm (revolutions per minute).

Reasoning and Proving
Representing · Selecting Tools
Problem Solving
Connecting · Reflecting
Communicating

a) Model the horizontal position, h, in centimetres, of the piston as a function of time, t, in seconds.

b) Sketch a graph of h versus t over two cycles.

c) If the pilot increases the engine speed to 2400 rpm, what changes need to be made to the model? Justify your answer.

✓ Achievement Check

21. Consider the function $y = 4\sin\left[2\left(x + \dfrac{2\pi}{3}\right)\right] - 5$.

a) What is the amplitude?

b) What is the period?

c) Describe the phase shift.

d) Describe the vertical translation.

e) Graph the function. Compare the graph to the properties in parts a) to d).

f) Describe the x-intercepts of the function. Explain your answer.

22. Use Technology Consider the function $y = \csc x$. Use a graphing calculator to investigate the effects of a, k, d, and c when these are used to transform the function in a manner similar to the transformations of the sine function that you studied in this section. Summarize your findings in a table.

23. The vertical position, h, in metres, of a gondola on a Ferris wheel is modelled using the function $h = 10 \sin\left[\dfrac{\pi}{15}(t - d)\right] + 12$, where t is the time, in seconds. The gondola must assume a vertical position of 7 m at $t = 0$ s and be on its way upward.

a) Determine the phase shift required for the desired operation of the Ferris wheel. Explain your method and show that your answer is correct.

b) Determine the phase shift using a different method. Explain your method and show that your answer is correct.

24. Use Technology Consider the function $y = 5 \sin(x + 1)$. By properly selecting values of a and b, the expression on the right side can be written as $a \sin x + b \cos x$.

a) Use technology to graph the function.

b) Select values for a and b, and graph the second expression. Then, adjust the values of a and b until the two graphs coincide.

c) Record the values of a and b.

d) Select a test value for x, and show that the two expressions result in the same answer.

e) Use technology to demonstrate that $\sin x + \cos x = \sqrt{2} \sin\left(x + \dfrac{\pi}{4}\right)$.

Technology Tip ⠒⠆

If you use *The Geometer's Sketchpad* ® to graph the function, you can construct sliders to control the values of a and b dynamically. You can find information on how to construct sliders by accessing the Help menu.

---

25. Math Contest Use Technology Refer to Section 5.1, question 24. You can use technology such as a graphing calculator to graph functions in polar form.

- Press MODE . Set the graphing calculator to Polar graphing mode and Radian angle mode.

- Press WINDOW . Use the following settings:

  $\theta\text{min} = 0$

  $\theta\text{max} = \pi$

  $\theta\text{step} = \dfrac{\pi}{6}$

  $X\text{min} = -2$

  $X\text{max} = 2$

  $X\text{scl} = 0.1$

  $Y\text{min} = -1$

  $Y\text{max} = 3$

  $Y\text{scl} = 0.1$

- Graph $r = 2 \sin \theta$.

a) Explore the θstep setting. Display the graph of $r = 2 \sin \theta$ using $\theta\text{step} = \dfrac{\pi}{10}$. Repeat for $\theta\text{step} = \dfrac{\pi}{100}$. Explain how the value of θstep affects the graph.

b) Graph each relation using window settings of your choice.

   i) $r = 6$

   ii) $r = 1 - \sin \theta$

   iii) $r = 2(1 - \sin \theta)$

   iv) $r = \theta$

   v) $r = \cos 2\theta$

   vi) $r = 3 + 5 \cos \theta$

Extension

Use a Graphing Calculator to Fit a Sinusoidal Regression to Given Data

Part 1: *Explore Sinusoidal Regression*

Tools

• graphing calculator

Sinusoidal regression is a statistical process, often implemented using technology, that determines a sinusoidal function that best represents a collection of data points.

1. A sinusoidal regression requires a minimum of five points. If you want an accurate regression, select points that cover a wide range of x- and y-values across a single cycle. If you pick five points that are too close together and do not cover a cycle adequately, the regression will match those points well but will diverge from the desired function as you move away from the five points. Since regression is a statistical process, care must be taken in extrapolating from the resulting model.

   a) As an example, select five values of x that represent special angles in the interval $x \in [0, 2\pi]$, as shown. Copy the table.

x	y
0	
0.5π	
π	
1.5π	
2π	

   b) Let $y = \sin x$. Complete the y-column of the table using your knowledge of special angles.

2. Clear the lists on the calculator. Enter the x-values in **L1** and the y-values in **L2**. Display the scatter plot.

3. Determine the equation of the curve of best fit.

   a) Press ⬚STAT. Cursor over to the **CALC** menu and select **C:SinReg**.

   b) Press ⬚2nd **1** for [L1], followed by ⬚,.

   c) Press ⬚2nd **2** for [L2], followed by ⬚,.

   d) Press ⬚VARS, cursor over to the **Y-VARS** menu, and then select **1:Function...** and **1:Y1**.

   e) Press ⬚ENTER.

4. Take note of the form of the equation. How is it different from the form you learned in Section 5.3?

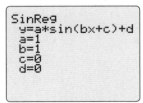

```
SinReg
 y=a*sin(bx+c)+d
 a=1
 b=1
 c=0
 d=0
```

5. Press (ZOOM) and select **7:Z Trig**. Inspect the graph.

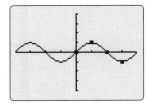

Technology Tip   ∴

The sinusoidal regression will yield an answer using radian measure, even if your calculator is set to degree mode.

6. Reflect Explain why the graph follows the familiar curve that you worked with in Section 5.1.

Part 2: *Apply Sinusoidal Regression to Real-World Data*

1. The times of sunrise in Fort Erie, Ontario, on the first of each month over 1 year are shown.

Sunrise in Fort Erie, ON	
Date	**Time**
Jan 1	7:47
Feb 1	7:31
Mar 1	6:52
Apr 1	5:58
May 1	5:10
Jun 1	4:40
Jul 1	4:40
Aug 1	5:06
Sep 1	5:40
Oct 1	6:12
Nov 1	6:49
Dec 1	7:26

a) Copy the table. Add a column to express the time of sunrise as a decimal value, rounded to two decimal places. Complete the table.

b) Enter the integers 1 to 12 in list **L1** to represent the months. Enter the decimal values of the sunrise times in list **L2**.

c) Display the scatter plot.

2. a) Perform a sinusoidal regression to fit a sine function to these data. Record the regression equation.

b) Determine the amplitude, the maximum value, the minimum value, the period, the phase shift, and the vertical translation of the regression model.

c) Use the values from part b) to determine appropriate window settings. Graph the regression model.

3. Use the graph to estimate the time of sunrise on June 15th.

4. Reflect Quito, the capital of Ecuador, lies on the equator. How would the amplitude of the regression model for Quito compare to the amplitude of the regression model for Fort Erie? How would the periods compare? Justify your answers.

Technology Tip   ∴

If you have worked with regression before, you may be surprised that the calculator did not display a value of the coefficient of determination, R^2. It will not display this value for sinusoidal regressions.

5.4 Solve Trigonometric Equations

The designer of a new model of skis must model their performance as a skier slides down a hill. The model involves trigonometric functions. Once the design is modelled, equations must be solved for various snow conditions and other factors to determine the expected performance of the skis. In this section, you will learn how to solve trigonometric equations with and without technology.

Investigate **How can you use trigonometric identities and special angles to solve a trigonometric equation?**

Tools

- Special Angles and Trigonometric Ratios table from Chapter 4
- graphing calculator

1. Consider the trigonometric equation $2 \sin x - 1 = 0$. Solve the equation for $\sin x$.

2. Refer to your Special Angles and Trigonometric Ratios table.

   a) Determine an angle x in the interval $[0, 2\pi]$ whose sine matches the sine in step 1. Use radian measure.

   b) Determine another angle x in the interval $[0, 2\pi]$ that matches this sine.

3. Use the left side/right side method to verify that your solutions are valid.

4. **Reflect** Are these the only angles in the interval $[0, 2\pi]$ that work? Justify your answer.

5. Graph the left side of the equation.

   - Ensure that the graphing calculator is in Radian mode.
   - Enter $2 \sin x - 1$ using ⬚Y=⬚.
   - Press ⬚ZOOM⬚ and select **7:ZTrig.**

6. **a)** Use the **Zero** operation to determine the first zero to the right of the origin.

   - Press ⬚2nd⬚ [CALC] to display the **CALCULATE** menu.
   - Select **2:zero.**
   - Move the cursor to locations for the left bound, right bound, and guess, pressing ⬚ENTER⬚ after each.

   b) How does this value compare to your solutions in step 2?

7. Use the **Zero** operation to determine any other solutions in the interval $[0, 2\pi]$. Compare them to your solutions in step 2.

8. Reflect Suppose that the right side of the equation in step 1 were not 0, but -2. Could you still find the solutions by graphing the left side? If so, explain how, and demonstrate using a graphing calculator. If not, how could you modify the procedure to yield the correct solutions? Demonstrate your modifications using the graphing calculator.

Example 1 | Solve a Quadratic Trigonometric Equation

Determine the exact solutions for the trigonometric equation $2\sin^2 x - 1 = 0$ in the interval $x \in [0, 2\pi]$.

Solution

Method 1: *Use Pencil and Paper*

$$2\sin^2 x - 1 = 0$$

$$2\sin^2 x = 1$$

$$\sin^2 x = \frac{1}{2}$$

$$\sin x = \pm\frac{1}{\sqrt{2}}$$

Case 1: $\sin x = \dfrac{1}{\sqrt{2}}$

The angles in the interval $[0, 2\pi]$ that satisfy $\sin x = \dfrac{1}{\sqrt{2}}$ are $x = \dfrac{\pi}{4}$ and $x = \dfrac{3\pi}{4}$.

Case 2: $\sin x = -\dfrac{1}{\sqrt{2}}$

The angles in the interval $[0, 2\pi]$ that satisfy $\sin x = -\dfrac{1}{\sqrt{2}}$ are $x = \dfrac{5\pi}{4}$ and $x = \dfrac{7\pi}{4}$.

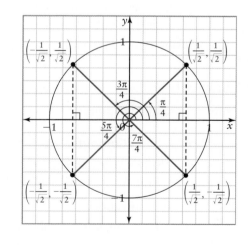

CONNECTIONS

In Chapter 4, Section 4.2, you learned how special triangles, the unit circle, and the CAST rule can be used to determine exact values for the trigonometric ratios of special angles and their multiples.

The solutions in the interval $[0, 2\pi]$ are $x = \dfrac{\pi}{4}$, $x = \dfrac{3\pi}{4}$, $x = \dfrac{5\pi}{4}$, and $x = \dfrac{7\pi}{4}$.

Check: $x = \dfrac{\pi}{4}$

L.S. $= 2\sin^2 x - 1$ **R.S.** $= 0$

$\qquad = 2\sin^2 \dfrac{\pi}{4} - 1$ Substitute $\dfrac{\pi}{4}$ for x.

$\qquad = 2\left(\dfrac{1}{\sqrt{2}}\right)^2 - 1$ Evaluate the sine ratio.

$\qquad = 2\left(\dfrac{1}{2}\right) - 1$

$\qquad = 1 - 1$

$\qquad = 0$

L.S. = R.S.

Therefore, $x = \dfrac{\pi}{4}$ is a solution. The check of the other solutions is left to the reader.

Method 2: *Use a Graphing Calculator*

Ensure that the graphing calculator is in Radian mode.

Enter the left side of the equation using $\boxed{\text{Y=}}$.

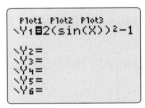

Display the graph using the ZTrig window settings.

Use the **Zero** operation to determine the first zero to the right of the origin.

The solution is $x = 0.785\ldots$, or $x = \dfrac{\pi}{4}$.

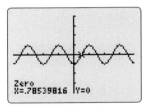

Technology Tip ⸫

Instead of typing $<=$, you can press $\boxed{\blacklozenge}$ **0** to obtain $\leq$. You can type the "and" operator using the $\boxed{\text{ALPHA}}$ key or select it from the **CATALOG** menu. The condition $0 \leq x \leq 2\pi$ restricts the domain of the answers.

To see all four of the answers, cursor up to the answer line and then right.

For approximate answers, you can set the **Exact/Approx** mode to **APPROXIMATE**, use the **approx(** operation from the **F2** menu before the **solve(** operation, or press $\boxed{\blacklozenge}$ $\boxed{\text{ENTER}}$ for $\approx$.

In a similar manner, you can determine the three remaining solutions in the interval $[0, 2\pi]$. The solutions are $x = \dfrac{\pi}{4}$, $x = \dfrac{3\pi}{4}$, $x = \dfrac{5\pi}{4}$, and $x = \dfrac{7\pi}{4}$.

Method 3: *Use a Computer Algebra System (CAS)*

Press $\boxed{\text{MODE}}$. Ensure that the **Angle** mode is set to **RADIAN** and that the **Exact/Approx** mode is set to **AUTO**.

Use the **solve(** operation.

- From the **F2** menu, select **1:solve(**.
- Type $2 \times (\sin(x)) \wedge 2 - 1 = 0, x) \,|\, 0 <= x$ and $x <= 2\pi$.
- Press $\boxed{\text{ENTER}}$.

The calculator returns the four answers between 0 and 2π:

$x = \dfrac{\pi}{4}$, $x = \dfrac{3\pi}{4}$, $x = \dfrac{5\pi}{4}$, and $x = \dfrac{7\pi}{4}$.

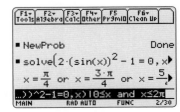

Example 2 | Solve a Trigonometric Equation by Factoring

Solve $\cos^2 x - \cos x - 2 = 0$ on the interval $x \in [0, 2\pi]$. Use a graphing calculator to illustrate your solutions.

Solution

Factor the trinomial.

$$\cos^2 x - \cos x - 2 = 0$$
$$(\cos x - 2)(\cos x + 1) = 0$$
$$\cos x - 2 = 0 \quad \text{or} \quad \cos x + 1 = 0$$

Case 1:

$$\cos x - 2 = 0$$
$$\cos x = 2$$

Since the maximum possible value for $\cos x$ is 1, there are no solutions.

Case 2:

$$\cos x + 1 = 0$$
$$\cos x = -1$$

The only solution in the given domain is $x = \pi$.

Graph $y = \cos^2 x - \cos x - 2$ using the ZTrig window settings.

The only solution in the interval $[0, 2\pi]$ is $x = \pi$.

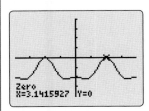

Zero
X=3.1415927 Y=0

CONNECTIONS

If the factoring step is not clear to you, try a substitution method. For example, to solve $\cos^2 x - \cos x - 2 = 0$, let $\cos x = u$ and rewrite the equation. Then, factor the trinomial. Finally, substitute $\cos x$ for u.

$$u^2 - u - 2 = 0$$
$$(u - 2)(u + 1) = 0$$
$$(\cos x - 2)(\cos x + 1) = 0$$

Example 3 | Solve an Equation Involving Reciprocal Trigonometric Ratios

Solve $2\csc^2 x + \csc x - 1 = 0$ on the interval $x \in [0, 2\pi]$.

Solution

Factor the trinomial.

$$2\csc^2 x + \csc x - 1 = 0$$
$$(2\csc x - 1)(\csc x + 1) = 0$$
$$2\csc x - 1 = 0 \quad \text{or} \quad \csc x + 1 = 0$$

Case 1:

$$2 \csc x - 1 = 0$$

$$\csc x = \frac{1}{2}$$

$$\sin x = 2 \qquad \csc x = \frac{1}{\sin x}$$

Since the maximum possible value for $\sin x$ is 1, there are no solutions.

Case 2:

$$\csc x + 1 = 0$$

$$\csc x = -1$$

$$\sin x = -1 \qquad \csc x = \frac{1}{\sin x}$$

The only solution in the given domain is $x = \frac{3\pi}{2}$.

Example 4	Solve a Trajectory Problem

The range of an arrow shot from a particular bow can be modelled by the equation $r = 100 \sin 2\theta$, where r is the range, in metres, and θ is the angle, in radians, above the horizontal that the arrow is released. A target is placed 80 m away.

a) What are the restrictions on the angle θ? Justify your answer.

b) Determine the angle or angles that the archer should use to hit the target, to the nearest hundredth of a radian.

Solution

a) The angle θ cannot exceed $\frac{\pi}{2}$, which is straight up. The maximum value of 2θ is $2 \times \frac{\pi}{2}$, or π.

You are looking for solutions for 2θ between 0 and π.

b) Substitute the desired range into the equation, and solve for the angle θ.

$$100 \sin 2\theta = 80$$

$$\sin 2\theta = 0.8$$

$$2\theta = \sin^{-1}(0.8)$$

$$2\theta \doteq 0.927$$

$$\theta \doteq 0.46$$

However, if 2θ lies in the second quadrant, then θ will lie in the first quadrant. Use the trigonometric identity $\sin x = \sin(\pi - x)$.

$$\pi - 2\theta \doteq 0.927$$

$$2\theta \doteq 2.214$$

$$\theta \doteq 1.11$$

The angles that result in a range of 80 m are approximately $\theta = 0.46$ and $\theta = 1.11$.

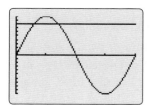

You can see that the graphs of $r = 100 \sin 2\theta$ and $r = 80$ intersect at two points in the interval $[0, \pi]$.

CONNECTIONS

An archer will always choose the lesser of the two angles. The arrow will travel faster, follow a flatter trajectory, and be more likely to hit the target on its way down.

Communicate Your Understanding

C1 Consider the trigonometric equation $\sin x = 1$. How many solutions do you expect in the interval $x \in [0, 2\pi]$? Justify your answer.

C2 Consider the quadratic trigonometric equation $4\cos^2 x - 1 = 0$. How many solutions do you expect in the interval $x \in [0, 2\pi]$? Justify your answer.

C3 Consider the trigonometric equation $\sin 3x - 2 = 0$. Use transformations to explain why there are no solutions.

C4 Consider the trigonometric equation $3\cos^2 x - 2\cos x = 0$. It is tempting to divide each side of the equation by $\cos x$ to simplify. Explain why this is not a valid procedure.

A   Practise

For help with questions 1 to 4, refer to the Investigate.

1. Determine approximate solutions for each equation in the interval $x \in [0, 2\pi]$, to the nearest hundredth of a radian.

   a) $\sin x - \dfrac{1}{4} = 0$ **b)** $\cos x + 0.75 = 0$

   c) $\tan x - 5 = 0$ **d)** $\sec x - 4 = 0$

   e) $3\cot x + 2 = 0$ **f)** $2\csc x + 5 = 0$

2. **Use Technology** Verify the answers to question 1 by graphing with technology.

3. Determine exact solutions for each equation in the interval $x \in [0, 2\pi]$.

   a) $\sin x + \dfrac{\sqrt{3}}{2} = 0$ **b)** $\cos x - 0.5 = 0$

   c) $\tan x - 1 = 0$ **d)** $\cot x + 1 = 0$

4. Illustrate the answers to question 3 by graphing.

For help with questions 5 to 12, refer to Examples 1 to 3.

5. Determine approximate solutions for each equation in the interval $x \in [0, 2\pi]$, to the nearest hundredth of a radian.

   a) $\sin^2 x - 0.64 = 0$

   b) $\cos^2 x - \dfrac{4}{9} = 0$

   c) $\tan^2 x - 1.44 = 0$

   d) $\sec^2 x - 2.5 = 0$

   e) $\cot^2 x - 1.21 = 0$

6. **Use Technology** Verify the answers to question 5 by graphing with technology.

7. Determine exact solutions for each equation in the interval $x \in [0, 2\pi]$.

   a) $\sin^2 x - \dfrac{1}{4} = 0$ **b)** $\cos^2 x - \dfrac{3}{4} = 0$

   c) $\tan^2 x - 3 = 0$ **d)** $3\csc^2 x - 4 = 0$

8. Use Technology Use a graphing calculator to illustrate the answers to question 7.

9. Solve $\sin^2 x - 2\sin x - 3 = 0$ on the interval $x \in [0, 2\pi]$.

10. Solve $\csc^2 x - \csc x - 2 = 0$ on the interval $x \in [0, 2\pi]$.

11. Solve $2\sec^2 x + \sec x - 1 = 0$ on the interval $x \in [0, 2\pi]$.

12. Solve $\tan^2 x + \tan x - 6 = 0$ on the interval $x \in [0, 2\pi]$. Round answers to the nearest hundredth of a radian.

For help with question 13, refer to Example 4.

13. Determine approximate solutions for each equation in the interval $2x \in [0, \pi]$, to the nearest hundredth of a radian.

a) $\sin 2x - 0.8 = 0$

b) $5\sin 2x - 3 = 0$

c) $-4\sin 2x + 3 = 0$

B Connect and Apply

For the remaining questions, determine exact solutions where possible. If exact solutions are not possible, determine approximate solutions, rounded to the nearest hundredth of a radian. Be sure to indicate whether a solution is exact or approximate.

14. Solve $2\tan^2 x + 1 = 0$ on the interval $x \in [0, 2\pi]$.

15. Solve $3\sin 2x - 1 = 0$ on the interval $x \in [0, 2\pi]$.

16. Solve $6\cos^2 x + 5\cos x - 6 = 0$ on the interval $x \in [0, 2\pi]$.

17. Solve $3\csc^2 x - 5\csc x - 2 = 0$ on the interval $x \in [0, 2\pi]$.

18. Solve $\sec^2 x + 5\sec x + 6 = 0$ on the interval $x \in [0, 2\pi]$.

19. Solve $2\tan^2 x - 5\tan x - 3 = 0$ on the interval $x \in [0, 2\pi]$.

20. Consider the trigonometric equation $3\sin^2 x + \sin x - 1 = 0$.

a) Explain why the left side of the equation cannot be factored.

b) Use the quadratic formula to obtain the roots.

c) Determine all solutions in the interval $x \in [0, 2\pi]$.

21. Use Technology

a) Refer to question 20. Use a graphing calculator or a CAS to check your solutions.

b) Explain how the technology can help you ensure that you have found all of the possible solutions in the domain of interest.

22. Chapter Problem The height, h, in metres, above the ground of a rider on a Ferris wheel can be modelled by the equation $h = 10\sin\left(\dfrac{\pi}{15}(t - 7.5)\right) + 12$, where t is the time, in seconds.

a) At $t = 0$ s, the rider is at the lowest point. Determine the first two times that the rider is 20 m above the ground, to the nearest hundredth of a second.

b) Use a graph to illustrate your solutions to part a).

23. Consider the trigonometric equation $4\sin x \cos 2x + 4\cos x \sin 2x - 1 = 0$ in the interval $x \in [0, 2\pi]$. Either show that there is no solution to the equation in this domain, or determine the smallest possible solution.

Reasoning and Proving

Representing — Selecting Tools

Problem Solving

Connecting — Reflecting

Communicating

24. The range of a "human-cannonball" act at a circus can be modelled by the equation $r = \dfrac{v^2}{g}\sin 2\theta$, where r is the range, in metres; v is the launch speed, in metres per second; g is the acceleration due to gravity, 9.8 m/s²; and θ is the angle above the horizontal that the cannon is aimed. The target net is placed 20 m away. If the human cannonball is launched at 15 m/s, determine the angle or angles at which the cannon could be aimed to hit the target.

25. Consider the equation $2\cos^2 x + \sin x - 1 = 0$.

a) Explain why the equation cannot be factored.

b) Suggest a trigonometric identity that can be used to remove the problem identified in part a).

c) Apply the identity and rearrange the equation into a factorable form.

d) Factor the equation.

e) Determine all solutions in the interval $x \in [0, 2\pi]$.

f) Use a graph to verify your answers to part e).

C Extend and Challenge

26. Determine solutions for $\tan x \cos^2 x - \tan x = 0$ in the interval $x \in [-2\pi, 2\pi]$.

27. The voltage, V, in volts, applied to an electric circuit can be modelled by the equation $V = 167\sin(120\pi t)$, where t is the time, in seconds. A component in the circuit can safely withstand a voltage of more than 120 V for 0.01 s or less.

a) Determine the length of time that the voltage is greater than 120 V on each half-cycle.

b) Is it safe to use this component in this circuit? Justify your answer.

28. Determine solutions for

$$\frac{\cos x}{1 + \sin x} + \frac{1 + \sin x}{\cos x} = 2$$

in the interval $x \in [-2\pi, 2\pi]$.

29. Math Contest Refer to Section 5.1, question 24. You can use symmetry to help you graph polar curves.

a) Investigate symmetry about the *polar axis* (x-axis) by replacing θ with $-\theta$ in the polar equation $r = 2\cos\theta$. Explain why there is symmetry.

b) Investigate symmetry about the *pole* (origin) by replacing r with $-r$ and by replacing θ with $\theta + \pi$ in the polar equation $r^2 = \tan\theta$. Explain why there is symmetry.

c) Investigate symmetry about $\theta = \dfrac{\pi}{2}$ (y-axis) by replacing θ with $\pi - \theta$ in the polar equation $r^3 \sin\theta = 2$. Explain why there is symmetry.

CAREER CONNECTION

Thomas completed a 4-year science degree in atmospheric science at York University. In his career as a meteorologist, he provides weather-consulting services for airports in the region. Thomas collects data on wind current, precipitation, and air pressure from weather satellites, radar, and meteorological stations. Then, he analyses the data using a complex computer model to predict the weather so that airplanes can take off and land safely.

Making Connections and Instantaneous Rate of Change

Sinusoidal models apply to many real-world phenomena that do not necessarily involve angles. In a vehicle that uses a steering system that moves back and forth easily, an oscillation known as a speed wobble, or shimmy, can occur if the amplitude of the oscillations is not reduced. Dangerous speed wobbles can occur in motorcycles, bicycles, tricycle-geared aircraft, jeeps, skateboards, in-line skates, and grocery carts. The speed wobble can be modelled using a sinusoidal function.

| **Investigate** | **How can you determine average and instantaneous rates of change for a sinusoidal function?** |

Tools

- computer with *The Geometer's Sketchpad* ®

Optional

- graph of sine function and mathematics construction set

1. a) Open *The Geometer's Sketchpad*®. From the **Edit** menu, choose **Preferences**, and click on the **Units** tab. Set the angle units to radians and the precision to ten thousandths for all measurements.

b) Turn on the grid, and plot the function $f(x) = \sin x$.

c) Plot points A and B on the function.

d) Measure the x- and y-coordinates of points A and B.

e) Construct a secant from B to A.

f) Measure the slope of secant BA.

2. a) Drag point A until its x-coordinate is approximately $\frac{\pi}{4}$, rounded to two decimal places. Drag point B until its x-coordinate is approximately $\frac{\pi}{6}$, rounded to two decimal places.

b) Calculate the average rate of change of the sine function from $x = \frac{\pi}{6}$ to $x = \frac{\pi}{4}$.

c) Drag point B toward point A. What type of line does secant AB approach as point B approaches point A? How is the slope of this line related to the rate of change of the function?

d) What is the instantaneous rate of change of the sine function when $x = \frac{\pi}{4}$?

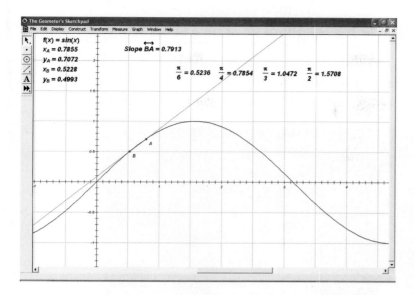

3. **a)** Copy the table and record your results. One line has already been filled in for you.

Angle x	$f(x) = \sin x$	Instantaneous Rate of Change
0		
$\dfrac{\pi}{6}$		
$\dfrac{\pi}{4}$	0.71	0.71
$\dfrac{\pi}{3}$		
$\dfrac{\pi}{2}$		

b) In a similar manner, determine the instantaneous rate of change of the sine function for the other values of x in the table.

c) Extend the table to multiples of the first quadrant angles up to, and including, 2π.

4. Add the instantaneous rates of change to the graph of the sine function. Sketch a smooth line through these points.

5. **Reflect**

a) Inspect the rate of change of the sine function at $x = \dfrac{\pi}{4}$. Explain why this value makes sense.

b) Inspect the rate of change of the sine function at $x = \dfrac{\pi}{2}$. Explain why this value makes sense.

c) Inspect the rate of change of the sine function at $x = \dfrac{3\pi}{4}$. Explain why this value makes sense.

d) Note that the graph of the instantaneous rate of change of the sine function is also periodic. Explain why this makes sense.

Example 1 | Height of a Car on a Ferris Wheel

The height, h, in metres, of a car above the ground as a Ferris wheel turns can be modelled using the function $h = 20\sin\left(\dfrac{\pi t}{60}\right) + 25$, where t is the time, in seconds.

a) Determine the average rate of change of h over each time interval, rounded to three decimal places.

   i) 5 s to 10 s

   ii) 9 s to 10 s

   iii) 9.9 s to 10 s

   iv) 9.99 s to 10 s

b) Estimate a value for the instantaneous rate of change of h at $t = 10$ s.

c) What physical quantity does this instantaneous rate of change represent?

d) Would you expect the instantaneous rate of change of h to be the same at $t = 15$ s? Justify your answer.

Solution

Use the formula Average rate of change $= \dfrac{h_2 - h_1}{t_2 - t_1}$.

a) i) Average rate of change $= \dfrac{\left[20\sin\left(\dfrac{\pi(10)}{60}\right) + 25\right] - \left[20\sin\left(\dfrac{\pi(5)}{60}\right) + 25\right]}{10 - 5}$

$\doteq 0.965$

   ii) Average rate of change $= \dfrac{\left[20\sin\left(\dfrac{\pi(10)}{60}\right) + 25\right] - \left[20\sin\left(\dfrac{\pi(9)}{60}\right) + 25\right]}{10 - 9}$

$\doteq 0.920$

iii) Average rate of change $= \dfrac{\left[20\sin\left(\dfrac{\pi(10)}{60}\right) + 25\right] - \left[20\sin\left(\dfrac{\pi(9.9)}{60}\right) + 25\right]}{10 - 9.9}$

$\doteq 0.908$

iv) Average rate of change $= \dfrac{\left[20\sin\left(\dfrac{\pi(10)}{60}\right) + 25\right] - \left[20\sin\left(\dfrac{\pi(9.99)}{60}\right) + 25\right]}{10 - 9.99}$

$\doteq 0.907$

b) The instantaneous rate of change at $t = 10$ s is about 0.907 m/s.

c) The instantaneous rate of change represents the vertical speed of the car at $t = 10$ s.

d) The instantaneous rate of change of h at $t = 15$ s is not expected to be the same as at $t = 10$ s. The graph of the sine function changes its slope continually and would not likely yield the same value at a different value of t.

Example 2   Seasonal Variation in Temperature

The variations in maximum daily temperatures for Moose Factory, Ontario, on the first of the month from January to December are shown.

Moose Factory Temperatures	
Month	**Temperature (°C)**
1	−14.0
2	−12.0
3	−4.9
4	3.2
5	11.0
6	19.1
7	22.4
8	20.6
9	15.9
10	8.3
11	−1.7
12	−10.0

Reasoning and Proving

Representing   Selecting Tools

Problem Solving

Connecting   Reflecting

Communicating

a) Write a sine function to model the data.

b) Make a scatter plot of the data. Then, graph your model on the same set of axes. How well does it fit the data?

c) Check your model using a sinusoidal regression. How does the regression equation compare to the model?

d) Explain why a sinusoidal function is an appropriate model for these data.

Solution

a) The data can be modelled by a sine function of the form
$T = a\sin[k(m - d)] + c$, where T represents the temperature, in degrees Celsius, and m represents the month number.

Determine values for a, c, k, and d.

In this situation, the amplitude is half the difference between the maximum and minimum temperatures.

$$a = \frac{22.4 - (-14.0)}{2}$$

$$= 18.2$$

The vertical translation is the average of the maximum and minimum temperatures.

$$c = \frac{22.4 + (-14.0)}{2}$$

$$= 4.2$$

The desired period is 12 months.

$$12 = \frac{2\pi}{k} \qquad \text{Determine the value of } k \text{ required for a period of 12 months.}$$

$$12k = 2\pi$$

$$k = \frac{\pi}{6}$$

If the period is 12, the maximum value of the sine function occurs at $\frac{1}{4}$ of a period, or $t = 3$.

However, the maximum temperature occurs at $t = 7$. The phase shift is $7 - 3$, or 4 months to the right. Therefore, $d = 4$.

A sine function that models the data is $T = 18.2\sin\left[\frac{\pi}{6}(m - 4)\right] + 4.2$.

b) Use a graphing calculator to display the scatter plot and graph of the model equation using the ZoomStat window settings. The equation seems to fit the data well.

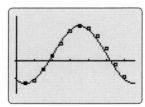

c) Store the result of the sinusoidal regression on a graphing calculator as **Y2**.

The sinusoidal regression equation is approximately

$$T \doteq 18.3\sin(0.5t - 2.1) + 4.1$$

$$= 18.3\sin(0.5(t - 4.2)) + 4.1$$

The values for a, c, k, and d compare well with those in the model.

d) Seasonal variations in temperature are periodic, varying between a maximum and a minimum, making a sinusoidal function an appropriate choice of model.

Example 3 **Predator and Prey Relationships**

The population, P, of wolves in a certain area can be modelled by the function $P(t) = 500 + 100 \sin t$, where t represents the time, in years. The population, p, of deer in the same area is given by $p(t) = 2000 + 500 \cos t$.

a) Graph these functions over a period of 20 years.

b) Compare the two graphs. What happens to the deer population when the wolf population is increasing? when it is decreasing?

Solution

a) Graph the functions using a graphing calculator.

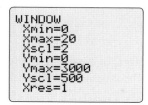

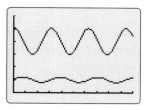

b) When the wolf population is increasing, the deer population stops growing and then decreases. When the wolf population is decreasing, the deer population stops declining and then increases.

⟪ KEY CONCEPTS ⟫

- The instantaneous rates of change of a sinusoidal function follow a sinusoidal pattern.

- Many real-world processes can be modelled with a sinusoidal function, even if they do not involve angles.

- Modelling real-world processes usually requires transformations of the basic sinusoidal functions.

Communicate Your Understanding

For questions C1 to C3, refer to your graphs of the sine function and the instantaneous rate of change of the sine function from the Investigate.

C1 As the value of x changes from 0 to $\frac{\pi}{2}$, what happens to the instantaneous rate of change of the sine function? Explain why this is happening.

C2 Inspect the graph of the sine function over the interval $x \in [0, 2\pi]$. For what values of x does the instantaneous rate of change equal 0? Explain why this happens.

C3 Inspect the graph of the instantaneous rate of change of the sine function over the interval $x \in [0, 2\pi]$. For what values of x does the instantaneous rate of change reach a maximum value? a minimum value? What are the maximum and minimum values? Explain why they occur.

A ▶ Practise

For help with questions 1 and 2, refer to the Investigate.

1. a) Sketch a graph of $f(x) = \cos x$ on the interval $x \in [0, 2\pi]$.

b) For what values of x does the instantaneous rate of change appear to equal 0?

c) For what values of x does the instantaneous rate of change appear to reach a maximum value? a minimum value?

2. a) Prepare a table similar to the one in the Investigate for the cosine function.

Angle x	$f(x) = \cos x$	Instantaneous Rate of Change

b) Plot the instantaneous rates of change on the same set of axes as the cosine function from question 1.

c) Do the instantaneous rates of change of the cosine function appear to follow a sinusoidal pattern? Justify your answer.

For help with question 3, refer to Example 1.

3. The height, h, in metres, of a car above the ground as a Ferris wheel turns can be modelled using the function $h = 15\cos\left(\frac{\pi t}{120}\right) + 18$, where t is the time, in seconds.

a) Determine the average rate of change of h in the following time intervals, rounded to three decimal places.

i) 15 s to 20 s

ii) 19 s to 20 s

iii) 19.9 s to 20 s

iv) 19.99 s to 20 s

b) Estimate a value for the instantaneous rate of change of h at $t = 20$ s.

c) What physical quantity does this instantaneous rate of change represent?

d) Would you expect the instantaneous rate of change of h to be the same at $t = 25$ s? Justify your answer.

For help with question 4, refer to Example 2.

4. The durations of daylight in Sarnia, Ontario, on the first of the month from January to December are shown.

Daylight in Sarnia, ON	
Month	Duration (h:min)
1	9:05
2	9:57
3	11:12
4	12:44
5	14:06
6	15:08
7	15:19
8	14:31
9	13:11
10	11:45
11	10:18
12	9:15

a) Copy the table. Add a column to express the durations of daylight as decimal values, to the nearest hundredth of an hour.

b) Write a sine function to model the data.

c) Make a scatter plot of the data. Then, graph your model on the same set of axes. How well does it fit the data?

d) **Use Technology** Check your model using a sinusoidal regression. How does the regression equation compare with the model?

e) Suppose that you wanted to model these data using a cosine function rather than a sine function. Describe how you would do this.

f) Carry out your procedure in part e).

CONNECTIONS

The number of daylight hours in a given day is known as the photo-period. The photoperiod is important for the development of animals and plants. For example, flowering plants use a pigment known as phytochrome to sense seasonal variations in photoperiods in order to determine when it is best to begin the flowering process. Go to the *Advanced Functions 12* page on the McGraw-Hill Ryerson Web site and follow the links to determine the photoperiod at different locations and dates.

5. Refer to the sine function that you developed in part b) of question 4. Use a method similar to that in Example 1 to estimate the rate of change of the number of hours of daylight on April 1.

6. A weight is suspended on a spring and set in motion such that it bobs up and down vertically. The graph shows the height, h, in centimetres, of the weight above a desk after time, t, in seconds. Use the graph to determine a model of the height versus time using a cosine function.

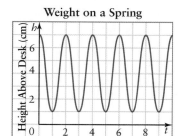

Weight on a Spring

7. a) Refer to question 6. Select a point on the graph where the instantaneous rate of change of the height appears to be a maximum.

b) Use a method similar to that in Example 1 to estimate the instantaneous rate of change of the height at this point.

c) What does this instantaneous rate of change of the height represent?

8. **Use Technology**

a) Go to the *Advanced Functions 12* page on the McGraw-Hill Ryerson Web site and follow the links to access Fisheries and Oceans Canada tide tables. Select a location. Obtain data on the water level at that location over the course of a 24-h day.

b) Graph the data you obtained in part a).

c) Write a sine function to model the data in part a).

d) Graph your model on the same set of axes as in part b).

e) Comment on the fit of your model.

9. a) Refer to question 8. Select a point on the graph where the instantaneous rate of change of the water level appears to be a minimum.

b) Use a method similar to that in Example 1 to estimate the instantaneous rate of change of the water level at this point.

c) What does this instantaneous rate of change of the water level represent?

10. An antique motorcycle is susceptible to a speed wobble that is modelled by $d = a \sin kt$, where d represents the deviation, in centimetres, of the front of the wheel from forward motion and t represents the time, in seconds. A graph of deviation versus time is shown.

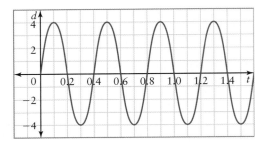

a) Use the graph to determine values for a and k.

b) Determine an equation for the speed wobble.

11. Chapter Problem A rollercoaster at a theme park starts with a vertical drop that leads into two pairs of identical valleys and hills, as shown.

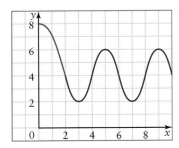

a) Write a quadratic function to model the first section of the rollercoaster.

b) Write a sinusoidal function to model the second section of the rollercoaster.

c) Graph your models and comment on the fit.

12. Refer to question 11.

a) Determine the instantaneous rate of change of the function that you used to model the first section of the rollercoaster at $x = 2$.

b) Determine the instantaneous rate of change of the function that you used to model the second section of the rollercoaster at $x = 2$.

c) How do the answers to parts a) and b) compare?

d) In the design of a rollercoaster, the instantaneous rates of change predicted at the junction of different models must match. Why is this important? What might happen if they were considerably different?

13. Use Technology

a) Go to the *Advanced Functions 12* page on the McGraw-Hill Ryerson Web site and follow the links to access E-STAT and navigate to the "Function Modelling Using Secondary Data from E-STAT" Web page. You may need to obtain a login and password from your teacher.

b) Scroll down to Sinusoidal. Select a table that interests you and download the data.

c) Graph the data you obtained in part b).

d) Write a sine function to model the data in part b).

e) Graph your model on the same set of axes as in part c).

f) Comment on the fit of your model.

14. a) Refer to question 13. Select a point on the graph.

b) Use a method similar to that in Example 1 to estimate the instantaneous rate of change at this point.

c) What does this instantaneous rate of change represent?

15. The volume, V, in millilitres, of air in the lungs of a cat as the cat breathes versus time, t, in seconds, is shown.

Time (s)	Volume of Air (mL)
0.0	131
0.5	134
1.0	141
1.5	150
2.0	156
2.5	154
3.0	148
3.5	137
4.0	132
4.5	133
5.0	140

a) Make a scatter plot of the data.

b) Use the table and the graph to write a sinusoidal function to model the data.

c) Graph your model on the same set of axes as the scatter plot. Comment on the fit.

d) **Use Technology** Check your model using a sinusoidal regression. How does the regression equation compare with the model?

e) How would the graph change if the cat breathed at a faster rate and increased the volume of air it took into its lungs, as if it were running?

C **Extend and Challenge**

16. a) Sketch a graph of the inverse trigonometric relation $y = \sin^{-1}(x)$ such that the range covers the interval $[0, 2\pi]$.

b) Is this relation a function in this range? If so, explain how you know. If not, show how it can be made into a function by restricting the range.

c) Determine a value of x where the instantaneous rate of change appears to be a maximum.

d) Estimate the instantaneous rate of change for the value of x in part c).

17. a) Sketch a graph of the tangent function on the interval $x \in [0, 2\pi]$.

b) For what values of x does the instantaneous rate of change appear to equal 0? reach a maximum value? reach a minimum value?

c) Prepare a table similar to the one in the Investigate for the tangent function.

d) Plot the instantaneous rates of change on the same set of axes as the tangent function.

e) Describe the pattern formed by the instantaneous rates of change of the tangent function.

18. a) Sketch a graph of the cosecant function on the interval $x \in [0, 2\pi]$.

b) For what values of x does the instantaneous rate of change appear to equal 0? reach a maximum value? reach a minimum value?

c) Prepare a table similar to the one in the Investigate for the cosecant function.

d) Plot the instantaneous rates of change on the same set of axes as the cosecant function.

e) Describe the pattern formed by the instantaneous rates of change of the cosecant function.

19. Math Contest Given $\left(\dfrac{w^2 + 1}{w}\right)^2 = 3$, determine the value of $w^2 + \dfrac{1}{w^2}$.

20. Math Contest In $\triangle PQR$, $3\sin P + 4\cos Q = 6$ and $4\sin Q + 3\cos P = 1$.

a) Find $\sin(P + Q)$.

b) Determine the measure of $\angle R$, in radians.

21. Math Contest Refer to Section 5.1, question 24. Show that the polar equation $r = a\sin\theta + b\cos\theta$, where $ab \neq 0$, represents a circle, and give its centre.

5.1 Graphs of Sine, Cosine, and Tangent Functions

1. The graph of a sine function has a maximum value of 6 and a minimum value of 2.

 a) Determine the amplitude of the function.

 b) Determine the vertical translation of the function.

2. Write an equation for a cosine function with a period of 3π and a phase shift of $+\dfrac{\pi}{3}$.

3. The piston in a lawn mower motor moves up and down 30 times in 1 s. Its total travel from the top position to the bottom position is 10 cm. The vertical position, y, in centimetres, versus time, t, in seconds, can be modelled using a sinusoidal function.

 a) Write an equation to model the motion of the piston.

 b) Is this the only possible equation? Justify your answer.

5.2 Graphs of Reciprocal Trigonometric Functions

4. Determine all values of x in the interval $[0, 2\pi]$ such that $\csc x = 4$. Round your answers to two decimal places.

5. a) Explain the difference between $\sec \dfrac{1}{\sqrt{2}}$ and $\cos^{-1}\left(\dfrac{1}{\sqrt{2}}\right)$.

 b) Determine a value for each expression in part a).

6. When the Sun is at an angle of elevation x, a tree with height 12 m casts a shadow of length s, in metres.

 a) Show that the length of the shadow can be modelled by the relation $s = 12\cot x$.

 b) Sketch a graph of $s = 12\cot x$ on the interval $x \in \left[0, \dfrac{\pi}{2}\right]$.

 c) Interpret the meaning of the graph as x approaches 0 and as x approaches $\dfrac{\pi}{2}$.

5.3 Sinusoidal Functions of the Form $f(x) = a\sin[k(x-d)] + c$ and $f(x) = a\cos[k(x-d)] + c$

7. Model the graph shown using a cosine function.

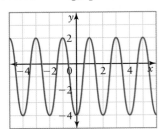

 a) From the graph, determine the amplitude, the vertical translation, the phase shift, and the period.

 b) Write an equation for the function.

 c) Graph the equation for the function.

 d) Compare the graph in part c) to the given graph and verify that the graphs match.

8. Consider the function $y = -3\sin[\pi(x+4)] - 1$.

 a) What is the amplitude?

 b) What is the period?

 c) Describe the phase shift.

 d) Describe the vertical translation.

 e) Graph the function. Compare the graph to the characteristics expected.

5.4 Solve Trigonometric Equations

9. Determine approximate solutions for each equation in the interval $x \in [0, 2\pi]$, to the nearest hundredth of a radian. Verify the answers by graphing.

 a) $\cos x - \dfrac{1}{4} = 0$ **b)** $\sin x - 0.6 = 0$

 c) $\cot x - 2 = 0$ **d)** $4\sec x + 3 = 0$

10. a) Determine all solutions for the equation $2\sin^2 x + \sin x - 1 = 0$ in the interval $x \in [0, 2\pi]$.

 b) Verify your solutions to part a) by graphing.

11. Determine an exact solution for the equation $\cos^2 x - \dfrac{3}{4} = 0$ in the interval $x \in [0, 2\pi]$.

12. A boat tied up at a dock bobs up and down with passing waves. The vertical distance between its high point and its low point is 1.8 m and the cycle is repeated every 4 s.

   a) Determine a sinusoidal equation to model the vertical position, in metres, of the boat versus the time, in seconds.

   b) Use your model to determine when, during each cycle, the boat is 0.5 m above its mean position. Round your answers to the nearest hundredth of a second.

5.5 Making Connections and Instantaneous Rate of Change

13. Refer to question 12. At what time or times during a cycle is the instantaneous rate of change of the vertical position of the boat equal to 0? At what times is it a maximum? Justify your answers.

14. The number of employees at the City Bicycle Company for each of the last 11 years is shown.

Year	Employees
1	228
2	241
3	259
4	233
5	226
6	209
7	212
8	225
9	240
10	251
11	261

   a) Make a scatter plot of the data.

   b) Use the table and the graph to write a sine function to model the data.

   c) Graph your model on the same set of axes as in part a). Comment on the fit.

   d) **Use Technology** Check your model using a sinusoidal regression. How does the regression equation compare with the model?

   e) Suggest reasons why the number of employees might fluctuate in this way.

PROBLEM WRAP-UP

In this chapter, you explored a number of applications of sinusoidal functions to the types of rides you would find in a theme park. As a wrap-up, you will integrate the concepts in this chapter with those from previous chapters to design a rollercoaster. Your coaster must meet the following conditions.

- The first part of the ride is modelled by a polynomial function. It includes a steep hill that starts at the origin, where the cars obtain their initial energy.

- The second part of the ride is modelled by a sinusoidal function with at least two cycles.

- The third part of the ride is modelled by a rational function that brings the cars back close to the ground.

- The rates of change where one part of the ride meets another part of the ride must not differ by more than 10%.

   a) Determine an equation for each part of the ride.

   b) Graph all three equations and show that they join each other.

   c) Show that the rates of change at the points at which the models join each other do not differ by more than 10%.

Chapter 5 PRACTICE TEST

For questions 1 to 7, choose the best answer.

1. What is the maximum value of the function $y = \cos x - 2$?

   A -3 **B** -1 **C** 1 **D** 3

2. A transformed sine function has a maximum value of 8 and a minimum value of -2. What is the vertical translation of the function?

   A -3 **B** 0 **C** 3 **D** 8

3. Consider the function $y = 2\sin[3\pi(x - 4)] - 1$. What is the period of the function?

   A $\dfrac{3\pi}{2}$ **B** $\dfrac{2\pi}{3}$ **C** $\dfrac{2}{3}$ **D** $\dfrac{3}{2}$

4. Consider the function $y = 3\cos\left(2x - \dfrac{\pi}{2}\right)$. What is the phase shift of the function?

   A $\dfrac{\pi}{4}$ to the right

   B $\dfrac{\pi}{4}$ to the left

   C $\dfrac{\pi}{2}$ to the right

   D $\dfrac{\pi}{2}$ to the left

5. Which of the following functions has vertical asymptotes at $x = \dfrac{\pi}{2}$ and $x = \dfrac{3\pi}{2}$ in the interval $[0, 2\pi]$?

   A $y = \tan x$

   B $y = \sec x$

   C $y = \csc x$

   D $y = \tan x$ and $y = \sec x$

6. Consider the graphs of $y = \csc x$ and $y = \cos\left(x - \dfrac{\pi}{2}\right)$. For which values of x in the interval $[0, 2\pi]$ will the graphs intersect?

   A none

   B 0, π, and 2π

   C $\dfrac{\pi}{2}$ and $\dfrac{3\pi}{2}$

   D 0 and 2π

7. Which of these is a possible solution for $\sin x - \dfrac{1}{\sqrt{2}} = 0$?

   A $x = \dfrac{3\pi}{4}$ **B** $x = \dfrac{3\pi}{2}$

   C $x = \dfrac{5\pi}{4}$ **D** $x = \dfrac{7\pi}{4}$

8. **a)** Explain the difference between $\csc\dfrac{\sqrt{3}}{2}$ and $\sin^{-1}\left(\dfrac{\sqrt{3}}{2}\right)$.

   b) Determine a value for each of the expressions in part a).

9. A sailboat has a single mast that is 4 m high. A wire of length l metres runs from the bow to the top of the mast. Let x represent the angle of inclination of the wire.

   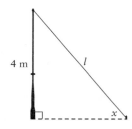

   a) Show that the length of the wire can be modelled by the function $l = 4\csc x$.

   b) Sketch a graph of $l = 4\csc x$ on the interval $x \in \left[0, \dfrac{\pi}{2}\right]$.

   c) Interpret the meaning of the graph as x approaches 0 and as x approaches $\dfrac{\pi}{2}$.

10. Consider the function $y = -2\cos\left[4\left(x + \dfrac{2\pi}{3}\right)\right] - 3$.

    a) What is the amplitude?

    b) What is the period?

    c) Describe the phase shift.

    d) Describe the vertical translation.

    e) Graph the function. Compare the graph to the given parameters.

11. A cosine function has a maximum value of 3, a minimum value of -1, a phase shift of 1 rad to the right, and a period of 4.

   a) Determine an equation for the function.

   b) Graph the function and verify that it satisfies the properties given.

12. A sine function has a maximum value of 4, a minimum value of -2, a phase shift of $\dfrac{5\pi}{6}$ rad to the left, and a period of π.

   a) Write an equation for the function.

   b) Graph the function and verify that it satisfies the properties given.

13. Determine approximate solutions for $\cos^2 x - 0.49 = 0$ in the interval $x \in [0, 2\pi]$, to the nearest hundredth of a radian.

14. Determine exact solutions for $2\sin^2 x - 3\sin x + 1 = 0$ in the interval $x \in [0, 2\pi]$.

15. Average monthly temperatures for the city of Hamilton, Ontario, from January to December are shown.

Month	Temperature (°C)
1	−4.8
2	−4.8
3	−0.2
4	6.6
5	12.7
6	18.6
7	21.9
8	20.7
9	16.4
10	10.5
11	3.6
12	−2.3

   a) Make a scatter plot of the data.

   b) Use the table and the graph to write a sinusoidal function to model the data.

   c) Graph your model on the same set of axes as your scatter plot. Comment on the accuracy of the fit.

16. Dates for the phases of the Moon during the first four months of 2007 are shown.

Phases of the Moon 2007	
Date	Phase
Jan 3	Full
Jan 11	Last Quarter
Jan 19	New
Jan 25	First Quarter
Feb 2	Full
Feb 10	Last Quarter
Feb 17	New
Feb 24	First Quarter
Mar 3	Full
Mar 12	Last Quarter
Mar 19	New
Mar 25	First Quarter
Apr 2	Full
Apr 10	Last Quarter
Apr 17	New
Apr 24	First Quarter

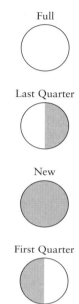

Full

Last Quarter

New

First Quarter

   a) Express the dates as days counted from the beginning of the year.

   b) Express the phases as a percent of the Moon illuminated.

   c) Determine a model for percent illumination versus day of the year using a sinusoidal function.

   d) Graph your model.

   e) **Use Technology** Check your model using a sinusoidal regression. How does the regression equation compare to the model?

17. a) Refer to question 16. Describe how you can estimate the instantaneous rate of change of the illumination of the Moon on January 25.

   b) Carry out your method in part a).

   c) What does this instantaneous rate of change represent?

Chapter 4 Trigonometry

1. a) Determine the exact radian measure of $100°$.

   b) Determine the exact degree measure of $\dfrac{7\pi}{12}$.

2. A gymnasium has a circular running track around the mezzanine with a radius of 20 m. A runner ran along the arc of the track for 60 m. What is the sector angle, in radians, from the start to the finish of his run?

3. Determine an exact value for $\sin\dfrac{3\pi}{4} - \tan\dfrac{5\pi}{6}$.

4. Two guy wires are attached to the top of a radio antenna 25 m in height. The wires make angles of $\dfrac{\pi}{6}$ and $\dfrac{\pi}{4}$ with the ground, as shown. Determine an exact expression for the distance between the two anchor points of the wires, A and B.

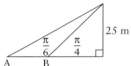

5. Given that $\cos\dfrac{7\pi}{15} \doteq 0.1045$, use an equivalent expression to determine $\sin\dfrac{29\pi}{30}$, to four decimal places.

6. If $\sin y = \cos 3y$, determine an exact value for angle y.

7. Angle a is located in the second quadrant such that $\sin a = \dfrac{12}{13}$. Angle b is located in the third quadrant such that $\cos b = -\dfrac{4}{5}$. Determine an exact value for $\sin(a + b)$.

8. An A-frame ski chalet is built with an extension shed, as shown. Show that the height, h, of the A-frame is equal to the expression $5\sin c\,(1 + 2\cos c)$.

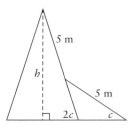

9. Consider the right triangle with sides as shown.

   a) Use the Pythagorean theorem to write an equation relating the lengths of the sides.

   b) Prove that the equation is an identity.

10. Prove $\dfrac{\sin 2x}{\sec x} = \dfrac{2\cos^2 x}{\csc x}$.

11. Prove $\sin(x + y)\cos(x - y) = \dfrac{\sin x}{\sec x} + \dfrac{\cos y}{\csc y}$.

Chapter 5 Trigonometric Functions

12. One cycle of a sine function begins at $x = -\dfrac{\pi}{4}$ and ends at $x = \dfrac{\pi}{3}$.

   a) Determine the period of the function.

   b) Determine the phase shift of the function.

13. The piston in a motorcycle engine moves up and down 100 times every second. It moves a total distance of 12 cm from its top position to its bottom position. The motion of the piston is modelled using a cosine function.

   a) What is the amplitude of the function?

   b) What is the period of the function?

   c) What is the value of k in the formula Period $= \dfrac{2\pi}{k}$ that will result in the required period?

   d) Assume that the bottom position and phase shift are equal to zero. Write the equation of the function.

   e) Graph the function over two cycles.

14. Consider the function $y = 3\sin\left[4\left(x - \dfrac{\pi}{4}\right)\right] + 2$.

   a) What is the amplitude?

   b) What is the period?

   c) Describe the phase shift.

   d) Describe the vertical shift.

   e) Graph the function. Compare the graph to the characteristics expected.

15. Contestants in a bicycle race start at A and finish at C, as shown. A contestant may stay on paved roads from A to B and B to C. Alternatively, she may turn off the road at any point P through an angle x, and ride cross-country a distance d directly to C. The speed possible cross-country is lower than that possible on the paved road.

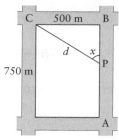

a) Show that $d = 500 \csc x$.

b) What are the upper and lower limits on d?

c) Suppose that a contestant can ride at 10 m/s on pavement, and 6 m/s cross-country. Would it be best to stay on pavement for the race, go cross-country all the way, or a combination of the two? Justify your answer.

16. a) A sine function has an amplitude of 3, a period of π, and a vertical translation of 1. If it passes through the point $\left(\frac{\pi}{3}, 1\right)$, what is the phase shift?

b) Sketch a graph to verify your answer.

17. Commercial bottling machines often use a circular drum as part of a mechanism to install tops on bottles.

One such machine has a diameter of 120 cm, and makes a complete turn once every 5 s. A sensor at the left side of the drum monitors its movement. Take the sensor position as zero.

a) Model the horizontal position of a point on the drum, h, in centimetres, as a function of time, t, in seconds.

b) Sketch a graph of h versus t over two cycles.

c) If the technician monitoring the machine increases the speed to complete a cycle in 3 s, what changes would occur in your model? Justify your answer.

18. Determine approximate solutions for each equation in the interval $x \in [0, 2\pi]$, to the nearest hundredth of a radian.

a) $\sec x - 5 = 0$

b) $12 \sin^2 x - \sin x - 1 = 0$

19. The owner of a beachfront ice-cream stand keeps records of the demand, d, in thousands of cones, versus time, t, in years, relative to a base year of 1990. She performs a sinusoidal regression on the data and arrives at the model $d = 4.2 \sin(0.72t + 0.2) + 6.3$.

a) Graph the model.

b) What was the demand in 1990, to the nearest cone?

c) Determine the average demand for ice-cream cones.

d) Determine the period of the model, to the nearest tenth of a year.

e) Predict two years in which the model forecasts a peak demand.

f) Suggest reasons why demand for ice cream might follow a sinusoidal model.

20. As a science project, Anwar monitored the content of carbon monoxide outside his house in the city over several days. He found that it reached a maximum of about 30 ppm (parts per million) at 6:00 P.M., and a minimum of 10 ppm at 6:00 A.M.

a) Model the concentration of carbon monoxide, C, in parts per million, as a function of time t, in hours. Use a sinusoidal function.

b) Sketch a graph of C versus t over three days.

21. Refer to question 20.

a) Select a point on the graph where the instantaneous rate of change of the carbon monoxide level appears to be a maximum.

b) Use a method similar to that in Example 1 of Section 5.5 to estimate the instantaneous rate of change of the carbon monoxide level at this point, to one decimal place.

TASK

Predators and Prey

Natural Resources personnel recorded data on deer and wolf populations in an area of Ontario.

Year	Number of Adult Deer	Number of Adult Wolves
1996	340	550
1997	315	480
1998	305	380
1999	330	300
2000	355	405
2001	305	560
2002	300	500
2003	320	445
2004	345	385
2005	365	455
2006	340	640
2007	310	560

a) With or without technology, plot the two sets of data on the same grid, one set for the prey (deer) and one set for the predators (wolves).

b) In your notebook, sketch a curve of best fit for each data set.

c) Find the equation of the curve of best fit for each data set.

d) Discuss the characteristics of each curve:
   • maximum and minimum populations
   • average increase in population from trough to peak

e) What is the phase shift between the two curves? What is the real-world explanation for this phase shift?

f) Why are sinusoidal models appropriate for this data?

g) The two curves intersect at various times. Interpret these points of intersection in terms of the populations.

h) Choose one point of intersection, and determine the instantaneous rate of change for each population at that time. Interpret your results.

i) Can you think of another real-world situation in which pairs are related in the same way? Justify your answer in writing.

Chapter **6**

Exponential and Logarithmic Functions

People have been fascinated by the universe for thousands of years. How many stars are there? How far away are they? How are they powered? Why are some brighter than others?

A number of these concepts are related to exponential growth and decay. Throughout this chapter, you will explore a variety of situations that can be modelled with an exponential function or its inverse, the logarithmic function. You will learn techniques for solving various problems, such as some of those posed above.

By the end of this chapter, you will

- recognize the logarithm of a number to a given base as the exponent to which the base must be raised to give the number (A1.1)
- determine the approximate logarithm of a number to any base (A1.2)
- make connections between related logarithmic and exponential equations (A1.3)
- make connections between the laws of exponents and the laws of logarithms, and verify and use the laws of logarithms to simplify and evaluate numerical expressions (A1.4)
- determine the key features of the graph of a logarithmic function (A2.1, D3.1)
- recognize the relationship between an exponential function and the corresponding logarithmic function to be that of a function and its inverse (A2.2)

- determine the roles of d, c, a, and k in functions of the form $f(x) = a \log [k(x - d)] + c$ (A2.3)
- pose and solve problems based on real-world applications of exponential and logarithmic functions (A2.4)
- solve problems involving exponential and logarithmic equations algebraically (A3.4)
- recognize examples of instantaneous rates of change arising from real-world situations, and make connections between instantaneous rates of change and average rates of change (D1.5)
- determine approximate instantaneous rates of change arising from real-world applications (D1.6)
- determine the approximate slope of the tangent to a given point on the graph of a function (D1.8)
- solve problems involving average and instantaneous rates of change (D1.9)

Prerequisite Skills

Graph an Exponential Function

1. Consider the function $y = 3(2)^x$.

   a) Sketch a graph of the function.

   b) Identify

   i) the domain

   ii) the range

   iii) an equation for the asymptote

2. A bacterial colony doubles every day. The equation relating population, P, and time, t, in days, is given by $P(t) = 300(2)^t$.

   a) What is the initial population? Explain how you can tell.

   b) Use the equation to find how many bacteria will be present after 3 days.

   c) Use the graph to estimate

   i) the length of time it will take for the population to reach 2000

   ii) the population 3 days ago

   Check your estimates by using the equation.

Apply the Exponent Laws

3. Simplify. Express your answers with positive exponents only.

   a) $x^2(x^5)$

   b) $\dfrac{m^5}{m^2}$

   c) $(k^3)^2$

   d) $(-2x^4)^3$

   e) $(2a^2b^{-1})(-a^{-3}b^2)$

   f) $\dfrac{4x^3y^2}{2x^5y^2}$

   g) $\dfrac{(3u^3v^5)(3u^2v)}{(-3u^3v^3)^2}$

4. Simplify, and then evaluate.

   a) $(2^{-3})(2^5)$

   b) $\dfrac{10^8 \times 10^{-5}}{10^2}$

   c) $\dfrac{\left(\frac{1}{3}\right)^2\left(\frac{1}{3}\right)^4}{\left[\left(\frac{1}{3}\right)^3\right]^3}$

   d) $\dfrac{(3^2)^3 \times 3^5}{3^4 \times 3^3} + 10^0$

Graph an Inverse

5. **a)** Graph the function $f(x) = \sqrt{x}$.

   b) What are the domain and range?

   c) Graph the line $y = x$ on the same grid.

   d) Graph the inverse f^{-1} by reflecting f in the line $y = x$.

   e) Is f^{-1} a function? Explain how you can tell.

   f) Identify the domain and range of f^{-1}.

6. Repeat question 5 for the function $g(x) = x^2 + 4$.

7. Are the functions f and g inverses? Justify your answer.

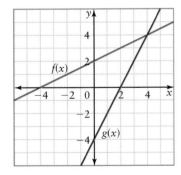

Apply Transformations to Functions

8. Identify the transformations required to map *f* onto *g*.

a)

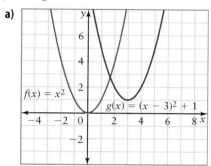

b)

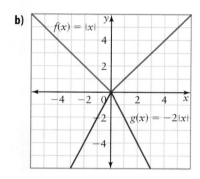

9. Identify the transformations required to map *f* onto *g*.

   a) $f(x) = x$, $g(x) = 3x - 4$

   b) $f(x) = \sin x$, $g(x) = \sin\left(-\dfrac{1}{2}x\right)$

10. Sketch a graph of $y = (x - 2)^2 - 7$ by first graphing $y = x^2$ and then applying horizontal and vertical translations.

11. Sketch a graph of $y = -\sqrt{2x}$ by first graphing $y = \sqrt{x}$ and then applying a horizontal compression and a reflection in the *x*-axis.

12. Sketch a graph of $f(x) = 3(2)^{-x}$ by first graphing $y = 2^x$ and then applying a vertical stretch and a reflection in the *y*-axis.

13. **Use Technology** Check your answers to questions 10 to 12 using graphing technology.

PROBLEM

Astronauts are faced with many mathematical problems during a journey to space. What kinds of problems are astronauts likely to encounter as they hurtle through space? In this chapter, you will see how exponents and logarithms can be used to help describe and solve problems involving some aspects of space travel.

6.1

The Exponential Function and Its Inverse

Exponential functions are useful for describing relationships. If the growth of a population is proportional to the size of the population as it grows, we describe the growth as exponential. Bacterial growth and compound interest are examples of exponential growth. Exponential decay occurs in nuclear reactions and in the depreciation in value of vehicles or equipment.

How can the inverse of an exponential function be found, and why is it useful? Graphing technology is useful for exploring the nature of the inverse of an exponential function. Applications of the inverse of an exponential function will appear throughout this chapter.

Investigate 1   What is the nature of the rate of change of an exponential function?

Tools

- computer with *The Geometer's Sketchpad*®
- graphing calculator (optional)
- grid paper

A: *Numerical Analysis: Average Rate of Change*

1. a) Copy and complete the table of values for the function $y = 2^x$. Leave room for three more columns.

x	y			
0	1			
1	2			
2				
3				
4				
5				
6				

b) Describe any patterns you see in the values of *y* as *x* increases.

2. a) Calculate values for $\Delta_1 y$, the first differences, and record them in the third column.

x	y	$\Delta_1 y$	$\Delta_2 y$	$\Delta_3 y$
0	1			
1	2			
2				
3				
4				
5				
6				

b) Explain how these values confirm your answer to step 1b).

3. a) Compare the pattern of values for y and $\Delta_1 y$. Explain what you notice.

b) Predict the pattern of values for the second differences, $\Delta_2 y$, of this function.

c) Calculate the second differences and record them in the fourth column of the table. Was your prediction correct? Explain.

4. Predict the values for the third differences, $\Delta_3 y$, and justify your prediction with mathematical reasoning. Test your prediction and enter these values in the last column.

5. Repeat steps 1 to 4 for the function $y = 3^x$.

6. Reflect What do these results illustrate about the rate of change of an exponential function?

B: *Graphical Analysis: Comparing Average and Instantaneous Rates of Change*

1. Open *The Geometer's Sketchpad*® and begin a new sketch.

2. a) Plot the function $y = 2^x$.

b) Construct two points on the graph and label them A and B.

c) Construct a secant through A and B and measure its slope.

Technology Tip   ∴

For instructions on how to plot a function and perform other basic functions using *The Geometer's Sketchpad*®, refer to the Technology Appendix on page 505.

Technology Tip   ∴

You can determine first differences with a graphing calculator:

Enter the values for x and y into **L1** and **L2** of the List Editor.

Place the cursor on **L3** in the table and press (2nd) (STAT) for [LIST].

From the **OPS** menu, choose **7:ΔList(** and type (2nd) **2** for [L2] and then a closing bracket.

Press (ENTER).

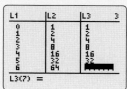

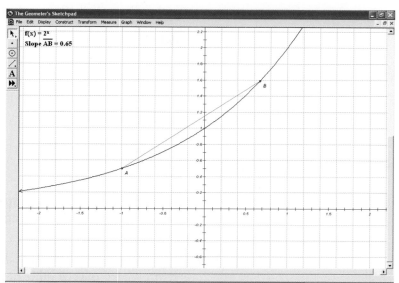

3. a) Click and drag the points so that A is at $x = 0$ and B is at $x = 1$.

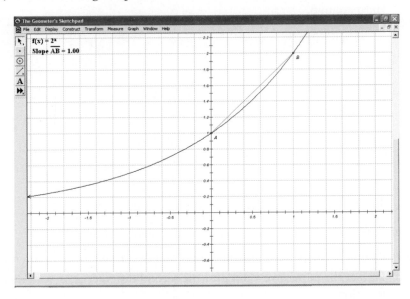

b) What is the average slope of the curve for the interval [0, 1], correct to one decimal place?

c) How is the average slope related to the first of the first differences you found in part A of this Investigate?

4. a) Drag point B until it is very close to A, first to the left, and then to the right, so that the line through A and B approximates a tangent to the curve at $x = 0$. Note the slope in each case and estimate the instantaneous rate of change when $x = 0$, correct to one decimal place.

b) Move both points very close to where $x = 1$ and estimate the instantaneous rate of change when $x = 1$, correct to one decimal place.

5. Repeat steps 3 and 4 for several points on the graph. Use whole-number values of x. Record all your results in a table like this one.

Interval		Average Rate of Change, m_{AB}	Instantaneous Rate of Change at A, m_A	Instantaneous Rate of Change at B, m_B
A	B			
$x = 0$	$x = 1$			
$x = 1$	$x = 2$			
$x = 2$	$x = 3$			
$x = 3$	$x = 4$			
$x = 4$	$x = 5$			

6. Reflect Compare the average rates of change to the first differences you found in part A of this Investigate. What do you notice? Explain this relationship.

7. a) How are consecutive values of the instantaneous rate of change, m_A and m_B, related to each other in each case?

b) Use linear interpolation (averaging) to estimate the instantaneous rate of change at $x = \dfrac{1}{2}$. Do you think this value is correct? Explain why or why not.

c) Drag A and B close to where $x = \dfrac{1}{2}$ and check your estimate. Was your estimate correct? If not, explain why not.

8. Reflect Explain how the results of step 7 illustrate that an exponential function has an instantaneous rate of change that is proportional to the function itself (i.e., also exponential).

9. Do these results hold true for different bases?

  a) Explore this question for exponential functions, $y = b^x$,

    i) with other values of $b > 1$

    ii) with values of b, where $0 < b < 1$

  b) Reflect Write a summary of your findings.

Example 1   Write an Equation to Fit Data

Write an equation to fit the data in the table of values.

x	y
0	1
1	4
2	16
3	64

Solution

Calculate $\Delta_1 y$ to determine if the data represent an exponential function.

x	y	$\Delta_1 y$
0	1	
1	4	3
2	16	12
3	64	48

Because y is increasing at a rate proportional to the function, the function is exponential.

Consider the equation $y = b^x$. Substitute the given values into this equation to find b.

$1 = b^0$ This statement is true for any value of b.
$4 = b^1$
$4^1 = b^1$
$4 = b$ The only valid value for b is 4.

Check the other values in the table to make sure 4 is the correct value for b.

$16 = b^2$
$4^2 = b^2$

$64 = b^3$
$4^3 = b^3$

An equation for a function that fits the data in the table is $y = 4^x$.

CONNECTIONS

The first differences are proportional to successive y-values because their ratios are equal. i.e.

$\dfrac{4}{16} = \dfrac{3}{12}$ and $\dfrac{16}{64} = \dfrac{12}{48}$

Tools

- computer with *The Geometer's Sketchpad®*
- grid paper

1. Begin a new sketch with *The Geometer's Sketchpad®*.

2. **a)** Plot the function $y = 2^x$.

   b) Identify the key features of the graph.

      i) domain and range

      ii) x-intercept, if it exists

      iii) y-intercept, if it exists

      iv) intervals for which the function is positive and intervals for which it is negative

      v) intervals for which the function is increasing and intervals for which it is decreasing

      vi) equation of the asymptote

3. **a)** Use the key features to sketch a graph of the function $y = 2^x$ in your notebook.

   b) Draw the line $y = x$ on the same graph. Explain how you can use this line to sketch a graph of the inverse, $x = 2^y$.

   c) Sketch a graph of the inverse function.

   d) Verify that your sketch is accurate by comparing points on the two graphs. The x-coordinates and y-coordinates should be switched.

4. Use *The Geometer's Sketchpad®* to verify your sketch by tracing the inverse of $y = 2^x$ as follows.

   - Select the graph of $f(x)$. From the **Construct** menu, choose **Point On Function Plot**.
   - Select the constructed point. From the **Measure** menu, choose **Abcissa (x)**. Repeat to measure **Ordinate (y)**.
   - Select the **Ordinate (y)** measure followed by the **Abcissa (x)** measure. From the **Graph** menu, choose **Plot as (x, y)**.
   - Select the image point that appears. From the **Display** menu, choose **Trace Plotted Point**.
   - Click and drag the original constructed point on $y = 2^x$ along the graph of $f(x)$ until a smooth curve is traced out.

5. **a)** Describe the shape of the pattern of points that appears.

   b) Identify the key features of the inverse graph.

      i) domain and range

      ii) x-intercept, if it exists

      iii) y-intercept, if it exists

      iv) intervals for which the function is positive and intervals for which it is negative

      v) intervals for which the function is increasing and intervals for which it is decreasing

      vi) equation of the asymptote

CONNECTIONS

The **abscissa** and **ordinate** are the x-coordinate and y-coordinate, respectively, of an ordered pair. For example, in $(1, -5)$, the abscissa is 1 and the ordinate is -5.

6. a) Copy and complete the table of values.

x	Calculation $2^x = y$	y	Inverse (y, x)
-4	$2^{-4} = \dfrac{1}{16}$	$\dfrac{1}{16}$	$\left(\dfrac{1}{16}, -4\right)$
-3	$2^{-3} = ?$		
-2			
-1			
0			
1			
2			
3			
4			

b) Verify that each ordered pair in the fourth column of the table is on your graph of the inverse function.

7. Reflect

a) How are the two graphs related?

b) When the image point was constructed from the constructed point on the graph of $y = 2^x$, why were the coordinates chosen in the order (y, x)?

8. a) Using graphing technology, explore the effect of changing the base of the function $y = b^x$ for values of b for

  i) $b > 1$

  ii) $0 < b < 1$

b) Reflect Describe what happens to the graphs of the function and its inverse in each case.

Example 2 | Graphing an Inverse Function

Consider the function $f(x) = 4^x$.

a) Identify the key features of the function.

   i) domain and range

   ii) x-intercept, if it exists

   iii) y-intercept, if it exists

   iv) intervals for which the function is positive and intervals for which it is negative

   v) intervals for which the function is increasing and intervals for which it is decreasing

   vi) equation of the asymptote

b) Sketch a graph of the function.

c) On the same set of axes, sketch a graph of the inverse of the function.

d) Identify the key features, as in part a) i) to vi), of the inverse of the function.

Solution

a)   **i)** domain $\{x \in \mathbb{R}\}$; range $\{y \in \mathbb{R}, y > 0\}$

   ii) no x-intercepts

   iii) y-intercept 1

   iv) positive for all values of x

   v) increasing for all intervals

   vi) horizontal asymptote with equation $y = 0$; no vertical asymptote

b), c)

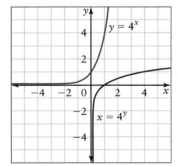

d)   **i)** domain $\{x \in \mathbb{R}, x > 0\}$; range $\{y \in \mathbb{R}\}$

   ii) x-intercept 1

   iii) no y-intercepts

   iv) positive for $x > 1$ and negative for $x < 1$

   v) increasing for all intervals

   vi) vertical asymptote with equation $x = 0$; no horizontal asymptote

KEY CONCEPTS

- An exponential function of the form $y = b^x$, $b > 0$, $b \neq 1$, has
  - a repeating pattern of finite differences
  - a rate of change that is increasing proportional to the function for $b > 1$
  - a rate of change that is decreasing proportional to the function for $0 < b < 1$

- An exponential function of the form $y = b^x$, $b > 0$, $b \neq 1$,
  - has domain $\{x \in \mathbb{R}\}$
  - has range $\{y \in \mathbb{R}, y > 0\}$
  - has y-intercept 1
  - has horizontal asymptote at $y = 0$

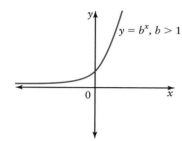

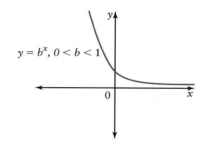

- is increasing on its domain when $b > 1$

- is decreasing on its domain when $0 < b < 1$

- The inverse of $y = b^x$ is a function that can be written as $x = b^y$. This function
  - has domain $\{x \in \mathbb{R}, x > 0\}$
  - has range $\{y \in \mathbb{R}\}$
  - has x-intercept 1
  - has vertical asymptote at $x = 0$
  - is a reflection of $y = b^x$ about the line $y = x$

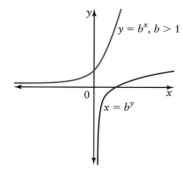

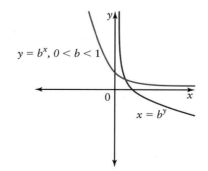

- is increasing on its domain when $b > 1$

- is decreasing on its domain when $0 < b < 1$

Communicate Your Understanding

C1 Explain how you can recognize whether or not a function is exponential by examining its

a) finite differences

b) graph

C2 Is the inverse of $y = 2^x$ a function? Explain your answer using

a) algebraic reasoning

b) graphical reasoning

C3 Consider the function $y = 2^x$ and its inverse. Describe the ways in which they are

a) alike

b) different

C4 **a)** What happens to the shape of the graph of $f(x) = b^x$ when $b = 1$?

b) What happens to the shape of its inverse?

c) Explain why this happens.

A) Practise

For help with questions 1 and 2, refer to Investigate 1, part A.

1. Which of the following functions are exponential? Explain how you can tell.

A

x	y
1	3
2	6
3	9
4	12

B

x	y
0	0
1	1
2	3
3	10
4	16

C

x	y
0	1
1	3
2	9
3	27
4	81

D

x	y
−3	27
−2	9
−1	3
0	1
1	$\frac{1}{3}$

2. Refer to question 1. For the exponential functions that you identified, write an equation to fit the data.

For help with questions 3 and 4, refer to Investigate 1, part B.

3. a) Use Technology Graph the function $y = 1.5^x$ over the domain $0 \le x \le 6$ using graphing technology.

b) Determine the average rate of change of y with respect to x for each interval.

i) $x = 1$ to $x = 2$

ii) $x = 2$ to $x = 3$

iii) $x = 3$ to $x = 4$

iv) $x = 4$ to $x = 5$

c) Estimate the instantaneous rate of change of y with respect to x at each of the endpoints in part b).

d) Describe how these rates are changing over the given domain.

4. Repeat question 3 for the function $y = \left(\frac{1}{2}\right)^x$ over the domain $-4 \le x \le 2$.

For part b) use the following intervals.
i) $x = -3$ to $x = -2$
ii) $x = -2$ to $x = -1$
iii) $x = -1$ to $x = 0$
iv) $x = 0$ to $x = 1$

For help with questions 5 to 8, refer to Investigate 2.

5. a) Copy the graph.

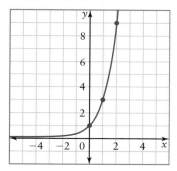

b) Write an equation for this exponential function.

c) Graph the line $y = x$ on the same grid.

d) Sketch a graph of the inverse of the function by reflecting its graph in the line $y = x$.

6. a) Copy the graph.

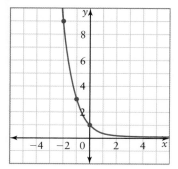

b) Write an equation for this function.

c) Graph the line $y = x$ on the same grid.

d) Sketch a graph of the inverse of the function by reflecting its graph in the line $y = x$.

7. Match each equation to its corresponding graph.

i) $y = 5^x$
ii) $y = \left(\frac{1}{2}\right)^x$
iii) $y = 2^x$
iv) $y = \left(\frac{1}{5}\right)^x$

a)

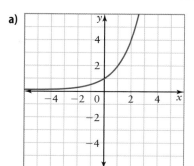

b)

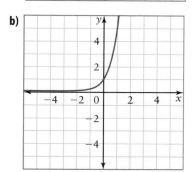

c)

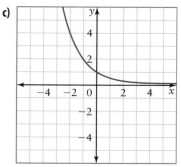

d)

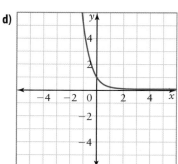

8. Tell which graph from question 7 each graph below is the inverse of.

a)

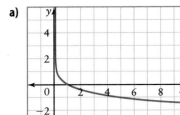

b)

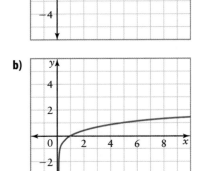

c)

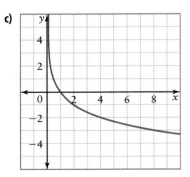

d)

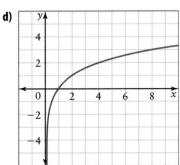

9. Consider the functions $f(x) = 3x$, $g(x) = x^3$, and $h(x) = 3^x$.

a) Graph each function.

b) Make a list of the key features for each function, as in Investigate 2, step 2 b). Organize the information in a table.

c) Identify key features that are common to each function.

d) Identify key features that are different for each function.

e) How do the instantaneous rates of change compare for these three functions?

10. An influenza virus is spreading through a school according to the function $N = 10(2)^t$, where N is the number of people infected and t is the time, in days.

a) How many people have the virus at each time?

   i) initially, when $t = 0$ **ii)** after 1 day

   iii) after 2 days   **iv)** after 3 days

b) Graph the function. Does it appear to be exponential? Explain your answer.

c) Determine the average rate of change between day 1 and day 2.

d) Estimate the instantaneous rate of change after

   i) 1 day   **ii)** 2 days

e) Explain why the answers to parts c) and d) are different.

Use the functions $f(x) = 4^x$ and $g(x) = \left(\dfrac{1}{2}\right)^x$ to answer questions 11 to 18.

11. a) Sketch a graph of f.

b) Graph the line $y = x$ on the same grid.

c) Sketch the inverse of f on the same grid by reflecting f in the line $y = x$.

12. Identify the key features of f.

a) domain and range

b) x-intercept, if it exists

c) y-intercept, if it exists

d) intervals for which the function is positive and intervals for which it is negative

e) intervals for which the function is increasing and intervals for which it is decreasing

f) equation of the asymptote

13. Repeat question 12 for the inverse of f.

14. a) Sketch a graph of the function g.

b) Graph the line $y = x$ on the same grid.

c) Sketch the inverse of g on the same grid by reflecting g in the line $y = x$.

15. Identify the key features of g.

a) domain and range

b) x-intercept, if it exists

c) y-intercept, if it exists

d) intervals for which the function is positive and intervals for which it is negative

e) intervals for which the function is increasing and intervals for which it is decreasing

f) equation of the asymptote

16. Repeat question 15 for the inverse of g.

17. Compare the graphs of f and g. Describe how they are

a) alike

b) different

18. Repeat question 17 for f^{-1} and g^{-1}.

19. a) Copy the graph.

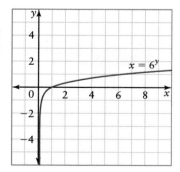

b) Graph the line $y = x$ on the same grid.

c) Graph the inverse of this function by reflecting it in the line $y = x$.

d) Write an equation for the inverse function.

20. Write an equation for the inverse of the function shown.

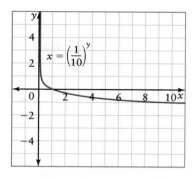

21. Consider the equation $f(x) = (-2)^x$.

a) Copy and complete the table of values.

x	y
0	
1	
2	
3	
4	

b) Graph the ordered pairs.

c) Do the points form a smooth curve? Explain.

d) Use technology to try to evaluate

  i) $f(-0.5)$ **ii)** $f(-2.5)$

  Use numerical reasoning to explain why these values are undefined.

e) Use these results to explain why exponential functions are defined only for functions with positive bases.

22. Chapter Problem A spaceship approaches Planet X and the planet's force of gravity starts to pull the ship in. To prevent a crash, the crew must engage the thrusters when the ship is exactly 100 km from the planet. The distance away from the planet can be modelled by the function $d(t) = (1.4)^t$, where d represents the distance, in hundreds of kilometres, between the ship and the planet and t represents the time, in seconds.

a) What is the ship's average velocity between 1 s and 2 s? between 3 s and 4 s?

b) What is the ship's instantaneous velocity at 3 s? at 4 s?

23. a) For the graph of any function $f(x) = b^x$ and its inverse, describe the points where the x-coordinates and y-coordinates are equal. Explain how the functions relate to the line $y = x$ at these points.

b) Does your answer to part a) differ when $b > 1$ versus when $0 < b < 1$?

24. Use Technology Open *The Geometer's Sketchpad*® and begin a new sketch.

a) From the **Graph** menu, choose **New Parameter**. Call the parameter b and set its initial value to 2.

b) Plot the function $f(x) = b^x$. Explore the shape of this graph and its inverse, using different values of b.

c) For which values of b is f

   i) a function?

   ii) undefined?

d) For which values of b is the inverse of f

   i) a function?

   ii) undefined?

e) Are the answers to parts c) and d) the same? Explain.

Technology Tip

To graph a function using a parameter, choose **Plot New Function** from the **Graph** menu, and double-click on the parameter b to change its value when the **Edit Parameter Value** box appears.

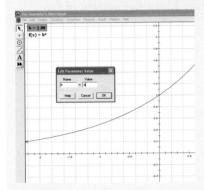

The parameter b can be adjusted manually either by right-clicking on it and choosing **Edit Parameter** or by selecting it and pressing $+$ or $-$.

The parameter b can be adjusted dynamically by right-clicking on it and choosing the **Animate Parameter** feature. This will enable the **Motion Controller**.

You can graph the inverse by following these steps:
- From the **Graph** menu, choose **New Function**.
- From the **Equation** menu, choose $x = f(y)$.
- Then, select parameter b and type **^y** and click on **OK**.
- From the **Graph** menu, choose **Plot Function**.

CAREER CONNECTION

Andre completed a 4-year bachelor of science degree in nuclear medicine at the Michener Institute for Applied Health Sciences. He now works in a hospital as a nuclear medicine technologist. After administering a dose of a radiopharmaceutical to a patient, he monitors the spread of the radioactive drug with a gamma scintillation camera. Andre saves the images on a computer. They will later be interpreted by a doctor. It is critical that Andre decide on the correct radioactive material to use, as well as calculating and preparing the proper dosage.

Suppose a new Web site becomes very popular very quickly. The number of visitors as a function of time can be modelled using an exponential function. What if you wanted to describe the time required for the number of visitors to reach a certain value? This type of functional relationship can be modelled using the inverse of an exponential function.

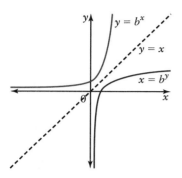

Because each x-value in the inverse graph gives a unique y-value, the inverse is also a function of x. In the inverse function, the y-value is the exponent to which the base, b, must be raised to produce x, $b^y = x$. In the mathematics of functions, we usually prefer to express the y-coordinate in terms of the x-coordinate, so we restate the relationship as y being the logarithm of x to the base b. This relationship is written as $y = \log_b x$.

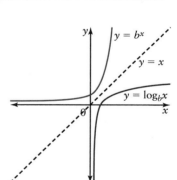

Any exponential relationship can be written using logarithm notation:

$$2^3 = 8 \quad \leftrightarrow \quad \log_2 8 = 3$$
$$5^2 = 25 \quad \leftrightarrow \quad \log_5 25 = 2$$
$$r^s = t \quad \leftrightarrow \quad \log_r t = s$$

The **logarithmic function** is defined as $y = \log_b x$, or y equals the logarithm of x to the base b.

This function is defined only for $b > 0$, $b \neq 1$.

Using this notation, the logarithm, y, is the exponent to which the base, b, must be raised to give the value x. The logarithmic function is the inverse of the exponential function with the same base. Therefore, any equation of the form $y = b^x$ can be written in logarithmic form.

Example 1 | Write an Exponential Equation in Logarithmic Form

Rewrite each equation in logarithmic form.

a) $16 = 2^4$

b) $m = n^3$

c) $3^{-2} = \dfrac{1}{9}$

Solution

a) $16 = 2^4$

$\quad 4 = \log_2 16$

b) $\quad m = n^3$

$\quad \log_n m = 3$

c) $\quad 3^{-2} = \dfrac{1}{9}$

$\quad \log_3 \left(\dfrac{1}{9}\right) = -2$

CONNECTIONS

$4 = \log_2 16$ is read as "4 equals the logarithm of 16 to the base 2."

Notice that in both forms of the equation, the base is 2:

$16 = 2^4 \qquad 4 = \log_2 16$

base

Note that logarithms can produce negative results, as in part c) above, but the base of a logarithm can never be negative, zero, or one. Why is this? A negative base with a non-integer exponent is undefined, $\log_0 0$ has an infinite number of solutions, and $\log_1 x$ only has meaning for $x = 1$, in which case it has an infinite number of values.

The logarithmic function is useful for solving for unknown exponents.

Example 2 | Evaluate a Logarithm

Evaluate.

a) $\log_3 81$

b) $\log_2 \left(\dfrac{1}{8}\right)$

c) $\log_{10} 0.01$

Solution

a) The logarithm is the exponent to which you must raise a base to produce a given value.

Let $y = \log_3 81$

Then, $3^y = 81$

$\qquad 3^y = 3^4$

$\qquad y = 4$

b) $\log_2\left(\dfrac{1}{8}\right)$

Method 1: *Mental Calculation*

$$\frac{1}{8} = \frac{1}{2^3}$$

$$= 2^{-3} \qquad \text{Think: To what exponent must 2 be raised to produce the value } \frac{1}{8}?$$

$$\log_2\left(\frac{1}{8}\right) = -3$$

c) Let $y = \log_{10} 0.01$.

Then $10^y = 0.01$

$\qquad 10^y = 10^{-2}$

$\qquad\quad y = -2$

Method 2: *Graphical Analysis*

Graph the function $y = 2^x$, and find the value of x that corresponds to $y = \dfrac{1}{8}$ or 0.125. A graphing calculator can be used for this.

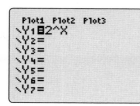 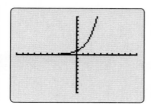 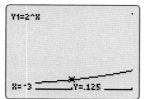

Technology Tip ∴

You can see from the graph in the standard viewing window that $y = 0.125$ at some point when $x < 0$. Adjust the viewing window and zoom in to find the point where $y = 0.125$.

Notice from Example 2a) and c) that $\log_a(a^b) = b$.

Logarithms to the base 10 are called **common logarithms**. When writing a common logarithm, it is not necessary to write the base; that is, log 100 is understood to mean the same as $\log_{10} 100$.

Example 3 Write a Logarithmic Equation in Exponential Form

Rewrite in exponential form.

a) $\log_4 64 = 3$ **b)** $y = \log x$

Solution

a) $\log_4 64 = 3$

The base is 4 and the exponent is 3. In exponential form, this equation is $4^3 = 64$.

b) $y = \log x$

Because there is no base written, this function is understood to be the common logarithm of x. In exponential form, this is $10^y = x$.

Example 4 | Approximate Logarithms

Find an approximate value for each logarithm.

a) $\log_2 10$ **b)** $\log 2500$

Solution

a) $\log_2 10$

Method 1: *Systematic Trial*

$\log_2 8 = 3$ and $\log_2 16 = 4$, so $\log_2 10$ must be between 3 and 4. Find the approximate exponent to which 2 must be raised to give 10. Try 3.50 first.

Estimate	Check	Analysis
3.50	$2^{3.50} \doteq 11.3$	Too high. Try a lower value.
3.10	$2^{3.10} \doteq 8.6$	Too low. Try 3.3.
3.30	$2^{3.30} \doteq 9.8$	Low, but very close.
3.35	$2^{3.35} \doteq 10.2$	A little high.
3.32	$2^{3.32} \doteq 10.0$	**This is a good estimate.**

Therefore, $\log_2 10 \doteq 3.32$.

Method 2: *Graphical Analysis of $y = 2^x$*

Trace the graph of $y = 2^x$ and find the value of x that produces $y = 10$. Graphing software can be used to do this.

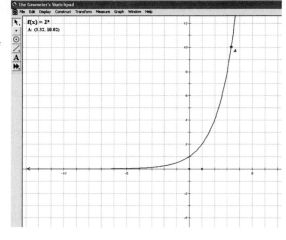

The graph shows that $y = 10$ when $x \doteq 3.32$, so $\log_2 10 \doteq 3.32$.

Method 3: *Intersection of Two Functions*

To find the value of x when $2^x = 10$, enter the left side and the right side into a graphing calculator, each as a separate function. Then, find their point of intersection.

Technology Tip ∴

To find the intersection point using a graphing calculator, press [2nd] [TRACE] for [CALC]. Choose **5:intersect**. Press [ENTER] three times.

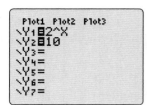
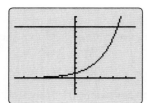
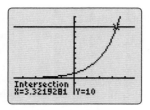

These graphs intersect when $x \doteq 3.32$, so $\log_2 10 \doteq 3.32$.

b) log 2500

While any of the methods illustrated above can be used here, a scientific or graphing calculator can be used to calculate common logarithms.

$\log 2500 \doteq 3.40$

Later in this chapter, you will analyse a technique for evaluating logarithms with any base, using a calculator.

KEY CONCEPTS

- The logarithmic function is the inverse of the exponential function.

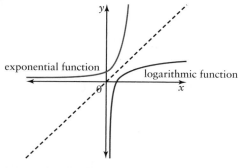

- The value of $\log_b x$ is equal to the exponent to which the base, b, is raised to produce x.

- Exponential equations can be written in logarithmic form, and vice versa.

$$y = b^x \qquad \leftrightarrow \qquad x = \log_b y$$
$$y = \log_b x \qquad \leftrightarrow \qquad x = b^y$$

- Exponential and logarithmic functions are defined only for positive values of the base that are not equal to one:

$$y = b^x, b > 0, x > 0, b \neq 1$$
$$y = \log_b x, b > 0, y > 0, b \neq 1$$

The logarithm of x to base 1 is only valid when $x = 1$, in which case y has an infinite number of solutions and is not a function.

- Common logarithms are logarithms with a base of 10. It is not necessary to write the base for common logarithms: $\log x$ means the same as $\log_{10} x$.

Communicate Your Understanding

C1 Is a logarithm an exponent? Explain.

C2 Consider an equation in logarithmic form. Identify each value in the equation and describe what it means. Discuss how this equation would appear in exponential form.

C3 Does $\log_2 (-4)$ have meaning? If so, explain what it means. If not, explain why it has no meaning.

For help with question 1, refer to Example 1.

1. Rewrite each equation in logarithmic form.

   a) $4^3 = 64$

   b) $128 = 2^7$

   c) $5^{-2} = \dfrac{1}{25}$

   d) $\left(\dfrac{1}{2}\right)^2 = 0.25$

   e) $6^x = y$

   f) $10^5 = 100\ 000$

   g) $\dfrac{1}{27} = 3^{-3}$

   h) $v = b^u$

For help with questions 2 and 3, refer to Example 2.

2. Evaluate each logarithm.

   a) $\log_2 64$

   b) $\log_3 27$

   c) $\log_2 \left(\dfrac{1}{4}\right)$

   d) $\log_4 \left(\dfrac{1}{64}\right)$

   e) $\log_5 125$

   f) $\log_2 1024$

   g) $\log_6 36^3$

   h) $\log_3 81$

3. Evaluate each common logarithm.

   a) $\log 1000$

   b) $\log \left(\dfrac{1}{10}\right)$

   c) $\log 1$

   d) $\log 0.001$

   e) $\log 10^{-4}$

   f) $\log 1\ 000\ 000$

   g) $\log \left(\dfrac{1}{100}\right)$

   h) $\log 10\ 000$

For help with question 4, refer to Example 3.

4. Rewrite in exponential form.

   a) $\log_7 49 = 2$

   b) $5 = \log_2 32$

   c) $\log 10\ 000 = 4$

   d) $w = \log_b z$

   e) $\log_2 8 = 3$

   f) $\log_5 625 = 4$

   g) $-2 = \log \left(\dfrac{1}{100}\right)$

   h) $\log_7 x = 2y$

5. Sketch a graph of each function. Then, sketch a graph of the inverse of each function. Label each graph with its equation.

   a) $y = 2^x$

   b) $y = 4^x$

For help with questions 6 to 8, refer to Example 4.

6. Estimate the value of each logarithm, correct to one decimal place, using a graphical method.

   a) $\log_2 6$

   b) $\log_4 180$

   c) $\log_3 900$

   d) $\log_9 0.035$

7. Pick one part from question 6. Use a different graphical method to verify your answer.

8. Evaluate, correct to two decimal places, using a calculator.

   a) $\log 425$

   b) $\log 0.000\ 037$

   c) $\log 9$

   d) $\log 0.2$

   e) $\log 17$

   f) $\log 99$

   g) $\log 183$

   h) $\log 1010$

9. Let $y = \log x$.

   a) Write the corresponding inverse function in exponential form.

   b) Sketch a graph of $y = \log x$ and its inverse on the same grid.

10. Evaluate each logarithm.

   a) $\log_3 3$

   b) $\log_2 2$

   c) $\log_{12} 12$

   d) $\log_{\frac{1}{2}}\left(\dfrac{1}{2}\right)$

11. a) Make a prediction about the value of $\log_x x$ for any value of $x > 0$, $x \neq 1$.

   b) Test your prediction by evaluating several cases.

   c) What can you conclude about the value of $\log_x x$? Explain your answer using algebraic, numerical, or graphical reasoning.

12. a) Compare the rate of change of a logarithmic function to that of its inverse (exponential) function.

Reasoning and Proving
Representing · Selecting Tools
Problem Solving
Connecting · Reflecting
Communicating

   b) How are their rates of change different? How are they alike? Use an example to illustrate and support your explanation.

13. The number of visitors to a popular Web site is tripling every day. The time, t, in days for a number, N, of visitors to see the site is given by the equation $t = \dfrac{\log N}{\log 3}$. How long will it take until the number of visitors to the Web site reaches each number?

   a) 1000

   b) 1 000 000

14. Fog can greatly reduce the intensity of oncoming headlights. The distance, d, in metres, of an oncoming car whose headlights have an intensity of light, I, in lumens (lm), is given by $d = -167\log\left(\dfrac{I}{125}\right)$.

   a) How far away is a car whose headlight intensity is 50 lm?

   b) If the headlight intensity doubles, does this mean the car is half as far away? Explain.

   c) What implications do these results have on recommended driver behaviour?

15. Chapter Problem Engineers of spacecraft take care to ensure that the crew is safe from the dangerous cosmic radiation of space. The protective hull of the ship is constructed of a special alloy that blocks radiation according to the equation $P = 100(0.2)^x$, where P is the percent of radiation transmitted through a hull with a thickness of x centimetres.

   a) What thickness of the hull walls will ensure that less than 1% of the radiation will pass through?

   b) By how much would the thickness of the walls need to be increased in order to reduce the harmful radiation transmission to 0.1%?

✔ **Achievement Check**

16. After hearing some mysterious scratching noises, four friends at a high school decide to spread a rumour that there are two hedgehogs living inside the school's walls. Each friend agrees to tell the rumour to two other students every day, and also to encourage them to do likewise. Assuming that no one hears the rumour twice, the time, t, in days, it will take for the rumour to reach N students is given by $t = \dfrac{\log\left(\dfrac{N}{4}\right)}{\log 3}$.

   a) Determine how long it will take for the rumour to reach

   i) 30 students

   ii) half of the student population of 1100

   iii) the entire student population

   b) Graph the function.

   c) Describe how the graph would change if the number of students who initially began the rumour were

   i) greater than 4

   ii) less than 4

   Explain your reasoning.

   d) Describe how the graph would change if some students were to hear the rumour more than once. Explain your reasoning.

17. Use Technology Graph the function $y = \log x$ using a graphing calculator or graphing software. Experiment with the **Zoom** and **Window** settings. Try to view the function over as large a range as possible.

a) Approximately how many integer values of y can be viewed at any one time?

b) Explain why it is difficult to view a broad range of this function.

18. Because logarithmic functions grow very slowly, it is difficult to see much of their range using normal graphing methods. One method of getting around this is to use semi-log graph paper, in which one variable is graphed versus the common logarithm of the other variable.

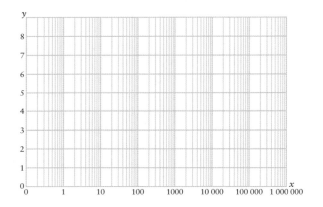

a) Create a table of values for the function $y = \log x$, using several powers of 10 for x.

b) Graph the function on semi-log graph paper. Describe the shape of the graph. Explain why it has this shape.

c) What are some advantages of using this technique to graph logarithmic relationships?

CONNECTIONS

In laboratory experiments, semi-logarithmic scatter plots can be used to determine an unknown parameter that occurs in the exponent of an exponential relationship. You will learn more about semi-log plots if you study physics or chemistry at university.

Log charts are also used in the stock market to track a stock's value over a period of time.

---

19. Use Technology Another technique that can be used to view logarithmic functions over a broad range is to linearize the relationship using spreadsheet software.

a) Enter the table of values from question 18 for the function $y = \log x$. Use column A for x and column B for y, starting at row 1.

	A	B	C	D
1	1	0		
2	10	1		
3	100	2		
4	1000	3		
5				
6				
7				

b) Create a scatter plot of the data. Describe the shape of the graph of $y = \log x$.

c) Use the formula $= \log(A1)$ in cell C1 and copy it to cells C2 to C4 to find the common logarithm of column A.

d) Create a scatter plot using the data in columns C and B. Describe the shape of this graph.

e) What are some advantages of using this technique to graph a logarithmic relationship?

20. Math Contest The ratio $\dfrac{10^{2006} + 10^{2008}}{10^{2007} + 10^{2007}}$ is closest to which of the following numbers?

A 0.1 **B** 0.2 **C** 1 **D** 5 **E** 10

21. Math Contest Two different positive numbers, m and n, each differ from their reciprocals by 1. What is the value of $m + n$?

6.3

Transformations of Logarithmic Functions

Transformations apply to logarithmic functions in the same way as they do to other functions. Recall the following transformations and their geometric effects on a graph:

- $f(x) \rightarrow f(x) + c$
- $f(x) \rightarrow f(x - d)$
- $f(x) \rightarrow af(x)$
- $f(x) \rightarrow f(kx)$

What type of transformation does each of these represent? Will these transformations produce the same effects on logarithmic functions?

Investigate | **How do transformations affect the graph of a logarithmic function?**

For this investigation, you will use the common logarithm function $f(x) = \log x$.

A: The Effects of c and d in $f(x) = \log(x - d) + c$

1. Graph the function $f(x) = \log x$.

2. Based on your knowledge of transformations, predict what the graph of $f(x) = \log x + c$ will look like. Verify your prediction using technology.

Tools

One or more of the following tools are recommended:

- computer with *The Geometer's Sketchpad*®
- graphing calculator

Technology Tip

If you are using *The Geometer's Sketchpad*®, parameters can be helpful. Follow these steps:

- From the **Graph** menu, choose **New Parameter**.
- In the name field, type **c** and click on **OK**.
- From the **Graph** menu, choose **Plot New Function**. A dialogue box will appear.
- From the **Functions** menu, choose **log** and type **x)+**. Click on the parameter **c** and click on **OK**.

A graph of the function $f(x) = \log x + c$ will appear.

You can change the value of c in the following ways:

- To enter a specific value, right-click on the parameter and type in the value.
- To increase or decrease by increments of one, click on the parameter and type the ⊕ or ⊖ key.
- To dynamically change continuously, right-click on the parameter and choose **Animate Parameter**. Use the various commands in the **Motion Controller**.

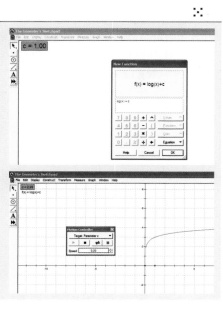

3. a) Repeat step 2 for the function $f(x) = \log(x - d)$.

   b) Reflect Why do you think a minus sign is normally used with this type of transformation?

4. a) Predict what will happen when these transformations are combined: $f(x) = \log(x - d) + c$.

   b) Reflect Test your prediction. Write a summary of the effects of these transformations on the graph of $f(x) = \log x$.

B: *The Effects of a and k in f(x) = a log (kx)*

1. Design and carry out an investigation to explore the effect of a on the graph of $f(x) = a \log x$. Include both positive and negative values. Take note of your observations.

2. Repeat step 1 for the effect of k on the graph of $f(x) = \log(kx)$.

3. Reflect Summarize the effects of translations, stretches, and reflections of the function $f(x) = \log x$, using algebraic and graphical reasoning.

Example 1 | Translations

a) Graph the function $y = \log(x - 2) - 5$.

b) State the key features of the function.

   i) domain and range

   ii) x-intercept, if it exists

   iii) y-intercept, if it exists

   iv) equation of the asymptote

Solution

a) This function can be graphed by applying a horizontal and a vertical translation to the graph of $y = \log x$.

$$y = \log(x - 2) - 5$$

translate right 2 units   translate down 5 units

Apply the horizontal translation first.

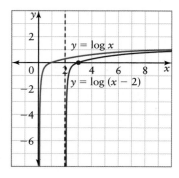

The vertical asymptote has shifted to the line $x = 2$. The x-intercept has become $x = 3$.

Now apply the vertical translation.

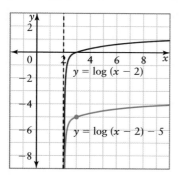

b) **i)** domain $\{x \in \mathbb{R}, x > 2\}$; range $\{y \in \mathbb{R}\}$

ii) The x-intercept occurs when $y = 0$:

$$y = \log(x - 2) - 5$$
$$0 = \log(x - 2) - 5$$
$$5 = \log(x - 2)$$
$$10^5 = x - 2 \qquad \text{Rewrite in exponential form.}$$
$$10^5 + 2 = x$$
$$100\ 002 = x$$

The x-intercept is 100 002.

iii) The y-intercept occurs when $x = 0$:

$$\begin{aligned}
y &= \log(x - 2) - 5 \\
&= \log(0 - 2) - 5 \\
&= \log(-2) - 5
\end{aligned}$$

Because $\log(-2)$ is undefined, there is no y-intercept.

iv) The vertical asymptote occurs when $x - 2 = 0$. Thus, the vertical asymptote is at $x = 2$.

Example 2 | Stretches, Reflections, and Translations

a) Sketch a graph of each function.

   i) $y = 5 \log(x + 3)$

   ii) $y = \log(-2x) + 4$

b) Identify the key features of each function.

Solution

a) When applying multiple transformations, it can be helpful to focus on certain anchor points, such as $(1, 0)$ and $(10, 1)$, as well as the position of the asymptote.

i) $y = 5 \log (x + 3)$

A graph of this function can be obtained by applying a vertical stretch and a horizontal translation to the graph of $y = \log x$.

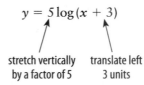

stretch vertically   translate left
by a factor of 5   3 units

Apply the vertical stretch first. Consider the anchor points as $y = \log x$ is transformed to $y = 5 \log x$:

$(1, 0) \to (1, 0)$

$(10, 1) \to (10, 5)$

The asymptote will remain at $x = 0$ at this stage.

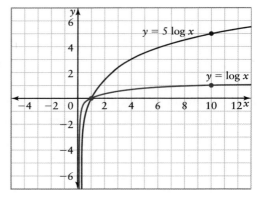

Now apply the horizontal shift from $y = 5 \log x$ to $y = 5 \log (x + 3)$. The anchor points and vertical asymptote will both shift 3 units to the left:

$(1, 0) \to (-2, 0)$

$(10, 5) \to (7, 5)$

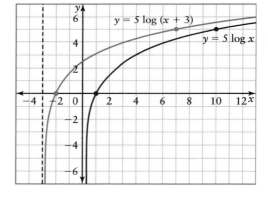

ii) $y = \log (-2x) + 4$

The graph of this function can be obtained by applying a horizontal compression, a horizontal reflection, and a vertical translation to the graph of $y = \log x$.

$$y = \log (-2x) + 4$$

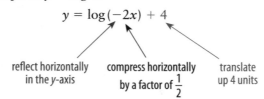

reflect horizontally   compress horizontally   translate
in the y-axis   by a factor of $\dfrac{1}{2}$ up 4 units

Apply the horizontal compression first from $y = \log x$ to $y = \log(2x)$. The anchor points move as follows:

$(1, 0) \rightarrow (0.5, 0)$

$(10, 1) \rightarrow (5, 1)$

The asymptote will remain at $x = 0$ at this stage.

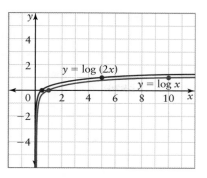

Now reflect the graph in the y-axis to transform $y = \log(2x)$ to $y = \log(-2x)$.

$(0.5, 0) \rightarrow (-0.5, 0)$

$(5, 1) \rightarrow (-5, 1)$

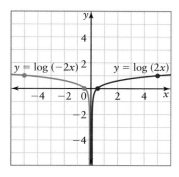

Finally, apply the vertical translation to transform $y = \log(-2x)$ to $y = \log(-2x) + 4$.

$(-0.5, 0) \rightarrow (-0.5, 4)$

$(-5, 1) \rightarrow (-5, 5)$

The vertical asymptote has remained unchanged throughout these transformations.

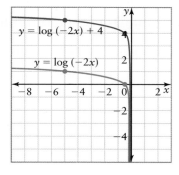

b) i) For the function $y = 5\log(x + 3)$:

domain $\{x \in \mathbb{R}, x > -3\}$; range $\{y \in \mathbb{R}\}$

The x-intercept occurs when $y = 0$:

$$y = 5\log(x + 3)$$
$$0 = 5\log(x + 3)$$
$$0 = \log(x + 3)$$
$$10^0 = x + 3 \qquad \text{Rewrite in exponential form.}$$
$$1 = x + 3$$
$$-2 = x$$

The x-intercept is -2.

The y-intercept occurs when $x = 0$:

$$y = 5\log(x + 3)$$
$$= 5\log(0 + 3)$$
$$= 5\log 3$$
$$\doteq 2.386$$

The y-intercept is approximately 2.386.

There is a vertical asymptote at $x = -3$.

ii) For the function $y = \log(-2x) + 4$:

domain $\{x \in \mathbb{R}, x < 0\}$; range $\{y \in \mathbb{R}\}$

The x-intercept occurs when $y = 0$:

$$y = \log(-2x) + 4$$
$$0 = \log(-2x) + 4$$
$$-4 = \log(-2x)$$
$$10^{-4} = -2x \qquad \text{Rewrite in exponential form.}$$
$$\left(-\frac{1}{2}\right)10^{-4} = x$$
$$(-0.5)10^{-4} = x$$
$$x = -0.000\ 05$$

The x-intercept is $-0.000\ 05$.

The y-intercept occurs when $x = 0$:

$$y = \log(-2x) + 4$$
$$= \log[-2(0)] + 4$$
$$= \log(0) + 4$$

Because $\log 0$ is undefined, there is no y-intercept.

There is a vertical asymptote at $x = 0$.

Example 3 | **Transformations**

Sketch a graph of the function $y = \log(2x - 4)$.

> **Solution**

The graph of this function can be obtained by applying a horizontal compression and a horizontal translation of the graph of $y = \log x$, but the argument must be factored first, to be in the form $y = \log[k(x - d)]$.

$$y = \log(2x - 4)$$
$$= \log[2(x - 2)]$$

$$y = \log[2(x - 2)]$$

compress horizontally by a factor of $\frac{1}{2}$ translate right 2 units

Apply the horizontal compression first from $y = \log x$ to $y = \log(2x)$. The anchor points move as follows:

$(1, 0) \rightarrow (0.5, 0)$

$(10, 1) \rightarrow (5, 1)$

The vertical asymptote will remain at $x = 0$ at this stage.

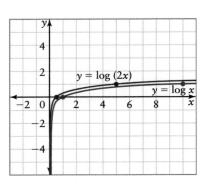

Then, apply the horizontal translation to transform $y = \log{(2x)}$ to $y = \log{[2(x - 2)]}$.

$(0.5, 0) \rightarrow (2.5, 0)$

$(5, 1) \rightarrow (7, 1)$

The vertical asymptote has also shifted to the right to $x = 2$.

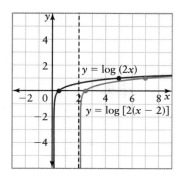

KEY CONCEPTS

- The techniques for applying transformations to logarithmic functions are the same as those used for other functions:

  - $y = \log{x} + c$ Translate up c units if $c > 0$.
    Translate down $|c|$ units if $c < 0$.

  - $y = \log{(x - d)}$ Translate right d units if $d > 0$.
    Translate left $|d|$ units if $d < 0$.

  - $y = a \log{x}$ Stretch vertically by a factor of $|a|$ if $|a| > 1$.
    Compress vertically by a factor of $|a|$ if $|a| < 1$.
    Reflect in the x-axis if $a < 0$.

  - $y = \log{(kx)}$ Compress horizontally by a factor of $\left|\dfrac{1}{k}\right|$ if $|k| > 1$.
    Stretch horizontally by a factor of $\left|\dfrac{1}{k}\right|$ if $|k| < 1$, $k \neq 0$.
    Reflect in the y-axis if $k < 0$.

- It is easier to perform multiple transformations in a series of steps:

  Step 1: Ensure that the function is in the form $f(x) = a \log{[k(x - d)]} + c$.

  Step 2: Apply any horizontal or vertical stretches or compressions.

  Step 3: Apply any reflections.

  Step 4: Apply any horizontal or vertical translations.

Communicate Your Understanding

C1 Explain how you could graph each function by applying transformations.

    a) $y = \log{(x - 2)} + 7$

    b) $f(x) = -3 \log{x}$

    c) $y = \log{(-3x)} - 5$

C2 Let $f(x) = \log{x}$, $g(x) = -\log{x}$, and $h(x) = \log{(-x)}$.

    a) How are the graphs of f and g related? Are these functions inverses of each other? Explain your answer.

    b) How are the graphs of f and h related? Are these functions inverses of each other? Explain your answer.

    c) Are g and h inverses of each other? Explain.

For help with questions 1 to 3, refer to Example 1.

1. Match each equation to its graph.

a) $y = \log(x - 3)$ **b)** $y = \log x - 3$

c) $y = \log(x + 3)$ **d)** $y = \log x + 3$

i)

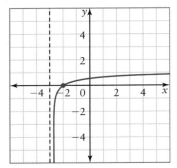

ii)

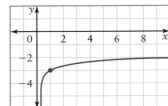

iii)

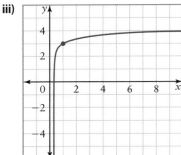

iv)

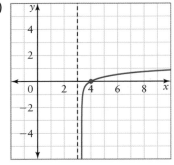

2. Let $f(x) = \log x$. Describe the transformations that would map f onto g in each case.

a) $g(x) = \log(x - 2)$

b) $g(x) = \log(x + 5) - 4$

c)

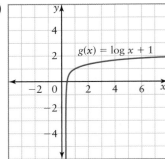

d)

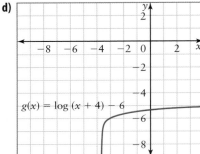

3. Sketch a graph of each function. Identify the key features of each.

a) $y = \log x + 2$

b) $f(x) = \log(x - 3)$

c) $y = \log(x - 3) + 4$

d) $f(x) = \log(x + 5) - 1$

For help with questions 4 to 8, refer to Examples 2 and 3.

4. Each of the following graphs can be generated by stretching or compressing the graph of $y = \log x$. Write an equation to correctly describe each graph.

a)

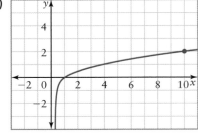

b)

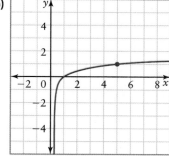

c)

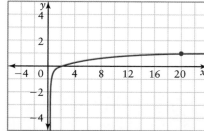

d)

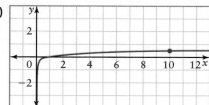

5. Let $f(x) = \log x$. Describe the transformation(s) that would map f onto g in each case.

a) $g(x) = \dfrac{1}{2} \log x$

b) $g(x) = \log(-5x)$

c)

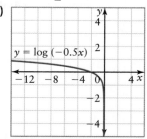

$y = \log(-0.5x)$

d)

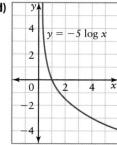

$y = -5 \log x$

6. Graph each function.

a) $y = 4 \log x$

b) $y = \log\left(\dfrac{1}{3}x\right)$

c) $f(x) = \dfrac{1}{3} \log x$

d) $y = \log(4x)$

7. Graph each function.

a) $y = -\log(x - 4)$

b) $y = \log(-x) - 3$

B   Connect and Apply

8. Refer to question 7. For each function, identify the

a) the domain

b) the range

c) an equation for the asymptote

9. a) Sketch by hand, or use technology to graph, $y = -2 \log x$ over the domain $10^{-3} \le x \le 10^{-1}$.

b) What is the range of this function over the restricted domain?

10. Describe what happens to the domain and range of a logarithmic function under a vertical reflection. Support your explanation with diagrams.

11. Refer to question 10. Does the same thing happen under a horizontal reflection? Explain using words and diagrams.

Reasoning and Proving
Representing — Selecting Tools
Problem Solving
Connecting — Reflecting
Communicating

12. Describe what happens to the domain and range of a logarithmic function under both a horizontal and a vertical translation. Support your explanation with diagrams.

13. Sketch a graph of each function.

a) $f(x) = 2\log[3(x + 4)] - 2$

b) $y = \log(-x)$

c) $f(x) = 5\log(2x - 4) - 6$

d) $y = -2\log\left(\frac{1}{2}x + 3\right) - 3$

14. Use Technology Check your answers to question 13 using graphing technology.

15. An operational amplifier (Op Amp) is a type of electronic circuit that transforms a voltage input, V_i, to produce a desired output, V_o. Suppose a particular Op Amp produces a voltage output signal according to the function $V_o = \log V_i + 5$, where both input and output voltages are measured in volts (V).

a) Graph this function.

b) What is the output voltage for an input signal of 10 V? 20 V?

c) What is the input voltage if the output is 25 V?

d) Determine the domain and range. Explain what these represent.

16. a) Graph the function
$$f(x) = -\frac{1}{2}\log\left(-\frac{1}{2}x + 3\right) + 2.$$

b) Identify the key features of f.

  i) domain

  ii) range

  iii) equation of the asymptote

c) Sketch a graph of the inverse function.

CONNECTIONS

An Op Amp is an example of an integrated circuit, such as the one pictured below.

Contained inside these little black chips are many tiny circuits, each designed to perform a specific function. Devices such as these are building blocks for many household electronic devices, such as personal computers, video cameras, and stereo equipment.

You will learn more about Op Amps and other integrated circuits if you decide to study solid-state electronics or digital logic at university or college.

C ▶ Extend and Challenge

17. a) Graph the function $f(x) = \frac{1}{2}\log x - 4$.

b) Graph the line $y = x$ on the same grid.

c) Graph the inverse function f^{-1} by reflecting f in the line $y = x$.

d) Determine the key features of f^{-1}.

  i) domain

  ii) range

  iii) equation of the asymptote

e) Determine an equation for f^{-1}.

18. Graph each function.

a) $y = \log_2(x - 2) + 1$

b) $y = -3\log_2(2x + 5) - 4$

19. Use Technology Suppose that an electronic signal generator produces a voltage output as a function of time that is given by $V_o = 0.4\log(\sin t) + 5$.

a) What are the domain and range of this function? Explain your reasoning.

b) Graph this function using graphing technology.

c) This Op Amp is called a pulsator. Why does this name make sense?

20. Math Contest For what value(s) of x does $\log_2(\log_3(\log_4 x)) = 0$?

Power Law of Logarithms

If you invested $100 today in an account that pays 5% interest, compounded annually, how long do you think it would take for your investment to double in value? This type of problem leads to an equation in which the unknown variable is an exponent. Because of the inverse relationship between exponential functions and logarithmic functions, logarithms provide a way to solve such equations.

Investigate 1 | How can you solve for an unknown exponent?

Suppose you invest $100 in an account that pays 5% interest, compounded annually. The amount, A, in dollars, in the account after any given time, t, in years, is given by $A = 100(1.05)^t$.

1. Predict how long it will take, to the nearest year, for the amount in this account to double in value. Give a reason for your estimate.

2. a) Design a method that will allow you to find an accurate answer to the question in step 1.

   b) Carry out your method. How long will it take for the investment to double in value?

   c) Compare this result with your prediction. How close was your prediction?

3. Suppose the initial amount invested is $250. How does this affect the answer to step 2b)? Explain, using mathematical reasoning.

4. **Reflect** How can you express the original equation, $A = 100(1.05)^t$, in logarithmic form?

Tools

One or more of the following tools are recommended:

- computer with *The Geometer's Sketchpad*®
- graphing calculator
- computer algebra system (CAS)

Logarithms are useful for solving for an unknown exponent in an equation. Consider the problem posed in Investigate 1.

$A = 100(1.05)^t$

To find the time after which the value has doubled, substitute $A = 200$, and try to solve for t.

$200 = 100(1.05)^t$

$\quad 2 = 1.05^t \qquad$ Divide both sides by 100.

You probably solved this equation, $2 = 1.05^t$, in step 2 of Investigate 1 using trial and error or by inspecting a graph. Can the equation be solved algebraically? What if the equation were written in logarithmic form to express it in terms of t?

$$t = \log_{1.05} 2$$

Most scientific calculators can only evaluate logarithms in base 10, so how can this expression be evaluated? Clearly, further study is needed.

Investigate 2 | What is the power law for logarithms?

Tools

One or more of the following tools are recommended:
- scientific calculator
- graphing calculator
- CAS
- spreadsheet software

Technology Tip ⸫

Spreadsheets and graphing calculators are useful tools for performing repeated calculations.

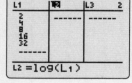

1. **a)** Evaluate each logarithm. Organize your results in a table.

   i) log 2   **ii)** log 4   **iii)** log 8   **iv)** log 16   **v)** log 32

   b) Look for a pattern in your results. How are these values related to log 2? Make a prediction for

   i) log 64   **ii)** log 1024

   c) Verify your predictions.

2. Write a rule for the general result of log 2^n.

3. Do you think the general result will work for other powers?

   a) Repeat the analysis in step 1 for powers of 3:

   i) log 3   **ii)** log 9   **iii)** log 27

   b) Write a rule for evaluating log 3^n.

   c) Verify your rule using a few cases.

4. **Reflect**

   a) Write a rule for evaluating log b^n for any base $b > 0$.

   b) Test your rule using several different cases.

To prove the rule you investigated above, apply algebraic reasoning.

Let $w = \log_b x$.

$$\begin{aligned}
w &= \log_b x \\
x &= b^w && \text{Write the equation in exponential form.} \\
x^n &= (b^w)^n && \text{Raise both sides to the exponent } n. \\
x^n &= b^{wn} && \text{Apply the power law of exponents.} \\
\log_b x^n &= wn && \text{Rewrite in exponential form.} \\
\log_b x^n &= n \log_b x && \text{Substitute } w = \log_b x \text{ to eliminate } w.
\end{aligned}$$

This result is known as the power law of logarithms.

Power Law of Logarithms

$\log_b x^n = n \log_b x,\ b > 0,\ b \neq 1,\ x > 0,\ n \in \mathbb{R}$

Example 1	**Apply the Power Law of Logarithms**

Evaluate.

a) $\log_3 9^4$

b) $\log_2 8^5$

c) $\log 0.001^2$

d) $\log_5 \sqrt{125}$

> **Solution**

a) Method *1: Simplify and Then Evaluate the Logarithm*

$$\begin{aligned}
\log_3 9^4 &= \log_3 (3^2)^4 \\
&= \log_3 3^8 \\
&= 8
\end{aligned}$$

Method 2: *Apply the Power Law of Logarithms*

$$\begin{aligned}
\log_3 9^4 &= 4 \log_3 9 \\
&= 4 \log_3 3^2 \\
&= 4(2) \\
&= 8
\end{aligned}$$

Note that both methods give the same answer, but Method 2 involves simpler calculations.

b) $$\begin{aligned}
\log_2 8^5 &= 5 \log_2 8 \\
&= 5 \log_2 2^3 \\
&= 5(3) \\
&= 15
\end{aligned}$$

c) $$\begin{aligned}
\log 0.001^2 &= 2 \log 0.001 \\
&= 2 \log 10^{-3} \\
&= 2(-3) \\
&= -6
\end{aligned}$$

d) $\log_5 \sqrt{125} = \log_5 125^{\frac{1}{2}}$ Rewrite the radical in exponential form.

$$= \frac{1}{2} \log_5 125$$ Apply the power law.

$$= \frac{1}{2}(3)$$

$$= \frac{3}{2}$$

The power law of logarithms can be applied to evaluate logarithms with bases other than 10.

> ## Example 2 | Compound Interest
>
> Recall the equation $2 = 1.05^t$, found after Investigate 1, the solution of which gives the doubling period for an investment at 5% interest, compounded annually. Determine this doubling period.
>
> ### Solution
>
> | | |
> |---|---|
> | $2 = 1.05^t$ | |
> | $\log 2 = \log 1.05^t$ | Take the common logarithm of both sides. |
> | $\log 2 = t \log 1.05$ | Apply the power law of logarithms and solve for t. |
> | $t = \dfrac{\log 2}{\log 1.05}$ | The expression on the right is a quotient of common logarithms. It can be evaluated with a scientific or graphing calculator. |
> | $t \doteq 14.2$ | |
>
> This should confirm the result you obtained in Investigate 1 that it would take approximately 14.2 years for the initial investment to double in value.

The technique used in Example 2 can be generalized to determine the value of logarithms of any base $b > 0$, $b \neq 1$.

Let $x = \log_b m$.

$x = \log_b m$	
$b^x = m$	Write in exponential form.
$\log b^x = \log m$	Take common logarithms of both sides.
$x \log b = \log m$	Apply the power law of logarithms.
$x = \dfrac{\log m}{\log b}$	Express in terms of x.

To calculate a logarithm with any base, express in terms of common logarithms using the **change of base formula** :

$$\log_b m = \frac{\log m}{\log b}, m > 0, b > 0, b \neq 1$$

Example 3 Evaluate Logarithms With Various Bases

Evaluate, correct to three decimal places.

a) $\log_5 17$

b) $\log_{\frac{1}{2}} 10$

Solution

```
log(17)/log(5)
          1.760374428
```

a) $\log_5 17 = \dfrac{\log 17}{\log 5}$ Express in terms of common logarithms.

$ \doteq 1.760$ Use a calculator to evaluate.

b) $\log_{\frac{1}{2}} 10 = \dfrac{\log 10}{\log \frac{1}{2}}$

$\phantom{\log_{\frac{1}{2}} 10} = \dfrac{1}{\log \frac{1}{2}}$ $\log 10 = 1$

$\phantom{\log_{\frac{1}{2}} 10} \doteq -3.322$

The change of base formula also provides a way to graph logarithmic functions with any base.

Example 4 Graph Logarithmic Functions With Various Bases

Graph the function $f(x) = \log_5 x$.

Solution

Reasoning and Proving
Representing · Selecting Tools
Problem Solving
Connecting · Reflecting
Communicating

Method 1: *Graph the Inverse of an Exponential Function*

The inverse function of f is $f^{-1}(x) = 5^x$.

Graph $f^{-1}(x) = 5^x$ and then reflect it in the line $y = x$ to produce the graph of $f(x) = \log_5 x$.

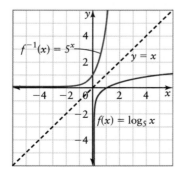

Method 2: *Use a Graphing Calculator or Graphing Software*

Express f in terms of common logarithms:

$$f(x) = \log_5 x$$
$$= \frac{\log x}{\log 5}$$

Choose reasonable values for the window settings.

 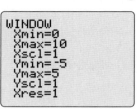 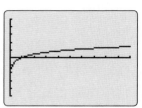

⟪ KEY CONCEPTS ⟫

- The power law of logarithms states that $\log_b x^n = n \log_b x$ for $b > 0$, $b \ne 1$, $x > 0$, and $n \in \mathbb{R}$. This property can be used to solve equations with unknown exponents.

- Any logarithm can be expressed in terms of common logarithms using the change of base formula:

$$\log_b m = \frac{\log m}{\log b}, \; b > 0, \, b \ne 1, \, m > 0$$

This formula can be used to evaluate logarithms or graph logarithmic functions with any base.

Communicate Your Understanding

C1 Explain how you could evaluate $\log_2 10$

    a) with a calculator

    b) without a calculator

C2 Refer to the change of base formula:
$$\log_b m = \frac{\log m}{\log b}, \; b > 0, \, b \ne 1, \, m > 0$$

    a) Describe two applications for which this formula is useful.

    b) Explain why the restrictions $b > 0$, $b \ne 1$, and $m > 0$ are necessary.

C3 **a)** Explain how you could evaluate $\dfrac{1}{\log_3 7}$.

    b) Evaluate the logarithm using your method.

For help with questions 1 and 2, refer to Example 1.

1. Evaluate.

   a) $\log_2 16^3$
   b) $\log_4 8^2$
   c) $\log 100^{-4}$
   d) $\log 0.1^{\frac{1}{2}}$

2. Evaluate.

   a) $\log_2 \sqrt{8}$
   b) $\log_3 \sqrt{243}$
   c) $\log_3 (\sqrt[3]{81})^6$
   d) $\log_4 (\sqrt[5]{16})^{15}$

For help with questions 3 and 4, refer to Example 2.

3. Solve for t to two decimal places.

   a) $10 = 4^t$
   b) $5^t = 250$
   c) $2 = 1.08^t$
   d) $500 = 100(1.06)^t$

4. An investment earns 7% interest, compounded annually. The amount, A, that the investment is worth as a function of time, t, in years, is given by $A(t) = 500(1.07)^t$.

   a) Use the equation to determine the value of the investment

      i) initially, when $t = 0$

      ii) after 2 years

      iii) after 4 years

   b) How long will it take for the investment to

      i) double in value?

      ii) triple in value?

CONNECTIONS

People in the financial sector estimate how long an investment will take to double by using the rule of 72. Dividing 72 by the annual interest rate as a percent gives the approximate number of years for the amount to double.

For help with questions 5 and 6, refer to Example 3.

5. Evaluate, correct to three decimal places.

   a) $\log_3 23$
   b) $\log_6 20$
   c) $\log_7 2$
   d) $-\log_{12} 4$
   e) $\log_{\frac{1}{2}} 30$
   f) $\log_{\frac{3}{4}} (8)$

6. Write as a single logarithm.

   a) $\dfrac{\log 8}{\log 5}$
   b) $\dfrac{\log 17}{\log 9}$
   c) $\dfrac{\log\left(\frac{1}{2}\right)}{\log\left(\frac{2}{3}\right)}$
   d) $\dfrac{\log(x + 1)}{\log(x - 1)}$

For help with questions 7 and 8, refer to Example 4.

7. a) Sketch a graph of the function $f(x) = \log_2 x$ by first graphing the inverse function $f^{-1}(x) = 2^x$ and then reflecting the graph in the line $y = x$.

   b) **Use Technology** Check your graph using graphing technology.

8. **Use Technology** Use graphing software or a graphing calculator to graph $f(x) = \log_{25} x$.

9. Solve for x, correct to three decimal places.

   a) $2 = \log 3^x$
   b) $100 = 10 \log 1000^x$
   c) $4 = \log_3 15^x$
   d) $12 = 2 \log_5 3^x$

10. An investment earns 9% interest, compounded annually. The amount, A, that the investment is worth as a function of time, t, in years, is given by $A(t) = 400(1.09)^t$.

    a) What was the initial value of the investment? Explain how you know.

    b) How long will it take for the investment to double in value?

11. Does $\log (mx) = m \log x$ for some constant m? Explain why or why not, using algebraic or graphical reasoning and supporting examples.

Reasoning and Proving

Representing · Selecting Tools

Problem Solving

Connecting · Reflecting

Communicating

12. Does $\log (x^n) = (\log x)^n$ for some constant n? Explain why or why not, using algebraic or graphical reasoning and supporting examples.

13. a) Evaluate $\log_2 8^5$ without using the power law of logarithms.

b) Evaluate the same expression by applying the power law of logarithms.

c) Which method do you prefer? Why?

14. Create an expression such as the one in question 13. Evaluate first using, and then without using, the power law.

15. Chapter Problem A spacecraft is approaching a space station that is orbiting Earth. When the craft is 1000 km from the space station, reverse thrusters must be applied to begin braking. The time, t, in hours, required to reach a distance, d, in kilometres, from the space station while the thrusters are being fired can be modelled by $t = \log_{0.5}\left(\dfrac{d}{1000}\right)$. The docking sequence can be initialized once the craft is within 10 km of the station's docking bay.

a) How long after the reverse thrusters are first fired should docking procedures begin?

b) What are the domain and range of this function? What do these features represent?

✓ **Achievement Check**

16. An investment pays 8% interest, compounded annually.

a) Write an equation that expresses the amount, A, of the investment as a function of time, t, in years.

b) Determine how long it will take for this investment to

  i) double in value

  ii) triple in value

c) Determine the percent increase in value of the account after

  i) 5 years

  ii) 10 years

d) Explain why the answers to parts b) and c) do not depend on the amount of the initial principal.

C   Extend and Challenge

17. Use algebraic reasoning to show that any logarithm can be written in terms of a logarithm with any base:

$\log_b x = \dfrac{\log_k x}{\log_k b}$ for any $x > 0$, $k > 0$, $b > 0$.

18. Use the result of question 17 to express each of the following in terms of base-2 logarithms.

a) $\log_3 9$ **b)** $\log 25$

19. A computer design contains 10 binary digits in 64 sequences. As a result, the number of codes is $(2^{10})^{64}$. Express this number in logarithmic form with base 2.

> **CONNECTIONS**
>
> You will learn about binary codes and how they are useful for programming computers if you study computer science or technology in university or college.

20. An investment pays 3.5% interest, compounded quarterly.

a) Write an equation to express the amount, A, of the investment as a function of time, t, in years.

b) Determine how long it will take for this investment to

  i) double in value

  ii) triple in value

21. Math Contest Given that $f(x) = \dfrac{1}{\sqrt{1-x}}$ and $f(a) = 2$, what is the value of $f(1-a)$?

22. Math Contest Given that e and f are integers, both greater than one, and $\sqrt{e\sqrt{e\sqrt{e}}} = f$, determine the least possible value of $e + f$.

Making Connections: Logarithmic Scales in the Physical Sciences

The number of hydronium ions in a typical substance indicates how acidic or alkaline it is. Amounts can range from about 1×10^{-15} mol/L (moles per litre) to 0.1 mol/L. In order to make it easier to compare such a vast range of quantities, logarithms are used. What effect does this have?

The pH scale is an example of the application of logarithmic functions in the field of chemistry. **Logarithmic scales** are often used in situations in which a variable ranges over several orders of magnitude, or powers of 10.

Example 1 | pH Scale

The **pH scale** is used to measure the acidity or alkalinity of a chemical solution. It is defined as pH = $-\log [H^+]$, where $[H^+]$ is the concentration of hydronium ions, measured in moles per litre.

Acidic   Neutral   Alkaline

pH 1.0   7.0   14.0

Concentration (mol/L) 10^{-1} 10^{-7} 10^{-14}

CONNECTIONS

You will learn more about pH, acids, and bases if you study chemistry.

a) Tomato juice has a hydronium ion concentration of approximately 0.0001 mol/L. What is its pH?

b) Blood has a hydronium ion concentration of approximately 4×10^{-7} mol/L. Is blood acidic or alkaline?

c) Orange juice has a pH of approximately 3. What is the concentration of hydronium ions in orange juice?

d) Which has a greater concentration of hydronium ions, orange juice or tomato juice, and by how much?

Solution

a) To find the pH of tomato juice, substitute its hydronium ion concentration into the equation.

$$pH = -\log [H^+]$$
$$= -\log 0.0001$$
$$= -(-4)$$
$$= 4$$

The pH of tomato juice is 4.

b) Substitute the hydronium ion concentration of blood into the equation, and use a scientific or graphing calculator to evaluate the common logarithm.

$$\begin{aligned} \text{pH} &= -\log[H^+] \\ &= -\log(4 \times 10^{-7}) \\ &\doteq 6.4 \end{aligned}$$

Blood has a pH of approximately 6.4, which is below the neutral value of 7.0. Therefore, blood is acidic.

c) The pH of orange juice is given. To find its concentration of hydronium ions, rearrange the equation to express it in terms of $[H^+]$.

$$\begin{aligned} \text{pH} &= -\log[H^+] \\ -\text{pH} &= \log[H^+] \qquad \text{Multiply both sides by } -1. \\ 10^{-\text{pH}} &= [H^+] \qquad \text{Rewrite in exponential form.} \end{aligned}$$

Substitute the known pH and solve for $[H^+]$.

$$\begin{aligned} [H^+] &= 10^{-3} \\ &= 0.001 \end{aligned}$$

Therefore, the hydronium ion concentration in orange juice is 0.001 mol/L.

d) The pH and hydronium ion concentrations in tomato juice and orange juice are summarized in the table.

	Tomato Juice	Orange Juice
pH	4	3
Hydronium Ion Concentration (mol/L)	0.0001	0.001

Orange juice has a greater concentration of hydronium ions than tomato juice, by a ratio of

$$\frac{0.001}{0.0001} = 10$$

Notice that a pH difference of -1 corresponds to a tenfold increase in hydronium ion concentration.

CONNECTIONS

A decibel is equal to one tenth of a bel (B).

There are several other areas in which logarithmic scales are applied in the physical sciences. For example, how the human ear perceives sound intensity can be described using a logarithmic scale. The decibel scale provides a convenient way of comparing sound levels that range over several orders of magnitude. Each increase of 10 decibels (dB) represents a tenfold increase in sound intensity, or loudness.

Example 2 | Decibel Scale

Some common sound levels are indicated on the decibel scale shown.

The difference in sound levels, in decibels, can be found using the equation

$$\beta_2 - \beta_1 = 10 \log\left(\frac{I_2}{I_1}\right),$$ where $\beta_2 - \beta_1$ is the

difference in sound levels, in decibels, and $\frac{I_2}{I_1}$

is the ratio of their sound intensities, where I is measured in watts per square metre (W/m^2).

a) How many times as intense as a whisper is the sound of a normal conversation?

b) The sound level in normal city traffic is approximately 85 dB. The sound level while riding a snowmobile is about 32 times as intense. What is the sound level while riding a snowmobile, in decibels?

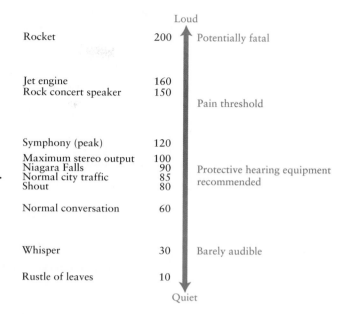

Loud

Rocket	200 — Potentially fatal
Jet engine	160
Rock concert speaker	150 — Pain threshold
Symphony (peak)	120
Maximum stereo output	100
Niagara Falls	90 — Protective hearing equipment
Normal city traffic	85 — recommended
Shout	80
Normal conversation	60
Whisper	30 — Barely audible
Rustle of leaves	10

Quiet

Solution

a) Substitute the given decibel levels for a normal conversation and a whisper, and solve for the ratio of their sound intensities.

$$\beta_2 - \beta_1 = 10 \log\left(\frac{I_2}{I_1}\right)$$

$$60 - 30 = 10 \log\left(\frac{I_2}{I_1}\right)$$

$$30 = 10 \log\left(\frac{I_2}{I_1}\right)$$

$$3 = \log\left(\frac{I_2}{I_1}\right) \qquad \text{Solve for } \frac{I_2}{I_1}.$$

$$10^3 = \frac{I_2}{I_1} \qquad \text{Rewrite in exponential form.}$$

$$1000 = \frac{I_2}{I_1}$$

The ratio of these intensities is 1000. This means that to the human ear, a normal conversation sounds 1000 times as intense as a whisper!

b) The ratio of the intensity of the sound while riding a snowmobile to the intensity of the sound of normal city traffic is given as 32. Substitute this and the given decibel level for normal city traffic into the equation and solve for the decibel level of the sound while riding a snowmobile.

$$\beta_2 - \beta_1 = 10 \log\left(\frac{I_2}{I_1}\right)$$

$$\beta_2 - 85 = 10 \log 32$$

$$\beta_2 = 10 \log 32 + 85$$

$$\beta_2 \doteq 100$$

```
10log(32)+85
        100.0514998
```

The sound level while riding a snowmobile is approximately 100 dB.

Example 3 | Richter Scale

The magnitude, M, of an earthquake is measured using the Richter scale, which is defined as $M = \log\left(\frac{I}{I_0}\right)$, where I is the intensity of the earthquake being measured and I_0 is the intensity of a standard, low-level earthquake.

a) How many times as intense as a standard earthquake is an earthquake measuring 2.4 on the Richter scale?

b) What is the magnitude of an earthquake 1000 times as intense as a standard earthquake?

Solution

a) Substitute $M = 2.4$ into the equation and solve for $\frac{I}{I_0}$:

$$M = \log\left(\frac{I}{I_0}\right)$$

$$2.4 = \log\left(\frac{I}{I_0}\right)$$

$$10^{2.4} = \frac{I}{I_0} \qquad \text{Rewrite in exponential form.}$$

$$251.19 \doteq \frac{I}{I_0}$$

An earthquake measuring 2.4 on the Richter scale is approximately 251 times as intense as a standard earthquake.

b) Substitute $\frac{I}{I_0} = 1000$ and solve for M:

$$M = \log\left(\frac{I}{I_0}\right)$$

$$= \log 1000$$

$$= 3$$

An earthquake that is 1000 times as intense as a standard earthquake has a magnitude of 3.

- Logarithmic scales provide a convenient method of comparing values that typically have a very large range.

- Several phenomena in the physical sciences can be described using logarithmic scales.

- The pH scale is defined as pH $= -\log [H^+]$, where H^+ is the hydronium ion concentration in a substance.

- The difference in sound levels, in decibels, can be found by using the equation $\beta_2 - \beta_1 = 10 \log \left(\dfrac{I_2}{I_1} \right)$, where I_1 and I_2 are the intensities of the two sounds, in watts per square metre.

Communicate Your Understanding

C1 **a)** In what types of situations are logarithmic scales used?

   b) Why are they used?

C2 How can you tell if a chemical is acidic, alkaline, or neutral? Use examples to illustrate your answer.

C3 Consider the following statement: "According to the decibel scale, a whisper is three times as loud as the rustle of leaves." Is this statement true? Explain.

A) Practise

For help with questions 1 to 5, refer to Example 1.

1. Determine the pH of a solution with each hydronium ion concentration.

   a) 0.01   **b)** 0.000 034

   c) 10^{-9} **d)** 1.5×10^{-10}

2. Determine the hydronium ion concentration, in moles per litre, of a solution with each pH.

   a) 11   **b)** 3

   c) 8.5   **d)** 4.4

3. The hydronium ion concentration of most chemicals varies from about 10^{-15} mol/L to 0.1 mol/L. Given this fact, why do you suppose that the pH scale was created

   a) in terms of a logarithmic function

   b) with a factor of -1

4. Determine the pH of a solution with a hydronium ion concentration of

   a) 0.000 01   **b)** 2.5×10^{-11}

5. **Use Technology** Acetic acid (vinegar) has a hydronium ion concentration of 1.9×10^{-3} mol/L. Suppose you want to use a graphing calculator to view the graph of the pH function.

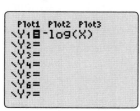

   a) What **window** settings would you choose in order to read the pH value of acetic acid from the graph?

   b) Use the graph to determine the pH level of acetic acid.

   c) Verify this result using the equation.

For help with questions 6 to 8, refer to Example 2.

6. How many times as intense is the sound of a shout as the sound of a

   a) conversation   **b)** whisper

7. A loud car stereo has a decibel level of 110 dB. How many times as intense as the sound of a loud car stereo is the sound of a rock concert speaker?

8. The sound intensity of a pin drop is about $\dfrac{1}{30\,000}$ of the sound intensity of a normal conversation. What is the decibel level of a pin drop?

B Connect and Apply

For help with questions 9 to 11, refer to Example 3.

9. On September 26, 2001, an earthquake in North Bay, Ontario, occurred that was 10 000 times as intense as I_0. What was the measure of this earthquake on the Richter scale?

10. On February 10, 2000, an earthquake happened in Welland, Ontario, that measured 2.3 on the Richter scale.

   a) How many times as intense was this as a standard low-level earthquake?

   b) On July 22, 2001, an earthquake in St. Catharines measured 1.1 on the Richter scale. How many times as intense as the St. Catharines earthquake was the Welland earthquake?

11. The most intense earthquakes measured have had a value of about 8.9 on the Richter scale. How do these earthquakes compare in intensity to a standard, low-level earthquake?

12. The stellar magnitude scale compares the brightness of stars using the equation

$$m_2 - m_1 = \log\left(\frac{b_1}{b_2}\right),$$

where m_1 and m_2 are the apparent magnitudes of the two stars being compared (how bright they appear in the sky) and b_1 and b_2 are their brightness (how much light they actually emit). This relationship does not factor in how far from Earth the stars are.

   a) Sirius is the brightest-appearing star in our sky, with an apparent magnitude of -1.5. How much brighter does Sirius appear than Betelgeuse, whose apparent magnitude is 0.12?

   b) The Sun appears about 1.3×10^{10} times as brightly in our sky as does Sirius. What is the apparent magnitude of the Sun?

✓ Achievement Check

13. How bright a star appears can depend on how much light the star actually emits and how far away it is. The stellar magnitude scale can be adjusted to account for distance as follows:

$$M_2 - M_1 = \log\left(\frac{b_1}{b_2}\right)$$

Here, M refers to a star's absolute magnitude, that is, how brightly it appears from a standard distance of 10 parsecs (or 32.6 light-years). The absolute brightness of Sirius is 1.4 and the absolute brightness of Betelgeuse is -8.1.

   a) Which of these two stars is brighter, in absolute terms, and by how much?

   b) Compare this result with your answer to question 12a). What does this suggest about these two stars' distance from Earth?

14. Refer to questions 12 and 13. Which physical property of stars do you think astronomers would be more interested in, apparent magnitude or absolute magnitude, and why?

15. Chapter Problem Astronauts in space have just encountered three unknown stars and assigned them temporary names. Their absolute magnitudes are recorded.

Star	Absolute Magnitude
Cheryl-XI	0.4
Roccolus-III	−1.8
Biffidus-V	3.2

a) How much brighter, in absolute terms, is the brightest of these three stars than the
  i) second brightest?
  ii) least bright?

b) Assuming that these stars have the same apparent brightness, rank them in order of distance away from the astronaut looking at them.

C Extend and Challenge

16. Conduct some research, either on the Internet or in a library, about earthquakes. Where and when have the most severe earthquakes occurred? What were their intensity levels? Have there ever been any earthquakes where you live? Write a brief report on your findings.

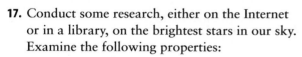

Reasoning and Proving
Representing — Selecting Tools
Problem Solving
Connecting — Reflecting
Communicating

17. Conduct some research, either on the Internet or in a library, on the brightest stars in our sky. Examine the following properties:

• apparent magnitudes
• absolute magnitudes
• distance from Earth

Are there any interesting trends or relationships? Write a brief report of your findings. Include in your report a short discussion of why stellar magnitudes include both positive and negative values and how they are related to each other.

18. There is a logarithmic relationship between how bright a luminous object is and how its brightness is perceived by the human eye. Conduct some research on this topic and summarize some of the mathematics behind it. Also discuss why this property may be advantageous to human existence.

19. Math Contest If $\log_{\sin x} (\cos x) = \frac{1}{2}$, and $0 < x < \frac{\pi}{2}$, what is the value of $\sin x$?

A $\dfrac{1}{\sqrt{3}}$

B $\dfrac{\sqrt{5} - 1}{2}$

C $\dfrac{2}{\sqrt{3}}$

D $\dfrac{\sqrt{5} + 1}{3}$

E $\dfrac{2\sqrt{3} - 1}{2}$

20. Math Contest A triangle is constructed so that its base is a diagonal of a certain square and its area is equal to that of the square. Express the length of the altitude of the triangle in terms of the square's side length, s.

21. Math Contest If $a + b = 3$ and $a^2 + b^2 = 7$, then what is the value of $a^4 + b^4$?

A 45 **B** 47 **C** 49 **D** 51 **E** 81

22. Math Contest If $\log_b (a^2) = 3$, which of the following is the value of $\log_a (b^2)$?

A $\dfrac{5}{3}$ **B** $\dfrac{3}{4}$ **C** $2\dfrac{2}{3}$ **D** $\dfrac{4}{3}$ **E** $\dfrac{3}{2}$

6.1 The Exponential Function and Its Inverse

1. a) Graph the function $f(x) = 3^x$. Identify the key features of the graph.

   i) domain and range

   ii) x-intercept, if it exists

   iii) y-intercept, if it exists

   iv) intervals for which the function is positive and intervals for which it is negative

   v) intervals for which the function is increasing and intervals for which it is decreasing

   vi) equation of the asymptote

   b) Graph the line $y = x$ on the same grid.

   c) Graph the inverse function f^{-1} by reflecting f in the line $y = x$. Identify the key features of f^{-1}.

2. Repeat question 1 for the function $g(x) = \left(\frac{1}{4}\right)^x$.

6.2 Logarithms

3. Rewrite each equation in logarithmic form.

   a) $4^3 = 64$ **b)** $28 = 3^x$

   c) $6^3 = y$ **d)** $512 = 2^9$

4. Rewrite each equation in exponential form.

   a) $7 = \log_2 128$

   b) $x = \log_b n$

   c) $5 = \log_3 243$

   d) $19 = \log_b 4$

5. Estimate the value of $\log_2 50$ without using a calculator. Justify your estimate with mathematical reasoning.

6. Evaluate.

   a) $\log_2 16$

   b) $\log_3 81$

   c) $\log_4 \left(\frac{1}{16}\right)$

   d) $\log 0.000\,001$

7. What is the value of $\log_x x$? For what values of x does your answer hold true? Justify your answer with mathematical reasoning.

6.3 Transformations of Logarithmic Functions

8. a) Graph the function $y = -\log(x - 5) + 2$.

   b) Identify the

   i) domain

   ii) range

   iii) equation of the asymptote

9. Repeat question 8 for the function $y = 3\log(-x)$.

10. Use Technology Check your graphs for questions 8 and 9 using graphing technology.

11. a) Create a logarithmic function that includes all of the following transformations of the function $y = \log x$:

   • a horizontal stretch

   • a translation to the left

   • a vertical translation

   • a reflection

   Write an equation for your function.

   b) Graph the function.

   c) Identify

   i) the domain

   ii) the range

   iii) an equation for the asymptote

6.4 Power Law of Logarithms

12. Evaluate.

   a) $\log_2 32^3$

   b) $\log 1000^{-2}$

   c) $\log 0.001^{-1}$

   d) $\log_{\frac{1}{4}} \left(\frac{1}{16}\right)^4$

13. Solve for x, correct to three decimal places.

   a) $x = \log_3 17$

   b) $\log_2 0.35 = x$

   c) $4^x = 10$

   d) $80 = 100\left(\frac{1}{2}\right)^x$

14. The intensity, I, of light, in lumens, passing through the glass of a pair of sunglasses is given by the equation $I(x) = I_0(0.8)^x$, where x is the thickness of the glass, in millimetres, and I_0 is the intensity of light entering the glasses. How thick should the glass be so that it will block 25% of the light entering the sunglasses?

15. a) Sketch a graph of the function $y = \log_3 x$ without using technology.

    b) Use graphing technology to check your sketch.

6.5 Making Connections: Logarithmic Scales in the Physical Sciences

16. Recall the pH scale, $pH = -\log [H^+]$. Chemical A has a pH of 6, while chemical B has a pH of 8. What does this suggest about their relative levels of hydronium ion concentration, $[H^+]$?

17. The magnitude, M, of an earthquake is measured using the Richter scale:

$$M = \log \left(\frac{I}{I_0} \right)$$

A "great" earthquake measures about 8 on the Richter scale, while a "light" earthquake measures about 4. Does this mean that a great earthquake is twice as intense as a light earthquake? If so, explain why, and if not, explain why not, using mathematical reasoning.

18. Welders use a logarithmic scale to identify protective eyewear. The shade number, n, is given by the equation

$$n = 1 - \frac{7 \log T}{3},$$

where T is the fraction of visible light that the glass transmits.

    a) What shade number should a welder use that will only transmit $\frac{1}{8}$ of the light entering the glass?

    b) Viewing a solar eclipse through #14 welding glasses is considered safe. What fraction of light do these glasses transmit?

    c) For doing furnace repairs, #2 welding glasses are sufficient. How many times as much visible light is transmitted by #2 welding glasses as by #14 welding glasses?

19. **Use Technology** Refer to question 18.

    a) Graph n versus T using graphing technology.

    b) Use the graph or algebraic reasoning to identify the domain and range of this function.

▪▪ PROBLEM WRAP-UP

CHAPTER 6

How are stars powered? Where does the energy come from? Do they ever burn out?

Stars are fuelled by various nuclear reactions, such as nuclear fission and nuclear fusion. The equation $N(t) = N_0 \left(\frac{1}{2} \right)^{\frac{t}{b}}$ is related to these processes.

Do some research on this equation and these topics. What is this equation called? What do the variables represent? Pose and solve two problems related to this equation. Write a brief report about anything interesting that you discover.

Chapter 6 PRACTICE TEST

For questions 1 to 4, choose the best answer.

1. The graph of $y = \left(\frac{1}{2}\right)^x$ is shown.

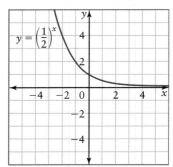

Which of the following is the graph of the inverse of this function?

A
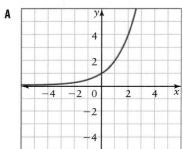

B
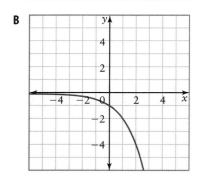

C
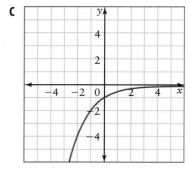

D
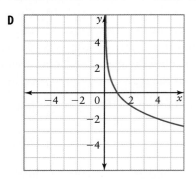

2. What is the value of $\log_5\left(\frac{1}{125}\right)$?

A -3 **B** -2 **C** 2 **D** 25

3. What is the value of $\log_4 16^{-3}$?

A $\frac{1}{8}$ **B** -6 **C** -12 **D** undefined

4. Which of the following graphs represents the function $y = \log(x + 3) - 5$?

A
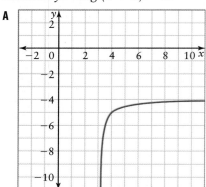

B
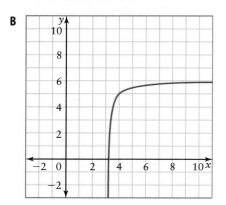

C

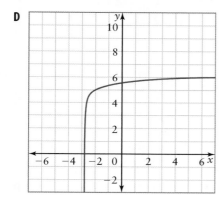

D

5. Evaluate, correct to three decimal places.

a) $\log_6 27$

b) $\log_{12} 6^3$

6. Consider the function $g(x) = \frac{1}{2}\log(-x - 3) + 6$.

a) Describe the transformations required to map $f(x) = \log x$ onto g.

b) Graph the function g.

c) Identify

i) the domain

ii) the range

iii) an equation for the asymptote

d) Sketch a graph of $g^{-1}(x)$. What type of function is the inverse?

7. Use Technology Refer to question 6. Use graphing technology to verify your answers.

8. $250 is put into an account that pays 6.5% interest, compounded annually. How long will it take for the amount in this account to double?

9. Use the pH formula, $\text{pH} = -\log[H^+]$, to answer the following.

a) Ammonia has a hydronium ion concentration of 3.2×10^{-12} mol/L. What is its pH level?

b) The pH of vinegar can range between 2 and 3.5. Determine the range of the hydronium ion concentration in vinegar.

c) Refer to the pH scale presented on page 349. Classify ammonia and vinegar as acidic, alkaline, or neutral. Explain your answers.

10. The atmospheric pressure, P, in kilopascals (kPa), as a function of altitude, d, in kilometres, above sea level can be modelled by the equation $P = 101.3(1.133)^{-d}$.

a) Graph this function for $0 < d < 10$.

b) Use the graph to estimate the atmospheric pressure at an altitude of 5 km.

c) Use the graph to estimate how high above sea level a mountain climber is who is feeling an atmospheric pressure of 85 kPa.

d) Provide algebraic solutions to parts b) and c) to check your answers.

11. Use the decibel scale, $\beta_2 - \beta_1 = 10\log\left(\frac{I_2}{I_1}\right)$, to answer the following.

a) The sound as a subway train passes is about 315 times as intense as normal city traffic, which has a decibel level of about 85. What is the decibel level of a passing subway train?

b) A worker using a power saw hears a decibel level of 118. How many times as intense as the sound of normal city traffic is the sound of a power saw?

12. Use Technology Design and carry out a method for demonstrating that the power law of logarithms holds using graphing technology and examples of your choice.

TASK

Not Fatal

Viral infections, while often quite severe and requiring admission to the hospital, are rarely fatal. Most people recover and go home.

In this task, you will simulate recovery from a viral infection for 100 people who contract the infection. Work in small groups.

Materials needed: 100 coins per group. Heads represents a person who has recovered, and tails represents a person who is still ill.

- Toss 100 coins.
- Remove all the coins that turn up heads. These are the people who have recovered after one week in the hospital, and get to go home.
- Record in a table of values the number of coins remaining (people still ill) versus the number of tosses.
- Repeat the process with the remaining coins until you have no coins left.

a) Use technology to construct a scatterplot of the data, with the number of tosses (days) as the independent variable and the number of people still ill as the dependent variable.

b) Determine an equation for the curve of best fit for your data. Explain how you determined the best model.

c) Predict how long it would take for 1600 people to get well and go home.

d) Justify your prediction algebraically.

e) Why does a logarithmic model work well for this situation?

f) For what other situations might this model be appropriate? Justify your answer.

Chapter 7

Tools and Strategies for Solving Exponential and Logarithmic Equations

Do you like music? What about rock music? Music has been around for thousands of years, but rock music is a relatively new form that has existed for only about half a century. The science and mathematics behind the inner workings of instruments, such as electric guitars, that rock musicians play involve exponential and logarithmic equations.

In this chapter, you will learn a variety of strategies for solving exponential and logarithmic equations. You will also apply modelling strategies to solve a variety of problems involving data that can be modelled by exponential and other types of curves.

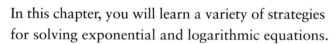

By the end of this chapter, you will

- make connections between the laws of exponents and the laws of logarithms, verify the product and quotient laws of logarithms with or without technology, and use the laws of logarithms to simplify and evaluate numerical expressions (A1.4)
- pose problems based on real-world applications of exponential and logarithmic functions and solve these and other such problems by using a given graph or a graph generated with technology from a table of values or from its equation (A2.4)
- recognize equivalent algebraic expressions involving logarithms and exponents, and simplify expressions of these types (A3.1)

- solve exponential equations in one variable by determining a common base and by using logarithms, recognizing that logarithms base 10 are commonly used (A3.2)
- solve simple logarithmic equations in one variable algebraically (A3.3)
- solve problems involving exponential and logarithmic equations algebraically, including problems arising from real-world applications (A3.4)
- solve problems arising from real-world applications by reasoning with functions (D3.3)

Prerequisite Skills

Apply the Exponent Laws

1. Simplify. Identify the exponent law that you used.

   a) $(x^2)(x^3)(x^4)$

   b) $(3a^2b^3)(2a^3b)$

   c) $(xy^3)(x^3y^2)$

   d) $(2r)(3rs^2)$

   e) $(5q)(qr)$

   f) $(vw)(w^3)(v^2)$

   g) $(2ab)(2b^3)$

2. Which exponent law would you use to simplify each expression? Simplify. Express answers using positive exponents.

   a) $\dfrac{k^6}{k^2}$

   b) $\dfrac{-24mn^3}{4mn^2}$

   c) $\dfrac{48x^4y^2}{8xy}$

   d) $\dfrac{2a^2b^3}{ab}$

   e) $\dfrac{(5q)(qr)}{(10r^2)}$

   f) $\dfrac{(vw)(w^3)(v^2)}{(vw^2)}$

   g) $\dfrac{(2ab)(2b^3)}{(4a)}$

3. Simplify, and identify the exponent law that you used.

   a) $(w^2)^4$

   b) $(-2uv^3)^2$

   c) $(a^2b)^3$

   d) $(x^3y^3)^2$

   e) $(2w^2)^3$

   f) $(ab^4)^2$

   g) $r(s^2)^3$

4. Simplify. Identify the exponent laws that you used. Express answers using positive exponents.

   a) $\dfrac{(ab^2)(4a^2b^{-2})}{2ab}$

   b) $(-3km^3)^3(2k^3m^2)^2$

   c) $\dfrac{(2x^3y)(-8xy^2)^2}{4x^5}$

   d) $\dfrac{(a^3)^2(ab^2)^3}{a^5b^5}$

Solve Quadratic Equations

5. Solve by factoring.

   a) $x^2 + 2x - 24 = 0$

   b) $2m^2 = 9m - 10$

   c) $4a^2 + 12a - 7 = 0$

   d) $q^2 - q = 20$

   e) $9b^2 = 1$

   f) $8y^2 + 6y + 1 = 0$

   g) $x^2 = x + 2$

   h) $2r^2 + 5r = 3$

   i) $q^2 + 5q + 4 = 0$

6. Solve by applying the quadratic formula.

   a) $y^2 + 6y - 5 = 0$

   b) $4q^2 = 2q + 10$

   c) $x^2 + x = 1$

   d) $2a^2 + 2a - 10 = 0$

   e) $x^2 = x + 7$

   f) $-r^2 + 5r = 3$

   g) $2m^2 + 6m + 3 = 0$

   h) $3a^2 = 3a + 4$

CONNECTIONS

The quadratic formula for the solutions of a quadratic equation in

the form $ax^2 + bx + c = 0$ is $x = \dfrac{-b \pm \sqrt{b^2 - 4ac}}{2a}$.

Simplify a Radical Expression

7. Simplify.

a) $\sqrt{8}$

b) $2\sqrt{20}$

c) $\sqrt{18}$

d) $3\sqrt{18}$

e) $\sqrt{75}$

f) $\dfrac{4 + \sqrt{48}}{2}$

g) $\dfrac{2 \pm \sqrt{24}}{2}$

Apply the Power Law of Logarithms

8. Evaluate, using the power law of logarithms.

a) $\log_4 16^3$

b) $\log_2 \sqrt[4]{32}$

c) $\log_3 27^2$

d) $\log_5 25^2$

e) $\log_2 32^2$

f) $\log_3 81$

g) $\log_4 16^2$

h) $\log_2 0.25$

9. Evaluate, correct to three decimal places.

a) $\log_3 10$

b) $\log_{\frac{1}{2}} \dfrac{1}{5}$

c) $\log_2 15$

d) $\log_4 17$

e) $\log_2 3$

f) $\log_3 8$

g) $\log_4 20$

h) $\log_2 19$

10. Solve for t, correct to two decimal places.

a) $5^t = 4$

b) $1.2^{2t} = 1.6$

c) $7^t = 2$

d) $\left(\dfrac{1}{4}\right)^{3t} = 2$

e) $3^t = 2$

f) $8^t = 3$

g) $2^t = 9$

h) $2^{3t} = 15$

11. Use algebraic reasoning to show that, if $y = b^x$, then $x = \dfrac{\log y}{\log b}$.

PROBLEM

Have you ever wondered how electric guitars work? When a note is struck, a coiled device called a pick-up transforms the sound into an electronic signal. This signal is then boosted by an amplifier, which creates the exciting sounds that music fans love!

In this chapter, you will apply techniques for solving equations related to the music of electric guitars.

CHAPTER

Equivalent Forms of Exponential Equations

How many names do people have? How many do you have? People can be identified in more ways than you may immediately realize. For example, consider how the names and terms on this visual could be used to describe the same person.

In this way, numbers are like people. They can be represented in a variety of ways, depending on the situation.

Think about powers. Can any number be written as a power of any other number? If so, how and why might this be useful?

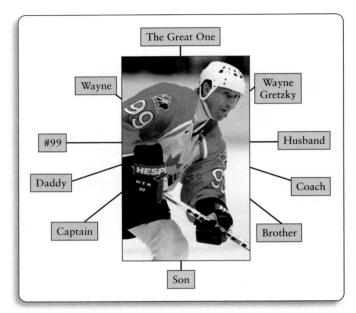

Investigate | How can exponential growth be modelled in different ways?

Tools

- linking cubes
- graphing calculator or computer with *The Geometer's Sketchpad®*

1. a) Use linking cubes to model the growth of bacteria in a petri dish.

b) Explain how these models illustrate the sequence 4^n, $n = 0, 1, 2, \ldots$.

c) Build a model to represent the next term in this pattern, 4^3.

2. a) Build or examine the following models.

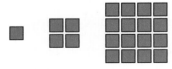

b) Explain how these models illustrate the sequence 2^{2n}, $n = 0, 1, 2, \ldots$.

c) Build a model to represent the next term in this pattern, $2^{2(3)}$.

3. a) Compare the number of cubes in each stage of both patterns. Are they the same?

b) How can you represent the next term in each pattern? Will this require the same number of cubes in each case?

4. Reflect

    a) What do these observations suggest about the functions $f(x) = 4^x$ and $g(x) = 2^{2x}$?

    b) Predict the results when f and g are graphed on the same set of axes. Use graphing technology to verify this relationship for $x \in \mathbb{R}$.

    c) Apply algebraic reasoning to prove this relationship.

Exponential functions can be represented in many different ways. It is often useful to express an exponential expression using a different base than the one that is given.

Example 1	**Change the Base of Powers**

Express in terms of a power with a base of 2.

a) 8   **b)** 4^3 **c)** $\sqrt{16} \times (\sqrt[5]{32})^3$ **d)** 12

Solution

a) $8 = 2^3$ 8 is the third power of 2.

b) $4^3 = (2^2)^3$ Write 4 as 2^2.

      $= 2^6$ Apply the power of a power law.

c)
$$\sqrt{16} \times (\sqrt[5]{32})^3 = 16^{\frac{1}{2}} \times 32^{\frac{3}{5}} \qquad \text{Write radicals in exponential form.}$$
$$= (2^4)^{\frac{1}{2}} \times (2^5)^{\frac{3}{5}} \qquad \text{Express the bases as powers of 2.}$$
$$= 2^{\frac{4}{2}} \times 2^{\frac{15}{5}} \qquad \text{Apply the power of a power law and simplify.}$$
$$= 2^2 \times 2^3$$
$$= 2^5$$

d) 12

     This cannot be solved by inspection as in part a). To express 12 as a power of 2, solve the equation $2^k = 12$ for k.

$$2^k = 12$$
$$\log 2^k = \log 12 \qquad \text{Take the common logarithm of both sides.}$$
$$k \log 2 = \log 12 \qquad \text{Apply the power law of logarithms.}$$
$$k = \frac{\log 12}{\log 2} \qquad \text{Divide both sides by log 2.}$$

     Therefore, 12 can be written as power of 2:

$$12 = 2^{\frac{\log 12}{\log 2}}$$

     This result can be verified by using a calculator.

```
2^(log(12)/log(2
)
                12
```

The result of Example 1d) suggests that any positive number can be expressed as a power of any other positive number.

| Example 2 | Solve an Equation by Changing the Base |

Solve each equation.

a) $4^{x+5} = 64^x$

b) $4^{2x} = 8^{x-3}$

Solution

a) $4^{x+5} = 64^x$

Method 1: *Apply a Change of Base*

$$4^{x+5} = 64^x$$

$$4^{x+5} = (4^3)^x \qquad \text{Express the base on the right side as a power with base 4.}$$

$$4^{x+5} = 4^{3x} \qquad \text{Apply the power of a power law.}$$

$$x + 5 = 3x \qquad \text{Equate exponents.}$$

$$5 = 2x$$

$$x = \frac{5}{2} \qquad \text{Solve for } x.$$

Method 2: *Use a Graphing Calculator*

Enter the left side of the equation as one function and the right side as another function and identify where the graphs intersect.

It may be necessary to experiment with the window settings in order to view the point of intersection.

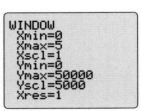 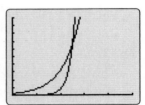

Use the **Intersect** operation to determine the coordinates of the point of intersection.

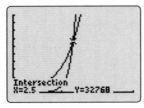

The solution is $x = 2.5$.

CONNECTIONS

$$x^a = x^b$$
$$\log x^a = \log x^b$$
$$a \log x = b \log x$$
$$a = b$$

Two exponents are equal if their exponential expressions have the same base and are equal.

b)

$$4^{2x} = 8^{x-3}$$

$$(2^2)^{2x} = (2^3)^{x-3} \qquad \text{Express bases as powers of 2.}$$

$$2^{4x} = 2^{3x-9} \qquad \text{Apply the power of a power law.}$$

$$4x = 3x - 9 \qquad \text{Equate exponents.}$$

$$x = -9 \qquad \text{Solve for } x.$$

⟪ KEY CONCEPTS ⟫

- Exponential functions and expressions can be expressed in different ways by changing the base.

- Changing the base of one or more exponential expressions is a useful technique for solving exponential equations.

- Graphing technology can be used to solve exponential equations.

Communicate Your Understanding

C1 **a)** Explain how you can write 16^2 with base 4.

b) Explain how you can write 16^2 with two other, different, bases.

C2 Examine these graphing calculator screens.

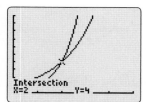

a) What exponential equation is being solved?

b) What is the solution? Explain how you know.

C3 Can any number be written as a power of any other number? If yes, explain how, with a supporting example. If not, explain why not, with a counterexample.

For help with questions 1 to 4, refer to Example 1.

1. Write each expression with base 2.

   a) 4^6 b) 8^3 c) $\left(\dfrac{1}{8}\right)^2$ d) 14

2. Write each expression with base 3.

   a) 27^2 b) $\left(\dfrac{1}{3}\right)^4$ c) 10   d) $\dfrac{1}{2}$

3. a) Write 2^8 as a power of a number other than 2.

   b) Write 2^8 as a power with a base that is different than the one you chose in part a).

   c) Use a calculator to check that these powers are equivalent.

4. Write each expression as a single power of 4.

   a) $(\sqrt{16})^3$ b) $\sqrt[3]{16}$
   c) $\sqrt{64} \times (\sqrt[4]{128})^3$ d) $(\sqrt{2})^8 \times (\sqrt[3]{2})^4$

For help with questions 5 and 6, refer to Example 2.

5. Solve. Check your answers using graphing technology.

   a) $2^{4x} = 4^{x + 3}$

   b) $25^{x - 1} = 5^{3x}$

   c) $3^{w + 1} = 9^{w - 1}$

   d) $36^{3m - 1} = 6^{2m + 5}$

6. Solve. Check your answers using graphing technology.

   a) $4^{3x} = 8^{x - 3}$

   b) $27^x = 9^{2x - 3}$

   c) $125^{2y - 1} = 25^{y + 4}$

   d) $16^{2k - 3} = 32^{k + 3}$

7. Consider the equation $10^{2x} = 100^{2x - 5}$.

   a) Solve this equation by expressing both sides as powers of a common base.

   b) Solve the same equation by taking the common logarithm of both sides, as shown in Chapter 6.

   c) Reflect on these techniques. Which do you prefer, and why?

8. a) Build or draw a concrete model that represents the first few terms of the sequence described by $f(n) = (2^3)^n$, $n = 0, 1, 2, \ldots$.

   b) Repeat part a) for the sequence described by $g(n) = 8^n$, $n = 0, 1, 2, \ldots$.

   c) Explain how your model illustrates that $f(n) = g(n)$.

   d) Use graphical or algebraic reasoning to prove that $f(n) = g(n)$, $n \in \mathbb{R}$.

9. a) Identify two equivalent exponential expressions that have different bases.

   b) Build or draw a concrete model that illustrates their equality.

   c) Use graphical or algebraic reasoning to prove their equality.

10. Solve. Check your answers using graphing technology.

    a) $(\sqrt{8})^x = 2^{x - 2}$

    b) $9^{k - 1} = (\sqrt{27})^{2k}$

11. Consider the equation $10 = 2^x$.

    a) Solve the equation for x by taking the common logarithm of both sides.

    b) Use this result to show that $10 = 2^{\frac{1}{\log 2}}$.

    c) Apply algebraic reasoning to show that $10 = 3^{\frac{1}{\log 3}}$.

12. Develop a formula that shows how 10 can be written as a power of any base $b > 0$.

13. Apply algebraic reasoning to show that $a = b^{\frac{\log a}{\log b}}$ for any $a, b > 0$.

14. Consider the equation $81^{2x} = 9^{x+3}$.

a) Solve this equation by expressing both sides as a power with base 3.

b) Solve the same equation by expressing both sides as a power with base 9.

c) **Use Technology** Solve the same equation using graphing technology.

d) Reflect on these methods. Which do you prefer, and why?

e) Create an exponential equation that can be solved by choosing more than one common base. Solve the equation using multiple strategies.

C **Extend and Challenge**

15. a) Solve each inequality.

i) $2^{3x} > 4^{x+1}$

ii) $81^{x-2} < 27^{2x+1}$

b) **Use Technology** Use a sketch to help you explain how you can use graphing technology to check your answers. Use your method and check the answers.

c) Create an inequality involving an exponential expression. Solve the inequality using graphing technology.

16. **Use Technology** The word *exponential* is often used to indicate very fast growth. But do exponential functions always grow faster than power functions?

a) Look at the following pairs of functions in different viewing windows and make a note of what you see.

i) $y = 2^x$ and $y = x^3$

ii) $y = 1.1^x$ and $y = x^{10}$

b) Use a graphing calculator to graph $p(x) = x^4$ and $q(x) = 3^x$. For what values of x is the exponential function growing faster than the quartic function?

CAREER CONNECTION

Rose is an electrical engineer. She works for a company that specializes in industrial and environmental noise control, vibration, and architectural acoustics. In her last project, she was involved in the design of a large performance theatre. Rose learned about ray tracing, sound transmission, and reverberation analysis. The new theatre was designed to have excellent acoustics and musical clarity. Rose trained for her career by taking a 4-year bachelor of engineering degree at Ryerson University.

Techniques for Solving Exponential Equations

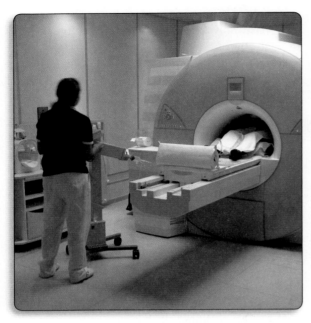

Radioactive decay is the process by which an unstable element transforms into a different element, typically releasing energy as it does so. The **half-life** of a radioactive substance is the time required for a sample of the material to decay to half its initial amount.

The amount, A, in milligrams, of a radioactive material remaining as a function of time, t, in years, can be modelled by the equation $A(t) = A_0\left(\dfrac{1}{2}\right)^{\frac{t}{h}}$, where A_0 is the initial amount, in milligrams, and h is the half-life, in years.

In practice, A, A_0, and t can be measured for an element. Once these values are known, they can be used to determine the half-life.

Example 1 | Radioactive Decay

CONNECTIONS

British physicist Ernest Rutherford (1871–1937) and others discovered that radioactivity was very complicated. Different types of decay can occur, but Rutherford was the first to realize that they all occur with the same approximately exponential formula, the half-life equation.

Polonium-218 is a radioactive substance that spontaneously decays into lead-214. One minute after a 100-mg sample of polonium-218 is placed into a nuclear chamber, only 80 mg remains.

a) Determine the half-life of polonium-218.

b) Graph the decay function for polonium-218.

Solution

a) Substitute $A_0 = 100$, $t = 1$, and $A(1) = 80$ into the decay equation and solve for h.

$$A(t) = A_0\left(\frac{1}{2}\right)^{\frac{t}{h}}$$

$$80 = 100\left(\frac{1}{2}\right)^{\frac{1}{h}}$$

$$0.8 = 0.5^{\frac{1}{h}} \qquad \text{Divide both sides by 100, and write } \frac{1}{2} \text{ as 0.5.}$$

$$\log 0.8 = \log 0.5^{\frac{1}{h}} \qquad \text{Take the common logarithm of both sides.}$$

$$\log 0.8 = \frac{1}{h} \log 0.5 \qquad \text{Apply the power law of logarithms.}$$

$$h \log 0.8 = \log 0.5 \qquad \text{Multiply both sides by } h.$$

$$h = \frac{\log 0.5}{\log 0.8}$$ Solve for h.

$$h \doteq 3.1$$

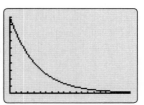
```
log(.5)/log(.8)
          3.10628372
```

The half-life of polonium-218 is approximately 3.1 min.

b) Substitute the initial amount and the half-life into the decay equation to graph the function.

$$A(t) = A_0 \left(\frac{1}{2}\right)^{\frac{t}{h}}$$

$$A(t) = 100\left(\frac{1}{2}\right)^{\frac{t}{3.1}}$$ $A_0 = 100$ and $h = 3.1$.

Use graphing technology. Choose appropriate window settings to view the graph.

```
Plot1 Plot2 Plot3
\Y1 ▫100(1/2)^(X/
3.1)
\Y2=
\Y3=
\Y4=
\Y5=
\Y6=
```

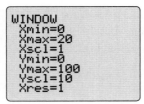
```
WINDOW
 Xmin=0
 Xmax=20
 Xscl=1
 Ymin=0
 Ymax=100
 Yscl=10
 Xres=1
```

Example 2 | Powers With Different Bases

Solve the equation $4^{2x - 1} = 3^{x + 2}$.

Solution

Method 1: *Apply Algebraic Reasoning*

Take the logarithm of both sides and apply the power law of logarithms to remove the variables from the exponents.

$$4^{2x - 1} = 3^{x + 2}$$

$$\log 4^{2x - 1} = \log 3^{x + 2}$$

$$(2x - 1)\log 4 = (x + 2)\log 3$$ Apply the power law of logarithms.

$$2x \log 4 - \log 4 = x \log 3 + 2 \log 3$$ Apply the distributive property.

$$2x \log 4 - x \log 3 = 2 \log 3 + \log 4$$ Collect variable terms on one side of the equation.

$$x(2 \log 4 - \log 3) = 2 \log 3 + \log 4$$ Factor x on the left side.

$$x = \frac{2 \log 3 + \log 4}{2 \log 4 - \log 3}$$ Solve for x.

This is an exact expression for the root of the equation. Use a calculator to determine an approximate value for this expression.

```
(2log(3)+log(4))
/(2log(4)-log(3)
)
         2.140722454
```

The solution to this equation is $x \doteq 2.14$.

Method 2: *Use a Graphing Calculator*

Enter the left side of the equation as one function and the right side as another function. Identify where the graphs of these functions intersect. Experiment with the window settings in order to view the point of intersection.

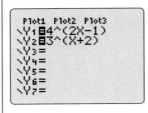 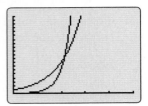 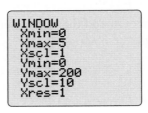

Use the **Intersect** operation to determine the coordinates of the point of intersection.

The graph shows that the expressions 4^{2x-1} and 3^{x+2} are equal when $x \doteq 2.14$, which confirms the result derived algebraically above.

Example 3 | Apply the Quadratic Formula

Solve the equation $2^x - 2^{-x} = 4$ algebraically, and then check the solution using a graphing calculator.

Reasoning and Proving

Representing · Selecting Tools

Problem Solving

Connecting · Reflecting

Communicating

> **Solution**

There is no immediately obvious method of solving this equation. Notice that if you multiply both sides of the equation by 2^x, then a quadratic equation is obtained in terms of 2^x.

$$2^x - 2^{-x} = 4$$
$$2^x(2^x - 2^{-x}) = 2^x(4)$$
$$2^x(2^x) - 2^x(2^{-x}) = 2^x(4) \qquad \text{Apply the distributive property.}$$
$$2^{2x} - 2^0 = 2^x(4) \qquad \text{Apply the product rule for exponents.}$$
$$2^{2x} - 1 = 2^x(4) \qquad \text{Recall that } a^0 = 1.$$

This is a quadratic equation in which the variable is 2^x. To see this more clearly, apply the power of a power law to the term 2^{2x}.

$$(2^x)^2 - 1 = 2^x(4)$$

$$(2^x)^2 - 4(2^x) - 1 = 0 \qquad \text{Write in standard form: } az^2 + bz + c = 0, \text{ where } z = 2^x.$$

The coefficients of the quadratic expression on the left side are $a = 1$, $b = -4$, and $c = -1$. This expression is not factorable. Apply the quadratic formula to determine the roots.

Method 1: *Solve for 2^x Directly*

$$2^x = \frac{-b \pm \sqrt{b^2 - 4ac}}{2a}$$

$$= \frac{-(-4) + \sqrt{(-4)^2 - 4(1)(-1)}}{2(1)}$$

$$= \frac{4 \pm \sqrt{20}}{2}$$

$$= \frac{4 \pm 2\sqrt{5}}{2} \qquad \text{Simplify the radical.}$$

$$= 2 \pm \sqrt{5} \qquad \text{Simplify the rational expression.}$$

Method 2: *Let k = 2^x and Solve for k*

$$k^2 - 4k - 1 = 0$$

$$k = \frac{-b \pm \sqrt{b^2 - 4ac}}{2a}$$

$$k = \frac{-(-4) \pm \sqrt{(-4)^2 - 4(1)(-1)}}{2(1)}$$

$$k = 2 \pm \sqrt{5}$$

Now substitute $2^x = k$.

$$2^x = 2 \pm \sqrt{5}$$

This equation appears to give two solutions. Explore each case.

Case 1

$$2^x = 2 + \sqrt{5}$$

$$\log 2^x = \log(2 + \sqrt{5}) \qquad \text{Take the common logarithm of both sides.}$$

$$x \log 2 = \log(2 + \sqrt{5}) \qquad \text{Apply the power law of logarithms.}$$

$$x = \frac{\log(2 + \sqrt{5})}{\log 2} \qquad \text{Divide both sides by log 2.}$$

Use a calculator to evaluate this expression.

One root of this equation is approximately 2.08.

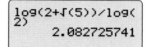

Case 2

$$2^x = 2 - \sqrt{5}$$

Note that $2 - \sqrt{5} < 0$. A power is always a positive number, so it cannot be equal to a negative number. Thus, this root is extraneous.

Use a graphing calculator to verify these results. Use reasonable window settings to view the point of intersection.

 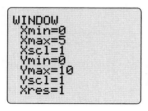 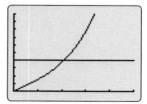

Use the **Intersect** operation to determine the coordinates of the point of intersection.

This confirms the algebraic result.
There is a single solution to the equation $2^x - 2^{-x} = 4$ and its value is $x \doteq 2.08$.

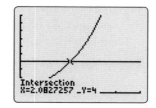

Example 3 illustrates an important point: when both sides of an equation are multiplied by the same non-constant factor, the possibility of obtaining extraneous roots is introduced. When this technique is used to solve an equation, the roots obtained must be checked to ensure that they are valid solutions to the original equation. Any extraneous roots should be rejected as invalid.

≪ KEY CONCEPTS ≫

- An equation maintains balance when the common logarithm is applied to both sides.
- The power law of logarithms is a useful tool for solving for a variable that appears as part of an exponent.
- When a quadratic equation is obtained, methods such as factoring and applying the quadratic formula may be useful.
- Some algebraic methods of solving exponential equations lead to extraneous roots, which are not valid solutions to the original equation.

Communicate Your Understanding

C1 Refer to the radioactive decay equation $A(t) = A_0 \left(\dfrac{1}{2}\right)^{\frac{t}{h}}$.

    a) Why is there a factor that contains the fraction $\dfrac{1}{2}$?

    b) Explain the significance of the fraction $\dfrac{1}{2}$ in the context of this question.

C2 The solution to the equation $5^{3x} = 4^{x+1}$ is given below, but in jumbled order.

$$x(3\log 5 - \log 4) = \log 4$$
$$5^{3x} = 4^{x+1}$$
$$3x\log 5 - x\log 4 = \log 4$$
$$\log 5^{3x} = \log 4^{x+1}$$
$$3x\log 5 = (x+1)\log 4$$
$$3x\log 5 = x\log 4 + \log 4$$
$$x = \frac{\log 4}{3\log 5 - \log 4}$$

    a) Copy the solution into your notebook, with the steps rearranged in the correct order.

    b) Write a brief explanation beside each step.

C3 Refer to Example 3. Could this equation be solved by taking the common logarithm of both sides? If so, provide a solution. If not, explain the problem with this method.

C4 **a)** What is an extraneous root?

    b) How can extraneous roots be identified?

    c) Give an example of an extraneous root for an exponential equation.

For help with questions 1 to 3, refer to Example 1.

1. Match each graph with its equation.

a)

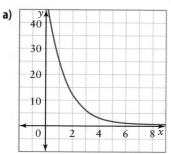

b)

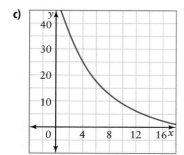

c)

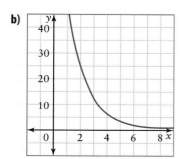

d)

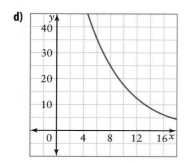

i) $y = 100\left(\frac{1}{2}\right)^x$ **ii)** $y = 50\left(\frac{1}{2}\right)^{\frac{x}{4}}$

iii) $y = 50\left(\frac{1}{2}\right)^x$ **iv)** $y = 100\left(\frac{1}{2}\right)^{\frac{x}{4}}$

2. Solve for t. Round answers to two decimal places.

a) $2 = 1.07^t$ **b)** $3 = 1.1^t$

c) $100 = 10(1.04)^t$ **d)** $5 = 1.08^{t+2}$

e) $0.5 = 1.2^{t-1}$ **f)** $10 = \left(\frac{1}{4}\right)^{3t}$

g) $15 = \left(\frac{1}{2}\right)^{\frac{t}{4}}$ **h)** $100 = 25\left(\frac{1}{2}\right)^{\frac{6}{t}}$

3. Use the decay equation for polonium-218, $A(t) = A_0\left(\frac{1}{2}\right)^{\frac{t}{3.1}}$, where A is the amount remaining after t minutes and A_0 is the initial amount.

a) How much will remain after 90 s from an initial sample of 50 mg?

b) How long will it take for this sample to decay to 10% of its initial amount of 50 mg?

c) Would your answer to part b) change if the size of the initial sample were changed? Explain why or why not.

For help with questions 4 and 5, refer to Example 2.

4. Solve each equation. Leave answers in exact form.

a) $2^x = 3^{x-1}$

b) $5^{x-2} = 4^x$

c) $8^{x+1} = 3^{x-1}$

d) $7^{2x+1} = 4^{x-2}$

5. Use Technology Find approximate values for your answers to question 4, correct to three decimal places.

For help with questions 6 and 7, refer to Example 3.

6. Consider the equation $2^{2x} + 2^x - 6 = 0$.

a) Write the equation in the form $az^2 + bz + c = 0$, where $z = 2^x$, and then identify the coefficients a, b, and c.

b) Solve the equation using the quadratic formula.

c) Identify any extraneous roots.

7. Consider the equation $8^{2x} - 2(8^x) - 5 = 0$.

a) Write the equation as a quadratic equation of 8^x, as in question 6, and then identify the coefficients a, b, and c.

b) Solve the equation using the quadratic formula.

c) Identify any extraneous roots.

8. A 20-mg sample of thorium-233 decays to 17 mg after 5 min.

a) Determine the half-life of thorium-233.

b) How long will it take for this sample to decay to 1 mg?

9. A 10-mg sample of bismuth-214 decays to 9 mg in 3 min.

Reasoning and Proving
Representing — Selecting Tools
Problem Solving
Connecting — Reflecting
Communicating

a) Determine the half-life of bismuth-214.

b) Graph the amount of bismuth-214 remaining as a function of time.

c) Describe how the graph would change if the half-life were

  i) shorter   **ii)** longer

Give reasons for your answers.

d) Describe how the graph would change if the initial sample size were

  i) greater   **ii)** less

Give reasons for your answers.

CONNECTIONS

The element bismuth is used in making chemical alloys, medicines, and transistors.

10. Does the equation $4^{2x} + 2(4^x) + 3 = 0$ have any real solutions? Explain your answer.

11. Solve and check for extraneous roots. Where necessary, round answers to 2 decimal places.

a) $3^{2x} = 7(3^x) - 12$

b) $5^x = 3 - 5^{2x}$

c) $8(3)^{2x + 3} = 24$

d) $18 = 2(9)^{2x - 1}$

e) $3^x + 1 + 56(3^{-x}) = 0$

f) $4^x = 3 + 18(4^{-x})$

12. Use Technology Check your solutions to question 11 using graphing technology.

13. Alchemy is the ancient study of turning substances into gold using chemical, or sometimes magical, means. When platinum-197 undergoes a nuclear process known as beta decay, it becomes gold-197, which is a stable isotope. The half-life of platinum-197 is 20 h.

a) How long would it take to turn 90% of a 1-kg sample of platinum-197 into gold?

b) Do you think this is a viable "get-rich-quick" scheme? Why or why not?

14. The probability, P, in percent, that a person will respond to a certain advertisement can be modelled by the equation $P(n) = 1 - 2^{-0.05n}$, where n is the number of days since the advertisement began on television. After how many days is the probability greater than 20%?

15. Lana has purchased a minivan for $24 000. The value, V, in dollars, of the minivan as a function of time, t, in years, depreciates according to the function $V(t) = 24\,000 \left(\dfrac{1}{2}\right)^{\frac{t}{3}}$. How long will it take for Lana's minivan to depreciate to

a) one quarter of its initial value?

b) 10% of its initial value?

16. Chapter Problem One important characteristic of an electric guitar is its *sustain*, which is related to the length of time a plucked string continues to sound before the sound dies out. One particular guitar can hold a certain note according to the relation $I(t) = I_0 \left(\dfrac{1}{2}\right)^{\frac{t}{12}}$, where I is the intensity of the note as a function of time, t, in seconds, and I_0 is the initial intensity of the note when it is struck.

a) How long will it take for the intensity of this note to decay to

  i) half of its initial value?

  ii) 10% of its initial value?

b) Sketch a graph of the sustain function.

c) Suppose that the design of the guitar is improved so that its sustain is increased. What effect will this have on the

  i) equation?   **ii)** graph?

✓ Achievement Check

17. One day, a controversial video is posted on the Internet that seemingly gives concrete evidence of life on other planets. Suppose that 50 people see the video the first day after it is posted and that this number doubles every day after that.

a) Write an expression to describe the number of people who have seen the video t days after it is posted.

b) One week later, a second video is posted that reveals the first as a hoax. Suppose that 20 people see this video the first day after it is posted and that this number triples every day after that. Write an expression to describe the number of people who have seen the second video t days after it is posted.

c) Set the two expressions from parts a) and b) equal and solve for t using tools and strategies of your choice. What does this solution mean?

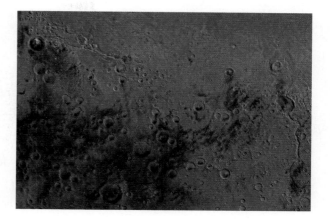

d) If you solved the equation in part c) algebraically, check your answer using graphing technology. If you solved it graphically, check your answer using algebraic reasoning.

C) Extend and Challenge

18. When platinum-197 undergoes beta decay, it becomes gold-197. The half-life of platinum-197 is 20 h.

a) Develop an equation for the amount of gold-197 produced as a function of time for the given scenario.

b) Find the domain and the range of this function.

19. a) Perform some research on the carbon fusion cycle. Describe the steps of the cycle and how energy is produced.

b) Pose and solve two problems related to the carbon fusion cycle that involve exponential equations.

20. Math Contest If $4^x - 4^{x-1} = 24$, what is the value of $(2x)^x$?

 A $5\sqrt{5}$ **B** 25 **C** 125 **D** $25\sqrt{5}$

21. Math Contest If $2^a = 5$ and $2^b = 3$, what is the value of $\log_3 10$?

 A $\dfrac{b+1}{a}$

 B $\dfrac{b+1}{a+1}$

 C $\dfrac{a+1}{b}$

 D $\dfrac{a}{b}$

 E $\dfrac{b}{a}$

22. Math Contest Given a function $h(x)$ that satisfies the equation $h(2x + 1) = 2h(x) + 1$ for all x, and $h(0) = 2$, what is the value of $h(3)$?

7.3

Product and Quotient Laws of Logarithms

Recall the exponent laws that you have already learned. How do you think these laws relate to logarithms, given that a logarithm is the inverse of an exponent?

The power law of logarithms introduced in Chapter 6 states that

$\log_b x^n = n \log_b x, b > 0, b \neq 1, x > 0$

What do the laws of logarithms have to do with music?

Investigate | **What is an equivalent expression for the logarithm of a product or of a quotient?**

Tools

- computer with *The Geometer's Sketchpad®*

or

- graphing calculator

or

- computer algebra system (CAS)

A: *Common Logarithm of a Product: Make Geometric and Algebraic Connections*

1. Evaluate the following.

   a) log 1   **b)** log 10   **c)** log 100   **d)** log 1000   **e)** log 10 000

2. **a)** Graph the following family of functions on the same grid.

   $f(x) = \log x$

   $g(x) = \log (10x)$

   $h(x) = \log (100x)$

   $i(x) = \log (1000x)$

   $j(x) = \log (10\ 000x)$

   b) Describe how these graphs are related to each other using vertical translations. To help recognize the translation, consider what happens to the points (1, 0) and (10, 1) in each case.

3. **a)** Copy and complete the table. Write each function in three different ways, as shown in the first row. The entry in the third column is found by converting the translation coefficient into a common logarithm.

Function	Vertical Translation of $f(x)$	Sum of Common Logarithms
$g(x) = \log (10x)$	$g(x) = \log x + 1$	$g(x) = \log x + \log 10$
$h(x) = \log (100x)$		
$i(x) = \log (1000x)$		
$j(x) = \log (10\ 000x)$		

   b) **Reflect** Describe any pattern you observe between the first and last columns.

B: *Extend the Pattern to Logarithms of Any Base*

Does the pattern observed in part A apply to logarithms of any base?

1. Copy and complete the table.

a	b	$\log_2 a$	$\log_2 b$	$\log_2 a + \log_2 b$	$\log_2 (a \times b)$
1	2	$\log_2 1 = 0$	$\log_2 2 = 1$	$0 + 1 = 1$	$\log_2 (1 \times 2)$ $= \log_2 2$ $= 1$
2	4				
4	4				
8	16				
Create at least two of your own examples.					

Technology Tip ∴

Spreadsheets, computer algebra systems, and graphing calculators are all useful tools for performing repeated calculations.

2. Look at the pattern of results in the table. What does this suggest about the base-2 logarithm of a product?

3. Make a conjecture about how a logarithm of a product with any base can be written in terms of a sum.

4. Repeat steps 1 and 2 for logarithms of various bases. Compare your results to your prediction in step 3, and determine whether your prediction is correct.

5. **Reflect**

   a) Is there a product law for logarithms? Write it down, using

   i) algebraic symbols

   ii) words

   b) Are there any restrictions or special considerations? If so, state them using

   i) algebraic symbols

   ii) words

C: *Explore the Common Logarithm of a Quotient*

1. Is there a quotient law for logarithms? Design and carry out an investigation that addresses this question using tools and strategies of your choice. Carry out the investigation.

2. **Reflect** Compare your results with those of your classmates. Write a brief report of your findings that includes

   • a quotient law for logarithms, written using words and symbols

   • three examples that illustrate the law

   • the values of the base for which the law holds true

The product law of logarithms can be developed algebraically as follows.

Let $x = \log_b m$ and $y = \log_b n$.

Write these equations in exponential form:

$b^x = m$ and $b^y = n$

$$mn = b^x b^y$$

$$mn = b^{x+y} \qquad \text{Use the product law of exponents.}$$

$$\log_b mn = x + y \qquad \text{Write in logarithmic form.}$$

$$\log_b mn = \log_b m + \log_b n \qquad \text{Substitute for } x \text{ and } y.$$

You will prove the quotient law in question 20.

Product Law of Logarithms

$\log_b (mn) = \log_b m + \log_b n$ for $b > 0$, $b \neq 1$, $m > 0$, $n > 0$.

Quotient Law of Logarithms

$\log_b \left(\dfrac{m}{n}\right) = \log_b m - \log_b n$ for $b > 0$, $b \neq 1$, $m > 0$, $n > 0$.

The product and quotient laws of logarithms, as well as the power law, are useful tools for simplifying algebraic expressions and solving equations.

Example 1 | **Simplify by Applying Laws of Logarithms**

Write as a single logarithm.

a) $\log_5 6 + \log_5 8 - \log_5 16$

b) $\log x + \log y + \log (3x) - \log y$

> **Solution**

a) $\log_5 6 + \log_5 8 - \log_5 16 = \log_5 \left(\dfrac{6 \times 8}{16}\right)$ 　　Apply the product and quotient laws of logarithms.

$$= \log_5 3$$

b) $\log x + \log y + \log (3x) - \log y$

Method 1: *Apply Laws of Logarithms Directly*

$\log x + \log y + \log (3x) - \log y = \log \left(\dfrac{xy(3x)}{y}\right)$ 　　Apply the product and quotient laws of logarithms.

$$= \log (3x^2), \ x > 0, \ y > 0$$

The power law of logarithms cannot be applied here, because the exponent 2 applies only to x, not to $3x$. Therefore, this is the simplest form of the expression.

Note the restrictions that must be placed on the variables, based on the nature of the original expression $\log x + \log y + \log(3x) - \log y$. The simplified expression is only defined for values of x and y for which each logarithmic term in the original expression is defined.

Method 2: *Simplify First, and Then Apply the Product Law*

$$\log x + \log y + \log(3x) - \log y = \log x + \log(3x) \quad \text{Collect like terms and simplify.}$$
$$= \log[(x)(3x)] \quad \text{Apply the product law of logarithms.}$$
$$= \log(3x^2), \; x > 0, \; y > 0$$

Example 2   Evaluate Using the Laws of Logarithms

Evaluate.

a) $\log_8 4 + \log_8 16$

b) $\log_3 405 - \log_3 5$

c) $2 \log 5 + \dfrac{1}{2} \log 16$

Solution

a) $\log_8 4 + \log_8 16 = \log_8 (4 \times 16) \quad$ Apply the product law of logarithms.
$$= \log_8 64$$
$$= 2 \qquad\qquad\qquad 8^2 = 64$$

b) $\log_3 405 - \log_3 5 = \log_3 \left(\dfrac{405}{5}\right) \qquad$ Apply the quotient law of logarithms.
$$= \log_3 81$$
$$= 4$$

c) $2 \log 5 + \dfrac{1}{2} \log 16 = \log 5^2 + \log 16^{\frac{1}{2}} \qquad$ Apply the power law of logarithms.
$$= \log 25 + \log \sqrt{16}$$
$$= \log 25 + \log 4$$
$$= \log(25 \times 4) \qquad \text{Apply the product law of logarithms.}$$
$$= \log 100$$
$$= 2$$

Example 3	Write the Logarithm of a Product or Quotient as a Sum or Difference of Logarithms

Write as a sum or difference of logarithms. Simplify, if possible.

a) $\log_3 (xy)$ **b)** $\log 20$ **c)** $\log (ab^2c)$ **d)** $\log \dfrac{uv}{\sqrt{w}}$

> **Solution**

a) $\log_3 (xy) = \log_3 x + \log_3 y, x > 0, y > 0$ Apply the product law of logarithms.

b) **Method 1:** *Use Factors 4 and 5*   **Method 2:** *Use Factors 2 and 10*

$\log 20 = \log 4 + \log 5$ $\log 20 = \log 10 + \log 2$

                                         $= 1 + \log 2$

c) $\log (ab^2c) = \log a + \log b^2 + \log c$

               $= \log a + 2 \log b + \log c, a > 0, b > 0, c > 0$ Apply the power law of logarithms.

d) $\log \left(\dfrac{uv}{\sqrt{w}} \right) = \log u + \log v - \log \sqrt{w}$ Apply the product and quotient laws of logarithms.

             $= \log u + \log v - \log w^{\frac{1}{2}}$ Write the radical in exponential form.

             $= \log u + \log v - \dfrac{1}{2} \log w, u > 0, v > 0, w > 0$ Apply the power law of logarithms.

Example 4	Simplify Algebraic Expressions

Simplify.

a) $\log \left(\dfrac{\sqrt{x}}{x^2} \right)$

b) $\log (\sqrt{x})^3 + \log x^2 - \log \sqrt{x}$

c) $\log (2x - 2) - \log (x^2 - 1)$

> **Solution**

a) **Method 1:** *Apply the Quotient Law of Logarithms*

     $\log \left(\dfrac{\sqrt{x}}{x^2} \right) = \log \sqrt{x} - \log x^2$ Apply the quotient law of logarithms.

              $= \log x^{\frac{1}{2}} - \log x^2$ Write the radical in exponential form.

              $= \dfrac{1}{2} \log x - 2 \log x$ Apply the power law of logarithms.

              $= \dfrac{1}{2} \log x - \dfrac{4}{2} \log x$

              $= -\dfrac{3}{2} \log x, x > 0$ Collect like terms.

Method 2: *Apply the Quotient Law of Exponents*

$$\log\left(\frac{\sqrt{x}}{x^2}\right) = \log\left(\frac{x^{\frac{1}{2}}}{x^2}\right)$$ Write the radical in exponential form.

$$= \log x^{\frac{1}{2}-2}$$ Apply the quotient law of exponents.

$$= \log x^{-\frac{3}{2}}$$

$$= -\frac{3}{2}\log x, \; x > 0$$ Apply the power law of logarithms.

b) $\log(\sqrt{x})^3 + \log x^2 - \log \sqrt{x} = \log x^{\frac{3}{2}} + \log x^2 - \log x^{\frac{1}{2}}$

$$= \log\left(\frac{\left(x^{\frac{3}{2}}\right)(x^2)}{\left(x^{\frac{1}{2}}\right)}\right)$$ Apply the product and quotient laws of logarithms.

$$= \log x^{\frac{3}{2}+2-\frac{1}{2}}$$ Apply the product and quotient laws of exponents.

$$= \log x^3$$

$$= 3\log x, \; x > 0$$ Apply the power law of logarithms.

c) $\log(2x - 2) - \log(x^2 - 1) = \log\left(\frac{2x - 2}{x^2 - 1}\right)$

$$= \log\left(\frac{2(x - 1)}{(x + 1)(x - 1)}\right)$$ Factor the numerator and denominator.

$$= \log\left(\frac{2}{x + 1}\right)$$ Simplify by dividing common factors.

To determine the restrictions on the variable x, consider the original expression:

$\log(2x - 2) - \log(x^2 - 1)$

For this expression to be defined, both logarithmic terms must be defined. This implies the following:

$2x - 2 > 0$	$x^2 - 1 > 0$
$2x > 2$	$x^2 > 1$
$x > 1$	$x > 1$ or $x < -1$

For both logarithmic terms to be defined, therefore, the restriction $x > 1$ must be imposed.

$\log(2x - 2) - \log(x^2 - 1) = \log\left(\frac{2}{x + 1}\right), \; x > 1$

Note that this restriction ensures that *all* logarithmic expressions in the equation are defined.

CONNECTIONS

A more concise way to write $x > 1$ or $x < -1$ is to use absolute value notation: $|x| > 1$.

KEY CONCEPTS

- The product law of logarithms states that $\log_b x + \log_b y = \log_b (xy)$ for $b > 0$, $b \neq 1$, $x > 0$, $y > 0$.

- The quotient law of logarithms states that $\log_b x - \log_b y = \log_b \left(\dfrac{x}{y}\right)$ for $b > 0$, $b \neq 1$, $x > 0$, $y > 0$.

- The laws of logarithms can be used to simplify expressions and solve equations.

Communicate Your Understanding

C1 Does $\log x + \log y = \log (x + y)$? If so, prove it. If not, explain why not. Use examples to support your answer.

C2 Does $\log \left(\dfrac{a}{b}\right) = \dfrac{\log a}{\log b}$? If so, prove it. If not, explain why not. Use examples to support your answer.

C3 Refer to the final line in the solution to Example 4. Why is the restriction on the variable $x > 1$ and not $|x| > 1$?

C4 Summarize the laws of logarithms in your notebook. Create an example to illustrate each law.

C5 Reflect on the domain and range of $y = \log x$. Why must x be a positive number?

A Practise

For help with questions 1 to 3, refer to Example 1.

1. Simplify, using the laws of logarithms.

   a) $\log 9 + \log 6$

   b) $\log 48 - \log 6$

   c) $\log_3 7 + \log_3 3$

   d) $\log_5 36 - \log_5 18$

2. **Use Technology** Use a calculator to evaluate each result in question 1, correct to three decimal places.

3. Simplify each algebraic expression. State any restrictions on the variables.

   a) $\log x + \log y + \log (2z)$

   b) $\log_2 a + \log_2 (3b) - \log_2 (2c)$

   c) $2 \log m + 3 \log n - 4 \log y$

   d) $2 \log u + \log v + \dfrac{1}{2} \log w$

For help with questions 4 to 6, refer to Example 2.

4. Evaluate, using the product law of logarithms.

   a) $\log_6 18 + \log_6 2$

   b) $\log 40 + \log 2.5$

   c) $\log_{12} 8 + \log_{12} 2 + \log_{12} 9$

   d) $\log 5 + \log 40 + \log 5$

5. Evaluate, using the quotient law of logarithms.

   a) $\log_3 54 - \log_3 2$

   b) $\log 50\ 000 - \log 5$

   c) $\log_4 320 - \log_4 5$

   d) $\log 2 - \log 200$

6. Evaluate, using the laws of logarithms.

   a) $3 \log_{16} 2 + 2 \log_{16} 8 - \log_{16} 2$

   b) $\log 20 + \log 2 + \dfrac{1}{3} \log 125$

For help with questions 7 and 8, refer to Example 3.

7. Write as a sum or difference of logarithms. Simplify, if possible.

a) $\log_7 (cd)$

b) $\log_3 \left(\dfrac{m}{n}\right)$

c) $\log (uv^3)$

d) $\log \left(\dfrac{a\sqrt{b}}{c^2}\right)$

e) $\log_2 10$

f) $\log_5 50$

8. Reflect on your answer to question 7f). Is there more than one possibility? Explain. Which solution gives the simplest result?

B Connect and Apply

For help with questions 9 and 10, refer to Example 4.

9. Simplify. State any restrictions on the variables.

a) $\log \left(\dfrac{x^2}{\sqrt{x}}\right)$

b) $\log \left(\dfrac{\sqrt{m}}{m^3}\right) + \log(\sqrt{m})^7$

c) $\log \sqrt{k} + \log (\sqrt{k})^3 + \log \sqrt[3]{k^2}$

d) $2 \log w + 3 \log \sqrt{w} + \dfrac{1}{2} \log w^2$

10. Simplify. State any restrictions on the variables.

a) $\log (x^2 - 4) - \log (x - 2)$

b) $\log (x^2 + 7x + 12) - \log (x + 3)$

c) $\log (x^2 - x - 6) - \log (2x - 6)$

d) $\log (x^2 + 7x + 12) - \log (x^2 - 9)$

11. Chapter Problem A certain operational amplifier (Op Amp) produces a voltage output, V_0, in volts, from two input voltage signals, V_1 and V_2, according to the equation $V_0 = \log V_2 - \log V_1$.

a) Write a simplified form of this formula, expressing the right side as a single logarithm.

b) What is the voltage output if

   i) V_2 is 10 times V_1?

   ii) V_2 is 100 times V_1?

   iii) V_2 is equal to V_1?

CONNECTIONS

Op Amps are tiny integrated circuits that can be used to perform various mathematical functions on voltage signals. Engineers combine Op Amps with other electronic circuit elements to create useful equipment such as electric guitar amplifiers, effects pedals, and signal processors.

12. a) Explain how you can transform the graph of $f(x) = \log x$ to produce $g(x) = \log (10nx)$, for any $n > 0$.

Reasoning and Proving
Representing · Selecting Tools
Problem Solving
Connecting · Reflecting
Communicating

b) Create two examples to support your explanation. Sketch graphs to illustrate.

13. Refer to question 12 part a). Can this process be applied when n is an integer? Explain.

14. Use Technology

a) Graph the functions $f(x) = 2 \log x$ and $g(x) = 3 \log x$.

b) Graph the sum of these two functions: $p(x) = f(x) + g(x)$.

c) Graph the function $q(x) = \log x^5$.

d) How are the functions $p(x)$ and $q(x)$ related? What law of logarithms does this illustrate?

CONNECTIONS

You will learn more about the sums of functions in Chapter 8.

Technology Tip ⠆⠆

To distinguish two graphs on a graphing calculator screen, you can alter the line style. Cursor over to the left of **Y2**= and press (ENTER). Observe the different line styles available. Press (ENTER) to select a style.

You can change colours and line thicknesses in *The Geometer's Sketchpad*® by right-clicking on the curve.

15. Use Technology

Refer to question 14.

Reasoning and Proving
Representing • Selecting Tools • Problem Solving • Connecting • Reflecting • Communicating

a) In place of $g(x) = 3 \log x$ use $g(x) = 4 \log x$. How should the function $q(x)$, in step c), change in order to illustrate the same property as in question 14?

b) Graph the functions $p(x)$ and $q(x)$.

c) You should observe something unusual about the graph of $q(x)$. Explain what is unusual about this graph and where the unusual portion comes from.

16. Use Technology Create a graphical example that illustrates the quotient law of logarithms using a graphing calculator with CAS or other graphing technology. Explain how your example works.

17. Use the power law of logarithms to verify the product law of logarithms for $\log 10^2$.

18. Renata, a recent business school graduate, has been offered entry-level positions with two firms. Firm A offers a starting salary of \$40 000 per year, with a \$2000 per year increase guaranteed each subsequent year. Firm B offers a starting salary of \$38 500, with a 5% increase every year after that.

a) After how many years will Renata earn the same amount at either firm?

b) At which firm will Renata earn more after

  i) 10 years?   **ii)** 20 years?

c) What other factors might affect Renata's choice, such as opportunities for promotion? Explain how these factors may influence her decision.

✓ Achievement Check

19. Express each as a single logarithm. Then, evaluate, if possible.

a) $\log_4 192 - \log_4 3$

b) $\log_5 35 - \log_5 7 + \log_5 25$

c) $\log_a (ab) - \log_a (a^3 b)$

d) $\log (xy) + \log \dfrac{y}{x}$

C) Extend and Challenge

20. Prove the quotient law of logarithms by applying algebraic reasoning.

21. a) Given the product law of logarithms, prove the product law of exponents.

b) Given the quotient law of logarithms, prove the quotient law of exponents.

22. Math Contest For what positive value of c does the line $y = -x + c$ intersect the circle $x^2 + y^2 = 1$ at exactly one point?

23. Math Contest For what value of k does the parabola $y = x^2 + k$ intersect the circle $x^2 + y^2 = 1$ in exactly three points?

24. Math Contest A line, l_1, has slope -2 and passes through the point $(r, -3)$. A second line, l_2, is perpendicular to l_1, intersects l_1 at the point (a, b), and passes through the point $(6, r)$. What is the value of a?

  A r **B** $\dfrac{2}{5}r$ **C** 1 **D** $2r - 3$ **E** $\dfrac{5}{2}r$

25. Math Contest A grocer has c pounds of coffee divided equally among k sacks. She finds n empty sacks and decides to redistribute the coffee equally among the $k + n$ sacks. When this is done, how many fewer pounds of coffee does each of the original sacks hold?

Techniques for Solving Logarithmic Equations

The sensitivity to light intensity of the human eye, as well as of certain optical equipment such as cameras, follows a logarithmic relationship. Adjusting the size of the aperture that permits light into the camera, called the f-stop, can compensate for poor lighting conditions. A good understanding of the underlying mathematics and optical physics is essential for the skilled photographer in such situations.

You have seen that any positive number can be represented as

- a power of any other positive base
- a logarithm of any other positive base

For example, the number 4 can be written as

- a power:

$$4^1 \qquad 2^2 \qquad 16^{\frac{1}{2}} \qquad 10^{\log 4}$$

- a logarithm:

$$\log_2 16 \qquad \log_3 81 \qquad \log 10\,000$$

Can any of these representations of numbers be useful for solving equations that involve logarithms? If so, how?

Investigate | **How can you solve an equation involving logarithms?**

1. **Use Technology** Consider the equation $\log(x + 5) = 2 \log(x - 1)$.

   a) Describe a method of finding the solution using graphing technology.

   b) Carry out your method and determine the solution.

2. **a)** Apply the power law of logarithms to the right side of the equation in step 1.

   b) Expand the squared binomial that results on the right side.

3. **Reflect**

   a) How is the perfect square trinomial you obtained on the right side related to $x + 5$, which appears on the left side of the equation? How do you know this?

   b) How could this be useful in finding an algebraic solution to the equation?

Tools

- graphing calculator
- grid paper

Find the roots of each equation.

a) $\log(x + 4) = 1$

b) $\log_5(2x - 3) = 2$

> **Solution**

a) Method 1: *Use Algebraic Reasoning*

$$\log(x + 4) = 1$$
$$x + 4 = 10^1 \qquad \text{Rewrite in exponential form, using base 10.}$$
$$x = 10 - 4 \qquad \text{Solve for } x.$$
$$x = 6$$

Method 2: *Use Graphical Reasoning*

Graph the left side and the right side as a linear-logarithmic system and identify the x-coordinate of their point of intersection.

Let $y_1 = \log(x + 4)$ and $y_2 = 1$.

Graph y_1 by graphing $y = \log x$ and applying a horizontal translation of 4 units to the left.

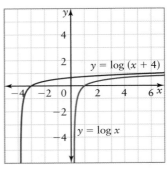

Graph the horizontal line $y_2 = 1$ on the same grid, and identify the x-coordinate of the point of intersection.

The two functions intersect when $x = 6$. Therefore, $x = 6$ is the root of the equation $\log(x + 4) = 1$.

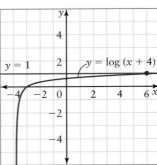

b) $\log_5(2x - 3) = 2$
$$\log_5(2x - 3) = \log_5 25 \qquad \text{Express the right side as a base-5 logarithm.}$$
$$2x - 3 = 5^2$$
$$2x = 25 + 3$$
$$2x = 28$$
$$x = 14$$

CONNECTIONS

If $\log_m a = \log_m b$, then $a = b$ for any base m, as shown below.

$\log_m a = \log_m b$

$\dfrac{\log_m a}{\log_m b} = 1$

$\log_b a = 1$ Use the change of base formula.

$b^1 = a$ Rewrite in exponential form.

$b = a$

Example 2 | **Apply Factoring Strategies to Solve Equations**

Solve. Identify and reject any extraneous roots.

a) $\log(x - 1) - 1 = -\log(x + 2)$

b) $\log \sqrt[3]{x^2 + 48x} = \dfrac{2}{3}$

Solution

a)
$$\log(x - 1) - 1 = -\log(x + 2)$$

$$\log(x - 1) + \log(x + 2) = 1 \qquad \text{Isolate logarithmic terms on one side of the equation.}$$

$$\log[(x - 1)(x + 2)] = 1 \qquad \text{Apply the product law of logarithms.}$$

$$\log(x^2 + x - 2) = \log 10 \qquad \text{Expand the product of binomials on the left side. Express the right side as a common logarithm.}$$

$$x^2 + x - 2 = 10$$
$$x^2 + x - 2 - 10 = 0$$
$$x^2 + x - 12 = 0 \qquad \text{Express the quadratic equation in standard form.}$$
$$(x + 4)(x - 3) = 0 \qquad \text{Solve the quadratic equation.}$$
$$x = -4 \text{ or } x = 3$$

Looking back at the original equation, it is necessary to reject $x = -4$ as an extraneous root. Both $\log(x - 1)$ and $-\log(x + 2)$ are undefined for this value because the logarithm of a negative number is undefined. Therefore, the only solution is $x = 3$.

b)
$$\log \sqrt[3]{x^2 + 48x} = \dfrac{2}{3}$$

$$\log(x^2 + 48x)^{\frac{1}{3}} = \dfrac{2}{3}$$

$$\dfrac{1}{3}\log(x^2 + 48x) = \dfrac{2}{3} \qquad \text{Write the radical as a power and apply the power law of logarithms.}$$

$$\log(x^2 + 48x) = 2 \qquad \text{Multiply both sides by 3.}$$

$$\log(x^2 + 48x) = \log 100 \qquad \text{Express the right side as a common logarithm.}$$

$$x^2 + 48x = 100$$
$$x^2 + 48x - 100 = 0$$
$$(x + 50)(x - 2) = 0$$
$$x = -50 \text{ or } x = 2$$

Check these values for extraneous roots. For a valid solution, the argument in green in the equation must be positive, and the left side must equal the right side: $\log \sqrt[3]{x^2 + 48x} = \dfrac{2}{3}$.

Check $x = -50$:

$$\sqrt[3]{x^2 + 48x} = \sqrt[3]{(-50)^2 + 48(-50)}$$
$$= \sqrt[3]{2500 - 2400}$$
$$= \sqrt[3]{100}$$

$$\begin{aligned} \text{L.S.} &= \log \sqrt[3]{x^2 + 48x} \\ &= \log \sqrt[3]{100} \\ &= \log 100^{\frac{1}{3}} \\ &= \frac{1}{3} \log 100 \\ &= \frac{1}{3}(2) \\ &= \frac{2}{3} \\ &= \text{R.S.} \end{aligned}$$

$\sqrt[3]{100} > 0$, and the solution satisfies the equation, so $x = -50$ is a valid solution.

Check $x = 2$:

$$\sqrt[3]{x^2 + 48x} = \sqrt[3]{(2)^2 + 48(2)}$$
$$= \sqrt[3]{100}$$

$$\begin{aligned} \text{L.S.} &= \log \sqrt[3]{100} \\ &= \frac{1}{3} \log 100 \\ &= \frac{1}{3}(2) \\ &= \frac{2}{3} \\ &= \text{R.S.} \end{aligned}$$

This is also a valid solution. Therefore, the roots of this equation are $x = -50$ and $x = 2$.

KEY CONCEPTS

- It is possible to solve an equation involving logarithms by expressing both sides as a logarithm of the same base: if $a = b$, then $\log a = \log b$, and if $\log a = \log b$, then $a = b$.

- When a quadratic equation is obtained, methods such as factoring or applying the quadratic formula may be useful.

- Some algebraic methods of solving logarithmic equations lead to extraneous roots, which are not valid solutions to the original equation.

Communicate Your Understanding

C1 Consider the equation $\log_4(x + 5) = 2$.

    a) Which of the following expressions are equivalent to the right side of the equation?

        $\log_2 4$ $\log_4 16$ $\log_5 25$ $\log 100$

    b) Which one would you use to solve the equation for x, and why?

C2 Examine these graphing calculator screens.

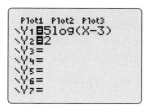 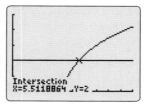

    a) What equation is being solved?

    b) What is the solution? Explain how you can tell.

C3 Consider the following statement: "When solving a logarithmic equation that results in a quadratic, you always obtain two roots: one valid and one extraneous."

    Do you agree or disagree with this statement? If you agree, explain why it is correct. If you disagree, provide a counterexample.

A) Practise

For help with questions 1 and 2, refer to Example 1.

1. Find the roots of each equation. Check your solutions using graphing technology.

    a) $\log(x - 2) = 1$

    b) $2 = \log(x + 25)$

    c) $4 = 2\log(p + 62)$

    d) $1 - \log(w - 7) = 0$

    e) $\log(k - 8) = 2$

    f) $6 - 3\log 2n = 0$

2. Solve.

    a) $\log_3(x + 4) = 2$

    b) $5 = \log_2(2x - 10)$

    c) $2 - \log_4(k - 11) = 0$

    d) $9 = \log_5(x + 100) + 6$

    e) $\log_8(t - 1) + 1 = 0$

    f) $\log_3(n^2 - 3n + 5) = 2$

For help with questions 3 and 4, refer to Example 2.

3. Solve. Identify and reject any extraneous roots. Check your solutions using graphing technology.

    a) $\log x + \log(x - 4) = 1$

    b) $\log x^3 - \log 2 = \log(2x^2)$

    c) $\log(v - 1) = 2 + \log(v - 16)$

    d) $1 + \log y = \log(y + 9)$

    e) $\log(k + 2) + \log(k - 1) = 1$

    f) $\log(p + 5) - \log(p + 1) = 3$

4. Use Technology Refer to Example 2b). Verify the solutions to the equation using graphing technology. Explain your method.

5. Solve. Check for extraneous roots. Check your results using graphing technology.

a) $\log \sqrt{x^2 - 3x} = \dfrac{1}{2}$ **b)** $\log \sqrt{x^2 + 48x} = 1$

6. Solve. Identify any extraneous roots.

a) $\log_2 (x + 5) - \log_2 (2x) = 8$

b) $\log (2k + 4) = 1 + \log k$

7. Use Technology Find the roots of each equation, correct to two decimal places, using graphing technology. Sketch the graphical solution.

a) $\log (x + 2) = 2 - \log x$

b) $3 \log (x - 2) = \log (2x) - 3$

8. Chapter Problem At a concert, the loudness of sound, L, in decibels, is given by the equation $L = 10 \log \dfrac{I}{I_0}$, where I is the intensity, in watts per square metre, and I_0 is the minimum intensity of sound audible to the average person, or 1.0×10^{-12} W/m^2.

a) The sound intensity at the concert is measured to be 0.9 W/m^2. How loud is the concert?

b) At the concert, the person beside you whispers with a loudness of 20 dB. What is the whisper's intensity?

c) On the way home from the concert, your car stereo produces 120 dB of sound. What is its intensity?

C O N N E C T I O N S
You used the decibel scale in Chapter 6. Refer to Section 6.5.

9. a) Is the following statement true?

$\log (-3) + \log (-4) = \log 12$

Explain why or why not.

b) Is the following statement true?

$-\log 3 - \log 4 = -\log 12$

Explain why or why not.

10. The aperture setting, or f-stop, of a digital camera controls the amount of light exposure on the sensor. Each higher number of the f-stop doubles the amount of light exposure. The formula $n = \log_2 \dfrac{1}{p}$ represents the change in the number, n, of the f-stop needed, where p is the amount of light exposed on the sensor.

a) A photographer wishes to change the f-stop to accommodate a cloudy day in which only $\dfrac{1}{4}$ of the sunlight is available. How many f-stops does the setting need to be moved?

b) If the photographer decreases the f-stop by four settings, what fraction of light is allowed to fall on the sensor?

11. a) Solve and check for any extraneous roots.

$\dfrac{2}{3} = \log \sqrt[3]{w^2 - 10w}$

b) Solve the equation in part a) graphically. Verify that the graphical and algebraic solutions agree.

12. Solve the equation $2 \log (x + 11) = \left(\dfrac{1}{2} \right)^x$. Explain your method.

13. Show that if $\log_b a = c$ and $\log_y b = c$, then $\log_a y = c^{-2}$.

14. Math Contest Find the minimum value of $1 \square 2 \square 3 \square 4 \square 5 \square 6 \square 7 \square 8 \square 9$, where $\square$ represents either $+$ or $\times$.

15. Math Contest Given that $3 = \sqrt{m} + \dfrac{1}{\sqrt{m}}$, determine the value of $m - \dfrac{1}{m}$.

16. Math Contest Let u and v be two positive real numbers satisfying the two equations $u + v + uv = 10$ and $u^2 + v^2 = 40$. What is the value of the integer closest to $u + v$?

A 4 **B** 5 **C** 6 **D** 7 **E** 8

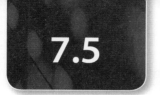

7.5

Making Connections: Mathematical Modelling With Exponential and Logarithmic Equations

Countless freshwater lakes, lush forests, and breathtaking landscapes make northern Ontario a popular summer vacation destination. Every year, millions of Ontarians go there to enjoy summer life in the peaceful setting of a cottage, a campground, or a small town.

Suppose you live and work in northern Ontario as an urban planner. As towns grow, you will need to pose and solve a variety of problems such as the following.

• How much commercial development should be encouraged or permitted?

• When and where should a highway off-ramp be built?

• Which natural landscapes should be left undisturbed?

These and other related problems may require applying and solving exponential and logarithmic equations.

Careful planning and development can ensure that the natural beauty of our northern landscape is preserved, while meeting the needs of a growing population.

Take a journey now to Decimal Point, a fictional town located somewhere in northern Ontario. You have been assigned to perform some urban planning for this friendly community.

Example 1 | Select and Apply a Mathematical Model

The population of Decimal Point has been steadily growing for several decades. The table gives the population at 5-year intervals, beginning in 1920, the year the town's population reached 1000.

Time (years)	Population
0	1000
5	1100
10	1180
15	1250
20	1380
25	1500
30	1600

a) Create a scatter plot to illustrate this growth trend.

b) Construct a quadratic model to fit the data.

c) Construct an exponential model to fit the data.

d) Which model is better, and why?

e) Suppose that it is decided that a recreation centre should be built once the town's population reaches 5000. When should the recreation centre be built?

Solution

Method 1: *Use a Graphing Calculator*

a) Clear all equations and Stat Plots from the calculator. Enter the data in lists **L1** and **L2** using the list editor.

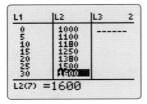

Turn **Plot1** on. From the **Zoom** menu, choose **9:ZoomStat** to display the scatter plot.

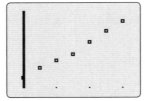

b) Use quadratic regression to determine a quadratic equation of best fit, and store it as a function, **Y1**, by following these steps:

- Press `STAT`.
- Choose **CALC**, and then select **5:QuadReg**.
- Press `2nd` 1 for [L1], followed by `,`.
- Press `2nd` 2 for [L2], followed by `,`.
- Press `VARS`. Cursor over to **Y-VARS**. Select **1:Function** and press `ENTER`.

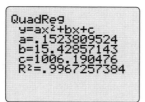

The equation of the curve of best fit is approximately
$y = 0.15x^2 + 15.4x + 1006$, where y is the population after x years.

c) To determine an exponential equation of best fit, follow the same steps as above, except choose **0:ExpReg** instead of **5:QuadReg**. Store the exponential equation of best fit in **Y2**.

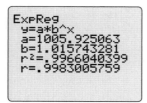

The equation of the exponential curve of best fit is approximately
$P = 1006(1.016)^t$, where P is the population after t years.

d) Note that both regression analyses yield equations with very high values of r^2, suggesting that both models fit the given data well. To examine the scatter plot and both model graphs, press `Y=` to open the graph editor. Then, ensure that **Plot1**, **Y1**, and **Y2** are all highlighted. For clarity, the line style of one of the functions can be altered (e.g., made thick).

Press `GRAPH` to see how well the two curves fit the given data.

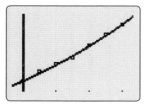

It appears that either model fits the data equally well, since the functions are virtually indistinguishable. Are these models equally valid? Zoom out to see how the models extrapolate beyond the given data.

Zoom out once:

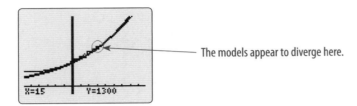

The models appear to diverge here.

Technology Tip ∴

When you press (TRACE), the cursor will trace the points of the scatter plot, the function **Y1**, or the function **Y2**. You can toggle between these by using the up and down cursor keys. Use the left and right cursor keys to trace along a function graph or set of points.

What meaning does the part of the graph to the left of the origin have? Do you think this a valid part of the domain for this problem? Zoom out again, and then use the **ZoomBox** operation to explore this region. Use the **TRACE** operation to track the coordinates of each model.

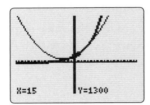
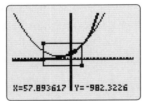
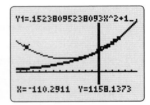

An anomaly occurs when extrapolating the quadratic model back in time. This model suggests that the population of the town was actually once larger than it was in year zero, and then decreased and increased again. This contradicts the given information in the problem, which states that the town's population had been growing for several decades.

The exponential model gives a more reasonable description of the population trend before year zero due to its nature of continuous growth. Therefore, the exponential model is better for describing this trend.

Method 2: *Use* Fathom®

a) Open a new collection and enter the data into a **Case Table**.

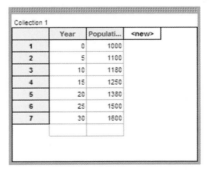

Create a scatter plot of **Year** versus **Population**.

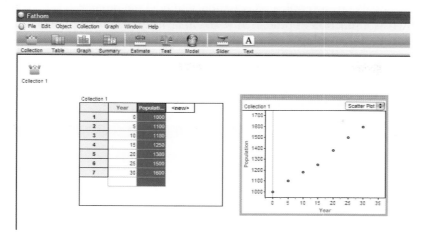

Technology Tip ∴

To create this **New Graph**:
- Click and drag the graph icon from the menu at the top.
- Click and drag the **Year** attribute onto the horizontal axis.
- Click and drag the **Population** attribute onto the vertical axis.

b) Create a dynamic quadratic model by following these steps:

- Click and drag three sliders from the menu at the top. Label them *a*, *b*, and *c*.
- Click on the graph. From the **Graph** menu, choose **Plot Function**.
- Enter the function a*Year^2 + b*Year + c and click on **OK**.

Adjust the sliders until a curve of best fit is obtained. Hint: What should the approximate value of *c* be (think about when $x = 0$)?

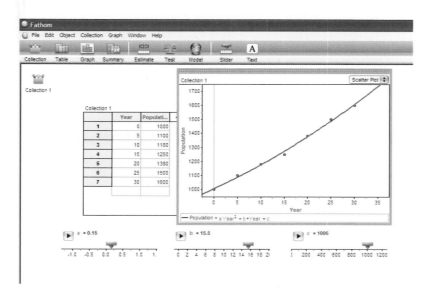

Technology Tip ∴

You can adjust the scales of the sliders by placing the cursor in various locations and then clicking and dragging. Experiment with this, noting the various hand positions that appear and what they allow you to do.

The quadratic curve of best fit is given approximately by $P = 0.15t^2 + 15.5t + 1006$, where *P* is the population after *t* years.

c) An exponential equation can be written in terms of any base. Therefore, it is possible to determine an equation to model the population, P, of this town as a function of time, t, in years, in terms of its initial population, 1000, and its doubling period, d:

$$P = 1000 \times 2^{\frac{t}{d}}$$

Create a dynamic exponential model with a single slider, d. Adjust d until the curve of best fit is obtained.

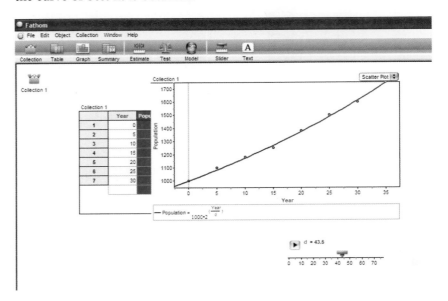

The doubling period is approximately 43.5 years. The exponential equation of the curve of best fit is approximately $P = 1000 \times 2^{\frac{t}{43.5}}$.

d) Note that both models fit the data well. To see how well they perform for extrapolation, adjust the axes of each graph.

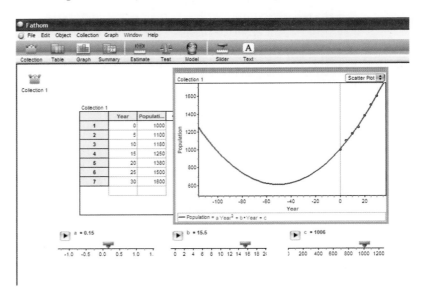

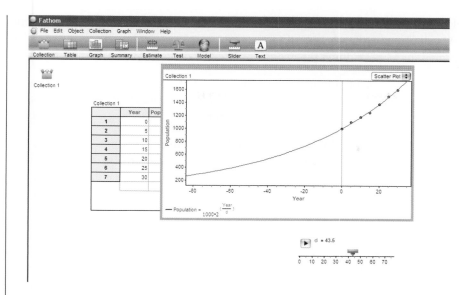

e) Use either exponential algebraic model to determine when the recreation centre should be built for Decimal Point by solving for t when $P = 5000$.

$$P = 1006(1.016)^t$$

$$5000 = 1006(1.16)^t$$

$$\frac{5000}{1006} \doteq 1.016^t \qquad \text{Divide both sides by 1006.}$$

$$\log\left(\frac{5000}{1006}\right) \doteq \log(1.016)^t$$

$$\frac{\log\left(\dfrac{5000}{1006}\right)}{\log 1.016} \doteq t \qquad \begin{array}{l}\text{Apply the power law of}\\ \text{logarithms and divide}\\ \text{both sides by log 1.016.}\end{array}$$

$$t \doteq 101 \qquad \begin{array}{l}\text{Use a calculator to}\\ \text{evaluate.}\end{array}$$

$$P = 1000 \times 2^{\frac{t}{43.5}}$$

$$5000 = 1000 \times 2^{\frac{t}{43.5}} \qquad \text{Divide both sides by 1000.}$$

$$5 = 2^{\frac{t}{43.5}}$$

$$\log 5 = \log\left(2^{\frac{t}{43.5}}\right) \qquad \begin{array}{l}\text{Take the common}\\ \text{logarithm of both sides.}\end{array}$$

$$\log 5 = \left(\frac{t}{43.5}\right)\log 2 \qquad \begin{array}{l}\text{Apply the power law}\\ \text{of logarithms.}\end{array}$$

$$43.5\left(\frac{\log 5}{\log 2}\right) = t \qquad \begin{array}{l}\text{Multiply both sides by}\\ \text{43.5 and divide both}\\ \text{sides by log 2.}\end{array}$$

$$t \doteq 101 \qquad \text{Use a calculator to evaluate.}$$

Both models indicate that the recreation centre should be built approximately 101 years after the population of Decimal Point reached 1000. Because the population reached 1000 in 1920, the recreation centre should be built in the year 2021.

Example 1 illustrates the important distinction between curve-fitting and modelling. A well-fit curve may be useful for interpolating a given data set, but such a model may break down when extrapolated to describe past or future trends.

The town of Decimal Point is enjoying a fiscal surplus, a pleasant situation in which financial revenues exceed expenses. How should the town's funds be invested in order to earn the best rate of return?

The **compound interest formula** modelling the future amount, A, of an investment with initial principal P is $A = P(1 + i)^n$, where i is the interest rate per compounding period, in decimal form, and n is the number of compounding periods.

Example 2 | **Investment Optimization**

Decimal Point has a surplus of $50 000 to invest to build a recreation centre. The two best investment options are described in the table.

Investment Option	Lakeland Savings Bond	Northern Equity Mutual Fund
Interest Rate	$6\frac{1}{4}$% compounded annually	6% compounded semi-annually
Conditions	2% of initial principal penalty if withdrawn before 10 years	none

a) Construct an algebraic model that gives the amount, A, as a function of time, t, in years, for each investment.

b) Which of these investment options will allow the town to double its money faster?

c) Illustrate how these relationships compare, graphically.

d) If the town needs $80 000 to begin building the recreation centre, how soon can work begin, and which investment option should be chosen?

Solution

a) Determine the number of compounding periods and the interest rate per compounding period for each investment. Then, substitute these values into the algebraic model. Use a table to organize the information.

	Lakeland Savings Bond	Northern Equity Mutual Fund
Number of compounding periods, n	$n = t$	$n = 2t$
Interest rate per compounding period, i	$6\frac{1}{4}$% per year $= 0.0625$	6% per year ÷ 2 periods per year $= 0.03$
$A = P(1 + i)^n$	$A = 50\ 000(1.0625)^t$	$A = 50\ 000(1.03)^{2t}$

b) To determine how long it will take for each investment to double in value, substitute $A = 100\ 000$ and solve for t.

Lakeland Savings Bond

$$A = 50\ 000(1.0625)^t$$

$$100\ 000 = 50\ 000(1.0625)^t$$

$$2 = (1.0625)^t$$

$\log 2 = \log(1.0625)^t$ Take the common logarithm of both sides.

$\log 2 = t \log 1.0625$ Use the power law of logarithms.

$t = \dfrac{\log 2}{\log 1.0625}$ Divide both sides by $\log 1.0625$.

$\doteq 11.4$

The Lakeland investment will take approximately 11.4 years to double in value.

Northern Equity Mutual Fund

$$100\ 000 = 50\ 000(1.03)^{2t}$$

$$2 = (1.03)^{2t}$$

$\log 2 = \log(1.03)^{2t}$ Take the common logarithm of both sides.

$\log 2 = 2t \log 1.03$ Use the power law of logarithms.

$t = \dfrac{\log 2}{2 \log 1.03}$ Divide both sides by $2 \log 1.03$.

$t \doteq 11.7$

The Northern Equity investment will take approximately 11.7 years to double in value.

Therefore, the Lakeland Savings Bond will allow the town to double its money slightly faster.

c) The two investment relationships can be compared graphically using graphing software.

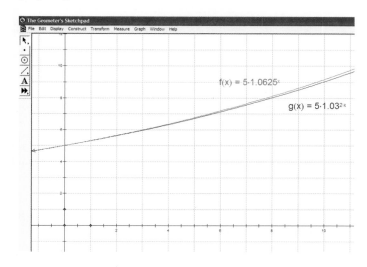

Note that $f(x)$ corresponds to Lakeland Savings Bond and $g(x)$ to Northern Equity Mutual Fund and that both are functions of x, measured in tens of thousands of dollars ($10 000).

d) The graph indicates that both accounts will reach $80 000 after about 8 years. The Lakeland account earns interest faster, but is it the best choice for preparing to build the recreation centre? The penalty for early withdrawal must be considered.

The exponential model can be adjusted for withdrawals that happen within the first 10 years by subtracting 2% of the initial principal. The adjusted equation becomes

$$A = 50\ 000(1.0625)^t - \underbrace{0.02(50\ 000)}$$

2% penalty for early withdrawal

or $A = 50\ 000(1.0625)^t - 1000$.

Applying a vertical shift to the original amount function can reveal the effect of this penalty.

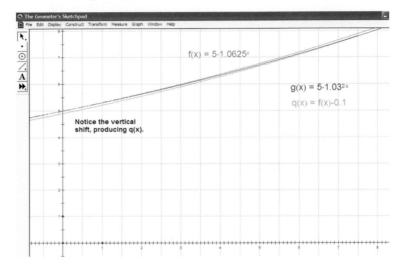

The function $q(x)$ represents the adjusted amount function for the Lakeland account. It is unclear from the graph which account will reach $80 000 first. Apply algebraic reasoning to decide.

Substitute $A = 80\ 000$ and solve for t.

Lakeland Savings Bond (penalty adjusted)

$A = 50\ 000(1.0625)^t - 1000$	
$80\ 000 = 50\ 000(1.0625)^t - 1000$	
$81\ 000 = 50\ 000(1.0625)^t$	Add 1000 to both sides.
$1.62 = (1.0625)^t$	Divide both sides by 50 000.
$\log 1.62 = \log(1.0625)^t$	Take the common logarithm of both sides.
$\log 1.62 = t \log 1.0625$	
$t = \dfrac{\log 1.62}{\log 1.0625}$	
$\doteq 7.96$	

The Lakeland account will reach \$80 000 in value after 7.96 years, after adjusting for the early withdrawal penalty.

Northern Equity Mutual Fund

$$A = 50\ 000(1.03)^{2t}$$

$$80\ 000 = 50\ 000(1.03)^{2t}$$

$$1.6 = 1.03^{2t}$$

$\log 1.6 = \log (1.03)^{2t}$ Take the common logarithm of both sides.

$$\log 1.6 = 2t \log 1.03$$

$$t = \frac{\log 1.6}{2 \log 1.03}$$

$$\doteq 7.95$$

The Northern Equity account will reach \$80 000 in value after 7.95 years.

Since the time difference between these two accounts is so small, it does not really matter which one is chosen, from a purely financial perspective. Other factors may be considered, such as the additional flexibility afforded by the Northern Equity account. If the township finds itself in a deficit situation (where expenses exceed revenues), for example, and if some of the money in reserve is required for other, more urgent, purposes, then the Northern Equity account may be preferable.

KEY CONCEPTS

- Different technology tools and strategies can be used to construct mathematical models that describe real situations.

- A good mathematical model
  - is useful for both interpolating and extrapolating from given data in order to make predictions
  - can be used, in conjunction with other considerations, to aid in decision making

- Exponential and logarithmic equations often appear in contexts that involve continuous growth or decay.

Communicate Your Understanding

C1 Refer to Example 1. Two regression models were proposed and one was found to be better.

    a) What was the basis for rejecting the quadratic model?

    b) Consider a linear model for the data. Is it possible to construct a line that fits the given data reasonably well?

    c) Would a linear model be valid for extrapolation purposes? Explain why or why not.

C2 Explain the difference between curve-fitting and mathematical modelling. Identify any advantages either procedure has over the other.

C3 Refer to Example 2. Suppose that instead of an early withdrawal penalty, the investment agency provids a bonus of 2% of the principal if it is not withdrawn before 10 years have elapsed. How could this be reflected using a transformation, and when will it apply?

A   Practise

For help with questions 1 to 3, refer to Example 1.

1. Plans for Decimal Point call for a highway off-ramp to be built once the town's population reaches 6500. When should the off-ramp be built?

2. The town historian is writing a newspaper article about a time when Decimal Point's population was only 100. Estimate when this was.

3. Refer to the two exponential models developed in Example 1:

$$P = 1006(1.016)^t \qquad P = 1000 \times 2^{\frac{t}{43.5}}$$

    a) Use both models to predict

        i) the town's population after 100 years

        ii) how long it will take for the town's population to reach 20 000

    b) Do these models generate predictions that are identical, quite close, or completely different? How would you account for any discrepancies?

B   Connect and Apply

For help with questions 4 and 5, refer to Example 2.

4. Suppose that the Lakeland Savings Bond group waives the early withdrawal penalty. How might this affect the investment decision for the town? Provide detailed information.

Reasoning and Proving

Representing   Selecting Tools

Problem Solving

Connecting   Reflecting

Communicating

5. Suppose two other investment options are available for Decimal Point's reserve fund:

Investment Option	Rural Ontario Investment Group	Muskoka Guaranteed Certificate
Interest Rate	$6\frac{1}{2}$% compounded semi-annually	6% compounded monthly
Conditions	no penalty	1% of initial principal penalty if withdrawn before 10 years

Should either of these investments be considered? Justify your reasoning.

6. Use Technology The table gives the surface area of seawater covered by an oil spill as a function of time.

Time (min)	Surface Area (m²)
0	0
1	2
2	4
3	7
4	11
5	14
6	29

a) Create a scatter plot of surface area versus time. Describe the shape of the curve.

b) Perform the following types of regression to model the data:

   i) linear

   ii) quadratic

   iii) exponential (omit time 0 for this regression)

   Record the equation for the line or curve of best fit in each case.

c) Assuming that the spill is spreading isotropically (equally in all directions), which model do you think makes the most sense for $t \geq 0$? Explain why.

d) Use the model that you chose in part c) to predict

   i) the size of the oil spill after 10 min

   ii) the length of time it will take for the spill to reach a diameter of 30 m

e) Describe any assumptions you must make.

7. A $1000 investment earns 8% interest, compounded quarterly.

a) Write an equation for the value of the investment as a function of time, in years.

b) Determine the value of the investment after 4 years.

c) How long will it take for the investment to double in value?

8. Refer to question 7. Suppose that a penalty for early withdrawal of 5% of the initial investment is applied if the withdrawal occurs within the first 4 years.

a) Write an equation for the adjusted value of the investment as a function of time.

b) Describe the effect this adjustment would have on the graph of the original function.

9. Use Technology

a) Prepare a cup of hot liquid, such as coffee, tea, or hot water. Carefully place the cup on a stable surface in a room at normal room temperature.

Reasoning and Proving

Representing — Selecting Tools

Problem Solving

Connecting — Reflecting

Communicating

b) Record the temperature of the liquid as it cools, in a table like the one shown. Collect several data points.

Time (min)	Temperature (°C)
0	
2	
4	

c) Create a scatter plot of temperature versus time. Describe the shape of the curve.

d) Create the following models for the data, using regression:

   i) quadratic

   ii) exponential

   Record the equation for each model.

e) Which of these is the better model? Justify your choice.

f) Use the model that you chose in part e) to estimate how long it will take for the liquid to cool to

   i) 40°C

   ii) 30°C

   iii) 0°C

   Justify your answers and state any assumptions you must make.

10. **Chapter Problem** Decimal Point is hosting Summer-Fest: a large outdoor concert to celebrate the start of summer. The headline act is a rising rock group from Australia.

> **Live, from Australia:**
>
> ## Koalarox!
>
> *Featuring*
> **Rocco Rox on lead guitar!**
> **Boom Boom Biff on drums!**
>
> **When:** July 1, 8:00 p.m.
>
> **Where:** Integer Island

During sound checks, the band's sound crew is responsible for setting various acoustic and electronic instruments to ensure a rich and balanced sound. The difference in two sound levels, β_1 and β_2, in decibels, is given by the logarithmic equation $\beta_2 - \beta_1 = 10 \log\left(\dfrac{I_2}{I_1}\right)$, where $\dfrac{I_2}{I_1}$ is the ratio of their intensities.

a) Biff's drum kit is miked to produce a sound level of 150 dB for the outdoor venue. The maximum output of Rocco's normal electric guitar amplifier is 120 dB. What is the ratio of the intensities of these instruments? Explain why Rocco's signal needs to be boosted by a concert amplifier.

b) After a few heavier songs, the band plans to slow things down a bit with a couple of power ballads. This means that Rocco will switch to his acoustic guitar, which is only one ten-thousandth as loud as his normally amplified electric guitar. By what factor should the sound crew reduce Biff's drums to balance them with Rocco's acoustic guitar?

CONNECTIONS

You first compared sound levels using the decibel scale in Chapter 6. Refer to Section 6.5.

✓ **Achievement Check**

11. **Use Technology** The table shows the population growth of rabbits living in a warren.

Time (months)	Number of Rabbits
0	16
1	18
2	21
3	24
4	32
5	37
6	41
7	50

CONNECTIONS

A warren is a den where rabbits live.

a) Create a scatter plot of rabbit population versus time.

b) Perform the following types of regression to model the data:
   i) linear
   ii) quadratic
   iii) exponential

   Record the equation for the line or curve of best fit in each case.

c) Assuming that the rabbit population had been steadily growing for several months before the collection of data, which model best fits the situation, and why?

d) Use the model to predict when the population will reach 100.

e) Do you think this trend will continue indefinitely? Explain why or why not.

12. a) Find some data on the Internet, or elsewhere, that could be modelled by one or more of the following:

    • a line of best fit

    • a quadratic curve of best fit

    • an exponential curve of best fit

   b) Describe the nature of the data.

   c) **Use Technology** Perform regression analysis for each type of curve. Record the equation in each case. How well does each line or curve fit the data?

   d) Which is the best model and why?

   e) Pose and solve two problems based on the data and your best model.

13. **Use Technology**

   a) Find some data on the Internet, or elsewhere, that could be modelled by a logistic curve.

   b) Describe the nature of the data.

   c) Perform logistical regression analysis. Record the equation. How well does each line or curve fit the data?

   d) Which is the best model and why?

   e) Pose and solve two problems based on the data and your best model.

14. Use your data from question 13. A piecewise linear function is a function made up of two or more connected line segments. Could the data be modelled using a piecewise linear function? If so, do so. If not, explain why not.

15. **Math Contest** A cyclist rides her bicycle over a route that is $\frac{1}{3}$ uphill, $\frac{1}{3}$ level, and $\frac{1}{3}$ downhill. If she covers the uphill part of the route at a rate of 16 km/h, and the level part at a rate of 24 km/h, what rate would she have to travel during the downhill part of the route in order to average 24 km/h for the entire route?

16. **Math Contest** A circle with radius $\sqrt{2}$ is centred at the point $(0, 0)$ on a Cartesian plane. What is the area of the smaller segment cut from the circle by the chord from $(-1, 1)$ to $(1, 1)$?

17. **Math Contest** The quantities x, y, and z are positive, and $xy = \frac{z}{4}$. If x is increased by 50%, and y is decreased by 25%, by what percent is z increased or decreased?

CONNECTIONS

Certain types of growth phenomena follow a pattern that can be modelled by a logistic function, which takes the form $f(x) = \dfrac{c}{1 + ae^{-bx}}$, where a, b, and c are constants related to the conditions of the phenomenon, and e is a special irrational number, like π. Its value is approximately 2.718. The logistic curve is sometimes called the S-curve because of its shape.

Logistic functions occur in diverse areas, such as biology, environmental studies, and business, in situations where resources for growth are limited and/or where conditions for growth vary over time.

Go to the *Advanced Functions 12* page on the McGraw-Hill Ryerson Web site and follow the links to learn more about logistic functions and logistic curves.

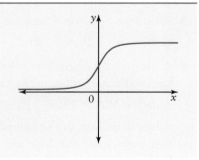

7.1 Equivalent Forms of Exponential Equations

1. Write each as a power of 4.

   a) 64   **b)** 4   **c)** $\dfrac{1}{16}$ **d)** $(\sqrt[3]{8})^5$

2. Write each as a power of 5.

   a) 20   **b)** 0.8

3. Solve each equation. Check your answers using graphing technology.

   a) $3^{5x} = 27^{x-1}$ **b)** $8^{2x+1} = 32^{x-3}$

7.2 Techniques for Solving Exponential Equations

4. A 50-mg sample of cobalt-60 decays to 40 mg after 1.6 min.

   a) Determine the half-life of cobalt-60.

   b) How long will it take for the sample to decay to 5% of its initial amount?

5. Solve exactly.

   a) $3^{x-2} = 5^x$ **b)** $2^{k-2} = 3^{k+1}$

6. **Use Technology** Refer to question 5.

   a) Use a calculator to find an approximate value for each solution, correct to three decimal places.

   b) Use graphing technology to check your solutions.

7. Solve each equation. Check for extraneous roots.

   a) $4^{2x} - 4^x - 20 = 0$ **b)** $2^x + 12(2)^{-x} = 7$

8. A computer, originally purchased for $2000, loses value according to the exponential equation $V(t) = 2000\left(\dfrac{1}{2}\right)^{\frac{t}{h}}$, where V is the value, in dollars, of the computer at any time, t, in years, after purchase and h represents the half-life, in years, of the value of the computer. After 1 year, the computer has a value of approximately $1516.

   a) What is the half-life of the value of the computer?

   b) How long will it take for the computer to be worth 10% of its purchase price?

7.3 Product and Quotient Laws of Logarithms

9. Evaluate, using the laws of logarithms.

   a) $\log_6 8 + \log_6 27$

   b) $\log_4 128 - \log_4 8$

   c) $2 \log 2 + 2 \log 5$

   d) $2 \log 3 + \log\left(\dfrac{25}{2}\right)$

10. Write as a single logarithm.

    a) $\log_7 8 + \log_7 4 - \log_7 16$

    b) $2 \log a + \log (3b) - \dfrac{1}{2} \log c$

11. Write as a sum or difference of logarithms. Simplify, if possible.

    a) $\log (a^2bc)$ **b)** $\log\left(\dfrac{k}{\sqrt{m}}\right)$

12. Simplify and state any restrictions on the variables.

    a) $\log (2m + 6) - \log (m^2 - 9)$

    b) $\log (x^2 + 2x - 15) - \log (x^2 - 7x + 12)$

7.4 Techniques for Solving Logarithmic Equations

13. Solve.

    a) $\log (2x + 10) = 2$ **b)** $1 - \log (2x) = 0$

14. Solve $\log_2 x + \log_2 (x + 2) = 3$. Check for extraneous roots.

15. **Use Technology** Check your answer to question 14 using graphing technology.

16. When you drink a cup of coffee or a glass of cola, or when you eat a chocolate bar, the percent, P, of caffeine remaining in your bloodstream is related to the elapsed time, t, in hours, by $t = 5\left(\dfrac{\log P}{\log 0.5}\right)$.

    a) How long will it take for the amount of caffeine to drop to 20% of the amount consumed?

    b) Suppose you drink a cup of coffee at 9:00 a.m. What percent of the caffeine will remain in your body at noon?

7.5 Making Connections: Mathematical Modelling With Exponential and Logarithmic Equations

17. A savings bond offers interest at a rate of 6.6%, compounded semi-annually. Suppose that a $500 bond is purchased.

a) Write an equation for the value of the investment as a function of time, in years.

b) Determine the value of the investment after 5 years.

c) How long will it take for the investment to double in value?

d) Describe how the shape of the graph of this function would change if

   i) a bonus of 1% of the principal were added after 3 years had passed

   ii) the size of the initial investment were doubled

▪ PROBLEM WRAP-UP

CHAPTER

The annual Summer-Fest concert in Decimal Point has been gaining popularity. Word of the combination of excellent performing acts and a picturesque concert site has spread quickly, even to some of the large cities in the south. Attendance figures at Summer-Fest are shown in the table.

Year	Number of Paid Admissions
2000	450
2001	512
2002	606
2003	718
2004	815
2005	956
2006	1092
2007	1220

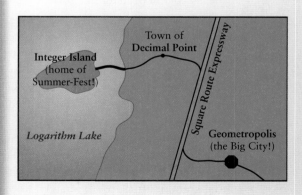

a) Create a scatter plot of the data.

b) Use regression to determine a curve of best fit. Explain why your choice of curve makes sense for this situation.

c) How many fans do you expect to attend the

   i) 2010 concert?

   ii) 2015 concert?

d) Integer Island has certain restrictions due to the physical limitations of the site:

- The concert venue has a capacity of 5000 people.
- Parking facilities can accommodate no more than 1800 vehicles.

Predict when the concert organizers will have to consider changing the location of Summer-Fest. Use mathematical reasoning to support your answer.

e) What other measures could be taken to keep Summer-Fest on Integer Island? Describe what you could do, as an urban planner, to preserve this popular northern tradition. Use mathematical reasoning to support your plans and to predict for how much longer Decimal Point can put off finding a new concert venue, without having to turn any fans away at the gate. Discuss any assumptions you must make.

For questions 1 to 4, select the best answer.

1. $\sqrt{8}$ is equivalent to

   A 4

   B $2^{\frac{2}{3}}$

   C $2^{\frac{3}{2}}$

   D $(2^2)^3$

2. What is the solution to $2^{x+1} = 4^x$?

   A 1

   B 2

   C 4

   D -1

3. Which is the product law of logarithms?

   A $\log a \times \log b = \log (ab)$

   B $\log a \times \log b = \log (a + b)$

   C $\log a + \log b = \log (a + b)$

   D $\log a + \log b = \log (ab)$

4. The expression $\log_2 5 + \log_2 10 - \log_2 25$ is equal to

   A $\log 2$

   B 0

   C 1

   D 2

5. Write as a single logarithm, and then evaluate.

   $\log_3 6 + \log_3 4 - \log_3 \left(\dfrac{8}{3}\right)$

6. Solve.

   a) $8^{x+2} = 4^{2x-1}$

   b) $3^x = 81^{x-4}$

   c) $\log 2 = \log (x + 5) - 1$

   d) $\log 8 = \log (x - 2) + 1$

7. **Use Technology** Check your answers to question 6 using graphing technology.

8. Consider the graphing calculator screens shown.

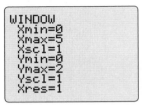

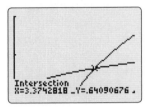

   a) What equation is being solved?

   b) What is the solution? Explain how you know.

   c) Verify this solution using algebraic reasoning.

9. A technician places 50 mg of a certain radioactive substance into a laboratory chamber. After 10 min, there are 41 mg remaining.

   a) Determine the half-life of the substance.

   b) How long will it take for the material to decay to 1% of its initial amount?

10. The carbon fusion cycle is one way that a star is fuelled. Through a series of processes, carbon atoms combine with hydrogen to form other elements such as nitrogen and oxygen, before returning back to carbon. Throughout this cycle, energy is released. In one step of the carbon fusion cycle, nitrogen-13 spontaneously decays into carbon-13. Suppose that in a laboratory simulation, a sample of nitrogen-13 is measured to be 10% of its initial amount after approximately 33 min. Determine the half-life of nitrogen-13.

11. a) Solve $2 \log (x - 1) = \log (x + 1)$ and identify any extraneous roots.

b) Check your answer using graphing technology.

12. Examine the scatter plot shown.

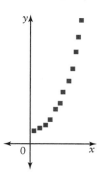

a) Could a quadratic curve of best fit be drawn through these points? Explain why or why not.

b) Could an exponential curve of best fit be drawn through these points? Explain why or why not.

c) Describe a scenario that these data might fit, in which the better model is

i) exponential

ii) quadratic

Justify your answers in each case.

13. Use Technology A cup of tea is placed on a counter and allowed to cool. The table shows the temperature of the tea over time.

Time (min)	Temperature (°C)
0	98
2	88
4	79
6	72
8	66
10	62
12	58

a) Create a scatter plot of temperature versus time.

b) Create a quadratic model to fit the data.

c) Create an exponential model to fit the data.

d) Which model is better, and why?

e) Use the better model to

i) predict the temperature of the tea after 15 min

ii) predict how long will it take for the tea to reach 38°C

f) Describe any assumptions you must make.

TASK

Make Your Own Slide Rule

Before the invention of the electronic calculator, solutions to long multiplication or division questions were tedious and error prone. John Napier (1550–1617) invented common logarithms, based on the exponent rules, as an aid to calculation. Using logarithms, addition replaces multiplication and subtraction replaces division, making calculations much easier! William Oughtred (1575–1660) invented a mechanical calculator called a slide rule to speed up the work with Napier's logarithms.

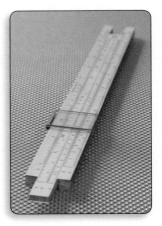

In this task, you will make your own slide rule and demonstrate how to use it to perform multiplication and division.

x	log x	30 log x
1	0	0
2	0.30	9.03
3		
4		
5		
6		
7		
8		
9		
10		

a) Copy and complete the table. Use a calculator and round to two decimal places. The first two entries have been done for you.

b) Cut two strips of cardstock, 3 cm wide and 30 cm long. Label the left end of each strip **1** and the right end of each strip **10**.

c) Along the bottom edge of one strip, carefully measure the distances in column three of your table, starting at the left edge each time. Label each distance with the value of *x* from column one. The distance from 1 to each value of *x* is now proportional to log *x*.

d) Repeat step c) along the top edge of the other strip.

e) You are now ready to use your slide rule. Slide the first strip along the second strip until the 1 on the first strip is above a number on the second strip. Now read along the first strip to any whole number. What number appears on the second strip below the whole number on the first strip? Write an explanation in your notebook identifying what mathematical operation you have performed, and why it worked.

f) Refine your slide rule by adding another logarithmic scale between the 1 and the 2 on each strip. Do the same between the 2 and the 3.

g) Explain in detail how to perform the operations of multiplication and division using your slide rule. Include several worked examples.

h) Use the Internet to investigate how slide rules were used to find square roots and cube roots. Explain your findings using the laws of logarithms.

Chapter **8**

Combining Functions

Throughout this course, you have learned advanced techniques for interpreting a variety of functions. Understanding functional relationships between variables is a cornerstone to further study at the university level in disciplines such as engineering, physical sciences, business, and social sciences.

Relationships between variables can become increasingly complex and may involve a combination of two or more functions. In this chapter, you will learn techniques to analyse various combinations of functions and solve real-world problems requiring these techniques.

By the end of this chapter, you will

- determine, through investigation using graphing technology, key features of the graphs of functions created by adding, subtracting, multiplying, or dividing functions, and describe factors that affect these properties (D2.1)
- recognize real-world applications of combinations of functions, and solve related problems graphically (D2.2)
- determine, through investigation, and explain some properties of functions formed by adding, subtracting, multiplying, and dividing general functions (D2.3)
- determine the composition of two functions numerically and graphically, with technology, for functions represented in a variety of ways, and interpret the composition of two functions in real-world applications (D2.4)
- determine algebraically the composition of two functions, verify that $f(g(x))$ is not always equal to $g(f(x))$, and state the domain and the range of the composition of two functions (D2.5)

- solve problems involving the composition of two functions, including problems arising from real-world applications (D2.6)
- demonstrate, by giving examples for functions represented in a variety of ways, the property that the composition of a function and its inverse function maps a number onto itself (D2.7)
- make connections, through investigation using technology, between transformations of simple functions $f(x)$ and the composition of these functions with a linear function of the form $g(x) = A(x + B)$ (D2.8)
- compare, through investigation using a variety of tools and strategies, the characteristics of various functions (D3.1)
- solve graphically and numerically equations and inequalities whose solutions are not accessible by standard algebraic techniques (D3.2)
- solve problems, using a variety of tools and strategies, including problems arising from real-world applications, by reasoning with functions and by applying concepts and procedures involving functions (D3.3)

Prerequisite Skills

Identify Linear, Quadratic, and Exponential Growth Models

Use the three patterns shown to answer questions 1 to 3.

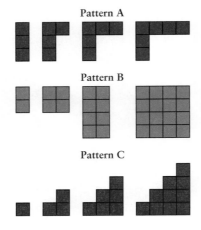

Pattern A

Pattern B

Pattern C

1. a) Build or draw the next stage in each pattern.

   b) Identify the nature of growth for each pattern as linear, quadratic, exponential, or other. Justify your reasoning in each case.

2. a) Create a scatter plot of the total number, C, of tiles as a function of the stage number, n, for each growing pattern.

   b) Do the shapes of the graphs confirm your answers to question 1b)? Explain why or why not.

3. Determine an equation relating C and n for each pattern in question 1. Verify that each equation holds true for the given pattern.

Graph and Analyse Power Functions

4. Sketch a graph of each power function and identify its domain and range.

   a) $y = x$

   b) $y = x^2$

   c) $y = x^3$

   d) $y = x^4$

5. Identify whether each function in question 4 is even or odd.

> ### CONNECTIONS
> You studied power functions in Chapter 1.
>
> Recall that an even function has line symmetry about the y-axis, and an odd function has point symmetry about the origin.
>
>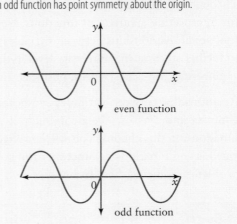
>
> even function
>
> odd function

6. Use Technology Verify your answers to question 5 using graphing technology.

Graph and Analyse Rational Functions

7. Sketch a graph of each rational function and identify its domain and range.

   a) $f(x) = \dfrac{1}{x}$

   b) $g(x) = \dfrac{1}{x - 4}$

8. Simplify each rational function. State any restrictions on the variables.

   a) $u(x) = \dfrac{x - 2}{x^2 - 4}$

   b) $v(x) = \dfrac{x^2 - x - 6}{x + 2}$

9. Refer to question 8. For each function,

   i) identify the domain and range

   ii) graph the function

   iii) identify any asymptotes or holes in the graph

10. Use Technology Verify your answers to question 9 using graphing technology.

11. Match each distance-time graph with the scenario that it best represents. Give reasons for your answers.

Graph

a)

b)

c)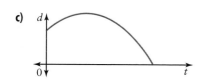

d)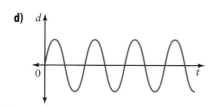

Scenario

i) the displacement of the tip of a metronome

ii) a rocket's height after being launched from a raised platform

iii) a girl's displacement on a swing after receiving a push from her big brother

iv) the height of a glider drifting to the ground

12. Refer to question 11. Suggest a reasonable scale and unit of measure for each scenario. Explain your choices.

Inverses

13. Find the inverse of each function.

a) $f(x) = x - 2$

b) $g(x) = 4x + 3$

c) $h(x) = x^2 - 5$

d) $k(x) = \dfrac{1}{x + 1}$

14. Which inverses in question 13 are functions? Explain.

PROBLEM

As a recent graduate of the business program of an Ontario university, you have been hired by Funky Stuff, a company that manufactures games and toys for kids of all ages. As a member of the marketing department, you will be given a number of scenarios and asked to identify marketing and pricing strategies to maximize profits for the company. Your understanding of functions and how they can be combined will be very useful as you begin your business career.

CHAPTER

Sums and Differences of Functions

Have you ever swum in a wave pool? If you have, you may have noticed that in some spots the waves can get quite high, while in other spots there is very little wave motion. Why do you suppose this happens? A sinusoidal function can be used to model a single wave, but when there are two or more waves interfering, the mathematics involved can get a little deeper.

Functions can be combined in a variety of ways to describe all sorts of complicated relationships. In many cases, such as the interference of two sine waves, addition and subtraction can be applied.

Investigate | **How can you represent the addition of functions in various ways?**

Tools

- coloured tiles or linking cubes
- graphing calculator or graphing software

Examine the pattern of tiles shown.

Stage 1   Stage 2   Stage 3   Stage 4

1. Copy the table. Complete the first four rows for the coloured tiles. Leave the last column blank for now.

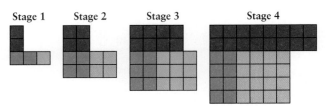

Stage Number, n	Blue Tiles, Y_1	Green Tiles, Y_2	Yellow Tiles, Y_3	
1				
2				
3				
4				
⋮	⋮	⋮	⋮	⋮
n				

2. a) Predict the number of each coloured tile required to build the next stage in the sequence.

b) Build or draw the next stage.

3. Examine the patterns in each tile column.

a) Identify which colour of tile is growing

   i) linearly

   ii) quadratically

   iii) exponentially

b) Write an equation to represent each coloured tile pattern in the last row of the table.

4. The ⬚superposition principle⬚ states that the sum of two or more functions can be found by adding the ordinates (*y*-coordinates) of the functions at each abscissa (*x*-coordinate).

Define Y_4 as the sum of Y_1, Y_2, and Y_3. Use the superposition principle to graph Y_4 on a graphing calculator.

First, use the **Y=** editor to enter the three functions as **Y1**, **Y2**, and **Y3**, respectively.

Then, do the following for **Y4**:

- Press VARS and cursor over to the **Y-VARS** menu.
- Select **1:Function...** and then **1:Y1**.
- Press + and repeat to enter the other functions, as shown.
- Change the line style of **Y4** to heavy.

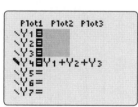

Use the window settings shown. Press GRAPH to view all four functions.

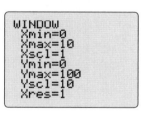

5. a) Determine the values of Y_4 when $x = 1$, $x = 2$, $x = 3$, and $x = 4$.

- Press 2nd [CALC] to display the **CALCULATE** menu, and select **1:value**.
- Enter one of the *x*-values and press ENTER.
- Use the up and down cursor keys to move from one graph to another, if necessary.

What meaning do these numbers have with respect to the growing pattern of tiles?

b) Complete the last column of the table. Use the heading "Total Number of Tiles, $Y_1 + Y_2 + Y_3$," and enter the values. Compare these values to those obtained in part a). Explain this result.

c) In the last row of the last column, write an equation to model the total number of tiles in any stage, *n*, of the pattern.

6. Reflect

a) View the graph representing the total tiles, Y_4, using the window settings shown.

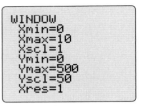

```
WINDOW
 Xmin=0
 Xmax=10
 Xscl=1
 Ymin=0
 Ymax=500
 Yscl=50
 Xres=1
```

Describe the shape of this graph. Explain why the graph looks the way it does.

b) Summarize the ways in which the total tiles pattern relationship is represented in this activity.

| Example 1 | **Apply the Superposition Principle** |

Determine an equation for the function $h(x) = f(x) + g(x)$ in each case. Then, graph $h(x)$ and state the domain and range of the function.

a) $f(x) = x^2$, $g(x) = 3$

b) $f(x) = x^2$, $g(x) = x$

Solution

a) An equation for $h(x)$ can be found by adding the expressions for $f(x)$ and $g(x)$.

$$h(x) = f(x) + g(x)$$
$$= x^2 + 3$$

To produce the graph of $h(x)$ using the superposition principle, first graph $f(x)$ and $g(x)$ on the same set of axes. Then, graph the sum of these functions, $h(x)$, by adding the y-coordinates at each point.

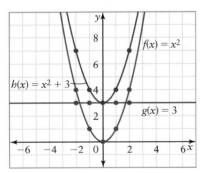

x	$f(x) = x^2$	$g(x) = 3$	$h(x) = x^2 + 3$
-2	4	3	$4 + 3 = 7$
-1	1	3	$1 + 3 = 4$
0	0	3	$0 + 3 = 3$
1	1	3	$1 + 3 = 4$
2	4	3	$4 + 3 = 7$

Note that this superposition can be thought of as a *constant* vertical translation of the parabola $y = x^2$ to produce the parabola $y = x^2 + 3$.

From the graph or the equation, it is clear that the domain of $h(x)$ is $\{x \in \mathbb{R}\}$ and the range is $\{y \in \mathbb{R}, y \geq 3\}$.

b) $h(x) = f(x) + g(x)$
$$= x^2 + x$$

First, graph $f(x)$ and $g(x)$ on the same set of axes.

Then, graph the sum of these functions, $h(x)$, by adding the y-coordinates at each point.

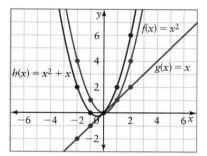

x	$f(x) = x^2$	$g(x) = x$	$h(x) = x^2 + x$
-2	4	-2	$4 + (-2) = 2$
-1	1	-1	$1 + (-1) = 0$
0	0	0	$0 + 0 = 0$
1	1	1	$1 + 1 = 2$
2	4	2	$4 + 2 = 6$

Note that this superposition can be thought of as a *variable* vertical translation of the parabola $y = x^2$ to produce the function $y = x^2 + x$.

The domain of $h(x)$ is $x \in \mathbb{R}$.

To identify the range, first find the vertex, which is the minimum point, since the parabola opens upward.

Method 1: *Apply Algebraic and Graphical Reasoning*

Locate the x-coordinate of the vertex, and then find the corresponding value of y at that point.

$y = x^2 + x$
$\quad = x(x + 1)$ Write in factored form.

The zeros of this function occur when $x = 0$ and $x + 1 = 0$, or $x = -1$. The zeros are 0 and -1. The minimum value will occur midway between these x-coordinates, due to symmetry.

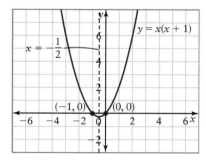

The minimum value occurs when $x = -\dfrac{1}{2}$. Evaluate y at this point.

$$y = x^2 + x$$
$$= \left(-\dfrac{1}{2}\right)^2 + \left(-\dfrac{1}{2}\right)$$
$$= \dfrac{1}{4} - \dfrac{1}{2}$$
$$= -\dfrac{1}{4}$$

The minimum value of y is $-\dfrac{1}{4}$. Therefore, the range of $h(x)$ is $\left\{y \in \mathbb{R}, y \geq -\dfrac{1}{4}\right\}$.

Method 2: *Use a Graphing Calculator*

Graph $h(x) = x^2 + x$. Use the **Minimum** operation.

- Press (2nd) [CALC] to display the **CALCULATE** menu, and then select **3:minimum**.
- Move the cursor to locations for the left bound, right bound, and guess, pressing (ENTER) after each.

  The minimum value of y is $-\dfrac{1}{4}$.

  Therefore, the range of $h(x)$ is $\left\{y \in \mathbb{R}, y \geq -\dfrac{1}{4}\right\}$.

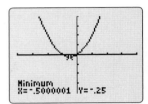

The superposition principle can be extended to the difference of two functions, because subtracting is the same as adding the opposite.

Example 2 | **The Profit Function**

Student Council is selling T-shirts to raise money for new volleyball equipment. There is a fixed cost of $200 for producing the T-shirts, plus a variable cost of $5 per T-shirt made. Council has decided to sell the T-shirts for $8 each.

a) Write an equation to represent
- the total cost, C, as a function of the number, n, of T-shirts produced
- the revenue, R, as a function of the number, n, of T-shirts produced

  Then, graph these functions on the same set of axes. Identify the point of intersection and explain the meaning of its coordinates.

b) Profit, P, is the difference between revenue and expenses. Develop an algebraic and a graphical model for the profit function.

c) Under what circumstances will Student Council lose money? make money?

d) Identify the domain and range of the cost, revenue, and profit functions in the context of this problem.

Solution

a) The total cost of producing the T-shirts is the sum of the fixed cost and the variable cost:

$C(n) = 200 + 5n$

The revenue is $8 per T-shirt multiplied by the number of T-shirts sold:

$R(n) = 8n$

Use a graphing calculator to graph these functions on the same set of axes. Use number sense to choose appropriate window settings.

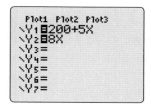  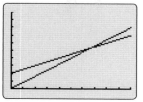

Determine the point of intersection.

Method 1: *Use Pencil and Paper*

To find the point of intersection, solve the following linear system.

$C(n) = 200 + 5n$
$R(n) = 8n$

The expressions on the right side above will have the same value when $R = C$.

$8n = 200 + 5n$

$3n = 200$

$n = \dfrac{200}{3}$

Find the corresponding value of R.

$R = 8n$ Substitute into either equation. Pick the easier one.

$\quad = 8\left(\dfrac{200}{3}\right)$

$\quad = \dfrac{1600}{3}$

The point of intersection is $\left(\dfrac{200}{3}, \dfrac{1600}{3}\right)$, or $\left(66\dfrac{2}{3}, 533\dfrac{1}{3}\right)$.

Method 2: *Use a Graphing Calculator*

Use the **Intersect** operation.

- Press (2nd) [CALC] to display the **CALCULATE** menu, and then select **5:intersect**.

- Use the cursor keys to select the first relation, the second relation, and guess, pressing (ENTER) after each.

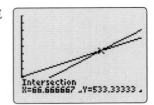

The point of intersection is $(66.\overline{6}, 533.\overline{3})$, or $\left(66\frac{2}{3}, 533\frac{1}{3}\right)$.

This means that if Student Council sells approximately 67 T-shirts, then the revenue and the cost will be equal, at approximately $533. This is known as the **break-even point**.

b) Profit is the difference between revenue and expenses.

$$
\begin{aligned}
P(n) &= R(n) - C(n) \\
&= 8n - (200 + 5n) \\
&= 8n - 200 - 5n \\
&= 3n - 200
\end{aligned}
$$

This equation represents the profit as a function of the number of T-shirts sold.

Use the superposition principle to develop a graphical model. Adjust the window settings to view the domain of interest.

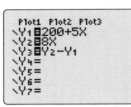 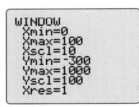 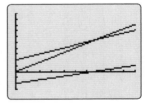

c) Student Council will lose money if profit is less than zero. This is modelled by the section of the graph of $P(n)$ that appears below the horizontal axis. Student Council will make money when $P(n) > 0$, or if more than 67 T-shirts are sold.

d) Although each linear function extends to the left of the vertical axis, it has no meaning for $n < 0$, because it is impossible to sell a negative number of T-shirts. Inspection of the graphs reveals the domain and range for these functions in the context of this problem.

Function	Practical Domain	Practical Range
$C(n) = 200 + 5n$	$\{n \in \mathbb{Z}, n \geq 0\}$	$\{C \in \mathbb{Z}, C \geq 200\}$
$R(n) = 8n$	$\{n \in \mathbb{Z}, n \geq 0\}$	$\{R \in \mathbb{Z}, R \geq 0\}$
$P(n) = 3n - 200$	$\{n \in \mathbb{Z}, n \geq 0\}$	$\{P \in \mathbb{Z}, P \geq -200\}$

Note that n is restricted to integer values greater than or equal to zero, while each of the dependent variables has different restrictions.

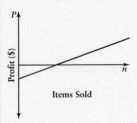

KEY CONCEPTS

- Some combined functions are formed by adding or subtracting two or more functions.

- The superposition principle states that the sum of two functions can be found by adding the y-coordinates at each point along the x-axis.

- The superposition principle also applies to the difference of two functions.

- The domain of the sum or difference of functions is the domain common to the component functions.

Communicate Your Understanding

C1 a) Explain how you can produce the graph of the combined function $y = f(x) + g(x)$ from the graph shown, where $f(x) = x$ and $g(x) = -2x + 5$.

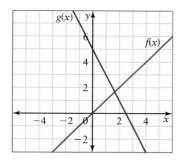

b) Explain how you can produce the graph of the combined function $y = f(x) - g(x)$.

C2 Refer to Example 1, part b). Explain what is meant by the term *variable vertical translation* in this situation.

C3 Refer to Example 2.

a) Why is it necessary to restrict the domain of n to integers greater than or equal to zero?

b) Why is this not necessary for the dependent variables, C and P?

C4 When dealing with a cost-revenue system of equations, what is meant by the break-even point? Why is this point important? Illustrate your answer with a sketch.

For help with questions 1 and 2, refer to the Investigate.

Use the pattern of tiles shown to answer questions 1 and 2.

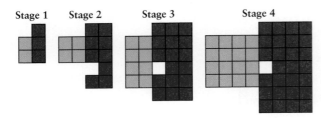

Stage 1   Stage 2   Stage 3   Stage 4

1. a) Identify the part of the pattern that is growing

  i) linearly

  ii) quadratically

  iii) exponentially

  b) Develop an equation for each of these parts, and verify that each equation holds true.

2. a) Develop an equation that gives the total number of tiles for each stage.

  b) Use this equation to predict the total number of tiles required for

  i) the fifth stage

  ii) the sixth stage

  c) Check your prediction by extending the model using concrete materials or a diagram.

For help with questions 3 to 9, refer to Examples 1 and 2.

3. For each pair of functions, find

  i) $y = f(x) + g(x)$

  ii) $y = f(x) - g(x)$

  iii) $y = g(x) - f(x)$

  a) $f(x) = 5x$ and $g(x) = x + 7$

  b) $f(x) = -2x + 5$ and $g(x) = -x + 9$

  c) $f(x) = x^2 + 4$ and $g(x) = 1$

  d) $f(x) = -3x^2 + 4x$ and $g(x) = 3x - 7$

4. Let $f(x) = 4x + 3$ and $g(x) = 3x - 2$.

  a) Determine an equation for the function $h(x) = f(x) + g(x)$. Then, find $h(2)$.

  b) Determine an equation for the function $j(x) = f(x) - g(x)$. Then, find $j(-1)$.

  c) Determine an equation for the function $k(x) = g(x) - f(x)$. Then, find $k(0)$.

5. Let $f(x) = -4x^2 + 5$ and $g(x) = 2x - 3$.

  a) Determine an equation for the function $h(x) = f(x) + g(x)$. Then, find $h(-3)$.

  b) Determine an equation for the function $j(x) = f(x) - g(x)$. Then, find $j(0)$.

  c) Determine an equation for the function $k(x) = g(x) - f(x)$. Then, find $k(3)$.

6. Copy each graph of $f(x)$ and $g(x)$. Then, apply the superposition principle to graph $f(x) + g(x)$. Give the domain and range of $f(x) + g(x)$.

a)

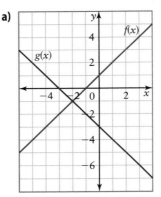

b)

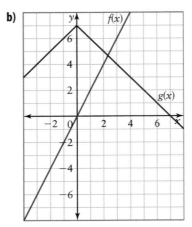

7. For each graph in question 6, use the superposition principle to graph $y = g(x) - f(x)$.

8. Let $f(x) = 2^x$ and $g(x) = 3$.

a) Graph each of the following.

   i) $y = f(x) + g(x)$

   ii) $y = f(x) - g(x)$

   iii) $y = g(x) - f(x)$

b) Explain how you could also produce each of these combined functions by applying transformations to the graph of $f(x) = 2^x$.

c) Give the domain and the range of each combined function.

9. Let $f(x) = \sin x$ and $g(x) = \log x$. Work in radians.

a) Sketch these functions on the same set of axes.

b) Sketch a graph of $y = f(x) + g(x)$.

c) Sketch a graph of $y = f(x) - g(x)$.

d) **Use Technology** Check your answers using graphing technology.

B **Connect and Apply**

For help with questions 10 and 11, refer to Example 2.

10. A hotdog vendor has fixed costs of $120 per day to operate, plus a variable cost of $1 per hotdog sold. He earns $2.50 per hotdog sold, in revenue. The maximum number of hotdogs that he can sell in a day is 250.

Reasoning and Proving • Representing • Selecting Tools • Problem Solving • Connecting • Reflecting • Communicating

a) Write an equation to represent

   i) the total cost, C, as a function of the number, h, of hotdogs sold

   ii) the revenue, R, as a function of the number, h, of hotdogs sold

b) Graph $C(h)$ and $R(h)$ on the same set of axes.

c) Identify the break-even point and explain what its coordinates mean.

d) Develop an algebraic and a graphical model for the profit function, $P(h) = R(h) - C(h)$.

e) Identify the domain and range in the context of this problem for $C(h)$, $R(h)$, and $P(h)$.

f) What is the maximum daily profit the vendor can earn?

11. Refer to question 10. The hotdog vendor has found a way to improve the efficiency of his operation that will allow him to either reduce his fixed cost to $100 per day *or* reduce his variable cost to $0.90 per hotdog.

a) Which of these two options has the most favourable effect on

   i) the break-even point?

   ii) the potential maximum daily profit?

b) What advice would you give the hotdog vendor?

12. An alternating current–direct current (AC-DC) voltage signal is made up of the following two components, each measured in volts (V):

$$V_{AC} = 10\sin t \qquad\qquad V_{DC} = 15$$

a) Sketch graphs of these functions on the same set of axes. Work in radians.

b) Graph the combined function $V_{AC} + V_{DC}$.

c) Identify the domain and range of $V_{AC} + V_{DC}$.

d) Use the range of the combined function to determine the following values of this voltage signal:

   i) minimum

   ii) maximum

   iii) average

13. **Use Technology** Consider the combined function $T(x) = f(x) + g(x) + h(x)$, where $f(x) = 2^x$, $g(x) = 2x$, and $h(x) = x^2$.

a) How is this function related to the total tiles pattern in the Investigate at the beginning of this section?

b) Graph $f(x)$, $g(x)$, and $h(x)$ on the same set of axes. Use colours or different line styles to easily distinguish the curves.

c) Graph the combined function $T(x)$.

d) Adjust the viewing window to explore what happens as the x- and y-values are increased by large quantities. The function $T(x)$ appears to converge with one of the three component functions. Which one is it?

e) Explain the result in part d) by considering the rates of change of the component functions.

14. a) Is $f(x) + g(x) = g(x) + f(x)$ true for all functions $f(x)$ and $g(x)$? Use examples to support your answer.

b) Is $f(x) - g(x) = g(x) - f(x)$ true for all functions $f(x)$ and $g(x)$? Use examples to support your answer.

c) What can you conclude about the commutative property of the sum of two functions? Does it hold true? What about the difference of two functions?

Reasoning and Proving
Representing — **Selecting Tools**
Problem Solving
Connecting — Reflecting
Communicating

15. **Use Technology**

a) Graph the function $f(x) = \sin x$ using *The Geometer's Sketchpad*® or a graphing calculator. Work in radians.

b) If you are using *The Geometer's Sketchpad*®, create a parameter c and set its initial value to zero. If you are using a graphing calculator, store the value zero in variable C.

c) Graph the function $g(x) = \sin(x - c)$. Explain how $f(x)$ and $g(x)$ are related when $c = 0$.

d) Predict the shape of $h(x) = f(x) + g(x)$. Sketch a graph of your prediction. Graph the function $h(x)$ and check your prediction. Use line colouring and/or bold to distinguish the graphs.

e) Give the domain and range of $h(x)$.

f) Predict the shape of $h(x)$ when the value of c is changed to each of these values:

i) $\dfrac{\pi}{2}$ ii) π iii) 2π

g) Adjust the value of c to check your predictions. Give the domain and range of $h(x)$ in each case. If you are using *The Geometer's Sketchpad*®, you can use the motion controller to view the effects of continuously varying the value of c.

h) Explain how these results may help explain the wave action of wave pools.

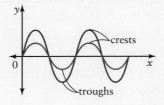
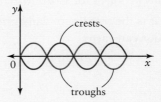

16. Let $f(x) = x + 5$ and $g(x) = x + 2$.

a) Write an expression for $-g(x)$.

b) Graph $f(x)$ and $-g(x)$ on the same set of axes.

c) Add these functions to produce $f(x) + [-g(x)]$.

d) Graph $f(x)$ and $g(x)$ together on another set of axes.

e) Subtract these functions to produce $f(x) - g(x)$. Compare this result to the one obtained in part c).

f) Explain how this illustrates that the superposition principle works for subtracting functions.

17. Refer to question 16. Develop an algebraic argument that illustrates the same concept.

Reasoning and Proving

Representing · Selecting Tools

Problem Solving

Connecting · Reflecting

Communicating

18. Chapter Problem The annual operating costs for Funky Stuff's Game Division are summarized in the table.

Operating Costs	
Fixed Costs	**Variable Costs (per game)**
Rent: $12 000	Material: $6
Taxes: $3 000	Labour: $9
Utilities: $5 000	
TOTAL:	TOTAL:

a) What are the total fixed costs? Graph this as a function of the number of games, and explain the shape of the graph. Call this function Y_1.

b) What are the total variable costs? Graph this as a function of the number of games, and explain the shape of the graph. Call this function Y_2.

c) Use the superposition principle to graph $Y_3 = Y_1 + Y_2$. Explain what this function represents.

d) The revenue earned from sales is $20 per game. Graph this as a function of the number of games, and explain the shape of the graph. Call this function Y_4.

e) Graph Y_3 and Y_4 on the same set of axes. Identify the point of intersection and explain the meaning of its coordinates. Why is this called the break-even point?

f) Use the superposition principle to graph $Y_5 = Y_4 - Y_3$. What does this function represent?

g) Explain the significance of Y_5

i) to the left of the x-intercept

ii) at the x-intercept

iii) to the right of the x-intercept

h) Describe what you expect to happen to the position of the break-even point if the game price is

i) increased

ii) decreased

Support your reasoning with graphs. Discuss any assumptions you must make.

✓ Achievement Check

19. Let $Y_1 = x^2$ and $Y_2 = 2$. Use graphs, numbers, and words, to determine

a) the function $Y_3 = Y_1 + Y_2$

b) the range of Y_3

20. Use Technology Let $f(x) = \tan x$ and $g(x) = x$.

a) Use graphing technology to graph $f(x)$ and $g(x)$ on the same set of axes. Work in radians.

b) Predict the shape of $h(x) = f(x) + g(x)$. Sketch a graph of your prediction.

c) Use graphing technology to check your prediction.

d) Hide $f(x)$ so that only $g(x)$ and $h(x)$ are visible. How many intersection points do there appear to be? You may need to adjust the viewing window.

e) Describe what you notice about where the line $g(x) = x$ intersects the graph of $h(x)$. Consider the curvature (up versus down) of $h(x)$. Explain why this is so.

CONNECTIONS

A point on a graph where the curvature changes from concave up to concave down, or vice versa, is called a *point of inflection*.

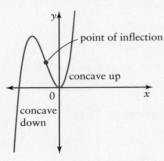

You will learn more about points of inflection and their significance if you study calculus.

---

21. Refer to question 20. Repeat the analysis for $g(x) = -x$.

22. Can the superposition principle be extended to the multiplication or division of two functions? Carry out an investigation using examples of your choice. Summarize your findings.

23. Use an example to help you generate a hypothesis about whether the sum of two even functions is even, odd, or neither. Verify algebraically with a second pair of functions. (Use at least three different types of functions, drawn from polynomial, trigonometric, exponential/logarithmic, and rational). Illustrate your results with graphs.

24. Math Contest Given a polynomial $f(x)$ of degree 2, where $f(x + 1) - f(x) = 6x - 8$ and $f(1) = 26$, then $f(2)$ is

A 23

B 24

C 25

D 26

E none of the above

25. Math Contest For which value of a does $\dfrac{2x + 5}{3x + 8} = a$ not have a solution for x?

A $-\dfrac{5}{8}$

B $\dfrac{5}{8}$

C $\dfrac{8}{5}$

D $\dfrac{2}{3}$

E none of the above

26. Math Contest If $x = \dfrac{1}{4 - y}$, evaluate $\dfrac{1}{x} + 4x + y - yx - 1$.

27. Math Contest If the roots of $Ax^2 + Bx + C = 0$ are negative reciprocals of each other, determine the relationship between A and C. What can you say about A and C if the roots are simply reciprocals of each other?

8.2

Products and Quotients of Functions

The superposition principle is a convenient way to visualize the sum or difference of two or more functions. When two functions are combined through multiplication or division, however, the nature of the resultant combined function is less obvious. In earlier chapters and courses, you learned various techniques for multiplying and dividing algebraic expressions. Many of these skills can be applied and extended to products and quotients of functions.

Products and quotients of functions can be combined to model and solve a variety of problems. How are these concepts related to the revenue generated at baseball games?

Investigate   What is the symmetrical behaviour of products and quotients of symmetrical functions?

A: *Products of Functions*

Tools
• grid paper

1. **a)** Sketch a graph of each power function.

   i) $f(x) = x$ **ii)** $g(x) = x^2$ **iii)** $p(x) = x^3$ **iv)** $q(x) = x^4$

   b) Classify each function as even, odd, or neither.

2. Use the functions from step 1. Prove each identity using algebraic reasoning.

   a) $f(x)g(x) = p(x)$ **b)** $f(x)p(x) = q(x)$

   c) $f(x)f(x) = g(x)$ **d)** $[g(x)]^2 = q(x)$

3. Examine the pattern of symmetry of the functions on the left side and right side of each identity in step 2. Copy and complete the table.

Identity	Symmetry of Factor Functions	Symmetry of Product Function
a) $f(x)g(x) = p(x)$	$f(x) = x$ (ODD) $g(x) = x^2$ (EVEN)	$p(x) = x^3$ (ODD)
b) $f(x)p(x) = q(x)$		
c) $f(x)f(x) = g(x)$		
d) $[g(x)]^2 = q(x)$		
Create an example of your own using power functions.		
Create an example of your own using power functions.		

4. Look for a pattern in the table. Write a conjecture about the nature of the symmetry of a combined function that consists of the product of

 a) two even functions

 b) two odd functions

 c) an even function and an odd function

5. Reflect

 a) Test your conjecture by exploring the graphs of various products of the following functions:

 $f(x) = \sin x$ $\qquad$ $g(x) = x$ $\qquad\qquad$ $h(x) = \cos x$

 $u(x) = x^2$ $\qquad$ $v(x) = \tan x$ $\qquad$ $w(x) = x^3$

 b) Based on your findings, write a summary of the symmetrical behaviour of the products of functions.

B: *Quotients of Functions*

 1. Design and carry out an investigation to determine the symmetric behaviour of combined functions formed by the quotient of two symmetric functions. Write a brief report of your findings that includes

 • a comparison to the symmetrical behaviour of products of symmetric functions

 • the conditions under which asymptotic behaviour occurs

To simplify a combined function formed by the product or quotient of functions, some previously learned algebraic skills can be useful.

| **Example 1** | **Product and Quotient of Functions** |

Let $f(x) = x + 3$ and $g(x) = x^2 + 8x + 15$. Determine an equation for each combined function. Sketch a graph of the combined function and state its domain and range.

 a) $y = f(x)g(x)$

 b) $y = \dfrac{f(x)}{g(x)}$

Solution

 a) To determine $y = f(x)g(x)$, multiply the two functions.

$$y = f(x)g(x)$$
$$= (x + 3)(x^2 + 8x + 15)$$
$$= x^3 + 8x^2 + 15x + 3x^2 + 24x + 45 \qquad \text{Apply the distributive property.}$$
$$= x^3 + 11x^2 + 39x + 45 \qquad\qquad\qquad \text{Collect like terms.}$$

Use the fact that $g(x)$ can be factored to help you sketch a graph of this cubic function.

$$y = (x + 3)(x^2 + 8x + 15)$$
$$= (x + 3)(x + 3)(x + 5)$$
$$= (x + 3)^2(x + 5)$$

The zeros of $y = (x + 3)^2(x + 5)$ are -3 (order 2) and -5. These are the x-intercepts. From the expanded form, $y = x^3 + 11x^2 + 39x + 45$, the y-intercept is 45. The leading coefficient is positive.

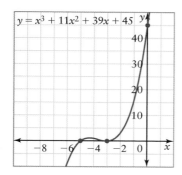

CONNECTIONS

You explored polynomial functions in depth in Chapter 1.

There are no restrictions on x or y. The domain is $x \in \mathbb{R}$ and the range is $y \in \mathbb{R}$.

b) To determine $y = \dfrac{f(x)}{g(x)}$, divide the two functions.

$$y = \frac{f(x)}{g(x)}$$
$$= \frac{x + 3}{x^2 + 8x + 15}$$
$$= \frac{\cancel{x + 3}}{\cancel{(x + 3)}(x + 5)} \qquad \text{Factor the denominator and simplify.}$$
$$= \frac{1}{x + 5}, x \neq -3$$

This is a rational function. A sketch of the graph can be produced by applying a horizontal translation of 5 units to the left of the function $y = \dfrac{1}{x}$.

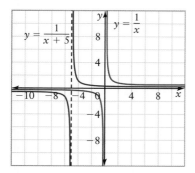

To identify the domain of this function, refer to the original form of the function, not the simplified one:

$$\frac{f(x)}{g(x)} = \frac{x + 3}{(x + 3)(x + 5)} \qquad x + 3 \neq 0 \text{ and } x + 5 \neq 0.$$

Note that this function is undefined for $x = -3$ and $x = -5$. Therefore, the domain is $\{x \in \mathbb{R}, x \neq -3, x \neq -5\}$. This is partly reflected in the graph by the asymptote that appears at $x = -5$. However, the graph of this function must be adjusted to reflect the discontinuity at $x = -3$. There is a hole at $\left(-3, \dfrac{1}{2}\right)$.

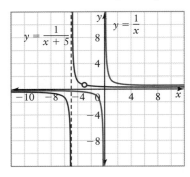

There is a horizontal asymptote at $y = 0$, so the range is $\left\{y \in \mathbb{R}, y \neq 0, \dfrac{1}{2}\right\}$.

CONNECTIONS

You explored rational functions in depth in Chapter 3.

These algebraic and graphing skills are useful for solving problems involving products and quotients of functions.

Example 2 | Baseball Marketing

In an effort to boost fan support, the owners of a baseball team have agreed to gradually reduce ticket prices, P, in dollars, according to the function $P(g) = 25 - 0.1g$, where g is the number of games that have been played so far this season.

The owners are also randomly giving away free baseball caps. The number, C, in hundreds, of caps given away per game can be modelled by the function $C(g) = 2 - 0.04g$.

Since these marketing initiatives began, the number, N, in hundreds, of fans in attendance has been modelled by the function $N(g) = 10 + 0.2g$.

a) Develop an algebraic and a graphical model for $f(g) = P(g)N(g)$ and explain what it means. Will the owners increase or decrease their revenue from ticket sales under their current marketing plan?

b) Develop an algebraic and a graphical model for $f(g) = \dfrac{C(g)}{N(g)}$ and explain what it means. How likely are you to receive a free baseball cap if you attend game 5?

Solution

a) Multiply $P(g)$ by $N(g)$ to produce the combined function $f(g) = P(g)N(g)$.

$$f(g) = P(g)N(g)$$
$$= (25 - 0.1g)(10 + 0.2g)$$
$$= 250 + 5g - g - 0.02g^2$$
$$= -0.02g^2 + 4g + 250$$

A graph of this function is shown. Note that these functions only have meaning for $g \geq 0$.

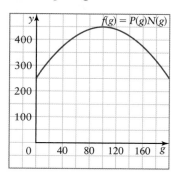

This combined function is the product of the ticket price and the number of fans attending, in hundreds. Therefore, $f(g) = P(g)N(g)$ represents the revenue from ticket sales, in hundreds of dollars. Note that the function is quadratic, increasing until about game 100, and then decreasing after that. Therefore, the owners will increase their revenue from ticket sales in the short term under their current marketing strategy, but eventually this strategy will no longer be effective.

b) Divide $C(g)$ by $N(g)$ to produce the combined function $f(g) = \dfrac{C(g)}{N(g)}$.

$$f(g) = \frac{C(g)}{N(g)}$$
$$= \frac{2 - 0.04g}{10 + 0.2g}$$

Use a graphing calculator to graph this function. Enter the equations $C(g) = 2 - 0.04g$ and $N(g) = 10 + 0.2g$ first. Then, use them to produce the graph of $f(g) = \dfrac{C(g)}{N(g)}$. To view only the quotient function, leave it turned on, but turn the other functions off. Apply number sense and systematic trial to set an appropriate viewing window.

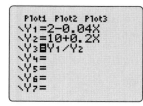

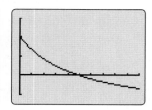

The combined function $f(g) = \dfrac{C(g)}{N(g)}$ represents the number of free caps randomly given out divided by the number of fans. Therefore, this function represents the probability that a fan will receive a free baseball cap as a function of the game number.

To determine the probability of receiving a free cap at game 5, evaluate $f(g) = \dfrac{C(g)}{N(g)}$ for $g = 5$.

Method 1: *Use a Graphing Calculator*

Use the **Value** operation to identify the function value when $x = 5$.

According to the graph, there is about a 16% chance of receiving a free baseball cap at game 5.

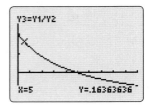

Method 2: *Use Pencil and Paper*

Substitute $g = 5$ into the equation for $f(g) = \dfrac{C(g)}{N(g)}$ and evaluate.

$$f(g) = \frac{2 - 0.04g}{10 + 0.2g}$$

$$f(5) = \frac{2 - 0.04(5)}{10 + 0.2(5)}$$

$$= \frac{2 - 0.2}{10 + 1}$$

$$= \frac{1.8}{11}$$

$$= 0.1\overline{63}$$

According to the equation, there is about a 16% chance of receiving a free baseball cap at game 5.

⟪ KEY CONCEPTS ⟫

- A combined function of the form $y = f(x)g(x)$ represents the product of two functions, $f(x)$ and $g(x)$.

- A combined function of the form $y = \dfrac{f(x)}{g(x)}$ represents the quotient of two functions, $f(x)$ and $g(x)$, for $g(x) \neq 0$.

- The domain of the product or quotient of functions is the domain common to the component functions. The domain of a quotient function $y = \dfrac{f(x)}{g(x)}$ is further restricted by excluding any values that make the denominator, $g(x)$, equal to zero.

- Products and quotients of functions can be used to model a variety of situations.

Communicate Your Understanding

C1 A damped harmonic oscillator is an object whose motion is cyclic, with a decaying (decreasing) amplitude, such as a released pendulum or a child on a swing after a single push. The motion of a damped harmonic oscillator can be modelled by a function of the form $y(t) = A\sin(kt) \times 0.5^{ct}$, where y represents distance as a function of time, t, and A, k, and c are constants.

a) What two component functions are combined to form this function? Sketch the shape of each component function.

b) Sketch the shape of the combined function.

C2 Refer to Example 1.

a) Will the graph of $y = \dfrac{g(x)}{f(x)}$ also produce a rational function or will it have a different shape? Explain your answer.

b) Will there be any asymptotes or holes in the graph? Justify your answer.

C3 Refer to Example 2. Suppose the owners took a more aggressive approach to reducing the ticket price. Predict the effect this would have on each function.

a) $P(g)$ **b)** $N(g)$ **c)** $C(g)$

Justify your answers with mathematical reasoning.

A   Practise

When graphing trigonometric functions, work in radians.

For help with questions 1 to 3, refer to the Investigate.

Use the graphs of the functions shown to answer questions 1 to 3.

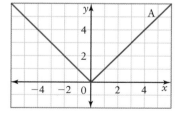

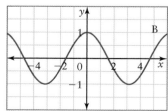

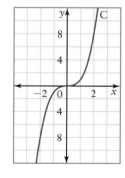

1. a) Which two of these functions will multiply to form a combined function that is even? odd?

b) Is there more than one answer in either case in part a)? Explain.

2. Is the product of all three functions even, odd, or neither? Explain.

3. Use Technology Check your answers to questions 1 and 2 using graphing technology and the equations $y = |x|$, $y = \cos x$, and $y = x^3$.

For help with questions 4 and 5, refer to Example 1.

4. Let $f(x) = x - 2$ and $g(x) = x^2 - 4$. Develop an algebraic and a graphical model for each combined function. Then, give the domain and range of the combined function. Identify any holes or asymptotes.

a) $y = f(x)g(x)$ **b)** $y = \dfrac{f(x)}{g(x)}$ **c)** $y = \dfrac{g(x)}{f(x)}$

5. Let $u(x) = \cos x$ and $v(x) = 0.95^x$. Develop an algebraic and a graphical model for each combined function. Then, give the domain and range of the combined function. Identify any holes or asymptotes.

a) $y = u(x)v(x)$

b) $y = \dfrac{u(x)}{v(x)}$

c) $y = \dfrac{v(x)}{u(x)}$

B   Connect and Apply

Use the following information to answer questions 6 and 7. Graphing technology is recommended.

A fish pond initially has a population of 300 fish. When there is enough fish food, the population, P, of fish grows as a function of time, t, in years, as $P(t) = 300(1.05)^t$. The initial amount of fish food in the pond is 1000 units, where 1 unit can sustain one fish for a year. The amount, F, of fish food is decreasing according to the function $F(t) = 1000(0.92)^t$.

6. a) Graph the functions $P(t)$ and $F(t)$ on the same set of axes. Describe the nature of these functions.

Reasoning and Proving

Representing   Selecting Tools

Problem Solving

Connecting   Reflecting

Communicating

b) Determine the mathematical domain and range of these functions.

c) Identify the point of intersection of these two curves. Determine the coordinates, to two decimal places, and explain what they mean. Call this point in time the crisis point.

d) Graph the function $y = F(t) - P(t)$. Explain the significance of this function.

e) What is the t-intercept, to two decimal places, of the function $y = F(t) - P(t)$? How does this relate to the crisis point?

f) Comment on the validity of the mathematical model for $P(t)$ for t-values greater than this intercept. Sketch how you think the curve should change in this region. Justify your answers.

For help with question 7, refer to Example 2.

7. a) Graph the function $y = \dfrac{F(t)}{P(t)}$ on a different set of axes. What does this function represent? Describe the shape of this function.

b) What are the coordinates of this function at the crisis point? Explain the meaning of these coordinates.

c) Describe the living conditions of the fish population before, at, and after the crisis point.

8. Let $f(x) = \sqrt{25 - x^2}$ and $g(x) = \sin x$.

a) Graph $f(x)$ and describe its shape. Is this function even, odd, or neither?

b) Graph $g(x)$ on the same set of axes. Is this function even, odd, or neither?

c) Predict the shape of $y = f(x)g(x)$. Sketch a graph of your prediction. Then, check your prediction using graphing technology.

d) Give the domain of $y = f(x)g(x)$. Estimate the range, to two decimal places, of $y = f(x)g(x)$. Explain why only an estimate is possible.

9. Refer to question 8.

a) Graph $y = \dfrac{g(x)}{f(x)}$. Is this function even, odd, or neither? Give the domain and range.

b) Graph $y = \dfrac{f(x)}{g(x)}$. Is this function even, odd, or neither? Give the domain and range.

Use the following information to answer questions 10 to 12.

Terra is a fictitious country. The population of Terra was 6 million in the year 2000 and is growing at a rate of 2% per year. The population, P, in millions, as a function of time, t, in years, can be modelled by the function $P(t) = 6(1.02)^t$.

Terra's government has put in place economic plans such that food production is projected to follow the equation $F(t) = 8 + 0.04t$, where F is the amount of food that can sustain the population for 1 year.

10. a) Graph $P(t)$ and $F(t)$ on the same set of axes and describe their trends.

b) Graph the function $y = F(t) - P(t)$, and describe the trend. Does the Terrian nation currently enjoy a food surplus or suffer from a food shortage? Explain. What about in the years to come?

c) Identify the coordinates of the maximum of $y = F(t) - P(t)$ and explain what they mean.

11. The food production per capita is the amount of food production per person.

Reasoning and Proving
Representing — Selecting Tools
Problem Solving
Connecting — Reflecting
Communicating

a) Graph the function $y = \dfrac{F(t)}{P(t)}$ and describe its trend. Use a separate grid, or adjust the viewing window to obtain a clear representation of the graph.

b) At what time is the food production per capita a maximum for Terra? Does this point coincide with the maximum that you found in question 10c)? Explain this result.

c) What does it mean when $\dfrac{F(t)}{P(t)} > 1$? $\dfrac{F(t)}{P(t)} < 1$? When are these conditions projected to occur for Terra?

12. Suppose that you are a cabinet minister in the Terrian government, with a portfolio in international trade and economic policy. What advice would you give your leader regarding projected food surpluses in the short to mid-term? What about shortages in the long term?

Use the following information to answer questions 13 and 14.

After the school dance on Thursday night, Carlos is thinking about asking Keiko out on a date, but his confidence is wavering. The probability, p_{Ask}, that Carlos will ask Keiko out as a function of time, t, in days following the dance, can be modelled by the function $p_{Ask}(t) = 0.45 \sin t + 0.5$. Keiko, meanwhile, is interested in dating Carlos, but less so if he appears too eager or too shy. The probability, p_{Yes}, that Keiko will agree to a date if Carlos asks her, as a function of time, can be modelled by the function $p_{Yes}(t) = -0.08t(t - 7)$.

13. a) Graph the functions $p_{Ask}(t)$ and $p_{Yes}(t)$ on the same set of axes. Describe each trend. Determine the domain and range of each function in the context of this problem.

b) When is Carlos most likely to ask Keiko, to the nearest tenth of a day? Explain your answer.

c) When is Keiko most likely to agree to a date with Carlo if he asks her? Explain.

d) Graph the function $y = p_{Ask}(t) - p_{Yes}(t)$. Suggest what this graph may reveal.

14. The likelihood of Carlos and Keiko agreeing to a date is the conditional probability that Carlos asks Keiko and that, given that he asks, Keiko says yes. This conditional probability is given by the combined function $y = p_{Ask}(t)p_{Yes}(t)$.

a) Develop an algebraic and a graphical model for this combined function.

b) After what amount of time, to the nearest tenth of a day, is it most likely that Carlos and Keiko will agree to a date? What is the probability that this will happen at this time, to two decimal places?

c) At what point does Carlos have no chance of dating Keiko?

d) Suppose that you are friends with both Carlos and Keiko. What advice would you give to Carlos?

15. Does the product of functions commute? A mathematical process is commutative if you can reverse the order of the operands and obtain the same result. Pick any two functions, $f(x)$ and $g(x)$, and see if $f(x)g(x) = g(x)f(x)$. Try several examples and summarize your findings.

CONNECTIONS
The commutative property holds over the real numbers for the multiplication of two numbers.
$2 \times (-4) = (-4) \times 2$
$a \times b = b \times a, a, b \in \mathbb{R}$

16. Refer to question 15. Repeat the analysis for the division of two functions.

17. Given the functions $f(x) = 2^{-x}$ and $g(x) = x^3$, sketch a graph of the function $y = f(x)g(x)$ and describe its key features. Explain its end behaviour.

✓ Achievement Check

18. Let $f(x) = x + 2$ and $g(x) = x^2 + 5x + 6$.

  a) Determine each combined function.

    i) $y = f(x)g(x)$

    ii) $y = \dfrac{f(x)}{g(x)}$

  b) State the domain and range of $y = \dfrac{f(x)}{g(x)}$.

C   Extend and Challenge

19. a) Given an even function $f(x)$, what is the symmetrical behaviour of a combined function that is

    i) the square of $f(x)$, $[f(x)]^2$?

    ii) the cube of $f(x)$, $[f(x)]^3$?

    iii) the nth power of $f(x)$, $[f(x)]^n$?

  Use algebraic reasoning with examples to justify your answers.

  b) Repeat the analysis for powers of odd functions.

  c) Use Technology Use graphing technology to verify your results.

20. The motion of a pendulum can be modelled by the function $x(t) = 10\cos(2t) \times 0.95^t$, where x is the horizontal displacement from the rest position, in centimetres, as a function of time, t, in seconds.

  a) Determine the length of the pendulum.

  b) Sketch how the shape of the graph would change if

    i) the air resistance were reduced

    ii) the pendulum were lengthened

  Justify your answers with mathematical reasoning.

21. Math Contest Increasing x by $y\%$ gives 12. Decreasing x by $y\%$ gives 8. Determine the value of x.

22. Math Contest A rectangle is divided into four smaller rectangles with areas of 4, 7, 15, and x, as shown. Determine the value of x.

7	15
4	x

23. Math Contest Given that $f(xy) = \dfrac{f(x)}{y}$ for all real numbers x and y and $f(500) = 3$, find $f(600)$.

24. Math Contest A rectangular container with base 9 cm by 11 cm has height 38.5 cm. Assuming that water expands 10% when it freezes, determine the depth to which the container can be filled so that the ice does not rise above the top of the container when the water freezes.

8.3 Composite Functions

You have learned four ways of combining functions—sums, differences, products, and quotients. Another type of combined function occurs when one function depends on another. For example, in a predator-prey relationship, the predator population is likely to depend on the prey population as its primary food source, which may fluctuate over time. Think about the effect on a predator population when its food source is plentiful versus when it is scarce.

Investigate | How can the composition of functions be used to model a predator-prey relationship?

1. The number, R, of rabbits in a wildlife reserve as a function of time, t, in years can be modelled by the function $R(t) = 50 \cos t + 100$.

   a) Graph this function. Describe the trend.

   b) Identify the following key features and their meanings.

       i) domain   **ii)** range   **iii)** period   **iv)** frequency

2. The number, W, of wolves in the same reserve as a function of time can be modelled by the function $W(t) = 0.2[R(t - 2)]$.

   a) Graph the function $W(t)$ on the same set of axes as in step 1. Adjust the viewing window to focus on this function.

   b) Identify the following key features and explain their meanings.

       i) domain   **ii)** range   **iii)** period   **iv)** frequency

3. Using the equation from step 1, substitute $R(t - 2)$ into the equation for $W(t)$ and develop a simplified equation to model the number of wolves as a function of time.

4. **Reflect**

   a) Set the viewing window so that you can see the graphs of both $R(t)$ and $W(t)$ simultaneously. Compare the graphs, and explain how they are

       i) alike

       ii) different

   b) Suggest possible reasons for the relationship between these two functions.

Tools

- graphing calculator or graphing software

Technology Tip ∴

If you are using *The Geometer's Sketchpad*®, you can graph one function in terms of another. For example, if the rabbit function is $f(x)$, you can graph the wolf population by entering $0.2*f(x - 2)$.

If you are using a graphing calculator, press VARS and use the **Y-VARS** secondary menu to enter $Y2 = 0.2*(Y1(X - 2))$.

A **composite function** is a function that depends on another function. It is formed when one function is substituted into another.

> $f(g(x))$ is the composite function that is formed when $g(x)$ is substituted for x in $f(x)$.
>
> $f(g(x))$ is read as "f of g of x."

Note that the order of the functions is important. As read from left to right, the second function is substituted into the first function. $(f \circ g)(x)$ is an alternative notation that means the same as $f(g(x))$.

Example 1 | Determine the Composition of Two Functions

Let $f(x) = x^2$ and $g(x) = x + 3$. Determine an equation for each composite function, graph the function, and give its domain and range.

a) $y = f(g(x))$ **b)** $y = g(f(x))$ **c)** $y = f(f(x))$

d) $y = g(g(x))$ **e)** $y = g^{-1}(g(x))$

Solution

a) To determine the composite function $y = f(g(x))$, substitute the function $g(x)$ for x in the function $f(x)$.

$$f(x) = x^2$$
$$f(g(x)) = (g(x))^2$$
$$= (x + 3)^2$$
$$= x^2 + 6x + 9 \qquad \text{Expand the perfect square trinomial.}$$

This is a quadratic function. There are no restrictions on the value of x in this equation. Therefore, the domain is $x \in \mathbb{R}$. This can be verified by inspecting the graph. Looking at the factored form, $f(g(x)) = (x + 3)^2$, the graph of this function is a horizontal translation of 3 units to the left of the graph of $y = x^2$.

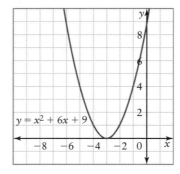

$y = x^2 + 6x + 9$

From the graph, it is clear that the range is $\{y \in \mathbb{R}, y \geq 0\}$.

b) To determine the composite function $y = g(f(x))$, substitute the function $f(x)$ for x in the function $g(x)$.

$$g(x) = x + 3$$
$$g(f(x)) = (f(x)) + 3$$
$$= (x^2) + 3$$
$$= x^2 + 3$$

This is a quadratic function. Its graph can be generated by vertically translating the graph of $y = x^2$ up 3 units.

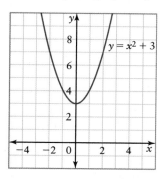

The domain of this function is $\{x \in \mathbb{R}\}$ and the range is $\{y \in \mathbb{R}, y \geq 3\}$.

Note that the different results for parts a) and b) suggest that the order of the component functions of a composite function is important: $f(g(x)) \neq g(f(x))$.

c) To determine the composite function $y = f(f(x))$, substitute the function $f(x)$ for x in the function $f(x)$.

$$f(x) = x^2$$
$$f(f(x)) = (f(x))^2$$
$$= (x^2)^2$$
$$= x^4$$

This is a quartic power function, and its graph is shown.

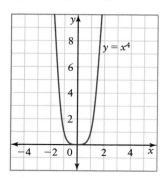

CONNECTIONS

You studied power functions in Chapter 1.

The domain of this function is $\{x \in \mathbb{R}\}$ and the range is $\{y \in \mathbb{R}, y \geq 0\}$.

d) To determine the composite function $y = g(g(x))$, substitute the function $g(x)$ for x in the function $g(x)$.

$$g(x) = x + 3$$
$$g(g(x)) = (g(x)) + 3$$
$$= (x + 3) + 3$$
$$= x + 6$$

This is a linear function.

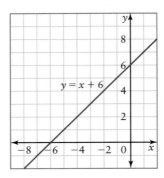

The domain of this function is $x \in \mathbb{R}$ and the range is $y \in \mathbb{R}$.

e) To determine an expression for $y = g^{-1}(g(x))$, it is necessary to determine the inverse function $y = g^{-1}(x)$.

$$y = x + 3 \qquad \text{Write } g(x) \text{ in terms of } x \text{ and } y.$$
$$x = y + 3 \qquad \text{Interchange } x \text{ and } y.$$
$$x - 3 = y \qquad \text{Isolate } y.$$
$$y = x - 3$$

Therefore, the inverse function is $g^{-1}(x) = x - 3$. To determine $g^{-1}(g(x))$, substitute $g(x)$ into $g^{-1}(x)$.

$$g^{-1}(g(x)) = (x + 3) - 3$$
$$= x + 3 - 3$$
$$= x$$

This is a linear function.

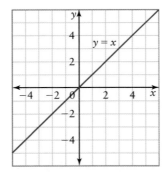

The domain of this function is $x \in \mathbb{R}$ and the range is $y \in \mathbb{R}$.

Example 2 | Evaluate a Composite Function

Let $u(x) = x^2 + 3x + 2$ and $w(x) = \dfrac{1}{x-1}$.

a) Evaluate $u(w(2))$.

b) Evaluate $w(u(-3))$.

Solution

a) Method 1: *Determine u(w(x)) and Then Substitute*

Determine an expression for $u(w(x))$.

$$u(w(x)) = \left(\frac{1}{x-1}\right)^2 + 3\left(\frac{1}{x-1}\right) + 2$$

Substitute $x = 2$.

$$u(w(2)) = \left(\frac{1}{2-1}\right)^2 + 3\left(\frac{1}{2-1}\right) + 2$$
$$= 1^2 + 3(1) + 2$$
$$= 6$$

Method 2: *Determine w(2) and Then Substitute*

Determine $w(2)$.

$$w(x) = \frac{1}{x-1}$$
$$w(2) = \frac{1}{2-1}$$
$$= 1$$

Substitute $w(2) = 1$ into $u(x)$.

$$u(w(2)) = u(1)$$
$$= 1^2 + 3(1) + 2$$
$$= 6$$

b) Determine $u(-3)$. Then, substitute the result into $w(x)$ and evaluate.

$$u(x) = x^2 + 3x + 2$$
$$u(-3) = (-3)^2 + 3(-3) + 2$$
$$= 2$$
$$w(u(-3)) = w(2)$$
$$= \frac{1}{2-1}$$
$$= 1$$

Example 3 | **Music Sales Revenue**

A music store has traditionally made a profit from sales of CDs and cassette tapes. The number, C, in thousands, of CDs sold yearly as a function of time, t, in years since the store opened, can be modelled by the function $C(t) = -0.03t^2 + 0.5t + 3$. The number, T, in thousands, of cassette tapes sold as a function of time can be modelled by the function $T(t) = 1.5 - 0.1t$. The store opened in 1990, at which point $t = 0$.

a) Graph both functions up to the year 2008 and describe their trends.

b) The total revenue, R, from sales of CDs and cassette tapes can be modelled by the composite function $R(t) = [3C(t) + 2T(t)](1.04^t)$. Develop an algebraic and a graphical model for the store's revenue, and interpret the trend.

> **Solution**

a) Use a graphing calculator. Apply number sense and systematic trial to set an appropriate viewing window.

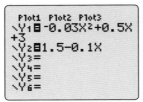 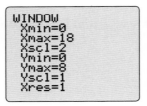 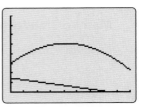

The graph indicates that the number of CDs sold increased from around 3000 per year to just over 5000 per year around 1999, after which it declined. To identify when this happened, use the **Maximum** operation. Press 2nd [CALC], select **4:maximum**, and follow the prompts.

About a third of the way through 1998, CD sales per year reached about 5083. Then, sales began decreasing.

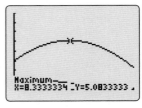

The number of cassette tapes sold has declined steadily from 1500 per year. In fact, the graph shows that the store stopped selling tapes after a certain time. To identify when this happened, use the **Zero** operation. Press 2nd [CALC], select **2:zero**, and follow the prompts.

Tape sales ceased when $t = 15$, which corresponds to the year 2005 $(1990 + 15 = 2005)$.

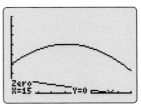

b) To develop the revenue function, substitute the CD and cassette tape sales functions into the revenue equation and simplify.

$$R(t) = [3C(t) + 2T(t)](1.04^t)$$
$$= [3(-0.03t^2 + 0.5t + 3) + 2(1.5 - 0.1t)](1.04^t)$$
$$= (-0.09t^2 + 1.5t + 9 + 3 - 0.2t)(1.04^t) \qquad \text{Apply the distributive property.}$$
$$= (-0.09t^2 + 1.3t + 12)(1.04^t) \qquad \text{Collect like terms.}$$

This simplified revenue function is the product of a quadratic function and an exponential function. To illustrate this, graph the revenue function on a new set of axes.

Method 1: *Graph the Composite Function in Terms of C(n) and T(n)*

Press (VARS) and cursor over to the **Y-VARS** menu to access **Y1** and **Y2**.

Turn off **Y1** and **Y2** to view **Y3** alone.

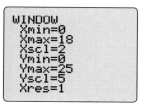

Method 2: *Graph the Simplified Revenue Function*

Clear all functions and enter the simplified revenue function.

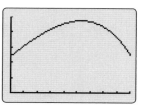

Use the window settings shown.

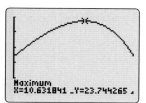

The trend in revenue from music sales steadily increased throughout the 1990s, peaking around the year 2001, after which revenues began to sharply decline.

Maximum revenues from sales of almost $24 000 were achieved in the eleventh year of business, for the year 2000–2001.

- $f(g(x))$ denotes a composite function, that is, one in which the function $f(x)$ depends on the function $g(x)$. This can also be written as $(f \circ g)(x)$.

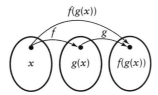

- To determine an equation for a composite function, substitute the second function into the first, as read from left to right. To determine $f(g(x))$, substitute $g(x)$ for x in $f(x)$.

- To evaluate a composite function $f(g(x))$ at a specific value, substitute the value into the equation of the composite function and simplify, or evaluate $g(x)$ at the specific value and then substitute the result into $f(x)$.

Communicate Your Understanding

C1 Does $f(g(x))$ mean the same thing as $f(x)g(x)$? Explain, using examples to illustrate.

C2 A predator-prey relationship is shown. Population levels are shown as functions of time.

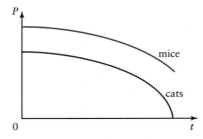

a) Is this a stable relationship? Explain why or why not.

b) What has happened to the cat population? Suggest some reasons why this may have happened.

c) Predict what will happen to the mouse population in the future. Justify your answer.

C3 Refer to the revenue function in Example 3, $R(t) = [3C(t) + 2T(t)](1.04^t)$.

a) What do the terms $3C(t)$ and $2T(t)$ represent?

b) Suggest a reason why the factor of 1.04^t is present.

For help with questions 1 to 3, refer to Example 1.

1. Let $f(x) = -x + 2$ and $g(x) = (x + 3)^2$. Determine a simplified algebraic model for each composite function.

a) $y = f(g(x))$ **b)** $y = g(f(x))$

c) $y = f(f(x))$ **d)** $y = g(g(x))$

e) $y = f^{-1}(f(x))$

2. Graph each composite function in question 1. Give the domain and range.

3. Use Technology Check your answers to question 2 using graphing technology.

For help with question 4, refer to Example 2.

4. Let $f(x) = x^2 + 2x - 4$ and $g(x) = \dfrac{1}{x + 1}$.

a) Evaluate $g(f(0))$.

b) Evaluate $f(g(-2))$.

c) Show that $g(f(x))$ is undefined for $x = 1$ and $x = -3$.

B **Connect and Apply**

For help with questions 5 to 7, refer to Example 3.

Use the following information to answer questions 5 to 7.

In an election campaign, the popularity, B, as a percent of voters, of the governing Blue party can be modelled by a function of time, t, in days throughout the campaign as $B(t) = 40 - 0.5t$. The popularity, $R(t)$, of the opposing Red party can be modelled by a composite function of $B(t)$, $R(B(t)) = 20 + 0.75[40 - B(t)]$.

5. a) Graph $B(t)$ and describe the trend.

b) What is the popularity of the Blue party at the beginning of the campaign?

c) What is the rate of change of this function, and what does it mean?

d) Can you tell if these are the only two parties in the election? If you can, explain how. If you cannot, describe what additional information is required.

6. a) Graph $R(t)$ and describe the trend.

b) What is the popularity of the Red party at the beginning of the campaign?

c) What is the rate of change of this graph, and what does it mean?

d) If it can be assumed that these are the only two parties running for election, which party do you think will win? Does your answer depend on something? Explain.

7. Assume that there are at least three parties running in the election.

Reasoning and Proving
Representing · Selecting Tools
Problem Solving
Connecting · Reflecting
Communicating

a) Graph the composite function $V(t) = 100 - [(B(t) + R(t)]$. What does this graph represent? Describe the trend.

b) Assuming that this is a three-party election, and that there are no undecided votes, can you tell who will win this election? Explain.

c) Repeat part b) assuming that there are four parties running.

8. Is $f(g(x)) = g(f(x))$ true for all functions $f(x)$ and $g(x)$? Justify your answer, using examples to illustrate.

9. Let $f(x) = x^3$.

a) Determine $f^{-1}(x)$.

b) Determine $f(f^{-1}(x))$.

c) Determine $f^{-1}(f(x))$.

d) Compare your answers to parts b) and c). Describe what you notice.

e) Determine $f(f^{-1}(3))$, $f(f^{-1}(5))$, and $f(f^{-1}(-1))$. What do you notice?

10. Refer to question 9. Does this result apply to all functions? Design and carry out an investigation to determine the answer. Use functions whose inverses are also functions. Write a conclusion based on your findings.

11. Let $f(x) = x^2$, $g(x) = x^3$, and $h(x) = \sin x$. Work in radians.

   a) Predict what the graph of $y = f(h(x))$ will look like, and sketch your prediction.

   b) **Use Technology** Check your prediction using graphing technology.

   c) Is the function in part a) periodic? Explain.

   d) Identify the domain and range.

12. a) Repeat question 11 for $y = g(h(x))$.

   b) Compare $y = f(h(x))$ and $y = g(h(x))$. How are these functions similar? different?

13. An environmental scientist measures the presence of a pollutant in a lake and models the concentration, C, in parts per million (ppm), as a function of the population, P, of the lakeside city, using the function $C(P) = 1.54P + 58.55$. The city's population, in thousands, can be modelled by the function $P(t) = 12.1 \times 2^{\frac{t}{52}}$, where t is the time, in years.

   a) Determine an equation for the concentration of pollutant as a function of time.

   b) Sketch a graph of this function.

   c) How long will it take for the concentration to reach 100 ppm, to the nearest year?

14. Is $(f \circ g)^{-1}(x) = (f^{-1} \circ g^{-1})(x)$, or is $(f \circ g)^{-1}(x) = (g^{-1} \circ f^{-1})(x)$, or is neither true? Verify using two examples involving at least two different types of functions.

Reasoning and Proving
Representing — *Selecting Tools*
Problem Solving
Connecting — *Reflecting*
Communicating

15. Chapter Problem Funky Stuff is releasing a new stuffed bear called "Funky Teddy Bear" in time for the winter holiday shopping rush. The number, N, in thousands, of Funky Teddy Bears sold is projected to be a function of the price, p, in dollars, as $N(p) = -0.1(p + 5)^2 + 80$. Revenue, R, from sales is given by the product of number sold and price: $R(p) = N(p) \times p$. Your task is to determine the optimum price that will maximize revenues.

   a) Graph $N(p)$. Describe and interpret the trend.

   b) Assuming a minimum price of \$5, what price domain will yield revenue?

   c) Can you tell the optimum price from this graph? Explain why or why not.

   d) Graph the function $R(p)$.

   e) At what price should Funky Stuff sell Funky Teddy Bears? How much revenue will this bring?

16. A manufacturer models its weekly production of office chairs since 2001 by the function $N(t) = 100 + 25t$, where t is the time, in years, since 2001, and N is the number of chairs. The size of the manufacturer's workforce can be modelled by the composite function $W(N) = 3\sqrt{N}$.

   a) Write the size of the workforce as a function of time.

   b) State the domain and range of the new function and sketch its graph.

✓ Achievement Check

17. Let $f(x) = x^2$, $g(x) = x - 2$, and $h(x) = \frac{1}{x}$.

   a) Determine a simplified algebraic model for each composite function.

   i) $f(g(x))$

   ii) $h(g(x))$

   iii) $g^{-1}(h(x))$

   b) Evaluate $f(h(2))$.

18. Let $f(x) = \log x$, $g(x) = \sin x$, and $h(x) = \cos x$. Work in radians.

a) What is the domain of $f(x)$?

b) Use this information to predict the shape of the graph of the composite function $y = f(g(x))$. Sketch your prediction.

c) **Use Technology** Check your prediction in part b) using graphing technology. Give the domain and range of $y = f(g(x))$.

d) Use your result in part c) to predict the shape of the graph of the composite function $y = f(h(x))$. Sketch your prediction.

e) **Use Technology** Check your prediction in part d) using graphing technology. Give the domain and range of $y = f(h(x))$.

19. Let $f(x) = x^2 - 9$ and $g(x) = \dfrac{1}{x}$.

a) Determine the domain and range of $y = f(g(x))$.

b) Determine the domain and range of $y = g(f(x))$.

c) **Use Technology** Use graphing technology to verify your answers in parts a) and b).

20. Two ships leave port at the same time. The first ship travels north at 4 km/h and the second ship travels east at 5 km/h. Write their distance apart as a function of time.

21. Math Contest Given that $f(x) = \dfrac{ax + b}{cx + d}$, find $f^{-1}(x)$.

22. Math Contest The mean of the nine numbers in the set $\{9, 99, 999, \ldots, 999\,999\,999\}$ is a nine-digit number n, all of whose digits are distinct. The number n does *not* contain what digit?

23. Math Contest Find all real numbers x such that $\sqrt{1 - \sqrt{1 - x}} = x$.

24. Math Contest The sum of two numbers is 7 and their product is 25. Determine the sum of their reciprocals.

25. Math Contest A number is called a decreasing number if each digit is less than the preceding digit. How many three-digit decreasing numbers are less than 500?

CAREER CONNECTION

After completing a 4-year bachelor of mathematics degree in actuarial sciences at the University of Waterloo, Farah works as an actuarial student for a large insurance agency. At the same time, she is studying for exams so that she can become a fully qualified actuary. In her job, Farah deals with probabilities and statistics, so that she can determine how much the insurance company should charge for its automobile insurance policies. Before the company insures an automobile, Farah helps to determine the risk of collisions. Her goal is to make sure that the policy is sold for a fair price that will be enough to pay claims and allow the company to make a profit.

8.4

Inequalities of Combined Functions

Suppose that you are a financial advisor for a building contractor. Your client has been offered a contract to build up to 500 new houses but is not sure how many she should build. If she builds too few, she might not make enough money to cover expenses. If she builds too many, market saturation might drive down prices, resulting in the risk of a loss. Is there an optimum number that you would advise your client to build?

Often, in business, as well as in other disciplines, analysing combined functions can lead to a range of acceptable solutions. In such cases, techniques for solving inequalities are often useful. Deeper analysis can also reveal conditions for an optimum solution.

Investigate | **If you build it, will they come?**

Tools

- graphing calculator and/or grid paper

A building developer can build up to 500 houses for a new subdivision for the following costs:

Fixed Cost: $8 000 000
Variable Cost: $65 000 per house

The developer earns revenue, R, in millions of dollars, from sales according to the function $R(n) = 1.6\sqrt{n}$, where n is the number of houses.

1. Write an equation to represent the total cost, C, in millions of dollars, as a function of the number, n, of houses built and sold.

2. Graph $R(n)$ and $C(n)$ on the same set of axes. Choose appropriate window settings so that sales of between 0 and 500 houses can be viewed.

3. Identify the region where $R(n) > C(n)$. Sketch the graph and shade in this region. What is its significance?

4. Identify the points of intersection of the two curves and determine their coordinates using a method of your choice. Explain the meaning of these coordinates.

5. a) Use the superposition principle to graph $y = R(n) - C(n)$. Adjust the viewing window, as needed.

   b) Describe at least three interesting things that this graph shows.

6. Reflect Write a brief letter to the housing developer, advising her about the subdivision contract. Include in your letter

- the minimum and maximum number of houses that she should agree to build
- the number of houses she would need to build and sell to yield a maximum profit
- suggestions on how she might be able to increase her profits

Support your advice with mathematical reasoning.

| Example 1 | Techniques for Illustrating Inequalities |

Let $f(x) = x$ and $g(x) = (x - 2)^2$.

a) Graph the functions on the same set of axes. Identify the points of intersection.

b) Illustrate the regions for which

    i) $f(x) > g(x)$ **ii)** $g(x) > f(x)$

Solution

a) The graph of $y = f(x)$ is a line with slope one, passing through the origin. The graph of $y = g(x)$ can be obtained by applying a horizontal translation of 2 units to the right of the graph of $y = x^2$.

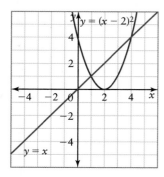

From the graph, the points of intersection appear to be $(1, 1)$ and $(4, 4)$. This can be verified algebraically by solving the linear-quadratic system of $f(x)$ and $g(x)$. Set the two functions equal and solve for x.

$$f(x) = g(x)$$
$$x = (x - 2)^2$$
$$x = x^2 - 4x + 4$$
$$x^2 - 5x + 4 = 0$$
$$(x - 1)(x - 4) = 0$$
$$x - 1 = 0 \quad \text{or} \quad x - 4 = 0$$
$$x = 1 \quad \text{or} \quad x = 4$$

To verify that the points of intersection are $(1, 1)$ and $(4, 4)$, mentally substitute each of these ordered pairs into $f(x) = x$ and $g(x) = (x - 2)^2$.

b) Method 1: *Compare the Functions Visually*

Using different colours or line styles is a useful technique for visualizing regions for which one function is greater than another. The graph of $y = f(x)$ is above the graph of $y = g(x)$ between $x = 1$ and $x = 4$. Therefore,

   i) $f(x) > g(x)$ on the interval $(1, 4)$

   ii) $g(x) > f(x)$ on the intervals $(-\infty, 1) \cup (4, \infty)$

Method 2: *Analyse the Difference Function*

Another way to illustrate where one function is greater than another is to subtract the functions and see where the graph of the difference is above the x-axis.

$f(x) > g(x)$

$f(x) - g(x) > 0$ Subtract $g(x)$ from both sides.

$$\begin{aligned} f(x) - g(x) &= x - (x - 2)^2 \\ &= x - (x^2 - 4x + 4) \\ &= -x^2 + 5x - 4 \end{aligned}$$

This function, $y = -x^2 + 5x - 4$, is positive on the intervals where $f(x) - g(x) > 0$ and therefore where $f(x) > g(x)$.

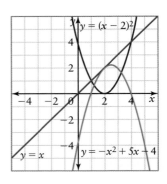

This function is positive on the interval $(1, 4)$. Therefore,

   i) $f(x) > g(x)$ on the interval $(1, 4)$

   ii) $g(x) > f(x)$ on the intervals $(-\infty, 1) \cup (4, \infty)$

Method 3: *Analyse the Quotient Function*

The functions $f(x)$ and $g(x)$ can also be compared by analysing their quotient. Graph the combined function $\dfrac{f(x)}{g(x)} = \dfrac{x}{(x - 2)^2}$ and identify the interval(s) for which this quotient is greater than one, which will correspond to where $f(x) > g(x)$.

To make this more clearly visible, graph the combined function using a graphing calculator with an appropriate viewing window. Include a graph of $y = 1$. Use the **Intersect** operation to identify the coordinates of the points of intersection.

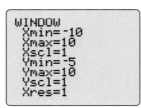

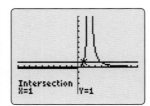

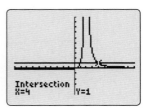

It appears that $\dfrac{f(x)}{g(x)} > 1$ on the interval $(1, 4)$. However, $\dfrac{f(x)}{g(x)}$ is not defined for $x = 2$. Determine $f(2)$ and $g(2)$ to decide what happens when $x = 2$.

$f(2) = 2$ and $g(2) = 0$.

Thus, $f(2) > g(2)$.

Therefore,

  i) $f(x) > g(x)$ on the interval $(1, 4)$

  ii) $g(x) > f(x)$ on the intervals $(-\infty, 1) \cup (4, \infty)$

Example 2 Solve an Inequality Graphically

Solve $\sin x > \log x$.

Solution

The solutions to this inequality cannot be found by algebraic techniques.

Graph $y = \sin x$ and $y = \log x$ on a graphing calculator. Ensure that the calculator is set to Radian mode. Use the window settings shown. Use the **Intersect** operation to find the approximate x-coordinates of any points of intersection.

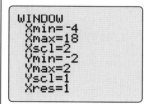 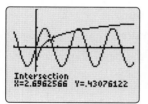 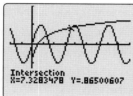 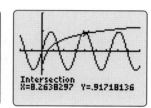

There is an asymptote at $x = 0$ and points of intersection at approximately $(2.70, 0.43)$, $(7.33, 0.87)$, and $(8.26, 0.92)$. The graph of $y = \sin x$ is above the graph of $y = \log x$ between $x = 0$ and $x \doteq 2.70$ and between $x \doteq 7.33$ and $x \doteq 8.26$. Therefore, $\sin x > \log x$ on the approximate intervals $(0, 2.70) \cup (7.33, 8.26)$.

You can verify this using the **TEST** menu of a graphing calculator.

- Enter the inequality in the **Y=** editor. For $>$, press ⟨2nd⟩ [TEST] to access the **TEST** menu and select **3: >.**

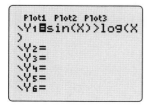

- Press (MODE) and set the calculator to Dot mode.
- Press (GRAPH).

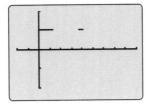

The graphing calculator plots the y-value 1 when the inequality is true and the y-value 0 when it is false. From the screen, you can see that $\sin x > \log x$ on the approximate intervals $(0, 2.70) \cup (7.33, 8.26)$.

Example 3 Inventory Control

A computer store's cost, C, for shipping and storing n computers can be modelled by the function $C(n) = 1.5n + \dfrac{200\,000}{n}$. The storage capacity of the store's warehouse is 750 units.

a) Graph this function and explain its shape. What is the domain of interest for this problem?

b) Determine the minimum and maximum number of computers that can be ordered at any one time to keep costs below $1500, assuming that inventory has fallen to zero.

c) What is the optimum order size that will minimize storage costs?

d) Why might this not be the best number to order?

Solution

a) Use a graphing calculator. Apply number sense to choose appropriate window settings.

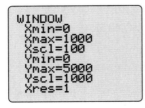 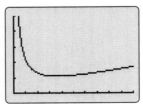

The shape of this graph can be understood if it is thought of as the superposition of a linear function and a rational function.

$$C(n) = 1.5n + \frac{200\,000}{n}$$

$$\underset{\text{linear}}{\nearrow} \qquad \underset{\text{rational}}{\nwarrow}$$

The domain of $C(n)$ is $\{n \in \mathbb{R}, n > 0\}$.

b) Determine the values of n that will keep costs below \$1500.

$$C(n) < 1500$$

$$1.5n + \frac{200\ 000}{n} < 1500$$

$$1.5n + \frac{200\ 000}{n} - 1500 < 0$$

Method 1: *Use a Graphing Calculator*

Graph the adjusted cost function $C = 1.5n + \dfrac{200\ 000}{n} - 1500$ and identify the region below the horizontal axis. Apply number sense to choose appropriate window settings to view the region of interest.

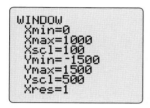
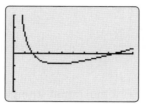

Notice that the adjustment term translates the original cost curve down 1500 units, making it easy to distinguish the region of interest. Locate the zeros by using the **Zero** operation.

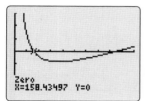
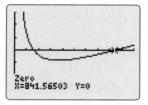

According to the graph, an inventory order of from 159 to 841 units will keep costs below \$1500. This region can be illustrated by setting **Y2** = 0 and then choosing shading above and below for the line styles of **Y1** and **Y2**, respectively.

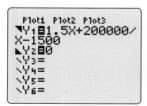
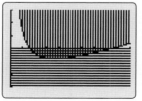

The region where the two shaded parts overlap shows the interval for which costs are below \$1500.

Method 2: *Use Pencil and Paper*

$1.5n^2 + 200\,000 - 1500n < 0$ Multiply both sides by n, since $n > 0$.

$1.5n^2 - 1500n + 200\,000 < 0$ Write the quadratic expression in standard form.

The quadratic expression on the left side corresponds to a quadratic function that opens upward. The region between the zeros will correspond to n-values for which $C < 0$. Solve for these zeros.

$1.5n^2 - 1500n + 200\,000 = 0$

$$n = \frac{-b \pm \sqrt{b^2 - 4ac}}{2a}$$ Apply the quadratic formula.

$$= \frac{-(-1500) \pm \sqrt{(-1500)^2 - 4(1.5)(200\,000)}}{2(1.5)}$$

$$= \frac{1500 \pm \sqrt{1\,050\,000}}{3}$$

$$\doteq 158 \text{ or } 842$$

Since the warehouse has a maximum storage capacity of 750 units, a shipment of from 159 to 750 computers will keep costs below \$1500.

c) To determine the optimum order size that will minimize shipping and storage costs, locate the minimum of the original cost function,

$C(n) = 1.5n + \dfrac{200\,000}{n}$.

Use the **Minimum** operation of a graphing calculator.

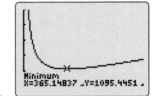

The minimum cost occurs when approximately 365 computers are ordered. The corresponding cost for this size of order is approximately \$1095.

d) The optimum order size may not be desirable, particularly if consumer demand is not aligned with this value. If demand significantly exceeds 365 units, then profit will be lost due to unfulfilled sales requests. On the other hand, if demand is significantly below 365 units, unnecessary shipping and storage costs will occur, as well as the cost of lost inventory space for other products.

KEY CONCEPTS

- Solutions to problems involving combined functions can sometimes lead to a range of acceptable answers. When this happens, techniques for solving inequalities are applied.

- There are a number of ways to graphically illustrate an inequality involving a combined function.

- Algebraic and graphical representations of inequalities can be useful for solving problems involving combined functions.

Communicate Your Understanding

C1 **a)** Refer to Example 1. List and summarize the methods for illustrating the inequality of two functions.

b) Describe at least one advantage and one disadvantage of each technique.

Use the following information to answer questions C2 and C3.

The cost, C, and revenue, R, functions for a business venture are shown on the graph. Assume that the independent variable is the number of units.

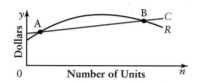

C2 **a)** Copy the graph. Shade the region where $R > C$. What is the meaning of this region?

b) Shade the region where $R < C$, using a different colour or shading style. What is the meaning of this region?

C3 **a)** Sketch a graph of the combined function $y = R - C$.

b) How would this graph change if the slope of the cost function were increased? decreased? What does each of these scenarios imply about potential profit?

A   Practise

For help with questions 1 and 2, refer to the Investigate.

Use the following information to answer questions 1 and 2.

The revenue and cost functions for the housing developer are shown on the graph.

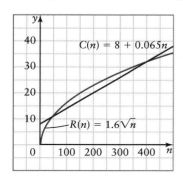

1. a) Suppose that the developer found a way to reduce her variable cost to $58 000 per house. How would this affect

i) the minimum and maximum number of houses she could build?

ii) her maximum potential profit?

b) Sketch a graph to illustrate your explanation.

2. a) Suppose that, instead of her variable costs being reduced, her fixed costs increase by $2 000 000. How would this affect

i) the minimum and maximum number of houses she could build?

ii) her maximum potential profit?

b) Sketch a graph to illustrate your explanation.

For help with questions 3 to 7, refer to Example 1.

3. The graphs of two functions are shown.

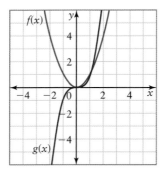

a) For what values of x is
  i) $f(x) > g(x)$?
  ii) $f(x) < g(x)$?

b) Sketch a graph of $y = f(x) - g(x)$ on the interval $(-2, 2)$.

c) For what region is $f(x) - g(x) > 0$? Explain how this corresponds to your answer to part a).

4. Let $u(x) = x + 5$ and $v(x) = 2^x$.

a) Graph these functions on the same set of axes.

b) Graph the combined function $y = \dfrac{u(x)}{v(x)}$.

c) Explain how $y = \dfrac{u(x)}{v(x)}$ can be used to identify the regions where
  i) $u(x) > v(x)$
  ii) $v(x) < u(x)$

5. Let $f(x) = x^3 + 8x^2 - 11x - 12$ and $g(x) = -x^2 - x + 12$.

a) Graph these functions on the same set of axes.

b) Identify, by inspecting the graphs, the intervals for which
  i) $f(x) > g(x)$
  ii) $g(x) > f(x)$

6. Solve question 5b) using two other methods.

7. Refer to Example 1.

a) Explain how you can determine an algebraic equation for $y = f(x) - g(x)$.

b) Find this equation.

c) Could the combined function $y = g(x) - f(x)$ be used to show where $f(x) > g(x)$ and $g(x) > f(x)$? Explain.

For help with questions 8 and 9, refer to Example 2.

8. Solve $\sin x < x$.

9. Solve $x^2 > 2^x$.

B **Connect and Apply**

For help with questions 10 to 12, refer to Example 3.

Use the following information to answer questions 10 to 12.

The owner of a small movie theatre needs to identify the optimum price for admission tickets to maximize her profits. The number, N, of people who attend a movie showing is a function of the price, p, in dollars, $N(p) = -(p + 7)(p - 15)$, assuming a minimum ticket price of $5.

10. a) Graph $N(p)$.

b) Identify the region for which $N(p) > 0$. What does this suggest about the maximum realistic ticket price? Explain your answer.

c) Identify the domain and range for which $y = N(p)$ has meaning.

11. Use Technology The revenue, R, in dollars, generated from ticket sales is given by $R(p) = N(p) \times p$, where p is the number of tickets sold.

a) Graph the function $R(p)$ on a graphing calculator.

b) For what region is $R(p) > 0$? Does this result agree with the one found in question 10b)? Explain.

c) Do the maxima of $N(p)$ and $R(p)$ occur at the same value of p? Explain why or why not.

d) What does $R(p)$ suggest that the optimum ticket price is? Explain.

12. Use Technology The cost, C, of showing a movie can be modelled by a composite function of $N(p)$, $C(p) = 150 + 5N(p)$.

a) Graph the function $C(p)$ on a graphing calculator.

b) Graph the combined function $y = R(p) - C(p)$. What does this function represent?

c) Identify the region for which $R(p) - C(p) > 0$. What is the significance of this region?

d) Do the maxima of $y = R(p)$ and $y = R(p) - C(p)$ occur for the same value of p? Explain why or why not.

e) Identify the optimum ticket price per movie and determine the maximum profit per showing.

13. A mass hanging from a spring is set into vertical motion. Its displacement, d, in centimetres, from the equilibrium point ($d = 0$) can be modelled by the function $d(t) = 5[\sin(6t) - 4\cos(6t)]$, where t is the time, in seconds. At what times during the first 2 s is the mass below the equilibrium position? Round answers to the nearest hundredth of a second.

14. Write two functions, $f(x)$ and $g(x)$, for which $f(x) > g(x)$ on the interval $(-\infty, \infty)$.

15. Chapter Problem It is with great fanfare that Funky Stuff announces their release of the vintage hula hoop!

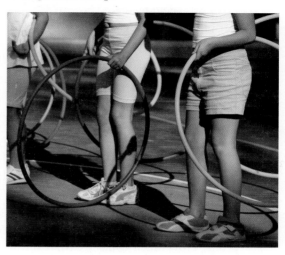

The marketing department needs to establish an acceptable range of prices for the hula hoop. Based on market research, the projected revenue, R, as a function of the number, n, in thousands, of units sold can be modelled by the function $R = -0.2n^2 + 3n$. The total cost, C, as a function of n can be modelled by the function $C = 0.1n^2 + 0.4n + 2$. R and C are amounts in thousands of dollars.

a) Graph R and C on the same set of axes.

b) How many points of intersection does this system of quadratic equations have? Explain their significance.

c) Identify the region where $R > C$. Why is this region important?

d) Maximum profit occurs when R exceeds C by the greatest amount. Use the superposition principle to graph the function $P = R - C$.

e) Use this function to determine

 i) the optimum number of units sold

 ii) the maximum profit per unit sold

 iii) the total profit, if the optimum number of units are sold

f) Reflect on the shapes of the revenue and cost curves. Suggest some reasons why they are shaped like this, instead of being linear functions.

16. Claire builds and sells birdhouses. Claire makes n birdhouses in a given week and sells them for $45 - n$ dollars per birdhouse. Her weekly costs include a fixed cost of $280 plus $8 per birdhouse made. Assume that Claire sells all of the birdhouses that she makes.

a) Write an equation to represent her total weekly cost.

b) Write an equation to represent her total weekly revenue.

c) Write an inequality to express the conditions for which Claire will make a profit.

d) How many birdhouses should Claire build each week in order to make a profit?

e) What is the optimum number of birdhouses Claire should build in order to earn maximum profit? How much will she earn if she does this?

✓ Achievement Check

17. The projected population, P, of a town can be modelled by the function $P(t) = 2000(1.025)^t$, where t is the time, in years, from now. The expected number, N, of people who can be supplied by local services can be modelled by the function $N(t) = 5000 + 57.5t$.

Reasoning and Proving
Representing — Selecting Tools
Problem Solving
Connecting — Reflecting
Communicating

a) Determine $y = N(t) - P(t)$ and sketch its graph.

b) Explain what the function in part a) represents.

c) When is $N(t) - P(t) < 0$? Explain what this means.

d) Determine $y = \dfrac{N(t)}{P(t)}$ and sketch its graph.

e) Explain what the function in part d) represents.

C   Extend and Challenge

18. Write two functions, $f(x)$ and $g(x)$, for which $f(x) > g(x)$ on regular periodic intervals.

19. a) Write two functions, $f(x)$ and $g(x)$, for which $f(x) > g(x)$ on the interval $(0, 4)$.

b) Determine a different solution to part a).

20. $f(x) > 0$ on the interval $(-3, 3)$ and $g(x) - f(x) > 0$ on the intervals $(-\infty, -3) \cup (2, \infty)$.

a) Determine possible equations for $f(x)$ and $g(x)$.

b) Is there more than one solution for part a)? Explain.

21. $f(x)$ is a quadratic function and $g(x)$ is a linear function for which $\dfrac{f(x)}{g(x)} > 1$ on the intervals $(-\infty, -3)$ and $(4, \infty)$. Determine possible equations for $f(x)$ and $g(x)$.

22. Math Contest A total of 28 handshakes are exchanged at the end of a party. Assuming that everyone shakes hands with everyone else at the party, how many people are at the party?

23. Math Contest Determine the value of $x + y + z$, given that $x^2 + y^2 + z^2 = xy + xz + yz = 3$.

24. Math Contest Bill has $1.64 in pennies, nickels, dimes, and quarters. If he has equal numbers of each coin, how many coins does he have?

25. Math Contest Prove that given any three consecutive numbers, one of these numbers will always be divisible by three.

Making Connections: Modelling With Combined Functions

Have you ever bungee jumped? If you were to bungee jump, how many bounces do you suppose you would make? When would you be travelling the fastest?

Many of these questions and others like it can be answered by mathematical modelling with combined functions. Are you ready to take the leap?

Investigate | **How can a combined function be used to model the path of a bungee jumper?**

The height versus time data of a bungee jumper are given in the table, for the first half minute or so of his jump. Heights are referenced to the rest position of the bungee jumper, which is well above ground level.

Tools

• computer with *Fathom*™

Time (s)	0	1	2	3	4	5	6	7	8	9	10	11	12
Height (m)	100	90	72	45	14	−15	−41	−61	−71	−73	−66	−52	−32
Time (s)	13	14	15	16	17	18	19	20	21	22	23	24	25
Height (m)	−11	11	30	44	53	54	48	37	23	6	−8	−23	−33
Time (s)	26	27	28	29	30	31	32	33	34	35	36	37	
Height (m)	−39	−39	−35	−27	−16	−4	6	17	24	28	29	26	

1. In *Fathom*™, open a new collection and enter the data in a case table.

2. **a)** Create a scatter plot of height versus time.

   b) Describe the shape formed by the points.

3. **a)** Describe how the graph exhibits sinusoidal features.

   b) Describe how the graph exhibits exponential features.

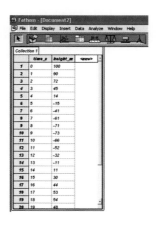

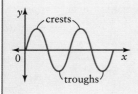

Technology Tip

To enter one of the attributes in a case table into a calculation, you can either type it in manually or select it from the **attributes** drop-down menu.

You can manipulate the scale of a slider by placing the cursor over different regions of the slider. Experiment to see how you can
- slide the scale
- stretch the scale
- compress the scale

4. a) Construct a cosine function that has the same period (or wavelength) as the scatter plot by following these steps:
- Create a slider and call it k.
- Click on the graph. From the **Graph** menu, choose **Plot Function**.
- Enter the function 100*cos(k*time_s).
- Adjust the slider until the crests and troughs of the function occur at the same times as for the scatter plot.

b) Note the value of k.

5. a) Construct an exponential function to model the decay in amplitude of the scatter plot by following these steps:
- Create a slider and call it c.
- Click on the graph. From the **Graph** menu, choose **Plot Function**.
- Enter the function 100*0.5^(c*time_s).
- Adjust the slider until the exponential curve just touches each crest of the scatter plot.

b) Note the value of c.

6. Construct a combined function to model the height-time relationship of the bungee jumper by following these steps:
- Click on the graph. From the **Graph** menu, choose **Plot Function**.
- Enter the function 100*cos(k*time_s)*0.5^(c*time_s).

Make any final adjustments to k or c, if necessary.

7. a) How far will the bungee jumper be above the rest position at his fourth crest?

b) For how long will the bungee jumper bounce before his amplitude has diminished to 10 m?

8. Reflect

a) What is the significance of the factor of 100?

b) Why was a cosine function chosen instead of a sine function?

c) When the cosine function and the exponential function are combined, only one factor of 100 is used. Why?

d) When is the magnitude of the rate of change of this function the greatest? What does this mean from a physical perspective?

Example 1 | Combining Musical Notes

Musical notes are distinguished by their pitch, which corresponds to the frequency of vibration of a moving part of an instrument, such as a string on a guitar. The table lists one octave of the frequencies of commonly used notes in North American music, rounded to the nearest hertz (Hz). This is called the chromatic scale.

Note	Frequency (Hz)	Note	Frequency (Hz)
C	262	F#	370
C#	277	G	392
D	294	G#	415
D#	311	A	440
E	330	A#	466
F	349	B	494
---	---	high C	524

The graph of a pure note can be modelled by the function $I(t) = \sin(2\pi ft)$, where I is the sound intensity; f is the frequency of the note, in hertz; and t is the time, in seconds.

According to music theory, notes sound good together when they cause constructive interference at regular intervals of time.

a) Graph the intensity functions for C and high C. Then, graph the combined function for these two notes struck together. Describe the resultant waveform.

b) A C-major triad is formed by striking the following notes simultaneously:

   C   E   G

   Graph the combined function for these notes struck together. Explain why these notes sound good together.

c) Graph the intensity functions for C and F# (F-sharp) and the combined function for these two notes struck together. Explain why these notes are discordant (do not sound good together).

Solution

a) Determine the waveforms for C and high C by substituting their frequencies into the intensity function.

$$I_C(t) = \sin[2\pi(262)t]$$
$$= \sin(524\pi t)$$

$$I_{high\ C}(t) = \sin[2\pi(524)t]$$
$$= \sin(1048\pi t)$$

Use a graphing calculator to graph these waveforms.

Ensure that the calculator is set to Radian mode. It may be necessary to experiment with the window settings to get a clear view of the waveforms.

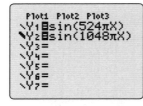 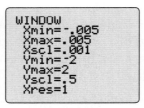 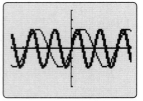

Note that high C has the same waveform as C, compressed by a horizontal factor of $\frac{1}{2}$, resulting in regular occurrences of constructive interference (their crests and troughs occur at nearly the same points).

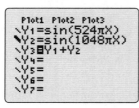

This suggests that these notes will sound good together. To view the combination of these two waveforms, apply the superposition principle. Turn off the functions for the two component waveforms for clarity.

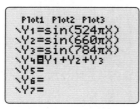 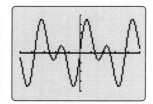

This waveform is periodic. It is basically sinusoidal with a slight variation at regular intervals. These notes will sound good together.

b) To graph the C-major triad, enter the waveforms for the C, E, and G notes, and then graph their sum using the superposition principle. Use the frequencies given in the table.

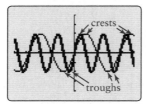 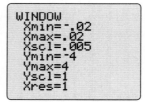 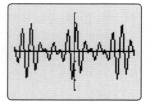

This waveform is considerably more complicated than a simple sinusoidal waveform. Note, however, that there is still a regular repeating pattern to the wave, which suggests that these notes will also sound good together. The multiple variations along the cycle actually give the chord its interesting character.

c) Use graphing technology to view the waveforms for the notes C and F#.

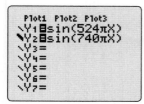
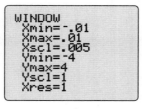
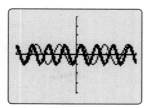

Notice that the crests and troughs of these two notes do not coincide at regular intervals, suggesting that these two notes will not sound good together. View the graph of their sum using the superposition principle to confirm this.

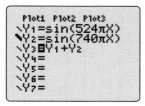
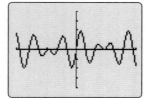

This waveform does not appear to be periodic, confirming that C and F# are discordant notes.

Example 2 | Path of a Skier

A skier is skiing down a 100-m hill at a constant speed of 1 m/s, through a series of moguls, or small hills. The constant slope of the hill is −1. Assuming that the moguls measure 1.5 m from crest to trough and are roughly 5 m apart, develop an algebraic and a graphical model of the height of the skier versus time.

Solution

Break the desired function into two parts. First, determine a function for the skier's height assuming that there are no moguls. Then, add the effect of the moguls.

Neglecting the effect of the moguls, the path of the skier, as a function of height versus time, can be modelled by a straight line.

The hill is 100 m high, and the rate of change of height versus time is -1 m/s. Therefore, the height of the skier can be approximated by the function $h(t) = -t + 100$. Using *The Geometer's Sketchpad®*, graph this function.

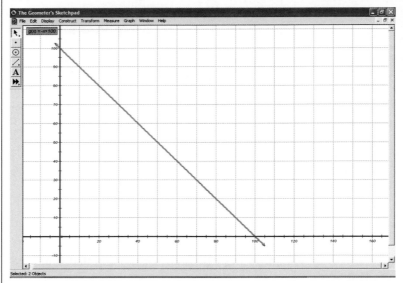

To model the skier's height through the moguls, ignoring the slope of the hill for the moment, generate a sinusoidal function to reflect the correct amplitude and wavelength.

Method 1: *Use Parameters*

Using *The Geometer's Sketchpad®*, create two parameters to represent the amplitude, A, and the horizontal compression, k. Then, construct the function $f(x) = A\sin(kx)$.

Adjust the parameters until the amplitude is $1.5 \div 2$, or 0.75 m, and the wavelength is 5 m.

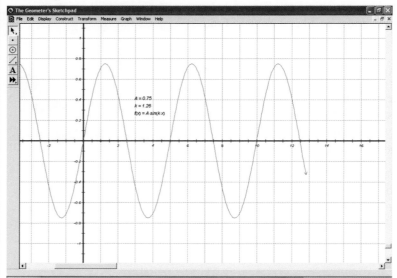

Therefore, the height, M, in metres, of the skier through the moguls, ignoring the slope of the hill, after t seconds, is $M(t) = 0.75\sin(1.26t)$.

Method 2: *Apply Algebraic Reasoning*

The crest-to-trough distance of the moguls is 1.5 m, and they are 5 m apart.

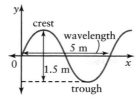

The amplitude, A, is half the crest-to-trough distance:

$A = 1.5 \div 2$
$\quad = 0.75$

CONNECTIONS

Jennifer Heil became the first female Canadian Olympic gold medal winner in mogul skiing in the freestyle moguls event at the 2006 Winter Games in Turin, Italy.

This Canadian hero, who is also a champion ski racer, then went on to become the 2007 CanWest athlete of the year.

The average speed of the skier is 1 m/s, so the frequency, f, is $\frac{1}{5}$, or 0.2 moguls per second.

Substitute these values for A and f into the function $M(t) = A\sin(2\pi f t)$, where M represents the height, in metres, within the mogul as a function of time, t, in seconds.

$M(t) = 0.75\sin(2\pi(0.2)t)$
$\quad\quad = 0.75\sin(0.4\pi t)$

Therefore, the height of the skier through the moguls, ignoring the slope of the hill, is $M(t) = 0.75\sin(0.4\pi t)$, or $M(t) \doteq 0.75\sin(1.26t)$.

To describe the skier's actual path of height versus time, add the two functions.

$P(t) = h(t) + M(t)$
$\quad\quad = -t + 100 + 0.75\sin(1.26t)$

The graph of this function is shown.

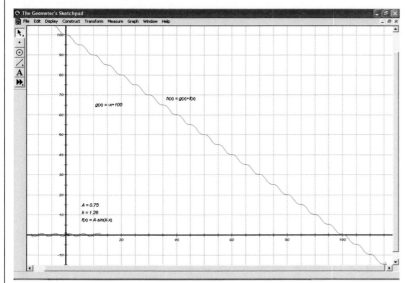

- A variety of real-world situations can be modelled using combined functions.

- To develop a model consisting of a combined function, consider

  - the component functions that could be combined to form the model
  - the nature of the rate of change of the component functions
  - the other key features of the graph or equation that fit the given scenario

Communicate Your Understanding

C1 Refer to the Investigate. A simple harmonic oscillator is an object that repeats a cyclic motion indefinitely, such as a pendulum on a clock. A damped harmonic oscillator is an object that repeats its cyclic motion, but whose amplitude decreases over time due to frictional forces.

   a) What is the difference between simple harmonic motion and damped harmonic motion?

   b) Is the motion of the bungee jumper an example of damped harmonic motion? Explain why or why not.

   c) Describe two other scenarios that are examples of damped harmonic motion.

C2 Each graph is made up of a sum or difference of two functions. Identify the types of functions that are combined in each case.

   a)

   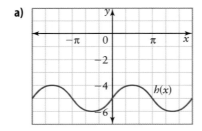

   b)

   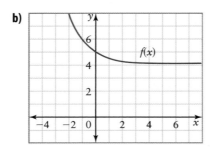

C3 Refer to question C2. Suggest a possible scenario that could be modelled by each graph.

For help with questions 1 to 3, refer to the Investigate.

Use this graph of the path of the bungee jumper to answer questions 1 to 3.

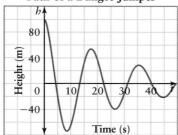

Path of a Bungee Jumper

1. Copy the graph of this curve. Sketch how the path of the jumper would change if she dropped from
   a) a greater height
   b) a lower height

2. Sketch how the path of the jumper would change if she were attached to
   a) a longer cord
   b) a shorter cord

3. Sketch how the path of the jumper would change if she were attached to
   a) a springier cord
   b) a stiffer cord

For help with questions 4 to 6, refer to Example 1.

4. A C-major triad can be expanded into other C-major chords by adding additional notes of the triad from the next octave.
   a) Graph the combined function formed by the following notes being struck simultaneously:
   C   E   G   high C   high E
   b) Compare this waveform to the one for the C-major triad.

5. A power chord is formed by dropping the major third (or E-note) from the C-major triad.
   a) Graph each C power chord.
   i) C   G
   ii) C   G   high C
   b) Compare these waveforms to those of the C-major triad and the C-major chord.

CONNECTIONS

Power chords are widely used in heavy metal music. In addition to generating a full, powerful sound, they are relatively easy to fret on a guitar, making it possible for even an amateur player to work quickly along the fret board to generate a blistering rhythm.

6. Bobby attempts to play a C-major triad on his guitar, but it is badly tuned. The C-note is correctly tuned to 262 Hz, but the E and G notes are flat (lower in frequency than they should be), as follows:

   E: 300 Hz
   G: 360 Hz

   a) Graph the C-major triad as played by Bobby's guitar.
   b) Discuss the sound quality of this chord, making reference to the waveform.

For help with questions 7 to 9, refer to Example 2.

7. Refer to Example 2. Sketch how the graph would change if the moguls were
   a) higher
   b) closer together

8. A skier is going up and down the same hill at regular intervals. On each run, she skis at an average speed of 1 m/s from the top of the hill to the bottom, waits in the chairlift line for about 1 min, and then travels up the chairlift at a speed of 0.5 m/s. Assume that this hill has no moguls.

a) Develop a graphical model of the skier's height versus time over the course of several ski runs.

b) Explain what is happening during each region of the graph for one cycle.

c) How might you develop an algebraic model to describe this motion?

9. Refer to question 8. Adjust your graph from part a) to illustrate the effect on the skier's height function in each scenario.

a) After her second run, she meets a friend and spends an extra minute chatting in the lift line.

b) On her third trip up the chairlift, the lift is stopped for 30 s so that other skiers can assist someone who is having trouble getting on the lift.

c) On her third trip down the hill, the skier doubles her speed.

B **Connect and Apply**

The number of teams in the National Hockey League (NHL) is given for the past several decades.

Year	Teams	Year	Teams	Year	Teams
1966	6	1980	21	1994	26
1967	12	1981	21	1995	26
1968	12	1982	21	1996	26
1969	12	1983	21	1997	26
1970	14	1984	21	1998	27
1971	14	1985	21	1999	28
1972	16	1986	21	2000	30
1973	16	1987	21	2001	30
1974	18	1988	21	2002	30
1975	18	1989	21	2003	30
1976	18	1990	21	2004	30
1977	18	1991	22	2005	30
1978	17	1992	24	2006	30
1979	21	1993	26	2007	30

Use this information to answer questions 10 to 12.

10. a) Using 1966 as year 0, create a scatter plot of the number, N, of teams versus time, t, in years.

b) Determine a line or curve of best fit, using a method of your choice (e.g., regression analysis, sliders, systematic trial). Justify the type of function that you chose.

c) Write an equation for $N(t)$.

d) There is an outlier in 1966 that does not appear to fit the trend very well. What effect does removing the outlier have on the model for $N(t)$? Does this effect appear to be significant?

| CONNECTIONS

You will study the effect of outliers on lines and curves of best fit if you study data management.

Use a line or curve of best fit for N(t) to answer questions 11 and 12.

11. According to one hockey analyst, the number of high-calibre players emerging from the junior ranks can be modelled by the function $D(t) = 25 + 0.4t$, where D is the number of drafted players who are considered talented enough to play at the NHL level as a function of time, t, in years.

   a) Graph this function and describe the trend. What does this suggest about the junior leagues?

   b) The number, R, of players retiring each year is a function of the number of teams and time given by $R(t) = 2[N(t)] - 0.53t$. Graph $R(t)$ on the same set of axes as in part a) and describe the trend.

   c) What does this suggest about the length of NHL players' careers?

   d) Graph the function $y = \dfrac{R(t)}{N(t)}$. Does this confirm your answer to part c)? Explain why or why not.

   e) Graph the function $P(t) = D(t) - R(t)$. What does this function describe?

   f) Describe the trend of $P(t)$, and discuss any implications it might have.

12. a) On a new set of axes, graph the function $y = \dfrac{P(t)}{N(t)}$. What does this function describe?

Reasoning and Proving
Representing — Selecting Tools
Problem Solving
Connecting — Reflecting
Communicating

   b) What is the significance of the t-intercept? What implications might this have for the quality of NHL hockey?

   c) Suppose that the function $D(t)$ is adjusted to recognize the increase in draftable players from foreign countries, such that the slope increases slightly. Discuss the effect this will have on the functions $y = P(t)$ and $y = \dfrac{P(t)}{N(t)}$. How might this affect your answers to part b)?

13. **Use Technology**

   a) Using a motion probe and a graphing calculator, capture the motion of a person on a swing as he or she moves back and forth relative to the sensor, while undergoing damped harmonic motion.

   b) Create a scatter plot of the data.

   c) Develop an equation to model the data. Explain how you determined the equation.

C) Extend and Challenge

14. A skier is skiing down a hill at a constant speed. Her height versus time graph is shown.

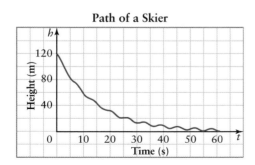
Path of a Skier

Develop an algebraic model for this relationship.

15. Perform research on the Internet or using other sources. Find an example of a real-world situation in which a combined function is, or could be, used to model a relationship. Explain

Reasoning and Proving
Representing — Selecting Tools
Problem Solving
Connecting — Reflecting
Communicating

   • the nature of the relationship being described

   • the types of component functions that are used

   • the way the functions are combined

   Pose and solve two problems based on your research.

8.1 Sums and Differences of Functions

1. a) Copy the graph.

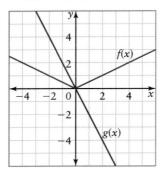

b) Use the superposition principle to generate a graph of each function.

i) $y = f(x) + g(x)$

ii) $y = f(x) - g(x)$

iii) $y = g(x) - f(x)$

2. Let $f(x) = x - 2$, $g(x) = x^2 + 3x - 3$, and $h(x) = 2^x$. Determine an algebraic and a graphical model for each combined function. Identify the domain and range in each case.

a) $y = f(x) + g(x)$

b) $y = f(x) + g(x) + h(x)$

c) $y = f(x) - h(x)$

3. Use Technology Use graphing technology to check your answers to question 2.

4. Max can earn \$6/h as a waiter, plus an additional \$9/h in tips.

a) Graph Max's earnings from wages as a function of hours worked.

b) Graph Max's earnings from tips as a function of hours worked.

c) Develop an algebraic and a graphical model for Max's total earnings.

d) How much can Max earn if he works 52 h in one week?

8.2 Products and Quotients of Functions

5. Let $u(x) = x^2$ and $v(x) = \cos x$. Work in radians.

a) What type of symmetry do you predict the combined function $y = u(x)v(x)$ will have? Explain your reasoning.

b) Use Technology Use graphing technology to check your prediction.

6. Let $f(x) = \sin x$ and $g(x) = \cos x$.

a) Graph $f(x)$ and $g(x)$ on the same set of axes.

b) Sketch a graph of the combined function $y = \dfrac{f(x)}{g(x)}$.

c) Identify the domain and range of this function.

d) Use your understanding of trigonometric identities to identify the graph of $y = \dfrac{f(x)}{g(x)}$.

7. Refer to question 6.

a) Graph the combined function $y = \dfrac{g(x)}{f(x)}$.

b) Identify the domain and range of this function.

c) How is $y = \dfrac{g(x)}{f(x)}$ related to $y = \dfrac{f(x)}{g(x)}$ in terms of transformations?

8.3 Composite Functions

8. Let $f(x) = x^2 + 3x$ and $g(x) = 2x - 5$. Determine an equation for each composite function, graph the function, and give its domain and range.

a) $y = f(g(x))$ **b)** $y = g(f(x))$

c) $y = g(g(x))$ **d)** $y = g^{-1}(g(x))$

9. Assume that a function $f(x)$ and its inverse $f^{-1}(x)$ are both defined for $x \in \mathbb{R}$.

a) Give a geometric interpretation of the composite function $y = f(f^{-1}(x))$.

b) Illustrate your answer to part a) with two examples.

8.4 Inequalities of Combined Functions

10. Let $f(x) = 1.2^x$ and $g(x) = 0.92^x + 5$.

  a) Identify the region for which

    i) $f(x) > g(x)$

    ii) $g(x) > f(x)$

  b) Illustrate this inequality graphically in two different ways.

11. Refer to question 10.

  a) Write a real-world scenario that these functions could model.

  b) Pose and solve two problems based on your scenario.

12. The cost, C, and revenue, R, as functions of the number of televisions sold by an electronics store are shown on the graph.

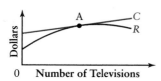

  a) Identify the region(s) for which

    i) $C > R$

    ii) $R > C$

  b) What can you conclude about this business venture?

  c) What suggestions would you give to the store owner in order to help him or her improve the situation?

8.5 Making Connections: Modelling with Combined Functions

Refer to the chromatic music scale on page 463.

13. A D-minor chord is formed by striking the following notes together:

    D   F   A   high D

  a) Double the frequency of D in the table to determine the frequency of high D.

  b) Graph the combined function formed by these four notes. Describe the waveform.

> **CONNECTIONS**
>
> Minor chords tend to have a sad sound to them. They combine with major chords (which sound happier) to create musical tension.

14. Experiment with various note combinations from the chromatic scale.

  a) Identify two chords that you think would make a good sound.

  b) Identify two chords that you think would make a discordant (unpleasant) sound.

  c) Use mathematical reasoning to justify your choices. Then, test your theories using a well-tuned guitar or piano. You may need to do a little research to identify the correct notes.

PROBLEM WRAP-UP

CHAPTER

The number, S, in thousands, of Funky Teddy Bears that can be supplied by Funky Stuff as a function of price, p, in dollars, can be modelled by the function $S(p) = p + 3$.

The demand, D, for the bears can be modelled by the function $D(p) = -0.1(p + 8)(p - 12)$.

  a) For what interval is $D(p) > S(p)$? What does this imply about the availability of Funky Teddy Bears?

  b) For what interval is $D(p) < S(p)$? What does this imply about the availability of Funky Teddy Bears?

  c) Graph these functions on the same set of axes. Identify their point of intersection. Explain what the coordinates of this point mean.

  d) Graph the function $y = S(p) - D(p)$ and explain what it shows.

For questions 1 to 4, choose the best answer.

1. Which function represents the composite function $y = f(g(x))$, where $f(x) = x + 2$ and $g(x) = x^2$?

   A $y = x^2 + 2$

   B $y = x^2 + 2x$

   C $y = x^2 + 4$

   D $y = x^2 + 4x + 4$

2. Let $u(x) = x - 1$ and $v(x) = x^2 - 1$. For which values of x is the combined function $y = \dfrac{u(x)}{v(x)}$ undefined?

   A $x \in \mathbb{R}$

   B $x = 1$

   C $x = -1$

   D $x = \pm 1$

3. Let $f(x) = (x - 2)^2$ and $g(x) = -x + 3$. Which function represents the combined function $y = f(x) + g(x)$?

   A $y = x^2 - x + 1$

   B $y = -x^2 + 3x - 7$

   C $y = x^2 + 3x + 7$

   D $y = x^2 - 5x + 7$

4. The graphs of two functions are shown.

   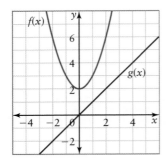

   Which is true for $x \in \mathbb{R}$?

   A $g(x) - f(x) < 0$

   B $\dfrac{f(x)}{g(x)} > 1, x \neq 0$

   C $f(x) < g(x)$

   D All of the above.

5. Let $f(x) = (x - 3)^2$ and $g(x) = x + 4$. Determine an algebraic and a graphical model for each combined function. Give the domain and range in each case.

   a) $y = f(x) + g(x)$

   b) $y = f(x) - g(x)$

   c) $y = f(g(x))$

   d) $y = g^{-1}(g(x))$

6. **Use Technology** Check your answers to question 5 using graphing technology.

7. **a)** Create a growing pattern of tiles to represent the sum of a linear function, a quadratic function, and another function of your choice. Draw several stages of the pattern.

   b) Develop an algebraic model to represent the total number of tiles required for the nth stage.

   c) Draw a separate graph for each part of the growing pattern as a function of n and a graph that represents the total number of tiles required for the nth stage.

8. Let $f(x) = x + 5$ and $g(x) = x^2 + 9x + 20$.

   a) Determine an algebraic and a graphical model for $y = \dfrac{f(x)}{g(x)}$ and identify its domain and range.

   b) Determine an algebraic and a graphical model for $y = \dfrac{g(x)}{f(x)}$ and identify its domain and range.

9. Express the volume of a sphere of radius r as a function of

   a) the circumference

   b) the surface area

   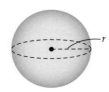

10. Is the difference of two odd functions odd or even? Justify your answer with two examples.

11. A pendulum is released and allowed to swing back and forth according to the equation $x(t) = 10\cos(2t) \times 0.95^t$, where x is the horizontal displacement from the rest position, in centimetres, as a function of time, t, in seconds.

  a) Graph the function. What type of motion is this? Identify the domain and range in the context of this problem.

  b) This combined function is the product of two component functions. Identify the component that is responsible for

   i) the periodic nature of the motion

   ii) the exponential decay of the amplitude

  c) At what horizontal distance from the rest position was the bob of the pendulum released?

  d) At what point on the graph is the magnitude of the rate of change the greatest? When does this occur with respect to the motion of the pendulum bob?

  e) At what point(s) is the rate of change zero? When does this occur with respect to the motion of the pendulum bob?

  f) After what elapsed time will the pendulum's amplitude diminish to 50% of its initial value?

12. A catenary is the shape of a hanging flexible cable or chain between two supports that is acted upon only by gravity. It looks like a parabola, but it is not. In reality, it is an exponential function, not a quadratic function. Once a load is applied, such as with a suspension bridge, the curve becomes parabolic.

  a) Sketch a graph of the catenary defined by $f(x) = \frac{1}{2}(e^x + e^{-x})$, where $e \doteq 2.718$, on the interval $x \in [-5, 5]$.

  b) Develop a quadratic function to closely model this catenary.

  c) Sketch both functions, labelling common points and showing where the functions diverge.

13. The number, S, in hundreds, of swimmers at Boulder Beach as a function of temperature, T, in degrees Celsius, can be modelled by the function $S(T) = -0.05(T - 28)(T - 34)$.

The number, I, of ice-cream sales made by the Boulder Beach ice-cream vendor can be modelled by the function $I(T) = 0.5S(T) \times T$.

  a) Graph $S(T)$ and $I(T)$ on the same set of axes and describe their trends.

  b) At what temperature will Boulder Beach attract the greatest number of swimmers? How many will come for a cooling dip?

  c) At what temperature will the Boulder Beach ice-cream vendor earn maximum profits? Is this the same temperature as the maximum found in part b)? Why or why not?

14. a) Determine two functions, $f(x)$ and $g(x)$, for which $f(x) < g(x)$ on the interval $(-1, 1)$ and $f(x) > g(x)$ on the intervals $(-\infty, -1) \cup (1, \infty)$.

  b) Illustrate graphically how your functions satisfy these criteria, using three different methods. Explain each method.

15. A skier's height, h, in metres, as a function of time, t, in seconds, can be modelled by the combined function $h(t) = [80(0.9)^t + 0.5] + 0.6\sin(3t)$.

  a) Graph this function.

  b) The skier encounters moguls at some point during her run. Assuming that she travels at a constant speed, at approximately what point in time does she encounter the moguls? Explain how you can tell.

  c) Assuming that the skier stops the first time her height reaches zero, find the domain and range relevant to this problem.

Chapter 6 Exponential and Logarithmic Functions

1. a) Copy and complete the table of values for the function $y = 4^x$.

x	y
-2	
-1	
0	
$\frac{1}{2}$	
1	
2	
3	

b) Graph the function.

c) Sketch a graph of the inverse of $y = 4^x$.

2. Evaluate each logarithm.

a) $\log_5 25$ **b)** $\log_2 128$

c) $\log_3 \left(\frac{1}{27} \right)$ **d)** $\log 1000$

e) $\log_7 7^4$ **f)** $\log 10^{-5}$

3. The intensity, I, of sunlight decreases exponentially with depth, d, below the surface of the ocean. The relationship is given by $I(d) = 100(0.39)^d$.

a) When the intensity of sunlight at the surface is 100 units, what is the intensity at a depth of 3 m, to the nearest tenth?

b) What is the intensity at a depth of 5 m, to the nearest tenth?

4. a) Graph the function $y = \log(2x - 4)$. Determine the domain, the range, the x- and y-intercepts, and the equations of any asymptotes.

b) Describe how a graph of the function $y = -\log(2x - 4)$ would differ from the graph in part a).

5. Evaluate.

a) $\log_6 36^5$

b) $\log_4 32 + \log_4 2$

6. Solve for x. Round answers to two decimal places, if necessary.

a) $4^x = 15$

b) $x = \log_2 18$

7. A vehicle depreciates by 25% each year. Its value, V, in dollars, as a function of time, t, in years, can be modelled by the function $V(t) = 28\,000(0.75)^t$.

a) What was the initial value of the vehicle? Explain how you know.

b) How long will it take for the vehicle to depreciate to half its initial value, to the nearest tenth of a year?

8. The decibel rating of a sound is $\beta = 10 \log \frac{I}{I_0}$, where $I_0 = 10^{-12}$ W/m².

a) Find the decibel rating of a rock concert with an intensity of 8.75×10^{-3} W/m².

b) A radio on very low, so it is just audible, has a decibel rating of 20 dB. What is the intensity of the sound from this radio?

Chapter 7 Tools and Strategies for Solving Exponential and Logarithmic Equations

9. Solve. Check your answers using graphing technology.

a) $27^{x+2} = 9^{5-2x}$

b) $10^{5x+4} = 1000^{3x}$

c) $64^{x+5} = 16^{2x-1}$

10. Solve for n. Round answers to two decimal places.

a) $8 = 3^n$ **b)** $5.8^n = 100$

c) $10^{n+5} = 7$ **d)** $2^{-n} = 6$

e) $278^{3n-7} = 21^{2n+5}$ **f)** $5^{2n} = 0.75^{n-4}$

11. Various radioactive substances are used in medical tests.

a) Iodine-131 is used in thyroid tests. A 20-mg sample decays to 16.85 mg in 48 h. What is the half-life of iodine-131, to the nearest hour?

b) Strontium-87 is used in some bone tests. After 1 h, a 100-mg sample decays to 78.1 mg. Determine the half-life of strontium-87, to the nearest tenth of an hour.

12. Simplify. State any restrictions on the variables.

a) $\log(x^2 - 1) - \log(x - 1)$

b) $\log\sqrt{x} + \log x^3 - 2\log x$

c) $\log\left(1 + \dfrac{2y}{x} + \dfrac{y^2}{x^2}\right) + 2\log x$

13. Solve. Identify and reject any extraneous roots. Check your solutions using graphing technology.

a) $\log_3(-3x + 5) = 2$

b) $\log(x + 5) - \log(x + 1) = \log(3x)$

c) $\log_5(x - 6) = 1 - \log_5(x - 2)$

14. According to the power law of logarithms, $\log x^2 = 2\log x$. Are the graphs of the functions $f(x) = \log x^2$ and $g(x) = 2\log x$ the same? Explain any differences.

15. The population of a city is increasing by 12% annually. The population is 38 000 now.

a) Write an equation to show the population as a function of time, t, in years.

b) How long will it take for the population to double, to the nearest tenth of a year?

c) After how many years will the population reach 100 000?

Chapter 8 Combining Functions

16. Given $f(x) = 2^x + 2$, $g(x) = x^2 - 1$, and $h(x) = 2x$, determine an algebraic and a graphical model for each function. Identify the domain and the range for each.

a) $y = f(x) + g(x)$

b) $y = f(x) - g(x) - h(x)$

c) $y = f(x)g(x)$

d) $y = \dfrac{f(x)}{g(x)}$

17. Kathy has a small business selling apple cider at the farmers' market. She pays \$35 per day to rent her space at the market, and each cup of cider costs her \$1. She sells the cider for \$2.50 per cup and brings enough cider and cups to sell a maximum of 200 cups in a day.

a) Write an equation to model each of the following for 1 day, as a function of the number, n, of cups of cider sold.

  i) her total cost, C

  ii) her revenue, R

b) Graph $C(n)$ and $R(n)$ on the same set of axes.

c) Identify the break-even point and explain what its coordinates mean.

d) Develop an algebraic and a graphical model for the profit function, $P(n)$.

e) What is the maximum daily profit Kathy can earn?

18. Consider $f(x) = x + 3$ and $g(x) = \cos x$, where x is in radians.

a) Describe and sketch a graph of $f(x)$. Is this function even, odd, or neither?

b) Describe and sketch a graph of $g(x)$. Is this function even, odd, or neither?

c) Predict the shape of $y = f(x)g(x)$. Sketch a graph of your prediction.

d) **Use Technology** Check your work by graphing the three functions in parts a) to c) using graphing technology.

e) Give the domain and the range of $y = f(x)g(x)$.

19. Let $f(x) = \sqrt{x - 9}$ and $g(x) = \dfrac{1}{x^2}$. Write a simplified algebraic model for each composite function. State the domain and the range of each.

a) $y = f(g(x))$

b) $y = g(f(x))$

20. Let $f(x) = x^3 - 3x^2 - 40x$ and $g(x) = 25 - x^2$.

a) Graph these functions on the same set of axes.

b) Identify, by inspecting the graphs, the interval(s) for which $f(x) > g(x)$.

c) Check your answer to part b) using another method.

TASK

Modelling a Damped Pendulum

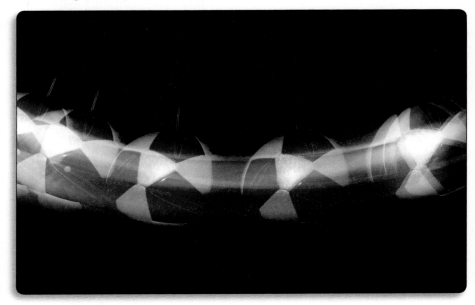

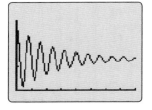

Jasmeet built a simple pendulum by fastening a soccer ball to a piece of string. She then swung the pendulum in front of a motion detector and obtained the graph shown on her graphing calculator. The horizontal scale is in 1-s intervals, and the vertical scale is in 1-m intervals.

a) Compare this graph to functions you have studied. Describe the similarities and the differences.

b) Use a trigonometric function to model the graph, with or without using technology. Match the initial amplitude and period. You will model the decreasing amplitude in the next two steps.

c) Locate the maximum values for the function. Construct a table of values for these maximum values. Subtract the vertical displacement from these values. Then, determine an exponential model for the maximum values, with or without using technology.

d) Use your model from step c) as part of the amplitude for your model from step b), and graph this blended model using technology. Add the appropriate vertical displacement. Discuss how well your model matches the real situation.

e) What physical factors explain the shape of the original graph? What other situations in the real world might give rise to a similar graph?

Chapter 1 Polynomial Functions

1. a) What is meant by even symmetry? odd symmetry?

b) Describe how to determine whether a function has even or odd symmetry.

2. Describe two key differences between polynomial functions and non-polynomial functions.

3. Compare the end behaviour of the following functions. Explain any differences.

$$f(x) = -3x^2 \qquad g(x) = 5x^4 \qquad h(x) = 0.5x^3$$

4. Determine the degree of the polynomial function modelling the following data.

x	y
−2	17
−1	−3
0	−3
1	−1
2	33
3	177

5. Determine an equation and sketch a graph of the function with a base function of $f(x) = x^4$ that has been transformed by $-2f(x - 3) + 1$.

6. Sketch the functions $f(x) = x^3$ and $g(x) = -\dfrac{1}{2}(x - 1)(x + 2)^2$ on the same set of axes. Label the x- and y-intercepts. State the domain and range of each function.

7. Consider the function $f(x) = 2x^4 + 5x^3 - x^2 - 3x + 1$.

a) Determine the average slope between the points where $x = 1$ and $x = 3$.

b) Determine the instantaneous slope at each of these points.

c) Compare the three slopes and describe how the graph is changing.

8. Determine an equation for each function.

a)

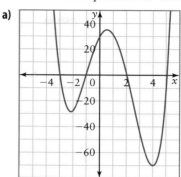

b)

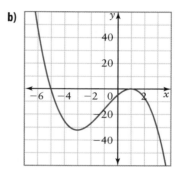

9. Given the function $f(x) = -2x^2 + 1$, describe the slope and the change in slope for the appropriate intervals.

Chapter 2 Polynomial Equations and Inequalities

10. Perform each division. Write the statement that can be used to check each division. State the restrictions.

a) $(4x^3 + 6x^2 - 4x + 2) \div (2x - 1)$

b) $(2x^3 - 4x + 8) \div (x - 2)$

c) $(x^3 - 3x^2 + 5x - 4) \div (x + 2)$

d) $(5x^4 - 3x^3 + 2x^2 + 4x - 6) \div (x + 1)$

11. Factor, if possible.

a) $x^3 + 4x^2 + x - 6$

b) $2x^3 + x^2 - 16x - 15$

c) $x^3 - 7x^2 + 11x - 2$

d) $x^4 + x^2 + 1$

12. Use the remainder theorem to determine the remainder for each.

a) $4x^3 - 7x^2 + 3x + 5$ divided by $x - 5$

b) $6x^4 + 7x^2 - 2x - 4$ divided by $3x + 2$

13. Use the factor theorem to determine whether the second polynomial is a factor of the first.

a) $3x^5 - 4x^3 - 4x^2 + 15; x + 5$

b) $2x^3 - 4x^2 + 6x + 5; x + 1$

14. Solve.

a) $x^4 - 81 = 0$

b) $x^3 - x^2 - 10x - 8 = 0$

c) $8x^3 + 27 = 0$

d) $12x^4 - 7x^2 - 6x + 16x^3 = 0$

15. A family of quartic functions has zeros -3, -1, and 1 (order 2).

a) Write an equation for the family. State two other members of the family.

b) Determine an equation for the member of the family that passes through the point $(-2, -6)$.

c) Sketch the function you found in part b).

d) Determine the intervals where the function in part b) is positive.

16. Solve each inequality, showing the appropriate steps. Illustrate your solution on a number line.

a) $(x - 4)(x + 3) > 0$

b) $2x^2 + x - 6 < 0$

c) $x^3 - 2x^2 - 13x \leq 10$

Chapter 3 Rational Functions

17. Determine equations for the vertical and horizontal asymptotes of each function.

a) $f(x) = \dfrac{1}{x - 2}$

b) $g(x) = \dfrac{x + 5}{x + 3}$

c) $h(x) = \dfrac{2}{x^2 - 9}$

d) $k(x) = \dfrac{-1}{x^2 + 4}$

18. For each function,

  i) determine equations for the asymptotes

  ii) determine the intercepts

  iii) sketch a graph

  iv) describe the increasing intervals and the decreasing intervals

  v) state the domain and the range

a) $f(x) = \dfrac{1}{x + 4}$

b) $g(x) = \dfrac{-4}{x - 2}$

c) $h(x) = \dfrac{x - 1}{x + 3}$

d) $i(x) = \dfrac{2x + 3}{5x + 1}$

e) $j(x) = \dfrac{10}{x^2}$

f) $k(x) = \dfrac{3}{x^2 - 6x - 27}$

19. Analyse the slope and the change in slope for the appropriate intervals of the function $f(x) = \dfrac{1}{x^2 - 4x - 21}$. Sketch a graph of the function.

20. Solve algebraically.

a) $\dfrac{5}{x - 3} = 4$

b) $\dfrac{2}{x - 1} = \dfrac{4}{x + 5}$

c) $\dfrac{6}{x^2 + 4x + 7} = 2$

21. Solve each inequality. Illustrate the solution on a number line.

a) $\dfrac{3}{x - 4} < 5$

b) $\dfrac{x^2 - 8x + 15}{x^2 + 5x + 4} \geq 0$

22. A lab technician pours a quantity of a chemical into a beaker of water. The rate, R, in grams per second, at which the chemical dissolves can be modelled by the function $R(t) = \dfrac{2t}{t^2 + 4t}$, where t is the time, in seconds.

a) By hand or using technology, sketch a graph of this relation.

b) What is the equation of the horizontal asymptote? What is its significance?

c) State an appropriate domain for this relation if a rate of 0.05 g/s or less is considered to be inconsequential.

Chapter 4 Trigonometry

23. Determine the exact radian measure for each angle.

a) $135°$ **b)** $-60°$

24. Determine the exact degree measure for each angle.

a) $\dfrac{\pi}{6}$ **b)** $\dfrac{9\pi}{8}$

25. A sector angle of a circle with radius 9 cm measures $\dfrac{5\pi}{12}$. What is the perimeter of the sector?

26. Determine the exact value of each trigonometric ratio.

a) $\cos\dfrac{5\pi}{6}$ **b)** $\sin\dfrac{3\pi}{2}$

c) $\tan\dfrac{4\pi}{3}$ **d)** $\cot\dfrac{11\pi}{4}$

27. Use the sum or difference formulas to find the exact value of each.

a) $\cos\dfrac{\pi}{12}$ **b)** $\sin\dfrac{11\pi}{12}$

28. Prove each identity.

a) $\sec x - \tan x = \dfrac{1 - \sin x}{\cos x}$

b) $(\csc x - \cot x)^2 = \dfrac{1 - \cos x}{1 + \cos x}$

c) $\sin 2A = \dfrac{2\tan A}{\sec^2 A}$

d) $\cos(x + y)\cos(x - y) = \cos^2 x + \cos^2 y - 1$

29. Given $\sin x = \dfrac{1}{5}$ and $\sin y = \dfrac{5}{6}$, where x and y are acute angles, determine the exact value of $\sin(x + y)$.

30. Given that $\cos\dfrac{5\pi}{8} = -\sin y$, first express $\dfrac{5\pi}{8}$ as a sum of $\dfrac{\pi}{2}$ and an angle, and then apply a trigonometric identity to determine the measure of angle y.

Chapter 5 Trigonometric Functions

31. a) State the period, amplitude, phase shift, and vertical translation for the function $f(x) = 3\sin\left[2\left(x - \dfrac{\pi}{2}\right)\right] + 4$.

b) State the domain and the range of $f(x)$.

32. Sketch a graph of each function for one period. Label the x-intercepts and any asymptotes.

a) $f(x) = \sin(x - \pi) - 1$

b) $f(x) = -3\cos\left[4\left(x + \dfrac{\pi}{2}\right)\right]$

c) $f(x) = \sec\left(x - \dfrac{\pi}{2}\right)$

33. Solve for $\theta \in [0, 2\pi]$.

a) $2\sin\theta = -\sqrt{3}$

b) $2\sin\theta\cos\theta - \cos\theta = 0$

c) $\csc^2\theta = 2 + \csc\theta$

34. The blade of a sabre saw moves up and down. Its vertical displacement in the first cycle is shown in the table.

Time (s)	Displacement (cm)
0	0
0.005	0.64
0.01	1.08
0.015	1.19
0.02	0.92
0.025	0.37
0.03	−0.30
0.035	−0.87
0.04	−1.18
0.045	−1.12
0.05	−0.71
0.055	−0.08
0.06	0.58
0.065	1.05
0.07	1.19

a) Make a scatter plot of the data.

b) Write a sine function to model the data.

c) Graph the sine function on the same set of axes as in part a).

d) Estimate the rate of change when the displacement is 0 cm, to one decimal place.

Chapter 6 Exponential and Logarithmic Functions

35. Express in logarithmic form.

a) $7^2 = 49$ **b)** $a^b = c$

c) $8^3 = 512$ **d)** $11^x = y$

36. a) Sketch graphs of $f(x) = \log x$ and $g(x) = \dfrac{1}{2}\log(x + 1)$ on the same set of axes. Label the intercepts and any asymptotes.

b) State the domain and the range of each function.

37. Express in exponential form.

a) $\log_3 6561 = 8$ **b)** $\log_a 75 = b$

c) $\log_7 2401 = 4$ **d)** $\log_a 19 = b$

38. Evaluate.

a) $\log_2 256$ **b)** $\log_{15} 15$

c) $\log_6 \sqrt{6}$ **d)** $\log_3 243$

e) $\log_{12} 12$ **f)** $\log_{11} \dfrac{1}{\sqrt{121}}$

39. Solve for x.

a) $\log_3 x = 4$ **b)** $\log_x 125 = 3$

c) $\log_7 x = 5$ **d)** $\log_x 729 = 6$

e) $\log_{\frac{1}{2}} 128 = x$ **f)** $\log_{\frac{1}{4}} 64 = x$

40. A culture begins with 100 000 bacteria and grows to 125 000 bacteria after 20 min. What is the doubling period, to the nearest minute?

41. The pH scale is defined as pH $= -\log[H^+]$, where $[H^+]$ is the concentration of hydronium ions, in moles per litre.

a) Eggs have a pH of 7.8. Are eggs acidic or alkaline? What is the concentration of hydronium ions in eggs?

b) A weak vinegar solution has a hydronium ion concentration of 7.9×10^{-4} mol/L. What is the pH of the solution?

Chapter 7 Tools and Strategies for Solving Exponential and Logarithmic Equations

42. Solve each equation. Check for extraneous roots.

a) $3^{2x} + 3^x - 21 = 0$

b) $4^x + 15(4)^{-x} = 8$

43. Use the laws of logarithms to evaluate.

a) $\log_8 4 + \log_8 128$ **b)** $\log_7 7\sqrt{7}$

c) $\log_5 10 - \log_5 250$ **d)** $\log_6 \sqrt[3]{6}$

44. Solve, correct to four decimal places.

a) $2^x = 13$ **b)** $5^{2x+1} = 97$

c) $3^x = 19$ **d)** $4^{3x+2} = 18$

45. Solve. Check for extraneous roots.

a) $\log_5(x + 2) + \log_5(2x - 1) = 2$

b) $\log_4(x + 3) + \log_4(x + 4) = \dfrac{1}{2}$

46. Determine the point(s) of intersection of the functions $f(x) = \log x$ and $g(x) = \dfrac{1}{2}\log(x + 1)$.

47. Bismuth is used in making chemical alloys, medicine, and transistors. A 10-mg sample of bismuth-214 decays to 9 mg in 3 min.

a) Determine the half-life of bismuth-214.

b) How much bismuth-214 remains after 10 min?

c) Graph the amount of bismuth-214 remaining as a function of time.

d) Describe how the graph would change if the half-life were shorter. Give reasons for your answer.

48. The volume of computer parts in landfill sites is growing exponentially. In 2001, a particular landfill site had 124 000 m³ of computer parts, and in 2007, it had 347 000 m³ of parts.

a) What is the doubling time of the volume of computer parts in this landfill site?

b) What is the expected volume of computer parts in this landfill site in 2020?

49. The value of a particular model of car depreciates by 18% per year. This model of car sells for $35 000.

a) Write an equation to relate the value of the car to the time, in years.

b) Determine the value of the car after 5 years.

c) How long will it take for the car to depreciate to half its original value?

d) Sketch a graph of this relation.

e) Describe how the shape of the graph would change if the rate of depreciation changed to 25%.

Chapter 8 Combining Functions

50. Consider $f(x) = 2^{-\frac{x}{\pi}}$ and $g(x) = 2\cos(4x)$ for $x \in [0, 4\pi]$. Sketch a graph of each function.

a) $y = f(x) + g(x)$ **b)** $y = f(x) - g(x)$

c) $y = f(x)g(x)$ **d)** $y = \dfrac{f(x)}{g(x)}$

51. Given $f(x) = 2x^2 + 3x - 5$ and $g(x) = x + 3$, determine each of the following.

a) $f(g(x))$ **b)** $g(f(x))$

c) $f(g(-3))$ **d)** $g(f(7))$

52. If $f(x) = \dfrac{1}{x}$ and $g(x) = 4 - x$, determine each of the following, if it exists.

a) $f(g(3))$ **b)** $f(g(0))$

c) $f(g(4))$ **d)** $g(f(4))$

53. Find expressions for $f(g(x))$ and $g(f(x))$, and state their domains.

a) $f(x) = \sqrt{x}$, $g(x) = x + 1$

b) $f(x) = \sin x$, $g(x) = x^2$

c) $f(x) = |x|$, $g(x) = x^2 - 6$

d) $f(x) = 2^{x+1}$, $g(x) = 3x + 2$

e) $f(x) = (x + 3)^2$, $g(x) = \sqrt{x - 3}$

f) $f(x) = \log x$, $g(x) = 3^{x+1}$

54. Consider $f(x) = -\dfrac{2}{x}$ and $g(x) = \sqrt{x}$.

a) Determine $f(g(x))$.

b) State the domain of $f(g(x))$.

c) Determine whether $f(g(x))$ is even, odd, or neither.

55. Verify, algebraically, that $f(f^{-1}(x)) = x$ for each of the following.

a) $f(x) = x^2 - 4$

b) $f(x) = \sin x$

c) $f(x) = 3x$

d) $f(x) = \dfrac{1}{x - 2}$

56. Solve. Illustrate each inequality graphically.

a) $\sin x < 0.1x^2 - 1$

b) $x + 2 \geq 2^x$

57. A Ferris wheel rotates such that the angle of rotation, θ, is defined by $\theta = \dfrac{\pi t}{15}$, where t is the time, in seconds. A rider's height, h, in metres, above the ground can be modelled by the function $h(\theta) = 20\sin\theta + 22$.

a) Write an equation for the rider's height in terms of time.

b) Sketch graphs of the three functions, on separate sets of axes, one above the other.

c) Compare the periods of the graphs of $h(\theta)$ and $h(t)$.

58. An office chair manufacturer models its weekly production since 2001 by the function $N(t) = 100 + 25t$, where t is the time, in years, since 2001, and N is the number of chairs. The size of the manufacturer's workforce can be modelled by the function $W(N) = 3\sqrt{N}$.

a) Write the size of the workforce as a function of time.

b) State the domain and range of the function in part a) that is relevant to this problem. Sketch its graph.

59. An environmental scientist measures the pollutant in a lake. The concentration, $C(P)$, in parts per million (ppm), of pollutant can be modelled as a function of the population, P, of the lakeside city, by $C(P) = 1.28P + 53.12$. The city's population, in ten thousands, can be modelled by the function $P(t) = 12.5 \times 2^{\frac{t}{20}}$, where t is the time, in years.

a) Determine an equation for the concentration of pollutant as a function of time.

b) Sketch a graph of this function.

c) How long will it take for the concentration to reach 100 ppm?

Prerequisite Skills Appendix

Angles From Trigonometric Ratios

Use inverse trigonometric operations on a calculator to find the corresponding angle measure given the value of the trigonometric ratio.

Ensure that the calculator is in Degree mode.

$$\sin x \doteq 0.8660$$
$$x = \sin^{-1}(0.8660)$$
$$x \doteq 60°$$

1. Find the measure of each angle x, to the nearest tenth of a degree.

   a) $\sin x = 0.3215$

   b) $\cos x = -0.7248$

   c) $\tan x = 2.7410$

   d) $\sin x = -0.6552$

   e) $\cos x = 0.2478$

   f) $\tan x = -3.5874$

Apply the Exponent Laws

To multiply powers with the same base, add the exponents.

$$x^2 \times x^3 = x^{2+3}$$
$$= x^5$$

To divide powers with the same base, subtract the exponents.

$$x^5 \div x^2 = x^{5-2}$$
$$= x^3$$

To raise a power to an exponent, multiply the exponents.

$$(x^2)^4 = x^{2 \times 4}$$
$$= x^8$$

a^{-n} means $\dfrac{1}{a^n}$, where $n > 0$ and $a \neq 0$.

$$2^{-5} = \frac{1}{2^5}$$
$$= \frac{1}{32}$$

$a^0 = 1$, where $a \neq 0$.

$$10^0 = 1$$

$a^{\frac{1}{n}}$ means $\sqrt[n]{a}$, where n is a positive integer and $a \geq 0$.

$$16^{\frac{1}{4}} = \sqrt[4]{16}$$
$$= 2$$

$a^{\frac{m}{n}}$ means $(\sqrt[n]{a})^m$, where n is a positive integer and m is an integer.

$$81^{\frac{3}{4}} = (\sqrt[4]{81})^3$$
$$= 3^3$$
$$= 27$$

$(ab)^n$ means $(a^n)(b^n)$.

$(5x)^2 = (5^2)(x^2)$
$= 25x^2$

$\left(\dfrac{a}{b}\right)^n$ means $\dfrac{a^n}{b^n}$, where $b \neq 0$.

$\left(\dfrac{3}{5}\right)^3 = \dfrac{3^3}{5^3}$

$= \dfrac{27}{125}$

1. Rewrite each expression using positive exponents only.

a) $5x^{-3}$ 　　　　　　　　　　**b)** $(3x)^{-4}$

c) $7 + x^{-6}$ 　　　　　　　　　**d)** $(5x^{-3})^{-2} - 6x^{-1} + 2x - x^3$

2. Expand and simplify each expression.

a) $x^{\frac{1}{2}}(3x^2 + 1)^2$ 　　　　　　**b)** $(3x^4 - 5)(2x + 3)$

c) $4x(x^2 - 1)(x^3 + 2)$ 　　　　　**d)** $\sqrt{x^2 + 5}\,\sqrt{2x - 4}$

3. Evaluate.

a) $(-3)^4$ 　　　　　　　　　　**b)** 4^{-5}

c) 21^0 　　　　　　　　　　　**d)** $36^{\frac{1}{2}}$

e) $625^{\frac{3}{4}}$

4. Simplify.

a) $(4x^3y^5)(5x^6y^2)$ 　　　　　**b)** $\dfrac{a^6b^7c^4}{(a^3b^2)^2c}$

c) $(m^2n^{-5})^2(m^{-3}n^4)^3$ 　　　**d)** $\dfrac{(x^2y^{-9})^{\frac{1}{3}}}{(x^{-2}y^6)^{\frac{1}{6}}}$

Apply Transformations to Functions

The graph of $f(x) + 5$ is a vertical translation of $f(x)$ by 5 units upward.

The graph of $f(x - 1)$ is a horizontal translation of $f(x)$ by 1 unit to the right.

The graph of $4f(x)$ is a vertical stretch (expansion) of $f(x)$ by a factor of 4.

The graph of $f(2x)$ is a horizontal stretch (compression) of $f(x)$ by a factor of $\dfrac{1}{2}$.

The graph of $-f(x)$ is a reflection of $f(x)$ in the x-axis.

The graph of $f(-x)$ is a reflection of $f(x)$ in the y-axis.

To graph $y = -2(x + 3)^2$, shift the graph of $y = x^2$ to the left by 3 units, then stretch it vertically by a factor of 2, and finally reflect in the x-axis.

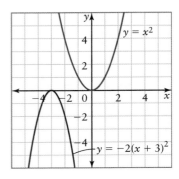

1. Determine whether the transformation of $f(x)$ is a vertical translation, a horizontal translation, a vertical stretch, a horizontal stretch, a vertical reflection, or a horizontal reflection.

   a) $f(x) + 2$ **b)** $5f(x)$ **c)** $f(6x)$ **d)** $-f(x)$

   e) $f(x - 4)$ **f)** $f(-x)$ **g)** $f(x + 7)$ **h)** $f\left(\dfrac{1}{4}x\right)$

   i) $f(x) - 5$ **j)** $10f(x)$

2. Describe the transformations being applied to $f(x)$.

   a) $3f(-x)$ **b)** $f(2x) - 3$

   c) $-f(x + 2)$ **d)** $\dfrac{1}{3}f(-5x)$

3. Graph each function by performing the indicated transformations on the graph of $y = x^2$.

   a) $y = x^2 + 4$ **b)** $y = 3(x + 1)^2$

   c) $y = (-2x - 5)^2 + 2$ **d)** $y = -4(3x + 2)^2 - 5$

Determine Equations of Quadratic Functions

To determine an equation for a quadratic function with zeros -1 and 3 that passes through the point $(5, 6)$, use the factored form of a quadratic equation, $f(x) = a(x - r)(x - s)$.

Substitute $r = -1$, $s = 3$, and $(x, f(x)) = (5, 6)$ then solve for a.

$f(x) = a(x - r)(x - s)$
$6 = a(5 - (-1))(5 - 3)$
$6 = a(6)(2)$
$6 = 12a$
$a = \dfrac{1}{2}$

An equation for the quadratic function is $f(x) = \dfrac{1}{2}(x + 1)(x - 3)$.

1. Determine an equation for the quadratic function with the given properties.

   a) zeros 1 and 5, passing through $(2, -6)$

   b) zeros -2 and 1, passing through $(-3, -4)$

   c) zeros -6 and -1, passing through $(1, 21)$

   d) zeros -3 and $\dfrac{1}{2}$, passing through $(-7, 15)$

Determine Intervals From Graphs

To determine the intervals for which the graph shown is above and the intervals for which it is below the x-axis, first identify the x-intercepts.

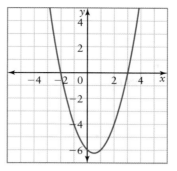

The x-intercepts are -2 and 3. The graph is above the x-axis for $x < -2$ and $x > 3$. The graph is below the x-axis for $-2 < x < 3$.

1. For each graph, identify the x-intercepts and write the intervals for which the graph is above the x-axis and the intervals for which the graph is below the x-axis.

a)
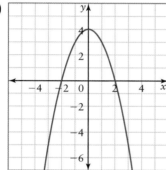

b)
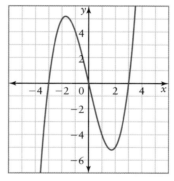

Distance Between Two Points

To determine the distance between the points $(x_1, y_1) = (2, -5)$ and $(x_2, y_2) = (-4, 3)$, substitute the x- and y-values into the formula

$$d = \sqrt{(x_2 - x_1)^2 + (y_2 - y_1)^2}.$$

$$d = \sqrt{(x_2 - x_1)^2 + (y_2 - y_1)^2}$$

$$= \sqrt{(-4 - 2)^2 + (3 - (-5))^2}$$

$$= \sqrt{(-6)^2 + 8^2}$$

$$= \sqrt{36 + 64}$$

$$= \sqrt{100}$$

$$= 10$$

The distance between the points is 10 units.

1. Determine the distance between the points in each pair.

a) $(2, 1)$ and $(5, 4)$ b) $(3, 6)$ and $(4, -2)$

c) $(1, -3)$ and $(-4, 4)$ d) $(-7, -2)$ and $(-1, -5)$

e) $(9, -3)$ and $(6, 3)$ f) $(2, 4)$ and $(3, -5)$

Domain and Range

The domain and range of a function can be determined from its graph.

Since x can be any real number, the domain is the set of real numbers.

Since y can be any real number, the range is the set of real numbers.

Since x can be any real number, the domain is the set of real numbers.

Since the value of y is always greater than or equal to zero, the range is $y \geq 0$.

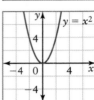

Since the value of x is always greater than or equal to zero, the domain is $x \geq 0$.

Since the value of y is always greater than or equal to zero, the range is $y \geq 0$.

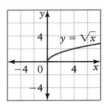

1. State the domain and range of each function. Justify your answer.

   a) $y = 2x - 3$

   b) $y = -3x + 1$

   c) $y = x^2 - 1$

   d) $y = (x - 1)^2 + 4$

   e) $y = \sqrt{x + 5}$

   f) $y = \sqrt{x - 2}$

   g) $y = \dfrac{1}{x + 2}$

   h) $y = \dfrac{1}{x - 1}$

Equation of a Line

To determine an equation of the line with slope 3 and y-intercept 2, substitute the slope for m and the y-intercept for b in the equation $y = mx + b$.

$$y = mx + b$$
$$= 3x + 2$$

An equation for the line is $y = 3x + 2$.

To determine an equation for the line with slope 2 that passes through the point $(4, -1)$, substitute the slope for m, the x-coordinate for x_1, and the y-coordinate for y_1 in the equation $y - y_1 = m(x - x_1)$. Then, simplify the equation.

$$y - y_1 = m(x - x_1)$$
$$y - (-1) = 2(x - 4)$$
$$y + 1 = 2x - 8$$
$$y = 2x - 9$$

An equation for the line is $y = 2x - 9$.

If the two points $(x_1, y_1) = (-2, 2)$ and $(x_2, y_2) = (1, 8)$ are given, the slope, m, of the line joining these points can be determined by substituting the x- and y-values into the formula $m = \dfrac{y_2 - y_1}{x_2 - x_1}$.

$$m = \frac{y_2 - y_1}{x_2 - x_1}$$

$$= \frac{8 - 2}{1 - (-2)}$$

$$= \frac{6}{3}$$

$$= 2$$

The slope of the line is 2. An equation of the line can be determined by substituting the slope m and the point $(x_1, y_1) = (-2, 2)$ into the formula $y - y_1 = m(x - x_1)$.

$$y - y_1 = m(x - x_1)$$
$$y - 2 = 2(x - (-2))$$
$$y - 2 = 2(x + 2)$$
$$y - 2 = 2x + 4$$
$$y = 2x + 6$$

1. Determine an equation for each line.

   a) slope 2 and y-intercept 1

   b) slope -4 and y-intercept 4

2. Determine an equation for each line.

   a) slope 3, passing through the point $(2, 5)$

   b) slope -1, passing through the point $(3, -6)$

3. Determine an equation of each line.

   a) passing through the points $(1, 5)$ and $(-1, -2)$

   b) passing through the points $(4, 4)$ and $(7, 1)$

4. Determine an equation for each line.

   a) x-intercept 1 and y-intercept 4

   b) x-intercept 3 and y-intercept -2

Evaluate Functions

To evaluate the function $f(x) = x^3 + 2x^2 + 5x + 6$ for $f(3)$, substitute 3 for x. Then, simplify.

$$f(x) = x^3 + 2x^2 + 5x + 6$$
$$f(3) = 3^3 - 2(3)^2 + 5(3) + 6$$
$$= 27 - 18 + 15 + 6$$
$$= 30$$

To determine if $f(2) > f(-1)$ for $f(x) = -x + 3$, evaluate $f(2)$ and $f(-1)$ and compare them.

$$f(x) = -x + 3 \qquad\qquad f(x) = -x + 3$$
$$f(2) = -2 + 3 \qquad\qquad f(-1) = -(-1) + 3$$
$$= 1 \qquad\qquad\qquad\qquad = 1 + 3$$
$$\qquad\qquad\qquad\qquad\qquad = 4$$

Since $1 < 4$, then $f(2) < f(-1)$. The statement $f(2) > f(-1)$ is false.

1. If $f(x) = x^3 + 3x^2 - 4x - 7$, determine the value of each.
   a) $f(0)$ b) $f(3)$ c) $f(-2)$ d) $f\left(-\dfrac{2}{3}\right)$
   e) $f(3.1)$ f) $f(n)$ g) $f(-3x)$ h) $f(x^2)$

2. If $f(x) = x^2 - 5$, determine the value of each.
   a) $f(2)$ b) $f(-5)$
   c) $f(\sqrt{7})$ d) $f(x + 2)$

3. If $f(x) = \sqrt{x - 3}$, determine the value of each.
   a) $f(3)$ b) $f(7)$
   c) $f(4)$ d) $f(x^2)$

4. If $f(x) = |x - 6|$, determine the value of each.
   a) $f(1)$ b) $f(8)$
   c) $f(-4)$ d) $f(6)$

5. Determine whether each statement is true or false for $f(x) = (x + 2)^2$.
   a) $f(1) > f(0)$ b) $f(2) < f(-1)$
   c) $f(-7) \le f(3)$ d) $f(-2) > f(-3)$

Exact Trigonometric Ratios of Special Angles

The Pythagorean theorem shows that the side lengths of a 30°–60°–90° triangle have a ratio of 1 to $\sqrt{3}$ to 2, as shown.

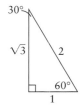

The side lengths of a 45°–45°–90° triangle have a ratio of 1 to 1 to $\sqrt{2}$, as shown.

These special triangles can be used to find the exact trigonometric ratios of special angles.

If applied in conjunction with a unit circle, with $r = 1$, the exact trigonometric ratios of multiples of special angles can be determined. If the terminal arm of an angle θ in standard position intersects the unit circle at $P(x, y)$, then $\cos \theta = x$ and $\sin \theta = y$.

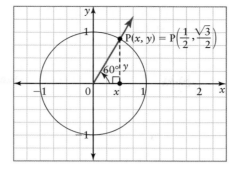

From the unit circle shown, the exact values of the six trigonometric ratios of 60° are

$$\sin 60° = y$$
$$= \frac{\sqrt{3}}{2}$$

$$\cos 60° = x$$
$$= \frac{1}{2}$$

$$\tan 60° = \frac{y}{x}$$
$$= \frac{\frac{\sqrt{3}}{2}}{\frac{1}{2}}$$
$$= \sqrt{3}$$

$$\csc 60° = \frac{1}{y}$$
$$= \frac{1}{\frac{\sqrt{3}}{2}}$$
$$= \frac{2}{\sqrt{3}}$$

$$\sec 60° = \frac{1}{x}$$
$$= \frac{1}{\frac{1}{2}}$$
$$= 2$$

$$\cot 60° = \frac{x}{y}$$
$$= \frac{\frac{1}{2}}{\frac{\sqrt{3}}{2}}$$
$$= \frac{1}{\sqrt{3}}$$

1. Determine the exact values of the six trigonometric ratios of 30°.

2. Use a unit circle to determine the exact values of the six trigonometric ratios for 150°, 210°, and 330°.

Factor Quadratic Expressions

To factor the difference of squares $16x^2 - 25$, use the equation $a^2 - b^2 = (a + b)(a - b)$. In this case, $a = 4x$ and $b = 5$.

$$a^2 - b^2 = (a + b)(a - b)$$
$$16x^2 - 25 = (4x + 5)(4x - 5)$$

To factor an equation of the form $x^2 + bx + c$, such as $x^2 - 8x + 12$, find two integers whose product is $c = 12$ and whose sum is $b = -8$. The only two integers with a product of 12 and a sum of -8 are -6 and -2.

Thus, $x^2 - 8x + 12 = (x - 6)(x - 2)$.

Product of 12		Sum
12	1	13
−12	−1	−13
6	2	8
−6	−2	−8
4	3	7
−4	−3	−7

To factor an equation of the form $ax^2 + bx + c$, where $a \neq 0$, such as $3x^2 + 13x + 10$, find two integers whose product is $a \times c = 30$ and whose sum is $b = 13$. The only two integers with a product of 30 and a sum of 13 are 10 and 3.

Product of 30		Sum
30	1	31
15	2	17
10	3	13
6	5	11

$$
\begin{aligned}
3x^2 + 13x + 10 &= 3x^2 + 3x + 10x + 10 \quad \text{Break up the middle term.}\\
&= (3x^2 + 3x) + (10x + 10) \quad \text{Group terms.}\\
&= 3x(x + 1) + 10(x + 1) \quad \text{Remove common factors.}\\
&= (3x + 10)(x + 1) \quad \text{Remove a common binomial factor.}
\end{aligned}
$$

Thus, $3x^2 + 13x + 10 = (3x + 10)(x + 1)$.

1. Factor.

a) $x^2 - 4$
b) $y^2 - 100$
c) $4n^2 - 49$
d) $25m^2 - 81$
e) $1 - 36x^2$
f) $4y^2 - 9x^2$

2. Factor.

a) $x^2 - x - 20$
b) $y^2 + 3y - 10$
c) $n^2 - 5n - 36$
d) $m^2 + 9m + 18$
e) $x^2 - 11x + 30$
f) $c^2 - 2c - 24$
g) $16 + 15y - y^2$
h) $x^2 + 12xy + 32y^2$
i) $c^2 - 3cd - 28d^2$

3. Factor.

a) $3x^2 - 2x - 8$
b) $2c^2 + 7c - 4$
c) $4m^2 - 11m + 6$
d) $5y^2 + 8y + 3$
e) $3n^2 + n - 2$
f) $6x^2 - 17x - 3$
g) $3x^2 - 5xy - 12y^2$
h) $5x^2 - 14x + 8$
i) $4x^2 + 23x + 15$
j) $2p^2 + pq - q^2$

Finite Differences

Finite differences are calculated from tables of values in which the x-coordinates are evenly spaced. First differences are found by subtracting consecutive y-coordinates. Second differences are found by subtracting consecutive first differences, and so on.

If the first differences are constant, the relation is linear. If the second differences are constant, the relation is quadratic. Otherwise, the relation is neither linear nor quadratic.

This relation is linear.

x	y	First Differences
1	3	
2	5	$5 - 3 = 2$
3	7	$7 - 5 = 2$
4	9	$9 - 7 = 2$
5	11	$11 - 9 = 2$

This relation is quadratic.

x	y	First Differences	Second Differences
1	50		
2	32	$32 - 50 = -18$	
3	18	$18 - 32 = -14$	$-14 - (-18) = 4$
4	8	$8 - 18 = -10$	$-10 - (-14) = 4$
5	2	$2 - 8 = -6$	$-6 - (-10) = 4$

This relation is neither linear nor quadratic.

x	y	First Differences	Second Differences
1	2		
2	4	$4 - 2 = 2$	
3	8	$8 - 4 = 4$	$4 - 2 = 2$
4	16	$16 - 8 = 8$	$8 - 4 = 4$
5	32	$32 - 16 = 16$	$16 - 8 = 8$

1. Use finite differences to determine whether each relation is linear, quadratic, or neither.

a)

x	y
1	5
2	8
3	11
4	14
5	17

b)

x	y
1	2
2	5
3	10
4	17
5	26

c)

x	y
1	9
2	7
3	5
4	3
5	1

d)

x	y
1	-33
2	-31
3	-27
4	-20
5	-9

e)

x	y
1	-3
2	-5
3	-3
4	3
5	13

f)

x	y
1	-1
2	1
3	-1
4	1
5	-1

Graph an Exponential Function

The graph of the exponential function $f(x) = a^x$, where $a > 1$, is always increasing (exponential growth), is asymptotic to the negative x-axis, and has y-intercept of 1.

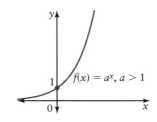

$f(x) = a^x, a > 1$

The graph of the exponential function $f(x) = a^x$, where $0 < a < 1$, is always decreasing (exponential decay), is asymptotic to the positive x-axis, and has y-intercept of 1.

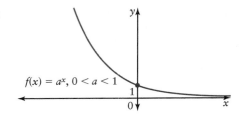

$f(x) = a^x, 0 < a < 1$

For the graph of the exponential function $y = 3^x$, the domain is $\{x \in \mathbb{R}\}$, the range is $\{y \in \mathbb{R}, y > 0\}$, and the equation of the asymptote is $x = 0$.

The graph can be used to estimate the value of x for a given function value. For example, when $y = 4$, the value of x is approximately 1.25.

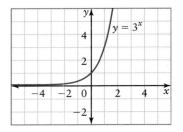

1. a) Sketch a graph of the function $y = 5^x$.

   b) Identify the domain, the range, and the equation of the asymptote.

   c) Use the graph to estimate
      i) the value of x when $y = 10$
      ii) the value of y when $x = -1$

Graph an Inverse

Given the graph of the function $f(x) = x^2 - 1$, the graph of its inverse $f^{-1}(x)$ can be found by reflecting the graph of $f(x)$ in the line $y = x$.

For $y = f(x)$, the domain is $\{x \in \mathbb{R}\}$ and the range is $\{y \in \mathbb{R}, \ y \geq -1\}$.

For $y = f^{-1}(x)$, the domain is $\{x \in \mathbb{R}, \ x \geq -1\}$ and the range is $\{y \in \mathbb{R}\}$.

Since the graph of the inverse does not pass the vertical line test, f^{-1} is not a function.

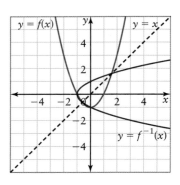

1. a) Graph the function $f(x) = x^2 + 2$.

   b) Identify the domain and the range of f.

   c) Graph f^{-1} by reflecting f in the line $y = x$.

   d) Identify the domain and range of f^{-1}.

   e) Is f^{-1} a function? Explain.

2. Repeat question 1 for the function $f(x) = \sqrt{x + 3}$.

Graphs and Transformations of Sinusoidal Functions Using Degree Measure

To graph two cycles of $y = 2\sin(x - 90°) + 1$, graph two cycles of $y = \sin x$ translated to the right 90° and up 1 unit, and stretched vertically by a factor of 2.

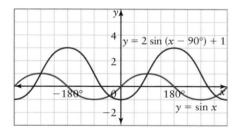

From the graph, the amplitude is $\dfrac{3 - (-1)}{2}$, or 2. The period is the horizontal length of one cycle, 360°. The phase shift, or horizontal translation, is 90° to the right. The vertical translation is 1 unit upward.

To graph two cycles of $y = \cos[2(x - 90°)] + 3$, graph two cycles of $y = \cos x$ translated to the right 90° and up 3 units, and stretched horizontally by a factor of 2.

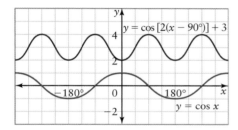

From the graph, the amplitude is $\dfrac{4 - 2}{2}$, or 1. The period is the horizontal length of one cycle, 180°. The phase shift, or horizontal translation, is 90° to the right. The vertical translation is 3 units upward.

1. Graph two cycles of each function. Identify the amplitude, period, phase shift, and vertical translation with respect to $y = \sin x$.

   a) $y = 3\sin x - 1$

   b) $y = \sin[2(x + 90°)]$

   c) $y = 4\sin(x - 60°) - 2$

2. Graph two cycles of each function. Identify the amplitude, period, phase shift, and vertical translation with respect to $y = \cos x$.

   a) $y = \cos x + 1$

   b) $y = 2\cos(x + 90°)$

   c) $y = \cos[3(x + 30°)] - 1$

Identify Linear, Quadratic, and Exponential Growth Models

A linear relation, such as $y = 2x + 1$, appears as a straight line when graphed. The first differences are constant.

A quadratic relation, such as $y = x^2 + 4$, appears as a parabola when graphed. The second differences are constant.

An exponential relation, such as $y = 3^x$, appears as an exponential curve when graphed. In a table of values with equally spaced x-values, there is a pattern of repeated multiplication between consecutive y-values.

1. Consider the first three stages of the pattern.

a) Draw the next two stages in the pattern.

b) Create a table of values in which n represents the stage number and t represents the total number of asterisks.

c) Use finite differences to determine whether the pattern is linear, quadratic, or exponential.

d) Create a scatter plot of the pattern.

e) Determine an equation to represent the pattern.

2. Repeat question 1 for the pattern of squares shown.

3. Repeat question 1 for the pattern of triangles shown.

Inverses

To find the inverse of $f(x) = 5x + 7$, first rewrite the function as $y = 5x + 7$. Then, interchange x and y and solve for y. x and y can be interchanged because a function and its inverse are reflections of each other in the line $y = x$.

$$x = 5y + 7$$
$$x - 7 = 5y$$
$$\frac{x - 7}{5} = y$$

Use the notation $f^{-1}(x)$ to express the inverse of $f(x)$. So, the inverse of $f(x) = 5x + 7$ is $f^{-1}(x) = \dfrac{x - 7}{5}$.

Since $f^{-1}(x)$ passes the vertical line test, that is, there is exactly one value of $f^{-1}(x)$ for each value of x, it is a function.

1. Find the inverse of each function, and determine whether the inverse is also a function.

   a) $f(x) = 3x - 1$

   b) $f(x) = 6x + 5$

   c) $f(x) = 4x^2 + 2$

   d) $f(x) = 3x^2 - 8$

   e) $f(x) = \dfrac{1}{x - 1}$

Primary Trigonometric Ratios and the CAST Rule

To determine the other primary trigonometric ratios for angle θ given $\tan \theta = \dfrac{5}{12}$ and $0° \leq \theta \leq 90°$, sketch the angle in standard position.

Since $\tan \theta = \dfrac{y}{x}$ and $\tan \theta = \dfrac{5}{12}$, then $x = 12$ and $y = 5$.

Determine the length of the hypotenuse, r.

$$r = \sqrt{x^2 + y^2}$$
$$= \sqrt{12^2 + 5^2}$$
$$= \sqrt{144 + 25}$$
$$= \sqrt{169}$$
$$= 13$$

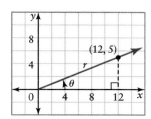

Now, determine the other two trigonometric ratios.

$$\sin \theta = \dfrac{y}{r} \qquad \cos \theta = \dfrac{x}{r}$$
$$= \dfrac{5}{13} \qquad\quad = \dfrac{12}{13}$$

To determine the sign of a trigonometric ratio, such as $\sin 125°$, use the CAST rule, which is a memory device for deciding when the three primary trigonometric ratios are positive.

	second quadrant	first quadrant
	S sine	**A** all
	third quadrant	fourth quadrant
	T tangent	**C** cosine

Since an angle of 125° is in the second quadrant, $\sin 125°$ is positive.

1. A trigonometric ratio is given. Find the exact value of the other two primary trigonometric ratios.

   a) $\tan \theta = \dfrac{8}{15}$, $0° \leq \theta \leq 90°$

   b) $\sin \theta = \dfrac{5}{13}$, $90° \leq x \leq 180°$

   c) $\cos \theta = -\dfrac{2}{3}$, $180° \leq \theta \leq 270°$

   d) $\tan \theta = -\dfrac{8}{5}$, $270° \leq \theta \leq 360°$

2. Use the CAST rule to determine the sign of each value. Then, use a calculator to evaluate each trigonometric ratio, rounded to four decimal places.

   a) $\tan 16°$ b) $\sin 110°$

   c) $\cos 125°$ d) $\tan 196°$

   e) $\cos 244°$ f) $\sin 305°$

Product of Two Binomials

To expand $(x - 3)(x + 4)$, multiply each term in the first binomial by each term in the second binomial. Then, collect like terms.

$$(x - 3)(x + 4) = (x - 3)(x + 4)$$
$$= x^2 + 4x - 3x - 12$$
$$= x^2 + x - 12$$

1. Expand and simplify.

   a) $(2a - 5)(a + 3)$ b) $(m + 4)(3m + 2)$

   c) $(x + 3y)(2x - 4y)$ d) $(2m - n)(5m - 3n)$

Quadratic Functions

The graph of $y = 2(x + 3)^2 - 8$ has vertex $(-3, -8)$, opens upward, and is vertically stretched by a factor 2 relative to the graph of $y = x^2$. The graph can be sketched using this information.

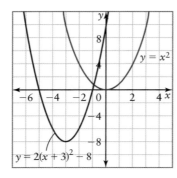

1. State the vertex, the direction of opening, and the vertical stretch factor relative to the graph of $y = x^2$ for each parabola. Then, sketch the graph.

a) $y = x^2 + 2$

b) $y = -x^2 - 1$

c) $y = 2x^2$

d) $y = 3(x + 4)^2$

e) $y = -2(x - 1)^2 + 4$

f) $y = 0.5(x + 2)^2 + 3$

g) $y = -(x + 1)^2 - 5$

h) $y = \frac{1}{4}(x - 3)^2 + 1$

Reciprocal Functions

To graph $f(x) = \dfrac{1}{x - 2}$, graph $f(x) = \dfrac{1}{x}$ translated 2 units to the right. The vertical asymptote has equation $x = 2$, since the function is undefined when the denominator equals zero. The equation of the horizontal asymptote is $y = 0$, since the numerator cannot equal zero.

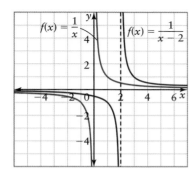

1. For each function, write equations for the vertical and horizontal asymptotes. Then, use transformations to sketch each graph relative to $f(x) = \dfrac{1}{x}$.

a) $f(x) = \dfrac{1}{x - 4}$

b) $f(x) = \dfrac{1}{x + 3}$

c) $f(x) = -\dfrac{2}{x - 1}$

d) $f(x) = \dfrac{1}{3x + 12}$

Reciprocal Trigonometric Ratios

The three reciprocal trigonometric ratios are defined as follows:

$$\text{cosecant} = \frac{1}{\text{sine}} \qquad \text{secant} = \frac{1}{\text{cosine}} \qquad \text{cotangent} = \frac{1}{\text{tangent}}$$

$$\csc \theta = \frac{r}{y} \qquad\qquad \sec \theta = \frac{r}{x} \qquad\qquad \cot \theta = \frac{x}{y}$$

Here, θ is any angle in standard position, (x, y) is a point on the terminal arm, and r is the length of the hypotenuse.

To determine the other reciprocal trigonometric ratios for angle θ given $\cot\theta = \dfrac{5}{12}$ and $0° \le \theta \le 90°$, sketch the angle in standard position.

Since $\cot\theta = \dfrac{x}{y}$ and $\cot\theta = \dfrac{5}{12}$, then $x = 5$ and $y = 12$.

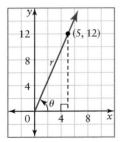

Determine the length of the hypotenuse, r.

$$r = \sqrt{x^2 + y^2}$$
$$= \sqrt{5^2 + 12^2}$$
$$= \sqrt{25 + 144}$$
$$= \sqrt{169}$$
$$= 13$$

Now, determine the values of the other two trigonometric ratios.

$$\csc\theta = \dfrac{r}{y} \qquad \sec\theta = \dfrac{r}{x}$$
$$= \dfrac{13}{12} \qquad\qquad = \dfrac{13}{5}$$

To determine the value of a trigonometric ratio such as $\csc 55°$, make sure your calculator is set to Degree mode and use the $\boxed{\text{SIN}}$ key.

$$\csc 55° = \dfrac{1}{\sin 55°}$$
$$\doteq 1.2208$$

To determine the value of θ if $\cot\theta = 1.15$, use the $\boxed{\text{TAN}^{\text{-1}}}$ key.

$$\cot\theta = 1.15$$
$$\dfrac{1}{\tan\theta} = 1.15$$
$$\tan\theta = \dfrac{1}{1.15}$$
$$\theta = \tan^{-1}\left(\dfrac{1}{1.15}\right)$$
$$\theta \doteq 41.0°$$

1. A reciprocal trigonometric ratio is given. Find the exact value of the other two reciprocal trigonometric ratios.

a) $\cot\theta = \dfrac{8}{15}$, $0° \le \theta \le 90°$ b) $\csc\theta = \dfrac{25}{24}$, $90° \le x \le 180°$

c) $\sec\theta = -\dfrac{8}{3}$, $180° \le \theta \le 270°$ d) $\cot\theta = -\dfrac{3}{2}$, $270° \le \theta \le 360°$

2. Evaluate each reciprocal trigonometric ratio, rounded to four decimal places.

   a) $\cot 37°$ **b)** $\csc 204°$

   c) $\sec 98°$ **d)** $\cot 317°$

   e) $\sec 126°$ **f)** $\csc 275°$

3. Determine the measure of each angle θ, rounded to the nearest degree.

   a) $\csc \theta = 2.05$ **b)** $\sec \theta = -3.86$

   c) $\cot \theta = -0.1763$ **d)** $\csc \theta = 2.54$

Simplify a Radical Expression

The following properties are used to simplify radicals.

$$\sqrt{ab} = \sqrt{a} \times \sqrt{b}, a \geq 0, b \geq 0$$

$$\sqrt{\frac{a}{b}} = \frac{\sqrt{a}}{\sqrt{b}}, a \geq 0, b > 0$$

$$\sqrt{75} = \sqrt{25} \times \sqrt{3} \qquad \sqrt{\frac{2}{9}} = \frac{\sqrt{2}}{\sqrt{9}} \qquad \frac{6 - \sqrt{45}}{3} = \frac{6 - \sqrt{9} \times \sqrt{5}}{3}$$

$$= 5\sqrt{3} \qquad\qquad\qquad = \frac{\sqrt{2}}{3} \qquad\qquad = \frac{6 - 3\sqrt{5}}{3}$$

$$= 2 - \sqrt{5}$$

1. Simplify.

   a) $\sqrt{12}$ **b)** $\sqrt{20}$

   c) $\sqrt{\frac{9}{16}}$ **d)** $-\sqrt{\frac{3}{25}}$

   e) $\frac{10 + \sqrt{20}}{2}$ **f)** $\frac{9 - \sqrt{54}}{3}$

Simplify Expressions

To simplify the expression $3(x + 2)(x - 4) - 2(x^2 - 3)$, expand to remove the brackets, and then collect like terms.

$$3(x + 2)(x - 4) - 2(x^2 - 3) = 3(x^2 - 2x - 8) - 2(x^2 - 3)$$

$$= 3x^2 - 6x - 24 - 2x^2 + 6$$

$$= x^2 - 6x - 18$$

1. Simplify.

   a) $2(x + 4) + 3(x + 4)$ **b)** $8(y - 3) - (y + 6)$

   c) $6(x - 4) + 2(3 + x)$ **d)** $2(w + 7) - (w - 3) + 3(w - 2)$

   e) $-5(y - 3) + 7(2 - y) + 6(y + 1)$ **f)** $4(x^2 + x - 5) + 3(x^2 - 2x + 8)$

   g) $3(x - 3)(x + 4) + (x - 2)(x + 5)$ **h)** $4(a - 1)(a - 4) + (a + 2)^2$

Slope

To determine the slope, m, of a line given two points on the line, (x_1, y_1) and (x_2, y_2), use the formula $m = \dfrac{y_2 - y_1}{x_2 - x_1}$.

The slope of the line passing through $(1, 2)$ and $(3, 5)$ is

$$m = \frac{5 - 2}{3 - 1}$$

$$= \frac{3}{2}$$

1. Determine the slope of the line passing through the points in each pair.

   a) $(-1, 5)$, $(3, 7)$

   b) $(2, 8)$, $(7, 5)$

   c) $(-2, -6)$, $(1, 5)$

   d) $(-5, -6)$, $(-1, -3)$

   e) $\left(\dfrac{1}{2}, 2\right)$ $(5, 1)$

   f) $\left(-\dfrac{4}{3}, \dfrac{3}{2}\right)$, $\left(\dfrac{2}{3}, 3\right)$

   g) $(0.9, 3.1)$, $(5.9, -6.9)$

   h) $(-3.0, 4.7)$, $(-1.7, 2.1)$

Slope and y-intercept of a Line

To determine the slope and the y-intercept of the line modelled by the equation $-3x + y + 4 = 0$, rewrite the equation in the form $y = mx + b$.

$$-3x + y + 4 = 0$$
$$y = 3x - 4$$

The slope is 3 and the y-intercept is -4.

1. Determine the values of the slope and the y-intercept for each line. Then, graph the line.

   a) $y = 4x + 1$

   b) $y = x - 2$

   c) $y = 3x + 5$

   d) $y = -7x + 3$

   e) $y = 3x$

   f) $y = -8$

   g) $y = 5x + 2$

   h) $4x - y = 3$

   i) $7x + 2y - 5 = 0$

   j) $y = x$

   k) $4(x + 3) - y = 8$

   l) $\dfrac{y - 4}{3x} = 2$

Solve Quadratic Equations

To solve $x^2 - 5x = 6$ by factoring, first write the equation in the form $ax^2 + bx + c = 0$.

$$x^2 - 5x = 6$$
$$x^2 - 5x - 6 = 0$$
$$(x - 6)(x + 1) = 0 \qquad \text{Factor the left side.}$$
$$x - 6 = 0 \quad \text{or} \quad x + 1 = 0 \qquad \text{Use the zero product property.}$$
$$x = 6 \quad \text{or} \qquad x = -1$$

The roots are 6 and -1.

To solve $x^2 - 3x = 1$ using the quadratic formula, write the equation in the form $ax^2 + bx + c = 0$.

$$x^2 - 3x = 1$$
$$x^2 - 3x - 1 = 0$$

Then, substitute $a = 1$, $b = -3$, and $c = -1$ into the quadratic formula

$$x = \frac{-b \pm \sqrt{b^2 - 4ac}}{2a} \text{ and simplify.}$$

$$x = \frac{-b \pm \sqrt{b^2 - 4ac}}{2a}$$

$$= \frac{-(-3) \pm \sqrt{(-3)^2 - 4(1)(-1)}}{2(1)}$$

$$= \frac{3 \pm \sqrt{13}}{2}$$

The exact roots are $\dfrac{3 + \sqrt{13}}{2}$ and $\dfrac{3 - \sqrt{13}}{2}$. The approximate roots are 3.3 and -0.3.

1. Solve by factoring.

   a) $x^2 + 9x + 20 = 0$ b) $y^2 + 2 = 3y$

   c) $b^2 + 7b = 30$ d) $a^2 + 8a + 15 = 0$

2. Solve by factoring.

   a) $3x^2 + x = 2$ b) $4x^2 - 20x = -25$

   c) $25y^2 - 9 = 0$ d) $9x^2 - 4x = 0$

3. Solve. Leave answers in exact form.

   a) $2x^2 - 3x + 1 = 0$ b) $10x^2 = 21x - 9$

   c) $3x^2 + 2 = 5x$

4. Solve using the quadratic formula. Express solutions as exact roots and as approximate roots, to one decimal place.

   a) $5x^2 + 2x - 2 = 0$ b) $3x^2 - 2x - 2 = 0$

   c) $2x^2 + 7 = 8x$ d) $4x^2 + 4x = 14$

   e) $10x^2 = 4x + 4$ f) $6x^2 + 5x = 3$

Trigonometric Identities

To prove the trigonometric identity $\sin x \tan x \cos x = 1 - \cos^2 x$, use the quotient identity, $\frac{\sin x}{\cos x} = \tan x$, and the Pythagorean identity, $\sin^2 x + \cos^2 x = 1$.

$$\text{L.S.} = \sin x \tan x \cos x \qquad\qquad \text{R.S.} = 1 - \cos^2 x$$
$$= \sin x \, \frac{\sin x}{\cos x} \, \cos x$$
$$= \sin^2 x$$
$$= 1 - \cos^2 x$$
$$\text{L.S.} = \text{R.S.}$$

Thus, $\sin x \tan x \cos x = 1 - \cos^2 x$.

1. Prove each trigonometric identity.

a) $\dfrac{\cos x}{\sin x} = \dfrac{1}{\tan x}$ **b)** $\dfrac{\sin^2 x}{\tan^2 x} = 1 - \sin^2 x$

c) $\cos x = \dfrac{\sin^3 x}{\tan x} + \cos^3 x$

Use Long Division

Long division is an algorithm for the division of two real numbers. One number, the dividend, is divided by another number, the divisor, with the result being the quotient.

$$
\begin{array}{r}
152 \\
3\overline{)457} \\
3\downarrow \\
\overline{15} \\
15\downarrow \\
\overline{07} \\
6 \\
\overline{1}
\end{array}
$$

The result of the quotient $457 \div 3$ is 152, with remainder 1.

$$
\begin{array}{r}
192 \\
13\overline{)2508} \\
13\downarrow \\
\overline{120} \\
117\downarrow \\
\overline{38} \\
26 \\
\overline{12}
\end{array}
$$

The result of the quotient $2508 \div 13$ is 192, with remainder 12.

1. Use long division to find each quotient. Write the remainder.

a) $143 \div 5$ **b)** $2187 \div 14$

c) $4689 \div 32$ **d)** $3567 \div 28$

Technology Appendix

Contents

The Geometer's Sketchpad® Geometry Software

Menu Bar

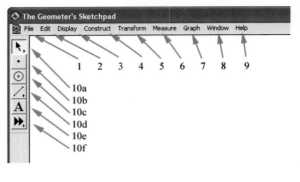

1 **File menu**—open/save/print sketches

2 **Edit menu**—undo/redo actions/set preferences

3 **Display menu**—control appearance of objects in sketch

4 **Construct menu**—construct new geometric objects based on objects in sketch

5 **Transform menu**—apply geometric transformations to selected objects

6 **Measure menu**—make various measurements on objects in sketch

7 **Graph menu**—create axes and plot measurements and points

8 **Window menu**—manipulate windows

9 **Help menu**—access the help system; this is an excellent reference guide

10 **Toolbox**—access tools for creating, marking, and transforming points, circles, and straight objects (segments, lines, and rays); also includes text and information tools

10a **Selection Arrow Tool** (Arrow)—select and transform objects

10b **Point Tool** (Dot)—draw points

10c **Compass Tool** (Circle)—draw circles

10d **Straightedge Tool**—draw line segments, rays, and lines

10e **Text Tool** (Letter A)—label points and write text

10f **Custom Tool** (Double Arrow)—create or use special custom tools

Saving a Sketch

If you are saving for the first time in a new sketch:

- Under the **File** menu, choose **Save As**. The **Save As** dialogue box will appear.
- You can save the sketch with the name assigned by *The Geometer's Sketchpad®*. Click on **Save**.

  OR

- Press the **Backspace** or **Delete** key to clear the name.
- Type whatever you wish to name the sketch file. Click on **Save**.

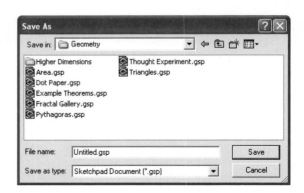

If you have already given your file a name:

- Choose **Save** from the **File** menu.

Setting Preferences

- From the **Edit** menu, choose **Preferences....**
- Click on the **Units** tab.
- Set the units and precision for angles, distances, and calculated values such as slopes and ratios.
- Click on the **Text** tab.
- If you check the auto-label box **For All New Points**, then *The Geometer's Sketchpad®* will label points as you create them.
- If you check the auto-label box **As Objects Are Measured**, then *The Geometer's Sketchpad®* will label any measurements that you define.

You can also choose whether the auto-labelling functions will apply only to the current sketch, or also to any new sketches that you create.

Be sure to click on **OK** to apply your preferences.

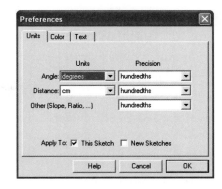

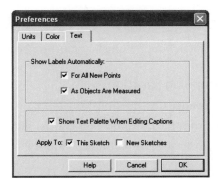

Selecting Points and Objects

- Choose the **Selection Arrow Tool**. The mouse cursor appears as an arrow.

To select a single point:

- Select the point by moving the cursor to the point and clicking on the point. The selected point will now appear as a darker point, similar to a bull's eye ⊙.

To select an object such as a line segment or a circle:

- Move the cursor to a point on the object until it becomes a horizontal arrow.
- Click on the object. The object's appearance will change to show that it is selected.

To select a number of points or objects:

- Select each object in turn by moving the cursor to the object and clicking on it.

To deselect a point or an object:

- Move the cursor over it and click the left mouse button.

To deselect all selected objects, click in an open area of the workspace.

Using a Coordinate System and Axes

- From the **Graph** menu, choose **Show Grid**.

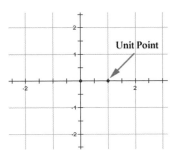

The default coordinate system has an origin point in the centre of the screen and a unit point at (1, 0). Drag the origin to relocate the coordinate system and drag the unit point to change the scale.

Plotting Points

- From the **Graph** menu, choose **Show Grid**.
- If you want points plotted exactly at grid intersections, also choose **Snap Points**.
- Choose the **Point Tool**.

If you have chosen **Snap Points,** a point will "snap" to the nearest grid intersection as you move the cursor over the grid.

- Click the left mouse button to plot the point.

Alternatively, you can plot points by typing in the desired coordinates.

- From the **Graph** menu, choose **Plot Points….** A dialogue box will appear. Type the desired x- and y-coordinates in the boxes. Then, click on **Plot**.
- When you are finished plotting points, click on **Done**.

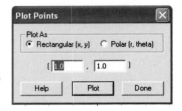

Graphing Functions

Consider the functions $f(x) = 2x - 1$ and $g(x) = -x^2 + 2$.

- From the **Graph** menu, choose **Show Grid**.
- From the **Graph** menu, choose **Plot New Function…**.

The calculator interface will appear.

- Enter the first function: $2 * x - 1$
- Click on **OK**.

The graph of $f(x)$ will be displayed, along with the equation in function notation. You can move the equation next to the line.

Use the same procedure to graph $g(x)$.

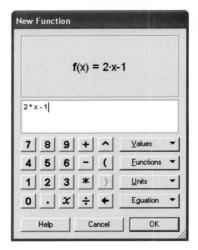

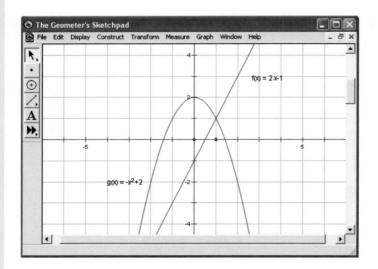

Tracing the Path of a Plotted Point and Using the Motion Controller

- Draw a point in the workspace.
- From the **Display** menu, choose **Trace Point**.
- From the **Display** menu, choose **Animate Point**.

The **Motion Controller** will appear. The point will move along a random path, leaving a trail.

You can use the **Motion Controller** to pause, stop, and start the motion, as well as to adjust the speed of the motion.

- You can erase the trail by pressing Ctrl-B.

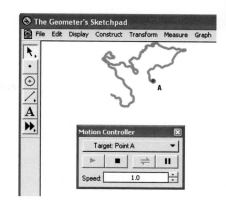

Creating and Using a Parameter

- From the **Graph** menu, **Show Grid**.
- From the **Graph** menu, choose **New Parameter....**

You can change the name or the value of the parameter. You can also specify units.

- Click on **OK**.

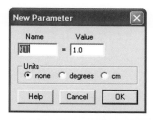

The parameter will be displayed in the workspace.

- From the **Measure** menu, choose **Calculate**.
- Enter $-2 * t_1$ and click on **OK**.
- Select t_1 and then $-2t_1$ in that order.
- From the **Graph** menu, choose **Plot As (x, y)**.

The point will be displayed.

- Select the point.
- From the **Display** menu, choose **Trace Plotted Point**.
- Deselect the point and then select the parameter t_1.
- From the **Display** menu, choose **Animate Parameter**.

When the motion controller appears, use it to control the motion, as well as to change the direction of the animation.

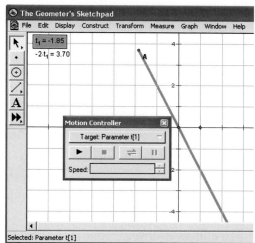

Hiding Objects

Open a new sketch. Draw several objects such as points and line segments.

To hide a point:

- Select the point.
- From the **Display** menu, choose **Hide Point**.

To hide more than one object:

- Select another point and a line segment.
- From the **Display** menu, choose **Hide Objects**.

Shortcut: You can hide any selected objects by pressing Ctrl-H.

You can make hidden objects reappear by choosing **Show All Hidden** from the **Display** menu.

Measuring the Abscissa, Ordinate, and Coordinates of a Point

- Plot a point in the workspace. Select the point.
- From the **Measure** menu, choose **Abscissa (x)**.
- Deselect the x_A measurement, and then select the point again. From the **Measure** menu, choose **Ordinate (y)**.
- Deselect the y_A measurement, and then select the point one more time. From the **Measure** menu, choose **Coordinates**.

Deselect the coordinates, and then drag the point around the workspace. Note how the measurements change.

You can use these measurements in other calculations.

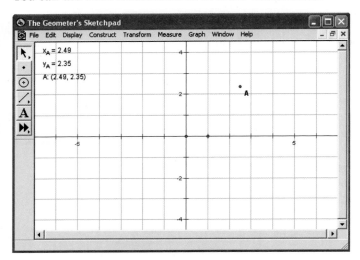

Changing Labels of Measures

- Right click on the measure and choose **Label Measurement** (or **Label Distance Measurement** depending on the type of measure) from the drop-down menu.
- Type the new label.
- Click on **OK**.

Constructing a Secant Line Through a Curve

- From the **Graph** menu, choose **Show Grid**.
- From the **Graph** menu, choose **Plot New Function**.
- Enter the function using the calculator that appears (for example, $f(x) = x^2 - 3x + 1$). Click on **OK** to plot the function.
- Select the function. From the **Construct** menu, choose **Point on Function Plot**.
- Select the new point. From the **Measure** menu, choose **Abscissa (x)**. Repeat for **Ordinate (y)**.
- Select the function. From the **Construct** menu, choose **Point on Function Plot**.
- Select both points on the function. From the **Construct** menu, choose **Line**.
- Select the new line. From the **Measure** menu, choose **Slope**.

- Select the new line again. From the **Measure** menu, choose **Equation**.
- Drag the second point you created on the line toward the first point and observe the secant line becoming a tangent line.

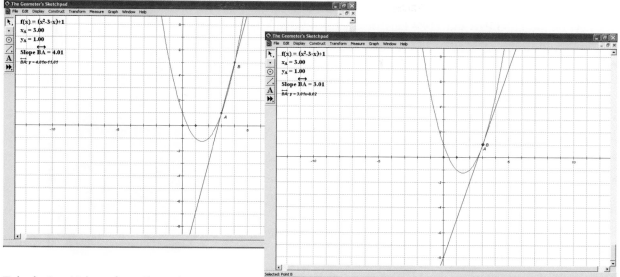

Tabulating Values for a Function

- From the **Graph** menu, choose **Show Grid**.
- From the **Graph** menu, choose **Plot New Function**.
- Enter the function using the calculator that appears (for example, $f(x) = x^2$). Click on **OK** to plot the function.
- Select the function. From the **Construct** menu, choose **Point on Function Plot**.
- Select the new point. From the **Measure** menu, choose **Abscissa** (x).
- From the **Measure** menu, choose **Calculate**.
- Select the equation and enter the Abscissa (x) value. Click on **OK**.
- Select the abscissa (x_A) value and the value of $f(x_A)$.
- From the **Graph** menu, choose **Tabulate**.
- Keeping the table of values selected, drag your selected point along the function. Double click on the table as you move along the function to collect data.

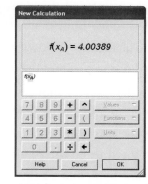

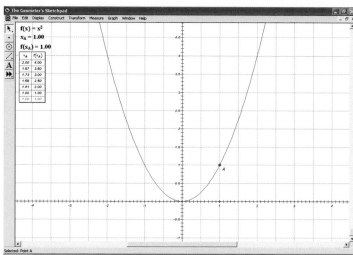

TI-83 Plus and TI-84 Plus Graphing Calculators

TI-83 Plus and TI-84 Plus Basics

The keys on the TI-83 Plus and TI-84 Plus are colour-coded to help you find the various functions. These descriptions apply to the TI-84 Plus calculator.

- The number keys, the decimal point key, and the negative sign key are white. When entering negative values, use the white $(-)$ key, not the grey $-$ key.
- The grey keys on the right side are the math operations.
- The grey keys across the top are used when graphing.
- The primary function of each key is printed on the key.
- The secondary function of each key is printed in blue above the key and is activated by pressing the blue 2nd key. For example, to find the square root of a number, press 2nd x^2 for $[\sqrt{}]$.
- The alpha function of each key is printed in green above the key and is activated by pressing the green ALPHA key.

Setting Window Variables

The WINDOW key defines the appearance of the graph. The standard (default) window settings are shown.

To change the window settings:

- Press WINDOW. Enter the desired window settings.

In the example shown,

- the minimum x-value is -47
- the maximum x-value is 47
- the scale on the x-axis is 10
- the minimum y-value is -31
- the maximum y-value is 31
- the scale on the y-axis is 10
- the resolution is 1, so equations are graphed at each horizontal pixel

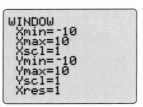

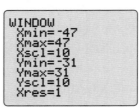

Changing the Appearance of a Graph

The default style is a thin solid line. The line style is displayed to the left of the equation.

There are seven options for the appearance of a line.

- Press Y= and clear any previously entered equations.
- Enter the function $f(x) = 3x + 5$ for **Y1**.
- Use the standard window settings.
- Press GRAPH.

Note the thin, solid line style.

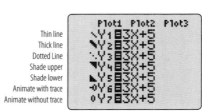

Thin line
Thick line
Dotted Line
Shade upper
Shade lower
Animate with trace
Animate without trace

- Press $\boxed{Y=}$. Cursor left to the slanted line.
- Press $\boxed{ENTER}$ repeatedly until the thick, solid line shows, as in **Y2** on the screen.
- Press $\boxed{GRAPH}$.

Note the thick, solid line.

- Press $\boxed{Y=}$. Cursor left to the slanted line.
- Press $\boxed{ENTER}$ repeatedly until the thin, dotted line shows, as in **Y3** on the screen.
- Press $\boxed{GRAPH}$.

Note the thin, dotted line.

- Press $\boxed{Y=}$. Cursor left to the slanted line.
- Press $\boxed{ENTER}$ repeatedly until the solid triangle with hypotenuse down shows, as in **Y4** on the screen.
- Press $\boxed{GRAPH}$.

Note that the graph is shaded above the line.

- Press $\boxed{Y=}$. Cursor left to the slanted line.
- Press $\boxed{ENTER}$ repeatedly until the solid triangle with hypotenuse up shows, as in **Y5** on the screen.
- Press $\boxed{GRAPH}$.

Note that the graph is shaded below the line.

- Press $\boxed{Y=}$. Cursor left to the slanted line.
- Press $\boxed{ENTER}$ repeatedly until the circle with a tail shows, as in **Y6** on the screen.
- Press $\boxed{GRAPH}$.

Note the flying ball tracing the graph.

- Press $\boxed{Y=}$. Cursor left to the slanted line.
- Press $\boxed{ENTER}$ repeatedly until the plain circle shows, as in **Y7** on the screen.
- Press $\boxed{GRAPH}$.

Note the flying ball that follows the graph, but does not leave a trace.

Graphing a Function Involving Absolute Value

Consider the function $f(x) = |x|$.

- Press $\boxed{Y=}$.
- Press $\boxed{MATH}$ and cursor over to the **NUM** menu. Then, select **1:abs(**.
- Type x) and press $\boxed{ENTER}$.
- Press $\boxed{ZOOM}$ and select **6:ZStandard**.

The graph will be displayed.

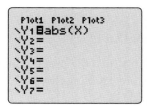
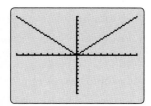

Graphing a Piecewise Function

Some graphs have different definitions on different domains.
Consider the function $f(x)$:

$$f(x) = \begin{cases} x, & x < 0 \\ x^2, & x \geq 0 \end{cases}$$

This is known as a piecewise function.

To graph this function, enter it as two functions, adjusting the domain of each function to the proper values.

- Press Y=. Enter $x(x < 0)$ in **Y1**. **Note:** You can insert $<$ and $\geq$ by pressing 2nd MATH for [TEST] to access the **TEST** menu.

- Enter $x^2(x \geq 0)$ in **Y2**.

- Press ZOOM and select **6:ZStandard**.

The graph will be displayed. Notice the two distinct sections of the graph.

Using Zoom

The ZOOM key is used to change the area of the graph that is displayed in the graphing window.

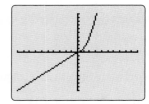

To set the size of the area you want to zoom in on:

- Press ZOOM. Select **1:ZBox**. The graph screen will be displayed, and the cursor will be flashing.

- If you cannot see the cursor, use the ◀, ▶, ▲, and ▼ keys to move the cursor until you can see it.

- Move the cursor to the edge of the area in which you would like a closer view. Press ENTER to mark that point as a starting point.

- Press the ◀, ▶, ▲, and ▼ keys as needed to move the sides of the box to enclose the area you want to look at.

- Press ENTER when you are finished. The area will now appear larger.

To zoom in on an area without identifying a boxed-in area:

- Press ZOOM. Select **2:Zoom In**.

To zoom out of an area:

- Press ZOOM. Select **3:Zoom Out**.

To display a viewing area in which the origin appears at the centre and the x- and y-axes intervals are equally spaced:

- Press ZOOM. Select **4:ZDecimal**.

To reset the axes ranges on your calculator to the standard window:

- Press ZOOM. Select **6:ZStandard**.

To display all data points in a STAT PLOT:

- Press ZOOM. Select **9:ZoomStat**.

Finding Friendly Windows

It is useful to have a "friendly window" to avoid distortion in the graph. The viewing window is 94 pixels across. When the calculator divides the pixels evenly into negative and positive integers, each pixel represents one tick mark. So, x-values can go from -47 to 47. The y-axis has 62 pixels vertically and stretches from -31 to 31.

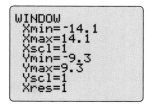

Multiples of the above values will also yield a friendly window.

For example, multiplying by 0.3 gives the first window shown.

Multiplying by 0.25 gives the second window shown.

Using the Tangent Operation

The **Tangent** operation will draw a tangent line to a function graph for a given value of the independent variable.

Consider the function $f(x) = x^2 - 5x + 4$. Suppose you want a tangent line at $x = 2$.

- Press $\boxed{\text{Y=}}$ and enter the function in **Y1**.
- Press $\boxed{\text{ZOOM}}$. Select **6:Standard**. The graph will be displayed.
- Press $\boxed{\text{2nd}}$ $\boxed{\text{PRGM}}$ to access the **DRAW** menu. Select **5:Tangent(**.
- Press **2**, then $\boxed{\text{ENTER}}$.

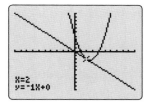

The tangent line will be drawn.

The equation of the tangent appears in the lower left corner of the screen.

Changing the Mode Settings

The mode settings are used to control the way the calculator displays and interprets numbers and graphs.

- Press $\boxed{\text{MODE}}$.

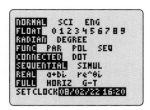

The first line controls the number display. Most of the time, you will use **Normal**. You can also select **Scientific** or **Engineering**.

The second line controls the number of decimal places that are displayed. If you choose **FLOAT**, the calculator will select the appropriate number. You can also choose the number of decimal places. For example, if you are working with money, you might want to have all numbers displayed with two decimal places.

To change a setting:
- Use the cursor keys to navigate to the desired setting.
- Press $\boxed{\text{ENTER}}$ to select the setting.

To leave the **Mode** screen:
- Press $\boxed{\text{2nd}}$ $\boxed{\text{MODE}}$ for [QUIT].

Entering Data Into Lists

To enter data:

- Press [STAT]. The cursor will highlight the **EDIT** menu.
- Press **1** or [ENTER] to select **1:Edit…**.

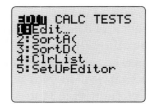

This allows you to enter new data, or edit existing data, in lists **L1** to **L6**. You can see the hidden lists by scrolling to the right using the cursor keys.

For example, press [STAT], select **1:Edit…** and then enter data in list **L1**.

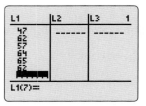

- Use the cursor keys to move around the editor screen.
- Complete each data entry by pressing [ENTER].
- Press [2nd] [MODE] for [QUIT] to exit the list editor when the data are entered.

You may need to clear a list before you enter data into it. For example, to clear list **L1**:

- Press [STAT] and select **4:ClrList**.
- Press [2nd] **1** for [L1] and press [ENTER].

OR

You can cursor up to the **L1** heading in the list editor, press [CLEAR], and then press [ENTER].

To clear all lists:

- Press [2nd] [+] for [MEM] to display the **MEMORY** menu.
- Select **4:ClrAllLists** and press [ENTER].

You can enter a formula into a list:

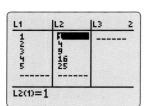

- Enter the integers 1 to 5 in list **L1**.
- Use the cursor keys to move to the title of list **L2**.
- Press [2nd] **1** for [L1]. Then, press $[x^2]$.
- Press [ENTER].

The squares of the entries in **L1** will be displayed in **L2**.

Finding Finite Differences

Enter the data:

- Press [STAT] and select **1:Edit**.
- Enter the x-values in **L1**.
- Enter the y-values in **L2**.

To determine the first differences, cursor over to select **L3**.

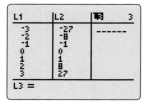

- Press [2nd] [STAT] and cursor over to **OPS**.
- Select **7:ΔList(**.

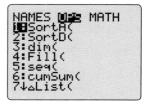

This will paste the command into the statistics screen.

- Press [2nd] **2** for [L2] and then press [ )].

This tells the calculator to find the changes between values in **L2** and place them into **L3**.

Notice, in the last screen, that the finite differences formula in list **L3** uses quotation marks, ", and the list name has a diamond (♦) beside it. The quotation marks make the finite differences dynamic so that the values in list **L3** will automatically update if list **L2** changes. The diamond indicates that the list is dynamic.

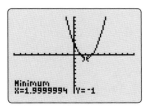

To insert quotation marks, press ⒜ˡᵖʰᵃ ⊞ for ["].

Finding the Maximum or Minimum

To find the maximum or minimum of a function such as $f(x) = x^2 - 4x + 3$:

- Press ⒠2ⁿᵈ ⒯ᴿᴬᶜᴱ to access the **CALCULATE** menu. Select **3:minimum**.
- Use the cursor keys to move the cursor to the left of the minimum. Press ⒠ɴᴛᴇʀ.
- Use the cursor keys to move the cursor to the right of the minimum. Press ⒠ɴᴛᴇʀ.
- Use the cursor keys to move the cursor close to your guess for the minimum. Press ⒠ɴᴛᴇʀ.

The coordinates of the minimum are displayed.

If the graph has a maximum, rather than a minimum, select **4:maximum** from the **CALCULATE** menu.

Finding Zeros

To find the zeros of a function such as $f(x) = x^2 - x - 6$:

- Press ⒴=. Enter the function.
- Press ⒵ᴏᴏᴹ. Select **6:ZStandard**.
- Press ⒠2ⁿᵈ ⒯ᴿᴬᶜᴱ to access the **CALCULATE** menu. Select **2:zero**.
- Use the cursor keys to move the cursor to the left of the left zero. Press ⒠ɴᴛᴇʀ.
- Use the cursor keys to move the cursor to the right of the left zero. Press ⒠ɴᴛᴇʀ.
- Use the cursor keys to move the cursor close to your guess for the left zero. Press ⒠ɴᴛᴇʀ.

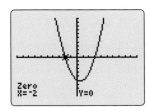

The coordinates of the zero are displayed.

Use a similar procedure to find the right zero.

Using the Value Operation

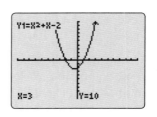

To find the corresponding y-value for any x-value for a function such as $f(x) = x^2 + x - 2$:

- Press $\boxed{Y=}$. Enter the function.
- Press $\boxed{ZOOM}$. Select **6:ZStandard**.
- Press $\boxed{TRACE}$.
- Enter a value for x, such as $x = 3$. Press $\boxed{ENTER}$.

The corresponding y-value, $y = 10$, is displayed.

Curve of Best Fit: Quadratic Regression and Exponential Regression

You can add a quadratic or an exponential curve of best fit to a scatter plot by using the **QuadReg** operation, or the **ExpReg** operation.

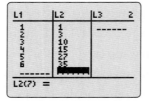
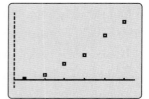

Create a scatter plot using the data shown.

- Press $\boxed{STAT}$. Cursor over to the **CALC** menu. Then, select **5:QuadReg**.
- Press $\boxed{2nd}$ **1** for **L1**, followed by $\boxed{,}$.
- Press $\boxed{2nd}$ **2** for **L2**, followed by $\boxed{,}$.
- Press $\boxed{VARS}$. Cursor over to the **Y-VARS** menu. Select **1:Function…** and then select **1:Y1**.
- Press $\boxed{ENTER}$ to obtain the **QuadReg** screen.

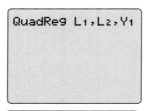

The equation of the quadratic curve is displayed.

Note: If the diagnostic mode is turned on, you will see values for r and r^2 displayed on the **QuadReg** screen.

To turn the diagnostic mode off:

- Press $\boxed{2nd}$ **0** for [CATALOG].
- Scroll down to **DiagnosticOff**. Press $\boxed{ENTER}$ to select this option.
- Press $\boxed{ENTER}$ again to turn off the diagnostic mode.
- Press $\boxed{GRAPH}$ to see the line of best fit overlaid on the scatter plot.

The quadratic regression equation is stored in the **Y=** editor.

- Press $\boxed{Y=}$ to display the equation generated by the calculator.

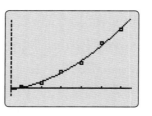

If you want to fit an exponential curve, select **0:ExpReg** from the **STAT CALC** menu rather than **5:QuadReg**.

Graphing the Inverse of a Function

You can use the **DRAW** menu to graph an inverse. For example, graph the function $y = 5^x$.

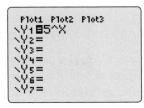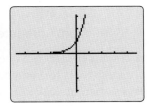

To graph the inverse of $y = 5^x$:

• Press ⟨2nd⟩ ⟨PRGM⟩ for [DRAW]. Select **8:DrawInv**.

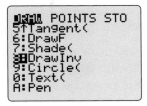

This will take you back to the **HOME** screen.

• Enter **Y1** by pressing ⟨VARS⟩, cursoring over to **Y-VARS**, selecting **1:Function**, and then selecting **1:Y1**.

• Press ⟨ENTER⟩.

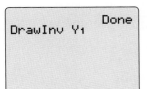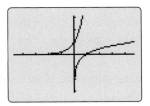

TI-89 Titanium Computer Algebra System

TI-89 Titanium Computer Algerbra System Basics

A computer algebra system, or CAS, is a program that contains tools for manipulation of symbolic expressions. It is sometimes called a symbolic manipulator. You can expand expressions, factor expressions, solve equations, check solutions, and perform many other operations with a CAS.

Keypad Tips: Use the 2nd key to access functions that are in **blue**. Use the ◆ key to access functions that are in **green**. Use the ALPHA key to access letters and other text characters. Use the (–) key to enter a negative, but use the – key for the subtraction operation.

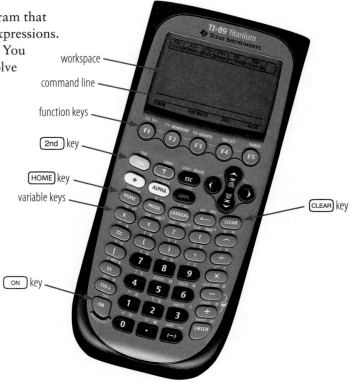

Changing the Mode Settings

The **Mode** settings are used to control the way the calculator displays and interprets numbers and other quantities.

* Press MODE.

The **Display Digits** line determines the number of decimal places that will be displayed. If you choose **FLOAT**, the calculator will select the appropriate number. You can also choose the number of decimal places.

Scroll down to **Exact/Approx**. Normally, you will set this to **AUTO**. The calculator will display an exact answer or an approximate answer, as appropriate.

You can also force the calculator to display either an exact or an approximate answer. For example, consider the equation $x^2 = 2$.

If you set the **Exact/Approx** mode to **EXACT**, the calculator will display the solution to this equation as $x\sqrt{2}$. If you set the **Exact/Approx** mode to **APPROXIMATE**, the calculator will display the solution as $x = 1.41421356237$, or to the accuracy you set in the **Display Digits** line.

* To leave the **Mode** screen, press ESC.

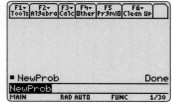

Starting a New Problem

Before you start using the calculator, it is wise to clear the memory. Otherwise, values that a previous user has entered may produce unexpected results.

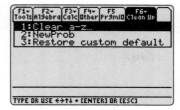

- Press (2nd) (F1) to access the **F6** menu. This is the **Clean Up** menu.
- Select **2:NewProb**. Then, press (ENTER).

Evaluating an Expression for a Given Value

You can evaluate an expression for a given value of the variable. For example, consider the expression $5x + 2$. To evaluate the expression for $x = 3$, type $5x + 2 \mid x = 3$

- Press (ENTER).

The calculator returns a value of 17.

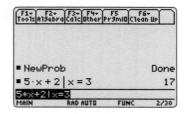

Defining a Function and Evaluating the Function for a Given Value

You can define and store a function in the CAS. You can then evaluate the function for different values of the independent variable, algebraically manipulate the function, or use it in other calculations.

Suppose that you want to store the function $f(x) = x^2 + 3x + 2$.

- Press (F4) and select **1:Define**.
- Enter $f(x) = x^2 + 3x + 2$. Use the (ALPHA) key to enter the letter f.
- Press (ENTER).

The function is now stored in the CAS.

To evaluate $f(3)$, type $f(3)$, and press (ENTER). The calculator will return a value of 20.

Solving an Equation for a Given Variable

Consider the equation $x^2 + 3x + 2 = 0$.

You can solve this equation for x using the CAS.

- Press (F2) and select **1:solve(**.
- Type $x^2 + 3x + 2 = 0, x)$.
  Note: you must tell the CAS which variable to solve for.
- Press (ENTER).

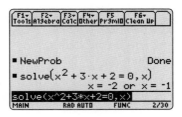

The CAS will display all possible solutions: $x = -2$ or $x = -1$.

Graphing the Inverse of a Function

You can graph the inverse of a given function.

- Press (APPS) to go to the main menu.
- Select **Y= Editor.**
- Press (ENTER).

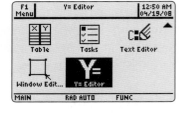

Suppose you want to graph the inverse of $y = 5^x$.

- Enter the function as **y1.**
- Press ◆ (F3) to graph the function.
- Press (2nd) (F1) to access the **F6** menu, and select **3:DrawInv.** This takes you to the **HOME** screen.

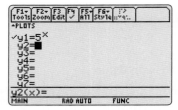
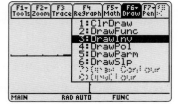

- Type 5^x next to **DrawInv.**
- Press (ENTER).

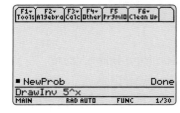
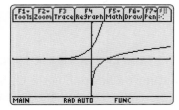

Solving Polynomial Inequalities Using Numerical Values

Consider solving the inequality $x^4 - 3x^2 - 4 < 0$.

You can determine the x-intercepts and then numerically verify the sign of the function within the intervals.

- Press (F2) and select **1:solve(.**
- Type $x^4 - 3x^2 - 4 = 0, x)$.

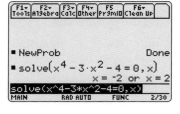

Select a value in each interval, $x < -2$, $-2 < x < 2$, and $x > 2$, and determine whether the value chosen makes the original inequality true or false.

For $x < 2$, choose $x = -3$.

- Type $x^4 - 3x^2 - 4 < 0 \mid x = -3$.

For $-2 < x < 2$, choose $x = 0$.

- Type $x^4 - 3x^2 - 4 < 0 \mid x = 0$.

Logical reasoning tells us the solution to the inequality is now found.

$x^4 - 3x^2 - 4 < 0$ for $-2 < x < 2$.

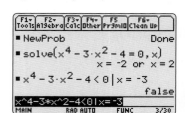
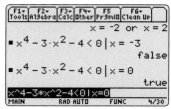

Dividing Polynomial Functions

You can use a CAS to do polynomial division of the type

$$\frac{2x^3 - 3x^2 + 8x - 12}{x - 1}.$$

Go to the **HOME** screen.

Method 1: *Use the Proper Fraction Function*

- Press F2 and select **7:propFrac(**.
- Type $2x^3 - 3x^2 + 8x - 12)/(x - 1))$.

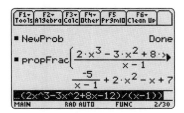

Method 2: *Use the Expand Function*

- Press F2 and select **3:Expand(**.
- Type $2x^3 - 3x^2 + 8x - 12)/(x - 1))$.

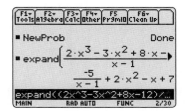

Finding Zeros

The real roots of the equation $x^4 - 13x^2 + 36 = 0$ are the x-intercepts or zeros of the graph of $f(x) = x^4 - 13x^2 + 36$.

- Press APPS and select **Y= Editor**.
- Type $y1 = x^4 - 13x^2 + 36$.
- Press ENTER.
- Press ◆ F3 to graph the function.
- Press APPS and select **HOME**.
- Press F2 and select **1:solve(**.
- Type $y1(x) = 0, x)$ to find the x-intercepts.

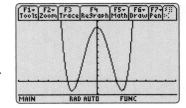
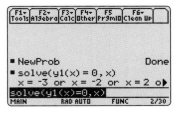

You can verify this on the graph.

- Press ◆ F3 to view the graph.
- Press F5 and select **2:Zero**.

Move the cursor close to each of the x-intercepts.

- Enter a **Lower Bound**.
- Enter an **Upper Bound**.
- The zero is displayed on the screen
- Find the other three zeros in the same way.

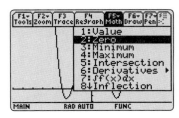
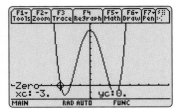

Answers

CHAPTER 1

Prerequisite Skills, pages 2–3

1. a) 7 **b)** −5 **c)** 11 **d)** 5 **e)** $8x + 7$ **f)** $-12x + 7$

2. a) 1 **b)** 10 **c)** 6 **d)** 0 **e)** $24x^2 - 18x + 3$ **f)** $18x^2 - 9x + 1$

3. a) $m = 3, b = 2$ **b)** $m = -\dfrac{1}{2}, b = \dfrac{3}{2}$ **c)** $m = 5, b = 7$

d) $m = -5, b = -11$ **e)** $m = -\dfrac{1}{2}, b = 1$

4. a) $y = 3x + 5$ **b)** $y = 4x + 4$ **c)** $y = -4x + 31$

d) $y = -7x + 12$

5. a) linear **b)** neither **c)** quadratic

6. a) $\{x \in \mathbb{R}\}, \{y \in \mathbb{R}, y \geq 1\}$ **b)** $\{x \in \mathbb{R}, x \neq -5\}, \{y \in \mathbb{R}, y \neq 0\}$

c) $\left\{x \in \mathbb{R}, x \leq \dfrac{1}{2}\right\}, \{y \in \mathbb{R}, y \geq 0\}$

7. Answers may vary. Sample answers:

a) $y = -3(x + 1)(x - 1)$ **b)** $y = -\dfrac{1}{2}x^2 + 3x - \dfrac{9}{2}$

c) $y = 4\left(x + \dfrac{1}{2}\right)(x - 2)$

8. a) x-intercepts $-6, \dfrac{5}{2}$; vertex $\left(-\dfrac{7}{4}, -\dfrac{289}{8}\right)$; opens up;

$\{x \in \mathbb{R}\}, \left\{y \in \mathbb{R}, y \geq -\dfrac{289}{8}\right\}$

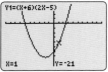

b) x-intercepts approximately 3.29, 4.71; vertex $(4, 1)$; opens down; $\{x \in \mathbb{R}\}, \{y \in \mathbb{R}, y \leq 1\}$

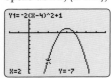

c) x-intercepts approximately $-1.47, 7.47$; vertex $(3, 5)$; opens down; $\{x \in \mathbb{R}\}, \{y \in \mathbb{R}, y \leq 5\}$

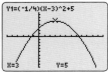

d) x-intercepts $-2, \dfrac{3}{5}$; vertex $\left(-\dfrac{7}{10}, -\dfrac{169}{20}\right)$; opens up;

$\{x \in \mathbb{R}\}, \left\{y \in \mathbb{R}, y \geq -\dfrac{169}{20}\right\}$

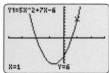

e) x-intercepts $1, \dfrac{2}{3}$; vertex $\left(\dfrac{5}{6}, \dfrac{1}{12}\right)$; opens down; $\{x \in \mathbb{R}\}$,

$\left\{y \in \mathbb{R}, y \leq \dfrac{1}{12}\right\}$

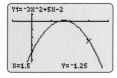

9. a) vertical stretch and a reflection in the x-axis **b)** vertical compression **c)** horizontal compression **d)** horizontal stretch and a reflection in the y-axis **e)** reflection in the y-axis

10. a) i) $f(x) = x + 5$

ii)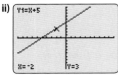

iii) $\{x \in \mathbb{R}\}, \{y \in \mathbb{R}\}$
b) i) $f(x) = -5(x + 1)^2 - 2$

ii)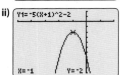

iii) $\{x \in \mathbb{R}\}, \{y \in \mathbb{R}, y \leq -2\}$

c) i) $f(x) = -3[2(x + 4)] + 6$

ii)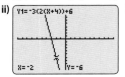

iii) $\{x \in \mathbb{R}\}, \{y \in \mathbb{R}\}$

11. a) i) vertical stretch by a factor of 2, reflection in the x-axis, translation 3 units left, translation 1 unit up **ii)** $y = -2(x + 3) + 1$ **b) i)** vertical compression by a factor of $\dfrac{1}{3}$, translation 2 units down **ii)** $y = \dfrac{1}{3}x^2 - 2$

12. vertical stretch by a factor of 3, horizontal stretch by a factor of 2, reflection in the y-axis, translation 1 unit right, translation 2 units up

1.1 Power Functions, pages 11–14

1. a) No. **b)** Yes. **c)** Yes. **d)** Yes. **e)** No. **f)** No.

2. a) 4, 5 **b)** 1, −1 **c)** 2, 8 **d)** 3, $-\dfrac{1}{4}$ **e)** 0, −5 **f)** 2, 1

3. a) i) even **ii)** negative **iii)** $\{x \in \mathbb{R}\}, \{y \in \mathbb{R}, y \leq 0\}$ **iv)** line **v)** quadrant 3 to quadrant 4 **b) i)** odd **ii)** positive **iii)** $\{x \in \mathbb{R}\}, \{y \in \mathbb{R}\}$ **iv)** point **v)** quadrant 3 to quadrant 1 **c) i)** odd **ii)** negative **iii)** $\{x \in \mathbb{R}\}, \{y \in \mathbb{R}\}$ **iv)** point **v)** quadrant 2 to quadrant 4 **d) i)** even **ii)** positive **iii)** $\{x \in \mathbb{R}\}, \{y \geq 0\}$ **iv)** line **v)** quadrant 2 to quadrant 1 **e) i)** odd **ii)** negative **iii)** $\{x \in \mathbb{R}\}, \{y \in \mathbb{R}\}$ **iv)** point **v)** quadrant 2 to quadrant 4

4.

End Behaviour	Function
Extends from quadrant 3 to quadrant 1	$y = 5x, y = 4x^5$
Extends from quadrant 2 to quadrant 4	$y = -x^3, y = -0.1x^{11}$
Extends from quadrant 2 to quadrant 1	$y = \dfrac{3}{7}x^2, y = 2x^4$
Extends from quadrant 3 to quadrant 4	$y = -x^6, y = -9x^{10}$

5. a)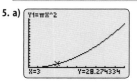

b) $\{r \in \mathbb{R}, 0 \leq r \leq 10\}; \{A \in \mathbb{R}, 0 \leq A \leq 100\pi\}$
c) Answers may vary. Sample answer: similarities—vertex $(0, 0)$, x-intercept, y-intercept, end behaviour; differences—domain, range, shape

6. a)

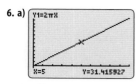

b) $\{r \in \mathbb{R}, 0 \le r \le 10\}$, $\{C \in \mathbb{R}, 0 \le C \le 20\pi\}$
c) Answers may vary. Sample answer: similarities—end behaviour; differences—domain, range, shape
7. a) power (cubic) **b)** exponential **c)** periodic **d)** power (constant)
e) none of these **f)** none of these **g)** power (quadratic)
8. a)

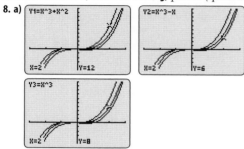

b) $\{x \in \mathbb{R}\}$, $\{y \in \mathbb{R}\}$, quadrant 3 to quadrant 1, point symmetry about $(0, 0)$; x-intercept 0, y-intercept 0
9. a)

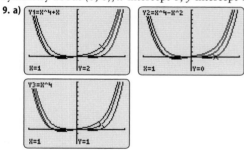

b) $\{x \in \mathbb{R}\}$, quadrant 2 to quadrant 1; x-intercept 0, y-intercept 0
10. Answers may vary. Sample answer: similarities—extend from quadrant 3 to quadrant 1 (positive leading coefficient), $\{x \in \mathbb{R}\}$, $\{y \in \mathbb{R}\}$, point symmetry about $(0, 0)$; differences— shape, extend from quadrant 2 to quadrant 4 (negative leading coefficient)

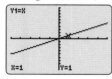 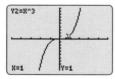

11. Answers may vary. Sample answer: similarities—extend from quadrant 2 to quadrant 1 (positive leading coefficient), domain, line symmetry; differences—shape, range, extend from quadrant 3 to quadrant 4 (negative leading coefficient)

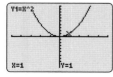 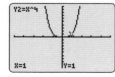

12. a) Answers may vary. Sample answer: similarities— quadrant 3 to quadrant 1, domain, range, point symmetry, shape; difference—shifted vertically

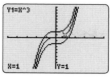

b) Answers may vary. Sample answer: similarities—quadrant 2 to quadrant 1, domain, line symmetry, shape; differences— range, shifted vertically

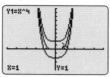

c) Second graph is a vertical shift of the first by c units
13. Answers may vary. Sample answer: path of a river: $y = x^3$, $\{x \in \mathbb{R}\}$, $\{y \in \mathbb{R}\}$; cross-section of a valley: $y = x^2$. $\{x \in \mathbb{R}\}$, $\{y \in \mathbb{R}, y \ge 0\}$
14. a) $y = (-x)^{2n}$ is the same graph as $y = x^{2n}$, n is a non-negative integer, $(-x)^{2n} = (-1)^{2n}(x)^{2n} = x^{2n}$
i)

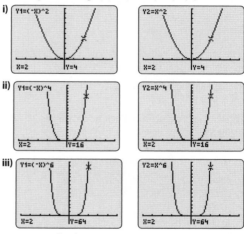

b) $y = (-x)^{2n+1}$ has the same graph as $y = -x^{2n+1}$, n is a non-negative integer, $(-x)^{2n+1} = (-1)^{2n+1}(x)^{2n+1} = -x^{2n+1}$

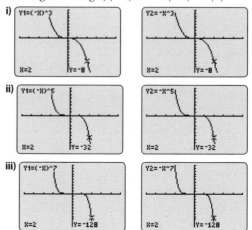

c) Answers may vary. Sample answer: $y = (-x)^{2n}$ has the same graph as $y = x^{2n}$, n is a non-negative integer, $(-x)^{2n} = (-1)^{2n}(x)^{2n} = x^{2n}$; $y = (-x)^{2n+1}$ has the same graph as $y = -x^{2n+1}$, n is a non-negative integer, $(-x)^{2n+1} = (-1)^{2n+1}(x)^{2n+1} = -x^{2n+1}$

15. a) Answers may vary. Sample answer: For the graph of $y = ax^n$, if $a > 0$, vertical stretch by a factor of a if $0 < a < 1$ vertical compression by a factor of a; if $-1 < a < 0$, vertical compression by a factor of a and a reflection in the x-axis; if $a < -1$, vertical stretch by a factor of a and a reflection in the x-axis

16. a) vertical stretch by a factor of 2, translation 3 units right, translation 1 unit up **b)** vertical stretch by a factor of 2, translation 3 units right, translation 1 unit up

c)
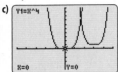

17. a) The second graph is a stretch (or compression) of factor a, a horizontal shift of units right, and a verticle shift of k units up

b) Answers may vary. Sample answers:
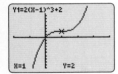
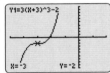

18. 124

19. $\left(4, \dfrac{8}{3}\right), \left(6, \dfrac{7}{3}\right)$

1.2 Characteristics of Polynomial Functions, pages 26–29

1. a) 4 **b)** 5 **c)** 4 **d)** 5 **e)** 3

2. a)–d)

	Sign of Leading Coefficient	End Behaviour (quadrants)	Symmetry	Number of Local Maximum Points	Number of Local Minimum Points
a)	+	2 to 1	none	1	2
b)	+	3 to 1	none	2	2
c)	−	3 to 4	none	2	1
d)	−	2 to 4	none	2	2
e)	−	2 to 4	point	1	1

d) If the function has a minimum or maximum point, the degree of the function is even. If the function has no maximum or minimum point, the degree is odd. The number of local maximums and local minimums is less than or equal to the degree of the function minus one.

3.

	i) End Behaviour (quadrants)	ii) Constant Finite Differences	iii) Value of Constant Finite Differences
a)	2 to 1	2nd	2
b)	2 to 4	3rd	−24
c)	3 to 4	4th	−168
d)	3 to 1	5th	72
e)	2 to 4	1st	−1
f)	3 to 4	6th	−720

4. a) 2, −4 **b)** 4, −2 **c)** 3, −2 **d)** 4, 1 **e)** 3, 6 **f)** 5, $\dfrac{1}{2}$

5. a) odd **b)** even **c)** odd **d)** even

6.

Graph	a) Least Degree	b) Sign of Leading Coefficient	c) End Behaviour (quadrants)	d) Symmetry
5a)	5	−	2 to 4	point
5b)	4	+	2 to 1	line
5c)	3	+	3 to 1	point
5d)	6	−	3 to 4	none

7. a) i) 3 **ii)** + **iii)** 1 **b) i)** 4 **ii)** − **iii)** −1

8. a) quartic **b)** fourth, 0.03 **c)** quadrant 2 to quadrant 1 **d)** $x \geq 0$ **e)** Answers may vary. Sample answer: They represent when the profit is equal to zero. **f)** $1 039 500

9. a) i) cubic (degree 3) **ii)** 2

b)
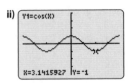

10. a) i)
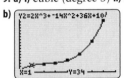
ii)
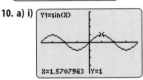

b) Answers may vary.

11. a) $x \geq 0$, $V(x) \geq 0$
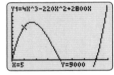

b) $V(x) = 4x(x - 35)(x - 20)$; x-intercepts 35, 20, 0 **c)** 24

12. a) cubic **b)** third, −4.2 **c)** quadrant 2 to 4 **d)** $\{d \in \mathbb{R}, d \geq 0\}$, $\{r \in \mathbb{R}, r \geq 0\}$

13. a) Answers may vary. Sample answer: quadrant 2 to quadrant 1, $\{x \in \mathbb{R}\}$, $\{P(t) \in \mathbb{R}, P(t) \geq 11\ 732\}$, no x-intercepts **b)** 144 **c)** 12 000 **d)** 69 000 **e)** 13 years

15. Answers may vary. Sample answers:

a)
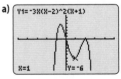
b)
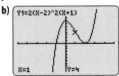

c)
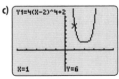
d)
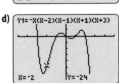

16. a) 1 to 5

b)
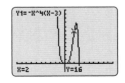

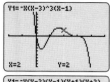

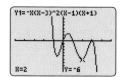

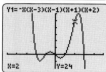

17. a) i) cubic **ii)** cubic **iii)** cubic

b)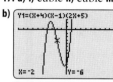

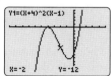

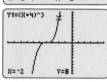

c) Answers may vary. Sample answer: The number of x-intercepts equals the number of roots of the equation.

18. a) i) $S(r) = 8\pi r^2$ **ii)** $V(r) = 3\pi r^3$ **b)** Answers may vary. Sample answer: $S(r)$ quadratic, has one x-intercept, $\{x \in \mathbb{R}, x \geq 0\}$, $\{y \in \mathbb{R}, y \geq 0\}$, from quadrant 2 to quadrant 1; $V(r)$ cubic, one x-intercept, $\{x \in \mathbb{R}\}$, $\{V \in \mathbb{R}\}$ from quadrant 3 to quadrant 1

19. a) 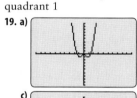 **b)**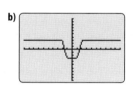

c)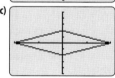

1.3 Equations and Graphs of Polynomial Functions, pages 39–41

1. a) i) 3, + **ii)** quadrant 3 to quadrant 1 **iii)** 4, -3, $\frac{1}{2}$

b) i) 4, $-$ **ii)** quadrant 3 to quadrant 4 **iii)** -2, 2, 1, -1

c) i) 5, + **ii)** quadrant 3 to quadrant 1 **iii)** $-\frac{2}{3}$, 4, -1, $\frac{3}{2}$

d) i) 6, $-$ **ii)** quadrant 3 to quadrant 4 **iii)** -5, 5

2. a) i) -4, $-\frac{1}{2}$, 1 **ii)** positive, $-4 < x < -\frac{1}{2}$, $x > 1$; negative $x < -4$, $-\frac{1}{2} < x < 1$ **iii)** no zeros of order 2 or 3

b) i) -1, 4 **ii)** negative $x < -1$, $-1 < x < 4$, $x > 4$ **iii)** could have zeros of order 2 **c) i)** -3, 1 **ii)** positive $x < -3$, $x > 1$; negative $-3 < x < 1$ **iii)** could have zeros of order 3 **d) i)** -5, 3 **ii)** positive $x < -5$, $-5 < x < 3$; negative $x > 3$ **iii)** could have zeros of order 2

3. a) i) -2, 3, $\frac{3}{4}$, all order 1 **ii)** -3, -1, 1, 3, all order 1 **iii)** order 2: -4, 1; order 1: -2, $\frac{3}{2}$ **iv)** order 3: $\frac{2}{3}$; order 2: 5; order 1: -6 **b)** graph in part ii) is even; others are neither

c) i) 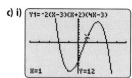 **ii)**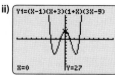

iii) 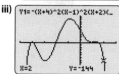 **iv)**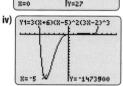

4. b) d) line, even; these functions have line symmetry about the y-axis because they are even functions. **a) c)** neither, neither; there is no symmetry about the origin or about the y-axis because these functions are neither even nor odd.

5. a) i) even **ii)** line **b) i)** odd **ii)** point **c) i)** neither **ii)** neither **d) i)** neither **ii)** neither **e) i)** even **ii)** line

6. a) $y = (x + 2)^3(x - 3)^2$ **b)** $y = -2(x + 3)(x + 1)(x - 2)$ **c)** $y = -3(x + 2)^2(x - 1)^2$ **d)** $y = 0.5(x + 2)^3(x - 1)^2$

7. a) $y = -\frac{3}{4}(x + 2)^2(x - 3)$, neither

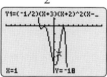

b) $y = 2(x + 1)^3(x - 1)$, neither

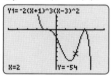

c) $y = -2(x + 1)^3(x - 3)^2$, neither

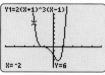

d) $y = -\frac{1}{2}(x + 3)(x + 2)^2(x - 2)^2$, neither

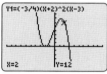

8. a) point **b)** line **c)** point **d)** point

9. Answers may vary. Sample answers:

a) 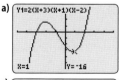 **b)**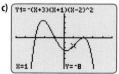

c) 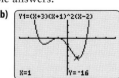 **d)**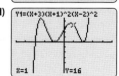

10. a) Answers may vary. **b)** Answers may vary. Sample answer: The equation provides information about the *x*-intercepts, the degree of the function, the sign of the leading coefficient, and the order of the zeros.

c)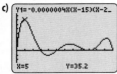

d) The maximum height is approximately 35.3 m above the platform. The minimum height is approximately 5.1 m below the platform.

11. a) $4, 1, -1, -\dfrac{1}{2}$

b)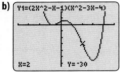

12. a) i) $3, 2, -2, -3$ **ii)** $0, -\dfrac{\sqrt{6}}{2}, \dfrac{\sqrt{6}}{2}$ **b) i)** even **ii)** odd

c) i) 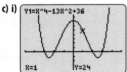 **ii)**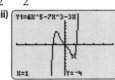

13. Answers may vary. Sample answers:

a) $c = -5$ **b)** $c = 0$

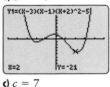

c) $c = 7$ **d)** $c \doteq 16.95$

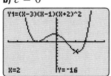

e) $c = 25$

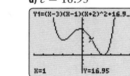

14. a) Answers may vary. Sample answer:
$f(x) = (3x - 2)(3x + 2)(x - 5)(x + 5)$,
$g(x) = 2(3x - 2)(3x + 2)(x - 5)(x + 5)$
b) $y = -3.2(3x - 2)(x - 5)$ **c)** $y = 3.2(3x - 2)(x - 5)$
15. Answers may vary. Sample answer: shifts from the origin, and an odd function must go through the origin.
16. a) 0.35 **b)** 2.517

1.4 Transformations, pages 49–52

1. a) $a = 4$ (vertical stretch by a factor of 4), $k = 3$
(horizontal compression by a factor of $\dfrac{1}{3}$), $d = -2$
(translation 2 units left), $c = -6$ (translation 6 units down)

b)

$y = x^4$	$y = (3x)^4$	$y = 4(3x)^4$	$y = 4[3(x + 2)]^4 - 6$
$(-2, 16)$	$(-2, 1296)$	$(-2, 5184)$	$(-2, -6)$
$(-1, 1)$	$(-1, 81)$	$(-1, 324)$	$(-1, 318)$
$(0, 0)$	$(0, 0)$	$(0, 0)$	$(0, 5178)$
$(1, 1)$	$(1, 81)$	$(1, 324)$	$(1, 26\ 238)$
$(2, 16)$	$(2, 1296)$	$(2, 5184)$	$(2, 82\ 938)$

c) 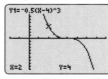 **d)** $\{x \in \mathbb{R}\}, \{y \in \mathbb{R}, y \geq -6\}$,
$(-2, -6), x = -2$

2. a) ii **b)** iv **c)** iii **d)** i
3. a) iii **b)** iv **c)** ii **d)** i
4. a) $k = $ (3 horizontal compression by a factor of $\dfrac{1}{3}$),
$c = -1$ (vertical translation 1 unit down), $n = 3$
b) $a = 0.4$ (vertical compression by a factor of 0.4), $d = -2$
(horizontal translation of 2 units left), $n = 2$ **c)** $c = 5$
(vertical translation of 5 units up), $n = 3$ **d)** $a = \dfrac{3}{4}$
(vertical compression by a factor of $\dfrac{3}{4}$), $k = -1$ (reflection
in the *y*-axis), $d = 4$ (horizontal translation 4 units right),
$c = 1$ (vertical translation 1 unit up), $n = 3$ **e)** $a = 2$
(vertical stretch by a factor of 2), $k = \dfrac{1}{3}$ (horizontal stretch
by a factor of 3), $c = -5$ (vertical translation 5 units down),
$n = 4$ **f)** $a = 8$ (vertical stretch by a factor of 8), $k = 2$
(horizontal compression by a factor of $\dfrac{1}{2}$), $c = 24$ (vertical
translation 24 units up), $n = 3$
5. a) ii **b)** iv **c)** i **d)** iii
6. a) 2 units left, 1 unit down, $y = (x + 2)^2 - 1$
b) 4 units right, 5 units up, $y = (x - 4)^3 + 5$
7. a) $a = -3, k = \dfrac{1}{2}, d = -4, c = 1$

b) *a*: vertical stretch by a factor of 3 and a reflection in the
x-axis; *k*: horizontal stretch by a factor of 2; *d*: 4 units left;
c: 1 unit up **c)** $\{x \in \mathbb{R}\}, \{y \in \mathbb{R}, y \leq 1\}, (-4, 1), x = -4$
d) vertical stretch, horizontal stretch, left, up; horizontal
stretch, vertical stretch, up, left
8. a) vertical compression by a factor of 0.5 and a reflection
in the *x*-axis, translation 4 units right; $f(x) = -0.5(x - 4)^3$
b) reflection in *x*-axis, horizontal compression by a factor
of $\dfrac{1}{4}$, translation 1 unit up; $f(x) = -(4x)^4 + 1$ **c)** vertical
stretch by a factor of 2, horizontal stretch by a factor of 3,
translation 5 units right, translation 2 units down;
$f(x) = 2\left[\dfrac{1}{3}(x - 5)\right]^3 - 2$
9. a) $f(x) = -0.5(x - 4)^3$ $f(x) = -(4x)^4 + 1$

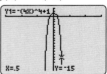

$f(x) = 2\left[\dfrac{1}{3}(x - 5)\right]^3 - 2$

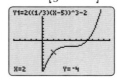

b) $f(x) = -0.5(x - 4)^3$, $\{x \in \mathbb{R}\}$, $\{y \in \mathbb{R}\}$; $f(x) = -(4x)^4 + 1$, $\{x \in \mathbb{R}\}$, $\{y \in \mathbb{R}, y \leq 1\}$, vertex $(0, 1)$, axis of symmetry $x = 0$; $f(x) = 2\left[\dfrac{1}{3}(x - 5)\right]^3 - 2$, $\{x \in \mathbb{R}\}$, $\{y \in \mathbb{R}\}$

10. a) i) $y = -x^4 + 3$ ii) $\{x \in \mathbb{R}\}$, $\{y \in \mathbb{R}, y \leq 3\}$, vertex $(0, 3)$, axis of symmetry $x = 0$ **b) i)** $y = -(x - 5)^3$ **ii)** $\{x \in \mathbb{R}\}$, $\{y \in \mathbb{R}\}$
c) i) $y = (x + 3)^4 - 5$ **ii)** $\{x \in \mathbb{R}\}$, $\{y \in \mathbb{R}, y \geq -5\}$, vertex $(-3, -5)$, axis of symmetry $x = -3$
11. $y = x^3$, $y = (x - 4)^3$, $y = (x + 4)^3$, $y = x^4 - 6$, $y = (x - 4)^4 - 6$, $y = (x + 4)^4 - 6$, $y = -x^4 + 6$, $y = -(x - 4)^4 + 6$, $y = -(x + 4)^4 + 6$
12. a) i) $f(x) = (x + 2)^4 + 3$ **ii)** $\{x \in \mathbb{R}\}$, $\{y \in \mathbb{R}, y \geq 3\}$, vertex $(-2, 3)$, axis of symmetry $x = -2$
b) i) $f(x) = \left[\dfrac{1}{5}(x + 12)\right]^5$ **ii)** $\{x \in \mathbb{R}\}$, $\{y \in \mathbb{R}\}$
c) i) $f(x) = -3(x + 1)^4 - 6$ **ii)** $\{x \in \mathbb{R}\}$, $\{y \in \mathbb{R}, y \leq -6\}$, vertex $(-1, -6)$, axis of symmetry $x = -1$
d) i) $f(x) = -\left[\dfrac{1}{5}(x - 1)\right]^6 - 3$ **ii)** $\{x \in \mathbb{R}\}$, $\{y \in \mathbb{R}, y \leq -3\}$, vertex $(1, -3)$, axis of symmetry $x = 1$
e) i) $f(x) = -7\left[\dfrac{5}{4}(x + 1)\right]^4 + 9$ **ii)** $\{x \in \mathbb{R}\}$, $\{y \in \mathbb{R}, y \leq 9\}$, vertex $(-1, 9)$, axis of symmetry $x = -1$

14. a) shift 2 right
b)

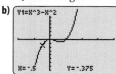 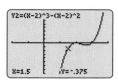

c) 0, 1; 3, 2
15. a) vertical stretch by a factor of 3, reflection in the x-axis, translation 4 units left, horizontal stretch by a factor of 2
b) 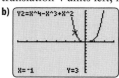 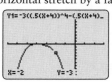 **c)** 0, -4

16. a) $h(x) = 3(x + 1)(x + 6)(x - 1) - 5$
b) $h(x) = -\dfrac{6}{5}(x + 1)(x + 6)(x - 1) + 2$

17. \$3.12
18. a) x^4, x^8, x^{16} **b)** $x^{2^{n+1}}$

1.5 Slopes of Secants and Average Rate of Change, pages 62–64

1. e)
2. a) constant and positive **b)** zero **c)** constant and negative
3. a) $\dfrac{7}{5}$ **b)** 0 **c)** $-\dfrac{4}{7}$
4. 3.89%/year
5. a) 6.45%/year
b) Answers may vary. **c)** 1999–2000: 11.1%/year; 2000–2001: 8.7%/year; 2001–2002: 2.8%/year; 2002–2003: 3.2%/year
d) greatest: between 1999 and 2000; least: between 2001 and 2002 **e)** Answers may vary.
6. a)

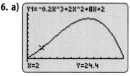

b) positive $0 \leq x < 8.28$; negative $8.28 < x \leq 13$; zero: $x = 8.28$ **c) i)** \$13/year **ii)** \$8.20/year **iii)** $-$\$4.80/year
iv) $-$\$17.40/year **d)** Answers may vary.
7. a) $V = \dfrac{4}{3}\pi r^3$, cubic, $\{x \in \mathbb{R}, x \geq 0\}$, $\{y \in \mathbb{R}, y \geq 0\}$; $S = 4\pi r^2$: quadratic, $\{x \in \mathbb{R}, x \geq 0\}$, $\{y \in \mathbb{R}, y \geq 0\}$

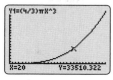 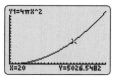

b) volume: **i)** 9529.50 **ii)** 6387.91; surface area:
i) 691.15
ii) 565.49 **c)** 314.16 cm² **d)** -570.07 **e)** Answers may vary.
8. Answers will vary.
9. a) $y = -0.2x(x - 28)$ **b)** secant **c)** 2.4, 1.6, 0.4, 0, 0, 0, -0.4, -1.6, -2.4; calculated using two points on the curve
d) steepness of the crossbeams **e)** have the same steepness in a different direction
10. a) i) -20 L/min **ii)** -50.66 L/min **iii)** -0.54 L/min
b) slows down
c)

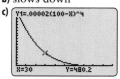

d) i) 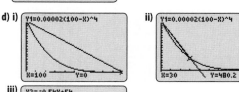 **ii)**

iii)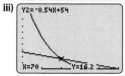

11. a) -1470, -1410, -1350, -1290, -1230, -1170, -1110, -1050, -990, -930 **b)** greatest: between 0 and 1; least: between 9 and 10 **c)** Type of polynomial function: quadratic

Time (h)	Amount of Water (L)	First Differences	Second Differences
0	18 750		
		-1470	
1	17 280		60
		-1410	
2	15 870		60
		-1350	
3	14 520		60
		-1290	
4	13 230		60
		-1230	
5	12 000		60
		-1170	
6	10 830		60
		-1110	
7	9 720		60
		-1050	
8	8 670		60
		-990	
9	7 680		60
		-930	
10	6 750		

d) The first differences are the same as the average rates of change for the same interval.

e)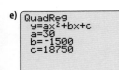

f)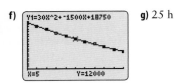

g) 25 h

12. a) velocity of the ball **b) i)** 5.3 **ii)** 7.75 **iii)** 9.71 **iv)** 10.151 **v)** 10.195 **vii)** 10.200 **c)** instantaneous rate at 1 s
d) Answers may vary.

13. $h(p) = \dfrac{p^2 - 100}{2p}$

1.6 Slopes of Tangents and Instantaneous Rate of Change, pages 71–73

1. a) (5, 3) **b)** (3, 7) **c)** −2 **d)** instantaneous rate of change at $x = 5$
2. a) A positive; B 0; C negative
b) A 4 m/s, C −6 m/s **c)** velocity at 2 s and 7 s
3. a)

Interval	Δh	Δt	$\dfrac{\Delta h}{\Delta t}$
$3 \le t \le 3.1$	−0.289	0.1	−2.89
$3 \le t \le 3.01$	−0.024 49	0.01	−2.449
$3 \le t \le 3.001$	−0.002 404 9	0.001	−2.4049

b) velocity is decreasing at a rate of approximately 2.4 m/s
4. 25 m/s
5. a) 3.9%/year **b) i)** between 5.9% and 6.2% per year
ii) between 1.3% and 2.2% per year **c)** Answers may vary.
6. a) 2.21 **b) i)** between 0.3 and 0.84 **ii)** between 3.66 and 4.52
iii) between 1.86 and 2.76 **c)** Answers may vary.
7. a) −2.7 m/s **b)** 2.2 m/s **d)** Answers may vary.
c)

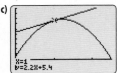 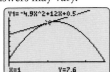

d) average velocity between 1 s and 2 s; velocity at 1 s is 2.2 m/s
8. a) Earth −14.7 m/s; Venus −13.35 m/s
b) Earth −29.4 m/s; Venus −26.7 m/s
c) a rock falls faster on Earth than on Venus
9. a) $110.50/MP3 **b)** $118/MP3 **c)** Answers may vary.
Sample answer: The cost of producing 200 MP3 players
is more than the average cost of between 100 and 200 MP3
players. **d)** No.
10. a) $327.25/MP3 **b)** $311/MP3 **c)** The average revenue
(between 100 and 200) is more than the revenue for 200 MP3
players. **d)** $P(x) = 250x - 0.000\,475x^3$ **e)** $216.75/MP3
f) $193/MP3 **g)** The average profit between 100 and 200 MP3
players is more than the profit for 200 MP3 players.
11. a) i) 19 440 **ii)** −10 800 **b)** Answers may vary. Sample
answer: The profits are increasing between 2000 and 6000
basketballs and decreasing between 16 000 and 20 000
basketballs.
c) i) 21 150 **ii)** −10 440 **d)** losing money
when making 18 000 basketballs
e)

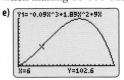

12. a) $0.5h^2 + 12h + 246$ **b) i)** 272 **ii)** 302 **iii)** 318.5 **c)** Average
rates of change between **i)** 8 and 10 years **ii)** 8 and 12 years
iii) 8 and 13 years **d)** when $h = 0$ **e)** 246

13. $\dfrac{1 + \sqrt{41}}{2}$

14. $|m| = 4\sqrt{5}$

Chapter 1 Review, pages 74–77

1. a) polynomial function, 4, 3 **b)** polynomial function, 2, −1
e) polynomial function, 3, 5
2. a) i) odd **ii)** negative **iii)** $\{x \in \mathbb{R}\}$, $\{y \in \mathbb{R}\}$ **iv)** quadrant 2 to
quadrant 4 **v)** point **b) i)** even **ii)** positive
iii) $\{x \in \mathbb{R}\}$, $\{y \in \mathbb{R}, y \ge 0\}$ **iv)** quadrant 2 to quadrant 1 **v)** line

3.

End Behaviour	Function	Reasons
Extends from quadrant 3 to quadrant 1	**c)** $y = 4x^3$	positive leading coefficient and odd degree
Extends from quadrant 2 to quadrant 4	**a)** $y = -x^5$	negative leading coefficient and odd degree
Extends from quadrant 2 to quadrant 1	**b)** $y = \dfrac{2}{3}x^4$, **d)** $y = 0.2x^6$	positive leading coefficient and even degree
Extends from quadrant 3 to quadrant 4	none	

4. a) ii **b)** iii **c)** i
5. i) a) fourth **b)** 12 **c)** none **ii) a)** fifth **b)** 120 **c)** point
iii) a) sixth **b)** −720 **c)** none
6. a) i) 1 **ii)** 5 **iii)** 4 **iv)** 2 **v)** 3 **vi)** 3

b) i) −5 **ii)** $-\dfrac{1}{2}$ **iii)** $\dfrac{3}{2}$ **iv)** 9 **v)** 7 **vi)** −3

7. a) i) 3 **ii)** negative **iii)** −4 **b) i)** 5 **ii)** positive **iii)** 2
8. a) quadratic **b) i)** 2nd **ii)** −9.8 **c)** quadrant 3 to quadrant 4
d) $0 \le t \le 26.73$

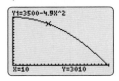

e) when the parachutist lands
9. a) i) 3, positive **ii)** 0, −2, 4 **iii)** positive $-2 < x < 0$, $x > 4$;
negative $x < -2$, $0 < x < 4$
b) i) 4, negative **ii)** $-2, \dfrac{1}{2}, 3$ **iii)** positive $-2 < x < \dfrac{1}{2}$;
negative: $x < -2$, $\dfrac{1}{2} < x < 3$, $x > 3$

10. a)

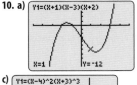

b)

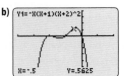

c)

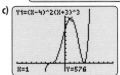

11. a) Answers may vary. Sample answer:
$y = (x + 3)(x + 1)(x - 2)^2$, $y = 2(x + 3)(x + 1)(x - 2)^2$
b) $y = \dfrac{1}{2}(x + 3)(x + 1)(x - 2)^2$

12. a) point symmetry **b)** line **c)** neither

13. a) $y = -(x + 2)(x - 4)^2$

b) $y = -\dfrac{10}{27}(x + 2)^2(x - 0.5)(x - 4)$

14. a) i) vertical compression by a factor of $\dfrac{1}{4}$, reflection in the x-axis, translation 2 units down; $y = -\dfrac{1}{4}x^3 - 2$

ii) $\{x \in \mathbb{R}\}$, $\{y \in \mathbb{R}\}$ **b) i)** vertical stretch by a factor of 5, horizontal stretch by a factor of $\dfrac{5}{2}$, translation 3 units right, translation 1 unit up; $y = 5\left[\dfrac{2}{5}(x - 3)\right]^4 + 1$ **ii)** $\{x \in \mathbb{R}\}$, $\{y \in \mathbb{R}, y \geq 1\}$, vertex $(3, 1)$, axis of symmetry $x = 3$

15. a) i) $y = \dfrac{3}{5}\left[-\dfrac{1}{2}(x + 4)\right]^4 + 1$ **ii)** $\{x \in \mathbb{R}\}$, $\{y \in \mathbb{R}, y \geq 1\}$, vertex $(-4, 1)$, axis of symmetry $x = -4$

b) i) $y = -5[4(x + 2)]^3 + 7$ **ii)** $\{x \in \mathbb{R}\}$, $\{y \in \mathbb{R}\}$

16. a), c), d)

17. a) $14, \$10 **b) i)** negative **ii)** positive **iii)** zero

c) i) $1.60/month **ii)** $2/month **iii)** $0/month

18. a) 5.7%/year **b)** between 6.7% and 6.9% in 2000; 4.6% in 2002 **c)** Answers may vary.

Practice Test, pages 78–79

1. Answers may vary. Sample answers for false:

A. False; $y = x^3 + x^2$

B. False; $y = x^2$

C. True

D. False; $y = x^4 + x$

2. Answers may vary. Sample answers for false:

A. False; $y = x^3$ has degree 3 and constant third differences

B. True

C. False; $y = x^2$ has line symmetry but not point symmetry

D. False; $y = (x - 1)^3(x - 2)(x - 3)(x - 4)$ has four x-intercepts and degree 6

3. Answers may vary. Sample answers for false:

A. False; $y = \dfrac{1}{3}x^2$ does not equal $y = \left(\dfrac{1}{3}x\right)^2$

B. False; stretches and compressions first

C. False; does not matter

D. False; reflection in the y-axis

E. True

4. a) i **b)** iii **c)** ii

5. i) a) third **b)** -12 **c)** point **ii) a)** fifth **b)** 120 **c)** point

iii) a) sixth **b)** -720 **c)** line

6. a) Answers may vary. Sample answers:

$y = 2x(x + 1)(x - 3)^2$, $y = -x(x + 1)(x - 3)^2$

b) $y = -3x(x + 1)(x - 3)^2$

c)

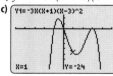

positive $-1 < x < 0$; negative $x < -1$, $0 < x < 3$, $x > 3$

7. $y = -x(x + 1)^2(x - 1)(x - 2)^3$

8. a) $a = \dfrac{1}{3}$ (vertical compression by a factor of $\dfrac{1}{3}$), $k = -2$ (horizontal compression by a factor of $\dfrac{1}{2}$, reflection in the y-axis), $d = -3$ (translation 3 units left), $c = -1$ (translation 1 unit down)

b) $\{x \in \mathbb{R}\}$, $\{y \in \mathbb{R}, y \geq -1\}$, vertex $(-3, -1)$, axis of symmetry $x = -3$

c) horizontal compression, vertical compression, reflection in the y-axis, 3 units left, 1 unit down; horizontal compression, vertical compression, reflection in the y-axis, 1 unit down, 3 units left

d)

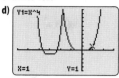

9. $y = -2(x - 3)^3 - 5$

10. Answers may vary. Sample answer: **a)** distance versus time at a constant rate **b)** drop in temperature versus time at a constant rate **c)** acceleration **d)** no change in revenue over a period of time

11. 4.66%/year

12. a) 3125 L **b) i)** -245 L/min **ii)** -20 L/min **c)** Answers may vary. Sample answer: Average rate of change of volume over time is negative and increasing.

d)

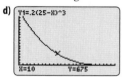

e) slopes of secants

13. a) 1 m/s **b)** 1.9 m/s **c)** speed is increasing

CHAPTER 2

Prerequisite Skills, pages 92–93

1. a) 124 R4 **b)** 161 R16 **c)** 147 R9 **d)** 358 R13

2. a) -22 **b)** -6 **c)** -51 **d)** -13.875 **e)** $-\dfrac{169}{27}$

3. a) $x^4 + x^3 - 7x^2 + 3x + 3$

b) $2x^4 + 4x^3 - 15x^2 + x - 19$

c) $3x^4 + 11x^3 - 7x^2 + 25x - 2$

d) $x^2 - 2$ **e)** $x^2 - 45$ **f)** $x^2 - 2x - 2$

4. a) $(x - 2)(x + 2)$ **b)** $(5m - 7)(5m + 7)$

c) $(4y - 3)(4y + 3)$ **d)** $3(2c - 3)(2c + 3)$

e) $2(x - 2)(x + 2)(x^2 + 4)$ **f)** $3(n^2 - 2)(n^2 + 2)$

5. a) $(x + 3)(x + 2)$ **b)** $(x - 4)(x - 5)$

c) $(b + 7)(b - 2)$ **d)** $(2x + 3)(x - 5)$

e) $(2x - 3)^2$ **f)** $(2a - 1)(3a - 2)$

g) $(3m - 4)^2$ **h)** $(m - 3)(3m - 1)$

6. a) $x = -3$ or $x = 5$ **b)** $x = -1$ or $x = \dfrac{3}{4}$

c) $x = -\dfrac{3}{2}$ or $x = \dfrac{3}{2}$ **d)** $x = \dfrac{1}{3}$ or $x = 5$

e) $x = -\dfrac{5}{2}$ or $x = 1$ **f)** $x = \dfrac{1}{7}$ or $x = \dfrac{1}{3}$

7. a) $x \doteq -1.3$ or $x \doteq 0.1$

b) $x \doteq 0.7$ or $x \doteq 2.8$

c) $x \doteq -1.2$ or $x \doteq 0.7$

d) $x \doteq -1.3$ or $x \doteq 2.5$

8. a) $y = -\dfrac{1}{3}(x + 4)(x - 1)$

b) $y = -3x(x - 3)$ **c)** $y = -4(x + 3)(x - 4)$

d) $y = 2(x + 1)(x - 5)$ **e)** $y = -3(2x + 1)(2x - 3)$

9. a) i) -4 and 1 **ii)** above the x-axis: $x < -4$ and $x > 1$; below the x-axis: $-4 < x < 1$ **b) i)** -1, 1, and 2 **ii)** above the x-axis: $-1 < x < 1$ and $x > 2$; below the x-axis: $x < -1$ and $1 < x < 2$ **c) i)** -2, -1, 1, and 2 **ii)** above the x-axis: $-2 < x < -1$ and $1 < x < 2$; below the x-axis: $x < -2$ and $-1 < x < 1$ and $x > 2$

2.1 The Remainder Theorem, pages 91–93

1. a) $\dfrac{x^3 + 3x^2 - 2x + 5}{x + 1} = x^2 + 2x - 4 + \dfrac{9}{x + 1}$ **b)** $x \neq -1$

c) $(x + 1)(x^2 + 2x - 4) + 9 = x^3 + 3x^2 - 2x + 5$

2. a) $\dfrac{3x^4 - 4x^3 - 6x^2 + 17x - 8}{3x - 4} = x^3 - 2x + 3 + \dfrac{4}{3x - 4}$

b) $x \neq \dfrac{4}{3}$

c) $3x^4 - 4x^3 - 6x^2 + 17x - 8 = (3x - 4)(x^3 - 2x + 3) + 4$

3. a) $\dfrac{x^3 + 7x^2 - 3x + 4}{x + 2} = x^2 + 5x - 13 + \dfrac{30}{x + 2}, x \neq -2$

b) $\dfrac{6x^3 + x^2 - 14x - 6}{3x + 2} = 2x^2 - x - 4 + \dfrac{2}{3x + 2}, x \neq -\dfrac{2}{3}$

c) $\dfrac{10x^3 - 9x^2 - 8x + 11}{5x - 2} = 2x^2 - x - 2 + \dfrac{7}{5x - 2}, x \neq \dfrac{2}{5}$

d) $\dfrac{-4x^4 + 11x - 7}{x - 3} = -4x^3 - 12x^2 - 36x - 97 - \dfrac{298}{x - 3}$, $x \neq 3$

e) $\dfrac{6x^3 + x^2 + 7x + 3}{3x + 2} = 2x^2 - x + 3 - \dfrac{3}{3x + 2}, x \neq -\dfrac{2}{3}$

f) $\dfrac{8x^3 + 4x^2 - 31}{2x - 3} = 4x^2 + 8x + 12 + \dfrac{5}{2x - 3}, x \neq \dfrac{3}{2}$

g) $\dfrac{8x^3 + 6x^2 - 6}{4x - 3} = 2x^2 + 3x + \dfrac{9}{4} + \dfrac{3}{4(4x - 3)}, x \neq \dfrac{3}{4}$

4. a) 27 **b)** -9 **c)** -2

5. $(x + 5)(x + 3)(2x + 1)$

6. $(3x - 2)$ cm by $(3x - 2)$ cm by $(x + 4)$ cm

7. a) 16 **b)** 31 **c)** 36 **d)** 211 **e)** 4

8. a) 16 **b)** -13 **c)** -23

9. a) 9 **b)** 15 **c)** 41 **d)** -4

10. a) $k = 3$ **b)** 123

11. a) $c = 4$ **b)** 28

12. $b = 11$

13. $k = 3$

14. a)–c) 8

15. a)–b) 15

16. a) $P\left(\dfrac{2}{3}\right) = 0$ **b)** $(3x - 2)$ is a factor of $6x^3 + 23x^2 - 6x - 8$.

c) $(3x - 2)(x + 4)(2x + 1)$

17. a) $\pi(9x^2 + 24x + 16)$; this result represents the area of the base of the cylindrical container, i.e., the area of a circle.
b) $\pi(3x + 4)^2(x + 3)$

c)

Value of x	Radius (cm)	Height (cm)	Volume (cm³)
2	10	5	1 571
3	13	6	3 186
4	16	7	5 630
5	19	8	9 073
6	22	9	13 685
7	25	10	19 635
8	28	11	27 093

18. a) $-5t^2 + 15t + 1 = (t - b)(-5t - 5b + 15) - 5b^2 + 15b + 1$

c) the slope of a secant between 2 points on the graph of the function

d) Q(+) is the average speed of the javelin between times t and b. If the value of b is close to the value of t Q(+) is close to the instantaneous speed of the javelin

19. a) $\dfrac{12}{5}$ **b)** At 1.5 s, the shot-put is 2.4 m above the ground.

20. $m = -\dfrac{11}{5}, n = \dfrac{59}{5}$

21. $a = -\dfrac{14}{3}, b = -\dfrac{2}{3}$

22. $k = -\dfrac{2}{3}$ or $k = 4$

23. 3

24. 8

2.2 The Factor Theorem, pages 102–103

1. a) $x - 4$ **b)** $x + 3$ **c)** $3x - 2$ **d)** $4x + 1$

2. a) No. **b)** Yes. **c)** Yes.

3. a) $(x - 2)(x + 1)(x + 4)$ **b)** $(x - 3)(x + 1)(x + 6)$

c) $(x - 4)(x - 2)(x + 3)$

4. a) $(x - 3)(x + 1)(x + 3)$ **b)** $(x - 4)(x - 1)(x + 4)$

c) $(x - 6)(x + 6)(2x - 1)$ **d)** $(x - 7)(x - 2)(x + 2)$

e) $(x - 5)(x + 5)(3x + 2)$ **f)** $x(x - 4)(x + 4)(2x + 3)$

5. a) $(x - 3)(x + 2)(3x + 4)$ **b)** $(x - 3)(x - 1)(2x - 1)$

c) $(x - 3)(2x - 1)(3x + 5)$ **d)** $(x - 1)(x + 1)(4x + 3)$

6. a) $(x - 1)(x + 1)(x + 2)$ **b)** $(x - 2)(x + 1)(x + 5)$

c) $(x - 5)(x - 2)(x + 2)$ **d)** $(x + 4)(x^2 + x - 1)$

e) $(x - 5)(x - 2)(x + 3)$ **f)** $(x - 3)(x + 2)(x - 1)(x - 2)$

g) $(x - 4)(x - 2)(x + 1)(x + 3)$

7. a) $(2x - 1)(2x + 1)^2$ **b)** $(x - 1)(x + 2)(2x + 3)$

c) $(x - 1)(x + 2)(5x - 2)$ **d)** $(x - 1)(x + 1)(2x - 1)(3x + 2)$

e) $(x - 2)(x + 2)(5x^2 + x - 2)$ **f)** $(x - 3)(x + 4)(3x + 1)$

g) $(x - 2)(2x - 1)(3x - 1)$

8. $(x + 4)(2x - 1)(3x + 2)$

9. $k = -3$

10. $k = -1$

11. a) $(x - 1)(x + 2)(2x + 3)$ **b)** $(x + 1)(2x - 3)(2x + 1)$

c) $(x - 1)(2x + 5)(3x - 2)$ **d)** $(x - 2)(4x^2 + 3)$

e) $(2x - 1)(x^2 + x + 1)$ **f)** $(x - 4)(x - 1)(x + 2)(x + 3)$

12. a) i) $(x - 1)(x^2 + x + 1)$ **ii)** $(x - 2)(x^2 + 2x + 4)$

iii) $(x - 3)(x^2 + 3x + 9)$ **iv)** $(x - 4)(x^2 + 4x + 16)$

b) $x^3 - a^3 = (x - a)(x^2 + ax + a^2)$ **c)** $(x - 5)(x^2 + 5x + 25)$

d) i) $(2x - 1)(4x^2 + 2x + 1)$ **ii)** $(5x^2 - 2)(25x^4 + 10x^2 + 4)$

iii) $(4x^4 - 3)(16x^8 + 12x^4 + 9)$

iv) $\left(\dfrac{2}{5}x - 4y^2\right)\left(\dfrac{4}{25}x^2 + \dfrac{8}{5}xy^2 + 16y^4\right)$

13. a) i) $(x + 1)(x^2 - x + 1)$ **ii)** $(x + 2)(x^2 - 2x + 4)$

iii) $(x + 3)(x^2 - 3x + 9)$ **iv)** $(x + 4)(x^2 - 4x + 16)$

b) $x^3 + a^3 = (x + a)(x^2 - ax + a^2)$ **c)** $(x + 5)(x^2 - 5x + 25)$

d) i) $(2x + 1)(4x^2 - 2x + 1)$ **ii)** $(5x^2 + 2)(25x^4 - 10x^2 + 4)$

iii) $(4x^4 + 3)(16x^8 - 12x^4 + 9)$

iv) $\left(\dfrac{2}{5}x + 4y^2\right)\left(\dfrac{4}{25}x^2 - \dfrac{8}{5}xy^2 + 16y^4\right)$

14. $(x^2 + x + 1)(x^2 - x + 1)$

15. a) $(x - 3)(x + 3)(2x - 1)(2x + 1)$

b) $(x - 4)(x + 4)(3x - 2)(3x + 2)$

17. a) $(x - 2)(x - 1)(x + 1)(x + 2)(2x + 3)$

b) $(x - 2)(x + 1)(x + 2)^2(2x - 1)(2x + 1)$

18. $m = -0.7, n = -5.1$

19. a) $(x + 4)(4x + 3)(2x - 1)$

b) $\dfrac{9}{10}(x - 3)(x + 1)(3x - 2)(2x + 3)$

20. a) i) $(x - 1)(x + 1)(x^2 + 1)$ **ii)** $(x - 2)(x + 2)(x^2 + 4)$

iii) $(x - 1)(x^4 + x^3 + x^2 + x + 1)$

iv) $(x - 2)(x^4 + 2x^3 + 4x^2 + 8x + 16)$

b) $x^n - a^n = (x - a)(x^{n-1} + ax^{n-2} + a^2x^{n-3} + ... + a^{n-3}x^2 + a^{n-2}x + a^{n-1})$, where n is a positive integer.

c) $(x - 1)(x^5 + x^4 + x^3 + x^2 + x + 1)$

d) i) $(x - 5)(x^2 + 25)$ **ii)** $(x - 3)(x^4 + 3x^3 + 9x^2 + 27x + 81)$

21. Yes, but only if n is odd. Let $n = 2k + 1$. Then, $x^{2k+1} + a^{2k+1} = (x - a)(x^{2k} - x^{2k-1}a + x^{2k-2}a^2 - x^{2k-3}a^3 + ... - xa^{2k-1} + a^{2k})$. If n is even, then $x^n + a^n$ is not factorable.

22. $7x - 5$

2.3 Polynomial Equations, pages 110–112

1. a) $x = 0$ or $x = -2$ or $x = 5$

b) $x = 1$ or $x = 4$ or $x = -3$

c) $x = -\dfrac{2}{3}$ or $x = -9$ or $x = 2$

d) $x = 7$ or $x = -\dfrac{2}{3}$ or $x = -1$

e) $x = 0.25$ or $x = 1.5$ or $x = -8$

f) $x = 2.5$ or $x = -2.5$ or $x = 7$

g) $x = 1.6$ or $x = -3$ or $x = 0.5$

2. a) $x = -3$ or $x = -1$ or $x = 1$

b) $x = -1$ or $x = 3$ or $x = 4$

c) $x = -2$ or $x = -1$ or $x = 2$ or $x = 3$

d) $x = -5$ or $x = -2$ or $x = 1$

e) $x = -3$ or $x = -1$ or $x = 0$ or $x = 2$

3. a) $x = 4$ **b)** $x = 1$ or $x = -1$ **c)** $x = 4$ or $x = -4$

d) $x = -1$ or $x = 1$ or $x = 5$ or $x = -5$

e) $x = 1.5$ or $x = -1.5$

f) $x = 7$ or $x = -7$ or $x = -3$ or $x = -4$

g) $x = -3$ or $x = 0.5$ or $x = 5$ or $x = -5$

4. a) $-5, 0, 9$ **b)** $-9, 0, 9$ **c)** $-\dfrac{1}{2}, 0, \dfrac{4}{3}$

d) $-2, -1, 2$ **e)** $-2, 2$ **f)** $-1, 0, 1, 2$ **g)** $-5, -2, 2, 5$

5. Answers may vary. Sample answers:

a) False. If the graph of a quartic function has four x-intercepts, then the corresponding quartic equation has four real roots.

b) True. **c)** True **d)** False. If a polynomial equation is not factorable, the roots can be determined by graphing. **e)** True.

6. a) $x = -2$ or $x = 3$ **b)** $x = 5$ or $x = -2$ or $x = 1$

c) $x = 1$ or $x = 3$ **d)** $x = -2$ or $x = 3$

e) $x = -2$ or $x = 2$ or $x = 3$ **f)** $x = -4$ or $x = 1$ **g)** $x = -1$

7. a) $x = -2$ or $x = -1$ or $x = 1.5$ **b)** $x = -0.5$ or $x = 3$

c) $x = -2$ or $x = -\dfrac{2}{3}$ or $x = \dfrac{2}{3}$

d) $x = -2$ or $x = 0.6$ or $x = 3$ **e)** $x = 0$ or $x = 2$

f) $x = -2$ or $x = 0$ or $x = 0.5$ or $x = 2$

g) $x = -3$ or $x = -1$ or $x = 2$ or $x = 3$

8. a) $x = -1$ or $x = 2$ or $x = 4$ **b)** $x = 3$

c) $x = 1$ **d)** $x = -1$ or $x = 2$ **e)** no real roots

9. a) $x \doteq -2.2$ or $x \doteq 0.5$ or $x \doteq 1.7$

b) $x \doteq -4.5$ or $x \doteq -0.6$ or $x \doteq 0.6$

c) $x \doteq -1.2$ or $x \doteq 1.2$ **d)** $x \doteq -1.3$

e) $x \doteq -1.4$ or $x \doteq 1.9$ **f)** $x = -1$ or $x \doteq 0.4$ or $x \doteq 1.4$

g) no real roots

10. 2 m by 2 m by 5 m

11. 13 m by 3 m by 3 m

12. Yes

13. No

14. 7 h

15. 0 m or 8 m or approximately 12.9 m from the end

16. a) $\{x \in \mathbb{R}, 0 \le x \le 9.92\}$ **b)** 22 000

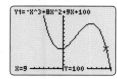

c) $x = 3$ or $x = 8$; If the selling price is \$3 per bottle or \$8 per bottle, then 17 200 bottles of sunscreen will be sold per month.

17. a) $x = 3$ **b)** $x \doteq -0.6$ or $x \doteq 0.1$ or $x \doteq 3.9$ or $x \doteq 4.6$

18. a) $k = 3$ **b)** $x \doteq -1.3$ or $x \doteq 0.8$

19. 24 cm by 20 cm by 4 cm, or 20 cm by 16 cm by 6 cm

20. a) $x = 3$ or $x = \dfrac{-3 + 3i\sqrt{3}}{2}$ or $x = \dfrac{-3 - 3i\sqrt{3}}{2}$

b) $x^3 - 2x^2 - 14x + 40$

21. 9 cm by 8 cm by 7 cm or 12 cm by 10 cm by 8 cm

22. $x^3 - 4x^2 - \dfrac{69}{4}x + \dfrac{63}{2} = 0$

23. $15°$

24. 20

2.4 Families of Polynomial Functions, pages 119–122

1. a) $y = k(x + 7)(x + 3), k \in \mathbb{R}, k \ne 0$

b) Answers may vary. Sample answer:

$y = 2(x + 7)(x + 3), y = -3(x + 7)(x + 3)$

c) $y = \dfrac{2}{5}(x + 7)(x + 3)$

2. C (has different zeros)

3. A, B and D (same zeros)

4. A, C, E (zeros are $-3, -2, 1$); B, D, F (zeros are $-1, 2, 3$)

5. a) $y = k(x + 5)(x - 2)(x - 3)$

b) $y = k(x - 1)(x - 6)(x + 3)$

c) $y = k(x + 4)(x + 1)(x - 9)$

d) $y = kx(x + 7)(x - 2)(x - 5)$

6. a) A: $y = (x + 2)(x - 1)(x - 3)$;

B: $y = -\dfrac{1}{2}(x + 2)(x - 1)(x - 3)$;

C: $y = -\dfrac{1}{2}(x + 2)(x - 2)(x - 3)$;

D: $y = 2(x + 2)(x - 1)(x - 3)$

7. a) $y = kx(x + 4)(x - 2)$ **b)** Answers may vary. Sample answer: $y = x(x + 4)(x - 2), y = -2x(x + 4)(x - 2)$

c) $y = \dfrac{1}{4}x(x + 4)(x - 2)$ **d)** Answers may vary.

Sample answers:

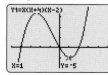
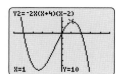

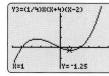

8. a) $y = k(x + 2)(x + 1)(2x - 1)$

b) Answers may vary. Sample answer:

$y = -(x + 2)(x + 1)(2x - 1), y = \dfrac{1}{2}(x + 2)(x + 1)(2x - 1)$

c) $y = -3(x + 2)(x + 1)(2x - 1)$

d) Answers may vary. Sample answer:

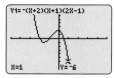
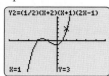

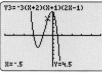

9. a) $y = k(x + 4)(x + 1)(x - 2)(x - 3)$

b) Answers may vary. Sample answer:

$y = 2(x + 4)(x + 1)(x - 2)(x - 3)$,

$y = -3(x + 4)(x + 1)(x - 2)(x - 3)$

c) $y = -\dfrac{1}{6}(x + 4)(x + 1)(x - 2)(x - 3)$

d) Answers may vary. Sample answer:

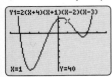
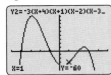

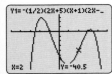

10. a) $y = k(2x + 5)(x + 1)(2x - 7)(x - 3)$
b) Answers may vary. Sample answer:
$y = -\dfrac{1}{2}(2x + 5)(x + 1)(2x - 7)(x - 3)$,
$y = 2(2x + 5)(x + 1)(2x - 7)(x - 3)$
c) $y = -\dfrac{5}{11}(2x + 5)(x + 1)(2x - 7)(x - 3)$
d) Answers may vary. Sample answer:

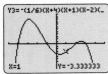

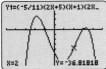

11. a) $y = k(2x^3 - 3x^2 - 4x - 1)$
b) $y = \dfrac{5}{2}(2x^3 - 3x^2 - 4x - 1)$
12. a) $y = k(x^4 + 2x^3 - 26x^2 - 6x + 117)$
b) $y = -\dfrac{1}{4}(x^4 + 2x^3 - 26x^2 - 6x + 117)$
13. a) $y = k(x^4 - 2x^3 - 10x^2 + 20x - 8)$
b) $y = 4(x^4 - 2x^3 - 10x^2 + 20x - 8)$
14. $y = -2(x + 2)(x - 1)(x - 3)$
15. $y = (x + 3)^2 (x - 1)(2x - 3)$
16. $y = -2x(2x + 7)(x + 2)(x - 1)$
17. Set A: no; Set B: yes
18. a) $V = x(48 - 2x)(30 - x)$ **b)** 44.31 cm by 28.16 cm
by 1.84 cm or 18.6 cm by 11.4 cm by 10.8 cm
c) volume doubles; volume triples; family of functions
with zeros 24, 30, 0 **d)** Answers may vary. Sample answer:

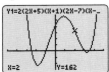
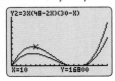

19. $y = kx(x - 30)(x - 60)(x - 90)(x - 120)(x - 150)$
20. a) $V = x(36 - 2x)(24 - 2x)$
b) i) $V = 2x(36 - 2x)(24 - 2x)$ **ii)** $V = 3x(36 - 2x)(24 - 2x)$
c) family of functions with the same zeros

d)

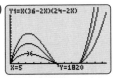
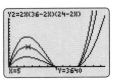

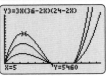

e) approximately 27.16 cm by 15.16 cm by 4.42 cm or
26 cm by 14 cm by 5 cm
22. a) Answers may vary. Sample answer:
$y = k(3x - 2)(x - 5)(x + 3)(x + 2)$
b) 4 **c)** Answers may vary. Sample answer:
$y = -\dfrac{8}{5}(3x - 2)(x - 5)(x + 3)(x + 2)$

d) $y = \dfrac{8}{5}(3x - 2)(x - 5)(x + 3)(x + 2)$

23. Answers may vary.
24. 24 cm
25. $g(x^2 - 1) = x^4 - x^2 - 3$

2.5 Solving Inequalities Using Technology, pages 129–131
1. a) $-7 < x \le -1$ **b)** $-2 \le x \le 6$ **c)** $x < -3, x \ge 4$
d) $x \le -1, x \ge 1$
2. a) $x < -1, -1 < x < 5, x > 5$
b) $x < -7, -7 < x < 0, 0 < x < 2, x > 2$
c) $x < -6, -6 < x < 0, 0 < x < 1, x > 1$
d) $x < -4, -4 < x < -2, -2 < x < \dfrac{2}{5}, \dfrac{2}{5} < x < 4.3, x > 4.3$

3.

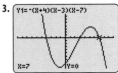

4. a) graph is below x-axis when $-2 < x < 1$ and when
$x > 6$
b) graph is on or above the x-axis when $x \le -3.6$ or $0 \le x$
≤ 4.7 or $x \ge 7.2$
5. a) i) $-6, 3$ **ii)** $-6 < x < 3$ **iii)** $x < -6, x > 3$
b) i) $-2, 5$ **ii)** $x < -2, x > 5$ **iii)** $-2 < x < 5$
c) i) $-4, 3, 5$ **ii)** $-4 < x < 3, x > 5$ **iii)** $x < -4, 3 < x < 5$
d) i) $-4, 1$ **ii)** $x < -4$ **iii)** $-4 < x < 1, x > 1$
6. a) $-3 < x < 4$ **b)** $-5 \le x \le -3$
c) $1 < x < 2, x > 3$ **d)** $-4 \le x \le -3, x \ge -1$
e) $x < -3, 2 < x < 3$ **f)** $x \le -4, -1 \le x \le 4$
7. a) $x \le -4$ or $x \ge 0.5$ **b)** $-0.5 < x < 3$
c) $x \le -4$ or $-2 \le x \le 1$ **d)** $-5 < x < -1$ or $x > 4$
e) $x < -5$ or $-2 < x < 7$ **f)** $x \le 7$
8. a) $-4.65 < x < 0.65$ **b)** $-2.43 < x < 1.10$
c) $x \le -2.17$ or $-0.31 \le x \le 1.48$
d) $-2.12 \le x \le -0.43$ or $x \ge 0.55$
e) $x < -1.93$ or $-0.48 < x < 1.08$
f) $-1.34 \le x \le 1.25$
9. a) approximately $x > -0.67$
b) $x \le -4$ or $-2 \le x \le 6$ **c)** $x \le -4$ or $-\dfrac{1}{3} \le x \le 3$

d) $x < -\dfrac{5}{3}$ or $-1 < x < 2$ **e)** $x < -2$ or $-\dfrac{1}{2} < x < 3$
f) $x < -3$ or $-1 < x < -\dfrac{1}{2}$ or $x > 4$

10. approximately $0.50 < t < 6.03$, or between about 0.5 s and 6.03 s.

11. a) approximately $2.73 < t < 5.51$, or between later in the second week and halfway through the fifth week **b)** There are no tent caterpillars left.

12. a) between 0 and approximately 4.47 years **b)** after approximately 4.91 years

13.–14. Answers may vary.

15. Answers may vary. Sample answers:
a) $(3x + 2)(5x - 4)(2x - 7) > 0$, $-30x^3 - 109x^2 - 2x - 56 < 0$
b) $x^3 - 2x^2 - 10x + 8 > 0$, $-x^3 + 2x^2 + 10x - 8 < 0$

16. approximately $-0.66 \le x \le 2.45$

17. a) $\{x \in \mathbb{R}, -1 \le x \le 0\}$, $\left\{y \in \mathbb{R}, 0 \le y \le \dfrac{1}{2}\right\}$
b) $\{x \in \mathbb{R}, x < -1, x > 1\}$, $\{y \in \mathbb{R}, y > 0\}$

19. $15:34$

20. $2\sqrt{6}$

2.6 Solving Factorable Polynomial Inequalities Algebraically, pages 138–139

1. a) $x \le 2$ **b)** $x > -\dfrac{5}{2}$ **c)** $x \le -\dfrac{1}{3}$ **d)** $x < 1$ **e)** $x < -2$ **f)** $x \ge \dfrac{10}{3}$

2. a) $x < -2$ or $x > 4$

b) $x \le -\dfrac{3}{2}$ or $x \ge 4$

3. a) $x < -3$ or $x > 2$

b) $6 \le x \le 9$

c) $-\dfrac{1}{4} \le x \le 2$

4. a) $-2 < x < -1$ or $x > 3$ **b)** $x \le -7$ or $\dfrac{1}{3} \le x \le 1$
c) $x < -2.5$ or $-\dfrac{2}{7} < x < 1$ **d)** $-4 \le x \le -2$ or $x \ge \dfrac{1}{3}$

5. a) $x \le 3$ or $x \ge 5$ **b)** $-3 < x < 5$ **c)** $-\dfrac{2}{5} \le x \le \dfrac{4}{3}$
d) $x < -2$ or $1 < x < 3$ **e)** $-\dfrac{3}{2} \le x \le -1$ or $x \ge 1$

6. a) approximately $x \ge -5.09$ **b)** $x < -4$ or $-3 < x < -2$
c) $x \le -1$ or $\dfrac{2}{5} \le x \le 3$ **d)** true for all intervals

7. a) $-5 \le x \le 1$ **b)** $-2 < x < -\dfrac{1}{2}$ or $x > 3$
c) $-1 < x < -\dfrac{1}{2}$ or $x > 1$
d) $\dfrac{-1 - \sqrt{17}}{2} \le x \le 1$ or $x \ge \dfrac{-1 + \sqrt{17}}{2}$

8. 22 cm by 24 cm by 10 cm

9. after 10 years (in 2009)

11. 8

12. approximately $x < 0.59$ or $1 < x < 3.41$

13. a) approximately $7 < n < 11$ or $19 < n < 20$, so between 7 and 11 years from today and between 19 and 20 years from today **b)** approximately $12 < n < 18.6$, so between 12 and 19 years from today **c)** Not valid beyond 20 years. 20 years from today the population will have fallen to 5560, and in the next year it would fall below 0, which is not possible.

14. $x^4 - 76x^2 + 1156 \le 0$, $-x^4 + 76x^2 - 1156 \ge 0$

15. $\sqrt{286}$

16. $y = \dfrac{4}{3}x - \dfrac{25}{3}$

Chapter 2 Review, pages 140–141

1. a) i) 37 **ii)** $\dfrac{x^3 + 9x^2 - 5x + 3}{x - 2} = x^2 + 11x + 17 + \dfrac{37}{x - 2}$, $x \ne 2$
b) i) -12 **ii)** $\dfrac{12x^3 - 2x^2 + x - 11}{3x + 1} = 4x^2 - 2x + 1 - \dfrac{12}{3x + 1}$, $x \ne -\dfrac{1}{3}$
c) i) $\dfrac{27}{2}$ **ii)** $\dfrac{-8x^4 - 4x + 10x^3 - x^2 + 15}{2x - 1}$
$= -4x^3 + 3x^2 + x - \dfrac{3}{2} + \dfrac{27}{2(2x - 1)}$, $x \ne \dfrac{1}{2}$

2. a) $k = -\dfrac{77}{27}$ **b)** 162

3. $b = -34$

4. a) $(x - 3)(x - 2)(x + 1)$ **b)** $(x - 4)(x + 2)(3x + 1)$
c) $(x - 3)(x - 1)(x + 6)(5x + 2)$

5. a) $-4(x - 2)(x + 1)(x + 2)$ **b)** $(x - 2)(5x - 3)(5x + 3)$
c) $x(x - 2)(x + 2)(2x + 5)$

6. a) $(2x - 1)$ metres by $(x + 3)$ metres by $(x + 1)$ metres
b) 4 m by 2 m by 1 m

7. $k = -2$

8. $x = -4$ or $x = -2$ or $x = 3$

9. a) $x = -4$ or $x = 4$ **b)** $x = \dfrac{1 - \sqrt{105}}{4}$ or $x = \dfrac{1 + \sqrt{105}}{4}$

10. a) $x = -1$ or $x \doteq -0.5$ or $x \doteq 0.8$
b) $x \doteq -0.7$ or $x \doteq 0.9$ or $x \doteq 8.8$

11. $V = l(l - 5)(2l + 1)$; approximately 8.55 cm by 3.55 cm by 18.10 cm

12. B (different zeros)

13. a) $y = k(x^3 - 4x^2 - x)$ **b)** $y = -2(x^3 - 4x^2 - x)$

14. $-3(x + 2)^2(x - 1)$

15. a) $x \le -4.2$ or $x \ge 1.2$ **b)** $-\dfrac{1}{2} < x < 3$ or $x > 4$
c) $x < -1.7$ or $0.4 < x < 3.3$ **d)** $x \le -4$ or $-\dfrac{1}{3} \le x \le 3$
e) $x < -2.2$ or $x > 2.2$

16. approximately between 0.8 s and 7.6 s and between 20 s and 23.6 s

17. a) $-\dfrac{4}{5} < x < 4$ **b)** $-\dfrac{3}{2} \le x \le \dfrac{2}{3}$ or $x \ge 1$
c) $x < -5$ or $x > 5$

18. a) $x \le -\dfrac{7}{3}$ or $x \ge \dfrac{1}{4}$ **b)** $x \le -4$ or $\dfrac{1}{3} \le x \le \dfrac{3}{2}$
c) approximately $x < -2.4$ or $x > 4.3$

Chapter 2 Practice Test, pages 142–143

1. C

2. C

3. D

4. a) $\dfrac{x^3 - 4x^2 + 3x - 7}{x + 3} = x^2 - 7x + 24 - \dfrac{79}{x + 3}$
b) $x \ne -3$ **c)** $(x + 3)(x^2 - 7x + 24) - 79$

5. a) $k = \dfrac{1}{2}$ **b)** 193

6. a) $(x - 4)(x - 2)(x + 1)$ **b)** $(x - 3)(x + 2)(x + 3)$
c) $(x - 2)(x + 3)(x + 4)$ **d)** $(x - 1)(x + 2)(5x + 2)$
e) $(x + 2)(x + 3)(x + 4)$ **f)** $(x + 1)(x + 2)(x + 3)(2x + 1)$
7. $x = -5$ or $x = 3$ or $x = -2$
8. a) $x = 2$ **b)** $x = -11$ or $x = 11$ **c)** $x = -5$ or $x = 5$
d) $x = -3$ or $x = 3$ or $x = -2$ or $x = 5$
9. a) $x = -2$ or $x = -1$ **b)** $x = -4$ or $x = 1$ or $x = 3$
c) $x = -1.75$ or $x = 1.5$ or $x = 1.75$
d) $x = -\dfrac{2}{3}$ or $x = 0$ or $x = \dfrac{3}{5}$ or $x = \dfrac{2}{3}$
10. Answers may vary.
11. a) $y = -\dfrac{1}{2}x(x + 3)(2x + 3)(x - 2)$
b) $x < -3, -\dfrac{3}{2} < x < 0, x > 2$
12. a) $y = k(x^4 - 6x^3 - 17x^2 + 120x - 50)$
b) $y = -\dfrac{2}{5}(x^4 - 6x^3 - 17x^2 + 120x - 50)$
13. a) $V = x(20 - 2x)(18 - x)$ **b)** approximately 16.7 cm
by 16.4 cm by 1.6 cm or 5.8 cm by 10.9 cm by 7.1 cm
c) $V = k(20 - 2x)(18 - x)x$
14. a) $x \le -0.9$ or $4 \le x \le 7.4$
b) $-2.0 < x < -0.6$ or $0.9 < x < 4.7$
15. a) approximately $x < -3.6$ or $-1.1 < x < 1.7$
b) $-1.5 \le x \le -1$ or approximately $x \le -1.7$ or
approximately $x \ge 1.7$
16. a) $-\dfrac{4}{3} < x < \dfrac{4}{3}$ **b)** $x < 0$ **c)** $x \le -3$ or $-\dfrac{5}{2} \le x \le 3$
d) $x \le -3$ or $-1 \le x \le -\dfrac{1}{2}$ or $x \ge 2$
17. a) $V = x(32 - 2x)(40 - 2x)$
b) i) $V = 2x(32 - 2x)(40 - 2x)$
ii) $V = \dfrac{1}{2}x(32 - 2x)(40 - 2x)$ **c)** family of functions
d) approximately $2 < x < 10.9$ or $x > 23.1$

CHAPTER 3

Prerequisite Skills, pages 146–147
1. Answers may vary. Sample answer: A line or curve that
the graph approaches more and more closely. For $f(x) = \dfrac{1}{x}$,
the vertical asymptote is $x = 0$.
2. a) $x = 3, y = 0$ **b)** $x = -4, y = 0$

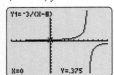
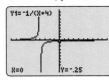

c) $x = 8, y = 0$ **d)** $x = 5, y = 0$

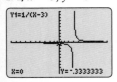
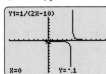

3. a) $\{x \in \mathbb{R}\}, \{y \in \mathbb{R}\}$ **b)** $\{x \in \mathbb{R}\}, \{y \in \mathbb{R}, y \ge 4\}$
c) $\{x \in \mathbb{R}\}, \{y \in \mathbb{R}\}$ **d)** $\{x \in \mathbb{R}, x \ne 0\}, \{y \in \mathbb{R}, y \ne 0\}$
e) $\{x \in \mathbb{R}, x \ne 4\}, \{y \in \mathbb{R}, y \ne 0\}$ **f)** $\{x \in \mathbb{R}, x \ne 0\}, \{y \in \mathbb{R}, y \ne 0\}$
4. a) -13 **b)** $\dfrac{1}{3}$ **c)** $-\dfrac{2}{9}$ **d)** -1 **e)** -13 **f)** $\dfrac{6}{5}$
5. a) 0.38 **b)** 0.71 **c)** 0.18 **d)** 0.38 **e)** 0.53 **f)** 0.35

6. a) $(x + 4)(x + 3)$ **b)** $(5x - 2)(x - 3)$ **c)** $(3x + 8)(2x - 1)$
d) $(x + 1)(x + 3)(x - 2)$ **e)** $(2x + 1)^2(3x - 2)$
f) $(3x - 4)(9x^2 + 12x + 16)$
7. a) $8, -4$ **b)** $-5, -1$ **c)** $3, \dfrac{3}{2}$ **d)** $-5, -\dfrac{1}{6}$ **e)** $-7, \dfrac{1}{2}$ **f)** $6, -\dfrac{5}{3}$
8. a) $-2 \pm \sqrt{2}$ **b)** $\dfrac{-4 \pm \sqrt{14}}{2}$ **c)** $\dfrac{5 \pm \sqrt{73}}{6}$ **d)** no x-intercepts
e) $\dfrac{-4 \pm \sqrt{10}}{3}$ **f)** $1 \pm 2\sqrt{2}$
9. a) $x > 6$ **b)** $x \le \dfrac{11}{2}$ **c)** $x > \dfrac{1}{2}$ **d)** $x > -5$ **e)** $x > -\dfrac{5}{2}$ **f)** $x > -9$
10. a) $-2 \le x \le 2$ **b)** $x < -3$ or $x > 6$ **c)** $-\sqrt{13} < x < \sqrt{13}$
d) $x < -5$ or $x > 2$ **e)** $-7 < x < -1$ **f)** $x < -6$ or $x > \dfrac{1}{2}$

3.1 Reciprocal of a Linear Function, pages 153–155
1. a)

As $x \to$	$f(x) \to$
2^+	$+\infty$
2^-	$-\infty$
$+\infty$	0
$-\infty$	0

b)

As $x \to$	$f(x) \to$
-5^+	$+\infty$
-5^-	$-\infty$
$+\infty$	0
$-\infty$	0

c)

As $x \to$	$f(x) \to$
8^+	$+\infty$
8^-	$-\infty$
$+\infty$	0
$-\infty$	0

2. a) i) $x = 2, y = 0$ **ii)** $x = -3, y = 0$
b) i) $y = \dfrac{1}{x - 2}$ **ii)** $y = \dfrac{1}{x + 3}$
3. a) i) $x = 5$ **ii)** $y = 0$ **iii)** $-\dfrac{1}{5}$ **b) i)** $x = -6$ **ii)** $y = 0$ **iii)** $\dfrac{1}{3}$
c) i) $x = 1$ **ii)** $y = 0$ **iii)** 5 **d) i)** $x = -7$ **ii)** $y = 0$ **iii)** $-\dfrac{1}{7}$
5. a) $y = \dfrac{1}{x - 3}$ **b)** $y = \dfrac{1}{x + 3}$ **c)** $y = \dfrac{1}{2x - 1}$ **d)** $y = -\dfrac{1}{x + 4}$
6. a)

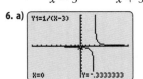

The slope is negative and
decreasing for $x < 3$.

The slope is negative and
increasing for $x > 3$.

b)

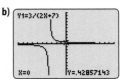

The slope is negative and
decreasing for $x < -\dfrac{7}{2}$.

The slope is negative and
increasing for $x < -\dfrac{7}{2}$.

c)

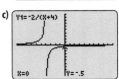

The slope is positive and
increasing for $x < -4$.

The slope is positive and
decreasing for $x > -4$.

d)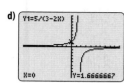

The slope is positive and increasing for $x < \dfrac{3}{2}$.

The slope is positive and decreasing for $x > \dfrac{3}{2}$.

7. a)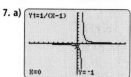

$\{x \in \mathbb{R}, x \neq 1\}$, $\{y \in \mathbb{R}, y \neq 0\}$, $x = 1, y = 0$

b)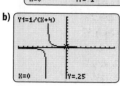

$\{x \in \mathbb{R}, x \neq -4\}$, $\{y \in \mathbb{R}, y \neq 0\}$, $x = -4, y = 0$

c)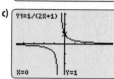

$\left\{x \in \mathbb{R}, x \neq -\dfrac{1}{2}\right\}$, $\{y \in \mathbb{R}, y \neq 0\}$, $x = -\dfrac{1}{2}, y = 0$

d)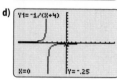

$\{x \in \mathbb{R}, x \neq -4\}$, $\{y \in \mathbb{R}, y \neq 0\}$, $x = -4, y = 0$

e)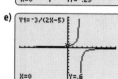

$\left\{x \in \mathbb{R}, x \neq \dfrac{5}{2}\right\}$, $\{y \in \mathbb{R}, y \neq 0\}$, $x = \dfrac{5}{2}, y = 0$

f)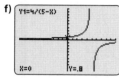

$\{x \in \mathbb{R}, x \neq 5\}$, $\{y \in \mathbb{R}, y \neq 0\}$, $x = 5, y = 0$

g)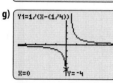

$\left\{x \in \mathbb{R}, x \neq \dfrac{1}{4}\right\}$, $\{y \in \mathbb{R}, y \neq 0\}$, $x = \dfrac{1}{4}, y = 0$

h)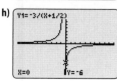

$\left\{x \in \mathbb{R}, x \neq -\dfrac{1}{2}\right\}$, $\{y \in \mathbb{R}, y \neq 0\}$, $x = -\dfrac{1}{2}, y = 0$

8. $y = \dfrac{1}{x - 1}$

9. $y = -\dfrac{1}{4x + 4}$

10. a) $t = \dfrac{3850}{v}$

b)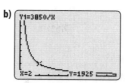

c) 7.7 h, or 7 h 42 min

d) As the speed increases, the rate of change of the time decreases.

11. a) Answers may vary.

b) The equation of the asymptote is $x = -\dfrac{2}{b}$. When $b = 1$, the asymptote is $x = -2$. When $b > 1$, $-2 < -\dfrac{2}{b} < 0$. When $0 < b < 1$, $-\dfrac{2}{b} < -2$. When $b < 0$, $-\dfrac{2}{b} > 0$.

12. a) 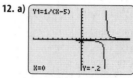 **b)**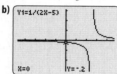

c)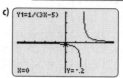

13. a) $F = \dfrac{600}{d}$ **b)**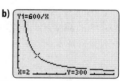

c) 300 N **d)** The force is halved.

14. a) 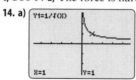 **b)**

c)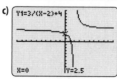

15.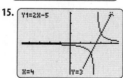

The x-intercept of $y = 2x - 5$ is $\dfrac{5}{2}$.

Answers may vary. Sample answer: The reciprocal of the y-coordinates on either side of the x-intercept of $y = 2x - 5$ are the y-coordinates of $f(x) = \dfrac{1}{2x - 5}$.

16. $x = \dfrac{yz}{y - z}$, $y \neq z, x \neq 0, y \neq 0, z \neq 0$

17. 14

18. E

Extension, page 156

2. a) no; does not divide pixels evenly
b) yes; divides pixels evenly
3. Answers may vary. Sample answer: Xmax = 47

3.2 Reciprocal of a Quadratic Function, pages 164–167

1. a)

As $x \rightarrow$	$f(x) \rightarrow$
3^-	$-\infty$
3^+	$+\infty$
1^-	$+\infty$
1^+	$-\infty$
$-\infty$	0
$+\infty$	0

b)

As $x \rightarrow$	$f(x) \rightarrow$
-4^-	$+\infty$
-4^+	$-\infty$
5^-	$-\infty$
5^+	$+\infty$
$-\infty$	0
$+\infty$	0

c)

As $x \rightarrow$	$f(x) \rightarrow$
-6^-	$-\infty$
-6^+	$-\infty$
$-\infty$	0
$+\infty$	0

2. a) $x = 4$; $\{x \in \mathbb{R}, x \neq 4\}$
b) $x = 2, x = -7$; $\{x \in \mathbb{R}, x \neq 2, x \neq -7\}$ **c)** $\{x \in \mathbb{R}\}$
d) $x = -5, x = 5$; $\{x \in \mathbb{R}, x \neq 5, x \neq -5\}$
e) $x = 3, x = 1$; $\{x \in \mathbb{R}, x \neq 3, x \neq 1\}$
f) $x = -4, x = -3$; $\{x \in \mathbb{R}, x \neq -4, x \neq -3\}$
g) $x = -2, x = \dfrac{4}{3}$; $\left\{x \in \mathbb{R}, x \neq -2, x \neq \dfrac{4}{3}\right\}$ **h)** $\{x \in \mathbb{R}\}$

3. a)

Interval	$x < 1$	$x > 1$
Sign of $f(x)$	+	+
Sign of Slope	+	−
Change in Slope	+	−

b)

Interval	$x < -2$	$-2 < x < 1$	$x = 1$	$1 < x < 4$	$x > 4$
Sign of $f(x)$	+	−	−	−	+
Sign of Slope	+	+	0	−	−
Change in Slope	+	−	−	−	+

c)

Interval	$x < -3$	$-3 < x < 0$	$x = 0$	$0 < x < 3$	$x > 3$
Sign of $f(x)$	−	+	+	+	−
Sign of Slope	−	−	0	+	+
Change in Slope	−	+	+	+	−

d)

Interval	$x < -4$	$x > -4$
Sign of $f(x)$	−	−
Sign of Slope	−	+
Change in Slope	−	−

4. a) $y = \dfrac{1}{(x - 1)^2}$ **b)** $y = \dfrac{1}{(x + 2)(x - 4)}$ **c)** $y = -\dfrac{1}{x^2 - 9}$
d) $y = -\dfrac{1}{(x + 4)^2}$

5. a) i) $\{x \in \mathbb{R}, x \neq -3, x \neq 3\}$ **ii)** $x = 3, x = -3, y = 0$
iii) y-intercept $-\dfrac{1}{9}$

iv)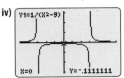

v)

Interval	$x < -3$	$-3 < x < 0$	$x = 0$	$0 < x < 3$	$x > 3$
Sign of $f(x)$	+	−	−	−	+
Sign of Slope	+	+	0	−	−
Change in Slope	+	−	−	−	+

vi) $\{y \in \mathbb{R}, y \neq 0\}$ **b) i)** $\{x \in \mathbb{R}, x \neq -3, x \neq 5\}$
ii) $x = -3, x = 5, y = 0$ **iii)** y-intercept $-\dfrac{1}{15}$

iv)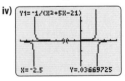

v)

Interval	$x < -3$	$-3 < x < 1$	$x = 1$	$1 < x < 5$	$x > 5$
Sign of $f(x)$	+	−	−	−	+
Sign of Slope	+	+	0	−	−
Change in Slope	+	−	−	−	+

vi) $\{y \in \mathbb{R}, y \neq 0\}$ **c) i)** $\left\{x \in \mathbb{R}, x \neq \dfrac{-5 \pm \sqrt{109}}{2}\right\}$
ii) $x = \dfrac{-5 \pm \sqrt{109}}{2}$, $y = 0$ **iii)** y-intercept $\dfrac{1}{21}$

iv)

Interval	Sign of $f(x)$	Sign of Slope	Change in Slope
$x < \dfrac{-5 - \sqrt{109}}{2}$	−	−	−
$\dfrac{-5 - \sqrt{109}}{2} < x < -2.5$	+	−	+
$x = -2.5$	+	0	+
$-2.5 < x < \dfrac{-5 + \sqrt{109}}{2}$	+	+	+
$x > \dfrac{-5 + \sqrt{109}}{2}$	−	+	−

vi) $\{y \in \mathbb{R}, y \neq 0\}$

d) i) $\left\{x \in \mathbb{R}, x \neq 2, x \neq -\dfrac{1}{3}\right\}$ **ii)** $x = 2$, $x = -\dfrac{1}{3}$, $y = 0$

iii) y-intercept $-\dfrac{1}{2}$

iv)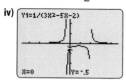

v)

Interval	$x < -\dfrac{1}{3}$	$-\dfrac{1}{3} < x < \dfrac{5}{6}$	$x = \dfrac{5}{6}$	$\dfrac{5}{6} < x < 2$	$x > 2$
Sign of $f(x)$	+	−	−	−	+
Sign of Slope	+	+	0	−	−
Change in Slope	+	−	−	−	+

vii) $\{x \in \mathbb{R}, y \neq 0\}$

e) i) $\{x \in \mathbb{R}\}$ **ii)** $y = 0$ **iii)** y-intercept $\dfrac{1}{2}$

iv)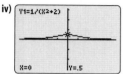

v)

Interval	$x < 0$	$x = 0$	$x > 0$
Sign of $f(x)$	+	+	+
Sign of Slope	+	0	−
Change in Slope	+	−	+

vi) $\left\{y \in \mathbb{R}, 0 < y \leq \dfrac{1}{2}\right\}$

6. Answers may vary. **a)** 0 **b)** 0.009 **c)** 0.011 **d)** 1.250 **e)** 0

7. a) $\{x \in \mathbb{R}, x \neq 0\}$; $\{y \in \mathbb{R}, y > 0\}$; asymptotes $x = 0$, $y = 0$; no x- or y-intercepts; for $x < 0$, the function is positive and increasing (positive slope); for $x > 0$, the function is positive and decreasing (negative slope) **b)** $\{x \in \mathbb{R}, x \neq 1\}$; $\{y \in \mathbb{R}, y > 0\}$; asymptotes $x = 1$, $y = 0$; y-intercept 1; for $x < 1$, the function is positive and increasing (positive slope); for $x > 1$, the function is positive and decreasing (negative slope) **c)** $\{x \in \mathbb{R}, x \neq -2\}$; $\{y \in \mathbb{R}, y > 0\}$; asymptotes $x = -2$, $y = 0$; y-intercept $\dfrac{1}{4}$; for $x < -2$, the function is positive and increasing (positive slope); for $x > -2$, the function is positive and decreasing (negative slope)

8. a) 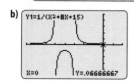 increasing for $x < -1$ and $-1 < x < 0$, decreasing for $0 < x < 1$ and $x > 1$

b) 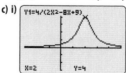 increasing for $x < -5$ and $-5 < x < -4$, decreasing for $-4 < x < -3$ and $x > -3$

c) 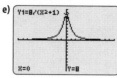 increasing for $x < -3$ and $-3 < x < -\dfrac{1}{2}$, decreasing for $-\dfrac{1}{2} < x < 2$ and $x > 2$

d) 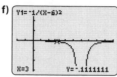 increasing for $\dfrac{1}{2} < x < \dfrac{3}{2}$ and $x > \dfrac{3}{2}$, decreasing for $x < -\dfrac{1}{2}$ and $-\dfrac{1}{2} < x < \dfrac{1}{2}$

e) 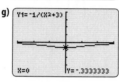 increasing for $x < 0$, decreasing for $x > 0$

f) 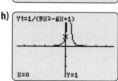 increasing for $x > 6$, decreasing for $x < 6$

g) 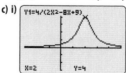 increasing for $x > 0$, decreasing for $x < 0$

h) 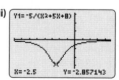 increasing for $x < \dfrac{1}{3}$, decreasing for $x > \dfrac{1}{3}$

9. a), b) Answers may vary.

c) i) 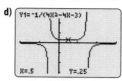 **ii)**

10. Answers may vary. Sample answers: **a)** $f(x)$ and $g(x)$ will have the same shape reflected in the x-axis.

b) $h(x) = \dfrac{2}{x^2 - 9}$ is a vertical stretch of $k(x) = \dfrac{1}{x^2 - 9}$ by a factor of 2.

c) $m(x)$ and $n(x)$ will have the same shape but different asymptotes.

11. Answers may vary. Sample answers: **a)** $y = \dfrac{1}{x^2 + x - 6}$

b) $y = \dfrac{1}{x^2 + 2}$ **c)** $y = -\dfrac{1}{(x + 3)^2}$

12. a) $I \doteq \dfrac{1368.9}{d^2}$

b) 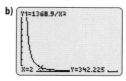 **c)** $I \doteq 1368.9$; rate of change is approximately -2737.8.

13. a)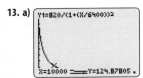

b)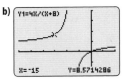

b) i) approximately 817.4 N **ii)** approximately 310.5 N
c) $h \geq 51\,554.5$ km

Interval	$x < -8$	$-8 < x < 0$	$x > 0$
Sign of $f(x)$	+	−	+
Sign of Slope	+	+	+
Change in Slope	+	−	−

14. a) 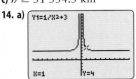   **b)**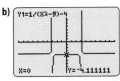

c)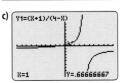

Interval	$x < -1$	$-1 < x < 4$	$x > 4$
Sign of $f(x)$	−	+	−
Sign of Slope	+	+	+
Change in Slope	+	+	−

16. a) 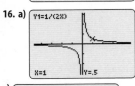   **b)**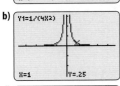

d)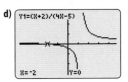

Interval	$x < -2$	$-2 < x < \frac{5}{4}$	$x > \frac{5}{4}$
Sign of $f(x)$	+	−	+
Sign of Slope	−	−	−
Change in Slope	−	−	+

c) 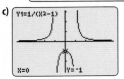   **d)**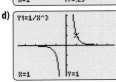

17. a) symmetric about the origin
b) symmetric about the y-axis
18. Explanations may vary.

a) 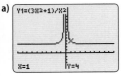   **b)**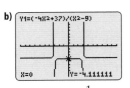

e)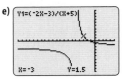

Interval	$x < -5$	$-5 < x < -1.5$	$x > -1.5$
Sign of $f(x)$	−	+	−
Sign of Slope	−	−	−
Change in Slope	−	+	+

19. Answers may vary. Sample answer: $y = \dfrac{1}{(x-a)(x-b)}$

20. $a < -27$ or $a > \dfrac{1}{2}$

21. 7

22. C

f)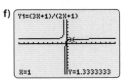

3.3 Rational Functions of the Form $f(x) = \dfrac{ax+b}{cx+d}$, pages 174–176

1. a) $x = 7$, $\{x \in \mathbb{R}, x \neq 7\}$ **b)** $x = -5$, $\{x \in \mathbb{R}, x \neq -5\}$
c) $x = -8$, $\{x \in \mathbb{R}, x \neq -8\}$ **d)** $x = \dfrac{1}{3}$, $\left\{x \in \mathbb{R}, x \neq \dfrac{1}{3}\right\}$
e) $x = -\dfrac{9}{4}$, $\left\{x \in \mathbb{R}, x \neq -\dfrac{9}{4}\right\}$ **f)** $x = 5$, $\{x \in \mathbb{R}, x \neq 5\}$
2. a) $y = 1$, $\{y \in \mathbb{R}, y \neq 1\}$ **b)** $y = 3$, $\{y \in \mathbb{R}, y \neq 3\}$
c) $y = 1$, $\{y \in \mathbb{R}, y \neq 1\}$ **d)** $y = \dfrac{5}{2}$, $\left\{y \in \mathbb{R}, y \neq \dfrac{5}{2}\right\}$
e) $y = -1$, $\{y \in \mathbb{R}, y \neq -1\}$ **f)** $y = 2$, $\{y \in \mathbb{R}, y \neq 2\}$

3. a)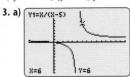

Interval	$x < -\frac{1}{2}$	$-\frac{1}{2} < x < -\frac{1}{3}$	$x > -\frac{1}{3}$
Sign of $f(x)$	+	−	+
Sign of Slope	+	+	+
Change in Slope	+	−	−

Interval	$x < 0$	$0 < x < 5$	$x > 5$
Sign of $f(x)$	+	−	+
Sign of Slope	−	−	−
Change in Slope	−	−	+

4. a) i) $m_{3.5} = -24$, $m_{20} = -0.02$ **ii)** $m_{2.5} = -24$, $m_{-20} = -0.02$
b) The function is decreasing for $x < 3$ and increasing for $x > 3$.

5. a) i) $y = \dfrac{1}{2}$ **ii)** $y = -\dfrac{5}{2}$

b) Answers may vary. Sample answer: The horizontal asymptote is equal to the coefficient of x in the numerator divided by the coefficient of x in the denominator.

c) $y = \dfrac{a}{c}$

6. a) $y = 1$, $x = 9$, $\{x \in \mathbb{R}, x \neq 9\}$, $\{y \in \mathbb{R}, y \neq 1\}$

b) $y = 3$, $x = -2$, $\{x \in \mathbb{R}, x \neq -2\}$, $\{y \in \mathbb{R}, y \neq 3\}$

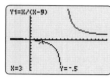

c) $y = 2$, $x = -\dfrac{1}{2}$, $\left\{x \in \mathbb{R}, x \neq -\dfrac{1}{2}\right\}$, $\{y \in \mathbb{R}, y \neq 2\}$

d) $y = \dfrac{1}{2}$, $x = \dfrac{5}{2}$, $\left\{x \in \mathbb{R}, x \neq \dfrac{5}{2}\right\}$, $\left\{y \in \mathbb{R}, y \neq \dfrac{1}{2}\right\}$

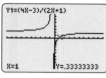 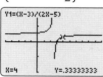

e) $y = -1$, $x = -5$, $\{x \in \mathbb{R}, x \neq -5\}$, $\{y \in \mathbb{R}, y \neq -1\}$

f) $y = -\dfrac{8}{3}$, $x = \dfrac{4}{3}$, $\left\{x \in \mathbb{R}, x \neq \dfrac{4}{3}\right\}$, $\left\{y \in \mathbb{R}, y \neq -\dfrac{8}{3}\right\}$

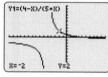 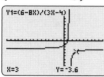

7. a) $y = \dfrac{2x - 3}{x - 3}$ **b)** $y = \dfrac{x - 4}{x + 1}$

8. $y = \dfrac{x + 4}{x - 2}$

9. $y = \dfrac{5x - 3}{2x + 1}$

10. a)

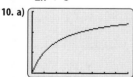

```
WINDOW
Xmin=0
Xmax=800000
Xscl=100000
Ymin=0
Ymax=30
Yscl=10
Xres=1
```

b) The amount of pollutant levels off at 30 g/L.
c) after approximately 333.9 min

11. a) $2 + \dfrac{7}{2x - 1}$ **b)** Answers may vary.

c)

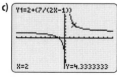

12. a)

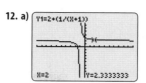

b)

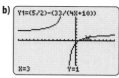

14. Answers may vary. Sample answer: As the mass of the club increases, the rate of change of the initial velocity also increases.

15.

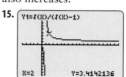

asymptotes $y = 1$, $x = 1$; $\{x \in \mathbb{R}, x \geq 0, x \neq 1\}$, $\{y \in \mathbb{R}, y \leq 0, y > 1\}$; y-intercept 0; for $0 < x < 1$, $f(x)$ is negative and decreasing and the slope is negative and decreasing; for $x > 1$, $f(x)$ is positive and decreasing and the slope is negative and increasing. Comparison: Answers may vary.

16. a)

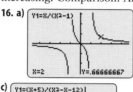

b)

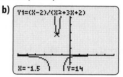

c)

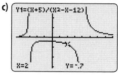

Common features: Answers may vary.

17. Answers may vary. Sample answer: When the degree of the polynomial in the numerator is greater than the degree of the polynomial in the denominator, you can expect to get an oblique asymptote.

18. A

19. a) quotient x, remainder -2 **b)** $x - \dfrac{2}{x}$

c) i) $y = x - 1$, $x = 2$ **ii)** $y = \dfrac{x + 3}{2}$, $x = 2$

iii) discontinuous at $x = -3$ (linear)

3.4 Solve Rational Equations and Inequalities, pages 183–185

1. a) -1 **b)** $-4, 3$ **c)** $\dfrac{3}{2}$ **d)** 0

2. a) $x = \dfrac{10}{3}$ **b)** $x = 4$ or $x = -2$ **c)** $x = \dfrac{11}{3}$ **d)** $x = 5$ or $x = -1$

e) $x = -34$ **f)** $x = 2$

3. a) $x = 0$ or $x \doteq 6.71$ **b)** $x \doteq -0.27$ or $x \doteq -18.73$

c) $x \doteq 4.34$ or $x \doteq 2.47$ or $x \doteq 0.19$ **d)** $x \doteq 1.28$ or $x \doteq -1.28$

4. a) $x < 3$ or $x > 7$

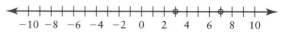

b) $-1 < x < 0$

c) $x < -4$ or $-1 < x \leq 1$

d) $-5 < x \le 2$ or $x > 4$

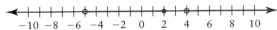

e) $x < -4$ or $-1 < x < 4$ or $x > 5$

f) $0 < x < 3$ or $x > 6$

5. a) $x < -7$ or $-2 < x < 1$ or $x > 5$ **b)** $-3 < x < \dfrac{1}{2}$

c) $-6 < x < -5$ or $-1 \le x \le 4$ **d)** $x < -\dfrac{1}{2}$ or $\dfrac{2}{3} \le x \le 2$ or $x > 5$

6. Answers may vary. Sample answer: $\dfrac{2x - 3}{(x - 3)(x + 5)} = 0$

7. $x < -4$ or $-1 < x < 0$ or $x > 2$; points of intersection $\left(-4, \dfrac{4}{3}\right)$ and $(0, 0)$

8. $-5 < x < 0$ or $3 < x < 7$

9. a) $x = \dfrac{1}{3}$ **b)** $x = \dfrac{-3 \pm \sqrt{14}}{5}$ **c)** $x = 2$ or $x = 6$

d) $\{x \in \mathbb{R}, x \ne 1\}$ **e)** $x = \dfrac{-3 \pm 3\sqrt{2}}{2}$ **f)** no solution

10. a) $x < 0$ or $x > 9$ **b)** $x < 0$ or $x > 3$

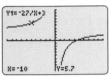
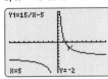

c) $0 < x < 2$ **d)** $x < 1$ or $x > 31$

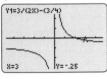
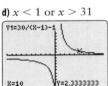

11. $x < -\dfrac{25}{2}$ or $x > 5$

12. $x < -7$ or $-3 < x < -2$ or $x > 5$ versus $-7 < x < -3$ or $-2 < x < 5$

13. $x < -5$ or $\dfrac{7}{13} \le x < 4$ versus $-1 < x \le \dfrac{7}{13}$ or $x > 3$

14. a) $\dfrac{1}{2a} + \dfrac{1}{2b} = \dfrac{1}{x}$ **b)** $\dfrac{40}{3}$ **c)** $b = \dfrac{2}{3}$

15. a) i) 3600 lux **ii)** 2.25 lux **b) i)** 141.4 m **ii)** $0 < d \le 2\sqrt{5}$

16. $2 < I < \dfrac{5}{2}$

18. a) $l \doteq 31.26$ cm, $w \doteq 0.74$ cm

b) $x = y = \dfrac{\sqrt{2}}{2}$ or $x = y = \dfrac{-\sqrt{2}}{2}$

19. a) $x = 2$ **b)** $x < -0.77$ or $2 < x < 4$

20. a)

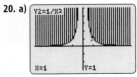

b)

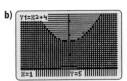
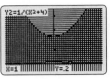

21. a) $\dfrac{3}{x - 1} + \dfrac{2}{x + 3}$ **b)** $\dfrac{27}{5(x - 3)} + \dfrac{8}{5(x + 2)}$

c) $\dfrac{1}{x + 2} + \dfrac{5}{x - 3} - \dfrac{3}{(x - 3)^2}$

3.5 Making Connections With Rational Functions and Equations, pages 189–191

1. a)

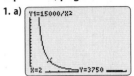

b) The light intensity is less.
c) When d is close to 0, the light intensity is very great.

2. a) $V = \dfrac{5000}{p}$

b)

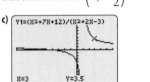
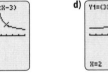
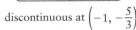

c) The volume is halved.

3. a) $x = 1$ **b)** $0 < x < 0.33$

4. a)

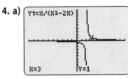

discontinuous at $\left(0, -\dfrac{1}{2}\right)$

b)

discontinuous at $\left(4, \dfrac{1}{9}\right)$

c)

discontinuous at $\left(-3, -\dfrac{1}{4}\right)$

d)

discontinuous at $\left(-1, -\dfrac{5}{3}\right)$

e)

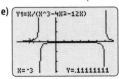

discontinuous at $\left(0, -\dfrac{1}{12}\right)$

f)

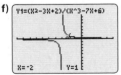

discontinuous at $\left(1, \dfrac{1}{4}\right)$ and $\left(2, \dfrac{1}{5}\right)$

5. a)

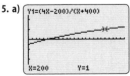
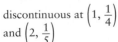

b) Answers may vary. Sample answer: Average profit is modelled by $\dfrac{P(x)}{x}$ = slope of secant.

c) The average profit is the greatest when $x = 200$.
d) 9.18×10^{-4}

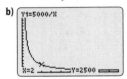
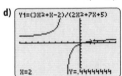

6. a) $R = \dfrac{0.64l}{d^2}$ **b)** $R = \dfrac{640}{d^2}$

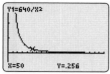

7. Answers may vary. Sample answers:

a)

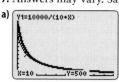

The cost is just slightly greater per person than the original model. The cost decreases at a greater rate at first.

b)

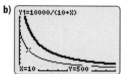

The cost is much greater per person. The gap between the graphs decreases as the number of passengers increases. The cost decreases at a slower rate.

c)

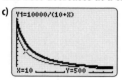

The cost per person is greater. As the number of passengers increases, the cost per person decreases and the graphs get closer. The cost decreases at a slightly slower rate.

8. a)

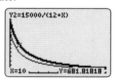

b) a slanting asymptote **c)** $x - 1 - \dfrac{6}{x - 1}$ **d)** $y = x - 1$

9. a)

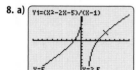

10. a)

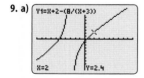

b) approximately 8.39 h **c)** approximately 5.85 h

11. a) $h = \dfrac{100\ 000}{\pi r^2}$

b)

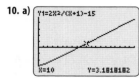

12. a)

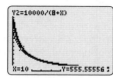

b) The systolic pressure decreases and gets closer to 25.
c) The rate of change decreases until $t \doteq 0.58$ s and then increases gradually, getting closer to 0.
d) The rate of change of $R(t)$ and $P(t)$ at $t = 5$ is -1.48
13. 1
14. a)

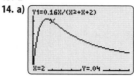

b) The curve increases to reach a maximum concentration of $C = 0.0418$ mg/cm^3 when $t \doteq 1.414$ min and then gradually decreases to C as time increases close to 0.
15. increasing for $0 < R < 0.40$
16. False because the function is discontinuous at the point $(2, 4)$.
17. A
18. $x = \dfrac{\pi}{3} + 2k\pi, k = 0, \pm 1, \pm 2, \pm 3, \ldots$
$\left(\text{i.e., } \ldots, -\dfrac{5\pi}{3}, \dfrac{\pi}{3}, \dfrac{7\pi}{3}, \ldots \right)$

Chapter 3 Review, pages 192–193
1. a) $x = 2, y = 0$ **b)** $x = -7, y = 0$ **c)** $x = 5, y = 0$
2. a) $y = \dfrac{2}{x - 1}$ **b)** $y = \dfrac{1}{x + 4}$
3. a)

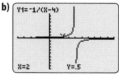

$\{x \in \mathbb{R}, x \neq 3\}, \{y \in \mathbb{R}, y \neq 0\}, -\dfrac{5}{3}, x = 3, y = 0$

b)

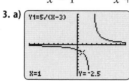

$\{x \in \mathbb{R}, x \neq 4\}, \{y \in \mathbb{R}, y \neq 0\}, \dfrac{1}{4}, x = 4, y = 0$

c)

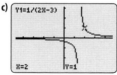

$\left\{x \in \mathbb{R}, x \neq \dfrac{3}{2}\right\}, \{y \in \mathbb{R}, y \neq 0\}, -\dfrac{1}{3}, x = \dfrac{3}{2}, y = 0$

d)

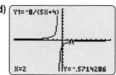

$\left\{x \in \mathbb{R}, x \neq -\dfrac{4}{5}\right\}, \{y \in \mathbb{R}, y \neq 0\}, -2, x = -\dfrac{4}{5}, y = 0$

4. a) $x = 3$, $x = -4$, $\{x \in \mathbb{R}, x \neq -4, x \neq 3\}$
b) $x = -3$, $\{x \in \mathbb{R}, x \neq -3\}$
c) $x = -6$, $x = -2$, $\{x \in \mathbb{R}, x \neq -6, x \neq -2\}$
5. a) i) $x = -5$, $x = -1$, $y = 0$ **ii)** $\dfrac{1}{5}$

iii)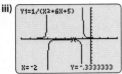

iv) increasing for $x < -5$ and $-5 < x < -3$, decreasing for $-3 < x < -1$ and $x > -1$
v) $\{x \in \mathbb{R}, x \neq -5, x \neq -1\}$, $\left\{y \in \mathbb{R}, y > 0, y \leq -\dfrac{1}{4}\right\}$

b) i) $x = 8$, $x = -3$, $y = 0$ **ii)** $-\dfrac{1}{24}$

iii)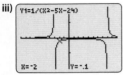

iv) increasing for $x < -3$ and $-3 < x < 2.5$, decreasing for $2.5 < x < 8$ and $x > 8$
v) $\{x \in \mathbb{R}, x \neq 8, x \neq -3\}$, $\left\{y \in \mathbb{R}, y > 0, y \leq -\dfrac{4}{121}\right\}$

c) i) $x = 3$, $y = 0$ **ii)** $-\dfrac{1}{9}$

iii)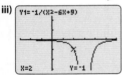

iv) increasing for $x > 3$, decreasing for $x < 3$
v) $\{x \in \mathbb{R}, x \neq 3\}$, $\{y \in \mathbb{R}, y < 0\}$

d) i) $y = 0$ **ii)** $-\dfrac{2}{5}$

iii)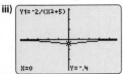

iv) increasing for $x > 0$, decreasing for $x < 0$
v) $\{x \in \mathbb{R}\}$, $\left\{y \in \mathbb{R}, -\dfrac{2}{5} \leq y < 0\right\}$

6.

Interval	Sign of Slope	Change in Slope
$x < -\dfrac{5}{2}$	$+$	$+$
$-\dfrac{5}{2} < x < -\dfrac{3}{4}$	$+$	$-$
$x = -\dfrac{3}{4}$	0	$-$
$-\dfrac{3}{4} < x < 1$	$-$	$-$
$x > 1$	$-$	$+$

7. $y = -\dfrac{1}{(x + 4)(x - 5)}$

8. a) $y = 1$ **b)** $y = -2$ **c)** $y = 1$
9. a) $x = 2$, $y = 1$, $\{x \in \mathbb{R}, x \neq 2\}$, $\{y \in \mathbb{R}, y \neq 1\}$, y-intercept 0; for $x < 0$, $f(x)$ is positive and decreasing and the slope is negative and decreasing; for $0 < x < 2$, $f(x)$ is negative and

decreasing and the slope is negative and decreasing; for $x > 2$, $f(x)$ is positive and decreasing and the slope is negative and increasing

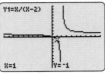

b) $x = -1$, $y = -3$, $\{x \in \mathbb{R}, x \neq -1\}$, $\{y \in \mathbb{R}, y \neq -3\}$
y-intercept 0; for $x < -1$, $f(x)$ is negative and decreasing and the slope is negative and decreasing; for $-1 < x < 0$, $f(x)$ is positive and decreasing and the slope is negative and increasing; for $x > 0$, $f(x)$ is negative and decreasing and the slope is negative and increasing

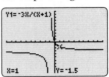

c) $x = -4$, $y = 1$, $\{x \in \mathbb{R}, x \neq -4\}$, $\{y \in \mathbb{R}, y \neq 1\}$, y-intercept $-\dfrac{1}{2}$, x-intercept 2; for $x < -4$, $f(x)$ is positive and increasing and the slope is positive and increasing; for $-4 < x < 2$, $f(x)$ is negative and increasing and the slope is positive and decreasing; for $x > 2$, $f(x)$ is positive and increasing and the slope is positive and decreasing

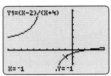

d) $x = \dfrac{1}{2}$, $y = 3$, $\left\{x \in \mathbb{R}, x \neq \dfrac{1}{2}\right\}$, $\{y \in \mathbb{R}, y \neq 3\}$; y-intercept -2, x-intercept $-\dfrac{1}{3}$; for $x < -\dfrac{1}{3}$, $f(x)$ is positive and decreasing and the slope is negative and decreasing; for $-\dfrac{1}{3} < x < \dfrac{1}{2}$, $f(x)$ is negative and decreasing and the slope is negative and decreasing; for $x > \dfrac{1}{2}$, $f(x)$ is positive and decreasing and the slope is negative and increasing

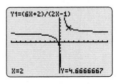

10. $f(x) = \dfrac{4x - 1}{3x + 2}$

11. a) $x = \dfrac{15}{2}$ **b)** $x = -9$ or $x = 3$
12. a) $x = 0$ or $x \doteq 0.86$ **b)** $x \doteq 40.88$ or $x \doteq 0.12$ **c)** $x \doteq 1.64$
13. a) $x < -5$ or $x > -\dfrac{7}{2}$
b) $-3 < x < -2$ or $x \geq 1$
c) $x < -4$ or $-2 < x < 5$ or $x > 6$
d) $-7 < x < -5$ or $x > -\dfrac{5}{3}$
14. a) $-4 < x < -1$ or $2 < x < 3$
b) $x < -8$ or $x > -\dfrac{1}{2}$ and $x \neq 3$

15. a)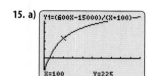

b) Profit increases as sales increase.
c) The rate of change of the profit at 100 t is 1.875 and approximately 0.208 at 500 t, so the rate of change is decreasing.

16. a) discontinuous at $\left(0, \frac{1}{5}\right)$ **b)** discontinuous at $\left(7, \frac{12}{11}\right)$

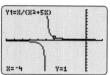 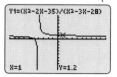

Chapter 3 Practice Test, pages 194–195

1. C
2. B
3. A
4. Answers may vary. Sample answers:
a) $y = \dfrac{1}{x + 2}$ **b)** $y = \dfrac{6}{(x + 4)(x - 3)}$
5. a) i) $\{x \in \mathbb{R}\}$, $\{y \in \mathbb{R}, -2 \le y < 0\}$ **ii)** y-intercept -2
iii) $y = 0$ **iv)** decreasing for $x < 0$, increasing for $x > 0$
b)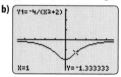

6. Yes; $\dfrac{1}{f(x)}$ will always have an asymptote at $y = 0$.

7. a) $x = -\dfrac{14}{5}$ **b)** $x = 3$

8. a) $x < -\dfrac{3}{2}, x > -\dfrac{7}{8}$ **b)** $x < -1$ or $2 < x < 5$

9. a) Answers may vary. Sample answer: $y = \dfrac{-x + 2}{2(x + 1)}$

b) Not possible.

10. a) $g = \dfrac{401\,800\,000}{d^2}$

b) 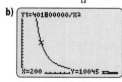   **c)** $d \doteq 8183.3$ km

11. a)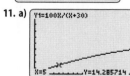

b) $\{t \in \mathbb{R}, t \ge 0\}$, $\{P \in \mathbb{R}, 0 \le P < 100\}$
c) The percent lost can get close to 100%, but not equal to 100%.

12. a)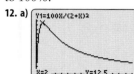

b) The power output increases from 0 Ω to 2 Ω. The power decreases from 2 Ω to 20 Ω.
c) The power is constant at $R = 2$ (not changing).

13. Answers may vary. Sample answer: $x = 0$, $y = 0$, slopes increasing and decreasing faster as n increases.
n even:
- For $x < 0$, $f(x)$ is positive and the slope is positive and increasing.
- For $x > 0$, $f(x)$ is positive and the slope is negative and increasing.

n odd:
- For $x < 0$, $f(x)$ is negative and the slope is negative and decreasing.
- For $x > 0$, $f(x)$ is positive and the slope is negative and increasing.

Chapter 1 to 3 Review, pages 196–197

1. a)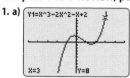

x-intercepts -1, 1, and 2; y-intercept 2

b)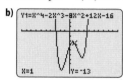

x-intercepts approximately -2.88 and 3.63; y-intercept -16
2. a) The graph extends from quadrant 2 to quadrant 1, thus, as $x \to -\infty$, $y \to \infty$, and as $x \to \infty$, $y \to \infty$.
The graph is not symmetric.
b) The graph extends from quadrant 3 to quadrant 1, thus, as $x \to -\infty$, $y \to -\infty$, and as $x \to \infty$, $y \to \infty$.
The graph is not symmetric.
3. a) i) -61 **ii)** -37 **b)** -49 approximates the instantaneous rate of change at $x = 2$.
4. a)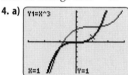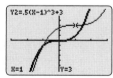

b)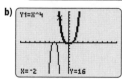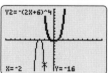

5. a)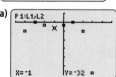

b) 4 **c)** $y = -2(x - 1)^2(x + 3)^2$
d) Answers may vary. Sample answer: Reflects and stretches the graph. Also, since the function has even degree, a negative leading coefficient means the graph extends from quadrant 3 to quadrant 4 and has at least one maximum point.
6. a) -4 **b)** 12 **c)** local minimum

7. a) maximum approximately (12.25, 9.64), minima approximately (3.14, −14.16), (26.61, −70.80)
b) between (3.14, −14.16) and (12.25, 9.64) approximately 2.61; between (12.25, 9.64), and (26.61, −70.80), approximately −5.60 **c)** $x = 32$
8. Answers may vary. Sample answers:
$y = 2x(x + 7)(x − 3)^2$; $y = -\frac{1}{3}x(x + 7)(x − 3)^2$
9. $y = k(x − 2)^2(x + 5)$. Answers may vary. Sample answers:
$y = 2(x − 2)^2(x + 5)$, y-intercept 40; $y = −3(x − 2)^2(x + 5)$, y-intercept −60
10. a) $4x^3 − 5x^2 + 6x + 2 = (2x + 1)\left(2x^2 − \frac{7}{2}x + \frac{19}{4}\right) − \frac{11}{4}$, $x \neq -\frac{1}{2}$
b) $3x^4 − 5x^2 − 28 = (x − 2)(3x^3 + 6x^2 + 7x + 14)$, $x \neq 2$
11. a) 38 **b)** $\frac{97}{9}$
12. a) No. **b)** Yes.
13. $k = -\frac{13}{2}$
14. a) $(x − 3)(x^2 + 3x + 9)$ **b)** $(x − 2)(2x^2 + 8x + 3)$
15. a) $x = −4$ or $x = 1$ or $x = 5$
b) $x = −3$ or $x = \frac{-4 − \sqrt{31}}{5}$ or $x = \frac{-4 + \sqrt{31}}{5}$
16. a) $x \leq 1$ or $x \geq 6$ **b)** $x < −3$ or $−2 < x < 2$
17. from 0 min to 10 min
18. A
19. a) $f(x) \to 0$ **b)** $f(x) \to 0$ **c)** $f(x) \to \infty$ **d)** $f(x) \to -\infty$
20. $\{x \in \mathbb{R}, x \neq −1\}$, $\{y \in \mathbb{R}, y \neq 1\}$
21. a) i) $\{x \in \mathbb{R}, x \neq 2\}$, $\{y \in \mathbb{R}, y \neq 3\}$; x-intercept $-\frac{1}{6}$, y-intercept $-\frac{1}{4}$; asymptotes $x = 2$, $y = 3$; negative slope $x < 2$, $x > 2$; decreasing $x < 2$; increasing $x > 2$
ii)
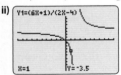
b) i) $\{x \in \mathbb{R}, x \neq −3, x \neq 3\}$, $\{y \in \mathbb{R}, y \neq 0, y \leq \frac{1}{9}, y > 0\}$; no x-intercept, y-intercept $-\frac{1}{9}$; asymptotes $x = −3$, $x = 3$, $y = 0$; positive slope $x < −3$, $−3 < x < 0$; negative slope $0 < x < 3$, $x > 3$; decreasing $0 < x < 3$, $−3 < x < 0$; increasing $x < −3$, $x > 3$
ii)
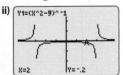
22. $f(x) = \frac{3x + 6}{x − 1}$
23. a) $x = −2.2$ **b)** $x \doteq 2.15$
24. a) $x < −2.75$ or $x > −2$ **b)** $−1 \leq x < 1$ or $x > 2$
25. a)
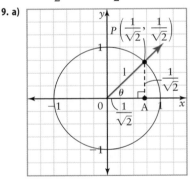
b) $\{x \in \mathbb{R}, x \geq 0\}$, $\left\{P(x) \in \mathbb{R}, -\frac{2}{3} \leq P(x) < 5\right\}$
c) The profit is always less than $5000.

26. Since t represents time, $t \geq 0$; $t \neq 10$ because the denominator cannot be zero.

CHAPTER 4

Prerequisite Skills, pages 200–201

1. a) $\cos \theta = \frac{4}{5}$, $\tan \theta = \frac{3}{4}$ **b)** $\sin \theta = -\frac{12}{13}$, $\tan \theta = -\frac{12}{5}$
c) $\sin x = \frac{7}{25}$, $\cos x = -\frac{24}{25}$ **d)** $\cos x = -\frac{15}{17}$, $\tan x = \frac{8}{15}$
2. a) 0.2588 **b)** 0.5592 **c)** 3.7321 **d)** 0.9848 **e)** −0.9205
f) 2.7475 **g)** −0.8480 **h)** 0.9781
3. a) 41° **b)** 65° **c)** 83° **d)** 117°
4. a) $\frac{1}{2}$ **b)** 3 **c)** $\frac{5}{3}$ **d)** $\frac{2}{\sqrt{3}}$
5. a) $\sec x = \frac{5}{3}$, $\cot x = \frac{3}{4}$ **b)** $\csc \theta = -\frac{13}{5}$, $\cot \theta = -\frac{12}{5}$
c) $\csc x = \frac{25}{7}$, $\sec x = -\frac{25}{24}$ **d)** $\sec \theta = -\frac{17}{8}$, $\cot \theta = \frac{8}{15}$
6. a) 1.7434 **b)** −1.2361 **c)** 2.1445 **d)** 1.1792 **e)** −1.2690
f) 1.0724 **g)** −1.5890 **h)** 1.0038
7. a) 53° **b)** 54° **c)** 18° **d)** 139°
8. a) $\sin \theta = \frac{1}{2}$, $\cos \theta = \frac{\sqrt{3}}{2}$, $\tan \theta = \frac{1}{\sqrt{3}}$
b) $\sin \theta = \frac{1}{\sqrt{2}}$, $\cos \theta = \frac{1}{\sqrt{2}}$, $\tan \theta = 1$
c) $\sin \theta = \frac{\sqrt{3}}{2}$, $\cos \theta = \frac{1}{2}$, $\tan \theta = \sqrt{3}$
9. a)
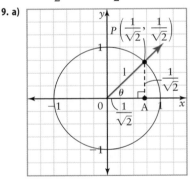
b) $x = \frac{1}{\sqrt{2}}$, $y = \frac{1}{\sqrt{2}}$ **c)** $\csc 45° = \sqrt{2}$, $\sec 45° = \sqrt{2}$, $\cot 45° = 1$
10. $\sin 135° = \frac{1}{\sqrt{2}}$, $\cos 135° = -\frac{1}{\sqrt{2}}$, $\tan 135° = −1$,
$\csc 135° = \sqrt{2}$, $\sec 135° = -\sqrt{2}$, $\cot 135° = −1$,
$\sin 225° = -\frac{1}{\sqrt{2}}$, $\cos 225° = -\frac{1}{\sqrt{2}}$, $\tan 225° = 1$,
$\csc 225° = -\sqrt{2}$, $\sec 225° = -\sqrt{2}$, $\cot 225° = 1$,
$\sin 315° = -\frac{1}{\sqrt{2}}$, $\cos 315° = \frac{1}{\sqrt{2}}$, $\tan 315° = −1$,
$\csc 315° = -\sqrt{2}$, $\sec 315° = \sqrt{2}$, $\cot 315° = −1$
11. a) 5 **b)** 13 **c)** 17 **d)** 10
12. a) $a^2 + 2ab + b^2$ **b)** $c^2 − d^2$ **c)** $6x^2 − xy − 2y^2$
d) $\sin^2 x + 2 \sin x \cos y + \cos^2 y$

4.1 Radian Measure, pages 208–210

1. a) $\frac{\pi}{3}$ **b)** $\frac{\pi}{2}$ **c)** $\frac{2\pi}{3}$ **d)** $\frac{5\pi}{6}$
2. a) $\frac{\pi}{12}$ **b)** $\frac{\pi}{18}$ **c)** $\frac{\pi}{24}$ **d)** $\frac{\pi}{36}$

3. a) $\dfrac{\pi}{2}$ **b)** $\dfrac{3\pi}{4}$ **c)** π **d)** $\dfrac{5\pi}{4}$

4. a) $\dfrac{\pi}{8}$ **b)** $\dfrac{\pi}{12}$ **c)** $\dfrac{\pi}{20}$ **d)** $\dfrac{\pi}{60}$

5. a) $\dfrac{2\pi}{9}$ **b)** $\dfrac{\pi}{18}$ **c)** $\dfrac{7\pi}{4}$ **d)** $\dfrac{7\pi}{6}$ **e)** $\dfrac{5\pi}{3}$ **f)** $\dfrac{5\pi}{12}$

6. a) 0.40 **b)** 0.89 **c)** 1.43 **d)** 2.23 **e)** 4.19 **f)** 5.76

7. a) 36° **b)** 20° **c)** 75° **d)** 50° **e)** 135° **f)** 270°

8. a) 134.1° **b)** 179.9° **c)** 301.9° **d)** 431.4° **e)** 39.0° **f)** 98.5°

9. 118.75 cm

10. a) 720°/s **b)** 4π rad/s

11. $\dfrac{\pi}{5}, \dfrac{2\pi}{5}, \dfrac{2\pi}{5}$

12. Answers may vary depending on speed.

13. a) 0.000 291 **b)** 1862 m **c)** Answers may vary.

14. b) 8 km

15. 0.009 053 rad, 0.5°

16. 0.5 rad, 28.6°

17. 400π rad/s, approximately 1256.6 rad/s

18. a) $\dfrac{80\pi}{3}$ m **b)** 83.8 m

19. a) It must follow the rotation of Earth. **b)** 24 h
c) 0.000 023π rad/s **d)** It is the same.

20. a) 100 grad **b)** $\dfrac{3\pi}{4}$

22. approximately 3076 m/s.

23. Using the modern definition of a nautical mile, 1852 m, the knots are approximately 15.4 m apart.

24. the same

25. a) $A = \dfrac{1}{2}r^2\theta$ **b)** 45.24 cm²

26. a) $A\!\left(1, \dfrac{\pi}{3}\right)$, $B\!\left(2, \dfrac{\pi}{4}\right)$, $C\!\left(2, \dfrac{7\pi}{4}\right)$, $D\!\left(2, \dfrac{3\pi}{2}\right)$

b) i) $\left(\sqrt{2}, \dfrac{\pi}{4}\right)$ **ii)** $(5, 2.21)$ **iii)** $\left(5, \dfrac{3\pi}{2}\right)$

4.2 Trigonometric Ratios and Special Angles, pages 216–219

1. a) i) 0.4226 **ii)** 0.3090 **iii)** −2.1445 **iv)** 0.2588 **b) i)** 0.4223
ii) 0.3087 **iii)** −2.1452 **iv)** 0.2586 **c)** The degree measures are approximately the same as the radian measures.

2. a) i) 0.9356 **ii)** −0.8187 **iii)** −0.0918 **iv)** 0.0076
b) i) 0.9336 **ii)** −0.8192 **iii)** −0.0875 **iv)** 0.0000
c) The degree measures are approximately the same as the radian measures.

3. a) 0.7071 **b)** 0.9010 **c)** −0.5774 **d)** 0.4142

4. a) 3.8637 **b)** 1.6243 **c)** −0.6745 **d)** −2.6695

5. a) 1.2123 **b)** −3.7599 **c)** 14.5955 **d)** 1.0582

6. a) −2.0000 **b)** 1.5270 **c)** −0.3249 **d)** −2.7475

7. a) $\sin\dfrac{2\pi}{3} = \dfrac{\sqrt{3}}{2}$, $\cos\dfrac{2\pi}{3} = -\dfrac{1}{2}$, $\tan\dfrac{2\pi}{3} = -\sqrt{3}$

b) $\sin\dfrac{5\pi}{6} = \dfrac{1}{2}$, $\cos\dfrac{5\pi}{6} = -\dfrac{\sqrt{3}}{2}$, $\tan\dfrac{5\pi}{6} = -\dfrac{1}{\sqrt{3}}$

c) $\sin\dfrac{3\pi}{2} = -1$, $\cos\dfrac{3\pi}{2} = 0$, $\tan\dfrac{3\pi}{2} =$ undefined

d) $\sin\dfrac{7\pi}{4} = -\dfrac{1}{\sqrt{2}}$, $\cos\dfrac{7\pi}{4} = \dfrac{1}{\sqrt{2}}$, $\tan\dfrac{7\pi}{4} = -1$

8. a) $\sin\dfrac{7\pi}{6} = -\dfrac{1}{2}$, $\cos\dfrac{7\pi}{6} = -\dfrac{\sqrt{3}}{2}$, $\tan\dfrac{7\pi}{6} = \dfrac{1}{\sqrt{3}}$,

$\csc\dfrac{7\pi}{6} = -2$, $\sec\dfrac{7\pi}{6} = -\dfrac{2}{\sqrt{3}}$, $\cot\dfrac{7\pi}{6} = \sqrt{3}$

b) $\sin\dfrac{4\pi}{3} = -\dfrac{\sqrt{3}}{2}$, $\cos\dfrac{4\pi}{3} = -\dfrac{1}{2}$, $\tan\dfrac{4\pi}{3} = \sqrt{3}$,

$\csc\dfrac{4\pi}{3} = -\dfrac{2}{\sqrt{3}}$, $\sec\dfrac{4\pi}{3} = -2$, $\cot\dfrac{4\pi}{3} = \dfrac{1}{\sqrt{3}}$

c) $\sin\dfrac{5\pi}{4} = -\dfrac{1}{\sqrt{2}}$, $\cos\dfrac{5\pi}{4} = -\dfrac{1}{\sqrt{2}}$, $\tan\dfrac{5\pi}{4} = 1$,

$\csc\dfrac{5\pi}{4} = -\sqrt{2}$, $\sec\dfrac{5\pi}{4} = -\sqrt{2}$, $\cot\dfrac{5\pi}{4} = 1$

d) $\sin\pi = 0$, $\cos\pi = -1$, $\tan\pi = 0$, $\csc\pi =$ undefined,
$\sec\pi = -1$, $\cot\pi =$ undefined

9. a) $20(\sqrt{2} - 1)$ m **b)** $20(\sqrt{3} - \sqrt{2})$ m **c)** 8.3 m horizontally,
6.4 m vertically

10. a) $(20\sqrt{2} - 30)$ m
b) The kite moves farther from Sarah, since the horizontal
distance at $\dfrac{\pi}{3}$ is now greater than at $\dfrac{\pi}{4}$.

c) $(30\sqrt{3} - 20\sqrt{2})$ m; the altitude increases since the
vertical distance of the kite at $\dfrac{\pi}{3}$ has increased.

d) 1.7 m horizontally, 23.7 m vertically

11. a) $\dfrac{\sqrt{2}}{2}$ **b)** 2

12. a) $\dfrac{\sqrt{6}}{6}$ **b)** 2

13. a) $30\sqrt{2}$ m **b)** $15\sqrt{6}$ m

14. a) $\dfrac{\pi}{2}$ **b)** $\dfrac{2\pi}{3}$ **c)** 9:00 **d)** 11:00 **e)** $\dfrac{5\pi}{4}$

15. b) 0.500π radians **d)** The values are approximately the same.

16. i) 0 **ii)** 1

17. i) 1 **ii)** 0

18. i) 0 **ii)** undefined

21. a) $\sin(150 \text{ grads}) = \dfrac{1}{\sqrt{2}}$, $\cos(150 \text{ grads}) = -\dfrac{1}{\sqrt{2}}$,

$\tan(150 \text{ grads}) = -1$, $\csc(150 \text{ grads}) = \sqrt{2}$,

$\sec(150 \text{ grads}) = -\sqrt{2}$, $\cot(150 \text{ grads}) = -1$
b) Answers may vary.

22. d) $0.00 \le x \le 0.31$ **e)** $0.000 \le x \le 0.144$

23. Answers may vary.

24. A

25. B

4.3 Equivalent Trigonometric Expressions, pages 225–227

1. $\sin\dfrac{\pi}{6} = \cos\left(\dfrac{\pi}{2} - \dfrac{\pi}{6}\right)$

2. $\cos\dfrac{\pi}{4} = \sin\left(\dfrac{\pi}{2} - \dfrac{\pi}{4}\right)$

3. $-\sin\dfrac{\pi}{6} = \cos\left(\dfrac{\pi}{2} + \dfrac{\pi}{6}\right)$

4. $-\csc\dfrac{\pi}{4} = \sec\left(\dfrac{\pi}{2} + \dfrac{\pi}{4}\right)$

5. $\dfrac{5\pi}{14}$

6. $\dfrac{\pi}{18}$

7. $\dfrac{2\pi}{9}$

8. $\dfrac{3\pi}{7}$

9. a) 0.6549 **b)** 0.6549

10. a) 0.8391 **b)** −0.8391

11. 0.12

12. 0.93

13. 2.32

14. 2.91

15. $\sin(\pi - x) = \sin x$, $\cos(\pi - x) = -\cos x$,
$\tan(\pi - x) = -\tan x$, $\csc(\pi - x) = \csc x$,
$\sec(\pi - x) = -\sec x$, $\cot(\pi - x) = -\cot x$

16. $\sin(\pi + x) = -\sin x$, $\cos(\pi + x) = -\cos x$,
$\tan(\pi + x) = \tan x$, $\csc(\pi + x) = -\csc x$,
$\sec(\pi + x) = -\sec x$, $\cot(\pi + x) = \cot x$

17. $\sin\left(\dfrac{3\pi}{2} - x\right) = -\cos x$, $\cos\left(\dfrac{3\pi}{2} - x\right) = -\sin x$,
$\tan\left(\dfrac{3\pi}{2} - x\right) = \cot x$, $\csc\left(\dfrac{3\pi}{2} - x\right) = -\sec x$,
$\sec\left(\dfrac{3\pi}{2} - x\right) = -\csc x$, $\cot\left(\dfrac{3\pi}{2} - x\right) = \tan x$

18. $\sin\left(\dfrac{3\pi}{2} + x\right) = -\cos x$, $\cos\left(\dfrac{3\pi}{2} + x\right) = \sin x$,
$\tan\left(\dfrac{3\pi}{2} + x\right) = -\cot x$, $\csc\left(\dfrac{3\pi}{2} + x\right) = -\sec x$,
$\sec\left(\dfrac{3\pi}{2} + x\right) = \csc x$, $\cot\left(\dfrac{3\pi}{2} + x\right) = -\tan x$

19. $\sin(2\pi - x) = -\sin x$, $\cos(2\pi - x) = \cos x$,
$\tan(2\pi - x) = -\tan x$, $\csc(2\pi - x) = -\csc x$,
$\sec(2\pi - x) = \sec x$, $\cot(2\pi - x) = -\cot x$

20. Answers may vary.

21. Answers may vary. Sample answer: $-\cos\dfrac{21\pi}{26}$

22. a) $r = \dfrac{v^2}{g}\tan\left(\dfrac{\pi}{2} - \theta\right) = \dfrac{v^2}{g}\cot\theta = \dfrac{v^2}{g\tan\theta}$ **b)** 255 m

24. Answers may vary. Sample answer: $\dfrac{\pi}{16}$

25. Answers may vary. Sample answer: $\dfrac{\pi}{2}$

26. Answers may vary.

28. a) i) $\left(1, \dfrac{\pi}{3}\right)$ **ii)** $\left(5, -\dfrac{\pi}{6}\right)$

b) i) $\left(\dfrac{3\sqrt{3}}{2}, \dfrac{3}{2}\right)$ **ii)** $(-4, 0)$

c) i) $\dfrac{\pi}{6} + 2\pi k$, $k \in \mathbb{Z}$ **ii)** $-\dfrac{\pi}{3} + 2\pi k$, $k \in \mathbb{Z}$

4.4 Compound Angle Formulas, pages 232–235

1. a) $\sin\left(\dfrac{\pi}{4} + \dfrac{\pi}{12}\right)$; $\dfrac{\sqrt{3}}{2}$ **b)** $\sin\left(\dfrac{\pi}{4} - \dfrac{\pi}{12}\right)$; $\dfrac{1}{2}$

c) $\cos\left(\dfrac{\pi}{4} + \dfrac{\pi}{12}\right)$; $\dfrac{1}{2}$ **d)** $\cos\left(\dfrac{\pi}{4} - \dfrac{\pi}{12}\right)$; $\dfrac{\sqrt{3}}{2}$

2. a) $\sin\left(\dfrac{3\pi}{5} + \dfrac{\pi}{15}\right)$; $\dfrac{\sqrt{3}}{2}$ **b)** $\sin\left(\dfrac{7\pi}{5} - \dfrac{\pi}{15}\right)$; $-\dfrac{\sqrt{3}}{2}$

c) $\cos\left(\dfrac{2\pi}{9} + \dfrac{5\pi}{18}\right)$; 0 **d)** $\cos\left(\dfrac{10\pi}{9} - \dfrac{5\pi}{18}\right)$; $-\dfrac{\sqrt{3}}{2}$

3. a) $\dfrac{\sqrt{3} + 1}{2\sqrt{2}}$ **b)** $\dfrac{1 - \sqrt{3}}{2\sqrt{2}}$ **c)** $\dfrac{-1 + \sqrt{3}}{2\sqrt{2}}$ **d)** $\dfrac{\sqrt{3} + 1}{2\sqrt{2}}$

4. a) $\dfrac{\sqrt{3} + 1}{2\sqrt{2}}$ **b)** $\dfrac{\sqrt{3} + 1}{2\sqrt{2}}$

5. a) $\dfrac{-1 - \sqrt{3}}{2\sqrt{2}}$ **b)** $\dfrac{-1 + \sqrt{3}}{2\sqrt{2}}$

6. a) $\dfrac{1 - \sqrt{3}}{2\sqrt{2}}$ **b)** $\dfrac{1 - \sqrt{3}}{2\sqrt{2}}$

7. a) $\dfrac{-\sqrt{3} - 1}{2\sqrt{2}}$ **b)** $\dfrac{1 + \sqrt{3}}{2\sqrt{2}}$

8. a) $\cos x = \dfrac{4}{5}$ **b)** $\sin y = \dfrac{12}{13}$

9. a) $\dfrac{63}{65}$ **b)** $-\dfrac{33}{65}$ **c)** $-\dfrac{16}{65}$ **d)** $\dfrac{56}{65}$

10. a) $\cos x = -\dfrac{12}{13}$ **b)** $\sin y = \dfrac{4}{5}$

11. a) $-\dfrac{33}{65}$ **b)** $\dfrac{63}{65}$ **c)** $-\dfrac{56}{65}$ **d)** $-\dfrac{16}{65}$

12. $\sin 2\theta = \sin(\theta + \theta)$

$= \sin\theta\cos\theta + \cos\theta\sin\theta$
$= 2\sin\theta\cos\theta$

13. $\cos 2x = \cos(x + x)$
$= \cos x\cos x - \sin x\sin x$
$= \cos^2 x - \sin^2 x$

15. a) $\dfrac{527}{625}$ **b)** $-\dfrac{336}{625}$ **c)** 2.86

16. For question 12:

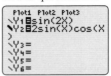

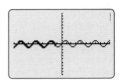

For question 13:

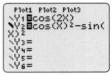

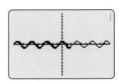

For question 14a):

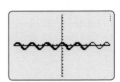

For question 14b):

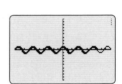

17. a) $h_1 = 12\sin x$

18. a) 66.5°; Answers may vary. The Sun is not seen at all at this latitude.

b) $-23.5°$; Answers may vary. The negative sign represents a latitude in the southern hemisphere. The Sun appears directly overhead at noon.

20. a) $\tan(x + y) = \dfrac{\sin x\cos y + \cos x\sin y}{\cos x\cos y - \sin x\sin y}$

c) Both sides of the equation equal $-\dfrac{\sqrt{3}}{3}$.

21. b) Both sides of the equation equal $\dfrac{\sqrt{3}}{3}$.

22. a) $\tan 2x = \dfrac{2\tan x}{1 - \tan^2 x}$

b)

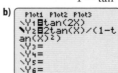

c) Both sides of the formula equal approximately 1.7036.

23. a) Both sides of the formula equal $\sqrt{3}$.

b) $\sin x - \sin y = 2\sin\left(\dfrac{x - y}{2}\right)\cos\left(\dfrac{x + y}{2}\right)$

25. 0.71 rad

27. a)

θ	0.01	0.05	0.10	0.15	0.25	0.35
$\theta - \dfrac{\theta^3}{6}$	0.01000	0.04998	0.09983	0.14944	0.24740	0.34285
$\sin\theta$	0.01000	0.04998	0.09983	0.14944	0.24740	0.34290

b)

θ	0.01	0.05	0.10	0.15	0.25	0.35
$1 - \dfrac{\theta^2}{2}$	0.99995	0.99875	0.99500	0.98875	0.96875	0.93875
$\cos\theta$	0.99995	0.99875	0.99500	0.98877	0.96891	0.93937

28. a) $\sin\theta = \theta - \dfrac{\theta^3}{6}$ **b)** $\cos\theta = 1 - \dfrac{\theta^2}{2}$ **c)** $\tan\theta = \theta + \dfrac{\theta^3}{3}$

4.5 Prove Trigonometric Identities, pages 240–241

9. b)

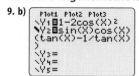

14. Answers may vary.
17. a) Yes, the graphs appear to be the same. **b)** identity
18. a) Answers may vary. Graphs are different.
b) While the left side results in both positive and negative values, the right side is restricted to positive values only.
20. a) Yes, the graphs appear to be the same. **b)** identity

22. $\tan 2x = \dfrac{2\tan x}{1 - \tan^2 x}$

Chapter 4 Review, pages 244–245

1. a) 0.58 **b)** 2.41 **c)** 4.40 **d)** 6.06
2. a) 71.0° **b)** 161.6° **c)** 273.9° **d)** 395.9°
3. a) $\dfrac{5\pi}{12}$ **b)** $\dfrac{\pi}{9}$ **c)** $\dfrac{\pi}{15}$ **d)** $\dfrac{\pi}{20}$
4. a) 72° **b)** 80° **c)** 105° **d)** 110°
5. a) 72°/s **b)** $\dfrac{2\pi}{5}$ rad/s

6. a), b)

Revolutions per Minute	16 rpm	$33\frac{1}{3}$ rpm	45 rpm	78 rpm
Degrees per Second	96°/s	200°/s	270°/s	468°/s
Radians per Second	$\dfrac{8\pi}{15}$ rad/s	$\dfrac{10\pi}{9}$ rad/s	$\dfrac{3\pi}{2}$ rad/s	$\dfrac{39\pi}{15}$ rad/s

7. $\sin\dfrac{4\pi}{11} \doteq 0.9096$, $\cos\dfrac{4\pi}{11} \doteq 0.4154$, $\tan\dfrac{4\pi}{11} \doteq 2.1897$,
$\csc\dfrac{4\pi}{11} \doteq 1.0993$, $\sec\dfrac{4\pi}{11} \doteq 2.4072$, $\cot\dfrac{4\pi}{11} \doteq 0.4567$

8. a) 2 **b)** $\dfrac{\sqrt{2}+1}{\sqrt{2}}$
9. $\dfrac{15\sqrt{3}}{4}$ m
10. $\dfrac{3\pi}{14}$
11. $\dfrac{\pi}{18}$
12. a) 5.6713; $\cot\dfrac{\pi}{18} = \cot\left(\dfrac{\pi}{2} - \dfrac{4\pi}{9}\right) = \tan\dfrac{4\pi}{9}$
b) 5.6713; $\tan\dfrac{13\pi}{9} = \tan\left(\dfrac{3\pi}{2} - \dfrac{\pi}{18}\right) = \cot\dfrac{\pi}{18}$
13. $\dfrac{17\pi}{22}$
14. a) $\sin\left(\dfrac{5\pi}{12} + \dfrac{\pi}{4}\right)$; $\dfrac{\sqrt{3}}{2}$ **b)** $\sin\left(\dfrac{5\pi}{12} - \dfrac{\pi}{4}\right)$; $\dfrac{1}{2}$

c) $\cos\left(\dfrac{5\pi}{12} + \dfrac{\pi}{4}\right)$; $-\dfrac{1}{2}$ **d)** $\cos\left(\dfrac{5\pi}{12} - \dfrac{\pi}{4}\right)$; $\dfrac{\sqrt{3}}{2}$
15. a) $\cos x = \dfrac{3}{5}$ **b)** $\sin y = \dfrac{24}{25}$ **c)** $\dfrac{4}{5}$
16. a) $\dfrac{527}{625}$ **b)** $\dfrac{336}{625}$
17. $\dfrac{-1 - \sqrt{3}}{2\sqrt{2}}$
19. b)

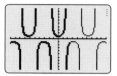

21. a) No; the graphs are not the same for all values.
b) Rewrite $3x$ as $2x + x$. Then, use the addition formula for cosine to expand $\cos(2x + x)$. Next, apply the appropriate double angle formulas and simplify.
22. Not an identity. Let $x = 0$; L.S. $\neq$ R.S.

Chapter 4 Practice Test, pages 246–247

1. B
2. C
3. C
4. D
5. B
6. C
7. A
8. a) 13°/day, 0.23 rad/day **b)** 88 471 km/day
9. $\dfrac{\sqrt{3}}{2}$
10. a) $\dfrac{80}{\sqrt{6}}$ m **b)** 32.7 m
11. a) 0.3420; $\sin\dfrac{\pi}{9} = \sin\left(\dfrac{\pi}{2} - \dfrac{7\pi}{18}\right) = \cos\dfrac{7\pi}{18}$
b) 0.3420; $\sin\dfrac{8\pi}{9} = \sin\left(\dfrac{\pi}{2} + \dfrac{7\pi}{18}\right) = \cos\dfrac{7\pi}{18}$
12. a) $\dfrac{-\sqrt{3} - 1}{2\sqrt{2}}$
13. a) $\cos x = -\dfrac{24}{25}$ **b)** $\sin y = \dfrac{12}{13}$ **c)** $-\dfrac{36}{325}$
14. Yes; the engine's maximum velocity (293.2 rad/s) is slower than the maximum velocity of the propeller (300 rad/s).
15. $\sqrt{5000 + 2500\sqrt{3}}$ km
18. Answers may vary. Sample answer: Let $x = 0$ and $y = \dfrac{\pi}{2}$.
20. $\dfrac{2.4(\sqrt{3} - 1)}{\sqrt{3}}$ m
21. a) $\dfrac{\pi}{2}$ **b)** $A\left(\dfrac{\pi}{3}, 0.5\right)$, $B\left(\dfrac{5\pi}{3}, 0.5\right)$; $\cos x = \cos(2\pi - x)$
c) $\cos x = -\sin\left(\dfrac{3\pi}{2} - x\right)$
d) No. An identity must be proven algebraically.

CHAPTER 5

Prerequisite Skills, pages 250–251
1. a) 0.5878 **b)** 0.9659 **c)** -5.6713 **d)** -0.4142
2. a) 5.9108 **b)** 32.4765 **c)** 0.3773 **d)** -1.4479
3. a) $-\dfrac{1}{\sqrt{2}}$ **b)** $\dfrac{\sqrt{3}}{2}$ **c)** -1 **d)** $\dfrac{1}{2}$ **e)** $\dfrac{1}{2}$ **f)** $\sqrt{3}$
4. a) $-\dfrac{2}{\sqrt{3}}$ **b)** $-\dfrac{2}{\sqrt{3}}$ **c)** -1 **d)** 1 **e)** 0 **f)** $\sqrt{2}$

5.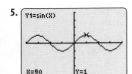

6.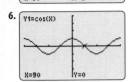

7. The graphs of sine and cosine are periodic because they repeat a pattern of y-values at regular intervals of their domain.
8. a) amplitude 3, period 180°, phase shift 30° to the right, vertical translation 1 unit downward **b)** maximum 2, minimum -4 **c)** 39.7°, 110.3°, 219.7° **d)** -3.6
9. a) amplitude 2, period 360°, phase shift 90° to the left, vertical translation 1 unit upward **b)** maximum 3, minimum -1 **c)** 30°, 150°, 390° **d)** 1
10. a) 31.3° **b)** 141.3° **c)** 74.3° **d)** 27.9°
11. a) 0.2 **b)** 2.3 **c)** 0.9 **d)** 0.2
12. a) $x = 1$, $x = -2$ **b)** $y = 0$
c)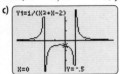

13. a) 3; the function is linear, so the rate of change is the slope of the line. **b)** same
14. 14.4 km/h
15. a) 17 m/s **b)** 15 m/s **c)** the speed at 0.5 s

5.1 Graphs of Sine, Cosine, and Tangent Functions, pages 258–260

1. a) maxima $\left(-\dfrac{3\pi}{2}, 5\right)$, $\left(\dfrac{\pi}{2}, 5\right)$;
minima $\left(-\dfrac{\pi}{2}, 3\right)$, $\left(\dfrac{3\pi}{2}, 3\right)$
b) maxima $(-2\pi, -4)$, $(0, -4)$, $(2\pi, -4)$; minima $(-\pi, -6)$, $(\pi, -6)$
c) maxima $\left(-\dfrac{3\pi}{2}, -1\right)$, $\left(\dfrac{\pi}{2}, -1\right)$;
minima $\left(-\dfrac{\pi}{2}, -3\right)$, $\left(\dfrac{3\pi}{2}, -3\right)$
d) maxima $(0, 2)$, $(2\pi, 2)$, $(-2\pi, 2)$; minima $(\pi, 0)$, $(-\pi, 0)$

2. a) 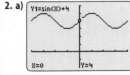 **b)**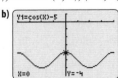
c) 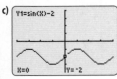 **d)**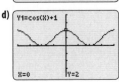

3. a) $y = 3 \sin x$ **b)** $y = 5 \cos x$ **c)** $y = -4 \sin x$ **d)** $y = -2 \cos x$

4. a) 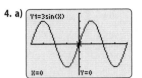 **b)**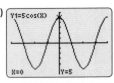
c) 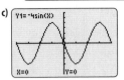 **d)**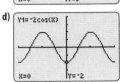

5. a) $y = \sin\left(x + \dfrac{\pi}{3}\right)$ **b)** $y = \cos\left(x - \dfrac{5\pi}{6}\right)$ **c)** $y = \sin\left(x + \dfrac{3\pi}{4}\right)$
d) $y = \cos\left(x - \dfrac{4\pi}{3}\right)$

6. a) 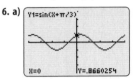 **b)**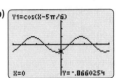
c) 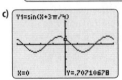 **d)**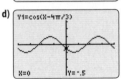

7. a) $y = \sin 4x$ **b)** $y = \cos \dfrac{4}{3}x$ **c)** $y = \sin \dfrac{1}{3}x$ **d)** $y = \cos 2x$

8. a) 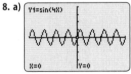 **b)**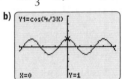
c) 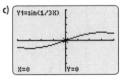 **d)**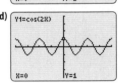

9. a) $y = 3 \sin 2x$
b) Window variables: $x \in [0, 2\pi]$, Xscl $\dfrac{\pi}{2}$, $y \in [-4, 4]$
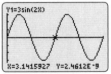

10. a) 5 **b)** 2 units upward
c) Window variables: $x \in [0, 4\pi]$, Xscl $\dfrac{\pi}{2}$, $y \in [-4, 8]$
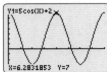

11. a) $\frac{\pi}{2}$ **b)** $\frac{\pi}{6}$ rad to the left **c)** $y = \sin\left[4\left(x + \frac{\pi}{6}\right)\right]$

d) Window variables: $x \in \left[-\frac{\pi}{6}, \frac{5\pi}{6}\right]$, Xscl $\frac{\pi}{4}$, $y \in [-4, 4]$

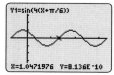

12. a) $\frac{1}{440}$ **b)** 880π

13. a) 120 **b)** $\frac{1}{60}$ **c)** $y = 120 \sin 120\pi x$

d) Window variables: $x \in \left[0, \frac{1}{30}\right]$, Xscl $\frac{1}{120}$, $y \in [-150, 150]$, Yscl 50

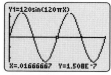

14. a) Odd. The graph of $y = \sin(-x)$ is equivalent to the graph of $y = -\sin x$.
b) Even. The graph of $y = \cos(-x)$ is equivalent to the graph of $y = \cos x$.
c) Odd. The graph of $y = \tan(-x)$ is equivalent to the graph of $y = -\tan x$.
15. Answers may vary.
16. g) For positive x_A, the amplitude gets larger as x_A gets larger. For negative x_A, the amplitude gets larger as x_A gets larger, but the graph of $y = \sin x$ is reflected in the x-axis.
h) The amplitude range changes.
17. a) $a = \frac{3}{2}$ **b)** $c = \frac{5}{2}$ **c)** The period is 60 s. **d)** $k = \frac{\pi}{30}$

18. a) $d = 0.6\sin\left(\frac{2\pi}{3}t\right)$
b) Window variables: $x \in [0, 6]$, $y \in [-1, 1]$

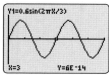

c) The waves will be closer together. The equation becomes $d = 0.6 \sin \pi t$.

20. a) Answers may vary. **b)**

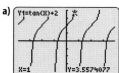

c) Yes; it passes the vertical line test.
d) Even; it is symmetric about the y-axis.
21. Window variables: $x \in \left[-\frac{47\pi}{24}, \frac{47\pi}{24}\right]$, Xscl $\frac{\pi}{2}$, $y \in [-4, 4]$

a) 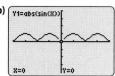 **b)**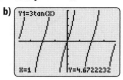

c) 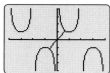 **d)**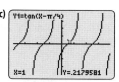

22. a) 3
b) Window variables: $x \in [-3\pi, 3\pi]$, Xscl $\frac{\pi}{2}$, $y \in [-2, 2]$

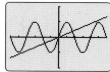

23. a) $\frac{\pi}{3}$ **b)** $\frac{\pi}{6}$ **c)** $\frac{\pi}{4}$ **d)** $\frac{3\pi}{4}$
24. a) i) $r = 2$ **ii)** $r = \dfrac{5}{3\cos\theta + 4\sin\theta}$ **iii)** $r = 4\sin\theta + 1$
b) i) $x^2 + y^2 = 36$ **ii)** $x^2 + y^2 = 3x$ **iii)** $x^2 + y^2 = 2x + 2y$

5.2 Graphs of Reciprocal Trigonometric Functions, pages 267–269

1. $x \doteq 0.20, x \doteq 2.94$
2. $x \doteq 1.05, x \doteq 5.24$
3. $x \doteq 2.90, x \doteq 6.04$
4. a) The cosecant function is the reciprocal of the sine function and $\sin^{-1}$ is the opposite operation of sine.
b) $\csc\dfrac{1}{\sqrt{2}} \doteq 1.5393$, $\sin^{-1}\left(\dfrac{1}{\sqrt{2}}\right) = \dfrac{\pi}{4}$
5. a) The secant function is the reciprocal function of the cosine function and $\cos^{-1}$ is the opposite operation of cosine.
b) $\sec\dfrac{\sqrt{3}}{2} \doteq 1.5425$, $\cos^{-1}\left(\dfrac{\sqrt{3}}{2}\right) = \dfrac{\pi}{6}$
6. a) The cotangent function is the reciprocal of the tangent function and $\tan^{-1}$ is the opposite operation of tangent.
b) $\cot 1 \doteq 0.6421$, $\tan^{-1}(1) = \dfrac{\pi}{4}$
7. a) $\sec x = \csc\left(x + \dfrac{\pi}{2}\right)$ or $\sec x = \csc\left(x - \dfrac{3\pi}{2}\right)$
b) Answers may vary. Yes; the phase shift can be increased or decreased by one period, 2π.
8. a) Window variables: $x \in [-2\pi, 2\pi]$, Xscl $\frac{\pi}{2}$, $y \in [-4, 4]$

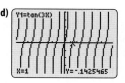

b) $x \doteq 0.944$ or $x \doteq -0.944$
9. b) The range is $0 \le x \le \tan^{-1}(2)$ or approximately $0 \le x \le 1.107$. **c)** Assuming the lifeguard swims a portion of the distance, $w \le d \le \sqrt{5}w$.
d) Answers may vary. **e)** Answers may vary. The total distance will be shorter.
10. b) 1.15 m
c)

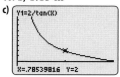

d) As x approaches 0, d approaches infinity. This means that the angle of elevation on the summer solstice approaches the horizon and so the length of the awning approaches infinity. As x approaches $\frac{\pi}{2}$, d approaches 0. This means that the angle of elevation on the summer solstice approaches an overhead location and the length of the awning approaches 0.

11. a) $x \doteq 0.70$ **b)** No; $x \doteq 0.40$. **c)** No; $x \doteq 1.28$.

12. a) Answers may vary. Sample answer: $\csc^2 x - 1 = \cot^2 x$.

13. a) $d = 500 \sec x$ **b)** $d = \dfrac{1000\sqrt{2}}{\sqrt{3} - 1}$

c)

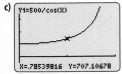

15. a) Window variables: $x \in \left[-\dfrac{47\pi}{24}, \dfrac{47\pi}{24}\right]$, Xscl $\dfrac{\pi}{2}$, $y \in [-4, 4]$

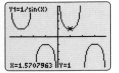

b) i)

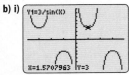
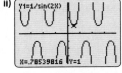

iii)
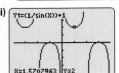
iv)
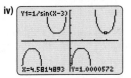

16. Window variables: $x \in \left[-\dfrac{47\pi}{24}, \dfrac{47\pi}{24}\right]$, Xscl $\dfrac{\pi}{2}$, $y \in [-4, 4]$

a)
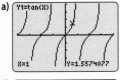
b) i)
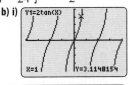

ii)
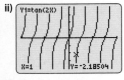
iii)
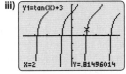

iv)
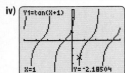

17. b) No; the equation is only true for $x \in \left[-\dfrac{\pi}{2}, \dfrac{\pi}{2}\right]$.

18. $\dfrac{3}{5}$

19. a)

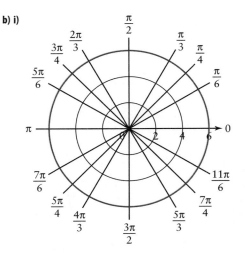

θ	$r = 2\cos\theta$	(r, θ)
0	2	$(2, 0)$
$\dfrac{\pi}{6}$	$\sqrt{3}$	$\left(\sqrt{3}, \dfrac{\pi}{6}\right)$
$\dfrac{\pi}{4}$	$\dfrac{2}{\sqrt{2}}$	$\left(\dfrac{2}{\sqrt{2}}, \dfrac{\pi}{4}\right)$
$\dfrac{\pi}{3}$	1	$\left(1, \dfrac{\pi}{3}\right)$
$\dfrac{\pi}{2}$	0	$\left(0, \dfrac{\pi}{2}\right)$
$\dfrac{2\pi}{3}$	-1	$\left(-1, \dfrac{2\pi}{3}\right)$
$\dfrac{3\pi}{4}$	$-\dfrac{2}{\sqrt{2}}$	$\left(-\dfrac{2}{\sqrt{2}}, \dfrac{3\pi}{4}\right)$
$\dfrac{5\pi}{6}$	$-\sqrt{3}$	$\left(-\sqrt{3}, \dfrac{5\pi}{6}\right)$
π	-2	$(-2, \pi)$

b) i)

ii)

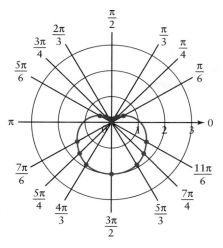

iii)

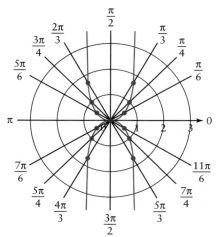

5.3 Sinusoidal Functions of the Form
$f(x) = a \sin[k(x - d)] + c$ and $f(x) = a \cos[k(x - d)] + c$,
pages 275–279

1. a) amplitude 5, period $\dfrac{2\pi}{3}$

Window variables: $x \in [-2\pi, 2\pi]$, Xscl $\dfrac{\pi}{2}$, $y \in [-6, 6]$

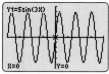

b) amplitude 3, period $\dfrac{3\pi}{2}$

Window variables: $x \in [-2\pi, 2\pi]$, Xscl $\dfrac{\pi}{2}$, $y \in [-4, 4]$

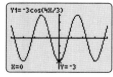

c) amplitude 3, period 2
Window variables: $x \in [-2\pi, 2\pi]$, Xscl $\dfrac{\pi}{2}$, $y \in [-4, 4]$

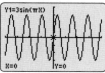

d) amplitude $\dfrac{1}{2}$, period 8π
Window variables: $x \in [-2\pi, 2\pi]$, Xscl $\dfrac{\pi}{2}$, $y \in [-2, 2]$

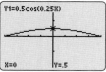

e) amplitude 1.5, period 10
Window variables: $x \in [-2\pi, 2\pi]$, Xscl $\dfrac{\pi}{2}$, $y \in [-4, 4]$

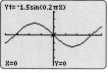

f) amplitude 0.75, period 2.5
Window variables: $x \in [-2\pi, 2\pi]$, Xscl $\dfrac{\pi}{2}$, $y \in [-2, 2]$

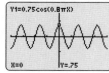

2. a) $y = 3 \sin 4x$ **b)** $y = \dfrac{1}{2} \cos 2\pi x$

3. a) 4 **b)** $\dfrac{2\pi}{3}$ **c)** $\dfrac{\pi}{3}$ rad to the left **d)** 2 units downward
e) Window variables: $x \in \left[0, \dfrac{4\pi}{3}\right]$, Xscl $\dfrac{\pi}{6}$, $y \in [-8, 4]$

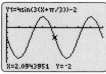

4. a) 3 **b)** 2 **c)** 2 rad to the left **d)** 1 unit downward
e) Window variables: $x \in [0, 4]$, $y \in [-6, 4]$

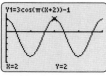

5. a) amplitude 3, period 2π, phase shift $\dfrac{\pi}{4}$ rad to the left, vertical translation 1 unit downward
Window variables: $x \in [0, 4\pi]$, Xscl $\dfrac{\pi}{2}$, $y \in [-6, 4]$

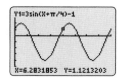

b) amplitude 2, period 4π, phase shift $\dfrac{5\pi}{6}$ rad to the right, vertical translation 4 units upward

Window variables: $x \in [0, 8\pi]$, Xscl $\dfrac{\pi}{2}$, $y \in [-2, 8]$

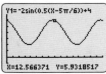

c) amplitude 2, period 1, phase shift 3 rad to the left, vertical translation 2 units downward

Window variables: $x \in [0, 2]$, Xscl 0.5, $y \in [-6, 4]$

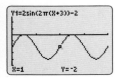

6. a) amplitude 3, period 2π, phase shift $\dfrac{\pi}{4}$ rad to the right, vertical translation 6 units upward

Window variables: $x \in [0, 4\pi]$, Xscl $\dfrac{\pi}{2}$, $y \in [-2, 12]$

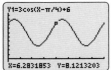

b) amplitude 5, period 8π, phase shift $\dfrac{4\pi}{3}$ rad to the left, vertical translation 5 units downward

Window variables: $x \in [0, 16\pi]$, Xscl $\dfrac{\pi}{2}$, $y \in [-12, 2]$

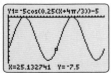

c) amplitude 7, period $\dfrac{2}{3}$, phase shift 2 rad to the right, vertical translation 7 units upward

Window variables: $x \in \left[0, \dfrac{4}{3}\right]$, Xscl $\dfrac{1}{6}$, $y \in [-2, 16]$

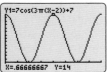

7. a) $h = 3\cos(0.4\pi t) + 4.5$

b)

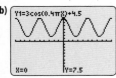

8. a) amplitude 3, period 4, phase shift 1 rad to the right, vertical translation 1 unit upward

b) $y = 3\sin\left[\dfrac{\pi}{2}(x - 1)\right] + 1$

c)

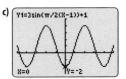

9. a) amplitude 2, period 12, phase shift 4 rad to the right, vertical translation 1 unit upward

b) $y = 2\cos\left[\dfrac{\pi}{6}(x - 4)\right] + 1$

c)

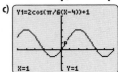

10. a) $y = 3\sin\left[2\left(x - \dfrac{\pi}{4}\right)\right] - 1$ **b)** $y = 2\sin\left[\dfrac{\pi}{3}(x + 2)\right] + 2$

11. a) $y = 4\cos\left[1.5\left(x + \dfrac{\pi}{3}\right)\right] + 1$ **b)** $y = 2.5\cos\left[\dfrac{\pi}{4}(x - 2)\right] - 1.5$

12. a) $y = 4\sin\left[4\left(x + \dfrac{3\pi}{4}\right)\right] + 3$

b) Window variables: $x \in [-\pi, \pi]$, Xscl $\dfrac{\pi}{2}$, $y \in [-2, 8]$

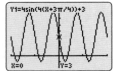

13. a) $y = 3\cos\left[\dfrac{2\pi}{3}(x - 2)\right] - 2$

b) Window variables: $x \in [-6, 6]$, $y \in [-8, 4]$

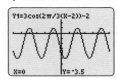

14. Answers may vary.

a) $y = 1.5\sin\left[2\left(x + \dfrac{\pi}{4}\right)\right] + 1.5$

b) Window variables: $x \in [-2\pi, 2\pi]$, Xscl $\dfrac{\pi}{2}$, $y \in [-4, 4]$

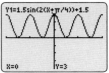

c) Yes. $y = 1.5\sin\left[2\left(x - \dfrac{7\pi}{4}\right)\right] + 1.5$

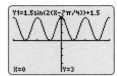

15. a) 2 **b)** $(0, 1)$, $\left(\dfrac{4\pi}{3}, -\dfrac{1}{2}\right)$

16. Answers may vary.

17. Answers may vary.

18. Answers may vary. Sample answer:

a) $x = 4\cos \pi t$ **b)** $y = 4\sin \pi t$

c) Window variables: $x \in [0, 4]$, $y \in [-6, 6]$

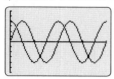

19. a) $v = -\dfrac{3}{4}\sin \dfrac{\pi}{3}x$

b) Window variables: $x \in [0, 12]$, $y \in [-2, 2]$

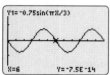

20. a) $h = 25\sin(70\pi t) + 50$

b) Window variables: $x \in \left[0, \dfrac{2}{35}\right]$, Xscl $\dfrac{1}{70}$, $y \in [0, 90]$

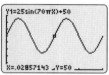

c) Only the period changes: $h = 25\sin(80\pi t) + 50$.

22. $y = a\csc[k(x - d)] + c$; a: multiply y-value by a;
k: changes the period to $\dfrac{2\pi}{k}$; d: phase shifts work the same as for sinusoidal functions; c: vertical translations work the same as for sinusoidal functions.

23. a), b) 2.5 s to the right

24. a) Window variables: $x \in [-2\pi, 2\pi]$, Xscl $\dfrac{\pi}{2}$, $y \in [-7, 7]$

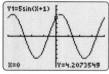

c) $a = 2.7$ and $b = 4.2$, to two decimal places.

25. a)

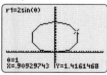

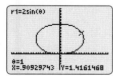

Smaller increments of θ step make the graph smoother (more circular).

b) i) Window variables: $\theta \in [0, 2\pi]$, θ step $\dfrac{\pi}{12}$, $x \in [-7, 7]$, $y \in [-7, 7]$

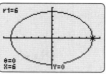

ii) Window variables: $\theta \in [0, 2\pi]$, θ step $\dfrac{\pi}{100}$, $x \in [-2, 2]$, $y \in [-3, 1]$

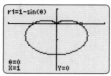

iii) Window variables: $\theta \in [0, 2\pi]$, θ step $\dfrac{\pi}{100}$, $x \in [-4, 4]$, $y \in [-6, 2]$

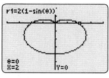

iv) Window variables: $\theta \in [-2\pi, 2\pi]$, θ step $\dfrac{\pi}{100}$, $x \in [-8, 8]$, $y \in [-8, 4]$

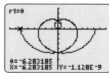

v) Window variables: $\theta \in [0, 2\pi]$, θ step $\dfrac{\pi}{100}$, $x \in [-2, 2]$, $y \in [-2, 2]$

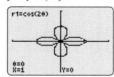

iv) Window variables: $\theta \in [0, 2\pi]$, θ step $\dfrac{\pi}{100}$, $x \in [-2, 10]$, $y \in [-6, 6]$

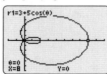

Extension, page 280

Part 1

1. a)

x	y
0	0
0.5π	1
π	0
1.5π	−1
2π	0

4. The k-value has not been factored out of the bracket.

6. Answers may vary.

Part 2

1. a)

Sunrise in Fort Erie, ON		
Date	Time	Time (decimals)
Jan 1	7:47	7.78
Feb 1	7:31	7.52
Mar 1	6:52	6.87
Apr 1	5:58	5.97
May 1	5:10	5.17
Jun 1	4:40	4.67
Jul 1	4:40	4.67
Aug 1	5:06	5.10
Sep 1	5:40	5.67
Oct 1	6:12	6.20
Nov 1	6:49	6.82
Dec 1	7:26	7.43

c)

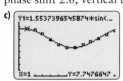

Window variables: $x \in [0, 12]$, $y \in [0, 10]$

2. a) $y = 1.553\ 739\ 6\ \sin(0.497\ 842\ 4x + 1.304\ 949\ 9)$
$+ 6.235\ 505\ 6$

b) amplitude 1.6, maximum 7.78, minimum 4.67, period 4π,
phase shift 2.6, vertical translation up 1.3

c)

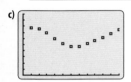

4. Answers may vary.

5.4 Solve Trigonometric Equations, pages 287–289

1. a) 0.25, 2.89 **b)** 2.42, 3.86 **c)** 1.37, 4.51 **d)** 1.32, 4.97
e) 2.16, 5.30 **f)** 3.55, 5.87

3. a) $\dfrac{4\pi}{3}, \dfrac{5\pi}{3}$ **b)** $\dfrac{\pi}{3}, \dfrac{5\pi}{3}$ **c)** $\dfrac{\pi}{4}, \dfrac{5\pi}{4}$ **d)** $\dfrac{3\pi}{4}, \dfrac{7\pi}{4}$

5. a) 0.93, 2.21, 4.07, 5.36 **b)** 0.84, 2.30, 3.98, 5.44
c) 0.88, 2.27, 4.02, 5.41 **d)** 0.89, 2.26, 4.03, 5.40
e) 0.74, 2.40, 3.88, 5.55

7. a) $\dfrac{\pi}{6}, \dfrac{5\pi}{6}, \dfrac{7\pi}{6}, \dfrac{11\pi}{6}$ **b)** $\dfrac{\pi}{6}, \dfrac{5\pi}{6}, \dfrac{7\pi}{6}, \dfrac{11\pi}{6}$ **c)** $\dfrac{\pi}{3}, \dfrac{2\pi}{3}, \dfrac{4\pi}{3}, \dfrac{5\pi}{3}$

d) $\dfrac{\pi}{3}, \dfrac{2\pi}{3}, \dfrac{4\pi}{3}, \dfrac{5\pi}{3}$

9. $\dfrac{3\pi}{2}$

10. $\dfrac{\pi}{6}, \dfrac{5\pi}{6}, \dfrac{3\pi}{2}$

11. π

12. 1.11, 1.89, 4.25, 5.03

13. a) 0.46, 1.11 **b)** 0.32, 1.25 **c)** 0.42, 1.15

14. no solution

15. 0.17, 1.40, 3.31, 4.54

16. 0.84, 5.44

17. $\dfrac{\pi}{6}, \dfrac{5\pi}{6}$

18. 1.91, 4.37, $\dfrac{2\pi}{3}, \dfrac{4\pi}{3}$

19. 1.25, 2.68, 4.39, 5.82

20. a) No two integers have a product of -3 and a sum of 1.

b) $\dfrac{-1 \pm \sqrt{13}}{6}$ **c)** 0.45, 2.69, 4.02, 5.41

21. b) Technology allows you to check all the zeros on the
graph within the domain.

22. a) 11.93 s, 18.07 s

b) Window variables: $x \in [0, 60]$, Xscl 5, $y \in [0, 30]$, Yscl 5

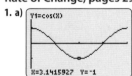

23. 0.08

24. 0.53, 1.04

26. $-2\pi, -\pi, 0, \pi, 2\pi$

27. a) 0.004 s **b)** No.

28. $-2\pi, 0, 2\pi$

29. Answers may vary.

**5.5 Making Connections and Instantaneous
Rate of Change, pages 296–299**

1. a)

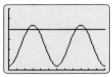

b) 0, π, 2π

c) maximum $\dfrac{3\pi}{2}$, minimum $\dfrac{\pi}{2}$

2. a)

Angle x	$f(x) = \cos x$	Instantaneous Rate of Change
0	1	0
$\dfrac{\pi}{6}$	0.87	-0.50
$\dfrac{\pi}{4}$	0.71	-0.71
$\dfrac{\pi}{3}$	0.50	-0.87
$\dfrac{\pi}{2}$	0	-1
$\dfrac{2\pi}{3}$	-0.50	-0.87
$\dfrac{3\pi}{4}$	-0.71	-0.71
$\dfrac{5\pi}{6}$	-0.87	-0.50
π	-1	0
$\dfrac{7\pi}{6}$	-0.87	0.50
$\dfrac{5\pi}{4}$	-0.71	0.71
$\dfrac{4\pi}{3}$	-0.50	0.87
$\dfrac{3\pi}{2}$	0	1
$\dfrac{5\pi}{3}$	0.50	0.87
$\dfrac{7\pi}{4}$	0.71	0.71
$\dfrac{11\pi}{6}$	0.87	0.50
2π	1	0

b)

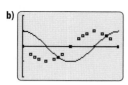

c) Yes.

3. a) i) -0.174 **ii)** -0.192 **iii)** -0.196 **iv)** -0.196
b) The instantaneous rate of change of h at $t = 20$ s is about -0.196 m/s.
c) The instantaneous rate of change represents the vertical speed of the car at $t = 20$ s.
d) No. The graph of the sine function changes its slope continually and would not likely yield the same value at a different value of t.

4. a)

Daylight in Sarnia, ON	
Month	Duration (decimal)
1	9.08
2	9.95
3	11.20
4	12.73
5	14.10
6	15.13
7	15.32
8	14.52
9	13.18
10	11.75
11	10.30
12	9.25

b) $T = 3.12 \sin\left[\dfrac{\pi}{6}(m - 4)\right] + 12.2$
c) Window variables: $x \in [0, 14]$, $y \in [0, 16]$

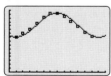

The equation fits the data well.
d) $T \doteq 3.11 \sin[0.51(m - 3.63)] + 12.14$
The values for a, k, c, and d compare well with those in the model.
e) phase shift
f) $T \doteq 3.11 \cos[0.51(m - 6.71)] + 12.14$
5. approximately 1.63 h/month
6. $h = 3 \cos(\pi t) + 4$
7. a) $(1.5, 4)$ **b)** 9.4 m/s **c)** speed of the spring
8. Answers may vary.
9. Answers may vary.
10. a) $a = 4$, $k = 5\pi$ **b)** $d = 4 \sin 5\pi t$
11. a) $y = -x^2 + 8$ **b)** $y = 2 \sin\left(\dfrac{\pi}{2}x\right) + 4$
12. a) -4 **b)** -3.14 **c)** different
d) Answers may vary. Sample answer: The cars may fall off the track.
13. Answers may vary.
14. Answers may vary.

16. a)

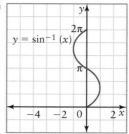

b) No. Restrict the range to the interval $\left(-\dfrac{\pi}{2}, \dfrac{\pi}{2}\right)$ **c)** 0 **d)** 1

17. a)

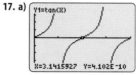

b) none; no maximum; no minimum

c)

Angle x	f(x) = tan x	Instantaneous Rate of Change
0	0	1
$\dfrac{\pi}{6}$	0.58	1.33
$\dfrac{\pi}{4}$	1	2
$\dfrac{\pi}{3}$	1.73	4
$\dfrac{\pi}{2}$	undefined	undefined
$\dfrac{2\pi}{3}$	-1.73	4
$\dfrac{3\pi}{4}$	-1	2
$\dfrac{5\pi}{6}$	-0.58	1.33
π	0	1
$\dfrac{7\pi}{6}$	0.58	1.33
$\dfrac{5\pi}{4}$	1	2
$\dfrac{4\pi}{3}$	1.73	4
$\dfrac{3\pi}{2}$	undefined	undefined
$\dfrac{5\pi}{3}$	-1.73	4
$\dfrac{7\pi}{4}$	-1	2
$\dfrac{11\pi}{6}$	-0.58	1.33
2π	0	1

d)

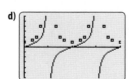

e) Answers may vary.

18. a)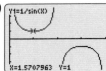

b) $\dfrac{\pi}{2}, \dfrac{3\pi}{2}$; no maximum; no minimum

c)

Angle x	f(x) = csc x	Instantaneous Rate of Change
0	undefined	undefined
$\dfrac{\pi}{6}$	2	−3.46
$\dfrac{\pi}{4}$	1.41	−1.41
$\dfrac{\pi}{3}$	1.15	−0.67
$\dfrac{\pi}{2}$	1	0
$\dfrac{2\pi}{3}$	1.15	0.67
$\dfrac{3\pi}{4}$	1.41	1.41
$\dfrac{5\pi}{6}$	2	3.46
π	undefined	undefined
$\dfrac{7\pi}{6}$	−2	3.46
$\dfrac{5\pi}{4}$	−1.41	1.41
$\dfrac{4\pi}{3}$	−1.15	0.67
$\dfrac{3\pi}{2}$	−1	0
$\dfrac{5\pi}{3}$	−1.15	−0.67
$\dfrac{7\pi}{4}$	−1.41	−1.41
$\dfrac{11\pi}{6}$	−2	−3.46
2π	undefined	undefined

d)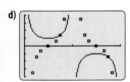

e) Answers may vary.
19. 1
20. a) $\dfrac{1}{2}$ **b)** $\angle R = \dfrac{\pi}{6}$
21. $r = a\sin\theta + b\cos\theta$ is a circle
$\left(x - \dfrac{b}{2}\right)^2 + \left(y - \dfrac{a}{2}\right)^2 = \dfrac{a^2 + b^2}{4}$ with center $\left(\dfrac{b}{2}, \dfrac{a}{2}\right)$ and
radius $\dfrac{\sqrt{a^2 + b^2}}{2}$.

Chapter 5 Review, pages 300–301
1. a) 2 **b)** 4
2. $y = \cos\left[\dfrac{2}{3}\left(x + \dfrac{\pi}{3}\right)\right]$
3. a) $y = 5\sin 60\pi t$ **b)** No. A phase shift can generate another possible equation.

4. 0.25, 2.89
5. a) The secant function is a reciprocal of the cosine function and $\cos^{-1}$ is the opposite operation of cosine.
b) $\sec\left(\dfrac{1}{\sqrt{2}}\right) \doteq 1.32,\ \cos^{-1}\left(\dfrac{1}{\sqrt{2}}\right) = \dfrac{\pi}{4}$

6. b)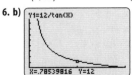

c) As x approaches 0, s approaches infinity. This means that the angle of elevation of the Sun approaches the horizon and so the length of the shadow approaches infinity. As x approaches $\dfrac{\pi}{2}$, s approaches 0. This means that the angle of elevation of the Sun approaches an overhead location and the length of the shadow approaches 0.
7. a) amplitude 3, vertical translation 1 unit downward, phase shift 1 rad to the right, period 2
b) $y = 3\cos[\pi(x - 1)] - 1$
c)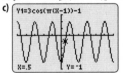

8. a) 3 **b)** 2 **c)** 4 rad to the left **d)** 1 unit downward
e) Window variables: $x \in [-\pi, \pi]$, Xscl $\dfrac{\pi}{2}$, $y \in [-5, 4]$

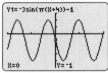

9. a) 1.32, 4.97 **b)** 0.64, 2.50 **c)** 0.46, 3.61 **d)** no solution
10. a) $\dfrac{\pi}{6}, \dfrac{5\pi}{6}, \dfrac{3\pi}{2}$
11. $\dfrac{\pi}{6}, \dfrac{5\pi}{6}, \dfrac{7\pi}{6}, \dfrac{11\pi}{6}$
12. a) $y = 0.9\sin\left(\dfrac{\pi}{2}t\right)$ **b)** 0.37 s, 1.63 s
13. 1 s, 3 s; maxima 0 s, 4 s
14. a) Window variables: $x \in [0, 12]$, $y \in [0, 300]$, Yscl 20

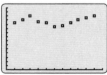

b) $y = 26\sin\left[\dfrac{\pi}{4}(x - 1)\right] + 235$
c) The equation fits the data reasonably well.

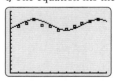

d) Using sinusoidal regression, an equation that better fits the data is $y \doteq 22.68\sin[0.83(x - 0.96)] + 230.61$.
e) Answers may vary.

Chapter 5 Practice Test, pages 302–303

1. B

2. C

3. C

4. A

5. D

6. C

7. A

8. a) The cosecant function is a reciprocal of the sine function and $\sin^{-1}$ is the opposite operation of sine.

b) $\csc\left(\dfrac{\sqrt{3}}{2}\right) \doteq 1.31$, $\sin^{-1}\left(\dfrac{\sqrt{3}}{2}\right) = \dfrac{\pi}{3}$

9. b)

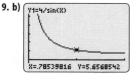

c) As x approaches 0, l approaches infinity. This means that the angle of inclination of the wire approaches horizontal and so the length of the wire approaches infinity. As x approaches $\dfrac{\pi}{2}$, l approaches 4. This means that the angle of inclination of the wire approaches vertical and the length of the wire approaches 4 m.

10. a) 2 **b)** $\dfrac{\pi}{2}$ **c)** $\dfrac{2\pi}{3}$ rad to the left **d)** 3 units downward

e) Window variables: $x \in [-\pi, \pi]$, Xscl $\dfrac{\pi}{2}$, $y \in [-8, 4]$

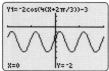

11. a) $y = 2\cos\left[\dfrac{\pi}{2}(x - 1)\right] + 1$

b) Window variables: $x \in [-\pi, \pi]$, Xscl $\dfrac{\pi}{2}$, $y \in [-4, 4]$

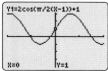

12. a) $y = 3\sin\left[2\left(x + \dfrac{5\pi}{6}\right)\right] + 1$

b) Window variables: $x \in [-\pi, \pi]$, Xscl $\dfrac{\pi}{2}$, $y \in [-4, 6]$

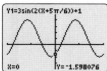

13. 0.80, 2.35, 3.94, 5.49

14. $\dfrac{\pi}{6}, \dfrac{\pi}{2}, \dfrac{5\pi}{6}$

15. a) Window variables: $x \in [0, 14]$, $y \in [-10, 30]$, Yscl 5

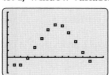

b) $y = 13.4 \sin\left[\dfrac{\pi}{6}(x - 4)\right] + 8.55$

c)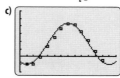

The model appears to fit the data well.

16. a), b)

Phases of the Moon 2007	
Date (days from beginning of year)	Phase (percent illumination)
3	100
11	50
19	0
25	50
33	100
41	50
48	0
55	50
62	100
71	50
78	0
84	50
92	100
100	50
107	0
114	50

c) $y = 50 \sin\left[\dfrac{\pi}{15}(x + 4.5)\right] + 50$

d) Window variables: $x \in [0, 150]$, Xscl 10, $y \in [-20, 120]$, Yscl 20

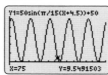

e) $y \doteq 49.75 \sin[0.21(x + 4)] + 52.74$; the values for a, k, c, and d compare well with those in the model.

17. a) Answers may vary. Sample Answer: Using your model, first find the average rate of change of the percent of illumination, and then estimate the instantaneous rate of change.

b) The instantaneous rate of change on January 25 is about 10.4%/day.

c) The instantaneous rate of change represents the percent change in illumination of the Moon on January 25.

Chapters 4 and 5 Review, pages 304–305

1. a) $\dfrac{5\pi}{9}$ **b)** $105°$

2. 3 radians

3. $\dfrac{\sqrt{3} + \sqrt{2}}{\sqrt{6}}$

4. $25(\sqrt{3} - 1)$ m

5. 0.1045

6. $\dfrac{\pi}{8}$

7. $-\dfrac{33}{65}$

9. a) $\dfrac{\sin^2 x}{\cot^2 x} + \sin^2 x = \tan^2 x$

12. a) $\dfrac{7\pi}{12}$ **b)** $\dfrac{\pi}{4}$ to the left

13. a) 6 cm **b)** $\dfrac{1}{100}$ s **c)** 200π **d)** $y = 6\cos(200\pi x) + 6$

e) Window variables: $x \in [0, 0.02]$, Xscl 0.01, $y \in [-4, 15]$

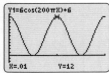

14. a) 3 **b)** $\dfrac{\pi}{2}$ **c)** $\dfrac{\pi}{4}$ to the right **d)** 2 units upward

e) Window variables: $x \in \left[-\dfrac{47\pi}{24}, \dfrac{47\pi}{24}\right]$, Xscl $\dfrac{\pi}{2}$, $y \in [-4, 6]$

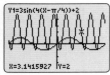

15. b) $0 \le d \le 250\sqrt{13}$ **c)** The total time will be a minimum when the contestant stays on the pavement.

16. a) $\dfrac{\pi}{3}$ to the right

b) Window variables: $x \in \left[-\dfrac{47\pi}{24}, \dfrac{47\pi}{24}\right]$, Xscl $\dfrac{\pi}{2}$, $y \in [-3, 5]$

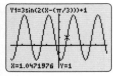

17. a) $h(t) = 60\sin\left(\dfrac{2\pi t}{5}\right)$

b) Window variables: $x \in [0, 10]$, $y \in [-80, 80]$, Yscl 10

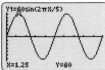

c) The value of k would change from $\dfrac{2\pi}{5}$ to $\dfrac{2\pi}{3}$, making the equation $h(t) = 60\sin\left(\dfrac{2\pi t}{3}\right)$.

18. a) 1.37, 4.91 **b)** 0.34, 2.80, 3.39, 6.03

19. a) Window variables: $x \in [0, 20]$, $y \in [-2, 14]$

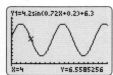

b) 7134 cones **c)** 6300 cones
d) 8.7 years **e)** Answers may vary. Sample answer: approximately Oct 1991 and June 2000
f) Answers may vary.

20. a) $C(t) = 10\sin\left[\dfrac{\pi}{12}(t - 12)\right] + 20$

b) Window variables: $x \in [0, 72]$, Xscl 3, $y \in [0, 40]$, Yscl 2

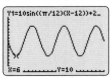

21. a) $t = 12$ **b)** 2.6 ppm/h

CHAPTER 6

Prerequisite Skills, pages 308–309

1. a)

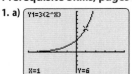

b) i) $\{x \in \mathbb{R}\}$ **ii)** $\{y \in \mathbb{R}, y > 0\}$ **iii)** $y = 0$
2. a) 300 **b)** 2400 **c) i)** approximately 2.74 days
ii) approximately 38 bacteria
3. a) x^7 **b)** m^3 **c)** k^6 **d)** $-8x^{12}$ **e)** $-\dfrac{2b}{a}$ **f)** $\dfrac{2}{x^2}$ **g)** $\dfrac{1}{u}$
4. a) 4 **b)** 10 **c)** 27 **d)** 82
5. a)

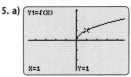

b) $\{x \in \mathbb{R}, x \ge 0\}$, $\{y \in \mathbb{R}, y \ge 0\}$
c)

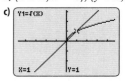

d)

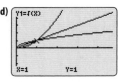

e) Yes. **f)** $\{x \in \mathbb{R}, x \ge 0\}$, $\{y \in \mathbb{R}, y \ge 0\}$
6. a)

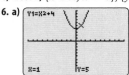

b) $\{x \in \mathbb{R},\}$, $\{y \in \mathbb{R}, y \ge 4\}$
c)

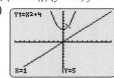

d)

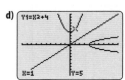

e) No. **f)** $\{x \in \mathbb{R}, x \ge 4\}$, $\{y \in \mathbb{R}\}$
7. Yes. Each curve is a reflection of the other in the line $y = x$.
8. a) translation of 3 units to the right and 1 unit up.
b) reflection in the x-axis, vertical stretch of factor 2
9. a) vertical stretch of factor 3 and then translated down 4 units
b) horizontal stretch of factor 2 and a reflection in the y-axis

10.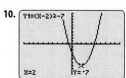

11.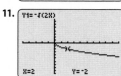

12.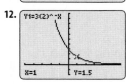

6.1 The Exponential Function and Its Inverse, pages 318–322

1. C, D

2. C: $y = 3^x$; D: $y = \left(\dfrac{1}{3}\right)^x$

3. a)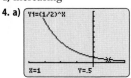

b) i) $m_{12} = 0.75$ **ii)** $m_{23} \doteq 1.13$ **iii)** $m_{34} \doteq 1.69$ **iv)** $m_{45} \doteq 2.53$
c) $m_1 \doteq 0.6$, $m_2 \doteq 0.9$, $m_3 \doteq 1.4$, $m_4 \doteq 2.1$, $m_5 \doteq 3.1$
d) increasing

4. a)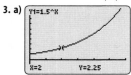

b) i) $m_{-3-2} = -4$ **ii)** $m_{-2-1} = -2$ **iii)** $m_{-10} = -1$ **iv)** $m_{01} = -0.5$
c) $m_{-3} \doteq -5.5$, $m_{-2} \doteq -2.8$, $m_{-1} \doteq -1.4$, $m_0 \doteq -0.7$,
$m_1 \doteq -0.35$
d) increasing

5. a) 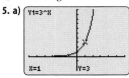   **b)** $y = 3^x$

c), d)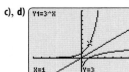

6. a) 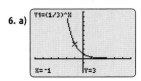   **b)** $y = \left(\dfrac{1}{3}\right)^x$

c), d)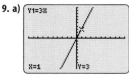

7. a) iii) **b)** i) **c)** ii) **d)** iv)
8. a) is inverse of 7d): $y = \left(\dfrac{1}{5}\right)^x$

b) is inverse of 7b): $y = 5^x$
c) is inverse of 7c): $y = \left(\dfrac{1}{2}\right)^x$
d) is inverse of 7a): $y = 2^x$

9. a)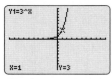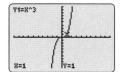

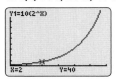

b)

Function	$f(x) = 3x$	$g(x) = x^3$	$h(x) = 3^x$
domain	$x \in \mathbb{R}$	$x \in \mathbb{R}$	$x \in \mathbb{R}$
range	$y \in \mathbb{R}$	$y \in \mathbb{R}$	$y \in \mathbb{R}, y > 0$
x-intercept	$(0, 0)$	$(0, 0)$	none
y-intercept	$(0, 0)$	$(0, 0)$	$(0, 1)$
function is negative	$x < 0$	$x < 0$	never
function is positive	$x > 0$	$x > 0$	$x \in \mathbb{R}$
function is increasing	$x \in \mathbb{R}$	$x \in \mathbb{R}$	$x \in \mathbb{R}$
equation of asymptote	none	none	$y = 0$

c) All three functions have the same domain and are increasing.
d) $h(x) = 3^x$ is different than the other two functions for range, x-intercept, y-intercept, $y = 0$ asymptote, and positive/negative intervals.
e) For $f(x) = 3x$, the instantaneous rate of change is constant. For $g(x) = x^3$, the instantaneous rate of change is decreasing and then increasing. For $h(x) = 3^x$, the instantaneous rate of change is increasing.
10. a) i) 10 **ii)** 20 **iii)** 40 **iv)** 80 **b)** Yes.

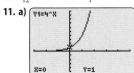

c) $m_{12} = 20$ **d) i)** $m_1 \doteq 13.9$ **ii)** $m_2 \doteq 27.7$ **e)** Answers may vary.
11. a) 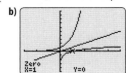   **b)**

12. a) $\{x \in \mathbb{R}\}$, $\{y \in \mathbb{R}, y > 0\}$ **b)** None. **c)** 1
d) The function is positive for all intervals. **e)** The function is increasing for all intervals. **f)** $y = 0$
13. a) $\{x \in \mathbb{R}, x > 0\}$, $\{y \in \mathbb{R}\}$ **b)** 1 **c)** None.
d) For $0 < x < 1$, the function is negative. For $x > 1$, the function is positive. **e)** The function is increasing for all intervals. **f)** $x = 0$.

14. a) 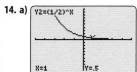 **b)**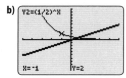

c)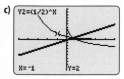

15. a) $\{x \in \mathbb{R}\}$, $\{y \in \mathbb{R}, y > 0\}$ **b)** None. **c)** 1
d) The function is positive for all intervals.
e) The function is decreasing for all intervals.
f) $y = 0$
16. a) $\{x \in \mathbb{R}, x > 0\}$, $\{y \in \mathbb{R}\}$ **b)** 1 **c)** None
d) For $0 < x < 1$, the function is positive. For $x > 1$, the function is negative.
e) The function is decreasing for $x > 0$ **f)** $x = 0$
17. a) same domain, range, y-intercept, positive intervals, and equations of asymptotes **b)** f increases and g decreases
18. a) same domain, range x-intercept, and equations of asymptotes **b)** f^{-1} increases and g^{-1} decreases, and they do not share the same positive and negative intervals

19. a)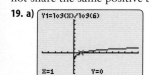

b), c)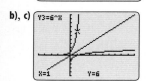

d) $y = 6^x$
20. $y = \left(\dfrac{1}{10}\right)^x$

21. a)

x	y
0	1
1	-2
2	4
3	-8
4	16

b)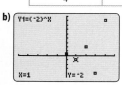

c) No. **d) i)** not real (square root of a negative value) **ii)** not real
e) Answers may vary.
22. a) $m_{12} \doteq 56$ km/s, $m_{34} \doteq 110$ km/s **b)** $m_3 \doteq 92$, $m_4 \doteq 129$
23. a) For $0 < b < 1$, f and f^{-1} have equal x- and y-coordinates at the point where they intersect the line $y = x$.
b) Yes; when $b > 1$, the graphs do not intersect the line $y = x$.
24. c) i) $b > 0$ **ii)** $b < 0$ **d) i)** $b > 0$ **ii)** $b < 0$ **e)** Yes.

6.2 Logarithms, pages 328–330

1. a) $\log_4 64 = 3$ **b)** $\log_2 128 = 7$ **c)** $\log_5\left(\dfrac{1}{25}\right) = -2$
d) $\log_{\frac{1}{2}} 0.25 = 2$ **e)** $\log_6 y = x$ **f)** $\log_{10} 100\,000 = 5$
g) $\log_3\left(\dfrac{1}{27}\right) = -3$ **h)** $\log_b v = u$
2. a) 6 **b)** 3 **c)** -2 **d)** -3 **e)** 3 **f)** 10 **g)** 6 **h)** 4
3. a) 3 **b)** -1 **c)** 0 **d)** -3 **e)** -4 **f)** 6 **g)** -2 **h)** 4
4. a) $7^2 = 49$ **b)** $2^5 = 32$ **c)** $10^4 = 10\,000$ **d)** $b^w = z$ **e)** $2^3 = 8$
f) $5^4 = 625$ **g)** $10^{-2} = \dfrac{1}{100}$ **h)** $7^{2y} = x$

5. a)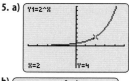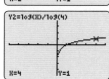

b)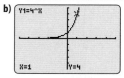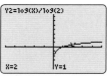

6. a) 2.6 **b)** 3.7 **c)** 6.2 **d)** -1.5
8. a) 2.63 **b)** -4.43 **c)** 0.95 **d)** -0.70 **e)** 1.23 **f)** 2.00 **g)** 2.26 **h)** 3.00
9. a) $y = 10^x$
b)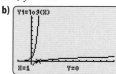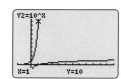

10. a) 1 **b)** 1 **c)** 1 **d)** 1
11. a) $\log_x x = 1$ for $x > 0$, $x \neq 1$. **b)** Answers may vary. Sample answer: $\log_{11} 11 = 1$ **c)** $\log_x x = 1$
12. a) Answers may vary. Sample answer: The logarithmic function has decreasing slope and the exponential function has increasing slope. **b)** Answers may vary.
13. a) approximately 6.3 days **b)** approximately 12.6 days
14. a) approximately 66.5 m **b)** No. $d \doteq 16.2$ m.
c) Answers may vary. Sample answer: Drive slower.
15. a) at least 5.72 cm **b)** increase by 1.43 cm
17. Answers may vary. Sample answer: **a)** 3 **b)** y is an integer but x is a power of 10.

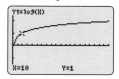

18. a) Answers may vary. Sample answer:

x	y
10^0	0
10^1	1
10^2	2
10^3	3
10^4	4
10^5	5
10^6	6

b)

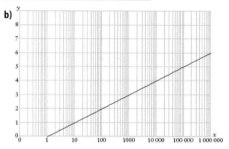

The graph is linear. The semi-log grid has turned each power into the exponent value.
c) To plot a greater range of values.
19. b) The graph is a curve with positive, decreasing slope.
c) Answers may vary. **d)** The graph is a line with positive, increasing slope.
20. D
21. $\sqrt{5}$

6.3 Transformations of Logarithmic Functions, pages 338–340

1. a) iv **b)** ii **c)** i **d)** iii
2. a) translate right 2 **b)** translate left 5 and down 4
c) translate up 1 **d)** translate left 4 and down 6
3. a)

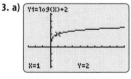

b)

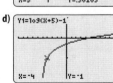

c)

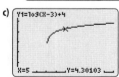

d)

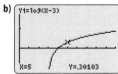

4. a) $y = 2\log x$ **b)** $y = \log(2x)$ **c)** $y = \log\left(\frac{1}{2}x\right)$ **d)** $y = \frac{1}{2}\log x$

5. a) vertical compression by a factor of $\frac{1}{2}$
b) horizontal compression by a factor of $\frac{1}{5}$ and a reflection in the y-axis **c)** horizontal stretch by a factor of 2 and a reflection in the y-axis **d)** vertical stretch by a factor of 5 and a reflection in the x-axis

6. a)

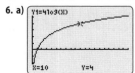

b)

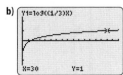

c)

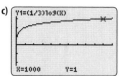

d)

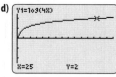

7. a)

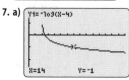

b)

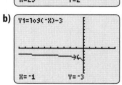

8. For $y = -\log(x - 4)$: **a)** $\{x \in \mathbb{R}, x > 4\}$ **b)** $\{y \in \mathbb{R}\}$ **c)** $x = 4$
For $y = \log(-x) - 3$: **a)** $\{x \in \mathbb{R}, x < 0\}$ **b)** $\{y \in \mathbb{R}\}$ **c)** $x = 0$
9. a)

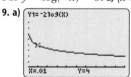

b) $\{y \in \mathbb{R}, 2 \le y \le 6\}$
10. Answers may vary. Sample answer: The domain and the range are the same.
11. Answers may vary. Sample answer: No; the domains are different, but the ranges are the same.
12. Answers may vary. Sample answer: The domains are different, but the ranges are the same.
13. a)

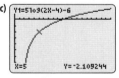

b)

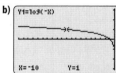

c)

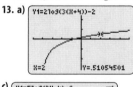

d)

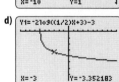

15. a)

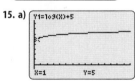

b) $V_o = 6$, $V_o \doteq 6.3$ **c)** $V_i = 10^{20}$ **d)** The domain is the input voltage, $V_i > 0$; the range is the output voltage, V_o, which can be any real number.
17. a)

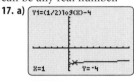

b)

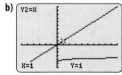

c)

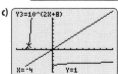

d) i) $\{x \in \mathbb{R}\}$ **ii)** $\{y \in \mathbb{R}, y > 0\}$ **iii)** $y = 0$ **e)** $y = 10^{2x + 8}$

18. a)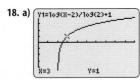

b)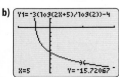

19. a) $\{t \in \mathbb{R}, 2n\pi < t < (2n + 1)\pi, n \in \mathbb{Z}\}$, $\{V_0 \in \mathbb{R}, V_0 \leq 5\}$

b)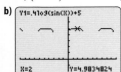

c) Answers may vary.
20. $x = 64$

6.4 Power Law of Logarithms, pages 347–348

1. a) 12 **b)** 3 **c)** -8 **d)** $-\dfrac{1}{2}$

2. a) $\dfrac{3}{2}$ **b)** $\dfrac{5}{2}$ **c)** 8 **d)** 6

3. a) $t \doteq 1.66$ **b)** $t \doteq 3.43$ **c)** $t \doteq 9.01$ **d)** $t \doteq 27.62$
4. a) i) \$500 **ii)** \$572.45 **iii)** \$655.40 **b) i)** $t \doteq 10.2$ years
ii) $t \doteq 16.2$ years
5. a) 2.854 **b)** 1.672 **c)** 0.356 **d)** -0.558 **e)** -4.907 **f)** -7.228
6. a) $\log_5 8$ **b)** $\log_9 17$ **c)** $\log_{\frac{2}{3}} \dfrac{1}{2}$ **d)** $\log_{(x-1)}(x + 1)$

7. a)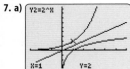

8.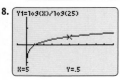

9. a) $x \doteq 4.192$ **b)** $x \doteq 3.333$ **c)** $x \doteq 1.623$ **d)** $x \doteq 8.790$
10. a) \$400; this is the amount when $t = 0$.
b) approximately 8 years
11. $\log(mx) = m\log x$ only when $m = 1$.
12. $\log x^n = (\log x)^n$ only when $n = 1$ and/or when $x = 1$.
13. a) 15 **b)** 15 **c)** Answers may vary.
14. Answers may vary.
15. a) approximately 6.6 h **b)** $\{d \in \mathbb{R}, 0 < d \leq 1000\}$,
$\{t \in \mathbb{R}, t \geq 0\}$
18. a) $\dfrac{\log_2 9}{\log_2 3}$ **b)** $\dfrac{\log_2 25}{\log_2 10}$
19. $\log_2 (2^{10})^{64} = 640$
20. a) $A = P(1.008\ 75)^{4t}$ **b) i)** approximately 19.9 years
ii) approximately 31.5 years

21. $\dfrac{2}{\sqrt{3}}$

22. 384

6.5 Making Connections: Logarithmic Scales in the Physical Sciences, pages 353–355
1. a) 2 **b)** approximately 4.5 **c)** 9 **d)** approximately 9.8
2. a) $[H^+] = 10^{-11}$ **b)** $[H^+] = 0.001$ **c)** $[H^+] \doteq 3.2 \times 10^{-9}$
d) $[H^+] \doteq 0.000\ 039\ 8$
3. a) Answers may vary. Sample answer: The pH scale varies
over several powers of 10. **b)** Answers may vary.
Sample answer: To ensure that the pH measurements
are positive.
4. a) 5 **b)** approximately 10.6
5. a) Answers may vary. Sample answer: $0 < x < 0.003$,
Xscl 1×10^{-4}, $0 < y < 5$, Yscl 1 **b)** approximately 2.7
6. a) 100 times **b)** 100 000 times
7. 10 000 times
8. approximately 15 dB
9. 4
10. a) approximately 199.53 times as intense
b) approximately 15.85 times as intense
11. approximately 794 328 235 times as intense
12. a) approximately 41.69 times brighter
b) approximately -11.61
14. Answers may vary. Sample answer: The absolute
magnitude takes distance into consideration.
15. a) i) approximately 158.5 times **ii)** 100 000 times
b) closest star is Biffidus-V, next is Cheryl-XI, farthest
away is Roccolus-III
16.–18. Answers may vary.
19. B
20. $\sqrt{2}s$
21. B
22. D

Chapter 6 Review, pages 356–357
1. a)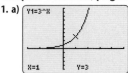

i) $\{x \in \mathbb{R}\}$, $\{y \in \mathbb{R}, y > 0\}$ **ii)** no x-intercept **iii)** 1
iv) positive for all intervals **v)** increasing for all intervals
vi) $y = 0$
b), c)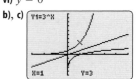

c) $\{x \in \mathbb{R}, x > 0\}$; $\{y \in \mathbb{R}\}$; x-intercept 1; no y-intercept;
f^{-1} is positive for $x > 1$ and negative for $0 < x < 1$;
f^{-1} is increasing for all intervals; vertical asymptote: $x = 0$
2. a)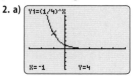

i) $\{x \in \mathbb{R}\}$, $\{y \in \mathbb{R}, y > 0\}$ **ii)** no x-intercept **iii)** 1
iv) positive for all intervals **v)** decreasing for all intervals
vi) $y = 0$

b), c)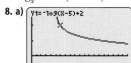

c) $\{x \in \mathbb{R}, x > 0\}$; $\{y \in \mathbb{R}\}$; x-intercept 1; no y-intercept; g^{-1} is positive for $0 < x < 1$ and negative for $x > 1$; g^{-1} is decreasing for all intervals; vertical asymptote; $x = 0$

3. a) $\log_4 64 = 3$ **b)** $\log_3 28 = x$ **c)** $\log_6 y = 3$ **d)** $\log_2 512 = 9$

4. a) $2^7 = 128$ **b)** $b^x = n$ **c)** $3^5 = 243$ **d)** $b^{19} = 4$

5. approximately 5.6

6. a) 4 **b)** 4 **c)** -2 **d)** -6

7. $\log_x x = 1, x > 0, x \neq 1$

8. a)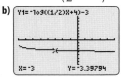

b) i) $\{x \in \mathbb{R}, x > 5\}$ **ii)** $\{y \in \mathbb{R}\}$ **iii)** $x = 5$

9. a)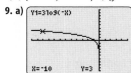

b) i) $\{x \in \mathbb{R}, x < 0\}$ **ii)** $\{y \in \mathbb{R}\}$ **iii)** $x = 0$

11. Answers may vary. Sample answer:

a) $y = -\log\left(\dfrac{1}{2}x + 4\right) - 3$

b)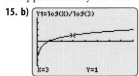

c) i) $\{x \in \mathbb{R}, x > -8\}$ **ii)** $\{y \in \mathbb{R}\}$ **iii)** $x = -8$

12. a) 15 **b)** -6 **c)** 3 **d)** 8

13. a) $x \doteq 2.579$ **b)** $x \doteq -1.515$ **c)** $x \doteq 1.661$ **d)** $x \doteq 0.322$

14. approximately 1.3 mm

15. b)

16. There is less hydronium ion concentration in Chemical B.

17. No; a great earthquake is 10 000 times as intense as a light earthquake.

18. a) 3 ($n \doteq 3.1$)

b) approximately $\dfrac{1}{372\ 717}$ ($T \doteq 2.683 \times 10^{-6}$)

c) approximately 138 950 times as much

19. a)

b) $\{T \in \mathbb{R}, 0 < T \leq 1\}$, $\{n \in \mathbb{R}, n \geq 1\}$

Chapter 6 Practice Test, pages 358–359

1. D

2. A

3. B

4. C

5. a) 1.839 **b)** 2.163

6. a) Compress vertically by a factor of $\dfrac{1}{2}$, translate 3 left, translate 6 up, and reflect in the y-axis.

b)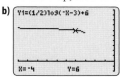

c) i) $\{x \in \mathbb{R}, x < -3\}$ **ii)** $\{y \in \mathbb{R}\}$ **iii)** $x = -3$

d)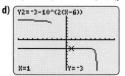

8. approximately 11 years

9. a) pH $\doteq 11.5$ **b)** approximately $0.000\ 32 < V < 0.01$

c) vinegar acidic, ammonia alkaline

10. a)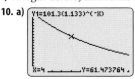

b) approximately 54.3 kPa **c)** approximately 1.4 km

11. a) approximately 110 dB **b)** approximately 1995 times

CHAPTER 7

Prerequisite Skills, pages 362–363

1. product law **a)** x^9 **b)** $6a^5b^4$ **c)** x^4y^5 **d)** $6r^2s^2$

e) $5q^2r$ **f)** v^3w^4 **g)** $4ab^4$

2. quotient law **a)** k^4 **b)** $-6n$ **c)** $6x^3y$ **d)** $2ab^2$ **e)** $\dfrac{q^2}{2r}$ **f)** v^2w^2 **g)** b^4

3. power law **a)** w^8 **b)** $4u^2v^6$ **c)** a^6b^3 **d)** x^6y^6 **e)** $8w^6$ **f)** a^2b^8 **g)** rs^6

4. a) $\dfrac{2a^2}{b}$, product and quotient laws **b)** $-108k^9m^{13}$, product and power laws **c)** $32y^5$, product, quotient, and power laws **d)** a^4b, product, quotient, and power laws

5. a) $x = -6$ or $x = 4$ **b)** $x = 2.5$ or $x = 2$ **c)** $x = \dfrac{1}{2}$ or $x = -\dfrac{7}{2}$

d) $q = 5$ or $q = -4$ **e)** $b = \dfrac{1}{3}$ or $b = -\dfrac{1}{3}$ **f)** $y = -\dfrac{1}{2}$ or $y = -\dfrac{1}{4}$

g) $x = 2$ or $x = -1$ **h)** $r = -3$ or $r = \dfrac{1}{2}$ **i)** $q = -4$ or $q = -1$

6. a) $y = -3 \pm \sqrt{14}$ **b)** $q = \dfrac{1 \pm \sqrt{41}}{4}$ **c)** $x = \dfrac{-1 \pm \sqrt{5}}{2}$

d) $a = \dfrac{-1 \pm \sqrt{21}}{2}$ **e)** $x = \dfrac{1 \pm \sqrt{29}}{2}$ **f)** $r = \dfrac{5 \pm \sqrt{13}}{2}$

g) $m = \dfrac{-3 \pm \sqrt{3}}{2}$ **h)** $a = \dfrac{3 \pm \sqrt{57}}{6}$

7. a) $2\sqrt{2}$ **b)** $4\sqrt{5}$ **c)** $3\sqrt{2}$ **d)** $9\sqrt{2}$ **e)** $5\sqrt{3}$

f) $2(\sqrt{3} + 1)$ **g)** $1 \pm \sqrt{6}$

8. a) 6 **b)** $\dfrac{5}{4}$ **c)** 6 **d)** 4 **e)** 10 **f)** 4 **g)** 4 **h)** -2

9. a) 2.096 **b)** 2.322 **c)** 3.907 **d)** 2.044 **e)** 1.585 **f)** 1.893
g) 2.161 **h)** 4.248
10. a) 0.86 **b)** 1.29 **c)** 0.36 **d)** −0.17 **e)** 0.63 **f)** 0.53 **g)** 3.17 **h)** 1.30

7.1 Equivalent Forms of Exponential Equations, pages 368–369

1. a) 2^{12} **b)** 2^9 **c)** 2^{-6} **d)** $2^{\frac{\log 14}{\log 2}}$

2. a) 3^6 **b)** 3^{-4} **c)** $3^{\frac{1}{\log 3}}$ **d)** $3^{\frac{\log \frac{1}{2}}{\log 3}}$

3. Answers may vary. Sample answers: **a)** 4^4 **b)** 16^2

4. a) 4^3 **b)** $4^{\frac{2}{3}}$ **c)** $4^{\frac{33}{8}}$ **d)** $4^{\frac{8}{3}}$

5. a) $x = 3$ **b)** $x = -2$ **c)** $w = 3$ **d)** $m = \frac{7}{4}$

6. a) $x = -3$ **b)** $x = 6$ **c)** $y = \frac{11}{4}$ **d)** $k = 9$

7. a) $x = 5$ **b)** $x = 5$ **c)** Answers may vary.

8. a)–d) Answers may vary.

9. Answers may vary.

10. a) $x = -4$ **b)** $k = -2$

11. a) $x = \dfrac{1}{\log 2}$

12. $10 = b^{\frac{1}{\log b}}$, $b > 0$

15. a) i) $x > 2$ **ii)** $x > -\frac{11}{2}$ **b)** Answers may vary. Sample answer for inequality i): Graph each side of the inequality as a separate function. Find their point of intersection. Test a point to the right of the point of intersection to ensure that the inequality is true.

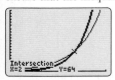 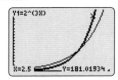

c) Answers may vary.

16. a) i) $x^3 > 2^x$ for $x > 1.37$ (correct to 2 decimal places).
ii) $1.1^x > x^{10}$ for $-0.99 < x < 1.01$.
b) $q(x)$ is growing faster for $x > 1.52$

7.2 Techniques for Solving Exponential Equations, pages 375–377

1. a) iii) **b)** i) **c)** ii) **d)** iv)

2. a) 10.24 **b)** 11.53 **c)** 58.71 **d)** 18.91 **e)** −2.80 **f)** −0.55
g) −15.63 **h)** −3

3. a) approximately 35.75 m **b)** approximately 10.3 min **c)** No.

4. a) $x = \dfrac{\log 3}{\log 3 - \log 2}$ **b)** $x = \dfrac{2\log 5}{\log 5 - \log 4}$

c) $x = \dfrac{\log 8 + \log 3}{\log 3 - \log 8}$ **d)** $x = \dfrac{\log 7 + 2\log 4}{\log 4 - 2\log 7}$

5. a) 2.710 **b)** 14.425 **c)** −3.240 **d)** −1.883

6. a) $a = 1$, $b = 1$, $c = -6$ **b)** $x = 1$ **c)** $2^x = -3$

7. a) $a = 1$, $b = -2$, $c = -5$ **b)** $x = \dfrac{\log(1 + \sqrt{6})}{\log 8}$

c) $8^x = 1 - \sqrt{6}$

8. a) approximately 21.3 min **b)** approximately 92.06 min

9. a) approximately 19.7 min

b)

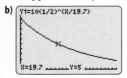

c) i) The graph is decreasing faster (shorter time). **c) ii)** The graph is decreasing at a slower rate (longer time to decay).
d) i) steeper slope (negative), more would decay in the same amount of time **ii)** slope is not as steep, less to decay in same amount of time

10. No.

11. a) $x = 1$ or $x \doteq 1.26$ **b)** $x \doteq 0.16$ **c)** $x = -1$ **d)** $x = 1$
e) no solution **f)** $x \doteq 1.29$

13. a) approximately 66.4 h **b)** Answers may vary.

14. approximately 6.44 days

15. a) 6 years **b)** approximately 10 years

16. a) i) 12 s **ii)** approximately 40 s

b)

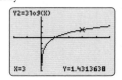

c) Answers may vary.

18. a) $y = A_0 - A_0 \left(\dfrac{1}{2}\right)^{\frac{t}{20}}$ **b)** $\{t \in \mathbb{R}, t \geq 0\}$, $\{y \in \mathbb{R}, 0 < y \leq A_0\}$

19. Answers may vary.

20. D

21. C

22. 11

7.3 Product and Quotient Laws of Logarithms, pages 384–386

1. a) $\log 54$ **b)** $\log 8$ **c)** $\log_3 21$ **d)** $\log_5 2$

2. a) 1.732 **b)** 0.903 **c)** 2.771 **d)** 0.431

3. a) $\log(2xyz)$, $x > 0$, $y > 0$, $z > 0$

b) $\log_2 \left(\dfrac{3ab}{2c}\right)$, $a > 0$, $b > 0$, $c > 0$

c) $\log \left(\dfrac{m^2 n^3}{y^4}\right)$, $m > 0$, $n > 0$, $y > 0$

d) $\log(u^2 v \sqrt{w})$, $u > 0$, $v > 0$, $w > 0$

4. a) 2 **b)** 2 **c)** 2 **d)** 3

5. a) 3 **b)** 4 **c)** 3 **d)** −2

6. a) 2 **b)** approximately 2.301

7. a) $\log_7 c + \log_7 d$ **b)** $\log_3 m - \log_3 n$ **c)** $\log u + 3\log v$

d) $\log a + \dfrac{1}{2}\log b - 2\log c$ **e)** $\log_2 2 + \log_2 5 = 1 + \log_2 5$

f) $\log_5 (25 \times 2) = 2 + \log_5 2$

8. Answers may vary.

9. a) $\dfrac{3}{2}\log x$, $x > 0$ **b)** $\log m$, $m > 0$ **c)** $\dfrac{8}{3}\log k$, $k > 0$

d) $\dfrac{9}{2}\log w$, $w > 0$

10. a) $\log(x + 2)$, $x > 2$ **b)** $\log(x + 4)$, $x > -3$

c) $\log\left(\dfrac{x + 2}{2}\right)$, $x > 3$ **d)** $\log\left(\dfrac{x + 4}{x - 3}\right)$, $x > 3$

11. a) $V_o = \log\left(\dfrac{V_2}{V_1}\right)$ **b) i)** $V_o = 1$ **ii)** $V_o = 2$ **iii)** $V_o = 0$

12. a) Translate $y = \log x$ up $(1 + \log n)$ units.
b) Answers may vary.

13. no, $n > 0$, positive integers only

14. a)

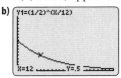 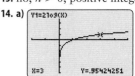

b) 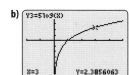 **c)**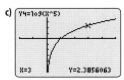

14. d) $p(x) = q(x)$; product law for logarithms.
15. a) $q(x) = \log x^6$

b)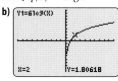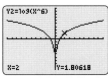

c) Answers may vary. Sample answer: The graph has values for $x < 0$ and $x > 0$ because x^6 is an even power; the graph has a discontinuity at $x = 0$.
16. Answers may vary.
18. a) approximately 6.7 years **b) i)** B **ii)** B **c)** Answers may vary.
22. $\sqrt{2}$
23. -1
24. B
25. $\dfrac{c}{k} - \dfrac{c}{k+n}$

7.4 Techniques for Solving Logarithmic Equations, pages 391–392
1. a) $x = 12$ **b)** $x = 75$ **c)** $p = 38$ **d)** $w = 17$
e) $k = 108$ **f)** $n = 50$
2. a) $x = 5$ **b)** $x = 21$ **c)** $k = 27$ **d)** $x = 25$ **e)** $t = \dfrac{9}{8}$
f) $n = 4$ or $n = -1$
3. a) $x = 2 + \sqrt{14}$ **b)** $x = 4$ **c)** $v = \dfrac{533}{33}$ **d)** $y = 1$
e) $k = 3$ **f)** $p = -\dfrac{995}{999}$
5. a) $x = -2$ or $x = 5$ **b)** $x = -50$ or $x = 2$
6. a) $x = \dfrac{5}{511}$ **b)** $k = \dfrac{1}{2}$
7. a) $x \doteq 9.05$ **b)** $x \doteq 2.16$

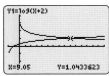 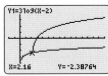

8. a) approximately 119.54 dB **b)** 1×10^{-10} W/m² **c)** 1 W/m²
9. a) No. **b)** Yes.
10. a) 2 **b)** $\dfrac{1}{16}$
11. a) $w = 5 \pm 5\sqrt{5}$

b)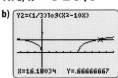

12. $x = -1$; graph each side of the equation as a function and find the point of intersection.

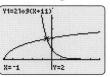

14. 44
15. $\pm 3\sqrt{5}$ or approximately 6.7 or -6.7
16. D

7.5 Making Connections: Mathematical Modelling With Exponential and Logarithmic Equations, pages 404–407
1. in June of 2037
2. in approximately the year 1774
3. a) for $P = 1006(1.016)^t$ **i)** $P \doteq 4920$ **ii)** $t \doteq 188.4$ years; for $P = 1000 \times 2^{\frac{t}{43.5}}$ **i)** $P \doteq 4921$ **ii)** $t \doteq 188$ years **b)** quite close
4. Answers may vary.
5. Answers may vary. Sample answer: Rural Ontario Investment Group takes a little less time to make $80 000 (7.35 years), so it could be considered. Muskoka Guaranteed Certificate takes the same amount of time, so it does not need to be considered.
6. a) Answers may vary. Sample answer: increasing in a curved pattern

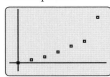

b) i) $y \doteq 4.21x - 3.07$ **ii)** $y \doteq 0.86x^2 - 0.93x + 1.2$
iii) $y \doteq 1.37(1.65)^x$
c) Answers may vary. Sample answer: exponential
d) Answers may vary. Sample answers:
i) approximately 207.8 m²
ii) $t \doteq 12.44$ min **e)** Answers may vary.
7. a) $A = 1000(1.02)^{4t}$ **b)** approximately $1372.79
c) approximately 8.75 years
8. a) $A = 1000(1.02)^{4t} - 50$ if $t < 4$.
b) shifts the graph down by 50
9. Answers may vary.
10. a) $1000 = \dfrac{I_2}{I_1}$ **b)** by 10 000 000 (or 10^7)
12.–14. Answers may vary.
15. 48 km/h
16. $A = \dfrac{\pi}{2} - 1$
17. z is increased by 12.5%.

Chapter 7 Review, pages 408–409

1. a) 4^3 **b)** 4^1 **c)** 4^{-2} **d)** $4^{\frac{5}{2}}$
2. a) $5^{\frac{\log 20}{\log 5}}$ **b)** $5^{\frac{\log 0.8}{\log 5}}$
3. a) $x = -\dfrac{3}{2}$ **b)** $x = -18$
4. a) approximately 5 min **b)** approximately 21.6 min
5. a) $x = \dfrac{2\log 3}{\log 3 - \log 5}$ **b)** $k = \dfrac{2\log 2 + \log 3}{\log 2 - \log 3}$
6. a) $x \doteq -4.301$, $k \doteq -6.129$

7. a) $x = \dfrac{\log 5}{\log 4}$ **b)** $x = 2$ or $x = \dfrac{\log 3}{\log 2}$

8. a) approximately 2.5 years **b)** approximately 8.3 years

9. a) 3 **b)** 2 **c)** 2 **d)** approximately 2.05

10. a) $\log_7 2$ **b)** $\log\left(\dfrac{3a^2 b}{\sqrt{c}}\right)$, $a > 0$, $b > 0$, $c > 0$

11. a) $2\log a + \log b + \log c$ **b)** $\log k - \dfrac{1}{2}\log m$

12. a) $\log\left(\dfrac{2}{m-3}\right)$, $m > 3$ **b)** $\log\left(\dfrac{x+5}{x-4}\right)$, $x > 4$, $x < -5$

13. a) $x = 45$ **b)** $x = 5$

14. $x = 2$

15.

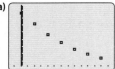

16. a) approximately 11.6 h **b)** approximately 66%

17. a) $A = 500(1.033)^{2t}$ **b)** approximately \$691.79
c) approximately 10.67 years
d) i) same shape translated up by 5 **ii)** above the original
function and increasing at a faster rate

Chapter 7 Practice Test, pages 410–411

1. C

2. A

3. D

4. C

5. 2

6. a) $x = 8$ **b)** $x = \dfrac{16}{3}$ **c)** $x = 15$ **d)** $x = 2.8$

8. a) $\log(x + 1) = 5\log x - 2$ **b)** $x \doteq 3.37$

9. a) approximately 35 min **b)** approximately 232.5 min
(or 3 h 52 min 30 s)

10. approximately 9.9 min

11. a) $x = 3$

12. a) Yes. **b)** Yes. **c)** Answers may vary.

13. a)

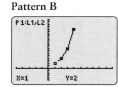

b) $y \doteq 0.17x^2 - 5.34x + 97.93$ **c)** $y \doteq 95.67(0.96)^x$
d) Answers may vary. Sample answer: Exponential, because
if predicting values for $x > 15.74$, the quadratic gives
increasing values, which is not realistic.
e) i) approximately 49.6°C **ii)** approximately 21.1 min
f) Answers may vary. Sample answer: The temperature of
the room was constant.

CHAPTER 8

Prerequisite Skills, pages 414–415

1. b) Pattern A: linear, Pattern B: exponential, Pattern C:
quadratic

2. a)

Pattern A	Pattern B

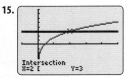

Pattern C

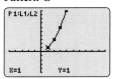

b) Yes.

3. A: $y = x + 2$; B: $y = 2^x$; C: $y = \dfrac{1}{2}x^2 + \dfrac{1}{2}x$

4. a) $\{x \in \mathbb{R}\}$, $\{y \in \mathbb{R}\}$

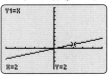

b) $\{x \in \mathbb{R}\}$, $\{y \in \mathbb{R}, y \geq 0\}$

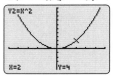

c) $\{x \in \mathbb{R}\}$, $\{y \in \mathbb{R}\}$

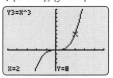

d) $\{x \in \mathbb{R}\}$, $\{y \in \mathbb{R}, y \geq 0\}$

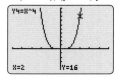

5. a) odd **b)** even **c)** odd **d)** even

7. a) $\{x \in \mathbb{R}, x \neq 0\}$, $\{y \in \mathbb{R}, y \neq 0\}$

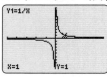

b) $\{x \in \mathbb{R}, x \neq 4\}$, $\{y \in \mathbb{R}, y \neq 0\}$

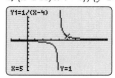

8. a) $u(x) = \dfrac{1}{x+2}$, $x \neq 2$, $x \neq -2$

b) $v(x) = x - 3$, $x \neq -2$

9. a) i) $\{x \in \mathbb{R}, x \neq 2, x \neq -2\}$, $\left\{y \in \mathbb{R}, y \neq 0, y \neq \dfrac{1}{4}\right\}$

ii)

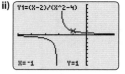

iii) asymptotes: $x = -2$, $y = 0$; hole: $\left(2, \frac{1}{4}\right)$

b) i) $\{x \in \mathbb{R}, x \neq -2\}$, $\{y \in \mathbb{R}, y \neq -5\}$

ii)

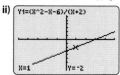

iii) hole: $(-2, -5)$

11. a) iv **b)** iii **c)** ii **d)** i

12. Answers may vary. Sample answers:
i) $0 \text{ s} \leq t \leq 8 \text{ s}$, $-5 \text{ cm} \leq d \leq 5 \text{ cm}$
ii) $0 \text{ s} \leq t \leq 3 \text{ s}$, $0 \text{ m} \leq d \leq 5 \text{ m}$
iii) $0 \text{ s} \leq t \leq 10 \text{ s}$, $-2 \text{ m} \leq d \leq 2 \text{ m}$
iv) $0 \text{ s} \leq t \leq 10 \text{ s}$, $0 \text{ m} \leq d \leq 3 \text{ m}$

13. a) $y = x + 2$ **b)** $y = \dfrac{x - 3}{4}$ **c)** $y = \pm\sqrt{x + 5}$, $x \geq -5$
d) $y = \dfrac{1}{x} - 1$, $x \neq 0$

14. The inverses of parts a), b), and d) are functions, since they pass the vertical line test.

8.1 Sums and Differences of Functions, pages 424–428

1. a) i) blue **ii)** red **iii)** yellow
b) i) $y = 3x$ **ii)** $y = x^2 - 1$ **iii)** $y = 2^x$
2. a) $y = 3x + x^2 - 1 + 2^x$ **b) i)** 71 **ii)** 117
3. a) i) $y = 6x + 7$ **ii)** $y = 4x - 7$ **iii)** $y = -4x + 7$
b) i) $y = -3x + 14$ **ii)** $y = -x - 4$ **iii)** $y = x + 4$
c) i) $y = x^2 + 5$ **ii)** $y = x^2 + 3$ **iii)** $y = -x^2 - 3$
d) i) $y = -3x^2 + 7x - 7$ **ii)** $y = -3x^2 + x + 7$
iii) $y = 3x^2 - x - 7$
4. a) $h(x) = 7x + 1$, $h(2) = 15$ **b)** $j(x) = x + 5$, $j(-1) = 4$
c) $k(x) = -x - 5$, $k(0) = -5$
5. a) $h(x) = -4x^2 + 2x + 2$, $h(-3) = -40$
b) $j(x) = -4x^2 - 2x + 8$, $j(0) = 8$
c) $k(x) = 4x^2 + 2x - 8$, $k(3) = 34$

6. a)

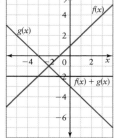

$\{x \in \mathbb{R}\}$, $\{y = 2\}$

b)

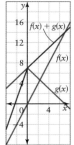

$\{x \in \mathbb{R}\}$, $\{y \in \mathbb{R}\}$

7. a)

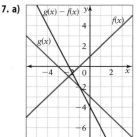

b)

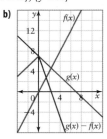

8. a) i)

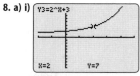

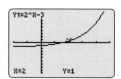

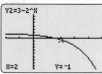

b) i) 3 units up **ii)** 3 units down
iii) reflection in the x-axis and 3 units up
c) i) $\{x \in \mathbb{R}\}$, $\{y \in \mathbb{R}, y > 3\}$
ii) $\{x \in \mathbb{R}\}$, $\{y \in \mathbb{R}, y > -3\}$
iii) $\{x \in \mathbb{R}\}$, $\{y \in \mathbb{R}, y < 3\}$

9. Window variables: $x \in [-\pi, 3\pi]$, Xscl $\dfrac{\pi}{2}$, $y \in [-2, 2]$

a)

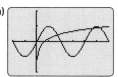

b)

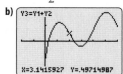

c)

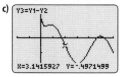

10. a) i) $C = 120 + h$ **ii)** $R = 2.5h$

b), c)

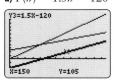

The break-even point is the point at which the revenue and cost are equal. When the vendor has sold 80 hotdogs, the cost and the revenue are both equal to $200.
d) $P(h) = 1.5h - 120$

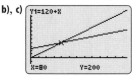

e) $C(h)$: $\{h \in \mathbb{Z}, 0 \leq h \leq 250\}$, $\{C \in \mathbb{R}, 120 \leq C \leq 370\}$
$R(h)$: $\{h \in \mathbb{Z}, 0 \leq h \leq 250\}$, $\{R \in \mathbb{R}, 0 \leq R \leq 625\}$
$P(h)$: $\{h \in \mathbb{Z}, 0 \leq h \leq 250\}$, $\{P \in \mathbb{R}, -120 \leq P \leq 255\}$
f) $255

11. a) i) If $C = 100 + h$, then the vendor only needs to sell about 67 hotdogs to break even.
ii) If $C = 120 + 0.9h$, then the potential daily profit becomes $280.
b) Answers may vary. Sample answer: Choose to reduce the variable cost.

12. a) Window variables: $x \in \left[-\frac{47\pi}{24}, \frac{47\pi}{24}\right]$, Xscl $\frac{\pi}{2}$, $y \in [-15, 30]$, Yscl 5

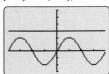

b)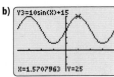

c) $\{t \in \mathbb{R}\}$, $\{y \in \mathbb{R}, 5 \le y \le 25\}$ **d) i)** 5 **ii)** 25 **iii)** 15
13. a) same **b)** Window variables: $x \in [-4, 4]$, $y \in [-4, 8]$

c)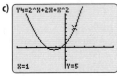

d) $f(x) = 2^x$ **e)** Answers may vary. The rate of change of the exponential function is continuously increasing at a greater rate than the other component functions.
14. a) Yes. **b)** No. **c)** The commutative property holds true for the sum of two functions, but not the difference of two functions.
15. a)   **c)** same

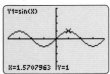   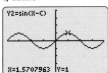

d)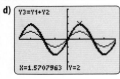

e) $\{x \in \mathbb{R}\}$, $\{y \in \mathbb{R}, -2 \le y \le 2\}$
f) i) shifted to the right and amplitude multiplied by $\sqrt{2}$
ii) horizontal line **iii)** same as when $c = 0$
g) i) $\{x \in \mathbb{R}\}$, $\{y \in \mathbb{R}, -\sqrt{2} \le y \le \sqrt{2}\}$
ii) $\{x \in \mathbb{R}\}$, $\{y \in \mathbb{R}, y = 0\}$ **iii)** $\{x \in \mathbb{R}\}$, $\{y \in \mathbb{R}, -2 \le y \le 2\}$
h) Answers may vary.
16. a) $y = -x - 2$
b)   **c)** $y = 3$

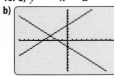

d)   **e)** $y = 3$, same

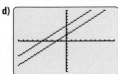

f) Subtracting the functions is the same as adding the opposite.

18. a) \$20 000; not affected by the number of games; $Y_1 = 20\,000$

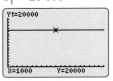

b) \$15/game; cost increases per game at a constant rate; $Y_2 = 15x$

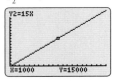

c) total operating costs; $Y_3 = 20\,000 + 15x$

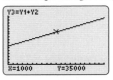

d) revenue increasing at a constant rate; $Y_4 = 20x$

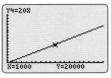   **e)**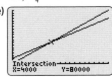

Break-even point: (4000, 80 000), cost equals revenue
f) profit; $Y_5 = 5x - 20\,000$

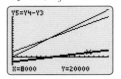

g) i) loss **ii)** break-even **iii)** profit
h) i) move to the left **ii)** move to the right
20. a) Window variables: $x \in \left[-\frac{47\pi}{24}, \frac{47\pi}{24}\right]$, Xscl $\frac{\pi}{2}$, $y \in [-4, 4]$

   **b)**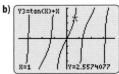

d) infinite number **e)** $g(x)$ intersects $h(x)$ at the point of inflection due to the variable vertical translation.
21. a) Window variables: $x \in \left[-\frac{47\pi}{24}, \frac{47\pi}{24}\right]$, Xscl $\frac{\pi}{2}$, $y \in [-4, 4]$

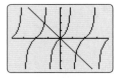   **b)**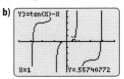

d) infinite number
e) $g(x)$ intersects $h(x)$ at the point of inflection due to the variable vertical translation.

22. Yes

23. The sum of two even functions is even.

24. B

25. D

26. 4

27. negative reciprocals: $A = -C$; reciprocals: $A = C$

8.2 Products and Quotients of Functions, pages 435–438

1. a) even: A and B; odd: A and C or B and C

b) Two combinations multiply to form an odd function.

2. odd

4. a) $y = x^3 - 2x^2 - 4x + 8$, $\{x \in \mathbb{R}\}$, $\{y \in \mathbb{R}\}$

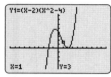

b) $y = \dfrac{1}{x + 2}$, $x \ne 2$, $x \ne -2$, $\{x \in \mathbb{R}, x \ne 2, x \ne -2\}$,

$\left\{y \in \mathbb{R}, y \ne \dfrac{1}{4}, y \ne 0\right\}$

hole: $\left(2, \dfrac{1}{4}\right)$, asymptotes: $x = -2$ and $y = 0$

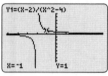

c) $y = x + 2$, $x \ne 2$, $\{x \in \mathbb{R}, x \ne 2\}$, $\{y \in \mathbb{R}, y \ne 4\}$, hole: (2, 4)

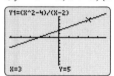

5. a) $y = 0.95^x \cos x$, $\{x \in \mathbb{R}\}$, $\{y \in \mathbb{R}\}$

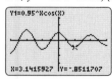

b) $y = \dfrac{\cos x}{0.95^x}$, $\{x \in \mathbb{R}\}$, $\{y \in \mathbb{R}\}$

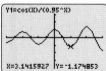

c) $y = \dfrac{0.95^x}{\cos x}$, $\cos x \ne 0$, $\left\{x \in \mathbb{R}, x \ne \dfrac{(2n + 1)\pi}{2}, n \in \mathbb{Z}\right\}$

$\{y \in \mathbb{R}, y \ne 0\}$, asymptotes: $x = \dfrac{(2n + 1)\pi}{2}$, $n \in \mathbb{Z}$, and $y = 0$

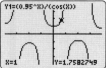

6. a) Both functions are exponential, with fish increasing and food decreasing.

Window variables: $x \in [0, 20]$, $y \in [0, 1500]$, Yscl 100

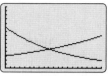

b) $P(t)$: $\{t \in \mathbb{R}\}$, $\{P \in \mathbb{R}, P \ge 0\}$

$F(t)$: $\{t \in \mathbb{R}\}$, $\{F \in \mathbb{R}, F \ge 0\}$

c) (9.11, 467.88); In 9.11 years, the number of fish and the amount of fish food both equal 467.88.

d) Answers may vary. Sample answer: The amount of fish food minus the number of fish. When the function is positive, there is a surplus of food. When the function is negative, there is not enough food.

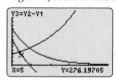

e) 9.11, same

f) Answers may vary. Sample answer: $P(t)$ should start to decrease since the amount of food is decreasing.

7. a) Answers may vary. Sample answer:
Ratio of food to fish. If the function is greater than one, there is more food. The graph is decreasing.

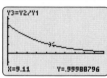

b) approximately (9.11, 1); After 9.11 years, the amount of food is equal to the number of fish.

c) plenty of food, enough food, not enough food

8. a) semi-circle, even   **b)** odd

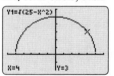   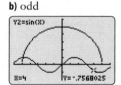

c)

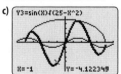

d) $\{x \in \mathbb{R}, -5 \le x \le 5\}$, $\{y \in \mathbb{R}, -4.76 \le y \le 4.76\}$

9. a) odd; $\{x \in \mathbb{R}, -5 < x < 5\}$, $\{y \in \mathbb{R}\}$

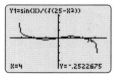

b) odd; $\{x \in \mathbb{R}, -5 \leq x \leq 5, x \neq -\pi, 0, \pi\}, \{y \in \mathbb{R}\}$

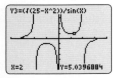

10. a) $P(t)$ is exponential and increasing, while $F(t)$ is linear and increasing.
Window variables: $x \in [0, 30]$, Xscl 2, $y \in [0, 15]$

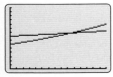

b) $y = 8 + 0.04t - 6(1.02)^t$; Answers may vary. Sample answers: In 2008, there is a surplus, since the function is positive. After 2019, there will be a food shortage.

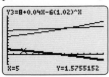

c) $(0, 2)$; In 2000, the maximum is 2, which is the amount of the surplus of food.

11. a) decreasing

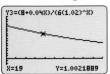

b) 2000; yes

c) When $\dfrac{F(t)}{P(t)} > 1$, there is a surplus of food. When $\dfrac{F(t)}{P(t)} < 1$, there is a shortage of food. For Terra, there is a surplus of food before 2019 and a shortage of food after 2019.

12. Answers may vary.

13. a) $p_{\text{Ask}}(t)$ is periodic, with domain $\{t \in \mathbb{R}, t \geq 0\}$ and range $\{p_{\text{Ask}} \in \mathbb{R}, 0.05 \leq p_{\text{Ask}} \leq 0.95\}$.
$p_{\text{Yes}}(t)$ is quadratic, increasing and then decreasing, with domain $\{t \in \mathbb{R}, 0 \leq t \leq 7\}$ and range $\{p_{\text{Yes}} \in \mathbb{R}, 0 \leq p_{\text{Yes}} \leq 0.98\}$.
Window variables: $x \in [0, 7]$, $y \in [0, 2]$, Yscl 0.5

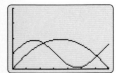

b) at the maximum values of $p_{\text{Ask}}(t)$, which occur at $\dfrac{\pi}{2}, \dfrac{5\pi}{2}, \dfrac{9\pi}{2}, \ldots$ days after the dance (approximately 1.6, 7.9, 14.1, . . . days after the dance)
c) at the maximum value of $p_{\text{Yes}}(t)$, which occurs 3.5 days after the dance

d) Answers may vary. Sample answer: The zeros of this graph are the points of intersection of the graphs of p_{Yes} and p_{Ask}.

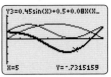

14. a) $y = -0.036t^2 \sin t + 0.252t \sin t - 0.04t^2 + 0.28t$

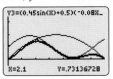

b) There is approximately a 73% chance of Carlos and Keiko agreeing to date 2.1 days after the dance.
c) after 7 days **d)** Answers may vary.
15. Yes.
16. No.
17. $\{x \in \mathbb{R}\}$, $\{y \in \mathbb{R}, y \leq 4.04\}$, x-intercept 0, y-intercept 0; $x < 0$, function is negative and increasing; $0 < x < 4.33$, function is positive and increasing; $x > 4.33$, function is positive and decreasing; as $x \rightarrow \infty$, $y \rightarrow 0$, and as $x \rightarrow -\infty$, $y \rightarrow -\infty$

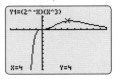

19. a) i) even **ii)** even **iii)** even **b) i)** even **ii)** odd **iii)** $[f(x)]^n$ is even if n is even and odd if n is odd when $f(x)$ is odd.
20. a) 245 cm
b) original function

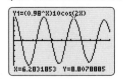

i) air resistance reduced

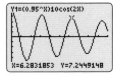

ii) pendulum lengthened

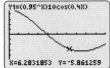

21. 10

22. $\dfrac{60}{7}$

23. $\dfrac{5}{2}$

24. 35 cm

8.3 Composite Functions, pages 447–449

1. a) $y = -x^2 - 6x - 7$ **b)** $y = x^2 - 10x + 25$ **c)** $y = x$
d) $y = x^4 + 12x^3 + 60x^2 + 144x + 144$ **e)** $y = x$
2. a) $\{x \in \mathbb{R}\}, \{y \in \mathbb{R}, y \leq 2\}$

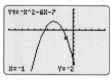

b) $\{x \in \mathbb{R}\}, \{y \in \mathbb{R}, y \geq 0\}$

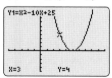

c) $\{x \in \mathbb{R}\}, \{y \in \mathbb{R}\}$

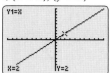

d) $\{x \in \mathbb{R}\}, \{y \in \mathbb{R}, y \geq 9\}$

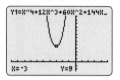

e) $\{x \in \mathbb{R}\}, \{y \in \mathbb{R}\}$

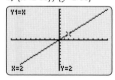

4. a) $-\dfrac{1}{3}$ **b)** -5
5. a) decreasing at a constant rate

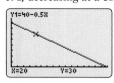

b) 40% **c)** decreasing by 0.5%/day
d) Answers may vary. Sample answer: No. Since the Blue party starts off with 40% and the Red party with 20%, there is a good possibility that there are more than two parties. Knowing the percent of undecided voters would help.
6. a) $R(t) = 20 + 0.375t$; increasing at a constant rate

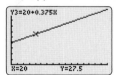

b) 20% **c)** increasing by 0.375%/day **d)** Answers may vary. Sample answer: If the election is held before 22.9 days, the Blue party will win. If the election is held after 22.9 days, then the Red party will win. 22.9 days is approximately when the two functions intersect. At least 40% of voters are undecided. We are assuming that these undecided voters do not vote.
7. a) $V(t) = 40 + 0.125t$; voters not decided on the Red or Blue party; increasing at a constant rate

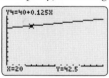

b) Answers may vary. Sample answer: The third party will win if the election is held before 80 days. At 80 days, both the Red party and the third party have 50% of the vote, while the Blue party has 0%. **c)** Answers may vary. Sample answer: If there were a fourth party, it would split the popularity in $V(t)$, and we can not tell who will win.
8. No
9. a) $y = x^{\frac{1}{3}}$ **b)** $y = x$ **c)** $y = x$ **d)** same
e) 3, 5, −1, $f(f^{-1}(x)) = x$ for all values of x.
10. Yes
11. a) $y = \sin^2 x$

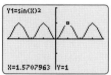

c) Yes **d)** $\{x \in \mathbb{R}\}, \{y \in \mathbb{R}, 0 \leq y \leq 1\}$
12. a) $y = \sin^3 x$; periodic; $\{x \in \mathbb{R}\}, \{y \in \mathbb{R}, -1 \leq y \leq 1\}$

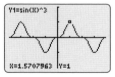

b) Answers may vary. Sample answer: The functions are both periodic and have a maximum value of 1. The functions differ in their minimum values (0 versus −1) and period (π versus 2π). One function is even, while the other is odd.
13. a) $C(P(t)) = 18.634 \times 2^{\frac{t}{52}} + 58.55$
b)

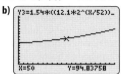

c) 60 years
14. $(f \circ g)^{-1}(x) = (g^{-1} \circ f^{-1})(x)$
15. a) parabolic, decreasing

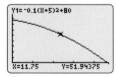

b) $\{p \in \mathbb{R}, 5 \le p \le 23.28\}$ c) No. d) $R(p) = [-0.1(p + 5)^2 + 80]p$

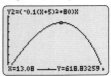

15. e) $13.08, $618.83
16. a) $W(N(t)) = 3\sqrt{100 + 25t}$
b) $\{t \in \mathbb{R}, t \ge 0\}, \{W \in \mathbb{R}, W \ge 30\}$

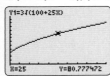

18. a) $\{x \in \mathbb{R}, x > 0\}$
b), c) $\{x \in \mathbb{R}, 2n\pi < x < (2n + 1)\pi, n \in \mathbb{Z}\}, \{y \in \mathbb{R}, y < 0\}$

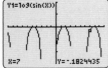

d), e) $\left\{x \in \mathbb{R}, \dfrac{(4n - 1)\pi}{2} < x < \dfrac{(4n + 1)\pi}{2}, n \in \mathbb{Z}\right\}$,
$\{y \in \mathbb{R}, y \le 0\}$

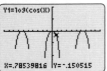

19. a) $\{x \in \mathbb{R}, x \ne 0\}, \{y \in \mathbb{R}, y > -9\}$
b) $\{x \in \mathbb{R}, x \ne -3, x \ne 3\}, \left\{y \in \mathbb{R}, y \le -\dfrac{1}{9}, y > 0\right\}$

20. $d(t) = \sqrt{41t}$
21. $f^{-1}(x) = \dfrac{b - dx}{cx - a}$
22. 0
23. 0, 1, $\dfrac{-1 + \sqrt{5}}{2}$
24. $\dfrac{7}{25}$
25. 10

8.4 Inequalities of Combined Functions, pages 457–460

1. a) i) The minimum number of homes will decrease and the maximum number of homes will increase. From the intersection points, the approximate number of homes becomes $44 \le n \le 442$.
ii) The maximum potential profit will increase. From the maximum of the difference function, the maximum potential profit becomes approximately $3.0 million.
1. b)

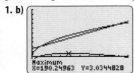

2. a) i) There will be no minimum or maximum number of homes, since the cost is higher than the revenue.
ii) There will be no profit, but a minimum loss of $153 846.
b)

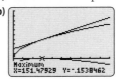

3. a) i) $x < 0, 0 < x < 1$ **ii)** $x > 1$
b)

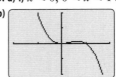

c) $x < 0, 0 < x < 1$, same
4. a)

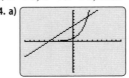

b)

c) i) When $y = \dfrac{u(x)}{v(x)} > 1$, $u(x) > v(x)$ for approximately
$-5 < x < 3$.
ii) When $y = \dfrac{u(x)}{v(x)} < 1$, $u(x) < v(x)$ for approximately
$x < -5, x > 3$.
5. a) Window variables: $x \in [-15, 10], y \in [-150, 150]$, Yscl 50

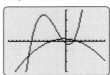

b) i) approximately $(-9.77, -1.23)$ or $(2, \infty)$
ii) approximately $(-\infty, -9.77)$ or $(-1.23, 2)$
7. a) Subtract $g(x)$ from $f(x)$. **b)** $y = -x^2 + 5x - 4$
c) Yes. When the graph is below the x-axis, $f(x) > g(x)$.
When the graph is above the x-axis, $g(x) > f(x)$.
8. $(0, \infty)$
9. approximately $(-\infty, -0.77)$ or $(2, 4)$
10. a)

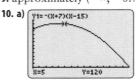

b) $5 \le p < 15$
c) $\{p \in \mathbb{R}, 5 \le p < 15\}, \{N \in \mathbb{R}, 0 < N \le 120\}$
11. a)

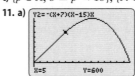

b) $5 \le p < 15$; yes
c) The $N(p)$ maximum is at $(4, 121)$, while the $R(p)$ maximum is at approximately $(9.16, 864.47)$.
The price affects where the maximum is. **d)** $9.16

12. a)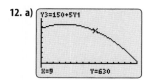

b) profit function

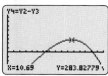

c) $6.30 < p < 14.24$; profit **d)** No. **e)** $10.69, $283.83
13. $0 \le t < 0.22$, $0.74 < t < 1.27$, and $1.79 < t \le 2$
14. Answers may vary. Sample answer: $f(x) = 5$ and
$g(x) = -1$
15. a) Window variables: $x \in [0, 16]$, Xscl 2, $y \in [-10, 30]$,
Yscl 2

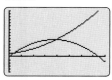

b) 2; where revenue equals cost **c)** $0.853 < n < 7.813$; profit
d)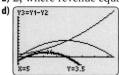

e) i) approximately 4333 **ii)** approximately $0.84/unit
iii) approximately $3633 **f)** Answers may vary.
16. a) $C(n) = 280 + 8n$ **b)** $R(n) = (45 - n)n$ **c)** $R(n) > C(n)$
d) $11 \le n \le 26$ **e)** 18 birdhouses at a profit of $62
18. Answers may vary. Sample answer:
$f(x) = \sin x$ and $g(x) = 0.5$
19. Answers may vary. Sample answers:
a) $f(x) = 2x$ and $g(x) = 0.5x^2$ **b)** $f(x) = 4x$ and $g(x) = x^2$
20. a) Answers may vary. Sample answer:
$f(x) = -(x - 3)(x + 3)$ and $g(x) = x + 3$ **b)** Yes.
21. Answers may vary. Sample answer:
$f(x) = (x + 3)(x - 4) + 1$ and $g(x) = 1$
22. 8
23. 3 or -3
24. 16

**8.5 Making Connections: Modelling With Combined
Functions, pages 461–471**
1. Window variables: $x \in [0, 50]$, Xscl 5, $y \in [-100, 140]$,
Yscl 20

a) 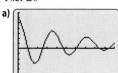 **b)**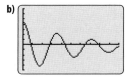

2. Window variables: $x \in [0, 50]$, Xscl 5, $y \in [-100, 140]$,
Yscl 20

a) 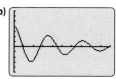 **b)**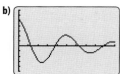

3. Window variables: $x \in [0, 50]$, Xscl 5, $y \in [-100, 140]$,
Yscl 20

a) 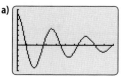 **b)**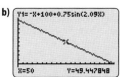

4. a)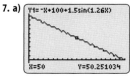

b) Answers may vary.
5. a) i) 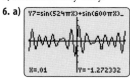 **ii)**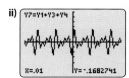

b) Answers may vary.
6. a)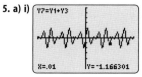

b) Answers may vary. Sample answer: This is not a pattern
like the others.
7. a) 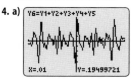 **b)**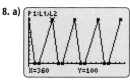

8. a)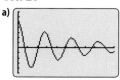

b) Answers may vary. Sample answer: $0 < x < 100$, skier
going down the hill; $100 < x < 160$, skier in line;
$160 < x < 360$, skier on lift **c)** Answers may vary.

9. a)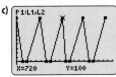
b)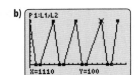

c)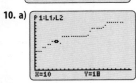

10. a)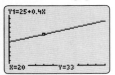

b) Answers may vary. Sample answer: Using regression on the graphing calculator, a curve of best fit that is quadratic has a greater R^2 value.
c) $N(t) \doteq -0.003x^2 + 0.621x + 11.003$
d) $N(t) \doteq -0.001x^2 + 0.505x + 12.216$; yes, it gives a better approximation for each value.
11. a) increasing, producing more high-calibre players

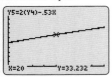

b) almost equal

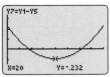

c) Answers may vary. Sample answer: It has stayed relatively constant over the years. **d)** confirm **e)** how many more draftees than retirees there are

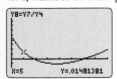

f) decreasing and then increasing; surplus, not enough, surplus
12. a) number of extra players per team over time

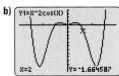

b) Years when there are no extra players; answers may vary.
c) Answers may vary. Sample answers: $P(t)$ increases;
$y = \dfrac{P(t)}{N(t)}$ increases so that it no longer crosses the t-axis;
surplus of players to draft
13. Answers may vary.

14. Answers may vary. Sample answer:
$y = 120(0.5^{0.1x}) + 2 \sin x$
15. Answers may vary.

Chapter 8 Review, pages 472–473

1. b) i) 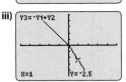   **ii)**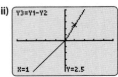

iii)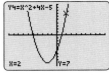

2. a) $y = x^2 + 4x - 5$; $\{x \in \mathbb{R}\}$, $\{y \in \mathbb{R}, y \geq -9\}$

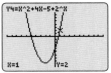

b) $y = x^2 + 4x - 5 + 2^x$; $\{x \in \mathbb{R}\}$, $\{y \in \mathbb{R}, y \geq -8.76\}$

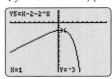

c) $y = x - 2 - 2^x$; $\{x \in \mathbb{R}\}$, $\{y \in \mathbb{R}, y \leq -2.9\}$

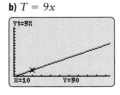

4. a) $W = 6x$ **b)** $T = 9x$

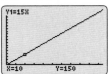

c) $E = 15x$

d) \$780
5. a) line symmetry about the y-axis; both $u(x)$ and $v(x)$ are even functions
b)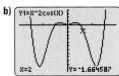

6. a) Window variables: $x \in \left[-\dfrac{47\pi}{24}, \dfrac{47\pi}{24}\right]$, Xscl $\dfrac{\pi}{2}$, $y \in [-4, 4]$

b)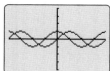

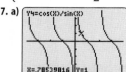

c) $\left\{ x \in \mathbb{R}, x \neq \dfrac{(2n-1)\pi}{2}, n \in \mathbb{Z} \right\}$, $\{y \in \mathbb{R}\}$ **d)** $y = \tan x$

7. a)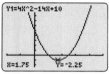

b) $\{x \in \mathbb{R}, x \neq n\pi, n \in \mathbb{Z}\}$, $\{y \in \mathbb{R}\}$
c) Answers may vary. Sample answer: reflection in the y-axis and shifted right $\dfrac{\pi}{2}$ units

8. a) $y = 4x^2 - 14x + 10$; $\{x \in \mathbb{R}\}$, $\{y \in \mathbb{R}, y \geq -2.25\}$

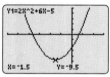

b) $y = 2x^2 + 6x - 5$; $\{x \in \mathbb{R}\}$, $\{y \in \mathbb{R}, y \geq -9.5\}$

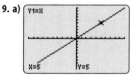

c) $y = 4x - 15$; $\{x \in \mathbb{R}\}$, $\{y \in \mathbb{R}\}$ **d)** $y = x$; $\{x \in \mathbb{R}\}$, $\{y \in \mathbb{R}\}$

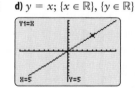

9. a)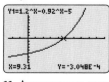

b) Answers may vary. Sample answer:
Given $f(x) = 2x - 3$, then $f^{-1}(x) = \dfrac{x+3}{2}$ and $f(f^{-1}(x)) = x$.
Given $f(x) = x^2$, then $f^{-1}(x) = \pm\sqrt{x}$ and $f(f^{-1}(x)) = x$.
10. a) i) approximately $x > 9.31$ **ii)** $x < 9.31$

b) i), ii)

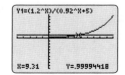

11. Answers may vary.

12. a) i) all values except at point A, where $C = R$
ii) no values **b)** not profitable **c)** Answers may vary.
Sample answer: The business owner should reduce costs.
13. a) 588 Hz

b)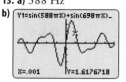

14. Answers may vary.

Chapter 8 Practice Test, page 474–475
1. A
2. D
3. D
4. A
5. a) $y = x^2 - 5x + 13$; $\{x \in \mathbb{R}\}$, $\{y \in \mathbb{R}, y \geq 6.75\}$

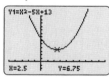

b) $y = x^2 - 7x + 5$; $\{x \in \mathbb{R}\}$, $\{y \in \mathbb{R}, y \geq -7.25\}$

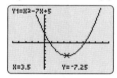

c) $y = x^2 + 2x + 1$; $\{x \in \mathbb{R}\}$, $\{y \in \mathbb{R}, y \geq 0\}$

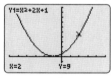

d) $y = x$; $x \in \mathbb{R}$, $y \in \mathbb{R}$

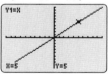

7. Answers may vary.
8. a) $y = \dfrac{1}{x+4}$, $x \neq -5$, $x \neq -4$; $\{x \in \mathbb{R}, x \neq -5, x \neq -4\}$, $\{y \in \mathbb{R}, y \neq 0, y \neq -1\}$

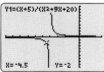

hole: $(-5, -1)$, asymptotes: $x = -4$ and $y = 0$

b) $y = x + 4$; $\{x \in \mathbb{R}, x \neq -5\}$, $\{y \in \mathbb{R}, y \neq -1\}$

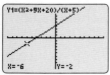

hole: $(-5, -1)$

9. a) $V(C) = \dfrac{C^3}{6\pi^2}$ **b)** $V(SA) = \dfrac{SA}{6}\sqrt{\dfrac{SA}{\pi}}$

10. odd

11. a) damped harmonic oscillation; $\{t \in \mathbb{R}, t \geq 0\}$, $\{x \in \mathbb{R}, -9.23 \leq x \leq 10\}$

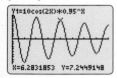

b) i) $10\cos(2t)$ **ii)** 0.95^t **c)** 10 cm **d)** at $x(t) = 0$; when the pendulum bob crosses the rest position the first time **e)** at crests and troughs; when the pendulum bob changes direction **f)** 12.7 s

12. a)

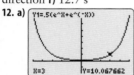

b) Answers may vary. Sample answer: $y \doteq 2.855x^2 - 7.217$ **c)** $(-4.73, 56.67)$, $(-1.94, 3.56)$, $(1.94, 3.56)$, $(4.73, 56.67)$ Window variables: $x \in [-5, 5]$, $y \in [-20, 100]$, Yscl 10

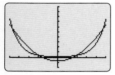

13. a) Window variables: $x \in [0, 40]$, Xscl 5, $y \in [-2, 10]$

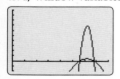

b) 31°C, 45 **c)** 31°C, yes

14. a) Answers may vary. Sample answer: $f(x) = (x - 1)(x + 1)$ and $g(x) = 0.5(x - 1)(x + 1)$

15. a)

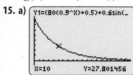

b) Answers may vary. Sample answer: The skier encounters moguls at 10 s, where the bumps start on the graph. **c)** $\{t \in \mathbb{R}, 0 \leq t \leq 64.3\}$, $\{h \in \mathbb{R}, 0 \leq h \leq 80\}$

Chapters 6 to 8 Review, pages 476–477

1. a)

x	y
-2	$\dfrac{1}{16}$
-1	$\dfrac{1}{4}$
0	1
$\dfrac{1}{2}$	2
1	4
2	16
3	64

b)

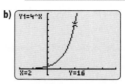

c)

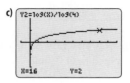

2. a) 2 **b)** 7 **c)** -3 **d)** 3 **e)** 4 **f)** -5
3. a) 5.9 units **b)** 0.9 units
4. a) $\{x \in \mathbb{R}, x > 2\}$, $\{y \in \mathbb{R}\}$ x-intercept 2.5, y-intercept none, asymptote $x = 2$

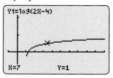

b) reflection in the x-axis
5. a) 10 **b)** 3
6. a) 1.95 **b)** 4.17
7. a) \$28 000, when $t = 0$ **b)** 2.4 years
8. a) 99 dB **b)** 10^{-10} W/m²
9. a) $\dfrac{4}{7}$ **b)** 1 **c)** 17

10. a) 1.89 **b)** 2.62 **c)** -4.15 **d)** -2.58 **e)** 5.06 **f)** 0.33
11. a) 194 h **b)** 2.8 h
12. a) $\log(x + 1)$, $x > -1$, $x \neq 1$ **b)** $\log\left(x^{\frac{3}{2}}\right)$, $x > 0$
c) $2\log(x + y)$, $x > -y$, $x \neq 0$
13. a) $-\dfrac{4}{3}$ **b)** 1, extraneous root $-\dfrac{5}{3}$ **c)** 7, extraneous root 1
14. Different; the domain of the graph of $g(x)$ is $\{x \in \mathbb{R}, x > 0\}$, while the domain of $f(x)$ is $\{x \in \mathbb{R}\}$.
15. a) $P(t) = 38\ 000(1.12)^t$ **b)** 6.1 years **c)** 8.5 years
16. a) $y = 2^x + x^2 + 1$; $\{x \in \mathbb{R}\}$, $\{y \in \mathbb{R}, y \geq 1.9\}$

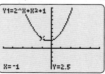

b) $y = 2^x - x^2 - 2x + 3$; $\{x \in \mathbb{R}\}$, $\{y \in \mathbb{R}\}$

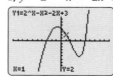

c) $y = (2^x + 2)(x^2 - 1)$; $\{x \in \mathbb{R}\}$, $\{y \in \mathbb{R}, y \geq -3.04\}$

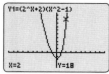

d) $y = \dfrac{2^x + 2}{x^2 - 1}$; $\{x \in \mathbb{R}, x \neq -1, x \neq 1\}$,
$\{y \in \mathbb{R}, y \leq -2.96, y > 0\}$

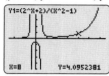

17. a) i) $C(n) = 35 + n$, $0 \leq n \leq 200$
ii) $R(n) = 2.5n$, $0 \leq n \leq 200$ **b)** Window variables:
$x \in [0, 200]$, Xscl 10, $y \in [0, 500]$, Yscl 50

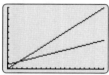

c) (23.33, 58.33); Kathy makes a profit if she sells 24 or more cups of apple cider. Kathy loses money if she sells 23 or fewer cups of apple cider.
d) $P(n) = 1.5n - 35$

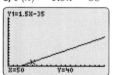

e) \$265
18. a) linear; neither   **b)** periodic; even

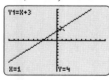 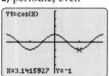

c)

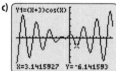

e) $\{x \in \mathbb{R}\}$, $\{y \in \mathbb{R}\}$
19. a) $y = \dfrac{\sqrt{1 - 9x^2}}{x}$; $\left\{x \in \mathbb{R}, -\dfrac{1}{3} \leq x < 0, 0 < x \leq \dfrac{1}{3}\right\}$,
$\{y \in \mathbb{R}\}$ **b)** $y = \dfrac{1}{x - 9}$; $\{x \in \mathbb{R}, x > 9\}$, $\{y \in \mathbb{R}, y > 0\}$
20. a) Window variables: $x \in [-20, 20]$, Xscl 2,
$y \in [-200, 100]$, Yscl 20

b) $[-5, -0.65)$ or $(7.65, \infty)$

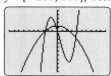

Course Review, pages 479–483
1. a) An even function is symmetric with respect to the y-axis. An odd function is symmetric with respect to the origin.
b) Substitute $-x$ for x in $f(x)$. If $f(-x) = f(x)$, the function is even. If $f(-x) = -f(x)$, the function is odd.
2. Answers may vary. Sample answer: A polynomial function has the form $f(x) = a_n x^n + a_{n-1} x^{n-1} + \ldots + a_1 x + a_0$. For a polynomial function of degree n, where n is a positive integer, the nth differences are equal (or constant).
3. $f(x)$ extends from quadrant 3 to quadrant 4; even exponent, negative coefficient
$g(x)$ extends from quadrant 2 to quadrant 1; even exponent, positive coefficient
$h(x)$ extends from quadrant 3 to quadrant 1; odd exponent, positive coefficient
4. 4
5. $y = -2(x - 3)^4 + 1$

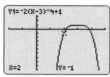

6. $f(x)$: x-intercept 0, y-intercept 0, $\{x \in \mathbb{R}\}$, $\{y \in \mathbb{R}\}$
$g(x)$: x-intercepts -2 and 1, y-intercept 2, $\{x \in \mathbb{R}\}$, $\{y \in \mathbb{R}\}$
Window variables: $x \in [-20, 20]$, Xscl 2, $y \in [-200, 100]$, Yscl 20

7. a) 138 **b)** 18; 342 **c)** The graph is increasing for $1 < x < 3$.
8. a) $y = (x + 3)(x + 1)(x - 2)(x - 5)$ **b)** $y = -(x + 5)(x - 1)^2$
9. For $x < 0$, the slope is positive and decreasing. For $x > 0$, the slope is negative and decreasing.
10. a) $\dfrac{4x^3 + 6x^2 - 4x + 2}{2x - 1} = 2x^2 + 4x + \dfrac{2}{2x - 1}$,
$x \neq \dfrac{1}{2}$
b) $\dfrac{2x^3 - 4x + 8}{x - 2} = 2x^2 + 4x + 4 + \dfrac{16}{x - 2}$, $x \neq 2$
c) $\dfrac{x^3 - 3x^2 + 5x - 4}{x + 2} = x^2 - 5x + 15 + \dfrac{-34}{x + 2}$, $x \neq -2$
d) $\dfrac{5x^4 - 3x^3 + 2x^2 + 4x - 6}{x + 1} = 5x^3 - 8x^2 + 10x - 6$, $x \neq -1$
11. a) $(x - 1)(x + 2)(x + 3)$ **b)** $(x - 3)(x + 1)(2x + 5)$
c) $(x - 2)(x^2 - 5x + 1)$ **d)** $(x^2 + x + 1)(x^2 - x + 1)$
12. a) 345 **b)** $\dfrac{44}{27}$
13. a) No. **b)** No.
14. a) -3, 3 **b)** -2, -1, 4 **c)** $-\dfrac{3}{2}$ **d)** $-\dfrac{3}{2}$, $-\dfrac{1}{2}$, 0, $\dfrac{2}{3}$
15. a) Answers may vary. Sample answer:
$y = k(x + 3)(x + 1)(x - 1)^2$; $y = 2(x + 3)(x + 1)(x - 1)^2$, $y = -(x + 3)(x + 1)(x - 1)^2$
b) $y = \dfrac{2}{3}(x + 3)(x + 1)(x - 1)^2$

c)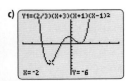

d) $x < -3$, $-1 < x < 1$, $x > 1$

16. a) $x < -3$ or $x > 4$ **b)** $-2 < x < \dfrac{3}{2}$

c) $x \leq -2$ or $-1 \leq x \leq 5$

17. a) $x = 2$, $y = 0$ **b)** $x = -3$, $y = 1$

c) $x = -3$, $x = 3$, $y = 0$ **d)** $y = 0$

18. a) i) $x = -4$, $y = 0$ **ii)** y-intercept $\dfrac{1}{4}$

iii)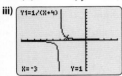

iv) decreasing for $x < -4$ and $x > -4$

v) $\{x \in \mathbb{R}, x \neq -4\}$, $\{y \in \mathbb{R}, y \neq 0\}$

b) i) $x = 2$, $y = 0$ **ii)** y-intercept 2

iii)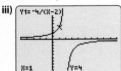

iv) increasing for $x < 2$ and $x > 2$

v) $\{x \in \mathbb{R}, x \neq 2\}$, $\{y \in \mathbb{R}, y \neq 0\}$

c) i) $x = -3$, $y = 1$ **ii)** y-intercept $-\dfrac{1}{3}$, x-intercept 1

iii)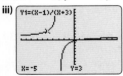

iv) increasing for $x < -3$ and $x > -3$

v) $\{x \in \mathbb{R}, x \neq -3\}$, $\{y \in \mathbb{R}, y \neq 1\}$

d) i) $x = -\dfrac{1}{5}$, $y = \dfrac{2}{5}$ **ii)** y-intercept 3, x-intercept $-\dfrac{3}{2}$

iii)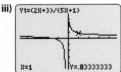

iv) decreasing for $x < -\dfrac{1}{5}$ and $x > -\dfrac{1}{5}$ **v)** $\left\{x \in \mathbb{R}, x \neq -\dfrac{1}{5}\right\}$, $\left\{y \in \mathbb{R}, y \neq \dfrac{2}{5}\right\}$

e) i) $x = 0$, $y = 0$ **ii)** no intercepts

iii)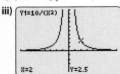

iv) increasing for $x < 0$, decreasing for $x > 0$

v) $\{x \in \mathbb{R}, x \neq 0\}$, $\{y \in \mathbb{R}, y > 0\}$

f) i) $x = -3$, $x = 9$, $y = 0$ **ii)** y-intercept $-\dfrac{1}{9}$

iii)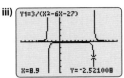

iv) increasing for $x < -3$ and $-3 < x < 3$, decreasing for $3 < x < 9$ and $x > 9$

v) $\{x \in \mathbb{R}, x \neq -3, x \neq 9\}$, $\left\{y \in \mathbb{R}, y \leq -\dfrac{1}{12}, y > 0\right\}$

19. positive increasing slope for $x < -3$, positive decreasing slope for $-3 < x < 2$, negative decreasing slope for $2 < x < 7$, negative increasing slope for $x > 7$

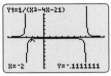

20. a) $\dfrac{17}{4}$ **b)** 7 **c)** -2

21. a) $x < 4$ or $x > \dfrac{23}{5}$ **b)** $x < -4$ or $-1 < x \leq 3$ or $x \geq 5$

22. a)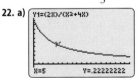

b) $R(t) = 0$; The chemical will not completely dissolve.

c) $\{t \in \mathbb{R}, 0 \leq t < 36\}$

23. a) $\dfrac{3\pi}{4}$ **b)** $-\dfrac{\pi}{3}$

24. a) 30° **b)** 202.5°

25. $\dfrac{15\pi + 72}{4}$

26. a) $-\dfrac{\sqrt{3}}{2}$ **b)** -1 **c)** $\sqrt{3}$ **d)** -1

27. a) $\dfrac{1 + \sqrt{3}}{2\sqrt{2}}$ **b)** $\dfrac{\sqrt{3} - 1}{2\sqrt{2}}$

29. $\dfrac{\sqrt{11} + 10\sqrt{6}}{30}$

30. $\dfrac{\pi}{8}$

31. a) period π, amplitude 3, phase shift $\dfrac{\pi}{2}$ rad to the right, vertical translation 4 units upward

b) $\{x \in \mathbb{R}\}$, $\{y \in \mathbb{R}, 1 \leq y \leq 7\}$

32. a) x-intercept $\dfrac{3\pi}{2}$ **b)** x-intercepts $\dfrac{\pi}{8}$, $\dfrac{3\pi}{8}$

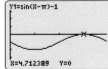 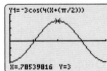

c) asymptotes $x = 0$, $x = \pi$, $x = 2\pi$

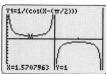

33. a) $\dfrac{4\pi}{3}, \dfrac{5\pi}{3}$ **b)** $\dfrac{\pi}{6}, \dfrac{\pi}{2}, \dfrac{5\pi}{6}, \dfrac{3\pi}{2}$ **c)** $\dfrac{\pi}{6}, \dfrac{5\pi}{6}, \dfrac{3\pi}{2}$

34. a)

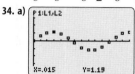

b) $y = 1.199 \sin(113.091x) - 0.002$

c)

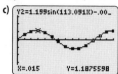

d) 135.6 cm/s

35. a) $\log_7 49 = 2$ **b)** $\log_a c = b$ **c)** $\log_8 512 = 3$ **d)** $\log_{11} y = x$

36. a) $f(x)$: x-intercept 1, asymptote $x = 0$
$g(x)$: x-intercept 0, y-intercept 0, asymptote $x = -1$
Window variables: $x \in [-2, 10]$, $y \in [-2, 3]$

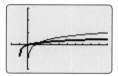

b) $f(x)$: $\{x \in \mathbb{R}, x > 0\}$, $\{y \in \mathbb{R}\}$; $g(x)$: $\{x \in \mathbb{R}, x > -1\}$, $\{y \in \mathbb{R}\}$

37. a) $3^8 = 6561$ **b)** $a^b = 75$ **c)** $7^4 = 2401$ **d)** $a^b = 19$

38. a) 8 **b)** 1 **c)** $\dfrac{1}{2}$ **d)** 5 **e)** 1 **f)** -1

39. a) 81 **b)** 5 **c)** 16 807 **d)** 3 **e)** -7 **f)** -3

40. 62 min

41. a) alkaline, 1.585×10^{-8} mol/L **b)** 3.1

42. a) $x \doteq 1.29$ **b)** $x \doteq 0.79$ or $x \doteq 1.16$

43. a) 3 **b)** $\dfrac{3}{2}$ **c)** -2 **d)** $\dfrac{1}{3}$

44. a) 3.7004 **b)** 0.9212 **c)** 2.6801 **d)** 0.0283

45. a) 3 **b)** -2

46. $(1.62, 0.21)$

47. a) $h \doteq 19.7$ min **b)** approximately 7.03 mg

c)

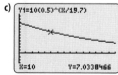

d) Answers may vary. Sample answer: The graph would decrease faster because the sample would be decreasing at a faster rate.

48. a) $d \doteq 4.04$ years **b)** approximately 3 229 660

49. a) $y = 35\,000(0.82)^t$ **b)** \$12 975.89
c) approximately 3.5 years

d)

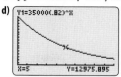

e) Answers may vary. Sample answer: The graph would decrease faster.

50. a)

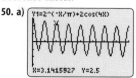

b)

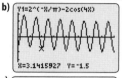

c)

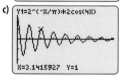

d)

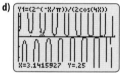

51. a) $2x^2 + 15x + 22$ **b)** $2x^2 + 3x - 2$ **c)** -5 **d)** 117

52. a) 1 **b)** $\dfrac{1}{4}$ **c)** does not exist **d)** $\dfrac{15}{4}$

53. a) $f(g(x)) = \sqrt{x + 1}$, $\{x \in \mathbb{R}, x \geq -1\}$;
$g(f(x)) = \sqrt{x} + 1$, $\{x \in \mathbb{R}, x \geq 0\}$
b) $f(g(x)) = \sin(x^2)$, $\{x \in \mathbb{R}\}$; $g(f(x)) = \sin^2 x$, $\{x \in \mathbb{R}\}$
c) $f(g(x)) = |x^2 - 6|$, $\{x \in \mathbb{R}\}$; $g(f(x)) = |x|^2 - 6$, $\{x \in \mathbb{R}\}$
d) $f(g(x)) = 2^{(3x + 3)}$, $\{x \in \mathbb{R}\}$; $g(f(x)) = 3(2^{x + 1}) + 2$, $\{x \in \mathbb{R}\}$
e) $f(g(x)) = 6\sqrt{x - 3} + x + 6$, $\{x \in \mathbb{R}, x \geq 3\}$;
$g(f(x)) = \sqrt{x^2 + 6x + 6}$, $\{x \in \mathbb{R}, x \leq -3 - \sqrt{3},$
$x \geq -3 + \sqrt{3}\}$ **f)** $f(g(x)) = (x + 1)\log 3$, $\{x \in \mathbb{R}\}$;
$g(f(x)) = 3^{\log x + 1}$, $\{x \in \mathbb{R}, x > 0\}$

54. a) $y = -\dfrac{2}{\sqrt{x}}$ **b)** $\{x \in \mathbb{R}, x > 0\}$ **c)** neither

56. a) approximately $(-\infty, -4.43)$ or $(-3.11, -1.08)$ or $(3.15, \infty)$

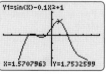

b) approximately $[-1.69, 2]$

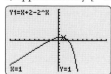

57. a) $h(t) = 20 \sin\left(\dfrac{\pi t}{15}\right) + 22$

b)

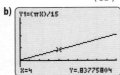

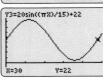

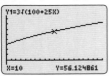

c) The period of $h(\theta)$ is 2π rad. The period of $h(t)$ is 30 s.

58. a) $W(t) = 3\sqrt{100 + 25t}$
b) $\{t \in \mathbb{R}, t \geq 0\}$, $\{W \in \mathbb{Z}, W \geq 30\}$

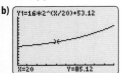

59. a) $C(t) = 16 \times 2^{\frac{t}{20}} + 53.12$

b)

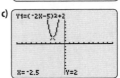

c) approximately 31 years

PREREQUISITE SKILLS APPENDIX ANSWERS

Angles From Trigonometric Ratios, page 484
1. a) $18.8°$ **b)** $136.5°$ **c)** $70.0°$ **d)** $-40.9°$ **e)** $75.7°$ **f)** $-74.4°$

Apply the Exponent Laws, pages 484–485
1. a) $\dfrac{5}{x^3}$ **b)** $\dfrac{1}{81x^4}$ **c)** $7 + \dfrac{1}{x^6}$ **d)** $\dfrac{1}{25}x^6 - \dfrac{6}{x} + 2x - x^3$
2. a) $9x^{\frac{9}{2}} + 6x^{\frac{5}{2}} + x^{\frac{1}{2}}$ **b)** $6x^5 + 9x^4 - 10x - 15$
c) $4x^6 - 4x^4 + 8x^3 - 8x$ **d)** $\sqrt{2x^3 - 4x^2 + 10x - 20}$
3. a) 81 **b)** $\dfrac{1}{1024}$ **c)** 1 **d)** 6 **e)** 125
4. a) $20x^9y^7$ **b)** b^3c^3, $a, b, c \neq 0$ **c)** $m^{-5}n^2$, $m, n \neq 0$
d) xy^{-4}, $x, y \neq 0$

Apply Transformations to Functions, pages 485–486
1. a) vertical translation **b)** vertical stretch **c)** horizontal
compression **d)** vertical reflection **e)** horizontal translation
f) horizontal reflection **g)** horizontal translation **h)** horizontal
stretch **i)** vertical translation **j)** vertical stretch
2. a) vertical stretch by a factor of 3 and horizontal reflection
in the y-axis
b) vertical translation downward by 3 units and horizontal
compression by a factor of $\dfrac{1}{2}$
c) horizontal translation left by 2 units and vertical reflection
in the x-axis
d) vertical compression by a factor of $\dfrac{1}{3}$, horizontal
compression by a factor of $\dfrac{1}{5}$, and horizontal reflection
in the y-axis

3. a)

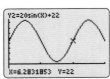

b)

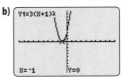

c)

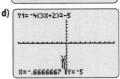

d)

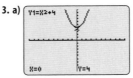

Determine Equations of Quadratic Functions, page 486
1. a) $f(x) = 2(x - 1)(x - 5)$ **b)** $f(x) = -(x + 2)(x - 1)$
c) $f(x) = 1.5(x + 6)(x + 1)$ **d)** $f(x) = 0.5(x + 3)(x - 0.5)$

Determine Intervals From Graphs, page 487
1. a) x-intercepts -2 and 2; above the x-axis for
$-2 < x < 2$; below the x-axis for $x < -2$ and $x > 2$
b) x-intercepts -3, 0, and 3; above the x-axis for $-3 < x < 0$
and $x > 3$; below the x-axis for $x < -3$ and $0 < x < 3$

Distance Between Two Points, page 487
1. a) $3\sqrt{2}$ **b)** $\sqrt{65}$ **c)** $\sqrt{74}$ **d)** $3\sqrt{5}$ **e)** $3\sqrt{5}$ **f)** $\sqrt{82}$

Domain and Range, page 488
1. a) $\{x \in \mathbb{R}\}$, $\{y \in \mathbb{R}\}$
b) $\{x \in \mathbb{R}\}$, $\{y \in \mathbb{R}\}$
c) $\{x \in \mathbb{R}\}$, $\{y \in \mathbb{R}, y \geq -1\}$
d) $\{x \in \mathbb{R}\}$, $\{y \in \mathbb{R}, y \geq 4\}$
e) $\{x \in \mathbb{R} \mid x \geq -5\}$, $\{y \in \mathbb{R}, y \geq 0\}$
f) $\{x \in \mathbb{R}, x \geq 2\}$, $\{y \in \mathbb{R}, y \geq 0\}$
g) $\{x \in \mathbb{R}, x \neq -2\}$, $\{y \in \mathbb{R}, y \neq 0\}$
h) $\{x \in \mathbb{R}, x \neq 1\}$, $\{y \in \mathbb{R}, y \neq 0\}$

Equation of a Line, pages 488–489
1. a) $y = 2x + 1$ **b)** $y = -4x + 4$
2. a) $y = 3x - 1$ **b)** $y = -x - 3$
3. a) $y = \dfrac{7}{2}x + \dfrac{3}{2}$ **b)** $y = -x + 8$
4. a) $y = -4x + 4$ **b)** $y = \dfrac{2}{3}x - 2$

Evaluate Functions, pages 489–490
1. a) -7 **b)** 35 **c)** 5 **d)** $-\dfrac{89}{27}$ **e)** 39.221 **f)** $n^3 + 3n^2 - 4n - 7$
g) $-27x^3 + 27x^2 + 12x - 7$ **h)** $x^6 + 3x^4 - 4x^2 - 7$
2. a) -1 **b)** 20 **c)** 2 **d)** $x^2 + 4x - 1$
3. a) 0 **b)** 2 **c)** 1 **d)** $\sqrt{x^2 - 3}$
4. a) 5 **b)** 2 **c)** 10 **d)** 0
5. a) true **b)** false **c)** true **d)** false

Exact Trigonometric Ratios of Special Angles, pages 490–491

1. $\sin 30° = \dfrac{1}{2}$, $\cos 30° = \dfrac{\sqrt{3}}{2}$, $\tan 30° = \dfrac{1}{\sqrt{3}}$, $\csc 30° = 2$,

$\sec 30° = \dfrac{2}{\sqrt{3}}$, $\cot 30° = \sqrt{3}$

2. $\sin 150° = \dfrac{1}{2}$, $\cos 150° = -\dfrac{\sqrt{3}}{2}$, $\tan 150° = -\dfrac{1}{\sqrt{3}}$,

$\csc 150° = 2$, $\sec 150° = -\dfrac{2}{\sqrt{3}}$, $\cot 150° = -\sqrt{3}$,

$\sin 210° = -\dfrac{1}{2}$, $\cos 210° = -\dfrac{\sqrt{3}}{2}$, $\tan 210° = \dfrac{1}{\sqrt{3}}$,

$\csc 210° = -2$, $\sec 210° = -\dfrac{2}{\sqrt{3}}$, $\cot 210° = \sqrt{3}$,

$\sin 330° = -\dfrac{1}{2}$, $\cos 330° = \dfrac{\sqrt{3}}{2}$, $\tan 330° = -\dfrac{1}{\sqrt{3}}$,

$\csc 330° = -2$, $\sec 330° = \dfrac{2}{\sqrt{3}}$, $\cot 330° = -\sqrt{3}$

Factor Quadratic Expressions, pages 491–492

1. a) $(x - 2)(x + 2)$ **b)** $(y - 10)(y + 10)$ **c)** $(2n - 7)(2n + 7)$
d) $(5m - 9)(5m + 9)$ **e)** $(1 - 6x)(1 + 6x)$ **f)** $(2y - 3x)(2y + 3x)$
2. a) $(x - 5)(x + 4)$ **b)** $(y + 5)(y - 2)$ **c)** $(n - 9)(n + 4)$
d) $(m + 3)(m + 6)$ **e)** $(x - 6)(x - 5)$ **f)** $(c - 6)(c + 4)$
g) $(16 - y)(1 + y)$ **h)** $(x + 4y)(x + 8y)$ **i)** $(c - 7d)(c + 4d)$
3. a) $(x - 2)(3x + 4)$ **b)** $(2c - 1)(c + 4)$ **c)** $(4m - 3)(m - 2)$
d) $(y + 1)(5y + 3)$ **e)** $(n + 1)(3n - 2)$ **f)** $(6x + 1)(x - 3)$
g) $(3x + 4y)(x - 3y)$ **h)** $(5x - 4)(x - 2)$ **i)** $(4x + 3)(x + 5)$
j) $(p + q)(2p - q)$

Finite Differences, pages 492–493

1. a) linear **b)** quadratic **c)** linear **d)** neither **e)** quadratic **f)** neither

Graph an Exponential Function, pages 493–494

1. a)

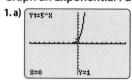

b) $\{x \in \mathbb{R}\}$, $\{y \in \mathbb{R}, y > 0\}$, asymptote $y = 0$
c) i) 1.4 **ii)** 0.2

Graph an Inverse, page 494

1. a)

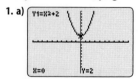

b) $\{x \in \mathbb{R}\}$, $\{y \in \mathbb{R}, y \geq 2\}$

c)

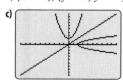

d) $\{x \in \mathbb{R}, x \geq 2\}$, $\{y \in \mathbb{R}\}$
e) Since the graph of the inverse does not pass the vertical line test, f^{-1} is not a function.

2. a)

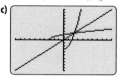

b) $\{x \in \mathbb{R}, x \geq -3\}$, $\{y \in \mathbb{R}, y \geq 0\}$

c)

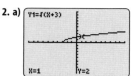

d) $\{x \in \mathbb{R}, x \geq 0\}$, $\{y \in \mathbb{R}, y \geq -3\}$
e) Yes. The graph of the inverse passes the vertical line test.

Graphs and Transformations of Sinusoidal Functions Using Degree Measure, page 495

1. a) Window variables: $x \in [-360, 360]$, Xscl 30, $y \in [-5, 5]$

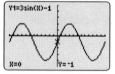

amplitude 3, period 360°, no phase shift, vertical translation 1 unit downward
b) Window variables: $x \in [-360, 360]$, Xscl 30, $y \in [-5, 5]$

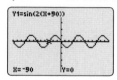

amplitude 1, period 180°, phase shift 90° to the left, no vertical translation

c)

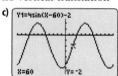

amplitude 4, period 360°, phase shift 60° to the right, vertical translation 2 units downward
2. Window variables: $x \in [-360, 360]$, Xscl 30, $y \in [-4, 4]$

a)

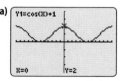

amplitude 1, period 360°, no phase shift, vertical translation 1 unit upward

b)

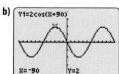

amplitude 2, period 360°, phase shift 90° to the left, no vertical translation

c)

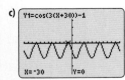

amplitude 1, period 120°, phase shift 30° to the left, vertical translation 1 unit downward

Identify Linear, Quadratic, and Exponential Growth Models, page 496

1. a)

b)

n	t
1	8
2	14
3	20
4	26
5	32

c) linear
d) Window variables: $x \in [0, 7]$, $y \in [0, 40]$, Yscl 5

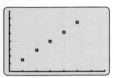

e) $t = 6n + 2$

2. a)

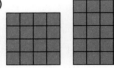

b)

n	t
1	1
2	4
3	9
4	16
5	25

c) quadratic
d) Window variables: $x \in [0, 7]$, $y \in [0, 40]$, Yscl 5

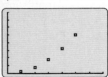

e) $t = n^2$

3.

b)

n	t
1	2
2	4
3	8
4	16
5	32

c) exponential
d) Window variables: $x \in [0, 7]$, $y \in [0, 40]$, Yscl 5

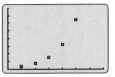

e) $t = 2^n$

Inverses, pages 496–497

1. a) $y = \dfrac{x + 1}{3}$; function **b)** $y = \dfrac{x - 5}{6}$; function

c) $y = \pm\sqrt{\dfrac{x - 2}{4}}$; not a function **d)** $y = \pm\sqrt{\dfrac{x + 8}{3}}$;

not a function **e)** $y = \dfrac{1}{x} + 1$; function

Primary Trigonometric Ratios and the CAST Rule, pages 497–498

1. a) $\sin \theta = \dfrac{8}{17}$, $\cos \theta = \dfrac{15}{17}$ **b)** $\cos \theta = -\dfrac{12}{13}$, $\tan \theta = -\dfrac{5}{12}$

c) $\sin \theta = -\dfrac{\sqrt{5}}{3}$, $\tan \theta = \dfrac{\sqrt{5}}{2}$ **d)** $\sin \theta = -\dfrac{8}{\sqrt{89}}$, $\cos \theta = \dfrac{5}{\sqrt{89}}$

2. a) positive, 0.2867 **b)** positive, 0.9397 **c)** negative, -0.5736
d) positive, 0.2867 **e)** negative, -0.4384 **f)** negative, -0.8192

Product of Two Binomials, page 498
1. a) $2a^2 + a - 15$ **b)** $3m^2 + 14m + 8$ **c)** $2x^2 + 2xy - 12y^2$
d) $10m^2 - 11mn + 3n^2$

Quadratic Functions, pages 498–499
1. a) vertex $(0, 2)$; opens upward; vertical stretch factor 1

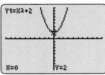

b) vertex $(0, -1)$; opens downward; vertical stretch factor 1

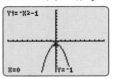

c) vertex $(0, 0)$; opens upward; vertical stretch factor 2

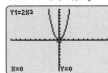

d) vertex $(-4, 0)$; opens upward; vertical stretch factor 3

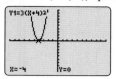

e) vertex $(1, 4)$; opens downward; vertical stretch factor 2

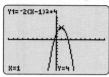

f) vertex $(-2, 3)$; opens upward; vertical stretch factor 0.5

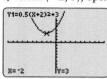

g) vertex $(-1, -5)$; opens downward; vertical stretch factor 1

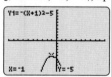

h) vertex $(3, 1)$; opens upward; vertical stretch factor $\frac{1}{4}$

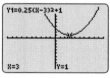

Reciprocal Functions, page 499
1. Window variables: $x \in [-6, 6]$, $y \in [-6, 6]$
a) vertical asymptote $x = 4$, horizontal asymptote $y = 0$

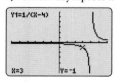

b) vertical asymptote $x = -3$, horizontal asymptote $y = 0$

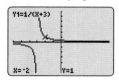

c) vertical asymptote $x = 1$, horizontal asymptote $y = 0$

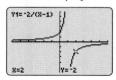

d) vertical asymptote $x = -4$, horizontal asymptote $y = 0$

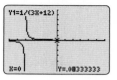

Reciprocal Trigonometric Ratios, pages 499–501
1. a) $\csc \theta = \frac{17}{15}$, $\sec \theta = \frac{17}{8}$ **b)** $\sec \theta = -\frac{25}{7}$, $\cot \theta = -\frac{7}{24}$
c) $\csc \theta = -\frac{8}{\sqrt{55}}$, $\cot \theta = \frac{3}{\sqrt{55}}$ **d)** $\csc \theta = -\frac{\sqrt{13}}{2}$, $\sec \theta = \frac{\sqrt{13}}{3}$
2. a) 1.3270 **b)** -2.4586 **c)** -7.1853 **d)** -1.0724 **e)** -1.7013
f) -1.0038
3. a) 29° **b)** 105° **c)** $-80°$ **d)** 23°

Simplify a Radical Expression, page 501
1. a) $2\sqrt{3}$ **b)** $2\sqrt{5}$ **c)** $\frac{3}{4}$ **d)** $-\frac{\sqrt{3}}{5}$ **e)** $5 + \sqrt{5}$ **f)** $3 - \sqrt{6}$

Simplify Expressions, page 501
1. a) $5x + 20$ **b)** $7y - 30$ **c)** $8x - 18$ **d)** $4w + 11$
e) $35 - 6y$ **f)** $7x^2 - 2x + 4$
g) $4x^2 + 6x - 46$ **h)** $5a^2 - 16a + 20$

Slope, page 502
1. a) $\frac{1}{2}$ **b)** $-\frac{3}{5}$ **c)** $\frac{11}{3}$ **d)** $\frac{3}{4}$ **e)** $-\frac{2}{9}$ **f)** $\frac{3}{4}$ **e)** -2 **f)** -2

Slope and y-intercept of a Line, page 502
1. a) slope 4; y-intercept 1 **b)** slope 1; y-intercept -2
c) slope 3; y-intercept 5 **d)** slope -7; y-intercept 3
e) slope 3; y-intercept 0 **f)** slope 0; y-intercept -8
g) slope 5; y-intercept 2 **h)** slope 4; y-intercept -3
i) slope -3.5; y-intercept 2.5 **j)** slope 1; y-intercept 0
k) slope 4; y-intercept 4 **l)** slope 6; y-intercept 4

Solve Quadratic Equations, page 503
1. a) $-4, -5$ **b)** $1, 2$ **c)** $3, -10$ **d)** $-3, -5$
2. a) $-1, \frac{2}{3}$ **b)** $\frac{5}{2}$ **c)** $\pm\frac{3}{5}$ **d)** $0, \frac{4}{9}$
3. a) $1, \frac{1}{2}$ **b)** $\frac{3}{2}, \frac{3}{5}$ **c)** $1, \frac{2}{3}$
4. a) $\frac{-1 \pm \sqrt{11}}{5}$; 0.5 or -0.9 **b)** $\frac{1 \pm \sqrt{7}}{3}$; 1.2 or -0.5
c) $\frac{4 \pm \sqrt{2}}{2}$; 2.7 or 1.3 **d)** $\frac{-1 \pm \sqrt{15}}{2}$; 1.4 or -2.4
e) $\frac{1 \pm \sqrt{11}}{5}$; 0.9 or -0.5 **f)** $\frac{-5 \pm \sqrt{97}}{12}$; 0.4 or -1.2

Trigonometric Identities, page 504
1. Answers may vary.

Use Long Division, page 504
1. a) 28 R3 **b)** 156 R3 **c)** 146 R17 **d)** 127 R11

Glossary

A

abscissa The first element of an ordered pair. In the ordered pair (x, y), x is the abscissa. See *ordinate*.

absolute value The distance from zero of a number on a number line.
$$|-5| = 5$$

absolute value function A piecewise function written as $y = |x|$, where $y = x$ for $x \geq 0$ and $y = -x$ for $x < 0$.

acceleration The rate of change of an object's velocity with respect to time.

acute angle An angle that measures less than 90°.

algebraic expression An expression that includes at least one variable.
$2t$, $3x^2 + 4x - 5$, and 2^x are algebraic expressions.

algebraic modelling The process of representing a relationship by an equation or a formula, or representing a pattern of numbers by an algebraic expression.

altitude The height of a geometric figure. In a triangle, an altitude is the perpendicular distance from a vertex to the opposite side.

amplitude Half the difference between the maximum and minimum values of a periodic funtion. $|a|$ for functions in the form $y = a \sin x$ or $y = a \cos x$. See *period*.

angle in standard position The position of an angle when its vertex is at the origin and its initial ray is on the positive x-axis. The angle is measured counterclockwise from the initial ray. For example, 45° is shown in standard position.

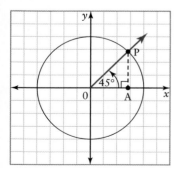

angular velocity (or speed) The rate at which the central angle is changing, often measured in radians per second.

arc A part of the circumference of a circle.

argument The value(s) assigned to the variable(s) in a function.

arithmetic sequence A sequence that has a common difference between consecutive terms.
1, 4, 7, 10, . . . is an arithmetic sequence.

astronomical unit (AU) The distance from Earth to the Sun, or approximately 150 000 000 km.

asymptote A line that a curve approaches more and more closely but does not intersect. The line may be a horizontal asymptote, a vertical asymptote, or a linear oblique asymptote.

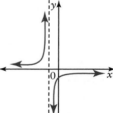

average rate of change The rate of change that is measured over an interval on a continuous curve. It corresponds to the slope of the secant between the two endpoints of the interval.

average rate of change of y with respect to x For a function $y = f(x)$, the average rate of change of y with respect to x over the interval $x \in [a, b]$ is $\dfrac{\Delta y}{\Delta x} = \dfrac{f(b) - f(a)}{b - a}$.

axis of symmetry A vertical mirror line that reflects every point on the graph of a function onto another point on the graph of the function. See *line of symmetry*.

B

base function For various functions, the simplest form of the function that others are related to by tranformations.
$y = x^2$ is the base function for quadratic functions.

base (of a power) The number that is repeatedly multiplied.
In 3^4, the base is 3.

binomial A polynomial with two terms.
$5x - 2$ is a binomial.

break-even point The point at which costs and revenue are equal.

C

capacity The greatest volume that a container can hold, usually measured in litres, millilitres, or kilolitres.

Cartesian coordinate system The system developed by René Descartes for graphing points as ordered pairs on a grid, using two perpendicular number lines. Also referred to as the Cartesian plane, the coordinate grid, or the *x-y* plane.

CAST rule A rule that tells which trigonometric ratios are positive in each quadrant.

S
sine

A
all

T
tangent

C
cosine

central angle An angle formed by two radii of a circle.

change of base formula $\log_b m = \dfrac{\log m}{\log b}$, $m > 0$, $b > 0$, $b \ne 1$

chord (of a circle) A line segment with its endpoints on a circle.

circle The set of all points in the plane that are equidistant from a fixed point called the centre.

coefficient The factor by which a variable is multiplied.
In the term $3x^2$, the coefficient is 3.

cofunction identities Relationships between pairs of trigonometric functions involving pairs of complementary angles that are true for all values of the variable. For example, $\sin x = \cos\left(\dfrac{\pi}{2} - x\right)$ and $\cos x = \sin\left(\dfrac{\pi}{2} - x\right)$.

common difference The difference between consecutive terms of an arithmetic sequence.
For 2, 5, 8, 11, . . ., the common difference is 3.

common factor Any factor that two or more numbers, or two or more terms of a polynomial, share.
2 is a common factor of 4, 6, and 18.
$3x$ is a common factor of $3x^2 - 12x$.

common logarithm A logarithm with base 10.

common ratio The ratio of consecutive terms of a geometric sequence.
For 2, 6, 18, 54, . . ., the common ratio is 3.

commutative property The property that the order of the operands in an expression does not matter. For example, for $a, b \in \mathbb{R}$, $a + b = b + a$ and $ab = ba$.

composite function A function made up of (composed of) other functions. The composition of f and g is defined by $f(g(x))$ and read as "f of g of x" or "f following g of x." In the composition $(f(g)(x))$, first apply the function g to x, and then apply the function f to the result.

compound angle expression A trigonometric expression that depends on two or more angles.

compound angle identities The following relationships are true for all values of x and y.
$\sin(x + y) = \sin x \cos y + \cos x \sin y$
$\sin(x - y) = \sin x \cos y - \cos x \sin y$
$\cos(x + y) = \cos x \cos y - \sin x \sin y$
$\cos(x - y) = \cos x \cos y + \sin x \sin y$

compound interest Interest that is calculated at regular compounding periods and then added to the principal for the next compounding period. The future amount, A, of an investment with initial principal P is $A = P(1 + i)^n$, where i is the interest rate per compounding period, in decimal form, and n is the number of compounding periods.

concurrent lines Two or more lines that have one point in common.

congruence The property of being congruent. Two geometric figures are congruent if they are equal in all respects.

conjecture A generalization, or educated guess, made from available evidence.

constant function A function of the form $f(x) = b$, where $b \in \mathbb{R}$.

constant rate of change The rate of change of a relation is constant when the average rate of change between any two points on the relation is equal to the average rate of change between any other two points on the relation. Linear relations have a constant rate of change.

constant term A term that does not include a variable. A numerical term.
In $x^2 + 5x - 1$, the constant term is -1.

coordinate plane A one-to-one pairing of all ordered pairs of real numbers with all points of a plane. Also called the Cartesian coordinate plane.

correlation coefficient A variable used to measure the strength of a relationship when regression is used to find an equation that approximates data.

cosecant ratio The reciprocal of the sine ratio.

cosine law See *law of consines*.

cosine ratio In a right triangle, for $\angle C$, the ratio of the length of the side adjacent to $\angle C$ and the length of the hypotenuse.

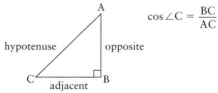

$\cos \angle C = \dfrac{BC}{AC}$

cotangent ratio The reciprocal of the tangent ratio.

coterminal angles Angles that have the same terminal arm.

counterexample An example that shows that a conjecture is not true.

cubic equation A polynomial equation of degree 3.

cubic function A polynomial function of degree 3.

curve of best fit A curve that approximates the distribution of points in a scatter plot.

cylinder A three-dimensional shape with two parallel faces that are congruent circles, and a curved surface connecting the two circles.

D

decibel scale A logarithmic scale used to compare sound levels.

decreasing function A function $f(x)$ such that $f(a) > f(b)$ for all $a < b$.

degree of a polynomial The greatest exponent of the variable in any one term.

The degree of $x^3 + 6x^2 - 1$ is 3.

dependent variable In a relation, the variable whose value depends on the value of the independent variable. On a coordinate grid, the values of the dependent variable are on the vertical axis.

In $d = 4.9t^2$, d is the dependent variable.

depreciation The amount by which an item decreases in value over time.

diagonal A line segment joining two non-adjacent vertices of a polygon.

diameter A chord that passes through the centre of a circle.

discontinuity A function has a discontinuity at $x = a$ if it is not continuous at $x = a$. For example, $f(x) = \frac{1}{x}$ has a discontinuity at $x = 0$.

discontinuous A function is discontinuous at $x = a$ if it has a discontinuity at $x = a$.

distributive property The property that, for all $a, b, c \in \mathbb{R}$, $a(b + c) = ab + ac$.

dividend A number, or expression, being divided.

In $30 \div 5 = 6$, 30 is the dividend.

divisor A number, or expression, that is dividing into another.

In $\dfrac{4x^2 + 10x + 25}{2x + 5}$, $2x + 5$ is the divisor.

domain of a function The set of numbers for which a function is defined. The set of all first coordinates of the ordered pairs in a function.

double root A solution of a polynomial equation that occurs twice. For example, in $(x - 2)^2(x + 1) = 0$, 2 is a double root.

dynamic geometry software Computer software that allows the user to plot points on a coordinate system, measure line segments and angles, construct two-dimensional shapes, create two-dimensional representations of three-dimensional objects, and transform constructed figures by moving parts of them.

E

elements The individual members of a set.

elimination method A method of solving a system of equations by addition or subtraction of the equations to eliminate one variable.

end behaviour The behaviour of the y-values of a function as x approaches $+\infty$ and x approaches $-\infty$.

equation A mathematical sentence formed by two equivalent expressions.

$5x - 3 = 2x + 6$ is an equation.

equilateral triangle A triangle with all sides equal.

equivalent algebraic expressions Expressions that are equal for all values of the variable.

$7t + 3t$ and $10t$ are equivalent algebraic expressions.

equivalent equations Equations that have the same solution.

evaluate To determine a value for.

even function A function $f(x)$ that satisfies the property $f(-x) = f(x)$ for all x in its domain. An even function is symmetric about the y-axis. See *odd function*.

expand To multiply, usually applied to polynomials.

$4(n - 3)$ expands to $4n - 12$.

exponent A raised number in a power that indicates repeated multiplication of the base.

In $(x + 3)^2 = (x + 3)(x + 3)$, the exponent is 2.

exponential decay Exponential decay occurs when a quantity decreases exponentially over time.

exponential equation An equation that has a variable in an exponent.

$3^x = 81$ is an exponential equation.

exponential form A shorthand method for writing repeated multiplication.

4^3 is the exponential form for $4 \times 4 \times 4$.

exponential function A function of the form $y = ab^x$, where $a \neq 0$, $b > 0$, and $b \neq 1$.

$f(x) = 3(2^x)$ is an exponential function.

exponential growth Exponential growth occurs when a quantity increases exponentially over time.

exponential regression A method of determining the exponential equation of a curve that fits the distribution of points on a scatter plot.

expression A mathematical phrase made up of numbers and/or variables.

$x^2 + x - 5$, $2x$, and $3n$ are expressions.

extraneous roots Roots that occur in a solution but that do not check in the orginal equation and so are invalid.

extrapolate Estimate values lying outside the range of the given data. To extrapolate from a graph means to estimate coordinates of a point beyond those that are plotted.

factor A number or an algebraic expression that is multiplied by another number or algebriac expression to give a product.
The factors of 12 are 1, 2, 3, 4, 6, and 12.
The factors of $4x^2 + 8xy$ are 4, x, and $x + 2y$.

factor theorem A polynomial $P(x)$ has $ax - b$ as a factor if and only if $P\left(\dfrac{b}{a}\right) = 0$, where $a, b \in \mathbb{R}$ and $a \neq 0$.

family of functions A group of functions with a common characteristic. For example, a family of polynomial functions has the same zeros.

finite differences Differences found from successive y-values in a table of values with evenly spaced x-values. See *first differences* and *second differences*.

first differences In a relation between two variables, the difference between successive values of the second variable for regular steps of the first variable.

$y = 2x + 1$		
x	y	First Differences
−2	−3	
−1	−1	$-1 - (-3) = 2$
0	1	$1 - (-1) = 2$
1	3	$3 - 1 = 2$
2	5	$5 - 3 = 2$

frequency The number of cycles per unit of time.

function A relation in which each element in the domain (or x-value) has only one corresponding element in the range (or y-value).
$y = (3x - 5)^2$ is a function.

half-life The time in which the mass of a radioactive substance decays to half its original mass.

hypotenuse The longest side of a right triangle.

image point A point that corresponds to an object point under a transformation.

increasing function A function $f(x)$ such that $f(a) < f(b)$ for all $a < b$.

independent variable In a relation, the variable whose value determines that of the dependent variable. On a coordinate grid, the values of the independent variable are on the horizontal axis.
In $d = 4.9t^2$, t is the independent variable.

inequality Two expressions related by an inequality symbol ($>, <, \geqslant, \leqslant, \neq$).
$4x + 5 > 8$ is an inequality.

instantaneous rate of change The rate of change that is measured at a single point on a continuous curve. Instantaneous rate of change corresponds to the slope of the tangent line at that point.

integer A number in the sequence
$\ldots, -3, -2, -1, 0, 1, 2, 3, \ldots$. Represented by the set symbol $\mathbb{Z}$.

integral zero theorem If $x - b$ is a factor of the polynomial function $P(x)$ with leading coefficient one and remaining coefficients that are integers, then b is a factor of the constant term.

intercept The distance from the origin of the Cartesian coordinate plane to the point at which a line or curve crosses a given axis. See *x-intercept* and *y-intercept*.

interest The amount earned on an investment or savings alternative, or the cost of borrowing money.

interest rate The rate, as a percent, at which an investment or savings alternative increases in value, or the cost of borrowing money, expressed as a percent.

interior angle An angle that is inside a polygon.

interpolate Estimate values for a relation that lie between given data points.

interval A set of real numbers having one of these forms where $a, b \in \mathbb{R}$: $x > a$, $x \geqslant a$, $x < a$, $x \leqslant a$, $a < x < b$, $a < x \leqslant b$, $a \leqslant x < b$, or $a \leqslant x \leqslant b$

interval notation Representations of intervals using brackets: (a, ∞), $[a, \infty)$, $(-\infty, a]$, (a, b), $(a, b]$, $[a, b)$, or $[a, b]$.

invariant point A point that is unchanged by a transformation.

inverse function The inverse function f^{-1} of a function f, if it exists, is found by writing the function in the form $y = f(x)$, exchanging x and y, and then solving for y.

inverse relation The relation formed by interchanging the domain and the range of a given relation.

inversely proportional If two variables, x and y, are inversely proportional, then $y = \dfrac{k}{x}$, where k is a constant.

irrational number A real number that cannot be expressed in the form $\dfrac{a}{b}$, where a and $b \in \mathbb{Z}$ and $b \neq 0$.

isosceles triangle A triangle with exactly two equal sides.

L

law of cosines The relationship between the lengths of the three sides and the cosine of an angle in any triangle.
$$a^2 = b^2 + c^2 - 2bc \cos \angle A$$

law of sines The relationship between the sides and their opposite angles in any triangle.
$$\frac{\sin A}{a} = \frac{\sin B}{b} = \frac{\sin C}{c}$$

leading coefficient The coefficient of the greatest power of x in a polynomial $P(x)$.

like terms Terms that have exactly the same variable(s) raised to exactly the same exponent(s).
$3x^2$, $-x^2$, and $-7x^2$ are like terms.

line of best fit The line that best describes the distribution of points in a scatter plot. The line passes through, or close to, as many of the data points as possible.

line of symmetry A mirror line that reflects an object onto itself.

line segment The part of a line that joins two points.

line symmetry A graph has line symmetry if there is a line $x = a$, called the axis of symmetry, that divides the graph into two parts such that each part is a reflection of the other in the line $x = a$.

linear equation An equation that represents the relationship between two variables that have a linear relationship and form a straight line when graphed.

linear function A function of the form $f(x) = mx + b$, where m and b are constants.

linear growth Growth represented by a linear equation and a straight-line graph. Arithmetic sequences and simple interest show linear growth.

linear regression A method for determining the linear equation that best fits the distribution of points on a scatter plot.

linear relation A relationship between two variables that forms a straight line when graphed.

local maximum The point on a function that has the greatest y-value on some interval close to the point.

local minimum The point on a function that has the least y-value on some interval close to the point.

logarithm The logarithm of a number is the value of the exponent to which a given base must be raised to produce the given number. For example, $\log_3 81 = 4$, because $3^4 = 81$.

logarithmic equation An equation that has a variable in a logarithm.
$\log_2 x = \log_2 3 + \log_2 5$ is a logarithmic equation.

logarithmic function The inverse of an exponential function. A function of the form $f(x) = \log_a x$, where $a > 0$, $a \neq 1$, and $x > 0$.
$y = \log_a x$ means $a^y = x$.

logarithmic scale A scale that uses powers of 10, for example, the decibel scale.

M

mathematical model A description of a real-life situation using a diagram, a graph, a table of values, an equation, a formula, a physical model, or a computer model.

mathematical modelling The process of describing a real-life situation in mathematical form.

mean The sum of a set of values divided by the number of values in the set.

N

$n!$ (n factorial) For any positive integer n, a short form for the product $n \times (n - 1) \times \ldots \times 2 \times 1$.
$$5! = 5 \times 4 \times 3 \times 2 \times 1$$
$$= 120$$

natural logarithm A logarithm in base e.

natural number The set, $\mathbb{N}$, of positive integers: 1, 2, 3, 4, ...

non-linear relation A relationship between two variables that does not form a straight line when graphed.

O

oblique asymptote An asymptote that is neither horizontal nor vertical.

oblique triangle A triangle that is not right-angled.

obtuse angle An angle that measures more than 90°, but less than 180°.

obtuse triangle A triangle containing one obtuse angle.

odd function A function that satisfies the property $f(-x) = -f(x)$ for all x in its domain. An odd function is symmetric about the origin. See *even function*.

order (of a zero) If a polynomial function has a factor $(x - a)$ that is repeated n times, then $x = a$ is a zero of order n. For example, the function $f(x) = (x - 2)(x + 1)^2$ has a zero of order 2.

ordered pair A pair of numbers, such as (3, 8), used to locate a point on a graph.

ordinate The second element in an ordered pair. In the ordered pair (x, y), y is the ordinate. See *abscissa*.

origin The point of intersection of the x-axis and the y-axis on a coordinate grid. It is described by the ordered pair (0, 0).

outlier A data point that does not conform to the pattern of the other data.

parabola The graph of a quadratic relation, which is U-shaped and symmetric about a line of symmetry.

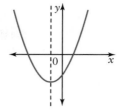

parameter A constant that can assume different values but does not change the form of the expression or function. In $y = mx + b$, m is a parameter that represents the slope of the line and b is a parameter that represents the y-intercept.

percent A number that represents a fraction or ratio with a denominator of 100.

$\frac{34}{100}$ as a percent is 34%.

perfect square A whole number that can be expressed as the square of a whole number.

25 is a perfect square.

perfect square trinomial A trinomial that can be factored as the square of a binomial.

$a^2x^2 + 2abx + b^2 = (ax + b)^2$

perimeter The distance around a two-dimensional shape.

period The magnitude of the interval of the domain over which a periodic function repeats itself.

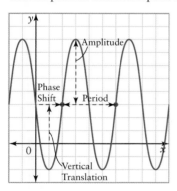

periodic function A function that repeats itself over an interval of its domain.

pH scale A logarithmic scale used to measure the acidity or alkalinity of chemical solutions. $pH = -\log[H^+]$, where $[H^+]$ is the concentration of hydronium ions, in moles per litre.

phase shift The horizontal translation of a trigonometric function. See *period* for diagram.

point of inflection A point P on a curve where the curve changes from concave upward to concave downward or from concave downward to concave upward.

point of intersection The point that is common to two non-parallel lines.

point of tangency The point of intersection of a tangent and a curve.

point symmetry A graph has point symmetry about a point (a, b) if each part of the graph on one side of (a, b) can be rotated 180° to coincide with part of the graph on the other side of (a, b).

polar coordinates A method of locating a point in a plane using its distance, r, from the origin and its angle in standard position.

polygon A two-dimensional closed shape whose sides are line segments.

polyhedron A three-dimensional object with faces that are polygons.

polynomial An expression of the form $a_nx^n + a_{n-1}x^{n-1} + \ldots + a_1x + a_0$, where $a_n, a_{n-1}, \ldots, a_0 \in \mathbb{R}$, $a_n \neq 0$, and $n \in \mathbb{Z}$, $n > 0$.

$3x^4 + 2x^3 + 5x^2 - x + 1$ is a polynomial.

polynomial function A function of the form $P(x) = a_nx^n + \ldots + a_2x^2 + a_1x + a_0$, where n is a whole number.

power An abbreviation for repeated multiplication. The power 5^3 means $5 \times 5 \times 5$ and has value 125.

power function A function of the form $f(x) = ax^n$, where $a \neq 0$ and n is a positive integer.

power law of logarithms $\log_b x^n = n\log_b x$, $b > 0$, $b \neq 1$, $x > 0$, $n \in \mathbb{R}$

primary trigonometric ratios The sine, cosine, and tangent ratios.

prime number A number with exactly two factors—itself and 1.

principal angle The least positive coterminal angle.

prism A three-dimensional shape with two parallel, congruent polygonal faces. The prism is named according to the shape of these two faces, for example, triangular prism.

probability The likelihood of an event occurring.

$P(\text{event}) = \frac{\text{number of favourable outcomes}}{\text{number of possible outcomes}}$.

product law of logarithms $\log_b(mn) = \log_b m + \log_b n$, $b > 0$, $b \neq 1$, $m > 0$, $n > 0$

proportion An equation that states that two ratios are equal.

$\frac{3}{5} = \frac{x}{80}$ is a proportion.

pyramid A polyhedron with one base in the shape of a polygon and the same number of lateral triangular faces as there are sides in the base.

Pythagorean identity The relationship $\sin^2 x + \cos^2 x = 1$, which is true for all values of x.

Pythagorean theorem In a right triangle, the square of the length of the hypotenuse is equal to the sum of the squares of the lengths of the other two sides.

Q

quadrant One of the four regions formed by the intersection of the x-axis and the y-axis.

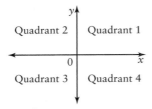

quadratic equation An equation that can be written in the form $ax^2 + bx + c = 0$, where a, b, and $c \in \mathbb{R}$ and $a \neq 0$.

quadratic formula The zeros, or solutions, of a quadratic equation of the form $ax^2 + bx + c = 0$, where $a \neq 0$, are given by $x = \dfrac{-b \pm \sqrt{b^2 - 4ac}}{2a}$.

quadratic function A relationship between two variables defined by an equation of the form $y = ax^2 + bx + c$, where a, b, and $c \in \mathbb{R}$ and $a \neq 0$. Its graph is a parabola.

quadrilateral A polygon with four sides.

quartic function A polynomial of degree four.

quintic function A polynomial of degree five.

quotient The result of a division.
In $\dfrac{30x^3}{6x} = 5x^2$, $5x^2$ is the quotient.

quotient function A function of the form $q(x) = \dfrac{f(x)}{g(x)}$, $g(x) \neq 0$.

quotient identity The relationship $\tan x = \dfrac{\sin x}{\cos x}$, which is true for all values of x.

quotient law of logarithms $\log_b\left(\dfrac{m}{n}\right) = \log_b m - \log_b n$, $b > 0$, $b \neq 1$, $m > 0$, $n > 0$

R

radian The measure of the angle formed by rotating the radius of a circle through an arc equal in length to the radius. There are 2π radians in one complete revolution (360°). In the diagram, θ measures 1 rad.

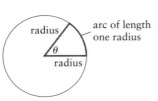

radical equation An equation that has a variable in the radicand.
$\sqrt{x + 1} + 3 = 8$ is a radical equation.

radical expression An expression that contains a radical.
$2\sqrt{3}$ and $3\sqrt{x}$ are radical expressions.

radical function A function that has a variable in a radicand.
$f(x) = \sqrt{x - 3}$ is a radical function.

radical sign The symbol $\sqrt{}$, which indicates the principal or non-negative square root of an expression.

radicand An expression under a radical sign.

random number A number chosen from a set of numbers in such a way that each number has an equally likely chance of being selected.

range of a function or relation The set of all second coordinates, or ordinates, of the ordered pairs of a relation.

range of data The difference between the greatest and the least values in a set of data.

rate A special type of ratio that compares two quantities with different units.
8.4 L/100 km is a rate.

rate of change See *instantaneous rate of change* and *average rate of change*.

ratio A comparison of quantities with the same unit.
3 cans of water to 1 can of juice is $3 : 1$.

rational equation An equation that contains one or more rational expressions.
$\dfrac{3}{x^2 - 4} = 5$ is a rational equation.

rational exponent An exponent that is a rational number.
$5^{\frac{1}{2}}$ has a rational exponent of $\dfrac{1}{2}$.

rational function A function of the form $f(x) = \dfrac{g(x)}{h(x)}$, where $g(x)$ and $h(x)$ are polynomials and $h(x) \neq 0$.
$f(x) = \dfrac{1}{2x - 5}$ is a rational function.

rational number A number that can be expressed in the form $\dfrac{a}{b}$, where a and $b \in \mathbb{Z}$ and $b \neq 0$.

rational zero theorem If $P(x)$ is a polynomial function with integer coefficients and $x = \dfrac{b}{a}$ is a zero of $P(x)$, where a and $b \in \mathbb{Z}$ and $a \neq 0$, then
• b is a factor of the constant term of $P(x)$
• a is a factor of the leading term of $P(x)$
• $ax - b$ is a factor of $P(x)$

real numbers All the rational and irrational numbers, represented by the set symbol $\mathbb{R}$.

reciprocal function A function, $g(x) = \dfrac{1}{f(x)}$ defined by $g(x) = \dfrac{1}{f(a)} = \dfrac{1}{b}$ if $f(a) = b$.

reciprocal trigonometric ratios The cosecant, secant, and cotangent ratios.

$$\text{cosecant} = \frac{1}{\text{sine}}, \text{secant} = \frac{1}{\text{cosine}}, \text{cotangent} = \frac{1}{\text{tangent}}$$

reciprocals Two non-zero numbers that have a product of one. x and $\frac{1}{x}$ are reciprocals.

regression A method for determining the equation of a curve or line that best fits the distribution of points on a scatter plot.

relation A relationship between variables that can be represented by a table of values, a graph, or an equation.

remainder theorem When a polynomial $P(x)$ is divided by $x - b$, the remainder is $P(b)$, and when it is divided by $ax - b$, the remainder is $P\left(\frac{b}{a}\right)$, where $a, b \in \mathbb{Z}$, and $a \neq 0$.

restriction A constraint on the value(s) of a variable. For example, in $\sqrt{x}$, the restriction is $x \geqslant 0$; in $f(x) = \frac{1}{x}$, the restriction is $x \neq 0$.

Richter scale A logarithmic scale used to measure the magnitude of earthquakes.

right angle An angle that measures 90°.

right triangle A triangle that contains a 90° angle.

roots The solutions of an equation.

S

scalene triangle A triangle with no sides equal.

scatter plot A graph showing two-variable data by means of points plotted on a coordinate grid.

secant A line passing through two different points on a curve.

secant ratio The reciprocal of the cosine ratio.

second differences The differences between consecutive first differences in a table of values with evenly spaced x-values. See *first differences*.

sector A part of a circle bounded by two radii and an arc of the circle.

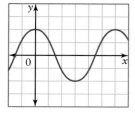

segment A part of a circle bounded by a chord and an arc of the circle.

sequence An ordered list of numbers or terms.

similar figures Figures having corresponding angles equal and corresponding lengths proportional.

simple interest Interest calculated only on the original principal using the simple interest formula $I = Prt$.

simplest form The form of a fraction or ratio that has no common factors.

simplest form of an algebraic expression An expression that has no like terms.

$5x + 3 - x + 2$ in simplest form is $4x + 5$.

sine law See *law of sines*.

sine ratio In a right triangle, for $\angle C$, the ratio of the length of the side opposite $\angle C$ and the length of the hypotenuse.

$$\sin \angle C = \frac{AB}{AC}$$

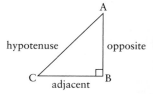

sinusoidal function A function that is used to model periodic data.

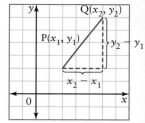

sinusoidal regression A statistical process that determines a sinusoidal function that best represents data.

slope A measure of the steepness of a line. The slope, m, of a line containing the points $P(x_1, y_1)$ and $Q(x_2, y_2)$ is

$$m = \frac{\Delta y}{\Delta x} = \frac{y_2 - y_1}{x_2 - x_1}, x_2 \neq x_1.$$

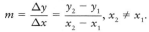

slope and y-intercept form of a linear equation A linear equation written in the form $y = mx + b$, where m is the slope and b is the y-intercept.

solve To find the value of a variable in an equation.

When $2x = 16$ is solved, $x = 4$.

standard form of a linear equation A linear equation written in the form $Ax + By + C = 0$, where A, B, and $C \in \mathbb{Z}$, A and B are not both zero, and x and $y \in \mathbb{R}$.

standard form of a quadratic function A quadratic function written in the form $y = ax^2 + bx + c$, where $a \neq 0$.

substitution method A method of solving a system of equations by solving one equation for one variable and then substituting that value into the other equation.

subtend An arc, AB, of a circle can subtend an angle at the centre, $\angle AOB$, or at the cirumference, $\angle ACB$.

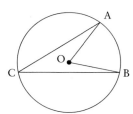

superposition principle The sum of two or more functions can be found by adding the *y*-coordinates of the function for each *x*-coordinate.

surface area The number of square units needed to cover the surface of a three-dimensional shape.

symmetric function A function that has either line symmetry or rotational symmetry.

tangent ratio In a right triangle, for $\angle C$, the ratio of the length of the side opposite $\angle A$ and the length of the side adjacent to $\angle A$.

$\tan \angle C = \dfrac{AB}{BC}$

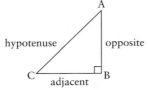

tangent to a curve A line that intersects a curve at exactly one point.

term A number or a variable, or the product or quotient of numbers and variables.

$3x^2 - 5$ has two terms: $3x^2$ and -5.

terminal arm The ray of an angle in standard position that is not on the positive *x*-axis.

transformation A mapping of points on a plane onto points on the same plane.

translation A transformation that maps an object onto its image so that each point in the object is moved the same distance in the same direction.

trigonometric equation An equation involving one or more trigonometric functions of a variable.

$\cos x - 2 \sin x \cos x = 0$ is a trigonometric equation.

trigonometric function A function involving a primary trigonometric ratio or a reciprocal trigonometric ratio.

$y = 2.8 \cos \dfrac{x}{3}$ is a trigomometric function.

trigonometric identity A trigonometric equation that is true for all values of the variable for which both sides of the equation are defined.

trinomial A polynomial with three terms.

unlike terms Terms that have different variables, or different powers of the same variable.

$2x^2$, $-x$, and $5y$ are unlike terms.

vertex A point at which two sides of a polygon meet.

vertex form of a quadratic function A quadratic equation expressed in the form $y = a(x - h)^2 + k$, where a, h, and $k \in \mathbb{R}$ and $a \neq 0$. The vertex of the parabola is (h, k).

vertex of a parabola The point where the axis of symmetry of the parabola intersects the parabola.

vertical line test A test for determining whether a given graph represents a function. If a vertical line intersects the graph more than once, then the relation is not a function.

vertical stretch A transformation where (x, y) on the graph of $y = f(x)$ is transformed into (x, ay) on the graph of $y = af(x)$. The stretch is an expansion when $a > 1$ and a compression when $0 < a < 1$.

volume The amount of space that an object occupies, measured in cubic units.

x approaches +∞ The values of x are positive and increasing in magnitude without bound; may be written $x \to +\infty$.

x approaches −∞ The values of x are negative and increasing in magnitude without bound; may be written $x \to -\infty$.

x-intercept The distance from the origin of the point where a line or curve crosses the *x*-axis.

y-intercept The distance from the origin of the point where a line or curve crosses the *y*-axis.

zero of a function A value of x (or the independent variable) that results in a *y*-value (or value of the dependent variable) of zero.

Index

Credits

p1 Sean McClean/Creative Commons License; p3 J. Solana/ IVY IMAGES; p4 HansChris/iStock; p15 Christian Waldegger/iStock; p29 KeyPix/Alamy; p30 James Phelps/ iStock; p53 D. Trask/IVY IMAGES; p65 David H. Lewis/ iStock; p80 Andrejs Zemdega/iStock; p81 Yoshikazu Tsuno/ AFP/Getty Images; p83 Nigel Silcock/iStock; p84 D. Trask/ IVY IMAGES; p93 David Tanaka; p94 Will Ivy/IVY IMAGES; p104 B. Lowry/IVY IMAGES; p113 Pamela Moore/iStock; p123 Jim Craigmyle/Corbis; p132 Alan Weintraub/Arcaid/Corbis; p144 Sarah Ivy/IVY IMAGES; p147 J. C.Whyte/IVY Images; p148 John Lund/Drew Kelly/ Getty Images; p168 Bill Ivy/IVY IMAGES; p176 Gabe Palmer/Corbis; p177 Rosenfeld Images Ltd./Photo Researchers, Inc.; p186 Lehtikuva/The Canadian Press (Seppo Samuli); p198 IVY IMAGES; p199 Photo courtesy of Bombardier Aerospace; p201 Alfred Pasieka/Photo Researchers, Inc; p202 Roger Ressmeyer/Corbis; p206 Richard Gunion/iStock; p210 Will Ivy/IVY IMAGES; p211 Leif Norman/iStock; p220 Kelly-Mooney Photography/Corbis; p227 TWPhoto/Corbis; p228 D. Trask/IVY IMAGES; p236 NASA; p243 Bill Ivy/ IVY IMAGES; p251 iStock; p252 The Canadian Press (Bill Becker); p259 top eStock/Alamy, bottom B.Lowry/ IVY IMAGES; p261 Purestock/Alamy; p270 PhotoTake Inc./Alamy; p273 iStock; p278 Donna Coleman/iStock; p281 Linda Matta/iStock; p282 Sami Suni/iStock; p286 Joe Gough/iStock; p289 Dana Hursey/Masterfile; p290 Slobo Mitic/iStock; p292 iStock; p295 Yan Gluzberg/ iStock; p301 Michal Rozanski/iStock; p305 Holt Studios International Ltd./Alamy; p306 David H. Lewis/iStock; p307–309 With permission Astrosurf; p310 Lida Caster/ iStock; p322 Caro/Alamy; p323 David Raymer/Corbis; p331, p340 Krzysztof Zmij/iStock; p341 Lisa F. Young/ iStock; p349 O. Bierwagon/IVY IMAGES; p360 N. Lightfoot/IVY IMAGES; p361 D. Trask/IVY IMAGES; p363 ron summers/iStock; p364 Canadian Olympic Committee/The Canadian Press (F. Scott Grant); p369 Bill Ivy/IVY IMAGES?; p370 Dr. Heinz Linke/iStock; p377 NASA; p378 Simon Podgorsek/iStock; p387 Bill Ivy/ IVY IMAGES; p393 J. Speijer; p412 David Ayers/iStock; p413 Jacob Wackerhausen/iStock; p416 B. Lowry/ IVY IMAGES; p429 David Rose/iStock; p439 Sharon Dominick/iStock; p449 Corbis; p450 Branko Miokovic/ iStock; p459 Vasiliki Varvaki/iStock; p461 Matej Michelizza/iStock; p465, p470 B. Lowry/IVY IMAGES; p478 David Tanaka

ALGEBRA

Factoring Special Polynomials

$x^2 \pm 2xy + y^2 = (x \pm y)^2$

$x^2 - y^2 = (x - y)(x + y)^2$

$x^3 \pm y^3 = (x \pm y)(x^2 \mp xy + y^2)$

Quadratic Formula

If $ax^2 + bx + c = 0$, then $x = \dfrac{-b \pm \sqrt{b^2 - 4ac}}{2a}$.

Rules for Exponents

Product	Quotient	Power
$(x^a)(x^b) = x^{a+b}$	$\dfrac{x^a}{x^b} = x^{a-b}$	$(x^a)^b = x^{ab}$
Power of a Product	**Rational Exponent**	**Negative Exponent**
$(xy)^a = x^a y^a$	$x^{\frac{1}{a}} = \sqrt[a]{x}$	$x^{-a} = \dfrac{1}{x^a}$

Logarithms

$y = \log_a x \Leftrightarrow a^y = x$

$\log_{10} x$ is usually written as $\log x$.

$\log_a a = 1$

$\log_a a^x = x$

$a^{\log_a x} = x$

$\log_a (xy) = \log_a x + \log_a y$

$\log_b x = \dfrac{\log_a x}{\log_a b}$

$\log_a \left(\dfrac{x}{y} \right) = \log_a x - \log_a y$

$\log_a x^n = n \log_a x$

ANALYTIC GEOMETRY

Distance Between Two Points

The distance between two points $P_1(x_1, y_1)$ and $P_2(x_2, y_2)$ is $P_1 P_2 = \sqrt{(x_2 - x_1)^2 + (y_1 - y_2)^2}$.

Linear Function

For a line through the points $P_1(x_1, y_1)$ and $P_2(x_2, y_2)$,

Slope: $m = \dfrac{y_2 - y_1}{x_2 - x_1}$

Slope y-intercept form of equation: $y = mx + b$, where b is the y-intercept

Point-slope form of equation: $y - y_1 = m(x - x_1)$

Quadratic Function

Equation for a parabola with vertex (p, q):

$y = a(x - p)^2 + q$

Circle

Equation for a circle centre (h, k) and radius r:

$(x - h)^2 + (y - k)^2 = r^2$

MEASUREMENT

In the following, P represents perimeter, C the circumference, A the area, V the volume, and SA the surface area.

Triangle

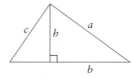

$P = a + b + c$

$A = \dfrac{1}{2} bh$

Trapezoid

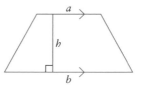

$A = \dfrac{1}{2}(a + b)h$

Circle

$$C = 2\pi r$$
$$A = \pi r^2$$

Cylinder

$$V = \pi r^2 h$$
$$SA = 2\pi rh + 2\pi r^2$$

Cone

$$V = \frac{1}{3}\pi r^2 h$$
$$SA = \pi r^2 + \pi rs$$

Sphere

$$V = \frac{4}{3}\pi r^3$$
$$SA = 4\pi r^2$$

TRIGONOMETRY

Angle Measure

$$1° = \frac{\pi}{180} \text{ rad}$$

$$1 \text{ rad} = \frac{180°}{\pi}$$

Primary Trigonometric Ratios

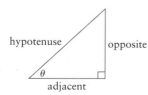

$$\sin\theta = \frac{\text{opposite}}{\text{hypotenuse}}$$

$$\cos\theta = \frac{\text{adjacent}}{\text{hypotenuse}}$$

$$\tan\theta = \frac{\text{opposite}}{\text{adjacent}}$$

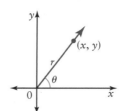

$$\sin\theta = \frac{y}{r}$$
$$\cos\theta = \frac{x}{r}$$
$$\tan\theta = \frac{y}{x}$$

Sine Law

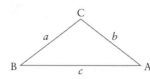

$$\frac{\sin A}{a} = \frac{\sin B}{b} = \frac{\sin C}{c}$$

$$\frac{a}{\sin A} = \frac{b}{\sin B} = \frac{c}{\sin C}$$

Cosine Law

$$a^2 = b^2 + c^2 - 2bc \cos A$$
$$b^2 = a^2 + c^2 - 2ac \cos B$$
$$c^2 = a^2 + b^2 - 2ab \cos C$$

Fundamental Identities

$$\sin^2\theta + \cos^2\theta = 1 \qquad \tan\theta = \frac{\sin\theta}{\cos\theta} \qquad \csc\theta = \frac{1}{\sin\theta}$$

$$\sec\theta = \frac{1}{\cos\theta} \qquad \cot\theta = \frac{1}{\tan\theta}$$

Compound Angle Formulas

$$\sin(A \pm B) = \sin A \cos B \pm \cos A \sin B$$
$$\cos(A \pm B) = \cos A \cos B \mp \sin A \sin B$$
$$\tan(A \pm B) = \frac{\tan A \pm \tan B}{1 \mp \tan A \tan B}$$

Double-Angle Formulas

$$\sin 2A = 2\sin A \cos A$$
$$\cos 2A = \cos^2 A - \sin^2 A$$
$$= 2\cos^2 A - 1$$
$$= 1 - 2\sin^2 A$$

$$\tan 2A = \frac{2\tan A}{1 - \tan^2 A}$$